BB 06-91

Computer Concepts

with Microsoft® Works Tutorial and Applications
IBM Version

GLORIA A. WAGGONER

JONATHAN PRICE

DC01AA3

PUBLISHED BY

SOUTH-WESTERN PUBLISHING CO.

CINCINNATI, OH   DALLAS, TX   LIVERMORE, CA

ISBN: 0-538-60863-3

Library of Congress Card Catalog Number: 89-64255

1 2 3 4 5 6 7 8 9 10 W 9 8 7 6 5 4 3 2 1 0

Printed in the United States of America

Special thanks to Bill Waggoner, whose years of computer industry experience contributed significantly to the content and quality of the Concepts material.

Microsoft Works, Microsoft, MS-DOS, and the Microsoft logo are registered trademarks of Microsoft Corporation.
IBM and Personal System/2 are registered trademarks of International Business Machines Corporation.
Tandy is a registered trademark of The Radio Shack Division of Tandy Corporation.
HyperGraphics is a registered trademark of HyperGraphics Corporation.

Credits for photos and illustrations appear on page I-1, which constitutes a continuation of the copyright page.

Acquisitions Editor: Robert First

Developmental Editor: Ronald W. Erickson

Associate Editor/Production: Anne Noschang

Editorial Associate: Mary Todd

Designer: Debbie Kokoruda

Photo Researchers: Paula Hickey and Devore Nixon

Marketing Manager: Gregory Getter

CONTENTS IN BRIEF

CONTENTS

CHAPTER 11   COMMERCIAL APPLICATION SOFTWARE   11.1

CHAPTER 12   THE INFORMATION SYSTEM DEVELOPMENT LIFE CYCLE   12.1

CHAPTER 13   PROGRAM DEVELOPMENT   13.1

Learning to Use Microsoft Works

UNIT V   INTEGRATION   MSW 237

PREFACE

Understanding the computer—how it works and how it can be used in the home, in school, and in business—is becoming more and more essential to be productive and successful in today's world. This textbook presents fundamental concepts in a manner that emphasizes their importance from the user's point of view. These concepts are reinforced by an appendix on the most widely used microcomputer applications—word processing, database, and spreadsheet. No previous experience with computers is required for this text.

ORGANIZATION OF THE TEXTBOOK

his textbook consists of fifteen concepts chapters, an introduction to DOS®, and a Microsoft®¹ Works tutorial.

The Concepts Chapters

We include fifteen chapters that cover a full range of computer and processing concepts. The concept of the information system is introduced in Chapter 1 and used throughout the text. The six elements of an information system—equipment, software, data, personnel, users, and procedures—are introduced in this chapter; subsequent chapters relate back to one or more of these six elements. The impact of microcomputers is addressed throughout the textbook. Chapter 2 presents a unique overview of the four most commonly used microcomputer applications—word processing, spreadsheet, database, and graphics. Chapter 3 discusses data—how it is organized in fields, records, files, and databases and how it is processed into information. The chapter also defines and describes the information processing cycle—input, process, output, and storage. Each of these operations is discussed in the next four chapters (Chapters 4–7).

Chapter 8 discusses file and database organization and emphasizes the significance and the advantages of relational database systems. Data communications, including networking, is discussed in Chapter 9.

Chapters 10 through 13 cover concepts relating to software, software acquisition, and software development: operating systems and systems software (Chapter 10), commercial applications software (Chapter 11), the information systems development life cycle (Chapter 12), and program development and popular programming languages (Chapter 13).

The concluding chapters point out career opportunities in the field of information processing (Chapter 14) and discuss some of the trends and issues in the information age (Chapter 15).

An Introduction to DOS

To use a computer effectively, students need a practical knowledge of operating systems. The MS-DOS operating system is covered in a separate appendix. This appendix presents the most commonly used DOS functions such as formatting a diskette and copying, renaming, and deleting files.

The Microsoft Works Tutorial

After an introduction to the most commonly used DOS functions, students are presented with an extensive 17-lesson tutorial about the Microsoft Works integrated software package. The tutorial consists of six units, starting with an introduction to Microsoft Works. Separate units are included for the Word Processor, Database, Spreadsheet, Integration, and Communications applications. The complete tutorial covers most of the features of this powerful, but easy-to-use, integrated program.

---

¹Microsoft Works, Microsoft, MS-DOS, and the Microsoft logo are registered trademarks of Microsoft Corporation.

The features of Microsoft Works are presented in a clear, step-by-step manner. First, a new command or concept is thoroughly explained. Then detailed instructions, combined with carefully labeled screens, illustrate the process of using the software. This hands-on approach provides an excellent way for your students to learn quickly how to use the software.

Each lesson is amplified by a list of key terms, a command summary, and several review questions and applications. The review questions emphasize the important concepts covered in the lesson. The applications offer the opportunity to practice the commands learned in the lesson. Students will become more proficient using the software by applying the skills they have learned to solve realistic problems.

SUPPLEMENTS TO ACCOMPANY THIS TEXT

 ight teaching and learning materials supplement this textbook. They are the Template Disk, Instructor's Manual, Study Guide and Applications, MicroExam, Transparency Masters, HyperGraphics, *Instructor's Manual to Accompany HyperGraphics*, and *ClassNotes and Study Guide*.

Template Disk

A special, copyable template disk contains documents that students will use to learn about the Word Processor, database files to use with the Data Base, and worksheets to use in the Spreadsheet lessons. Files are also included for the lessons in the integration unit. The purpose of this required template is to facilitate the process of learning how to use Microsoft Works. Students do not have to spend valuable class time keying information before they can begin practicing new skills. After a command is introduced, they can simply retrieve the appropriate file and practice the new command.

Instructor's Manual

This manual includes Lesson Plans, and Answers and Solutions. The Lesson Plans include: chapter behavioral objectives, chapter overviews, chapter outlines that are annotated with textbook page numbers on which the outlined material is covered, notes, teaching tips, additional activities, and a key for using the Transparency Masters. Complete answers and solutions for all exercises, projects, and controversial issues are included.

Study Guide and Applications

The Study Guide and Applications workbook provides an opportunity for students to review the concepts presented in the text. In addition, the workbook includes applications for word processing, database, and spreadsheet. These applications can be used by your students to master the skills they have already learned. The applications have been designed so that they can be completed using almost any software program that includes a word processor, database, or spreadsheet.

MicroExam II

This easy-to-use, computerized test generating system is available for use with this textbook. MicroExam II is menu-driven and allows the creation of custom testing documents plus answer keys. It provides testing flexibility and customizing of testing documents. The test bank is comprised of three types of questions—true/false, multiple choice, and fill-in. Each chapter has approximately 50 true/false, 25 multiple choice, and 35 fill-ins. MicroExam will run on the IBM® PC and Tandy®1000 systems with two diskette drives.

Transparency Masters

A Transparency Master is included for *every* figure in the textbook.

HyperGraphics®

How instructors teach has changed very little in the last few decades. After all the flag waving about computer tutorials, CAI, and the like, we have learned that the human instructor is neither replaceable by a machine nor by someone who is untrained. HyperGraphics is a tool that acknowledges these facts.

What Is HyperGraphics? HyperGraphics is an instructional delivery system; it is a piece of software that presents the content of the fifteen concepts chapters by using graphics, color, animation, and interactivity. It is a state-of-the-art, computer-based teaching and learning environment that promotes interactive learning and self-study.

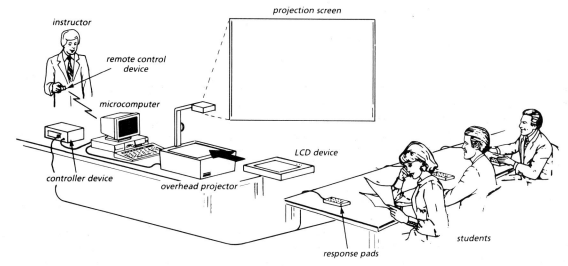

What Hardware Do You Need for HyperGraphics? You need three pieces of hardware to run HyperGraphics; two additional pieces are optional.

1. An IBM Personal Computer or Personal System/2 computer (or compatible) with a standard CGA graphics card.
2. A standard overhead projector and projection screen.
3. A standard projection device, such as a color projector or a liquid crystal display (LCD), that fits on the projection area of the overhead projector. The projection device is connected to the personal computer, resulting in the projection of the computer's screen.
4. A hand-held remote control device (*optional*) that allows the instructor to navigate throughout the presentation materials and still move freely around the classroom.
5. A set of response pads (*optional*), small pads consisting of 10 digit keys, that can be pressed to indicate a student's response. (These pads are linked to the microcomputer by a controller device.)

How Does the Instructor Use HyperGraphics? HyperGraphics is very easy to use. The instructor presses the appropriate keys on the hand-held remote control device or the keyboard and thereby controls the screen display. This display is projected through the LCD to the overhead projector. The instructor has complete control over the order and pacing of how the lessons are taught. By pushing one or more keys he or she can do such things as:

- View and select from the lesson menu
- Deliver the lesson's instructional materials in sequence
- Repeat any portion of a lesson to reinforce or review material
- Move ahead to specific portions of the lesson
- View the chapter objectives at any time

- View one or more questions about the lesson at any time
- Have students respond to one or more questions via the response pads
- Log students' responses to questions
- Randomly select students to respond to a question
- End a lesson
- Return directly to that point in the lesson where he or she stopped in the previous class meeting

What Are the Benefits of Using the Student Response Pads? Instructors can access student comprehension and retention of class instruction immediately and accurately if they use HyperGraphics with the student response pads. Suppose the instructor presents a multiple choice question on the screen at the end of a segment of a lesson. Students see an indication light illuminate on their response pads, and they have a period of time (controlled by the instructor) to press the button corresponding to the answer of their choice. Answers are tabulated by the microcomputer, and an optional aggregate bar chart of the answers selected is immediately available for viewing by the entire class. Each student's answer is also available on disk for later analysis or review. Thus, the progress of the entire class as well as each student can be tracked throughout the course.

Instructor's Manual to Accompany HyperGraphics

This manual contains teaching tips and guidelines for enhancing your classroom instruction using HyperGraphics and easy to implement installation instructions.

ClassNotes and Study Guide

The *ClassNotes and Study Guide* provides a chance for students to review and study independently. If used with Hyper-Graphics, this supplement relieves students from laborious and tedious notetaking responsibilities, freeing them to concentrate on the instruction.

# CHAPTER 1

An Introduction to Computers

An Introduction to Computers

OBJECTIVES

- Explain what a computer is and how it processes data to produce information.
- Identify the four operations of the information processing cycle: input, process, output, and storage.
- Explain how the operations of the information processing cycle are performed by computer hardware and software.
- Identify the major categories of computers.
- Describe the six elements of an information system: equipment, software, data, personnel, users and procedures.
- Identify the qualities of information.
- Describe the evolution of the computer industry.

FIGURE 1-1
This microcomputer chip contains the electronic circuits that perform the operations of a computer.

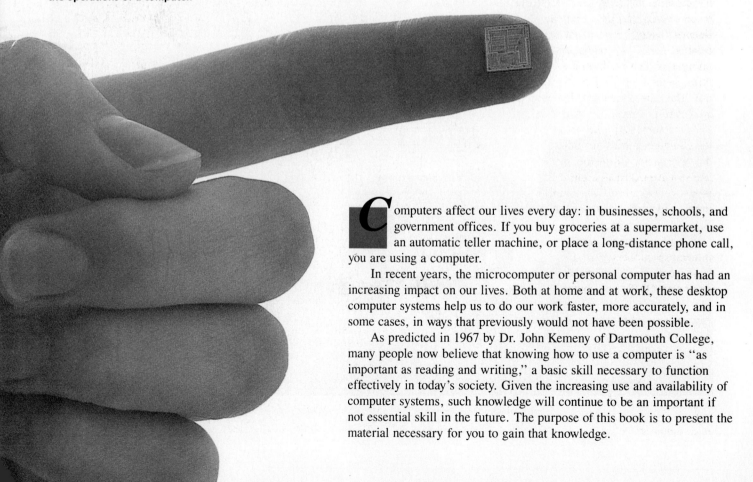

*C*omputers affect our lives every day: in businesses, schools, and government offices. If you buy groceries at a supermarket, use an automatic teller machine, or place a long-distance phone call, you are using a computer.

In recent years, the microcomputer or personal computer has had an increasing impact on our lives. Both at home and at work, these desktop computer systems help us to do our work faster, more accurately, and in some cases, in ways that previously would not have been possible.

As predicted in 1967 by Dr. John Kemeny of Dartmouth College, many people now believe that knowing how to use a computer is "as important as reading and writing," a basic skill necessary to function effectively in today's society. Given the increasing use and availability of computer systems, such knowledge will continue to be an important if not essential skill in the future. The purpose of this book is to present the material necessary for you to gain that knowledge.

WHAT IS A COMPUTER?

*T*he most obvious question related to understanding computers and their impact on our lives is, "What is a computer?" A **computer** is an electronic device, operating under the control of instructions stored in its own memory unit, that can accept data (input), process data arithmetically and logically, produce output from the processing, and store the results for future use. This definition of a computer encompasses devices of many different sizes and capabilities. While a microcomputer chip such as the one shown in Figure 1-1 may fulfill the definition of a computer, the term is generally used to describe a collection of devices that function together to process data. An example of the devices that make up a computer is shown in Figure 1-2.

WHAT DOES A COMPUTER DO?

*W*hether they are small or large, computers are capable of performing four general operations. These operations comprise the **information processing cycle**. They are input, process, output, and storage. Collectively, these operations describe the storage capabilities of a computer and the procedures that a computer performs in order to process data into information.

Data is required for all computer processing. It refers to the raw facts, including numbers and words, given to a computer during the input operation. In the processing phase, the computer manipulates the data in a predetermined manner to create information. **Information** refers to data that has been processed into a form that has meaning and is useful. The production of information by processing data on a computer is called **information processing**, or sometimes **electronic data processing**. During the output operation, the information that has been created is put into some form, such as a printed report, that people can use. The information can also be stored in an electronic format for future use.

The people who either use the computer directly or utilize the information it provides are called **computer users**, **end users**, or sometimes just simply **users**. Figure 1-3 shows a computer user and demonstrates how the four operations of the information processing cycle can take place on a personal computer. (1) The computer user inputs data by pressing the keys on the keyboard. (2) The data is then processed or manipulated by the unit called the processor.

FIGURE 1-2
The devices that comprise a microcomputer. ▶

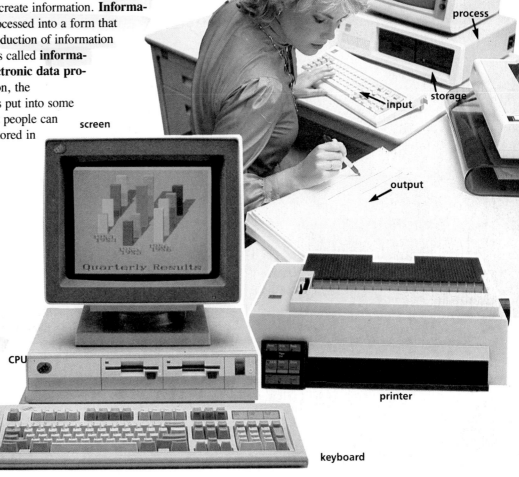

FIGURE 1-3 ⁄
The use of this personal computer illustrates the four operations of the information processing cycle: input, process, output, and storage. ▼

process

input   storage

output

screen

CPU

printer

keyboard

(3) The output or results from the processing are displayed on the screen or printed on the printer, providing information to the user. (4) Finally, the output may be stored on a disk for future reference.

WHY IS A COMPUTER SO POWERFUL?

*T*he input, process, output, and storage operations that a computer performs may seem very basic and simple. However, the computer's power derives from its ability to perform these operations very quickly, accurately, and reliably. In a computer, operations occur through the use of electronic circuits contained on small chips as shown in Figure 1-4. When data flows along these circuits it travels at close to the speed of light. This allows processing to be accomplished in billionths of a second. The electronic circuits in modern computers are very reliable and seldom fail.

Storage capability is another reason why computers are so powerful. They can store enormous amounts of data and keep that data readily available for processing. This capability combined with the factors of speed, accuracy, and reliability are why a computer is considered to be such a powerful tool for information processing.

FIGURE 1-4
Inside a computer are boards containing the chips and other electronic components that process data in billionths of a second.

HOW DOES A COMPUTER KNOW WHAT TO DO?

*F*or a computer to perform the operations in the information processing cycle, it must be given a detailed set of instructions or steps that tell it exactly what to do. These instructions can be called a **computer program**, **program instructions**, or **software**.

Before the information processing cycle for a specific job begins, the computer program corresponding to that job is stored in the computer. Once it is stored, the computer can begin to process data by executing the program's first instruction. The computer proceeds to execute one program instruction after another until the job is complete.

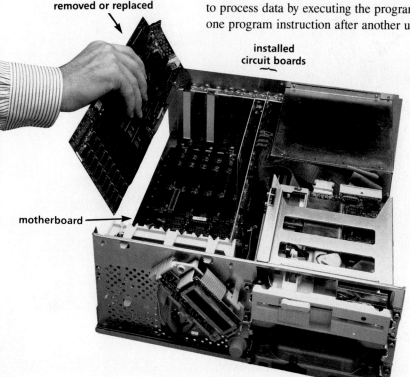

board being
removed or replaced

installed
circuit boards

motherboard

INFORMATION PROCESSING: A BUSINESS APPLICATION

*T*he example in Figure 1-5 illustrates the use of a computer to produce varied information from data contained on a sales invoice. Once the appropriate computer program has been loaded into the computer, processing occurs as follows:

1. The computer user enters data on the sales invoice into the computer.
2. The data entered into the computer is processed to create information.

3. Output from the processing is generated in three forms:

    a. A bar chart illustrates the daily sales, using a different color to represent each day of the week.

    b. A monthly sales report shows the monthly sales. The report displays the total sales for each week, together with the total sales for the month.

    c. The screen displays the name of the salesperson who generated the most sales during the month. In this example, Joan Rice had total sales of $1,250.00, which was the highest for the month.

4. The data entered and information created are stored for future use.

A key point of this example is that several different forms of information can be produced from a single set of data. Without the computer's ability to manipulate the data, the information produced would be difficult, costly, and time consuming to obtain.

FIGURE 1-5
The data contained on the sales invoices is entered into the computer. After the data is processed, information in the form of a graph, a report, and a screen display is produced.

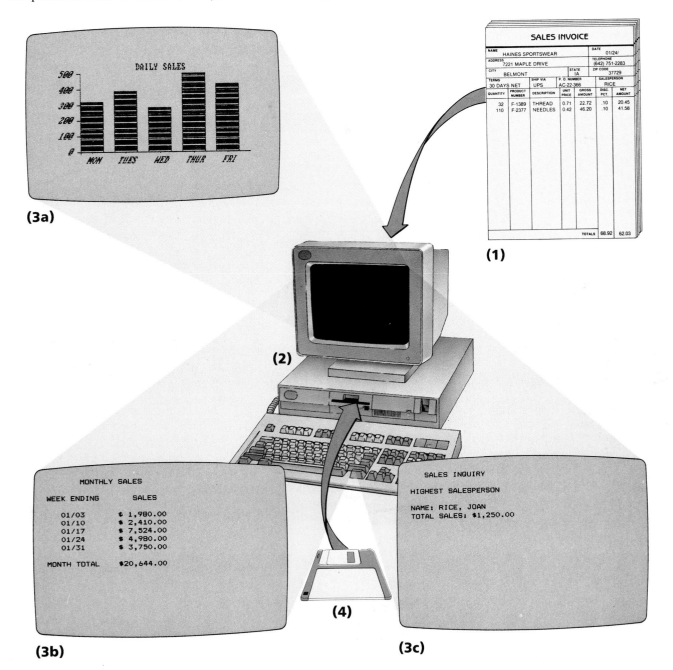

THE INFORMATION PROCESSING CYCLE

Your understanding of the information processing cycle introduced in this chapter is fundamental to understanding computers and how they process data into information. To review, the information processing cycle consists of four operations. They are: input, process, output, storage.

The first three of these operations, **input**, **process**, and **output**, describe the procedures that a computer performs in order to process data into information. The fourth operation, **storage**, describes a computer's electronic storage capability. As you learn more about computers you will see that these four operations apply to both the computer equipment and the computer software. The equipment or devices of a computer are classified according to the operations that they perform. Computer software is made up of instructions that describe how the operations are to be performed.

WHAT ARE THE COMPONENTS OF A COMPUTER?

Processing data on a computer is performed by specific equipment that is often referred to as computer **hardware** (Figure 1-6). This equipment consists of: input devices, processor unit, output devices, auxiliary storage units.

FIGURE 1-6
A computer is composed of input devices through which data is entered into the computer; the processor that processes data stored in main memory; output devices on which the results of the processing are made available; and auxiliary storage units that store data for future processing.

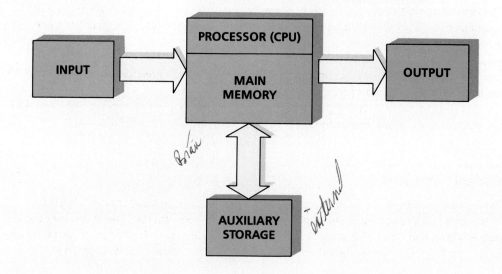

Input Devices

Input devices are used to enter data into a computer. A common input device is the **keyboard** (Figure 1-7a). As the data is entered or **keyed**, it is displayed on a screen and stored in the computer.

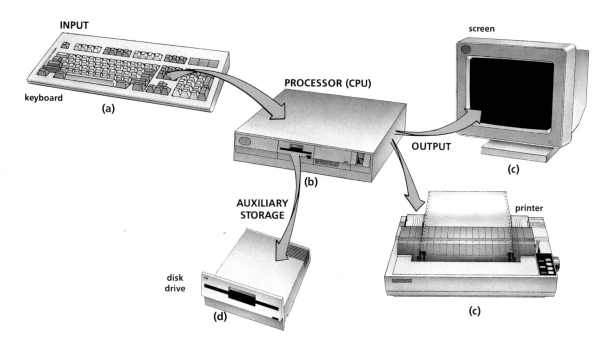

INPUT

keyboard

(a)

PROCESSOR (CPU)

(b)

AUXILIARY
STORAGE

disk
drive

(d)

screen

OUTPUT

(c)

printer

(c)

Processor Unit

The **processor unit** (Figure 1-7b) of a computer contains the electronic circuits that actually cause the processing of data to occur. All arithmetic and logical data processing takes place in the processor. Numeric calculations such as addition, subtraction, multiplication, and division are called **arithmetic operations**. Comparisons of data to see if one value is greater than, equal to, or less than another are called **logical operations**. The processor is sometimes called the **central processing unit** or **CPU**.

Main memory, also called **primary storage**, is a part of the processor unit. Main memory electronically stores data and program instructions when they are being processed.

Output Devices

Output from a computer can be presented in many forms. Where the computer is used for business applications or business-related personal applications, the two most commonly used **output devices** are the **printer** and the computer **screen** (Figure 1-7c). Other frequently used names for the screen are the **monitor** or the **CRT**, which stands for **cathode ray tube**.

Auxiliary Storage Units

Auxiliary storage units store instructions and data when they are not being used by the processor unit. A common auxiliary storage device on personal computers is a disk drive (Figure 1-7d), which stores data as magnetic spots on a small plastic disk called a **diskette** or **floppy disk**. Another auxiliary storage device is called a **hard disk drive**. Hard disk drives contain nonremovable metal disks and provide larger storage capacities than floppy disk drives.

Each computer component plays an important role. The processing unit is where the actual processing of data occurs. The input devices, output devices, and auxiliary storage units that surround the processing unit are sometimes referred to as **peripheral devices**.

connected
not part of

FIGURE 1-7
This figure illustrates the components of a computer that perform the four operations of the information processing cycle.

CATEGORIES OF COMPUTERS

Figure 1-8 shows the following four major categories of computers: microcomputers, minicomputers, mainframe computers, and supercomputers.

Computers are generally classified according to their size, speed, processing capabilities, and price. However, because of rapid changes in technology, firm definitions of these categories do not exist. This year's speed, performance, and price classification of a mainframe might fit next year's classification of a minicomputer. Even though they are not firmly defined, the categories are frequently referred to and should be generally understood.

Microcomputers (Figure 1-8a), also called **personal computers** or **micros**, are the small desktop-size systems that have become so widely used in recent years. These machines are generally priced under $10,000. This category also includes laptop, portable, and supermicro computers.

FIGURE 1-8
(a) Microcomputers are small desktop-sized computers. These machines have become so widely used that they are sometimes called "desktop appliances."

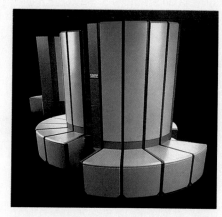

(b) Minicomputers can perform many of the functions of a mainframe computer, but on a smaller scale.

(c) Mainframe computers are large, powerful machines that can handle many users concurrently and process large volumes of data.

(d) Supercomputers are the most powerful and expensive computers.

# of people

Minicomputers (Figure 1-8b) are more powerful than microcomputers and can support a number of users performing different tasks. Originally developed to perform specific tasks such as engineering calculations, their use grew rapidly as their performance and capabilities increased. These systems can cost from approximately $25,000 up to several hundred thousand dollars. The most powerful "minis" are called superminicomputers.

size price speed # of users —

Mainframe computers (Figure 1-8c) are large systems that can handle numerous users, store large amounts of data, and process transactions at a very high rate. Mainframes usually require a specialized environment including separate air conditioning and electrical power. Raised flooring is often built to accommodate the many cables connecting the system components underneath. The price range for mainframes is from several hundred thousand dollars to several million dollars.

all over country

Supercomputers (Figure 1-8d) are the most powerful category of computers and, accordingly, the most expensive. The ability of these systems to process hundreds of millions of instructions per second is used for such applications as weather forecasting, space exploration, and other jobs requiring long, complex calculations. These machines cost several million dollars.

large powerful.

COMPUTER SOFTWARE

As previously mentioned, a computer is directed by a series of instructions called a computer program (see Figure 1-9), which specifies the sequence of operations to be performed. To do this, the program must be stored in the main memory of the computer. Computer programs are commonly referred to as **computer software**.

COMPUTER PROGRAM LISTING

```
100 REM TELLIST           SEPTEMBER 22          SHELLY/CASHMAN
110                                                          REM
120 REM THIS PROGRAM DISPLAYS THE NAME, TELEPHONE AREA CODE
130 REM AND PHONE NUMBER OF INDIVIDUALS.
140                                                          REM
150 REM VARIABLE NAMES:
160 REM    A.....AREA CODE
170 REM    T$....TELEPHONE NUMBER
180 REM    N$....NAME
190                                                          REM
200 REM ***** DATA TO BE PROCESSED *****
210                                                          REM
220 DATA 714, "749-2138", "SAM HORN"
230 DATA 213, "663-1271", "SUE NUNN"
240 DATA 212, "999-1193", "BOB PELE"
250 DATA 312, "979-4418", "ANN SITZ"
260 DATA 999, "999-9999", "END OF FILE"
270                                                          REM
280 REM ***** PROCESSING *****
290                                                          REM
300 READ A, T$, N$
310                                                          REM
320 WHILE N$<> "END OF FILE"
330    PRINT N$, A, T$
340    READ A, T$, N$
350 WEND
360                                                          REM
370 PRINT " "
380 PRINT "END OF TELEPHONE LISTING"
390 END
```

FIGURE 1-9
A computer program contains instructions that specify the sequence of operations to be performed. This program is written in a language called BASIC. It allows the user to generate a telephone directory of names, area codes, and telephone numbers.

Many instructions can be used to direct a computer to perform a specific task. For example, some instructions allow data to be entered from a keyboard and stored in main computer memory; some instructions allow data in main memory to be used in calculations, such as adding a series of numbers to obtain a total; some instructions compare two values stored in main memory and direct the computer to perform alternative operations based on the results of the comparison; and some instructions direct the computer to print a report, display information on the screen, draw a color graph on a screen, or store data on a disk.

Computer programs are written by people with specialized training. They determine the instructions necessary to process the data and place the instructions in the correct sequence so that the desired results will occur. Complex programs may require hundreds or even thousands of program instructions.

Computer software is the key to productive use of computers. Without the proper software, a computer cannot perform the desired tasks. With the correct software, a computer can become a valuable tool.

Application Software Packages

Most end users do not write their own programs. In large corporations, the information processing department develops programs for unique company applications. In addition, programs required for common business and personal applications can be purchased from software vendors or stores that sell computer products (Figure 1-10). Purchased programs are often referred to as **application software packages** or simply **software packages**.

Microcomputer Applications Software Packages

Personal computer users often use application software packages. The four most commonly used packages, shown in Figure 1-11, are: word processing software, electronic spreadsheet software, computer graphics software, and database software.

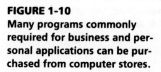

FIGURE 1-10
Many programs commonly required for business and personal applications can be purchased from computer stores.

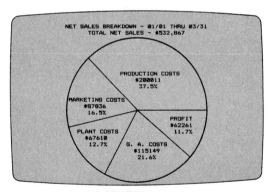

```
LETTER                                      01/14
Space 01   Line 07   Page 01      Letter to Johnson
........1.........2.........3.........4.........5
January 14

Harold A. Johnson
Yonnet Mfg. Co.
3342 Halliard Ave.
Hillsboro, UT 77531

Dear Mr. Johnson:

    I have received your letter concerning the
YT-9975 metal fasteners. We are interested in
testing the part. Would you please send one dozen
of the YT-9975 fasteners. Upon receipt, we shall
begin testing and let you know our decision in
two weeks.

          Sincerely,


          James L. Honnecut
          Vice President, Manufacturing
```

(a) word processing

```
        JOHNSON MANUFACTURING CORPORATION
                 BUDGET FORECAST

          FOR THE PERIOD 01/01 THRU 03/31

ITEM            JAN       FEB       MAR      TOTAL

SALES         112560    213450    211347    537357
RETURNS         1778       331      2381      4490
NET SALES     110782    213119    208966    532867

PROD COST      42773     85380     71858    200011
MARKETING      13587     36287     38042     87836
PLANT          21889     22229     23492     67610
G.A.           31227     41783     42139    115149
TOTAL COSTS   109396    185679    175531    470606

GROSS PROFIT    1386     27440     33435     62261
PROFIT %        .013      .129      .160      .117
```

(b) electronic spreadsheet

```
      NET SALES BREAKDOWN - 01/01 THRU 03/31
           TOTAL NET SALES - $532,867

                  PRODUCTION COSTS
                     $200011
                      37.5%
   MARKETING COSTS
     $87836
     16.5%
                              PROFIT
                              $62261
                              11.7%
      PLANT COSTS
       $67610
       12.7%      G. A. COSTS
                   $115149
                    21.6%
```

(c) computer graphics

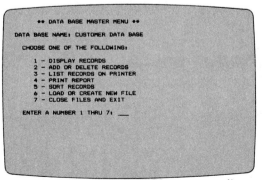

```
      ** DATA BASE MASTER MENU **

DATA BASE NAME: CUSTOMER DATA BASE

  CHOOSE ONE OF THE FOLLOWING:

     1 - DISPLAY RECORDS
     2 - ADD OR DELETE RECORDS
     3 - LIST RECORDS ON PRINTER
     4 - PRINT REPORT
     5 - SORT RECORDS
     6 - LOAD OR CREATE NEW FILE
     7 - CLOSE FILES AND EXIT

  ENTER A NUMBER 1 THRU 7: __
```

(d) database

FIGURE 1-11
Commonly used microcomputer applications software packages.

(a) **Word processing** is used to write letters, memos, and other documents. As the user keys in words and letters, they display on the screen. The user can easily add, delete, and change any text entered until the document is exactly as desired. When the text is correct, the user can save the document on auxiliary storage and can also print it on a printer.

(b) **Electronic spreadsheet** software is frequently used by people who work with numbers. The user enters the data and the formulas to be used on the data; then the program applies the formulas to the data and calculates the results. A powerful feature of electronic spreadsheet software is the ability to ask "what if" questions by changing the data and quickly recalculating the new results. For example, the user could direct the software to recalculate the profits based on a percentage increase in sales and a percentage decrease in costs.

(c) **Computer graphics** software provides the ability to transform a series of numeric values into graphic form for easier analysis and interpretation. In this example, the cost values from the electronic spreadsheet have been transformed into a pie chart. The chart makes it easier to see the various cost elements. Using graphics software, these graphs can be produced in seconds instead of the days that were required for a graphic artist to hand draw each graph.

(d) **Database** software allows the user to enter, retrieve, and update data in an organized and efficient manner. This screen shows a menu created with a database package. A menu is a list of processes that can be selected by the user and then performed by the program. The user chooses the number corresponding to the processing desired. In this example, the user can display records from the database, add or delete records, list and print data on a printer, sort records, and perform other database maintenance functions.

Word processing software (Figure 1-11a) is used to create and print documents that would otherwise be prepared on a typewriter. A key advantage of word processing software is its ability to make changes easily in documents, such as correcting spelling, changing margins, and adding, deleting, or relocating entire paragraphs. These changes would be difficult and time consuming to make on a typewriter. Once created, the documents can be printed quickly and accurately.

Electronic spreadsheet software (Figure 1-11b) allows the user to add, subtract, and perform user-defined calculations on rows and columns of numbers. These numbers can be changed and the **spreadsheet** quickly recalculates the new results. Electronic spreadsheet software eliminates the tedious recalculations required with manual methods.

Graphics software (Figure 1-11c) converts numbers and text into graphic output that visually conveys the relationships of the data. Some graphics software allows the use of color to further enhance the visual presentation. Line, bar, and pie charts are the most frequent forms of graphics output. Spreadsheet information is frequently converted into a graphic form, such as these charts. In fact, graphics capabilities are included in many spreadsheet packages.

Database software (Figure 1-11d) allows the user to enter, retrieve, and update data in an organized and efficient manner. These software packages have flexible inquiry and reporting capabilities that allow users to access the data in different ways.

A Typical Application: Budget Spreadsheet

FIGURE 1-12
After the floppy disk is inserted in the disk drive, the spreadsheet program is copied into main memory. The program illustrated in this example is shown as English statements for ease of understanding.

Electronic spreadsheets are one of the most widely used software applications. In the following example, a user develops a budget spreadsheet for the first quarter of a year. The user enters the revenues and the costs for the first three months of the year. Then the spreadsheet program calculates the total revenues and total costs, the profit for each month (calculated by subtracting costs from revenues), and the profit percentage (obtained by dividing the profit by the revenues). In addition, the spreadsheet program calculates the total profit and the total profit percentage.

The diagrams in Figures 1-12, 1-13, and 1-14 show the steps that occur in order to obtain the spreadsheet output. A more complete description of these steps follows.

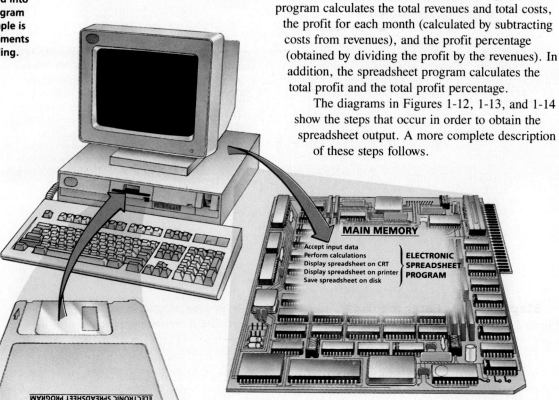

MAIN MEMORY

Accept input data
Perform calculations
Display spreadsheet on CRT
Display spreadsheet on printer
Save spreadsheet on disk

ELECTRONIC SPREADSHEET PROGRAM

ELECTRONIC SPREADSHEET PROGRAM

Loading the Program For processing to occur, a computer program must first be stored in the main memory of the computer. The process of getting the program into memory is called loading the program. The spreadsheet program in this example is stored on a floppy disk. To load the program into the main memory of the computer, a copy of the spreadsheet program is transferred from the floppy disk into main memory.

In Figure 1-12, the floppy disk on which the program is stored is inserted into the floppy disk drive. The user then issues the command to load the program from the floppy disk into main memory. After the program is loaded into main memory, the user directs the computer to begin executing the program.

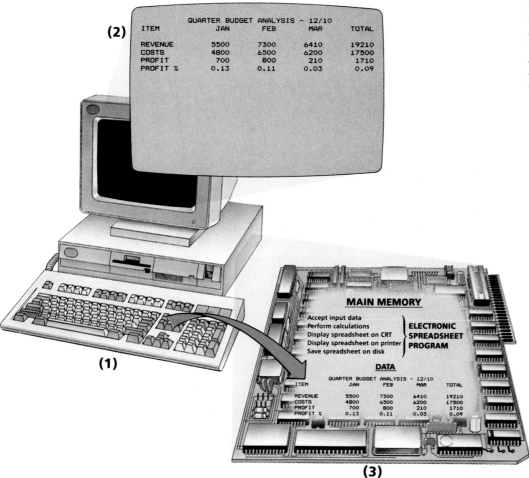

FIGURE 1-13
In this example, the user enters a report heading, column and row headings, the revenues for January, February, and March, and the costs for the three months.

Step 1—Input: Enter the Data The first step in the program is to input the data (Figure 1-13). This is accomplished by using a keyboard. As the data is entered on the keyboard (1), it is displayed on the screen (2) and stored in main memory (3).

The data for this application consists of not only the numbers on which calculations are to be performed, but also some words indicating the contents of each of the columns and rows on the screen.

Step 2—Process: Perform the Calculations As Figure 1-14 shows, the user has entered the data (1) and the program will direct the processor to perform the required calculations (2). In this example, the program calculates the profit for each month, the total revenue, costs, and profit for the quarter, the profit percent for each month, and the total profit percent.

FIGURE 1-14
After the data has been entered, the program specifies the following processing steps: (1) All calculations are performed. (2) The entire spreadsheet, with the calculation results, is displayed on the screen. (3) The spreadsheet is printed on the printer. (4) The spreadsheet data and results are stored on auxiliary storage.

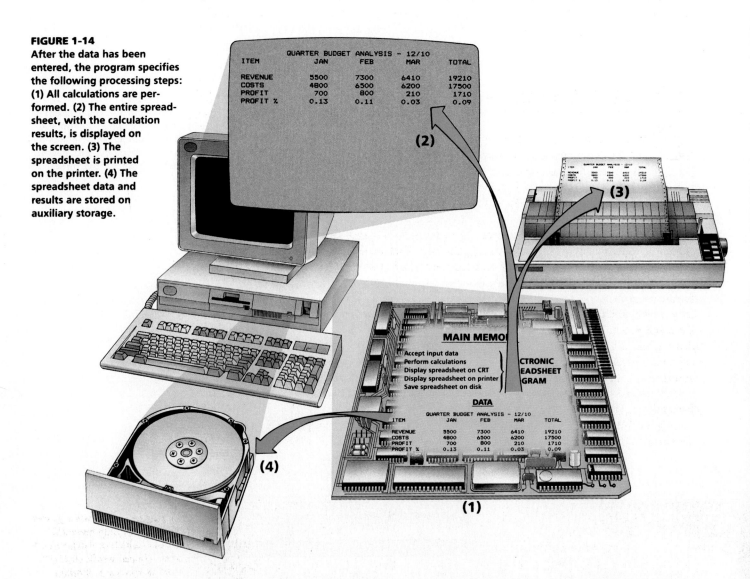

The preceding operations illustrate the calculating ability of computers. Whenever any calculations are performed on data, the data must be stored in main memory. The results of the calculations are also stored in main memory. If desired, the program can issue instructions to store the results on an auxiliary storage device, such as a hard or floppy disk.

Step 3—Output: Display the Results After the calculations have been completed, the program specifies that the spreadsheet, with the results of the calculations, is to be displayed on the screen. The program also specifies that the results are to be printed on the printer (3). When this instruction is executed, the spreadsheet is printed on paper so that the results of the processing can be used by someone other than the computer user.

Step 4—Storage: Save the Program and Data   The spreadsheet is also stored on a disk, in this example a hard disk, so that at a later time it can be retrieved and utilized again (4).

WHAT ARE THE ELEMENTS OF AN INFORMATION SYSTEM?

*O*btaining useful and timely information from computer processing requires more than just the equipment and software described so far. Other elements required for successful information processing include accurate data, trained information systems personnel, knowledgeable users, and documented procedures.

The equipment must be reliable and capable of handling the expected work load. The software must have been carefully developed and tested, and the data entered to be processed must be accurate. If the data is incorrect, the resulting information produced from it will be incorrect. Properly trained data processing personnel are required to run most medium and large computer systems. Users are sometimes overlooked as an important element of an information system, but with expanding computer use, users are taking increasing responsibility for the successful operation of information systems. This includes responsibility for the accuracy of both input and output information. In addition, users are taking a more active role in the development of computer applications. They work closely with information systems department personnel in the development of computer applications that relate to their areas of expertise. Finally, all information processing applications should have documented procedures covering not only the computer operations but any other related procedures as well.

To summarize, the six elements of an information system are: equipment, software, data, personnel, users, and procedures.

Figure 1-15 shows an example of each of the elements. The following section illustrates the elements as they occur in a large multiuser computer environment.

FIGURE 1-15
An information system requires (1) computer equipment; (2) software, which runs the equipment; (3) data, which the computer manipulates; people, including both (4) computer personnel who manage the equipment and (5) users who use the information that the equipment produces; and finally (6) procedures, which help the entire system run efficiently.

A TOUR OF AN INFORMATION SYSTEMS DEPARTMENT

Many organizations use computers that concurrently process requests from more than one user. For example, one or more accounts receivable clerks could be entering cash receipts at the same time that one or more accounts payable clerks are entering invoices. Such systems are usually referred to as **multiuser computers**. Multiuser computers are generally under the control of a separate department of the company called the **information systems department**, the **data processing department**, or sometimes just the **computer department**.

The discussion that follows illustrates the elements of an information system by touring a typical information systems department.

Equipment

We identified the hardware components of a computer system as input devices, processor, output devices, and auxiliary storage. These general classifications apply to the multiuser computer system discussed in this example.

FIGURE 1-16
A terminal contains a keyboard and a screen. The screen displays the data entered via the keyboard. ▼

Input Devices   The primary input device on a multiuser system is a terminal (Figure 1-16). A **terminal** is a device consisting of a keyboard and a screen, which is connected through a communication line or cable to a computer.

Processor   The processor unit of a multiuser computer (Figure 1-17) allocates computer resources to the programs that are being processed. Modern computer processors are so fast that they can usually handle numerous users and still provide very quick response time.

Output Devices   The most commonly used output devices for a multiuser computer are a printer (Figure 1-18) and a terminal (Figure 1-19). When large volumes of printed output must be produced, high-speed printers are used. The terminal can display both text material and graphics in either monochrome or color.

◀ **FIGURE 1-17**
This mainframe computer processes data for numerous users. Such a computer is usually placed in a room designed specifically for the machine. Special air conditioning, humidity control, electrical wiring, and flooring are required for many of these installations.

Auxiliary Storage   The two major types of auxiliary storage for a multiuser computer are magnetic disk and magnetic tape.

Magnetic disk is the most widely used auxiliary storage on multiuser computers. When using magnetic disk, data is recorded on an oxide-coated metal platter (the disk) as a series of magnetic spots. Disk drives can store data on either removable disks or fixed disks. **Removable disks** refer to disk packs that can be taken out of the disk drive. In Figure 1-20, the blue containers for the removable disk packs can be seen sitting on the disk drives. **Fixed disk** drives utilize nonremovable disk packs enclosed in sealed units that prevent contamination of the disk surface.

Magnetic tape (Figure 1-21) stores data as magnetic spots on one-quarter to one-half-inch tape on cassettes or reels. On systems with disk drives, tape is most often used to store data that does not have to be accessed frequently. Another common use of tape is for backup storage. The contents of the disk drives are regularly copied to tape to protect against data loss such as in the case of disk drive failure.

◄ FIGURE 1-18
High-speed printers are necessary to print the large volume of reports generated by a multiuser computer system.

FIGURE 1-19
A terminal is both an input and an output device. In this picture, the user is viewing a color graphics display. ▼

◄ FIGURE 1-20
Removable disk packs are mounted on the disk drives in this picture. The multiple disk drives shown here are common in large computer installations.

FIGURE 1-21
This photo shows a magnetic tape drive that uses reels of half-inch tape. Tape is often used to back up the data stored on disk drives. ▼

When a disk pack or tape is not in use, it is stored in a **data library** (Figure 1-22). These disk packs and tapes must be catalogued so that when they are required, they can be located quickly and taken to the computer room for use.

FIGURE 1-22
The data library stores disk packs and tapes when they are not in use.

Software

The information systems department keeps its software on either disks or tapes. Once the disk or tape containing the software is mounted on the disk or tape drive, the processor can run the software by reading it into main memory and executing the program instructions. Depending on the amount of disk storage available and how frequently a program is used, some software applications are always available for processing. An example would be order processing software that enters orders into the computer while the sales clerk is on the phone with the customer. Because a phone call can come in at any time, this software application must always be available for processing.

Data

Data exists throughout an organization and comes to the information systems department in many forms. Often data is in the form of **source documents**, which are original documents such as sales invoices. Sometimes there are no source documents. Then data can be entered directly into the system by users or it can be entered by machines that read special codes or labels. In all cases, the accuracy of the data is important because it will affect the usefulness of the resulting information.

Personnel

In order to implement applications on a computer, the information systems department usually employs people who have specialized training in computers and information processing. These employees may include data entry personnel to prepare and enter data into the computer; computer operators to run the computer; programmers to write specialized programs; systems analysts to design the software applications; a database administrator to control and manage data; and management to oversee the use of the computer.

Data Entry Personnel Data entry personnel (Figure 1-23) are responsible for entering large volumes of data into the computer system. Data is usually entered on terminals from source documents.

Computer Operators

The **computer operator** is responsible for a number of different tasks. When the computer is running, messages are displayed on the **operator's console** (Figure 1-24) indicating the status of the system. For example, a message may indicate that a special form, such as a check, must be placed in a printer. The operator responds to these messages in order to keep the computer running. In many instances, more than one operator is required to run a large computer.

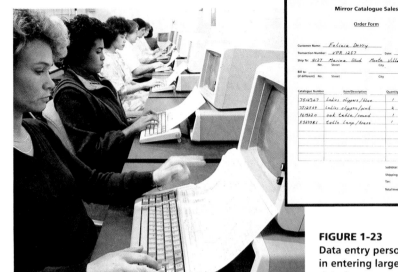

FIGURE 1-23
Data entry personnel specialize in entering large amounts of data from source documents.

Computer Programmers Computer programmers design, write, test, and implement specialized programs that process data on a computer. The design specifications from the systems analyst tell the programmer what processing needs to be accomplished. It is the programmer's job to develop the specific programs of computer instructions that process the data and create the required information. The analyst specifies "what" is to be done; the programmer decides "how" to do it.

FIGURE 1-24
The console allows the computer operator to monitor the processing.

Systems Analysts Systems analysts are called upon to review current or proposed applications within a company to determine if the applications should be implemented using a computer. Applications are considered for computer implementation if, among other things, productivity can be increased or more timely information can be generated to aid in the management of the company. If an application is to be "computerized," the analyst studies the application to identify the data used, how the data is processed, and other aspects of the application that are pertinent to the new system. The analyst then designs the new system by defining the data required for the computer application, developing the manner in which the data will be processed in the new system, and specifying the associated activities and procedures necessary to implement the application using the computer. Analysts work closely with both the people who will be using and benefiting from the new system and the programmers in the information systems department who will be writing the computer programs (Figure 1-25).

Database Administrator An important function within the information systems department is the management of data. In many companies, this task is the responsibility of the **database administrator**. Among other things, the database administrator must develop procedures to ensure that correct data is entered into the system, that confidential company data is not lost or stolen, that access to company data is restricted to those who need the data, and that data is available when needed. This function is very important to most companies where billions of pieces of data are processed on the computer, and the loss or misappropriation of that data could be detrimental to business.

Information Systems Department Management Management within an information systems department is found at varying levels, depending on the size and complexity of the department. Most information systems departments have operations management, systems management, programming management, and a manager of the entire department. The **systems manager** oversees the activities in the systems analysis and design area of the department. The **programming manager** is in charge of all programmers within the department. Each of the previously mentioned managers may also have **project managers** within their area. The **operations manager** oversees the operational aspects of the department, including the scheduling, maintenance, and operation of the equipment. The information systems department manager is in charge of the entire department and may have the title **vice president of information systems** or **chief information officer**.

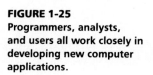

FIGURE 1-25
Programmers, analysts, and users all work closely in developing new computer applications.

Users

Users interact with the information systems department in several ways. They are often the first to request that a specific application be computerized. When a systems analyst is assigned to study the application, the analyst will rely on the users' knowledge of the requirements to determine if computerization is feasible. Once an application is implemented, users usually maintain an ongoing relationship with the information systems department. They may request special reports or processing and make suggestions about improving the application.

Procedures

Written procedures are an important part of any information system. Procedures should be documented for all steps in the processing cycle, including those steps that are not computerized. Accurate, up-to-date procedures minimize processing errors, reduce training time for new employees, and serve as a guide for future changes to the application.

Summary of the Tour of an Information Systems Department

During the tour of the information systems department we have seen the six elements of an information system: equipment, software, data, personnel, users, and procedures. Each of these elements directly affects an organization's ability to successfully process data into useful information.

SUMMARY OF AN INTRODUCTION TO COMPUTERS

*T*his chapter presented a broad introduction to concepts and terminology that are related to computers. You now have an understanding of what a computer is, how it processes data into information, and which elements are necessary for a successful information system. The following photo essay is a time line that shows the evolution of modern computers.

CHAPTER SUMMARY

1. A **computer** is an electronic device, operating under the control of instructions stored in its own memory unit, that can accept data (input), process data arithmetically and logically, produce output from the processing, and store the results for future use.
2. A computer can perform **input**, **process**, **output**, and **storage** operations. These operations are called the **information processing cycle**.
3. **Data** refers to the raw facts, including numbers and words, that are processed on a computer.
4. **Information** is data that has been processed into a form that has meaning and is useful.
5. The production of information by processing data on a computer is called **information processing**.
6. **Computer users** are the people who either directly use the computer or utilize the information it provides.
7. A computer is a powerful tool because it is reliable and can process data quickly and accurately.
8. A **computer program** is a detailed set of instructions that tells the computer exactly what to do.

9. Computer processing can produce many different forms of information from a single set of data.
10. Processing data on a computer is performed by computer equipment including input devices, the processor unit, output devices, and auxiliary storage units. Computer equipment is often referred to as **hardware**.
11. **Input devices** are used to enter data into a computer.
12. The **processor unit** contains the electronic circuits that cause processing to take place.
13. **Arithmetic operations** are numeric calculations such as addition, subtraction, multiplication and division that take place in the processor.
14. **Logical operations** are comparisons of data in the processor to see if one value is greater than, equal to, or less than another value.
15. The processor is sometimes called the **central processing unit (CPU)**.
16. **Main memory** consists of components that electronically store data and program instructions.
17. **Output devices** are used to print or display data and information.
18. **Auxiliary storage units** are used to store program instructions and data when they are not being used in the main memory of the computer.
19. The four major categories of computers are microcomputers, minicomputers, mainframes, and supercomputers.
20. Types of **microcomputers** include laptop, portable, desktop, and supermicro computers.
21. **Minicomputers** address the needs of users who want more processing power than a microcomputer but do not need the power of a mainframe. Minicomputers can support a number of users performing different tasks.
22. **Mainframe** computers are large systems that can handle numerous users, store large amounts of data, and process transactions at a very high rate.
23. **Supercomputers**, the most powerful and expensive category of computers, can process hundreds of millions of instructions per second and perform long, complex calculations.
24. **Computer software** is another name for computer programs.
25. A computer program must first be loaded into main memory before it can be executed.
26. Programs purchased from computer stores or software vendors are called **application software packages**.
27. Four commonly used personal computer software packages are word processing, electronic spreadsheet, graphics, and database software.
28. **Word processing software** is used to create and print documents.
29. **Electronic spreadsheet software** performs calculations on rows and columns of numeric data based on formulas entered by the user.
30. **Graphics software** provides the ability to transform numbers and text into a graphic format.
31. **Database software** allows the user to enter, retrieve, and update data efficiently.
32. The elements of an information system are equipment, software, data, personnel, users and procedures.
33. **Multiuser computers** can concurrently process requests from more than one user.
34. A **terminal**, consisting of a keyboard and screen, is the most commonly used input device for a large computer.
35. Modern computer processors are so fast that they can usually handle numerous users and still provide very quick response time.
36. The most commonly used output devices for large computers are terminals and high-speed printers.
37. Auxiliary storage devices used on a large computer include **magnetic disk** and **magnetic tape**.
38. A **data library** stores disk packs and tapes when they are not in use.
39. Data can be entered directly into the computer by users or by machines.
40. **Source documents** are original documents, such as sales invoices, from which data can be entered.
41. **Data entry personnel** prepare and enter data into the computer.
42. **Computer operators** run the computer equipment and monitor processing operations.
43. **Computer programmers** design, write, test, and implement programs that process data on a computer.
44. **Systems analysts** review and design computer applications. Analysts work closely with users and programmers.
45. A **database administrator** is responsible for managing a company's data.
46. Management within an information systems department includes a **systems manager**, **programming manager**, **operations manager**, and a department manager, sometimes called the **vice president of information systems** or **chief information officer**.
47. **Users** play an important role in the development of computer applications.
48. Procedures should be documented for all steps in the processing cycle, including those steps that are not computerized.

KEY TERMS

Application software packages *1.10*
Arithmetic operations *1.7*
Auxiliary storage units *1.7*
Cathode ray tube (CRT) *1.7*
Central processing unit (CPU) *1.7*
Chief information officer *1.20*
Computer *1.3*
Computer department *1.16*
Computer operator *1.19*
Computer program *1.4*
Computer programmers *1.19*
Computer software *1.9*
Computer users *1.3*
CPU (central processing unit) *1.7*
CRT (cathode ray tube) *1.7*
Data *1.3*
Data entry personnel *1.19*
Data library *1.18*
Data processing department *1.16*
Database administrator *1.20*
Database software *1.12*
Diskette *1.7*
Electronic data processing *1.3*
Electronic spreadsheet software *1.12*
End users *1.3*

Fixed disk *1.17*
Floppy disk *1.7*
Graphics software *1.12*
Hard disk drive *1.7*
Hardware *1.6*
Information *1.3*
Information processing *1.3*
Information processing cycle *1.3*
Information systems department *1.16*
Input *1.6*
Input devices *1.6*
Keyboard *1.6*
Keyed *1.6*
Logical operations *1.7*
Magnetic disk *1.17*
Magnetic tape *1.17*
Main memory *1.7*
Mainframe *1.9*
Micro *1.8*
Microcomputers *1.8*
Minicomputer *1.9*
Monitor *1.7*
Multiuser computers *1.16*
Operations manager *1.20*
Operator's console *1.19*

Output *1.6*
Output devices *1.7*
Peripheral devices *1.7*
Personal computers *1.8*
Primary storage *1.7*
Printer *1.7*
Process *1.6*
Processor unit *1.7*
Program instructions *1.4*
Programming manager *1.20*
Project managers *1.20*
Removable disks *1.17*
Screen *1.7*
Software *1.4*
Software packages *1.10*
Source documents *1.18*
Spreadsheet *1.12*
Storage *1.6*
Supercomputers *1.9*
Systems analysts *1.20*
Systems manager *1.20*
Terminal *1.16*
Users *1.3*
Vice president of information systems *1.20*
Word processing software *1.12*

REVIEW QUESTIONS

1. What is the definition of a computer?
2. Identify the four operations a computer can perform, and explain operation.
3. What is data? What is information? How is information derived from data?
4. What is the information processing cycle?
5. What are the four specific hardware units found on a computer? Describe each of them.
6. What is the difference between main memory and auxiliary storage? Why are both necessary?
7. What is computer software? Why is it critical to the operation of a computer?
8. Identify the four software packages most often used with personal computers.
9. Describe the processing of a typical application on a personal computer.
10. What are the six elements of an information system?
11. Identify some of the differences among microcomputers, minicomputers, mainframe computers, and supercomputers.
12. Who are some of the personnel who work in an information systems department?
13. What is the role of a systems analyst? How does that position differ from the job of a computer programmer?
14. What is the user's role in an information system?
15. List the key developments in the evolution of the modern computer.

CONTROVERSIAL ISSUES

1. When Dr. Kemeny made his prediction in 1967 that learning how to use a computer would be as important as learning how to read and write, few people had access to computers. Since that time, millions of computers have been sold. Do you feel that it is necessary for all students to study computers and their uses? If so, at what grade levels: elementary school, high school, or college?

2. Some people believe that the computer is replacing people in the workforce. Based on what you have learned about computers in Chapter 1, do you think this is a valid statement, or do you think that computers help people do a better job?

3. You learned in this chapter that accurate data is required in order to provide meaningful information. What are some of the consequences if management decisions are based on incorrect data? What obligation does management have to ensure that decisions are based on correct data?

RESEARCH PROJECTS

1. Write or call a manufacturer of a mini or mainframe computer (IBM, Honeywell, DEC, HP, etc.) and ask for a brochure describing one of their popular models. Prepare a report for your class based on what you learned.

2. Prepare a report for your class describing the use of computers at your school. You may focus on a single department or prepare a general report about computer use throughout the school.

3. Prepare a detailed report on an individual who made a contribution to the history of the computer industry.

The Evolution of the Computer Industry

The electronic computer industry began about fifty years ago. This time line summarizes the major events in the evolution of the computer industry.

During the years 1943 to 1946, Dr. John W. Mauchly and J. Presper Eckert, Jr., completed the ENIAC (Electronic Numerical Integrator and Computer), the first large-scale electronic digital computer. The ENIAC weighed thirty tons, contained 18,000 vacuum tubes, and occupied a thirty by fifty foot space.

In 1952, the public awareness of computers increased when the UNIVAC I correctly predicted that Dwight D. Eisenhower would win the presidential election after analyzing only 5% of the tallied vote.

| 1930 | 1937 | 1940 | 1945 | 1950 | 1952 |

Dr. John V. Atanasoff and his assistant, Clifford Berry, designed and began to build the first electronic digital computer during the winter of 1937-38. Their machine, the Atanasoff-Berry-Computer or ABC, provided the foundation for the next advances in electronic digital computers.

Dr. John von Neumann is credited with writing a report in 1945 describing a number of new hardware concepts and how to use stored programs. This brilliant breakthrough laid the foundation for the digital computers that have been built since then.

In 1951-52, after much discussion, IBM made the decision to add computers to their line of business equipment products. This led IBM to become a dominant force in the computer industry.

1.25

FORTRAN (FORmula TRANslator) was introduced in 1957. This programming language proved that efficient, easy-to-use computer languages could be developed. FORTRAN is still in use.

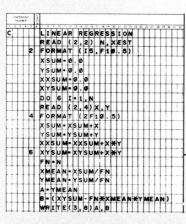

In 1952, Dr. Grace Hopper, a mathematician and commodore in the U.S. Navy, wrote a paper describing how to program a computer with symbolic notation instead of the detailed machine language that had been used.

Dr. Hopper became instrumental in developing high-level languages such as COBOL, a business applications language that was introduced in 1960. COBOL uses English-like phrases and can be run on most brands of computers, making it one of the most widely used languages in the world.

By 1959, over 200 programming languages had been created.

1952   1955   1957   1958   1959   1960

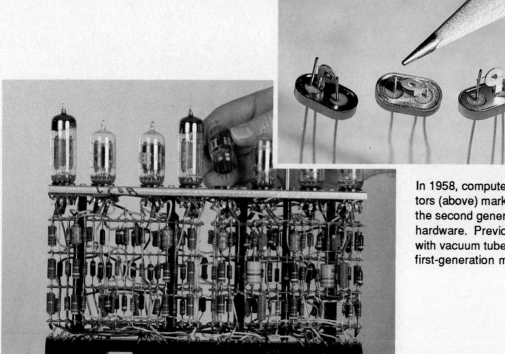

In 1958, computers built with transistors (above) marked the beginning of the second generation of computer hardware. Previous computers built with vacuum tubes (left) are called first-generation machines.

Dr. Ted Hoff of Intel Corporation is credited with developing the first microprocessor or microprogrammable computer chip, the Intel 4004, in 1969.

Third-generation computers were introduced in 1964. Their controlling circuitry is stored on chips. The family of IBM System/360 computers were the first third-generation machines.

1964   **1965**   **1968**   **1969**

From 1958 to 1964, it is estimated, the number of computers in the U.S. grew from 2,500 to 18,000.

The 1960s saw the birth of the software industry. In 1968, Computer Science Corporation became the first software company to be listed on the New York Stock Exchange.

Digital Equipment Corporation (DEC) introduced the first minicomputer in 1965.

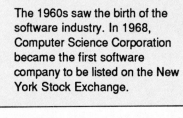

In 1969, under pressure from the industry, IBM announced that some of its software would be priced separately from the computer hardware. This "unbundling" opened up the industry to emerging software firms.

In 1965, Dr. John Kemeny of Dartmouth led the development of the BASIC programming language. BASIC is the most commonly used language on microcomputers. More people know how to program in BASIC than any other language.

Fourth-generation computers emerged in 1970. These machines were built with chips that utilized LSI (large-scale integration). The chips used in 1965 could contain as many as 1,000 circuits. By 1970, the LSI chip could contain as many as 15,000.

The VisiCalc spreadsheet program written by Dan Bricklin and Bob Frankston was introduced in 1979. This product was originally written to run on Apple II computers. Together, VisiCalc and Apple II computers became rapidly successful in the business community. Most people consider VisiCalc to be the single most important reason why microcomputers gained acceptance in the business world.

1970　　　　　　　　　　　**1975**　　　　　　　　　　　**1980**

The MITS, Inc., Altair computer was the first commercially successful microcomputer. It sold in kit form for less than $500.

In 1976, Steve Jobs and Steve Wozniak built the first Apple computer.

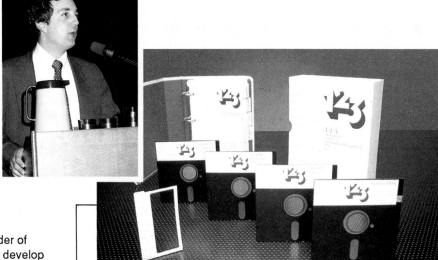

In 1980, IBM offered Bill Gates, the founder of Microsoft Corporation, the opportunity to develop the operating system for the soon-to-be-announced IBM personal computer. Microsoft developed MS-DOS, the product that helped them achieve tremendous growth and success.

The Lotus 1-2-3 integrated software package, developed by Mitch Kapor, was introduced in 1983. It combined spreadsheet, graphics, and database programs in one package.

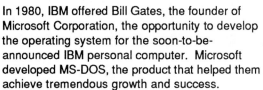

| 1981 | 1982 | 1983 | 1985 |

It is estimated that 313,000 microcomputers were sold in 1981. In 1982, the number jumped to 3,275,000.

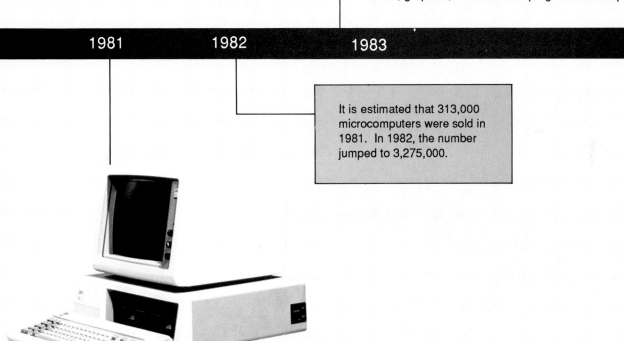

The IBM PC was introduced in 1981, signaling IBM's entrance in the microcomputer marketplace. The IBM PC quickly garnered the largest share of the personal computer market and became the personal computer most often used in business.

The IBM Application System 400, introduced in 1988, made a significant impact on the minicomputer and main-frame market, allowing users to expand their computing capabilities more easily.

1987   1988   1990

OS/2, an IBM microcomputer operating sys-tem, will enable microcomputers to be as powerful as many of today's minicomputers. Further, it will allow microcomputers to become multiuser systems, that is, multiple keyboards and screens can be attached to the same computer.

Several microcomputers utilizing the powerful Intel 80386 microprocessor were introduced in 1987. These machines can handle processing that previously only large systems could perform.

The computer industry will continue to evolve as improved technology and innovation lead to a variety of new computer applications.

Microcomputer Applications: User Tools

Microcomputer Applications: User Tools

OBJECTIVES

- Identify the four most widely used general microcomputer software applications.
- Describe how each of the four applications can help users.
- Explain the key features of each of the four major microcomputer applications.
- Describe the key features of data communications and desktop publishing software.
- Explain integrated software and its advantages.
- List and describe five guidelines for purchasing software application packages.
- Discuss tips for using each of the four major microcomputer applications.

Computer literate is a term you might have heard used to describe people who have an understanding of computers and how they are used in our modern world. Today, understanding the common applications used on microcomputers is often considered a part of being computer literate. In fact, a knowledge of these applications is now considered by many educators and employers to be more important than a knowledge of programming. Because of this, we place an introduction to microcomputer applications focusing on the four most widely used applications early in this book. Learning the features of each application will help you understand how microcomputers are used by people in our modern world and provide a foundation to help you learn.

AN INTRODUCTION TO GENERAL MICROCOMPUTER APPLICATIONS

The applications discussed in this chapter are sometimes referred to as **general microcomputer applications**. This software is called "general" because it is useful to a broad range of users. Word processing is a good example of a general application. Regardless of the type of business a company does, word processing can be used as a tool to help employees generate documents.

An important advantage of general applications is that you don't need any special technical skills or ability to use them. These programs are designed to be **user friendly**, in other words, easy to use. You do not need detailed computer instructions as you would if you were programming. Instead, you operate the software through simple commands. **Commands** are the instructions that you use to operate the software. For example, when you are finished using an application and you want to save your work, you issue an instruction called a "save" command. To use this command you might type SAVE WORKFILE. The word SAVE is the command and WORKFILE is the name under which your work will be stored.

User interfaces (Figure 2-1) are methods and techniques that make using an application simpler. They include function keys, screen prompts, menus, and icons. The **function keys** that are included on computer keyboards are a type of user interface. Pressing a function key in an applications program is a shortcut that takes the place of entering a command. The software defines exactly what the function key causes to happen. If you used a function key to perform the SAVE command described above, pressing one key instead of several could generate the entire command SAVE WORKFILE.

FIGURE 2-1
User interfaces.

(a) Function keys are programmed to execute commonly used instructions.

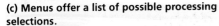
(c) Menus offer a list of possible processing selections.

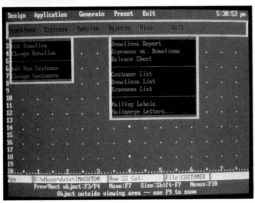

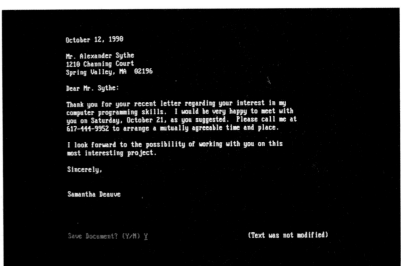

(b) Screen prompts, such as the red question in the lower left of this screen, indicate that the software is waiting for the user to respond.

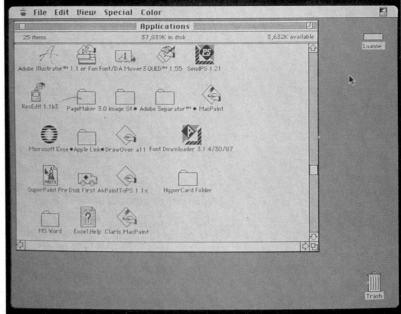

(d) Icons are symbols that represent a computer activity.

Screen **prompts** are the messages that the program displays to help you while you are using an application. **Menus**, a special kind of screen prompt, are used in applications to provide a list of processing options. You make a selection from the menu by pressing the number or letter key that corresponds with the desired option. **Icons** refer to pictures instead of words that are displayed on the screen to show you various program options.

These are some of the features included in general applications packages that help to make them user friendly. These aids minimize the need for technical computer knowledge when you are using general applications packages.

THE FOUR MOST COMMON GENERAL APPLICATIONS

While there are many kinds of general applications available, four software applications packages are the most widely used. They are:

1. word processing software
2. electronic spreadsheet software
3. database software
4. graphics software

Although we will discuss these four applications on microcomputers, they are actually available on computers of all sizes. The concepts you will learn about each application package on microcomputers will also apply if you are working on a larger system.

WORD PROCESSING SOFTWARE: A DOCUMENT PRODUCTIVITY TOOL

Probably the most widely used general application is word processing. If you need to create **documents**, such as letters or memos, you can increase your productivity by learning to use this software tool. Some of the popular packages used today include WordPerfect, WordStar, and Microsoft Word. This section discusses using a word processor to create a document.

Word processing software is used to prepare documents electronically (Figure 2-2). It allows you to enter text on the computer keyboard in the same manner as documents are created on a typewriter. As you enter the characters, they are displayed on the screen and stored in the computer's main memory. Because this is an electronic format, it is easy to **edit** the document by making changes and corrections to the text. Errors may be corrected and words, sentences, paragraphs, or pages may be added or deleted. When the document is complete, you enter a command and have the computer send the document to the printer. The document's format is also under your control. You can specify the margins, define the page length, and select the print style. The document can be printed as many times as you like. Each copy is an original and looks the same as the other copies. The computer's storage capability allows you to store your documents so that they can be used again. It is an efficient way to file documents because many documents can fit on one disk. If you wish, previously stored documents can be combined to make new documents, and you do not have to reenter the text as you would on a typewriter.

The value of word processing is that it reduces the time required to prepare and produce written documents. Any editing you wish to do in the document is easy because the software allows you to make changes quickly and efficiently. In addition, the tedious task of typing a final draft is eliminated.

FIGURE 2-2
Word processing using a computer is faster, more accurate, and less tedious than using a typewriter.

Most word processing packages include additional support features such as spelling checkers, a thesaurus, and some limited grammar checking.

Spelling Checkers

Spelling checker software allows you to check individual words or the entire document for correct spelling. To check individual words, you position the cursor at the start of the word and press a key defined by the software to indicate that the spelling is to be checked. The word in the text will then be checked against an electronic dictionary stored on a disk that is part of the spelling checker software. Some spelling checker dictionaries contain over 100,000 words.

When the entire document is checked for spelling, each word is compared against entries in the dictionary. If an exact match is not found, the word is highlighted. A menu is then superimposed on the screen, giving you a list of similar words that may be the correct spelling. You may select one of the words displayed on the menu, edit the highlighted word, leave the word unchanged, or add the word to the dictionary. Many users customize their software dictionaries by adding company, street, city, and personal names to the dictionary so that the software can check the correct spelling of those words.

Thesaurus

Thesaurus software allows you to look up synonyms for words in a document while you are using your word processor. Using a thesaurus is similar to using a spelling checker. When you want to look up a synonym for a word, you place the cursor on the word that you want to check, enter a command through the keyboard, and the thesaurus software displays a menu of possible synonyms. If you find a word you want to use, you select the desired word from the list and the software automatically incorporates it in the document by replacing the previous word.

Grammar Checkers

Grammar checker software can be used to check for certain grammar, writing style, and sentence structure errors. These programs can check documents for excessive usage of a word or phrase and can identify sentences that are too long. They can also show you words that have been repeated such as "and and" or words used out of context such as "four example."

A Word Processing Example

Figures 2-3 through 2-10 illustrate the following word processing example. Let's say the vice president of sales of a company wants to send a memo announcing a meeting of all sales personnel. She remembers that last month she sent a similar memo to just the sales managers. Thus, the first thing she does is load last month's memo into main memory so it will appear on the screen (Figure 2-3). This memo might be stored on a hard disk or on a floppy diskette.

FIGURE 2-3
Last month's memo that will be changed for this month's meeting.

FIGURE 2-4 ▶
The shaded areas
indicate text
to be deleted.

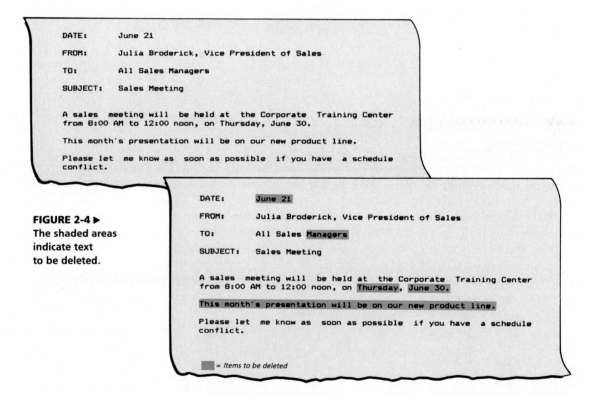

Word processing changes are usually of three types: to **insert** data, **delete** data, or **move** data. Often it makes sense to do your insertions and deletions at the same time; as you edit your document, you delete the existing word or phrase and insert the new one. **Replace** is a combination of the delete and insert commands. With replace, you can scan a document for a single or multiple occurrence of a word or phrase and replace it with another or delete it entirely. Figure 2-4 shows the document with the text to be deleted. Figure 2-5 shows the document after the new text has been inserted.

The **move** command allows you to either cut (remove) or copy a sentence, paragraph, page, or block of text. In our example, the VP of sales, Julia Broderick, decided she wanted to move the existing paragraph 3 in front of the existing paragraph 2 (Figure 2-6). First she would highlight or somehow signify the text to be moved. Next she would indicate that she wants to "cut" and not "copy" the marked text. With a **cut**, you are removing text from an area. With a **copy**, the word processor makes a copy of the marked text but leaves the marked text where it was. After you perform either the cut or the copy, the word processor needs to know where you want to place or **paste** the text. This is usually done by moving the cursor to the point where you want the moved text to begin. You then give a command to execute the move. Figure 2-7 shows the cut text "pasted" into a position that now makes it the second paragraph.

After the text changes are made, Julia runs a spelling checker. The spelling checker matches each word in the document against its spelling dictionary and discovers an unrecognized word: "personel." Figure 2-8 shows how a spelling checker might present two alternatives for the correct spelling of the word. Julia merely has to enter the letter B and the word processor will change "personel" to "personnel" (Figure 2-9).

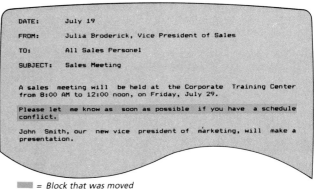

= Block that was moved

▲
FIGURE 2-7
Memo after third paragraph was moved to second paragraph.

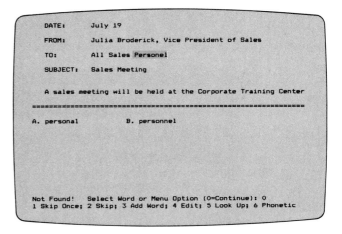

= Block that was moved

▲
FIGURE 2-8
Spelling checker highlighting unrecognized word and showing two possible spellings.

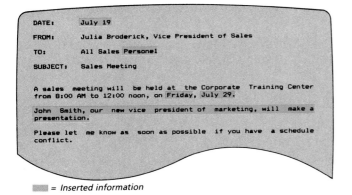

= Inserted information

▲
FIGURE 2-5
The shading on the computer screen shows the new text inserted into last month's memo.

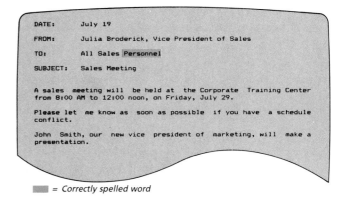

= Correctly spelled word

▲
FIGURE 2-9
Correct spelling of "personnel" inserted into text by spelling checker.

= Block to be moved to second paragraph

▲
FIGURE 2-6
The shading shows the text to be moved from third to second paragraph.

Before printing the memo, Julia reviews its format. She decides that the document is too wide and increases the margins. Figure 2-10 shows the document with the wider, 1 1/2-inch, margins.

FIGURE 2-10
Memo after margins are changed.

```
DATE:       July 19

FROM:       Julia Broderick, Vice President of Sales

TO:         All Sales Personnel

SUBJECT:    Sales Meeting


A sales meeting  will be held at  the Corporate Training
Center from 8:00 AM to 12:00 noon, on Friday, July 29.

Please let  me know as  soon as  possible if you  have a
schedule conflict.

John Smith,  our new  vice president of  marketing, will
make a presentation.
```

Now that the text and format are correct, Julia will save the document before printing it in case a system or power failure occurs during printing. Once saved, the document can be printed as often as necessary and is available for use or modification at a later date.

Word processing software is a productivity tool that allows you to create, edit, format, print, and store documents. Each of the many word processing packages available may have slightly different capabilities, but most have the features summarized in Figure 2-11.

FIGURE 2-11
Common features of word processing software.

WORD PROCESSING FEATURES	
INSERTION AND MOVING Insert character Insert word Insert line Move sentences Move paragraphs Move blocks Merge text **DELETE FEATURES** Delete character Delete word Delete sentence Delete paragraph Delete entire text **SCREEN CONTROL** Scroll up and down by line Scroll by page Word wrap Uppercase and lowercase display Underline display Screen display according to defined format Bold display Superscript display Subscript display	**SEARCH AND REPLACE** Search and replace word Search and replace character strings **PRINTING** Set top and bottom margins Set left and right margins Set tab stops Print columns Single, double, triple space control Variable space control within text Right justify Center lines Subscripts Superscripts Underline Boldface Condensed print Enlarged print Special type fonts Proportional spacing Headers Footers Page numbering Print any page from file

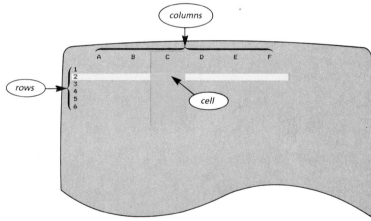

	A	B	C	D	E
3		31-Mar	30-Jun	30-Sep	31-Dec
4					
5	Depreciation	$6,200	$6,216	$6,249	$5,880
6	Telephone	15,150	14,880	18,630	19,290

B

	A	B	C	D	E
1	PLANNING DEPT. OFFICE EXPENSES				
2					
3		31-Mar	30-Jun	30-Sep	31-Dec
4					
5	Depreciation	$30,000	$13,977	$8,053	$14,747
6	Telephone	28,363	28,069	29,968	42,928

A

	A	B	C	D	E
1	OFFICE EXPENSES: CONSOLIDATION				
2					
3		31-Mar	30-Jun	30-Sep	31-Dec
4					
5	Depreciation	$41,149	$25,944	$17,467	$25,731
6	Telephone	55,602	52,994	56,232	80,175

FIGURE 2-12
The electronic spreadsheet on the right still uses the row and column format of the manual spreadsheet on the left.

ELECTRONIC SPREADSHEET SOFTWARE: A NUMBER PRODUCTIVITY TOOL

Electronic spreadsheet software allows you to organize numeric data in a worksheet or table format called an **electronic spreadsheet** or **spreadsheet**. Manual methods have long been used to organize numeric data in this manner (Figure 2-12). You will see that the data in an electronic spreadsheet is organized in the same manner as it is in a manual spreadsheet, one that is done by hand. Within a spreadsheet, data is organized horizontally in **rows** and vertically in **columns**. The intersection where a row and column meet is called a **cell** (Figure 2-13).

Cells may contain three types of data: labels (text), values (numbers), and formulas. The text, or **labels** as they are sometimes called, are used to identify the data and to document the worksheet. Good spreadsheets are well documented and contain descriptive titles. The rest of the cells in a spreadsheet may appear to contain numbers or **values**. However, some of the cells actually contain formulas. The **formulas** perform calculations on the data in the spreadsheet and display the resulting value in the cell containing the formula.

In a manual spreadsheet, each of the totals would have to be calculated by hand. In an electronic spreadsheet, the user enters a formula into a cell. Then the result for that cell is calculated and displayed automatically. Once a formula is entered into a cell, it can be copied to any other cell that requires a similar formula. As the formula is copied, the formula calculations are performed automatically.

One of the most powerful features of the electronic spreadsheet occurs when the data in a spreadsheet changes. To appreciate the capabilities of spreadsheet software, let's discuss how a change is handled in a manual system. When a value in a manual spreadsheet changes, it must be erased and a new value written into the cell. All cells that contain formulas referring to the value that changed must also be erased, recalculated, and the result reentered. For example, the row totals and column totals would be updated to reflect changes to any values within their areas. In large manual spreadsheets, accurately posting changes and updating the values affected can be time consuming. But posting changes on an electronic spreadsheet is

FIGURE 2-13
In a spreadsheet, rows refer to the horizontal lines of data and columns refer to the vertical lines of data. Note that rows are identified by numbers and columns are identified by letters. The intersection of a row and column is called a cell. The highlighted cell is the cursor. You can move the cursor by pressing the arrow keys on the keyboard.

FIGURE 2-14
The "what if" testing capability of electronic spreadsheets is a powerful tool used to aid managers in making decisions.

easy. You change data in a cell by simply typing in the new value. All other values that are affected are updated *automatically*. While the updating happens very quickly, if you watch the screen closely you can sometimes see the values change. As row and column totals are updated, the changes are said to *ripple* through the spreadsheet.

An electronic spreadsheet's ability to recalculate when data is changed makes it a valuable tool for management personnel. This capability allows managers to perform "what if" testing by changing the numbers in a spreadsheet (Figure 2-14). The resulting values that are calculated by the spreadsheet software provide management with valuable decision support information based on the alternatives tested.

To illustrate this powerful tool, we will show you how to develop the spreadsheet that was used as an example in Chapter 1. You may remember that the completed spreadsheet contains revenues, costs, profit, and profit percentage for three months and the totals for the three months. By following Figures 2-15 through 2-19, you can see that the first step in creating the spreadsheet is to enter the labels or titles. These should be short but descriptive, to help you organize the layout of the data in your spreadsheet. The next step is to enter the data or numbers in the body of the spreadsheet, and finally the formulas. At this point you can give commands to print the spreadsheet and to store it on a disk.

An electronic spreadsheet is a productivity tool that organizes and performs calculations on numeric data. Spreadsheets are one of the most popular software applications. They have been adapted to a wide range of business and nonbusiness applications. Some of the popular packages used today are Lotus 1-2-3, Excel, SuperCalc, and VP-Planner. Most of the packages available will have the features shown in Figure 2-20.

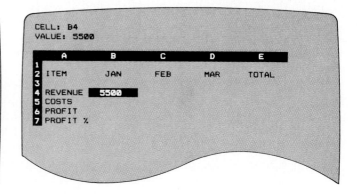

FIGURE 2-15
Labels identify rows and columns in a spreadsheet. The prompt line at the top left of the screen has two parts: CELL, which identifies the column and row being referenced; and VALUE, which identifies the value in the cell. The cursor, is located in cell B4, the intersection of column B and row 4. No value has been entered into B4.

FIGURE 2-16
The value 5500 is entered and stored at cell B4. Note the entries in the display at the top left corner of the screen, identifying which value (in this case a number) has been entered into which cell.

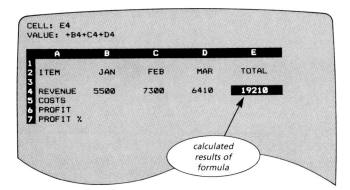

FIGURE 2-17
The arrow keys are used to move the cursor to cells in the spreadsheet. The values 7300 and 6410 are entered in cells C4 and D4. A formula is entered in cell E4. The formula specifies that the content of cell E4 is to be the sum of the values in cells B4, C4, and D4. The spreadsheet itself displays the numeric sum. The prompt line at the top of the screen, however, shows the formula used to calculate the value.

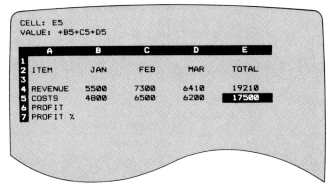

FIGURE 2-18
The formula required for cell E5 is similar to the one entered for cell E4; it totals the amounts in the three previous columns. When we copy the formula from E4 into E5, the software automatically changes the cell references from B4, C4, and D4 to B5, C5, and D5.

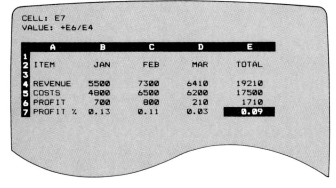

FIGURE 2-19
This screen shows the completed spreadsheet. The value in cell E7 is derived from the formula illustrated on the prompt line, which specifies that the value in cell E6 is to be divided by the value in cell E4. (The slash character indicates division.) Since the value in E6 is the total profit and the value in E4 is the total revenue, the result of the division operation is the profit percentage.

SPREADSHEET FEATURES	
WORKSHEET	**MOVE**
Global format	Move from cells
Insert column	Move to cells
Insert row	**FILE**
Delete column	Save
Delete row	Retrieve
Set up titles	Erase
Set up windows	List
RANGE	**PRINT**
Format range of data	Set up margins
Erase cells	Define header
COPY	Define footer
Copy from cells	Specify range to print
Copy to cells	Define page length
	Condensed print

FIGURE 2-20
Common features of spreadsheet software

DATABASE SOFTWARE: A DATA MANAGEMENT TOOL

Database software allows you to create electronic files on your computer and to retrieve, manipulate, and update the data you store in the files. Just as in a manual system, a **file** is a collection of related data. For example,.a file might consist of customer's names and addresses. In a manual system (Figure 2-21), the data might be recorded on paper and stored in a filing cabinet. On the computer, the data will be stored in an electronic format on an auxiliary storage device such as a disk. Another term that is used to reference data is record. A **record** is a collection of related facts or data items. In our name and address file example, all the information that relates to one person would be considered a record. Each of the facts or data items within a record is called a **field**.

Sometimes the word database is used interchangeably with the word file. However, the term **database** usually refers to a collection of data that is organized in multiple files. Understanding the difference between the terms file and database will help you to understand the difference between file management software and database software. In general, **file management software** allows you to work with one file at a time, while database software allows you to work with multiple files.

The screens in Figures 2-22 through 2-26 present the development of a personal checking account file and inquiry system using a file management system. The file management main menu (Figure 2-22) presents 5 choices: to create a file, enter data, update the file, display data, and terminate the processing of the file management system. To begin, you would select option 1, CREATE FILE.

When you select option 1, the FILE MANAGEMENT CREATE FILE information shown in Figure 2-23 is displayed. A prompt asks you to enter a file name, the name under which the file being created will be stored on disk. In this example, you would enter the name CHECKING.

You are then asked to enter descriptions for each field in the records to be stored in the file. A field description consists of a field name, the type of data to be stored in the field (A for alphanumeric, N for numeric data), and the number of characters in the field. In a numeric field, if digits are to appear to the right of the decimal point, you must specify the number of digits to the right. Thus, for the amount field, the designation 6.2 means there are six numeric digits in the field with two of those digits to the right of the decimal point.

Once you have defined the fields in the records, you enter data into the records. Therefore, you would choose main menu entry 2, ENTER DATA and Figure 2-24 would appear. The file management system prompts you to enter data for each record by typing the data to be stored in the field. Thus, after the field name NUMBER, you enter the check number. You complete each field in the same manner, and continue to enter data until all data is entered for the checking account file.

After the file has been defined and data has been stored in it, you can use the file to produce information. Therefore you would choose option 4, DISPLAY DATA, from the main menu. You are then asked to enter the commands that specify what should be displayed and how the data should be processed prior to being displayed. As Figure 2-25 shows, you stated that the data should be sorted on the field called NUMBER, and that all fields in the record should be displayed.

FIGURE 2-21
An electronic database is similar to a manual system; related data items are stored in files.

In Figure 2-26, you direct the system to display only those records where the class is equal to UTILITY and to print a total for the field AMOUNT. As a result, the report shows only those records for which the classification is UTILITY. The values in the amount field are totalled and printed after all records have been processed.

In addition to creating, retrieving, and storing data, most database and file management software provide for the manipulation of the data. This includes sorting the data in ascending or descending sequence by specifying a few simple English-like commands. Figure 2-27 lists some features of popular database software, such as dBASE III PLUS.

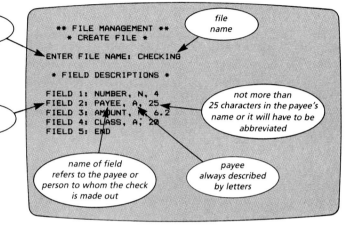

FIGURE 2-23
CREATE FILE screen showing definition of fields for records in the CHECKING file.

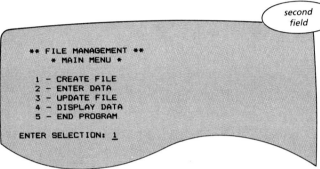

FIGURE 2-22
A typical main menu of file management software.

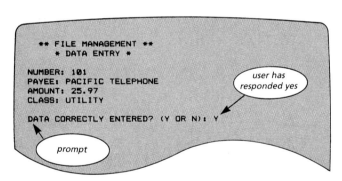

FIGURE 2-24
Data entry screen.

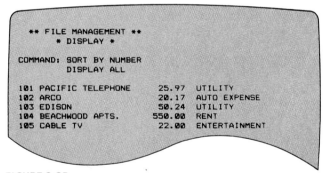

FIGURE 2-25
Display of all records sorted by record number.

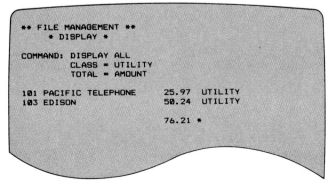

FIGURE 2-26
Display of only the UTILITY class records with a total calculated on the amount.

DATABASE FEATURES	
OPERATIONS	**ARITHMETIC**
Create database	Compute the average
Copy data	Count the records
Delete data	Sum data fields
Sort data	**OUTPUT**
EDITING	Retrieve data
Display data	Produce a report
Update data	

FIGURE 2-27
Common features of database software.

Note again that when using this microcomputer application, you do not need to have any special technical knowledge. Database software and file managers are general application tools that are designed to help you easily and efficiently manage data electronically.

GRAPHICS SOFTWARE: A DATA PRESENTATION TOOL

Information presented in the form of a graph or a chart is commonly referred to as **graphics**. Studies have shown that information presented in graphic form can be understood much faster than information presented in writing. Three common forms of graphics are **pie charts**, **bar charts**, and **line diagrams** (Figure 2-28).

FIGURE 2-28

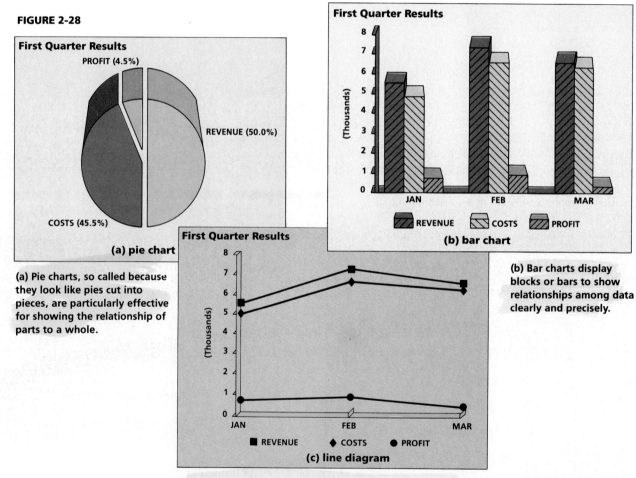

(a) Pie charts, so called because they look like pies cut into pieces, are particularly effective for showing the relationship of parts to a whole.

(b) Bar charts display blocks or bars to show relationships among data clearly and precisely.

(c) Line diagrams are particularly effective for showing movement or a change in the condition of the data.

Today, there are many software packages of different capabilities that can create graphics, including most spreadsheet packages. The graphics capabilities of these packages can be grouped into two categories: analytical graphics and presentation graphics. Both kinds can transform numeric data into graphic form.

Analytical graphics is widely used by management personnel when reviewing information and when communicating information to others within their organization (Figure 2-29).

For example, a production manager who is planning a meeting with the president of the company may use color graphics to depict the expenditures of the production department. This graphic display would have more impact and lead to better understanding than would a printed column of production figures.

As its name implies, **presentation graphics** goes beyond analytical graphics by offering the user a wide choice of presentation effects. These include three-dimensional displays, background patterns, multiple text fonts, and image libraries that contain illustrations of factories, people, coins, dollar signs and other symbols that can be incorporated into the graphic (Figure 2-30). Figure 2-31 shows an example of presentation graphics projected in front of an audience and one of the devices that can be used to project presentation graphics.

To create graphics on your computer, you must follow the directions that apply to your graphics software package. Most packages will prompt you to enter the data the graph will represent, and then ask you to select the type of graph you would like. After entering the data, you can select several different graphic forms to see which one will best convey your message. When you decide on a graph, you can print it and also store it for future reference.

Using graphics software as a presentation tool allows you to efficiently create professional-quality graphics that can help you communicate information more effectively.

▲ **FIGURE 2-29**
Color can enhance the presentation of graphic information.

FIGURE 2-30
An example of presentation graphics.▼

◀ **FIGURE 2-31**
Presentation graphics can be an effective way to communicate information to a large group. Presenters can use devices such as the computer projection device shown. When this device is connected to a microcomputer and placed over a standard projector, it can project everything on the microcomputer screen onto a large screen.

OTHER POPULAR MICROCOMPUTER APPLICATIONS

he four applications discussed so far, word processing, spreadsheet, database, and graphics, are the most widely used microcomputer applications. Two other packages that are finding increasing use are data communications and desktop publishing.

Data Communications

Data communications software is used to transmit data from one computer to another. It gives users access to online databases such as stock prices and airline schedules, and services such as home banking and shopping.

Microcomputer data communications software often involves using a telephone line connected to special communication equipment either inside or attached to the computer. Similar equipment must be present at the other computer that will be accessed. The data communications software is used to dial the other system and establish the communication connection. Once the connection is established, the user enters commands and responses that control the transmission of data from one computer to the other.

Desktop Publishing

Desktop publishing software allows the user to combine text and graphics to produce high-quality printed documents. Desktop publishing systems go far beyond the capabilities of typical word processing systems by providing many different type sizes and styles and the ability to merge charts, pictures, and illustrations with the text. Numerous special effects such as borders and backgrounds can also be used to enhance the appearance of a document. Businesses of all sizes are increasingly using desktop publishing systems to produce better-looking brochures and communications and to control the production of work that previously could only be done by graphic artists. Figure 2-32 is an example of a document produced on a desktop publishing system.

FIGURE 2-32
High-quality printed documents can be produced with desktop publishing software.

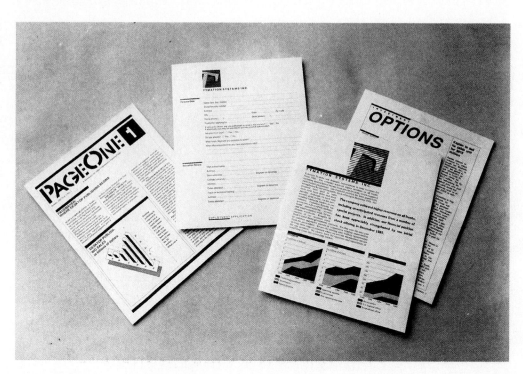

INTEGRATED SOFTWARE

Software packages such as electronic spreadsheet and word processing are generally used independently of each other. But what if you wanted to place information from a spreadsheet into a word processing document? The spreadsheet data would have to be reentered in the word processing document. This would be time consuming and errors could be introduced as you reentered the data. The inability of separate programs to communicate with one another and use a common set of data has been overcome through the use of integrated software.

Integrated software refers to packages that combine applications such as word processing, electronic spreadsheet, database, graphics, and data communications into a single, easy-to-use set of programs. Application packages that are included in integrated packages are designed to have a consistent command structure; that is, common commands such as those used to SAVE or LOAD files are the same for all the applications in the package. Besides the consistent presentation, a key feature of integrated packages is their ability to pass data quickly and easily from one application to another. For example, revenue and cost information from a database on daily sales could be quickly loaded into a spreadsheet. The spreadsheet could be used to calculate gross profits. Once the calculations are completed, all or a portion of the spreadsheet data can be passed to the graphics program to create pie, bar, line, or other graphs. Finally, the graphic (or the spreadsheet) can be transferred to a word processing document. A possible disadvantage of an integrated package is that individual integrated programs may not have all the features that are available in nonintegrated packages.

Integrated programs frequently use windows. A **window** is a rectangular portion of the screen that is used to display information. Windows can display help information about the commands of the program you are using or, with integrated packages, they can actually display data from another application. Many programs today can display multiple windows on the screen (Figure 2-33) and allow the user to move from one application window to another. Although they are called "windows" because of their ability to "see" into another part of the program, many people consider windows to be more like multiple sheets of paper on top of a desk. The papers can be shuffled, placed side by side, or moved entirely off the desk until needed again.

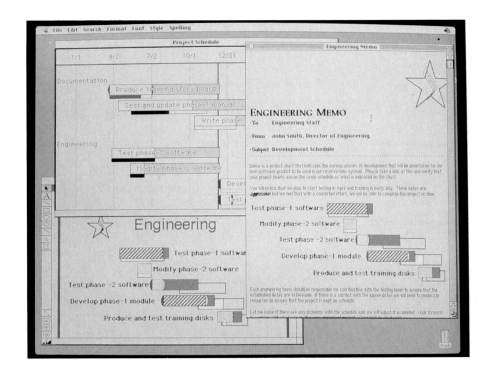

FIGURE 2-33
Windows on the Macintosh computer let you see several applications at one time. In this example the user can plan projects using project management software (top left), pictorially present the plan using graphics software (bottom left), and write about the plan using word processing software (right).

GUIDELINES FOR PURCHASING MICROCOMPUTER APPLICATIONS SOFTWARE

Whenever you purchase applications software (Figure 2-34), you should make sure that the software will meet your needs. Do this by following these five steps:

FIGURE 2-34
Shop carefully for software, evaluating the available packages and suppliers. Many people spend more on software than they do on their computer equipment.

1. **Verify that the software performs the task you desire.** In some cases, software that is supposed to perform particular functions either does not perform the functions or performs them in a manner that will be unacceptable to you. The best method of verifying that the software performs satisfactorily is to try it out prior to purchase. Many computer stores and software vendors will allow you to try software to see if it meets your needs before you purchase it. Some software developers even have special demonstration versions that allow you to try package features on a limited-use basis.

2. **Verify that the software will run on your computer.** The best way to verify this is to run the software on a computer that is the same as yours. Such factors as the number of disk drives, whether the software can run on a computer without a hard disk, main memory requirements, and graphics capabilities or requirements must be evaluated before you buy. For example, it would be unwise to purchase a package that is incompatible with your printer or one with graphics capabilities that your computer cannot handle.

3. **Make sure that the software is adequately documented.** The written material that accompanies the software is known as **documentation**. Even the best software may be unusable if the documentation does not clearly and completely describe what the software does, how it does it, how to recover from errors, and how to back up data.

4. **Purchase the software from a reputable store, distributor, or vendor.** Regardless of the care taken, software often contains errors. A reputable store or vendor will do everything possible to correct those errors. Admittedly, it can be hard to check on a company's reputation. Asking for references is probably the best method if you are not familiar with the prospective supplier.

5. **Obtain the best value, but keep in mind that that might not mean the lowest price.** Different stores or distributors will sell the same software package for different prices. Be sure to compare prices, but also ask about product support. Sometimes a store will offer training on products that you buy from them; other vendors provide no support or training. Also, some vendors offer telephone service so that you can call to ask questions about the software.

If you keep these factors in mind when buying application software packages, you are likely to be pleased with the software you buy.

A good place to look when shopping for microcomputer applications software is in computer magazines such as *InforWorld* and *PC World*. These magazines regularly review applications packages and publish articles and charts to help you choose the package best suited to your needs.

LEARNING AIDS AND SUPPORT TOOLS FOR APPLICATION USERS

*L*earning to use an application software package involves time and practice. Fortunately, several support tools are available to help you: tutorials, online help, trade books, and keyboard templates (Figure 2-35).

Tutorials are step-by-step instructions using real examples that show you how to use an application. Some tutorials are written manuals, but more and more, tutorials are in the software form, allowing you to use your computer to learn about a package.

Online help refers to additional instructions that are available within the application. In most packages, a function key or special combination of keys are reserved for the help feature. When you are using an application and have a question, pressing the designated "help" key will temporarily overlay your work on the screen with information on how to use the package. When you are finished using the help feature, pressing another key allows you to return to your work.

The documentation that accompanies software packages is frequently organized as reference material. This makes it very useful once you know how to use a package but difficult to

FIGURE 2-35
This figure shows four ways to learn application software packages.

Software **tutorials** help you learn an application while using the actual software on your computer.

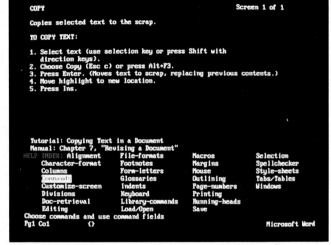

Online help gives you assistance without your having to leave the application.

Many **trade books** are available for the popular software applications.

Keyboard templates give you quick reference to software commands.

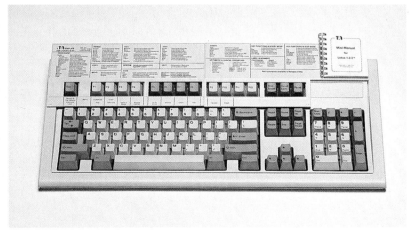

use when you are first learning it. For this reason, many **trade books** are available to help users learn to use the features of microcomputer application packages. These books can usually be found where software is sold and are frequently carried in regular bookstores.

Keyboard templates are plastic sheets that fit around a portion of your keyboard. The keyboard commands to select the various features of the application programs are printed on the template. Having these prompts readily available is helpful for both beginners and experienced users.

TIPS FOR USING MICROCOMPUTER APPLICATIONS

The following tips are listed under specific applications. Some of them will make sense now and will be useful to new users. Others may not be clear now but will be useful as you increase your proficiency with each application. Using this section for reference will help you develop good techniques as you learn microcomputer applications. Remember, it may take up to twenty hours or more of use before you become familiar with a package's capabilities. Don't expect to be an "instant expert."

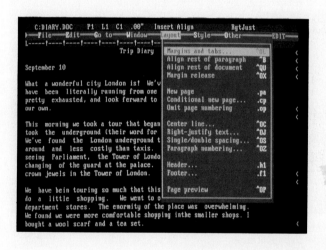

Tips for Using Word Processing

1. **Learn how to move the cursor.** Some people only learn the simplest methods of moving around inside a document: one character at a time sideways, and one line at a time up or down. But most word processors have a number of methods to move faster, such as a word at a time, to the end of a line, to the end of a sentence, to the top or bottom of the screen, to the top or bottom of a page, to a specific page, etc. Learn these movement commands and you'll save yourself a lot of editing time.

2. **Think about how your document "looks" as well as what it "says."** The use of underlining, boldface, indentation, borders, titles, and other stylistic features can enhance your document and help get your message across. After you get your words right, review your document one more time just to improve the visual presentation.

3. **Use a spelling checker.** Even if you're a champion speller, you still probably make a typo every once in a while. Get in the habit of running the spelling checker on all documents you create after every time you've added text.

4. **File your document under a meaningful name.** The main reason for a meaningful name is so you can recognize the document at a later date. If possible, place the name on the document itself. You've probably noticed document name or number references on letters from attorneys, accountants, and others who generate large volumes of correspondence.

5. **Create document templates for frequently used documents.** A **document template** is a document with the title, headings, footings, spacing, and other features that you want to have in frequently generated documents. The template usually contains everything except the text of the document. An example would be an interoffice memo template that contains the title (Interoffice Memorandum) and the TO:, FROM:, SUBJECT:, and DATE: headings. Using a document template reduces the time to prepare a document and results in a consistent format.

6. **When working on a document, save it frequently.** Nothing is more frustrating than entering a large amount of text and then losing it because of a system or power failure or an accidental mistake. Get in the habit of saving your document frequently, say every ten minutes or so, to minimize any data loss.

Tips for Using Electronic Spreadsheets

1. **State your assumptions explicitly in the upper portion of your spreadsheet. Assumptions** are data elements such as the unit selling price or an interest rate that are used in spreadsheet calculations. Instead of placing these items in formulas, put them in a separate cell and reference the cell in your formula. This not only makes your calculations more obvious but makes subsequent changes and "what if" testing easier.

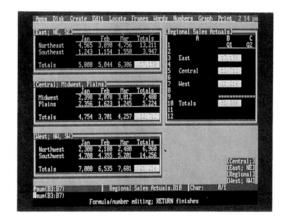

2. **Use range names for key cells.** Rather than referring to the cell that contains the unit price assumption by its cell number, use the option to give that cell a name, such as PRICE. Using named cells minimizes reference errors and makes your formulas more meaningful.

3. **Use meaningful names for your row and column descriptions.** Give some thought to the text you use to label rows and columns, especially if your spreadsheet will be used by others. A few extra characters can go a long way to helping someone understand the data being presented.

4. **Leave room for expansion.** Even the best designed spreadsheets can grow as you add additional data elements, rows, or columns. Anticipate the areas of your spreadsheet that may expand and structure them accordingly by providing blank rows and columns.

5. **Highlight your results.** Remember that your spreadsheet is also a visual document. If the main purpose of the spreadsheet is to calculate a single number such as net profit, try to highlight the result by using underlines, asterisks, or white space to set it apart from the other data.

6. **Document your spreadsheet in your spreadsheet.** A description of the spreadsheet and the assumptions helps other users understand the spreadsheet's purpose and can help you if you haven't worked with it for a while.

Tips for Using Database Software

1. **Before you start, take time to design your file.** Although data elements can be added later, it's desirable to have all necessary elements provided for at the beginning.

2. **Use meaningful names for the files and data fields.** Meaningful names are a good practice for all applications but especially in a database, where it's likely that you'll be working with multiple files and a large number of data fields.

3. **Avoid the use of significant identification numbers (IDs).** A significant ID is the identifying field or key field of a record in which two or more data elements are combined, thus building "significance" into the ID. An example would be an inventory parts file ID in which the ID is the part number plus a code indicating the part type. The problem with significant ID schemes is that they grow increasingly more

complicated and eventually break down; sooner or later you'll encounter an item that won't fit the scheme. Avoid this confusion by establishing separate fields for each data item.

4. **Have the system generate IDs whenever possible.** This tip is closely related to the last tip discussing significant IDs. Obviously the system shouldn't generate the ID for files where the ID is something like a social security number. But when the ID is merely an identifier to be used to distinguish between the records, such as a transaction number, have the system generate it.

5. **Create an index file if you frequently access a file by something other than the file ID field.** Let's say you have an employee file that you normally access by its ID, the employee number. Occasionally, however, you need to access records by employee name. You could sort the file by name each time but a faster way would be to create and maintain an index to the file based on employee name.

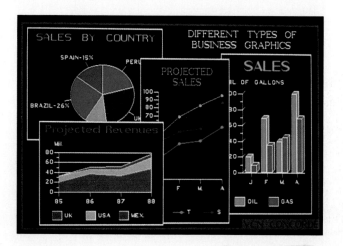

Tips for Using Graphics

1. **Keep in mind that a graphic is a visual presentation.** Before you start, give some thought to the arrangement ("composition") of the information to be presented.

2. **Don't try to present too much information.** If you do, you'll wind up with a cluttered look that will make the information difficult to understand.

3. **Choose the most appropriate type of graphic.**

   a. Bar charts show the relationship between variables such as the amount of sales (variable 1) for each month (variable 2).

   b. Pie charts are excellent for showing the relationship between individual variables (the pie slices) and the total of all variables (the whole pie). The effectiveness of pie charts is lessened if some of the variables are too small in relation to the others (resulting in pie slices too thin) or if there are too many variables.

   c. Line diagrams link a set of variables with a connecting line and are excellent for showing a trend as indicated by a rising or falling line.

4. **Use words sparingly.** Use text to title the graphic and identify the variables but don't overdo the use of words. If you have a choice of type styles, choose one that's simple and easy to read. Leave space around text so that it will stand out and can be easily read.

5. **Use colors carefully.** If you have a choice of colors, choose them carefully. The right colors can enhance the presentation while the wrong ones can confuse and distract. Lighter colors should be on top of darker, "heavier" colors.

6. **Be consistent.** If you're making a series of graphics, the type style, graphic size, headings, borders, use of colors, etc., should be the same for all items.

7. **Projected graphics should be simple.** If your graphic is going to be projected in front of an audience, you can't display as much information as you can if the graphic is going to be read by an individual. Remember, the audience can't see the projected graphic as well as someone holding a printed copy and they will only have a limited amount of time to look at it.

CHAPTER SUMMARY

1. **Computer literate** is a term used to describe people who have an understanding of computers and how they are used in our modern world.
2. Software that is useful to a broad range of users is sometimes referred to as **general microcomputer applications software**.
3. The four most widely used microcomputer software applications are word processing, electronic spreadsheet, database, and graphics.
4. **Word processing software** is used to prepare documents electronically.
5. Additional support features for a word processing application can include a spelling checker, thesaurus, and grammar checker.
6. **Spelling checker software** allows you to check individual words or an entire document for correct spelling.
7. **Thesaurus software** allows you to look up synonyms for words in a document while you are using your word processor.
8. **Grammar checker software** identifies possible grammar, writing style, and sentence structure errors.
9. Word processing software is a document productivity tool that allows you to create, edit, format, print, and store documents.
10. **Electronic spreadsheet software** allows you to organize numeric data in a worksheet or table format.
11. A spreadsheet is composed of **rows** and **columns**. Each intersection of a row and column is a **cell**.
12. A spreadsheet cell can contain one of the following: a **label**, a **value**, or a **formula**.
13. The "what if" capability of electronic spreadsheet software is a powerful tool that is widely used by management personnel for decision support information.
14. **Database software** and **file management software** are used to organize, retrieve, manipulate, and update data that is stored in files.
15. In general, database software can work with data that is stored in multiple files. File management software is designed to work with one data file at a time.
16. Information presented in the form of a graph or a chart is commonly referred to as **graphics**. Three popular graphics used to present information include **pie, bar, and line charts**.
17. **Data communications software** allows you to transmit data from one computer to another.
18. **Desktop publishing software** can combine text and graphics to produce high-quality printed documents.
19. **Integrated software** packages combine several applications in one package and allow data to be shared between the applications.
20. When you purchase software, you should perform the following steps: (1) Verify that the software performs the task desired. (2) Verify that the software runs on your computer. (3) Make sure the software documentation is adequate. (4) Purchase the software from a reputable store, distributor, or vendor. (5) Obtain the best value.
21. Aids such as tutorials, online help, trade books, and keyboard templates are useful in learning and using microcomputer applications.

KEY TERMS

Analytical graphics *2.14*	Database software *2.12*	File *2.12*
Assumptions *2.21*	Data communications software *2.16*	File management software *2.12*
Bar chart *2.14*	Delete *2.6*	Formula *2.9*
Cell *2.9*	Desktop publishing software *2.16*	Function keys *2.3*
Columns *2.9*	Document *2.4*	General microcomputer applications *2.2*
Commands *2.2*	Document template *2.20*	Grammar checker software *2.6*
Computer literate *2.2*	Edit *2.4*	Graphics *2.14*
Copy *2.7*	Electronic spreadsheet *2.9*	Icons *2.4*
Cut *2.7*	Electronic spreadsheet software *2.9*	Insert *2.6*
Database *2.12*	Field *2.12*	Integrated software *2.17*

REVIEW QUESTIONS

1. Define the term computer literate.
2. What is general microcomputer applications software?
3. List the four most widely used microcomputer application packages and describe how each application helps users.
4. What is a spelling checker? Describe a typical procedure when a misspelled word is found.
5. Explain how management personnel use the "what if" capability of electronic spreadsheets. Why is this capability useful for decision support?
6. What is the difference between database software and file management software?
7. List the three most commonly used charts. Draw an example of each.
8. Describe the advantage of using integrated software. What is a possible disadvantage? What are windows and how are they used in integrated software packages?
9. List the five steps that should be performed when purchasing software. Describe each of them.
10. List and describe four learning aids that can help you use general microcomputer application packages.

CONTROVERSIAL ISSUES

1. Some organizations insist that their employees use an integrated package so that data can be easily transferred between users. Other organizations let their users make individual decisions on which package they want to use for a particular application. Discuss the advantages and disadvantages of both policies.
2. Spreadsheets are increasingly used to support and justify management decisions. Sometimes these spreadsheets are very complex and are based on hundreds of calculations and assumptions. Discuss the responsibility of the person presenting the spreadsheet to document and explain the assumptions used by the spreadsheet.

RESEARCH PROJECTS

1. Interview a person who uses a word processing package on a regular basis. Write a report on the types of documents he or she prepares. Include the person's comments on the different word processing features.
2. Find someone who has developed an electronic spreadsheet no larger than a single page. Make a manual (hand-prepared) copy of the spreadsheet. Change one value in each data row and record the time it takes you to recalculate the spreadsheet totals. Report your findings.
3. Assume that you have decided to use a database package to record all the things you own. Define the fields that would make up your database record.

# CHAPTER 3

Processing Data Into Information

Processing Data Into Information

OBJECTIVES

- Explain the four operations of the information processing cycle: input, process, output, and storage.
- Define data and explain the terms used to organize data in an information processing system: field, record, file, database.
- Discuss data management and explain why it is needed.
- Explain arithmetic and logical processing.
- Describe interactive processing and batch processing.
- List and explain the qualities of information.

---

*T*he information processing cycle is basic to all computers, large or small. It is important that you understand this cycle, for much of your success in understanding computers and what they do depends on having an understanding or "feeling" for the movement of data as it flows through the information processing cycle and becomes information. This chapter discusses the information processing cycle, examines the nature of data—how it is organized for processing on a computer and how it is managed—and describes the qualities of information. Reading this chapter will give you a more detailed understanding of the input, processing, output, and storage operations that a computer performs to process data into information.

Also, this chapter summarizes the general types of processing that computers perform and discusses interactive and batch processing methods. Each processing method has advantages and is appropriate for certain types of applications. Business examples demonstrate the use of each processing method.

OVERVIEW OF THE INFORMATION PROCESSING CYCLE

*A*s seen in Chapter 1, the **information processing cycle** consists of four operations: input, processing, output, and storage. Regardless of the size and type of computer, these operations are used to process data into a meaningful form called information.

The operations in the information processing cycle are carried out through the combined use of computer equipment, also called computer hardware, and computer software. The computer software, or programs, contain instructions that direct the computer equipment to perform the tasks necessary to process data into information.

The diagram in Figure 3-1 illustrates some of the various devices used in conjunction with computer software to carry out the information processing cycle. Input devices are used to enter both the computer programs and the data into main memory. The primary input devices are keyboards on microcomputers and terminals on larger machines. Disk drives and tape drives can also be used to input data that has been stored on these auxiliary storage devices. The function of the input devices is to place into the main memory of the computer the program that is to be executed and the data that is to be processed. Both the program that is to control the processing and the data that is to be processed must be in main memory for processing to occur. Once the computer program is stored in main memory, the person using the computer gives a command to start the program. The processor executes each instruction in the program. These instructions direct the computer to perform the input, processing, output, and storage operations that will process the data into information.

The primary output devices on computers are printers and screens. The format of a report on a printer or a screen is under the control of the program stored in main memory. The program will format the data to be printed or displayed and then issue the commands that cause the output to occur.

Auxiliary storage devices, also called secondary storage devices, commonly used with computers are magnetic disk and magnetic tape. The programs and data not being used by the computer are stored on auxiliary storage until they are needed. Then they are loaded from auxiliary storage into main memory.

Note that some input and output devices can be used for more than one type of operation in the information processing cycle. For example, disk and tape units are used as auxiliary storage devices to store data, but when a disk or tape is receiving data from the main memory of the computer, it is operating as an output device. This process is described as writing or sending data to the auxiliary storage. When data is copied from disk or tape to the main memory of the computer, the disk or tape is operating as an input device. This process is described as reading data into the main memory of the computer. Terminals are also used as both input and output devices. Thus, to understand what is occurring in the information processing cycle, it is important for you to focus on the type of operation being performed rather than the device that is being used.

As we have discussed, the purpose of an information processing system is to process data into information. Data is the prime ingredient in this cycle. Without data, the computer hardware and software have nothing to manipulate. Because data is such an important part of the information cycle, it is important for you to understand what data is, how it is organized, and how it is managed.

FIGURE 3-1
A computer consists of input devices, the processor, output devices, and auxiliary storage units. This equipment or hardware is used to perform the operations of the information processing cycle.

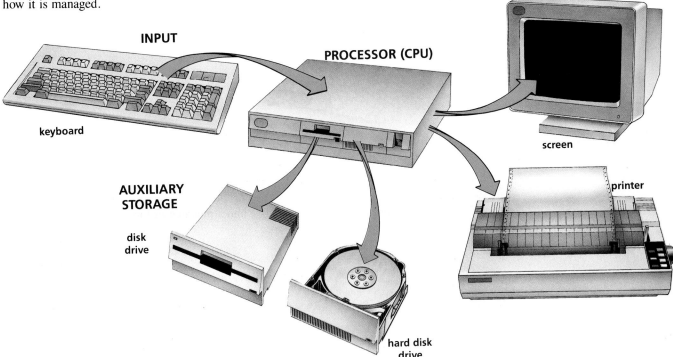

INPUT

PROCESSOR (CPU)

OUTPUT

keyboard

screen

AUXILIARY
STORAGE

printer

disk
drive

hard disk
drive

WHAT IS DATA AND HOW IS IT ORGANIZED?

Data is the raw facts, including numbers and words, that a computer receives during the input operation and processes to produce information. For example, in a monthly sales application (Figure 3-2), the value 01/31, identifying a month and day, is data. In a payroll application (Figure 3-3), the social security number 332-98-8776 is data. The name HAYNES is data.

Data is comprised of **characters**. These characters are classified as **alphabetic** (A–Z), **numeric** (0–9) or **special** (all characters other than A–Z and 0–9, such as , ? / ! % & : ;). The raw facts that we refer to as data are made up of a combination of these three kinds of characters. In the previous example, the date 01/31 is made up of the numeric characters 0 1 3 and the special character /. The social security number contains numeric characters and the special character -. The name Haynes contains only alphabetic characters.

Each fact or unique piece of data is referred to as a **data item**, **data field**, or just a **field**. Fields are classified by the characters that they contain. For example, a field that contains only alphabetic characters, such as the name field containing Haynes, is called an **alphabetic field**. A field that contains numeric characters is called a **numeric field**. Numeric fields may also contain some special characters that are commonly used with numbers, such as a decimal point (.) and the plus (+) and minus (–) signs. Even with the plus sign (+) and decimal point (.) the number + 500.00 is still called a numeric field. Fields that contain a combination of character types, such as the date 01/31 (numeric and special characters), are called **alphanumeric** fields. Even though the word "alphanumeric" implies only alphabetic and numeric characters, it also includes fields that contain special characters. The term alphanumeric is used to describe all fields that do not fall into the alphabetic or numeric classifications.

A field is normally most meaningful when combined with related fields. To illustrate, the month and day 01/31 by itself is not as useful as when it is related to monthly sales (Figure 3-2). Also, the social security number 332-98-8776 is more useful when it is related to the name HAYNES and to the paycheck amount $327.00 (Figure 3-3). Because related fields are more meaningful if they are together, fields are organized into groups called records.

A **record** is a collection of related fields. Each record normally corresponds to a specific unit of information. For example, a record that could be used to produce the payroll report in Figure 3-3 is illustrated in Figure 3-4. The fields in the record are the social security number, employee name, and paycheck amount. This example shows that the data in each record is used to produce a line on the payroll report. The first record contains all the data concerning the employee named Haynes. The second record contains all the data concerning the employee named Johnston. Each subsequent record contains all the data for a given employee. Thus, you can see how related data items are grouped together to form a record.

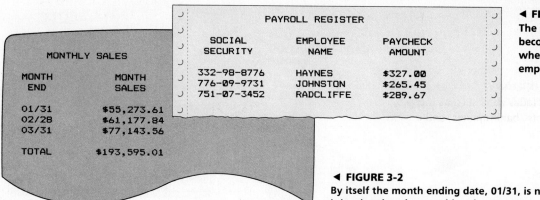

MONTHLY SALES	
MONTH END	MONTH SALES
01/31	$55,273.61
02/28	$61,177.84
03/31	$77,143.56
TOTAL	$193,595.01

PAYROLL REGISTER

SOCIAL SECURITY	EMPLOYEE NAME	PAYCHECK AMOUNT
332-98-8776	HAYNES	$327.00
776-09-9731	JOHNSTON	$265.45
751-07-3452	RADCLIFFE	$289.67

◀ **FIGURE 3-3**
The social security number becomes more meaningful when it is related to an employee name and pay rate.

◀ **FIGURE 3-2**
By itself the month ending date, 01/31, is not as useful as when it is related to the monthly sales amount.

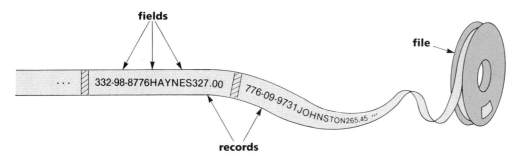

A collection of records is called a **file**. The payroll file in Figure 3-4, for example, contains all the records required to produce the payroll register report. Files are stored on some medium, such as magnetic tape or magnetic disk. Records on tape are usually arranged in a **sequential** manner. This means that the records in the file are arranged in some sequence such as employee number order or product number order. In the payroll file, for example, records could be arranged alphabetically by employee name or numerically by employee number. The field that is used to arrange the records in a specific order is called the **key field**. The records in files stored on disk can be arranged sequentially or randomly. In a **random** file, records are not arranged in any sequence or specific order.

Data is frequently organized in a **database**. As we discussed in Chapter 2, a database provides an efficient way to establish a relationship between data items and implies that a relationship has been established between multiple files. Data that has been organized in a database can be efficiently manipulated and retrieved by a computer.

Summary of Data Organization

In this section we have defined data as the raw facts that are processed by a computer system. We have also defined the terms used to describe how data is organized. We have seen that the smallest elements of data are alphabetic, numeric, and special characters and that these characters are used to build the fields, records, files, and databases that are manipulated by an information system to create information.

DATA MANAGEMENT

For data to be useful in the processing cycle, it must have certain attributes such as accuracy. **Data management** refers to techniques, methods, and procedures that are used to manage these attributes and provide for the security and maintenance of data. The purpose of data management is to ensure that data required for an application will be available in the correct form and at the proper time for processing.

To illustrate data management, we use an example of a credit checking bureau (Figure 3-5). A summary of the application follows:

1. Data entered into the database of the credit bureau is acquired from numerous sources such as banks and stores. The data relates to people's credit ratings and includes facts such as income, history of paying debts, bankruptcies, and certain personal information.
2. The database is stored on auxiliary storage.

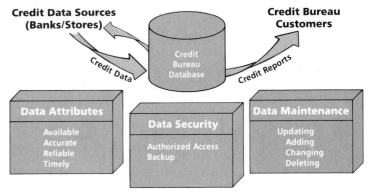

3. Customers of the credit bureau can call the bureau and request an individual's credit rating. The credit bureau employee uses a terminal to retrieve information concerning the credit rating from the database and gives the caller a brief credit history of the person in question. The system also generates a record that causes a complete credit history to be printed that night. The report will be mailed to the customer the following day.

Data Attributes

One attribute of data is that it must be *available*. In the credit bureau application, it would not be possible to implement the system if banks, stores, and other organizations were not willing to provide information about account holders. Therefore, prior to implementing an application on a computer, there must be assurance that the data required will be available.

Another important attribute of data in this application or any other is its integrity. **Data integrity** affects the confidence a user has in processing that data. The three primary elements of data integrity are: (1) data accuracy, (2) reliable data entry, and (3) timeliness.

For a user to have confidence in the information provided by a computer system, he or she first must be confident that the data used to create the information is *accurate*. This means that the source of the data is reliable and the data is correctly reported. For example, if someone incorrectly reports to the credit bureau that an individual did not pay a bill and this information becomes part of the database, a responsible customer could be denied credit unjustly. Users must be confident that the people and organizations providing data to the credit bureau provide accurate data.

A second element of data integrity is *reliable data entry*. Data entered for processing must be entered correctly. In the credit bureau example, if a bank reports that the balance on a credit card account is $200.00, but the balance is incorrectly entered as $20,000.00, the information generated would be invalid.

The third element of data integrity is timeliness. *Timeliness* means that data to be processed has not lost its usefulness or accuracy because time has passed. For example, assume that two years ago a salary of $15,000.00 was entered for an individual. Today, that data is not timely because two years have passed and the person may be earning either less or more.

Data integrity is critical. Before an application is implemented on a computer, all the criteria for valid data must be defined and checks for valid data should be placed in the programs.

Data Security

Data management also includes managing data security. **Data security** refers to protecting data to keep it from being misused or lost. This is an important issue because misuse or loss of data can have serious consequences. In the credit bureau example, a person's credit rating and history of financial transactions are confidential. People do not want their credit information made available to unauthorized organizations. Therefore, the credit bureau must develop systems and procedures that allow only authorized personnel to access the data stored in the database. In addition, if the data in the database should be tampered with or lost, the credit bureau must have some method for recovering the correct data. Therefore, data in an information system is periodically copied or backed up. **Backup** refers to making copies of data files so that if data is lost or destroyed, a timely recovery can be made and processing can continue.

Data Maintenance

Data maintenance, another aspect of data management, refers to the procedures used to maintain data accuracy by keeping data current. These procedures are called **updating** and include **adding** new data, such as creating a record for a new person to include in the credit bureau database; **changing** existing information, such as posting a change of address to an existing record; and **deleting** obsolete information, such as removing inactive records after some designated period of time.

Summary of Data Management

Management of data is critical if an application is to be successfully processed on a computer. Data management includes managing data attributes, data security, and data maintenance. If inadequate attention is given to managing data, the information processing system will not perform as intended and the output will have little value.

HOW THE INFORMATION PROCESSING CYCLE WORKS

ow that you have learned about data, and how it is organized and managed, we can discuss the input, process, output and storage operations of the information processing cycle and show the role that data plays in each of the four operations.

Input Operations

Input operations transfer data from an input device to main memory. We have already identified many input devices—including keyboards, terminals, magnetic disk, and magnetic tape. There are many other specialized types of input devices. Some of these devices can interpret special bar codes on products, numbers on checks, and handwritten characters. Some input devices even understand the human voice.

Regardless of the input device used, the principle is the same: data entered from the input device is electronically stored in main memory. Once in main computer memory, the data can be processed under the control of a computer program.

Figure 3-6 on the next page shows the input operation required to build employee files on a personal computer. Such files are common to all companies. The user enters, or inputs, the employee's name and social security number into the main memory by pressing the appropriate keys on the keyboard.

The steps involved in entering the data into main memory and forming the employee identification number are as follows:

1. A computer program is stored in main memory. When the program begins to process, it displays a message on the screen directing the user to enter the employee's name. When the user types the name on the keyboard of the computer, the name is stored in the NAME field in main memory.
2. The program then displays a message requesting that the user enter the employee's social security number. As the digits in the social security number are entered, they are stored in main memory in a SOCIAL SECURITY field that has been defined by the program. After both the name and the social security number have been entered and stored in main memory, the input operations are complete.

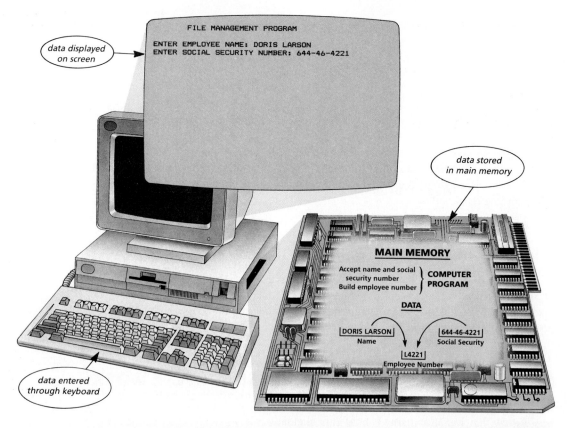

Important points illustrated by this portion of the example are: (1) Operations that occur on a computer are under the control of a program stored in the main memory of the computer. (2) The data entered from the input device (in this example, a keyboard) is electronically stored in main computer memory.

The input operation is important, because data must first be entered into main computer memory before it can be processed.

Processing Operations

Processing operations define how the data will be manipulated into a usable form. In the employee file example, the user wants to process data in order to build an employee identification number. The employee identification number consists of the first letter of the employee's last name and the last four digits of the social security number.

The processing operations are directed by instructions within the program. These instructions specify that the first letter of the last name and the last digits of the social security number are to be moved to the EMPLOYEE NUMBER field that has been defined by the program.

When data is moved from one location to another in main memory, the data in the sending location is copied or duplicated to the receiving location. Thus, in Figure 3-6, when the first letter of the last name is moved to the EMPLOYEE NUMBER field, the last name in the NAME field is not affected. Similarly, when the last four digits of the social security number are moved to the EMPLOYEE NUMBER field, the social security number in that field is not affected. The data is now located in both the sending and receiving memory locations.

As shown in the previous example, moving data from one location to another in main memory is considered a processing operation. Two other types of processing that are performed with computers include arithmetic and logical processing. The next two sections discuss these operations.

FIGURE 3-6
In this example of an input operation, the software directs the user to enter the employee's name and social security number. When the user enters this data on the keyboard, the data is electronically stored in main computer memory. The program then builds the employee number by moving the first letter of the last name and the last four digits of the social security number to the EMPLOYEE NUMBER field.

ARITHMETIC OPERATIONS

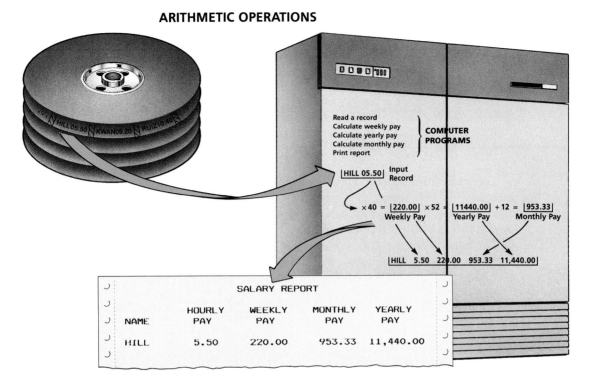

Arithmetic Operations   Business and scientific applications frequently require that **arithmetic operations** such as addition, subtraction, multiplication, and division be performed. On many computers, millions of arithmetic operations can be performed in one second. The ability to perform arithmetic operations rapidly and accurately is an important characteristic of all computers.

To illustrate the arithmetic capabilities of the computer, Figure 3-7 shows an application developed to determine a person's weekly, monthly, and yearly pay, based on hourly pay.

The first program instruction reads a record from the disk into main memory. The record contains the employee name and the hourly pay rate. These two data fields are contained in each employee's record. The file stored on disk contains a record for each of the employees.

When the record is read into main memory, program instructions direct that the weekly, yearly, and monthly pay are to be calculated. The weekly pay is determined by multiplying the hourly rate times 40 hours. The yearly pay is obtained by multiplying the weekly rate by 52 weeks. The monthly pay is calculated by dividing the yearly pay by 12. Note that when the yearly and monthly pay are calculated, answers from the previous calculations are used. Any numeric data stored in main memory, including results of previous calculations, can be used in arithmetic operations. After the calculations are completed, instructions in the program describe the output operations that will print a report.

In Figure 3-7, the first record in the file for the employee Hill has been processed. The file contains subsequent records for Kwan, Ruiz, and others. The same operations that were performed to calculate the weekly, yearly, and monthly pay for Hill are required for each subsequent employee. Thus, the program instructions will be repeated for each employee record. The computer will input the data from each record one at a time and then repeat the instructions "Read a Record, Calculate Weekly Pay, Calculate Yearly Pay, Calculate Monthly Pay, Print Report" for each record so long as there are more records in the file to be processed.

The ability to repeat the instructions in a program is very important because it allows a computer to process any number of records with a single set of instructions. It is similar to the method you would use if you were computing the weekly pay for each employee by hand. You

FIGURE 3-7
In this example of arithmetic processing, the program first reads an input record containing an employee name and hourly pay rate. The program then calculates the weekly, monthly, and yearly pay. The results of the calculations are printed in the salary report.

would compute the weekly pay for each employee one at a time and write the result in the report. You would follow the same steps for each employee. In a similar manner, the computer processes one employee, or record, at a time and repeats the same steps, or instructions, for each employee.

Important points illustrated by this example are: (1) The program stored in main memory can perform arithmetic operations on numeric data. (2) Answers derived from arithmetic operations can be used in other calculations and can also be used as output from a program. (3) The computer is processing one record at a time. (4) One set of program instructions can be repeated any number of times.

Logical Operations   The **logical operations** are the computer's ability to *compare* data stored in main memory. All computers have instructions that can compare numeric, alphabetic, and special characters. Based on the results of the comparison, different types of processing can be performed. It is this logical ability of computers that allows them to compute overtime pay, play games such as chess, perform medical diagnoses, make hotel reservations, and perform any other task that is based on comparing data.

Three types of logical operations are performed by computer programs. They are:

1. Comparing to determine if two values are *equal to* each other.
2. Comparing to determine if one value is *greater than* another value.
3. Comparing to determine if one value is *less than* another value.

Each of these logical operations is explained in the following paragraphs.

FIGURE 3-8
The program that creates the grade report uses the computer's ability to compare values. It compares a student's GPA (grade point average) to the value 4.0. If the GPA is equal to 4.0, the message HONOR STUDENT is printed on the report, along with the student's name and grade point average. If the comparison is not equal, no message is printed.

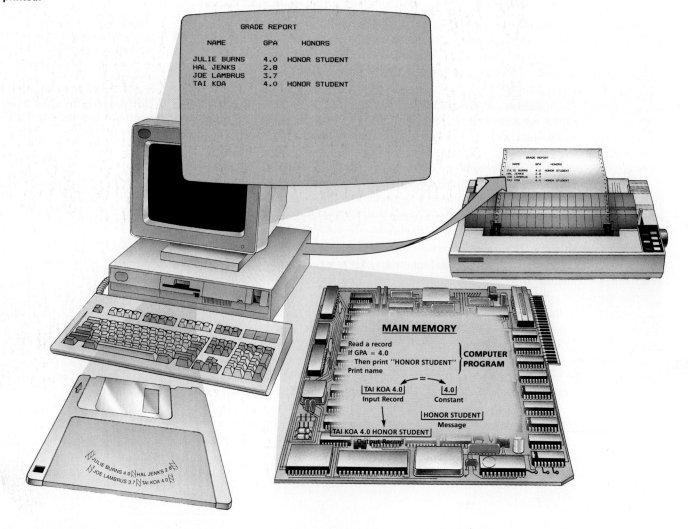

The example in Figure 3-8 illustrates the computer's ability to compare two values to determine if they are equal. This example shows a program whose function is to create a grade report. In order to make this report, an input record containing the student's name and grade point average is read. The grade point average is then compared to the value 4.0. If the grade point average is equal to 4.0, the message HONOR STUDENT is printed on the report. If the grade point average is not equal to 4.0, the message is not printed on the report.

When comparing two values, the program will specify what processing should occur when the condition tested is true and when it is false. In this example, when the condition is true (the grade point average is equal to 4.0), the processing is to print the message on the report together with the student name and average. When the condition is false (the grade point average is not equal to 4.0), the processing is not to print the message. Note that when comparing for an equal condition, the program essentially compares for an unequal condition as well.

A second type of comparison is to determine if one value is greater than another value. In the example in Figure 3-9, a database menu is displayed and the user is asked to enter a choice specifying which of the five functions is to be performed. The user should enter a value from 1 to 5. If, however, the value entered is greater than 5, an entry error has been made and the user is directed by the program to reenter the menu choice. How does the program cause the processing to occur? The program stored in main memory first displays the menu on the screen for the user. It then accepts the menu choice that the user enters. Next, the value entered by the user is compared to the value 5. If the choice entered by the user is greater than 5, the program displays the message, "Please reenter a value from 1 to 5." If the value entered by the user is not greater than five, processing will continue with another comparison to determine if the value is from 1 to 5.

The third type of comparison that is commonly performed on a computer is to determine if one value is less than another value. To illustrate this, the example in Figure 3-9 continues in Figure 3-10 on the next page, to check if the menu choice entered by the user is less than 1. If so, the user has entered an invalid value. The program will display an error message asking the user to reenter the choice and then will accept the new choice. If the value entered by the user is not less than 1, the program will continue with its processing.

An important point to note in each of the three comparison operations is that the program must specify the different types of processing that the computer is to perform. In other words, the program must specify what to do for both true and false comparison conditions. The ability of a computer to compare data and then select one of two processing paths is a simple but powerful feature that is used in programs of all levels of complexity.

FIGURE 3-9
When the user enters a menu choice, the program compares the value entered to 5, the number of valid selections. If the value entered is greater than 5, an error message is displayed and the user must reenter the choice. In this example, the user entered the value 6, the program displayed an error message, and the user was asked to reenter the choice.

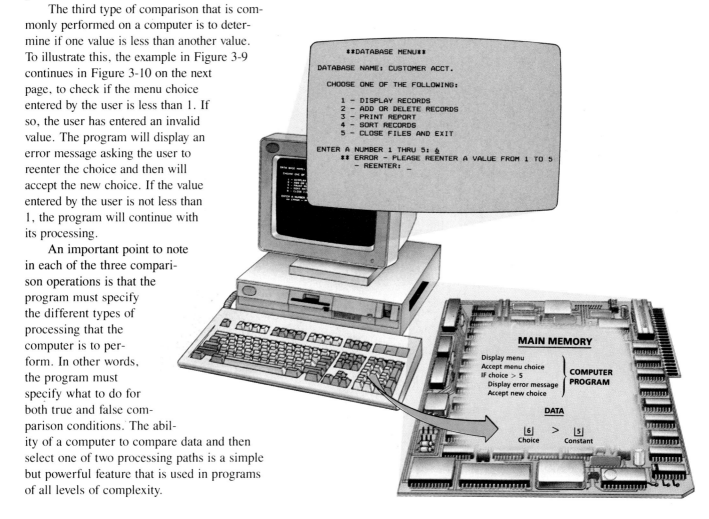

FIGURE 3-10
The value entered by the user
is compared to the value 1.
Because the value entered is
less than 1, an error message is
displayed and the user was
asked to reenter a choice.

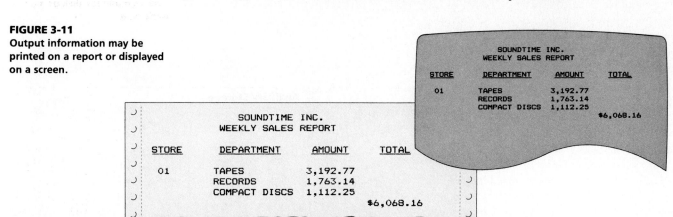

```
        **DATABASE MENU**

DATABASE NAME: CUSTOMER ACCT.

   CHOOSE ONE OF THE FOLLOWING:

      1 - DISPLAY RECORDS
      2 - ADD OR DELETE RECORDS
      3 - PRINT REPORT
      4 - SORT RECORDS
      5 - CLOSE FILES AND EXIT

ENTER A NUMBER 1 THRU 5: 0
      ** ERROR - PLEASE REENTER A VALUE FROM 1-5
            REENTER: _
```

MAIN MEMORY

Display menu
Accept menu choice
IF choice > 5
    Display error message
    Accept new choice   **COMPUTER**
IF choice < 1   **PROGRAM**
    Display error message
    Accept new choice

DATA

| 0 | > | 1 |
 Choice   Constant

Output Operations

The purpose of the input operations is to provide data and of the processing operations is to produce information. **Output operations** refer to the operations that take the information produced and put it in a form that can be used by a person or a machine. Reports are a common form of output that are often used by business people. Reports may be printed on the printer or displayed on a screen (Figure 3-11). There are many other types of output, including graphics and sound.

The type of output produced by an application depends on several factors. Some of these factors include the intended use of the output, the speed with which output delivery must take place (i.e., does the user need it right now or can it wait until later), and whether the output is to be permanently kept or used only at the moment. Whenever an application is designed for implementation on a computer, the format of the output and the way it will be presented must be defined. Users work closely with information processing personnel during the development of applications to define the best method and format of presentation.

FIGURE 3-11
Output information may be
printed on a report or displayed
on a screen.

```
           SOUNDTIME INC.
         WEEKLY SALES REPORT

STORE     DEPARTMENT      AMOUNT      TOTAL

  01      TAPES           3,192.77
          RECORDS         1,763.14
          COMPACT DISCS   1,112.25
                                     $6,068.16
```

```
              SOUNDTIME INC.
            WEEKLY SALES REPORT

STORE       DEPARTMENT       AMOUNT       TOTAL

  01        TAPES            3,192.77
            RECORDS          1,763.14
            COMPACT DISCS    1,112.25
                                          $6,068.16
```

Storage Operations

The first three operations of the information processing cycle, input, process, and output, describe the procedures that a computer performs in order to process data into information. The fourth operation, storage, refers to the electronic storage capability of a computer. To be more specific, **storage operations** refer to the transfer of programs, data, and information from main memory to an auxiliary storage device such as magnetic disk and magnetic tape (Figure 3-12 on the next page). Storage operations allow programs, data, and information that are not currently needed in main memory to be saved in an electronic format for future use. Programs and data are usually stored in this manner. Sometimes information, or the result of processing, is stored on auxiliary storage. An example of information storage would be storing on disk or tape a copy of a report that is to be printed at a later time.

Summary of the Information Processing Cycle

As you have seen, the information processing cycle consists of input, processing, output, and storage operations. These operations are controlled by a computer program. When a program begins to execute, it first directs the input operation by specifying how the data that is to be processed should be entered into main memory. Both the program directing the processing and the data to be processed must be in main memory for processing to occur. Next, the computer program directs the processing operation. Processing consists of arithmetic and logical operations and includes moving data from one location to another in main memory. As the program continues executing, it directs the output operation. This phase of the information processing cycle organizes the information produced into some form that can be used by people or other machines. Finally, program instructions direct the storage operation. Programs, data, and information that may be needed for future use are stored on auxiliary storage devices for subsequent retrieval.

STORAGE OPERATIONS

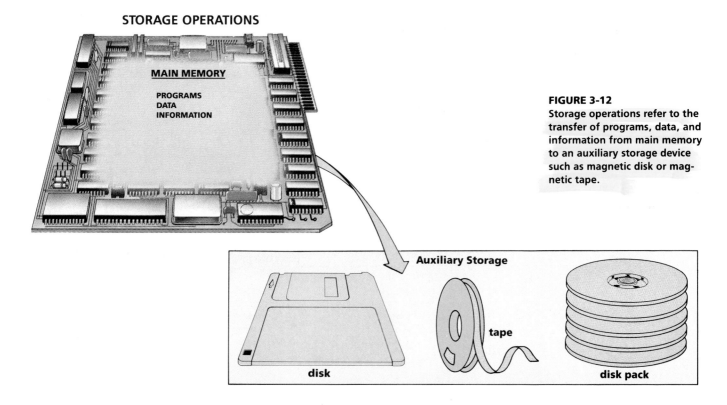

FIGURE 3-12
Storage operations refer to the transfer of programs, data, and information from main memory to an auxiliary storage device such as magnetic disk or magnetic tape.

METHODS OF PROCESSING DATA INTO INFORMATION

*T*he information processing cycle is usually implemented on a computer in one of two ways. These two methods are called interactive processing and batch processing. **Interactive processing** means that data is processed upon entry and output is produced immediately. In **batch processing**, data is collected and at some later time, all the data that has been gathered is processed as a group or "batch." Examples of these methods are given in the following sections.

FIGURE 3-13
This is an example of interactive processing to calculate the value of a savings account. After the user enters the beginning year, yearly deposit amount, and the interest rate, the program calculates and displays what the value of the account would be for the next 20 years.

Interactive Processing

The example in Figure 3-13 illustrates interactive processing. The program used in a bank accepts a beginning year, a yearly deposit amount, and an interest rate. It then calculates and displays the annual value of the savings account. This program is interactive because after the user enters the year, deposit amount, and interest rate, the program immediately performs the calculations and produces output for the user. This example illustrates the use of a personal computer for interactive processing. But large computers, such as minicomputers and mainframes, can also be used for interactive processing.

One type of interactive processing is called transaction processing. In **transaction processing**, the computer user enters all the data pertaining to a complete transaction. After all the data is entered, the program performs the processing required for that particular transaction.

The example in Figure 3-14 illustrates transaction processing as it could be used in a car rental agency. When a car is returned, the rental clerk enters on the terminal all the data required to prepare the final auto rental agreement. The program immediately retrieves the car's record from the disk (based on the license number), performs the necessary calculations, and writes the final rental agreement on the printer. The clerk then gives a copy to the customer. In addition to printing the final rental agreement, the program changes the car's record on disk by placing the ending mileage in the record. After this processing is done, the entire auto rental transaction is completed.

INTERACTIVE PROCESSING

```
ENTER YEAR: 1990
ENTER YEARLY DEPOSIT: 1000
ENTER INTEREST RATE: 10.5

YEAR    SAVINGS      YEAR    SAVINGS

1990    1,105.00     2000    21,037.72
1991    2,326.03     2001    24,351.60
1992    3,675.26     2002    28,013.61
1993    5,166.16     2003    32,060.03
1994    6,013.61     2004    36,531.34
1995    8,634.04     2005    41,472.13
1996    10,645.61    2006    46,931.70
1997    12,868.40    2007    52,964.53
1998    15,324.58    2008    59,638.81
1999    18,038.66    2009    66,997.04

PERFORM ANOTHER CALCULATION?
ENTER YES OR NO:
```

MAIN MEMORY

Accept year
Accept deposit amount
Accept interest rate
Calculate yearly savings amount
Print savings amounts

COMPUTER PROGRAM

DATA

| 1990 | | 1000.00 | | 10.5 |
| Year | | Yearly Deposit | | Interest Rate |

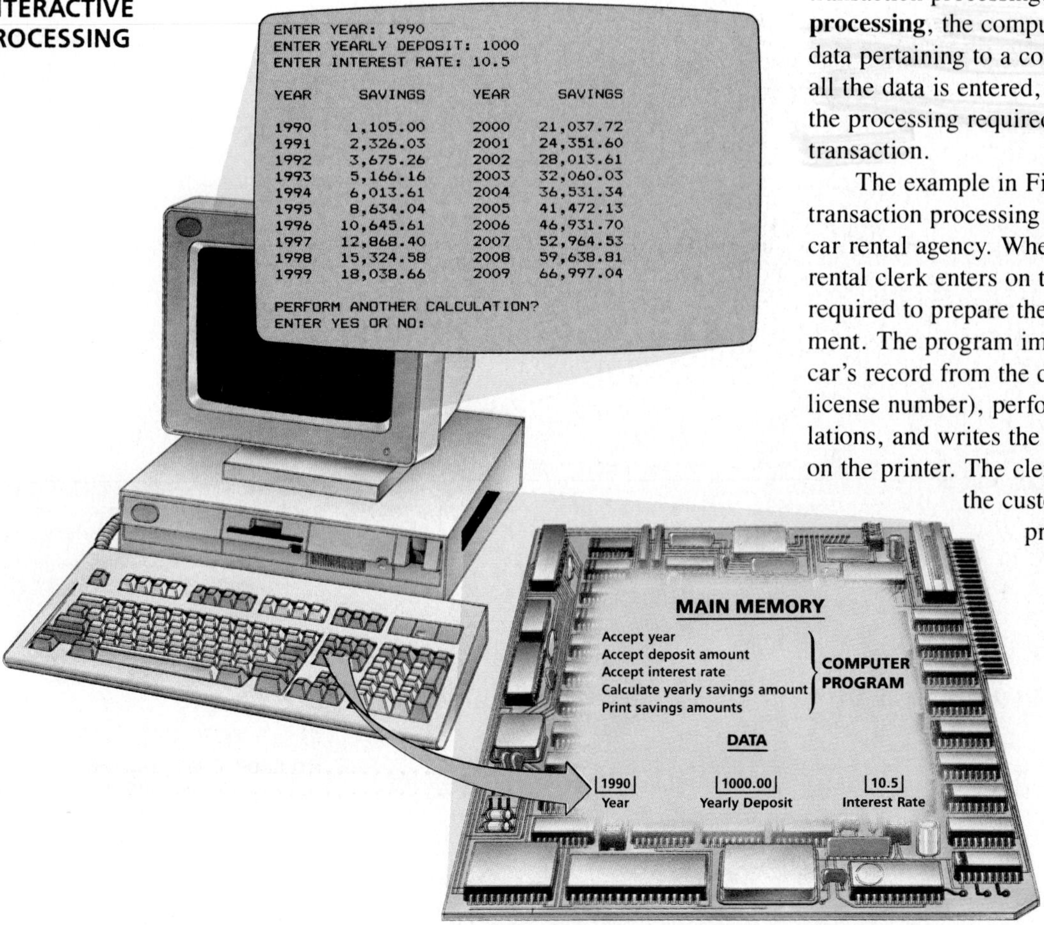

Note that the entire transaction was completed immediately after the user entered the input data. The key to understanding interactive processing is to realize that as soon as the required input data has been entered, the program performs the processing and generates output.

TRANSACTION PROCESSING

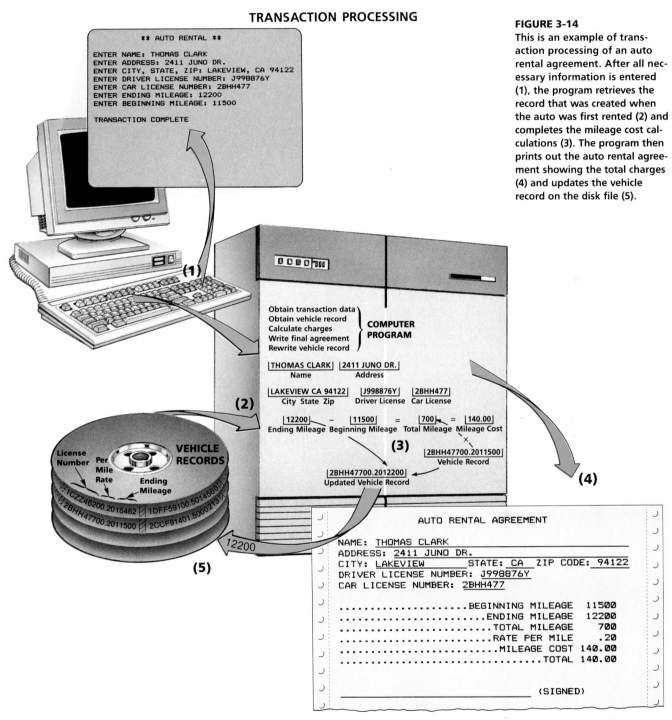

FIGURE 3-14
This is an example of transaction processing of an auto rental agreement. After all necessary information is entered (1), the program retrieves the record that was created when the auto was first rented (2) and completes the mileage cost calculations (3). The program then prints out the auto rental agreement showing the total charges (4) and updates the vehicle record on the disk file (5).

After the updated record is rewritten, the ending mileage (12200) would be in the record. This is not shown in the record stored on disk.

Batch Processing

Batch processing was used extensively when computers were first used in business. In many cases, source documents containing the data to be processed were brought to a central location where the data was punched on cards or placed on magnetic tape. All the data, in one single group or batch, was then read into the computer for processing. Many of the early applications implemented on computers, such as payroll or billing operations, were best processed in a batch environment.

Today, interactive processing is the most prominent method of processing because it provides immediate results and keeps data current. However, batch processing is still the best way to implement some applications. Applications that require periodic processing of a large number of records are good possibilities for batch processing. Payroll applications that create paychecks periodically, such as every other week, normally operate using a batch method of processing. Other users of batch processing include utility companies, which must send out thousands of bills each month, and credit card companies, which process thousands of charges and payments each month.

As shown in Figure 3-15, the following steps take place in batch processing.

1. The consumer uses a credit card to purchase an item from a store. A sales receipt is produced and becomes the source document.
2. The sales receipt is transmitted to the data entry section of the information systems department at the bank or company processing the credit card purchase. In this example, it is the First Federal Bank.
3. At a terminal, a data entry clerk enters the data from the sales receipt into a disk file. Several data entry personnel could be entering sales receipts at the same time.
4. When all the sales receipts for a given day have been entered, the file of data stored on disk is read into main memory and processed one record at a time. This is batch processing, where all records have been batched into one input file and then processed together.
5. When the input record is read from the batch input file, the corresponding customer record from the account file is also retrieved. The account file contains a record for each cardholder. The record contains the account number, the cardholder's name and address, and the account balance. In the example, the customer's name is Hal Dukes, the address is 613 Acorn Drive, Plain, Wyoming 83742, and the account balance prior to processing the purchase record is $265.40. When the account record is retrieved, it is updated to reflect the latest status of the account by adding the purchase amount from the input record to the account balance found in the account record.
6. After the account record is updated, it is rewritten in the account file. Thus, the next time Hal Dukes makes a purchase, the new balance, $309.39, will be in his account record.
7. After all the sales receipts are processed, another program might be run to prepare the account statements. Account statements are usually sent out once a month and contain the previous statement balance, the current charges, the current balance, the minimum payment (calculated by the program), and the payment due date.

This example illustrated each step that could occur when a purchase is made with a credit card. The important point of the example is that the input records are all batched together into a single input file. They are then processed as a group, updating the account file. At some later time, all account file records are processed as a batch to provide account statements. In applications of this type, hundreds or even thousands of records would be processed in one run of the program. Batch processing is the most appropriate method for processing this application because it provides the information when it is needed and it is cheaper than interactive processing.

BATCH PROCESSING

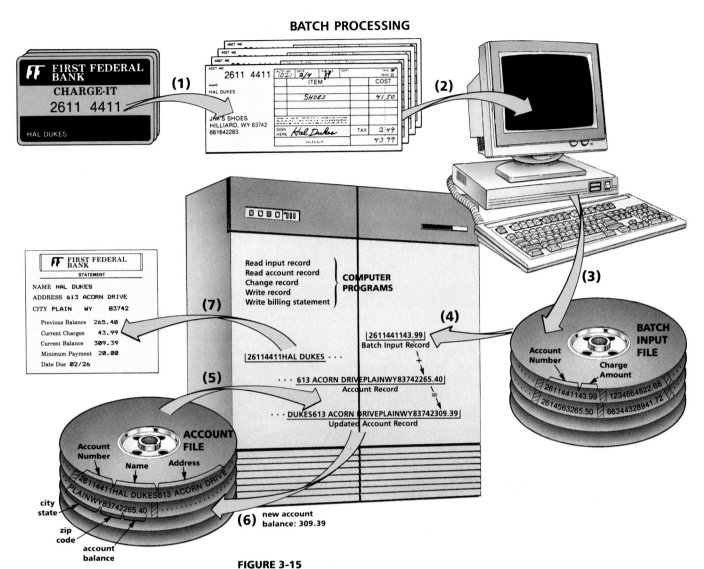

FIGURE 3-15
In this example of batch processing, a customer uses a credit card to make a purchase (1). A copy of the sales receipt is entered into the computer system (2) and recorded in a batch input file with charges for other customers (3). At the end of the day, when all charges have been entered into the file, the file is read by a program (4) and processed in a batch mode to update customer account balances stored on another file (5). New account balance amounts are written on the account file (6). At a later time, another program is run to produce customer account statements (7).

Combined Interactive and Batch Processing

Interactive and batch processing can be combined in a single application. This is illustrated in Figure 3-16, which shows a sales transaction in a retail store. The following steps occur:

1. The store clerk enters the details of the sale on a **point of sale terminal**, a special cash register that is connected to a computer. The sales data includes the department number where the sale took place (14), the item number of the item purchased (A437), and the quantity of items purchased (01).
2. As soon as the sales information (input data) is stored in main memory, the program directs the computer to retrieve the record corresponding to the item number (A437) from the item file. The record retrieved contains the item number (A437), the quantity of the item in inventory (0527), and the unit price for the item (14.95).
3. The program reduces the quantity in the item record (527) by the quantity purchased (1), giving the new inventory quantity (526). It also multiplies the quantity purchased (1) by the unit price (14.95) to determine the total sales amount (14.95). The total sales amount is sent back to the point of sale terminal, where the clerk can complete the transaction with the customer.
4. The item record with the new quantity (526) is written back into the item file. Interactive processing has been used in steps 1 through 4.
5. The program also adds a record to the sales transaction file. The sales transaction file contains a record for each sale that is made during the day at the store. These records will be used at the end of the day in batch processing.
6. After the store is closed and all transactions have been completed, the sales transaction file is input to a program that produces the daily sales report. This report contains the department and sales amount for each sale, the total dollar sales amount for each department of the store, and the total sales in the store for the day. Batch processing has been used in steps 5 and 6.

This application illustrates both interactive processing and batch processing of data generated from a single transaction. When the sales clerk enters the sale on the point of sale terminal and the program responds with the total sales amount, interactive processing has occurred. As soon as the data was entered, the program processed the data by performing the calculations, updating the item file, and producing output on the point of sale terminal. At the same time, input data for batch processing was created when the program wrote a record in the sales transaction file. When these transactions were used to produce the daily sales report, batch processing occurred. All the transaction records were batched together to be processed at one time. It would make little sense to produce the daily sales report until all the sales transactions for the day had been completed. Thus, batch processing is the appropriate method to use to prepare the daily sales report. Because each sale must be processed as it occurs, interactive processing is the appropriate method for the sales and item record processing.

Summary of Processing Methods

Interactive and batch processing are the two main methods for processing data on a computer. Generally, most processing that is performed on personal computers is interactive processing. On larger computers, the trend is toward more interactive processing, although batch processing is still appropriate for some applications. In addition, some processing involves a combination of both interactive and batch processing.

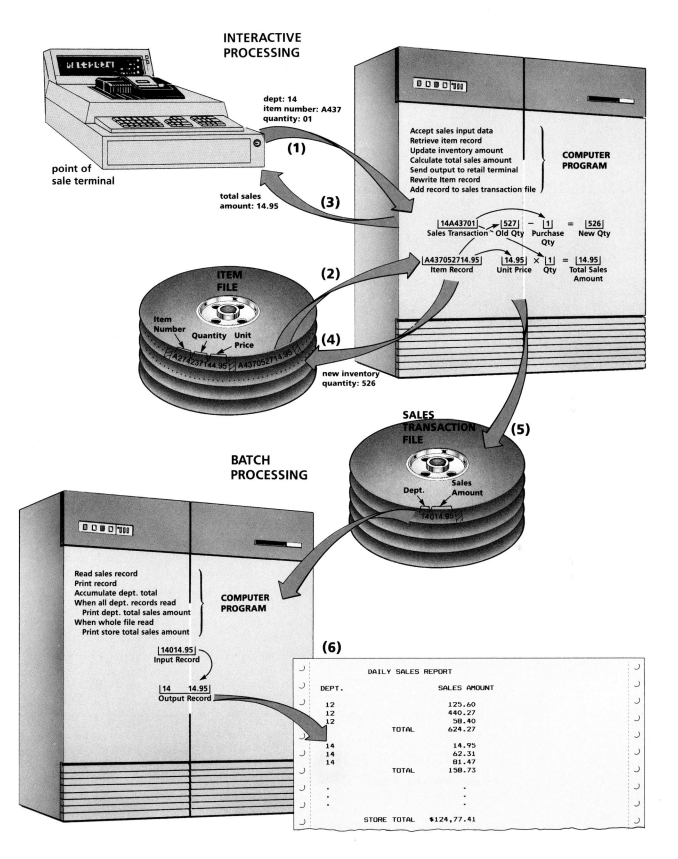

INTERACTIVE PROCESSING

point of sale terminal

dept: 14
item number: A437
quantity: 01

total sales amount: 14.95

(1)
(3)
(2)
(4)

Accept sales input data
Retrieve item record
Update inventory amount
Calculate total sales amount
Send output to retail terminal
Rewrite Item record
Add record to sales transaction file

COMPUTER PROGRAM

|14A43701| → |527| − |1| = |526|
Sales Transaction Old Qty Purchase Qty New Qty

|A437052714.95| → |14.95| × |1| = |14.95|
Item Record Unit Price Qty Total Sales Amount

ITEM FILE

Item Number   Quantity   Unit Price
A274237144.95   A437052714.95

new inventory quantity: 526

SALES TRANSACTION FILE

(5)

Dept.   Sales Amount
14014.95

BATCH PROCESSING

Read sales record
Print record
Accumulate dept. total
When all dept. records read
  Print dept. total sales amount
When whole file read
  Print store total sales amount

COMPUTER PROGRAM

|14014.95|
Input Record

|14   14.95|
Output Record

(6)

```
        DAILY SALES REPORT

DEPT.                SALES AMOUNT

12                      125.60
12                      440.27
12                       58.40
        TOTAL           624.27

14                       14.95
14                       62.31
14                       81.47
        TOTAL           158.73

.                          .
.                          .
.                          .

STORE TOTAL    $124,77.41
```

FIGURE 3-16
This example illustrates both interactive and batch processing resulting from a single sales transaction. The inventory balance is updated interactively but the sales report is prepared by batch processing at the end of the day.

QUALITIES OF INFORMATION

As we have discussed, the purpose of processing data is to create information. Just as data should have certain characteristics, so too should information. These characteristics are often called the "qualities of information." Terms used to describe these qualities include the following: accurate, verifiable, timely, organized, meaningful, useful, and cost effective.

Although it may seem obvious, the first quality of information is that it should be *accurate*. Inaccurate information is often worse than no information at all. As you may recall, accuracy was also a characteristic of data. And although accurate data does not guarantee accurate information, it is impossible to produce accurate information from erroneous data. The computer jargon term **GIGO** states this point very well; it stands for "Garbage In, Garbage Out."

Closely related to accuracy is the quality of information being *verifiable*. This means that if necessary, the user can confirm the information. For example, before relying on the amounts in a summary report, an accountant would want to know that the totals could be supported by details of transactions.

Another quality of information is that it must be *timely*. Although most information loses its value with time, some information, such as trends, becomes more valuable as time passes and more information is obtained. The important point here is that the timeliness must be appropriate for any decisions that will be made based on the information. Up-to-the-minute information may be required for some decisions while older information may be satisfactory or more appropriate for others.

To be of the most value, information should be *organized* to suit users' requirements. For example, a sales representative assigned to sell only to companies in a specific area would prefer to have a prospect list organized by zip code rather than a list that was only in alphabetical order.

Meaningful information means that the information is relevant to the person who receives it. Much information is only meaningful to specific individuals or groups within an organization. Extraneous and unnecessary information should be eliminated and the "audience" of the information should always be kept in mind.

To be *useful*, information should result in an action being taken or specifically not taken, as the case may be. Often, this quality can be improved through **exception reporting**, which focuses only on the information that exceeds certain limits. An example of exception reporting would be an inventory report showing items whose balance on hand is less than a predetermined minimum quantity. Rather than looking through an entire inventory report to find such items, the exception report would quickly bring these items to the attention of the persons responsible for inventory management.

Last, but not least, information must be *cost effective*. In other words, the cost to produce the information must be less than the "value" of the information. This can sometimes be hard to determine. If the value of the information cannot be determined, perhaps the information should only be produced as required instead of regularly. Many organizations periodically review the information they produce in reports to determine if the reports still have the qualities discussed above and their production cost can still be justified or possibly reduced.

Although the qualities of information have been discussed in conjunction with computer systems, these qualities apply to all information regardless of how it is produced. Knowing these qualities will help you evaluate the information you receive and provide every day.

SUMMARY OF PROCESSING DATA INTO INFORMATION

*T*he concepts presented in this chapter concerning data, the information processing cycle, interactive and batch processing, and the qualities of information apply to all information processing systems. By now you have developed an understanding and a "feeling" for the way a computer processes data into information. Your increased understanding should help you to feel more comfortable with computers and how they can be used.

CHAPTER SUMMARY

1. The **information processing cycle** consists of input, processing, output, and storage operations.
2. Regardless of the size and type of computer, the information processing cycle is used to process data into information.
3. The operations in the information processing cycle are carried out through the combined use of computer equipment, also called computer hardware, and computer software.
4. Computer software, or programs, contain the instructions that direct the computer equipment to perform the four types of operations.
5. The primary input devices are keyboards on microcomputers and terminals on larger machines.
6. Input devices are used to enter both computer programs and data into main memory.
7. Both the program that is to control the processing and the data to be processed must be in main memory for processing to occur.
8. Program instructions are executed by the processor.
9. The primary output devices on computers are printers and screens.
10. Auxiliary storage devices commonly used with computers are magnetic tape and magnetic disk.
11. Some devices are used for more than one purpose in the information processing cycle. For example, disks can be used for both input and output.
12. Data is the prime ingredient of an information processing system.
13. **Data** is defined as raw facts and consists of the numbers and words that a computer receives and processes to produce information.
14. Data is composed of **characters**. These include **alphabetic** (A–Z), **numeric** (0–9), and **special** characters, such as ( ) * & % # @ , .
15. Individual facts are referred to as **data items**, **data fields**, or **fields**.
16. Fields may be classified as **numeric**, **alphabetic**, or **alphanumeric**.
17. A field is often more useful when it is combined with other related fields.
18. A **record** is a collection of related fields.
19. A collection of related records is called a **file**.
20. Files are stored on some medium, such as magnetic tape or magnetic disk.
21. In a **sequential** file, records are arranged in alphabetical or numerical order by a **key field**.
22. The records in a **random** file are not arranged in any sequence or order.
23. A **database** provides an efficient way to establish a relationship between data items and implies that a relationship has been established between multiple files.
24. Data is organized into fields, records, files, and databases for processing on a computer.
25. **Data management** refers to techniques and procedures that ensure that the data required for an application will be available in the correct form and at the proper time for processing.
26. Data management includes the management of data attributes, data security, and data maintenance.
27. Data attributes include data availability and data integrity.
28. Data that is required for input must be available.
29. **Data integrity** determines the confidence a user can have in the processing of that data. The three elements of data integrity are data accuracy, reliable data entry, and timeliness.

30. Accurate data depends on a reliable source.
31. Reliable data entry must occur for the information generated to be valid.
32. Timeliness means that data has not lost its usefulness or accuracy because time has passed.
33. **Data security** is an important issue because misuse or loss of data can have serious consequences.
34. **Backup** procedures provide for maintaining copies of data so that in the event of loss data can be recovered.
35. **Data maintenance** refers to **updating** data. This includes **adding, changing** and **deleting** data in order to keep it current.
36. **Input operations** cause the data that is to be processed to be stored in main memory.
37. Once data is stored in main memory, it can be processed under the control of a computer program.
38. **Processing operations** define how the data will be manipulated into a usable form.
39. When data is moved from one location in memory to another, it is not destroyed but is duplicated in the new location.
40. Two main types of processing operations include arithmetic and logical processing of data.
41. Many computers are able to perform millions of **arithmetic operations** in one second, including addition, subtraction, multiplication, and division.
42. The results of arithmetic operations can be used in subsequent arithmetic operations, moved to other locations in main memory, and used for output.
43. **Logical operations** allow a computer to compare two data fields to determine if one is **equal to, greater than,** or **less than** the other.
44. Logical operations are performed on a computer by the execution of program instructions that direct the computer to compare data fields that are currently stored in main memory.
45. The result of a logical operation determines which of the processing paths of a program will be performed.
46. The ability of a computer to compare data and then select one of two processing paths is a powerful feature that is used in programs of all levels of complexity.
47. The process of repeating the instructions in a program allows a single set of program instructions to process any number of records.
48. **Output operations** take the information produced and put it in a form that can be used by a person or a machine. A common form of output are reports that are displayed on the screen or printed on the printer.
49. **Storage operations** refer to the transfer of programs, data, and information from main memory to an auxiliary storage device such as magnetic disk and magnetic tape.
50. The two methods used for processing data on a computer are interactive processing and batch processing.
51. **Interactive processing** means that data is processed upon entry and output is produced immediately.
52. **Transaction processing** is a type of interactive processing in which the user enters all the data pertaining to a complete transaction and the program immediately performs all the processing required for that particular transaction.
53. In **batch processing**, data is collected and at some later time, all the data that has been gathered is processed as a group or batch.
54. Batch and interactive processing can be combined in a single application.
55. The terms used to describe the qualities of information include accurate, verifiable, timely, organized, meaningful, useful, and cost effective.
56. **GIGO** is an acronym that stands for "Garbage In, Garbage Out."

KEY TERMS

Adding (data) *3.7*
Alphabetic (characters) *3.4*
Alphabetic field *3.4*
Alphanumeric field *3.4*
Arithmetic operations *3.9*
Backup *3.6*
Batch processing *3.14*
Changing (data) *3.7*
Characters *3.4*
Data *3.4*
Database *3.5*
Data field *3.4*
Data integrity *3.6*
Data item *3.4*

Data maintenance *3.7*
Data management *3.5*
Data security *3.6*
Deleting (data) *3.7*
Exception reporting *3.20*
Field *3.4*
File *3.5*
GIGO *3.20*
Information processing cycle *3.2*
Input operations *3.7*
Interactive processing *3.14*
Key field *3.5*
Logical operations *3.10*
Meaningful *3.20*

Numeric (characters) *3.4*
Numeric field *3.4*
Output operations *3.12*
Point of sale terminal *3.18*
Processing operations *3.8*
Random *3.5*
Record *3.4*
Sequential *3.5*
Special (characters) *3.4*
Storage operations *3.13*
Transaction processing *3.14*
Updating *3.7*

REVIEW QUESTIONS

1. What are the four elements of the information processing cycle? What types and sizes of computers can be used to implement the information processing cycle?
2. What is the definition of data? What terms are used to describe how data is organized for processing?
3. Why is data management important?
4. What is data integrity? What are the three elements of data integrity?
5. What is meant by 'data security? How does it relate to the privacy of an individual?
6. What is the input operation on a computer? What happens when the input operation takes place?
7. Why is the ability to repeat instructions in a program important?
8. Name three logical operations that can be performed on data.
9. Describe the purpose of the output operations. What is the most common form of output used by people?
10. Why are storage operations necessary? What are the primary devices used for auxiliary storage?
11. What is interactive processing? Give an example.
12. What is transaction processing?
13. What is batch processing? When is its use appropriate?
14. Is it possible to have batch processing and interactive processing in the same application? Why wouldn't just one processing method be used?
15. Describe the qualities of information.

CONTROVERSIAL ISSUES

1. In this chapter, we noted that computers can perform millions of arithmetic operations in a single second. Some people claim that much greater speed is needed for computers so that applications such as weather prediction and space flight simulation can be accurately performed within a reasonable time period. These people think research money should be spent to find ways to develop faster computers. Other people argue that computers process data fast enough and that research money should be spent in other areas, such as developing privacy safeguards. Take a side in this debate and defend your position.

2. Software is currently available that lets medical patients inform a computer of their symptoms by answering a series of questions. The program then compares the answers to symptoms retrieved from auxiliary storage. When equal conditions are found, a possible diagnosis will be given and, perhaps, a treatment suggested. Is the computer doing the same type of "thinking" that a doctor does when analyzing symptoms? Take a position and defend it.

3. In the past few years, some have advocated that all applications placed on a computer should use the interactive processing method. These people state that such features as the inherent delays when processing data in a batch method make batch processing obsolete. Other experts dispute this, saying that for some applications, batch is the best means for processing data. Take a position on this disagreement and defend your position.

RESEARCH PROJECTS

1. A banking application was described in this chapter. Visit a bank or savings and loan in your area. Determine the techniques they use to enter a new customer, make changes in account records for deposits and withdrawals, and close an account. Write a report for your class.

2. Obtain a manual for a programming language such as BASIC or COBOL. List and describe all the instructions that are used to compare data and the comparisons they can make. Include in your report the rules for comparing numeric data to numeric data and alphabetic data to alphabetic data.

Input to the Computer

Input to the Computer

OBJECTIVES

- Define the four types of input and how the computer uses each type.
- Describe the standard features of keyboards and explain how to use the cursor control and function keys.
- Identify the two types of terminals and how to use each type.
- Describe several input devices other than the keyboard and terminal.
- Define user interface and explain how it has evolved.
- Define the term menu and describe various forms of menus.
- Discuss some of the features that should be included in a good user interface.
- Discuss the differences between interactive and batch processing data entry.
- Describe online and offline data entry and the uses for each.
- List and explain the systems and procedures associated with data entry.
- Explain the term ergonomics and describe some of the changes that have occurred in equipment design.

*I*n the information processing cycle, the input operation must take place before any data can be processed and any information produced. Without valid input data, a computer is not capable of producing any useful information.

When they were first utilized for business applications, nearly all computers used punched cards as input. The data was recorded on cards using a device called a keypunch. A keypunch is a machine that contains a keyboard and a punching mechanism. As the operator presses the keys, holes representing numbers, letters of the alphabet, or special characters are punched into the card. The cards are then collected together and read into main memory by a card reader.

Today, punched cards are not as often used as input to a computer. In addition, the user has more choices concerning the type of input device or devices to be used for an application. This chapter examines some of the devices used for input, the ways that both hardware and software are designed to make input operations easier for the user, and the various methods of entering data into the computer.

WHAT IS INPUT?

Input refers to the process of entering programs, commands, user responses, and data into main memory. Input can also refer to the media (e.g., tapes, cards, documents, etc.) that contain these input types. These four types of input are used by a computer in the following ways:

- **Programs** are the sets of instructions that direct the computer to perform the necessary operations to process data into information. The program that is loaded and stored in main memory determines the processing that the computer will perform. When a program is first entered into a computer it is input by way of a keyboard. Once the program has been entered and stored on auxiliary storage, it can be transferred to main memory by a command.
- **Commands** are key words and phrases that the user inputs to direct the computer to perform certain activities. For example, if you wanted to use a payroll program, you might issue a command such as LOAD "PAYROLL" to load the program named PAYROLL into main memory from auxiliary storage. To begin the execution of the program you would enter another command such as RUN (Figure 4-1).
- **User responses** refer to the data that a user inputs in response to a question or message from the software. Usually these messages display on a screen and the user responds through a keyboard. One of the most common responses is to answer "Yes" or "No" to a question. Based on the answer, the computer program will perform specific actions. For example, in a spreadsheet program, typing the letter Y in response to the message "Do you want to save this file?" will result in the spreadsheet file being saved (written) to the auxiliary storage device.
- **Data** is raw facts; it is the source from which information is produced. It must be entered and stored in main computer memory for processing to occur. For example, data entered from sales orders can be processed by a computer program to produce sales reports useful to management. Data is the most common type of input.

Regardless of the type, input will be entered through some kind of input device. The next section of this chapter discusses the various types of available input devices.

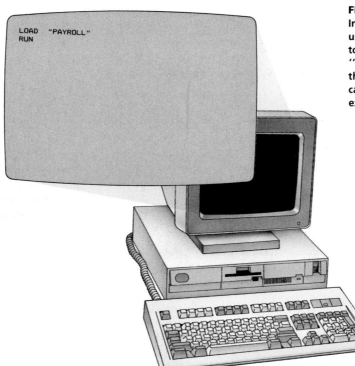

FIGURE 4-1
In this example, the computer user first entered a command to load the program called "PAYROLL" and then issued the command RUN, which will cause the program to be executed.

THE KEYBOARD

Keyboards are the most commonly used input devices. Users input data to a computer by pressing the keys on the keyboard. Keyboards are connected to other devices, such as a personal computer or a terminal, that have screens. As the user enters data on the keyboard, it displays on the screen.

The keyboards used for computer input are very similar to the keyboards used on the familiar office machine, the typewriter (Figure 4-2). They contain numbers, letters of the alphabet, and some special characters. In addition, many computer keyboards are equipped with a special **numeric keypad** on the right-hand side of the keyboard. These numeric keys are arranged in an adding machine or calculator format and aid the user with data entry.

FIGURE 4-2

The IBM PS/Model 30 keyboard shown in the picture contains a numeric keypad, cursor control keys, and function keys. The keys on the numeric keypad are arranged in the same order as the keys on an adding machine or a calculator. This arrangement allows those skilled in entering numbers to input numeric data at a much faster rate than if the number keys were across the top of the keyboard as they are on a typewriter. The four cursor control keys are identified by up ↑, down ↓, left ←, and right → arrows. When the user presses one of these keys, the cursor moves one position in the direction indicated by the arrow. Function keys are used for specific commands that are either programmed by the user or determined by the application software. Function keys can be located in different places, but on most keyboards they are either on the left side or along the top.

Keyboards also contain keys that can be used to position the cursor on the screen. A **cursor** is a symbol, such as a highlighted rectangle or an underline character, that indicates where on the screen the next character entered will be displayed. The keys that move the cursor are called **arrow keys** or **cursor control keys**. When pressed, the keys move the cursor in the direction where the arrow points. Cursor control keys have an up arrow, a down arrow, a left arrow, and a right arrow. When you press any of these keys, the cursor moves one space in the direction specified by the arrow. In addition, many keyboards contain other cursor control keys such as the HOME key, which when pressed sends the cursor to the upper left position of the screen or document.

Some computer keyboards also contain keys that are used to alter or edit the text displayed on the screen. For example, the INSERT and DELETE keys allow characters to be inserted into or deleted from data that appears on the screen.

Function keys are keys that can be programmed to accomplish certain tasks that will assist the user. For example, a function key might be programmed for use as a help key when a terminal is used for word processing. Whenever the key is pressed, messages will appear that give instructions pertaining to the word processor. Another use of function keys is to save keystrokes. Sometimes several keystrokes are required to accomplish a certain task, for example, printing a document. Some application software packages are written so that the user can either enter the individual keystrokes or press a function key and obtain the same result.

The disadvantage of using a keyboard as an input device is that training is required to use it efficiently. Users who do not know how to type are at a disadvantage because of the time they spend looking for the appropriate keys. While there are other input devices that are appropriate in some situations, users should be encouraged to develop their keyboard skills.

TERMINALS

*T*erminals, sometimes called **display terminals** or **video display terminals (VDTs),** consist of a keyboard and a screen. They fall into two basic categories: dumb terminals and intelligent terminals (sometimes called programmable terminals). We explain the features of each type in the following paragraphs. Figure 4-3 shows an example of each type of terminal.

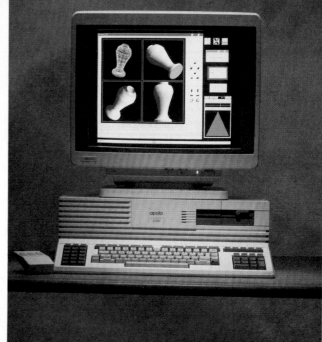

FIGURE 4-3
Terminals can be classified into two broad categories: dumb terminals and intelligent terminals. From appearance alone, it is often difficult to tell in which category a terminal belongs. In these photos the dumb terminal on the left lacks a CPU.

Dumb Terminals

A **dumb terminal** consists of a keyboard and a display screen that can be used to enter and transmit data to or receive and display data from a computer to which it is connected. A dumb terminal has no independent processing capability or auxiliary storage and cannot function as a stand-alone device.

Intelligent Terminals

Intelligent terminals are terminals whose processing capabilities are built in. These terminals are also known as **programmable terminals** because they can be programmed by the user to perform many basic tasks, including both arithmetic and logic operations. Personal computers are frequently used as intelligent terminals (Figure 4-4).

FIGURE 4-4
This WYSE pc 286 personal computer can function as both a stand-alone computer or as a terminal when it is connected to another computer system.

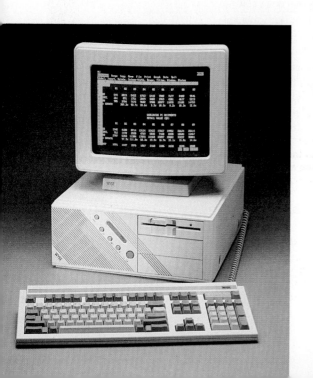

Intelligent terminals often contain not only the keyboard and screen associated with other terminals, but also are supported with disk drives and printers, so they can perform limited processing tasks when not communicating directly with the central computer. In some instances, when the user enters data, the data will be checked for errors and some type of report will be produced. In addition, the valid data that is entered will be stored on the disk connected to the terminal. After the data has been entered and stored on disk, it will be transmitted over communication lines to the central computer. This operation is sometimes called **uploading**, because the data is loaded from the smaller terminal "up" to the bigger main computer. Uploading is used most often when the data entered is to be processed in a batch processing mode.

As the amount of processing power that is incorporated into intelligent terminals increases, more processing can occur at the site of the terminal prior to sending the data to the central computer. This means that the large minicomputer or mainframe at the central site can perform the main processing and serve multiple users faster, rather than having to use its resources to perform tasks that can be performed by the intelligent terminal.

Special Purpose Terminals

Terminals are found in virtually every environment that generates data for processing on a computer. While many are standard terminals like those previously described, others are designed to perform specific jobs and contain features uniquely designed for use in a particular industry.

The terminal shown in Figure 4-5 is called a point of sale terminal. **Point of sale terminals** allow data to be entered at the time and place where the transaction with a customer occurs, such as in fast-food restaurants or hotels, for example. Point of sale terminals serve as input to either minicomputers located at the place of business or larger computers located elsewhere. The data entered is used to maintain sales records, update inventory, make automatic calculations such as sales tax, verify credit, and perform other activities associated with the sales transactions and critical to running the business. Point of sale terminals are designed to be easy to operate, requiring little technical knowledge.

FIGURE 4-5
This point of sale terminal is specially designed for grocery store item entry. The checker can press separate keys to process the prices of produce, meat, and other items.

OTHER INPUT DEVICES

*B*esides keyboards and terminals, there is an increasing variety of other input devices. This section describes some of the devices used for general purpose applications.

The Mouse

The mouse, initially designed by Xerox, is a unique device used with personal computers and some computer terminals. A **mouse** is a small, lightweight device that easily fits in the palm of your hand. You move it across a flat surface such as a desktop (Figure 4-6) to control the movement of the cursor on a screen. The mouse is attached to the computer by a cable. On the bottom of the mouse are one or more wheels or balls. As the mouse moves across the flat surface, the computer electronically senses the movement of the wheels. The movement of the cursor on the screen corresponds to the movement of the mouse (Figure 4-7). When you move the mouse left on the surface of the table or desk, the cursor moves left on the screen. When you move the mouse right, the cursor moves right, and so on.

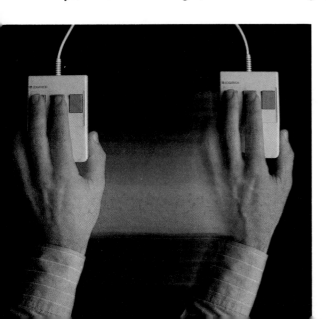

FIGURE 4-6 ▶
The mouse can be moved to control the cursor on the screen. Press the button at the top of the mouse to make selections or perform functions, depending on the software being used. The ball on the underside of the mouse moves as the user pushes the mouse around on a hard, flat surface. The movement of the ball causes the cursor to move correspondingly on the screen.

◀ **FIGURE 4-7**
This drawing illustrates using a mouse. The index finger, which rests on the top of the mouse, acts as a pointer to guide the movement of the mouse and the related movement of the cursor on the screen.

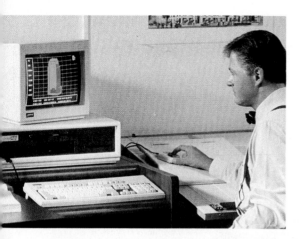

FIGURE 4-8
Notice that some amount of clear desk space is required for moving the mouse.

On top of the mouse are one or more buttons. By moving the cursor on the screen and pressing the buttons, you can make menu choices, choose letters or words in a word processing application for addition or deletion, move data from one point on the screen to another, and perform many other actions that move and rearrange information displayed on the screen.

The primary advantage of a mouse is that it is easy to use. Proponents of the mouse say that with a little practice, a person can use a mouse to point to locations on the screen just as easily as using a finger. For some applications such as desktop publishing, a mouse is indispensable.

There are two major disadvantages of the mouse. The first is that it requires empty desk space where it can be moved about (Figure 4-8). The second disadvantage is that the user must remove a hand from the keyboard and place it on the mouse whenever the cursor is to be moved or a command is to be given. Some keyboard experts have noted that taking hands from the keyboard slows the effective data entry speed considerably. Thus, some people have said the mouse is not an effective tool in those environments where keying must be performed rapidly, such as in word processing applications. Others, however, say that using a mouse is far superior to using the cursor control keys on a keyboard.

Touch Screens

Touch screens allow users to merely touch areas of the screen to enter data. They let the user interact with a computer by the touch of a finger, rather than typing on a keyboard or moving a mouse. The user enters data by touching words or numbers, or locations identified on the screen (Figure 4-9).

Several electronic techniques change a touch on the screen into electronic impulses that can be interpreted by the computer software. One of the most common techniques utilizes beams of infrared light, that are projected across the surface of the screen. A finger or other utensil touching the screen interrupts the beams, generating an electronic signal. This signal identifies the location on the screen where the touch occurred. The software interprets the signal and performs the required function.

FIGURE 4-9
Touch screens allow the user to make choices and execute commands by actually touching areas of the screen. Touch screens require special software that determines where the user touched the screen and what action should be taken.

Touch screens are not used to enter large amounts of data. They are used, however, for applications in which the user must issue a command to the software to perform a particular task or must choose from a list of options to be performed.

There are both advantages and disadvantages of touch screens. A significant advantage is that they are very "natural" to use; that is, people are used to pointing to things. With touch screens, they can point to indicate the processing they want performed by the computer. In addition, touch screens are usually easy for the user to learn. As quickly as pointing a finger, the user's request is processed. Finally, touch screens allow absolute cursor movement; that is, the user can point a finger at the location where the cursor is to appear and it will. This can be considerably faster than repeatedly pressing arrow keys to move the cursor from one location on the screen to another.

Two major complaints are lodged against touch screens. First, the resolution of the touching area is not precise. Thus, while a user can point to a box or a fairly large area on the screen and the electronics can determine the location of the touch, it is difficult to point to a single character in a word processing application, for example, and indicate that the character should be deleted. In cases such as these, a keyboard is easier to use. A second complaint is that after a period of reaching for the screen, the user's arm may become tired.

Graphic Input Devices

Graphic input devices are used to translate graphic input data, such as photos or drawings, into a form that can be processed on a computer. Three major devices that are used for graphic input are light pens, digitizers, and graphics tablets. A **light pen** is used by touching it on the display screen to create or modify graphics (Figure 4-10). A **digitizer** converts points, lines, and curves from a sketch, drawing, or photograph to digital impulses and transmits them to a computer (Figures 4-11 and 4-12). A **graphics tablet** works in a manner similar to a digitizer, but it also contains unique characters and commands that can be automatically generated by the person using the tablet (Figure 4-13).

FIGURE 4-11
The device in this aerospace engineer's hand reads and translates the coordinates on the printed wiring board layout into coordinates that can be stored in the computer and later used to reproduce the drawing on a screen or a printer. ▼

FIGURE 4-10
Placing the light pen at a point on the screen activates a sensing device within the pen. The activated pen transmits the location of the light to the computer, where the program can perform the desired tasks. ▼

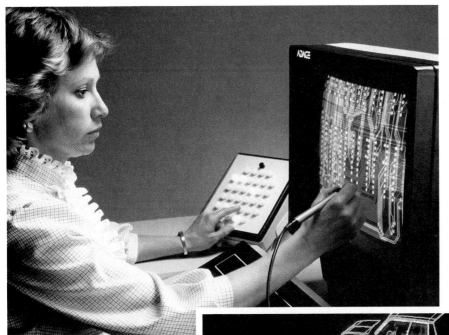

FIGURE 4-12
Digitizers are used in business to create original art or to trace and reproduce existing art quickly and accurately. ▼

◀ FIGURE 4-13
The graphics tablet in this picture is used by an automotive design engineer for the development and definition of a car body. The stylus, held in the engineer's right hand, is used to input commands by touching specific sections of the tablet.

Voice Input

One of the more exciting developments is the use of voice input, sometimes referred to as voice or speech recognition. As the name implies, **voice input** allows the user to enter data and issue commands to the computer with spoken words (Figure 4-14).

Most systems require the user to "train" the system first by speaking the words that will be used a number of times. As the words are spoken, they are digitized by the system; that is, they are broken down into digital components that the computer can recognize. After each word has been spoken several times, the system has developed a digital pattern for the word that can be stored on auxiliary storage. When the user later speaks a word to the system to request a particular action, the system compares the word to words that were previously entered and that it can "understand." When it finds a match, the software performs the activity associated with the word. For example, in voice-controlled word processing systems, spoken words can be used to control such functions as single and double spacing, choosing type styles, and centering text.

The major advantage of voice input is that the user does not have to key, move, or touch anything in order to enter data into the computer. It is expected that voice input will be a significant factor in the years to come.

FIGURE 4-14
This manager has just used his voice input system to request that sales data be presented in a bar graph. Often such systems have to be "trained" to recognize a particular user's voice.

INPUT DEVICES DESIGNED FOR SPECIFIC PURPOSES

Some input devices have been designed to perform specific tasks. Here we illustrate a few of these devices.

FIGURE 4-15
The characters at the bottom of a check can be read by MICR devices. All the banks in the United States and in many foreign countries use these codes for checks.

Magnetic Ink Character Recognition

Magnetic ink character recognition or **MICR** is a type of machine-readable data. This type of data is read into the computer by input devices called **MICR readers**. MICR is found almost exclusively in the banking industry. In the 1950s, the industry chose MICR as the method to be used to encode and read the billions of checks written each year.

When MICR is used, special characters encoded on checks identify such items as the bank number and the account number. When a check is processed, the amount is also encoded on it by a bank operator. The items are encoded in special MICR characters (Figure 4-15) using a special ink that can be magnetized during processing. MICR readers interpret the electronic signals generated from the magnetized characters so checks can be sorted and processed to prepare bank statements for customers. MICR devices can process over 1,000 checks per minute (Figure 4-16). MICR also is used in utility companies, credit card companies, and other industries that must process large volumes of data.

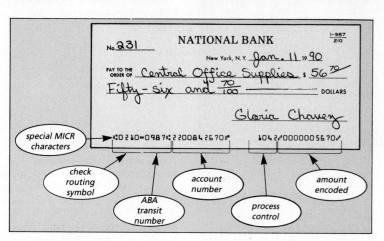

Scanners

Scanners include a variety of devices that "read" printed codes, characters, or images and convert them into a form that can be processed by the computer. This section describes several different types of scanning devices.

Optical Character Readers   Optical character recognition (OCR) devices are scanners that read typewritten, computer-printed, and in some cases hand-printed characters from ordinary documents. OCR devices range from large machines that can automatically read thousands of documents per minute to hand-held wands (Figure 4-17).

An OCR device scans the shape of a character on a document, compares it with a predefined shape stored in its memory, and converts the character read into a corresponding bit pattern for storing in main memory. The standard OCR typeface, called OCR-A, is illustrated in Figure 4-18 on the next page. The characters can be read easily by both humans and machines. OCR-B is a set of standard characters widely used in Europe and Japan.

FIGURE 4-16 ▲
This MICR reader-sorter can process up to 1,200 documents per minute. After the documents are read, they are sorted into the vertical bins shown in the top center portion of the machine. This device can be connected directly to a computer to allow the documents to be processed as they are read.

◀ FIGURE 4-17
This hand-held optical character recognition device is being used to read a typed document. Such wands can be used for both interactive and batch data entry.

ABCDEFGHIJKLMNOPQRSTUVWXYZ
abcdefghijklmnopqrstuvwxyz

Ψ♪⌐$%|&*{}—+∎:″¬.?
1234567890-=∎;',./

FIGURE 4-18
In the full OCR-A standard character set shown above. Characters such as B and 8, S and 5, and zero and the letter O are designed so the reading device can easily distinguish between them.

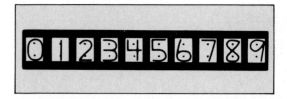

FIGURE 4-19
These hand-printed characters can be read by some types of OCR devices. The two small dots in each square identify where certain portions of each numeric digit must be placed.

Some optical character readers can read hand-printed characters. Building a machine able to read and interpret hand-printed characters is a challenging task even in this era of high technology. The characters must be carefully printed according to a strict set of rules regarding their shapes. The example in Figure 4-19 illustrates the shape of hand-printed characters that can be read with an OCR device.

The most widespread application for OCR devices is for reading turn-around documents prepared by computer printers. A **turn-around document** is designed to be returned to the organization that originally issued it. When the document is returned ("turned around"), the data on it is read by an OCR device. For example, many utility bills, department store bills, insurance premium statements, and so on request that the consumer return the statement with a payment (Figure 4-20). The statement is printed with characters that can be read by OCR devices. When the customer returns it, the machine reads it to give proper credit for the payment received. Some OCR devices, such as the one shown in Figure 4-20, are small enough to fit on top of a desk.

Optical Mark Readers   An **Optical mark reader (OMR)** is a scanning device that can read carefully placed pencil marks on specially designed documents. The pencil marks on the form usually indicate responses to questions and can be read and interpreted by a computer program. Optical mark readers are frequently used to score tests.

FIGURE 4-20
In this picture, utility company payment receipts are being read by an OCR device. These receipts are examples of turn-around documents because they were designed to be returned to the utility with the customer's payment.

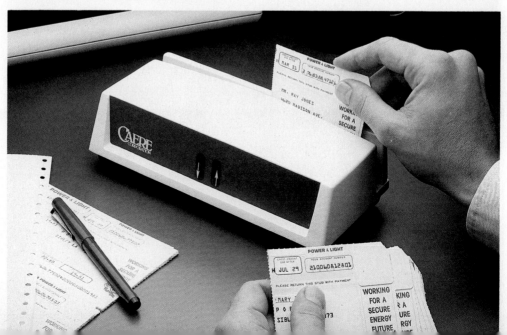

Laser Scanners A scanning device often used by modern grocery stores at checkout counters is a **laser scanner** (Figure 4-21). These devices use a laser beam to scan and read the special bar code printed on the products.

Page Scanners A **page scanner** is a type of scanner that can convert an entire page of printed material into the individual characters and words that can be processed by a word processing program. Other types of scanners can convert images such as photos and art work for eventual use with desktop publishing systems (Figure 4-22).

Image Processing As we've previously discussed, much of the information input to the computer is taken from source documents. Usually, only a portion of the information on the source document is input. But sometimes the entire source document is needed for data, such as a signature or a drawing. In these situations, organizations often implement image processing systems. **Image processing systems** use software and special equipment, including scanners, to input and store an actual image of the source document. These systems are like giant electronic filing cabinets that allow users to rapidly access and review exact reproductions of the original documents (Figure 4-23).

FIGURE 4-22
The scanner at the left can input text, graphics, or photographs for use in word processing or desktop publishing applications.

FIGURE 4-23
Image processing systems record and store an exact copy of a document. These systems are often used by insurance companies that may need to refer to any of hundreds of thousands of documents.

Data Collection Devices

Data entry is not confined to office environments or restricted to dedicated data entry personnel. **Data collection devices** are designed and used for obtaining data at the site where the transaction or event being reported takes place. For example, in Figure 4-24 a man is taking inventory in a warehouse. Rather than write down the number and type of items and then enter this data, he uses a portable data collection device to record the inventory count in the device's memory. After he takes the inventory, the data can be transmitted to a computer for processing.

Unlike most terminals, data collection equipment is designed to be used in environments where heat, humidity, and cleanliness are difficult or impossible to control (Figure 4-25). In addition, data collection devices are often used by people whose primary task is not to enter the data. Entering the data is only a small portion of their job duties. Therefore, the terminals must be easy to operate in any environment.

Using data collection devices can provide important advantages over alternative methods of input preparation. Because the data is entered as it is collected, clerical costs and transcription errors are reduced or eliminated. If the data collection devices are directly connected to the computer, the data is immediately available for processing.

Data collection devices range from portable devices that can be carried throughout a store or factory (such as in Figure 4-24) to sophisticated terminal systems with multiple input stations that feed directly into a central computer. These devices will continue to improve and find increased use in data entry applications.

Figure 4-26 summarizes the most commonly used input devices. While each device has advantages and disadvantages, each is appropriate for specific applications. Several of these devices incorporate a user interface to be more efficient.

FIGURE 4-24
This portable data collection device is being used to take an inventory in a warehouse. The data is stored in memory and can later be transferred to a computer system for processing.

FIGURE 4-25
This photograph illustrates a data collection terminal that has been designed to accommodate the user. Data collection devices should be simple and quick to operate, so that entering the data does not interfere with the main job of the person using the terminal.

DEVICE	DESCRIPTION
Keyboard	Most commonly used input device. Special keys may include numeric keypad, cursor control keys, and function keys.
Terminal	Video display terminals are dumb or intelligent.
Mouse	Small input device used to move the cursor on a screen and select options.
Touch screens	User interacts with the computer by touching the screen.
Graphic input	Light pens, digitizers, and graphics tablets translate graphic data into a form that can be processed by a computer.
Voice input	User enters data and issues commands with spoken words.
MICR reader	Used primarily in banking to read the magnetic ink characters printed on checks.
Scanner	A variety of devices that read printed codes, characters, or images.
Data collection	Used to input data where it is generated.

FIGURE 4-26 This table summarizes some of the more common data input devices.

USER INTERFACES

With the widespread use of terminals and personal computers, input operations are performed by many types of users whose computer knowledge and experience varies greatly. Some users have a limited knowledge of computers and others have many years of experience. In addition, some users interact with computers daily, while others use them only occasionally. Information systems need to provide all users with a means of interacting with the computer efficiently. This is done through user interfaces.

A **user interface** is the combination of hardware and software that allows a user to communicate with a computer system. Through a user interface, users are able to input values that will: (1) respond to messages presented by the computer; (2) control the computer; and (3) request information from the computer. Thus, a user interface provides the means for communication between an information system and the user.

Both the hardware and software working together form a user interface. A terminal is an example of hardware that is frequently part of a user interface. The screen on the terminal displays messages to the user. The devices used for responding to the messages and controlling the computer include the keyboard, the mouse, and other types of input devices. The software associated with an interface are the programs. These programs determine the messages that are given to the user, the manner in which the user can respond, and the actions that will take place based on the user's responses.

EVOLUTION OF USER INTERFACE SOFTWARE

In most instances, the software determines the quality of the user interface. To help you understand user interfaces we examine how user interface software has evolved and where the user interface software technology is today.

When computers were first used for business processing, users did not interact with the computer. Programmers and computer operators were the only people allowed to control the computer processing. While some programmers were also users (for example, scientists who wrote programs so they could use the results in their own work), there was generally little need to worry about the interface with nontechnical users. All that was required was a means for technicians such as operators and programmers, who were familiar with the computer and its operations, to communicate with the software.

In addition, during the early years of computer usage, computers executed programs much more slowly than they do today and memory was very expensive. Therefore, when software was developed, the ease of using a program was secondary to the fact that software had to execute quickly and use as little memory as possible. This dictated that commands and messages be as brief as possible.

When terminals first became available and gave users direct access to the central computer, most software was still difficult to use. Frequently, users had to learn detailed commands to direct the computer to perform the desired tasks. These commands normally consisted of special characters, words, and cryptic abbreviations that made them difficult to learn and remember. Infrequent users often had to retrain themselves each time they wanted to use the machine.

The example in Figure 4-27 illustrates a typical procedure and commands that a user might have used in the 1960s to communicate with the computer. First, users had to "log on" to the computer by identifying themselves. The software would determine if the person was an authorized user and if access to the computer should be allowed. While this is still common today, the procedures for logging on are much easier now than in earlier years. Note that the user had to begin the message with a single slash (/) followed by the word LOGON. This entry was followed immediately by a comma, open quotation marks, a name, and closed quotation marks. A comma was entered next and then the date. This format and spacing had to be followed exactly. A missing comma, quotation mark, slash, or even any one of these in the wrong position would cause the software to issue an error message. Thus, the user needed to know not only the data to be entered, but also the exact format to be followed.

The example in Figure 4-27 shows the additional lines that were required. The entry /T.1 means that terminal 1 was being used. The next entry designated the program to be executed, and the last entry informed the software that the user had entered all the commands. When the /END command was entered, the software would begin performing the processing requested by the user.

FIGURE 4-27
The entries illustrated here represent the type of commands that were required when users first began to have access to computers. Spacing and punctuation also had to be correct for the commands to be accepted. Understandably, many users found it difficult and frustrating to use the computer.

```
/LOGON, "JACOB" ,12/15/67
/T.1
/EXEC.TXT.EDT
/END
```

The entries illustrated in this example were acceptable for computer specialists, but such commands were not easy for the general user to master. Both users and computer professionals recognized that there was considerable room for improvement in the software that communicated with users.

The following sections discuss some of the user interface techniques that have been developed, such as prompts and menus, and how they have improved communication between the user and the computer.

Prompts

One of the first steps in improving user interface software was to display prompts on the screen. A **prompt** is a message to the user that displays on the screen and provides helpful information or instructions regarding some entry to be made or action to be taken.

The example in Figure 4-28 illustrates the use of prompts. On the first line, the prompt ENTER LAST NAME: appears on the screen. This message tells the user to enter his or her last name.

After the user enters his or her last name, a second prompt displays. This prompt, ENTER DATE (MM/DD/YY), indicates not only what is to be entered but also the exact format it should have. MM/DD/YY means to enter the date as a two-digit month number followed by a slash (/), a two-digit day number followed by a slash, and a two-digit year number. Thus, the entry 04/05/90 is valid, but 4/5/90 is not.

To help ensure that the user inputs valid data, the software should use **data editing**, the ability to check the data for proper format and acceptable values. When data is entered incorrectly, a message should be displayed so that the user becomes aware of the error and can reenter the data. The example in Figure 4-29 illustrates what might occur when the data is not entered in the correct format. Note that an error message displays and requests the user to reenter the date.

Prompts, combined with data editing, were a great stride forward in developing user interfaces. Today, prompts are widely used to assist users in entering valid input and communicating with computer systems.

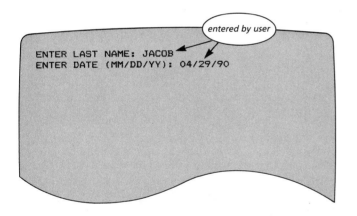

FIGURE 4-28
Prompts aid the user in entering data. They can tell the user what data to enter as well as the required format (as shown for the date entry). Prompts were one of the first types of interfaces designed to assist the user in utilizing the computer.

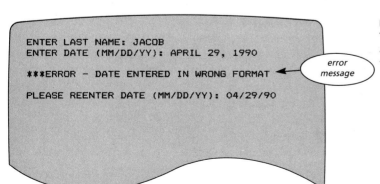

FIGURE 4-29
The software used for this screen checks the date entered and gives an error message if the date is entered in the wrong format.

Menus

As user interfaces continued to develop, people who wrote software recognized that much of the data entry users required was involved with choosing alternatives. For example, the user might have to choose which of four software programs to execute, which of five documents to use during word processing, or which function to perform in an electronic spreadsheet application. To allow the user to make an easy choice from various alternatives, menus were developed.

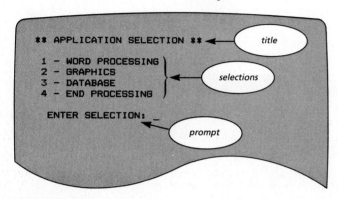

FIGURE 4-30
A menu consists of a title, the selections that can be made, and a prompt for the user to make an entry.

A **menu** is a display on a screen that allows a user to make a selection from multiple alternatives. A menu generally consists of three parts (Figure 4-30): a title, the selections, and a prompt. The title identifies the menu and orients the user to the choices that can be made. The selections consist of both a means for identifying the choices and the words that describe them. The prompt asks the user to enter one of the selections.

The screens in Figure 4-31 illustrate several ways in which a user can choose word processing from menus.

Sequential Number   In Example 1, each of the selections is identified by a number. The user enters the numbers 1, 2, 3, or 4 to select the desired processing operation. Entering a 1 means that the word processing program will be retrieved from auxiliary storage and brought into main memory for execution. Entering a 2 executes the graphics program, and entering a 3, the database program. Menus should always contain an entry that lets the user exit. In Example 1, this is entry 4.

Alphabetic Selection   In Example 2 letters of the alphabet identify the various processing options. The user makes a selection by entering the letter next to the processing description. Sometimes the letters used are simply A, B, C, and D but the person who designed this menu chose to make the letters significant. Thus, entering W will select word processing; entering G selects graphics; D, database; and E ends the processing.

Cursor Positioning   Example 3 illustrates a menu in which the choice is made by using the arrow or cursor control keys to position the cursor adjacent to the desired selection. Then the Enter key is pressed to make the choice.

Reverse Video   Example 4 illustrates using reverse video to highlight the selection. **Reverse video** means that the normal screen display pattern, such as amber on black, is reversed to highlight and draw attention to a certain character, word, or section of the screen. In the example, the directions instruct the user to move the reverse video from one selection to another by pressing the space bar. Pressing the space bar once moves the reverse video from the word processing option to graphics; pressing it again highlights the database option. If the space bar was pressed when reverse video was highlighting the end processing option, the reverse video would move to word processing. This is called **wraparound**. It is a shortcut that allows users to go quickly from the bottom to the top or from the top to the bottom of a menu. To make a selection in reverse video, the user highlights the desired procedure and presses the Return key.

Icon Selection   In Example 5, the same reverse video method is used to highlight the choices, but the choices are also identified by graphic images or icons. An **icon** is a pictorial representation of a function to be performed on the computer. Pressing the space bar highlights each of the words under the graphic in reverse video. Pressing the Return key executes the chosen function.

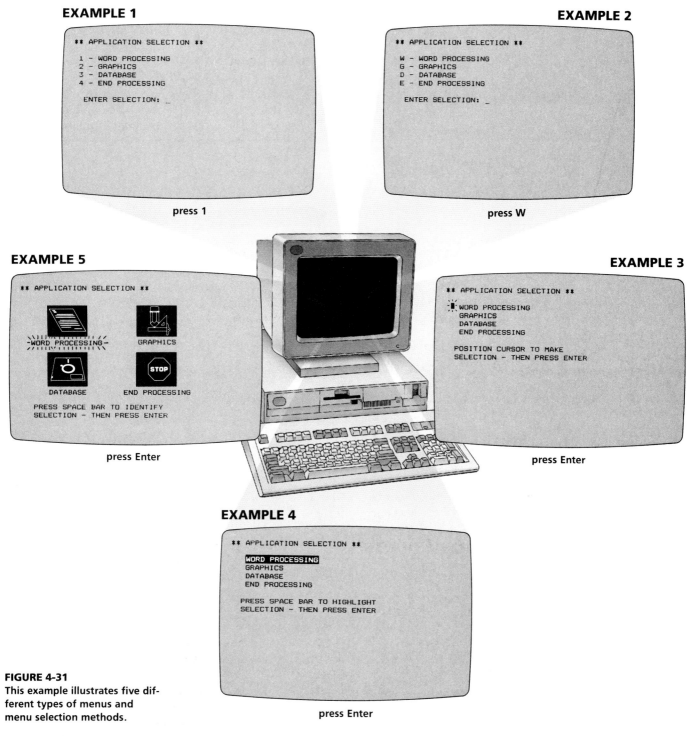

FIGURE 4-31
This example illustrates five different types of menus and menu selection methods.

From these examples, it is clear that a variety of methods can be used to identify and choose the selections in a menu.

Submenus

Some applications require the use of several related menus. Menus that further define the operations that can be performed are called **submenus**.

The example in Figure 4-32 illustrates the main menu from Example 1 in Figure 4-31,

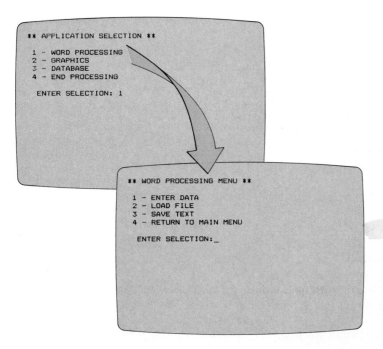

```
** APPLICATION SELECTION **

1 - WORD PROCESSING
2 - GRAPHICS
3 - DATABASE
4 - END PROCESSING

  ENTER SELECTION: 1
```

```
** WORD PROCESSING MENU **

1 - ENTER DATA
2 - LOAD FILE
3 - SAVE TEXT
4 - RETURN TO MAIN MENU

  ENTER SELECTION:_
```

FIGURE 4-32
A submenu is used when additional selections can be made within an application. In this example, the submenu displays additional word processing selections.

which allows the user to select word processing, graphics, or database. When the word processing function is selected, a submenu appears. This submenu contains more detailed functions. Depending on the submenu selection, additional menus could be displayed. For example, if the user selected option 1, enter data, from the submenu shown in Figure 4-32, a third menu could appear that would display selections relative to margin settings, page length, and other word processing functions.

Menus: Advantages and Disadvantages

Menus are a type of user interface that is used with all sizes and types of computers. There are both advantages and disadvantages to menus. Some of the advantages are:

1. The user does not have to remember special commands. He or she merely chooses a selection from a list of possible operations or functions.
2. The user can become productive with a minimum of training. Instead of having to learn a lot of technical computer information, he or she merely needs to understand the application and the results of choosing a particular option from the menu.
3. The user is guided through the application because only the options that are available are presented.

The disadvantage most often associated with menus, according to some experienced users, is that they can be slow and restrictive. For example, the menus illustrated in Figure 4-32 are good for the novice or infrequent computer user because they take him or her step-by-step through the possible operations that can be performed. The experienced user, however, knows what processing is required. Therefore, he or she may prefer to enter a few quick commands and immediately begin work instead of having to view and respond to two or more menus.

GRAPHICS

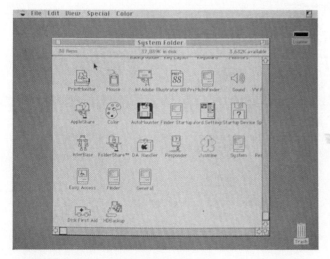

FIGURE 4-33
This screen illustrates icons representing functions or data that the user can select. In the upper right corner, for example, the icon of a speaker refers to the turning off or turning on of sounds the computer can make to signal errors and other messages to the user. Icons allow the user to quickly identify the processing options available.

Graphics can play an important role in aiding the user to effectively interact with a computer. For example, in Figure 4-33, the user's option to choose color is represented by the icon (picture) of an artist's palette. An icon representing functions to be performed on a computer is helpful because people not familiar with computer terminology can still use the machine.

FEATURES OF A USER INTERFACE

*T*he following list identifies some features that should be included in a good user interface.

1. System responses to the user—**System responses** are those messages and actions taken by the computer when a user enters data into the computer. In a well-designed system, the user receives a response for every action taken. A response can be shown in two ways. First, a message can be displayed that tells the user something is happening. For example, when a large program is being loaded into main memory from auxiliary storage, the message "Program Loading" would appear on the screen. A second type of feedback occurs when the screen changes based on an entry by the user. For example, in Figure 4-32, when the user chose selection 1 from the main menu, a submenu immediately displayed on the screen. This action told the user that the data had been accepted by the computer and was being operated on. Without a response from the computer, the user does not know if the input was accepted. A response from the system avoids user confusion.

   A second issue with respect to user response is response time. **Response time** is the elapsed time between the instant a user enters data and the instant the computer responds. A common guideline for response time is that it should never be greater than two seconds. When the activity requested by the user will require more than two seconds for the computer to accomplish, a message such as "Processing—Please Wait" should be displayed.

2. Screen design—The design of the messages and pictures that appear on the screen can have a significant impact on the usability of the system. The most important rule is to keep the screen uncluttered and simple. Each message and each action that a user must take should be clear and easily understood. All messages, menus, and prompts within a system should follow a consistent format. This reduces the time needed for users to learn how to use a system and increases ease of use for experienced users.

3. User responses—In general, the simpler the entry required from the user, the better the user interface. Users are seldom skilled typists. Thus, if the user does not have to enter a large number of characters, data entry will be faster and fewer errors will occur.

4. Error recovery—Because errors are inevitable, it should be as easy as possible for a user to recover from one. Whenever the user makes an error, three user interface activities should take place: (1) the user should be alerted that an error has been made; (2) the error should be identified as specifically as possible; and (3) the user should be told how to recover from the error. In general, error recovery can take place in three ways: (1) the user can reenter the data that caused the error; (2) the user can "back up" to a previous operation; or (3) the user can exit from the operation where the error was made.

5. Control and security—Many multiuser computer systems require users to "sign on" to the computer by entering an identification, such as a name or account number followed by a password. A **password** is a value, such as a word or number, which identifies the user. Unless the user enters the password, the computer will not allow access to the machine. These procedures help to ensure that only authorized users obtain access to the computer.

The systems and procedures listed on the previous page should be kept in mind by computer professionals when designing and developing user interfaces, and by users when they are evaluating software or hardware for purchase.

The question that must be asked when designing or deciding on a user interface is, Who will be using it and what is their level of computer experience? A good user interface must be appropriate for the people who are going to be using it.

DATA ENTRY FOR INTERACTIVE AND BATCH PROCESSING

s discussed in Chapter 3, computer applications use either interactive or batch processing methods to process data into information. The methods used to enter data for interactive and batch processing differ. We explain them in the following paragraphs.

Data Entry for Interactive Processing

Data entered in the interactive processing mode generates immediate output. In most interactive data entry, the person entering the data is communicating directly with the computer that will process the data. Therefore, data entry for interactive processing is said to be **online data entry**, meaning that the device from which the data is being entered is connected directly to the computer.

FIGURE 4-34
In this example of data entry for interactive processing, the data is entered by a terminal operator in the order entry department. The output generated, a picking slip, is printed in the warehouse. In addition, a record of the order is stored on disk.

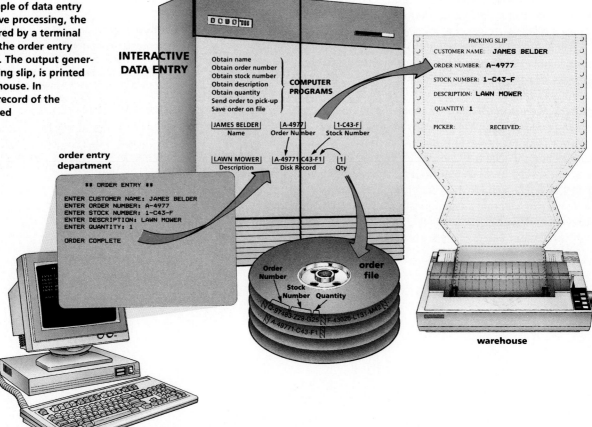

The output generated from interactive data entry processing is not always produced at the location where the data was entered. In Figure 4-34, for example, the data is entered from a terminal located in the order entry department. The data entered concerns a purchase by a customer. After the data is entered, a picking slip is printed in the warehouse. The worker in the warehouse would then retrieve the item purchased (in this case, a lawn mower) and package it for shipping. The terminal operator in the order entry department never sees the output generated, yet this is interactive processing because the data entered is processed immediately.

The person entering the order in the order entry department may enter hundreds of such orders each day. When large amounts of data are entered by a terminal operator whose only job is to enter the data, the data entry function is said to be **production data entry**.

Data Entry for Batch Processing

When data is entered for processing in the batch processing mode, it is stored on a storage medium (usually tape or disk) for processing at a later time. Data for batch processing can be entered in either an online or offline manner. As noted previously, online data entry means that the device from which the data is being entered is connected directly to the computer that will process it (Figure 4-35).

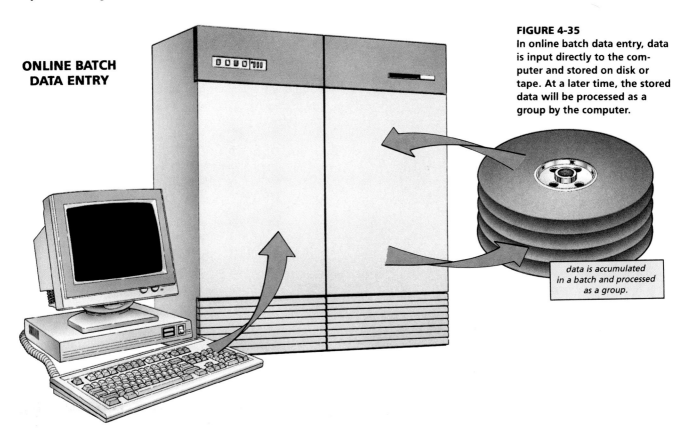

ONLINE BATCH DATA ENTRY

FIGURE 4-35
In online batch data entry, data is input directly to the computer and stored on disk or tape. At a later time, the stored data will be processed as a group by the computer.

data is accumulated in a batch and processed as a group.

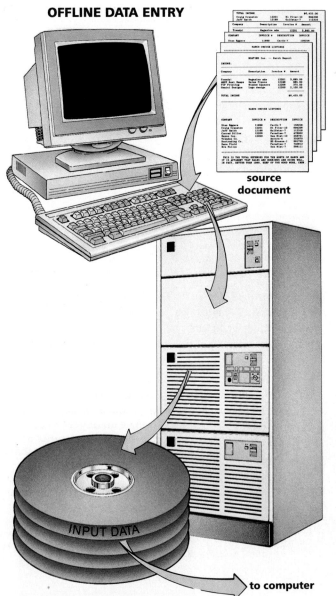

OFFLINE DATA ENTRY

source document

INPUT DATA

to computer

Offline data entry means that the device from which the data is being entered is not connected to the computer that will process it (Figure 4-36). Instead, the data is entered using a dedicated computer or other device devoted to the data entry function. This computer or special device accepts the input data and stores it on disk or tape. At a later time, the disk or tape can be transported to the site where the data will be entered for processing in a batch mode to produce information. An example of such a system is the key-to-disk shared processor system shown in Figure 4-37.

When offline data entry is used, source documents must be accumulated prior to entering the data. For example, in a payroll application, timecards for hourly employees would be the source documents from which the hours worked would be entered by the data entry operators.

In many applications, controls are established to ensure that data is entered and processed accurately. In a credit card payment application, for example, payments are usually divided into batches for processing. The payments for each batch are added manually and recorded prior to data entry. When the payment batches are processed on the computer, the total amount of the payments calculated by the computer for each batch is compared to the total determined from the manual addition performed prior to data entry. If the totals are the same, it is evidence that the data was input to the computer accurately. If the totals are not the same, however, then further checking must be performed to determine if the data was entered incorrectly or if the manually determined batch total was wrong. This technique of balancing to a predetermined total is called a **batch control**.

FIGURE 4-36
In offline data entry, the data is input to a computer other than the one that will eventually process it. Often computers used for offline data entry are dedicated to data input functions and perform little if any processing. The data entered is later transferred to another computer for processing.

Summary of Interactive and Batch Data Entry

Entering data to produce information can take place online or offline. Online data entry is always used for interactive processing and often for batch processing as well. Offline data entry is used for batch processing. When using offline data entry, source documents from which the data is obtained must be gathered prior to the data being entered. Regardless of the processing method, producing information often requires a large amount of data entry.

AN EXAMPLE OF ONLINE DATA ENTRY

Many types of devices can be used to enter data but by far the most common device is the terminal. We illustrate using terminals for online data entry with an order entry example. Order entry is the process followed when an order is received from a customer. An order entry application usually proceeds in the following manner:

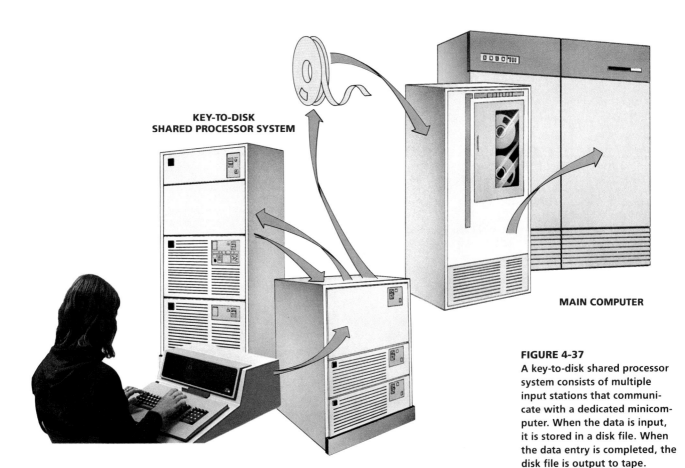

KEY-TO-DISK
SHARED PROCESSOR SYSTEM

MAIN COMPUTER

FIGURE 4-37
A key-to-disk shared processor system consists of multiple input stations that communicate with a dedicated minicomputer. When the data is input, it is stored in a disk file. When the data entry is completed, the disk file is output to tape. The tape is then physically transferred to another computer that will process the data.

1. The order is received from the customer, either through the mail or over the telephone, and the data concerning the customer and the order is entered into the computer by the data entry operator.
2. When the order is entered, the order entry program performs a credit check by retrieving credit data from a credit file stored on disk. The order is stored in the open order disk file so that a record of it is retained.
3. In addition, when the order is entered, the order entry program controlling the data entry operation determines if the item ordered is in inventory by reading a record from an inventory file or database. If the item ordered is in inventory, a picking slip is printed in the warehouse. A picking slip alerts warehouse personnel that an order has been received and specifies who the customer is and what items are to be shipped. Then, or at a later time, the warehouse personnel retrieve the item and package it for shipping. When the item is shipped, they will enter that information into the computer. Then the record for the order will be removed from the open order file and placed in the shipped file.
4. If the item ordered is not in the warehouse inventory, the order record will be placed in the backorder file and the customer will be notified that the item is not available. A backorder is an order for an item that is not currently in inventory. The order will be held until the item is available, at which time the order will be filled.

The following sections explain the data entry procedure that could be followed by a person entering orders using an online entry system.

Order Entry Menu

The data entry process for the sample order entry system begins with the Order Entry menu (Figure 4-38). In this example, the function to be performed is entering orders. Therefore, the data entry operator enters the value 1 to choose the option ENTER ORDERS.

FIGURE 4-38
The Order Entry menu specifies the options available for processing sales orders. Option 1 allows orders to be entered. Option 2 provides for order confirmations and inquiries into the order file. Option 3 allows certain changes to be made to orders, such as revising the ship to address. Option 4 provides for changes to backorders, orders for products that were not in inventory when the order was entered. Option 5 would be selected if the user wanted to end the order processing function.

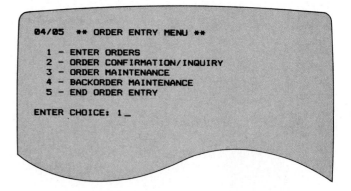

```
04/05   ** ORDER ENTRY MENU **

  1 - ENTER ORDERS
  2 - ORDER CONFIRMATION/INQUIRY
  3 - ORDER MAINTENANCE
  4 - BACKORDER MAINTENANCE
  5 - END ORDER ENTRY

ENTER CHOICE: 1_
```

Enter Orders

The following six steps are illustrated in Figure 4-39.

In Step 1, when the data entry operator chooses option 1 on the main menu, the first of two screens required to enter orders displays. The screen contains colors to designate different types of information. The blue characters are either headings or prompts that identify the fields to be processed. Each area where data will be displayed or entered is shown in reverse video. The white areas indicate fields that must be entered by the data entry operator. The red areas will contain fixed data based on the operator's entries. These fixed areas cannot be changed by the data entry operator. The yellow areas indicate **default values**, data that will be automatically displayed but which can be changed by the operator if needed.

In Step 2, the operator enters the data for the first field, the customer number. Here the value AE-1073 is the number for the customer ordering items. Note that instead of reverse video when the data is entered, the actual characters display in the same color as the reverse video; that is, the customer number displays in white because the reverse video was in white. The process of entering the data is shown in Figure 4-40 on the next page, where the first character (A) has been entered. The character is white but the rest of the input area on the screen where data has not yet been entered retains the reverse video. This technique is commonly used on terminals where reverse video identifies input fields.

Step 3 shows what the screen would look like after the operator enters the customer number. The order number is generated by the order entry computer program. It displays in red because the terminal operator cannot reference or change the order number. The bill to data also displays in red because it will not be changed. The bill to data, which is the name of the company and the address to which the bill for the items will be sent, was obtained from a customer file based on the customer number that was entered. The ship to data identifies the place to which the items will be sent. The company name displays in red because it will not be changed. The ship to address, however, displays reversed on a yellow background because the data is default data. It is used in data entry so that the operator does not have to spend time entering data that normally does not change. In this case, the address shown is the same as the bill to address because most of the time, items ordered by Hinkle Ltd. are shipped to the same address. This is the default address, so the operator would merely press the Enter key and continue to the next field. In this example, however, the ship to address is to be changed. Therefore, the operator must key in the new ship to address. Step 4 shows how the new ship to address displays.

STEP 1

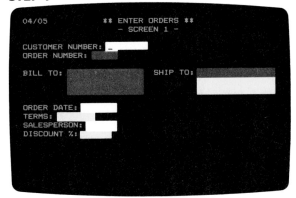

Step 1: Each field is identified by color. The blue fields are titles and prompts. The red fields will contain data that cannot be changed. The white fields must be entered by the operator. The yellow fields are default fields.

STEP 2

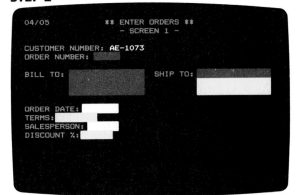

Step 2: In this step, the data entry operator has entered the customer number. The customer number is displayed in white letters because the operator had to enter the data. The operator would then press the Enter key to continue.

STEP 3

Step 3: Data retrieved from a customer file based on the customer number is displayed on the screen. The cursor is placed on the ship to address. The operator can enter data here if it is different from the default values.

STEP 4

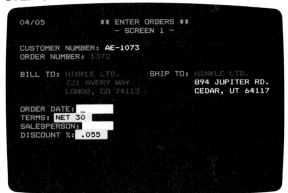

Step 4: The order date must be entered by the operator. Therefore, it is displayed in white. The default values in the ship to field have been changed to yellow characters because they have now been entered.

STEP 5

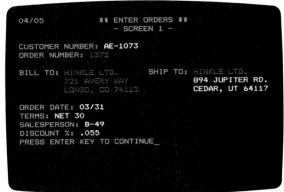

Step 5: The salesperson must be entered by the data entry operator. The default value in the terms field specified net 30. The operator accepted the default value by pressing the Enter key instead of entering new data.

STEP 6

Step 6: After the data entry operation for the first screen has been completed, all data is displayed as color characters on a black screen. The reverse video is not necessary because no data remains to be entered.

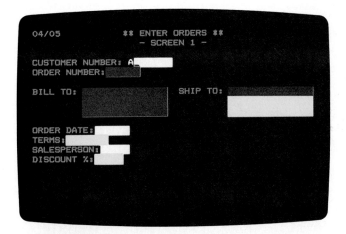

FIGURE 4-40
When a value is entered in a reverse video field, the normal technique is to display the character in the color of the reverse video field and to remove the reverse video field for that character. Here, the letter A has been entered into a white field; therefore, the letter is displayed in white on a black background.

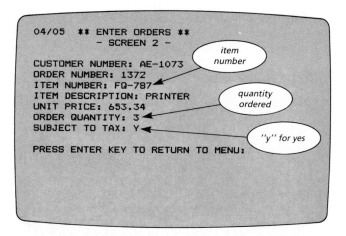

FIGURE 4-41
On the second order entry screen, the operator enters the item number and the quantity ordered. The program uses the item number to look up and display the item description and the unit price. The subject to tax default value is Y, but the operator can change it.

Next, the controlling program places the cursor at the order date field (Step 5) and the operator enters the order date (03/31). The order date field is white because the operator must always enter the order date.

In Step 5, by pressing the Enter key, the operator has accepted the default terms that the program displayed. The salesperson data, however, must be entered by the operator because it is in white. The default value for the discount percent is also accepted by the operator.

Step 6 shows how the screen would look after all data entry has been completed for the first order entry screen.

Next, the operator presses the Enter key to display the second screen required for the order entry operation (Figure 4-41). On this screen, the operator must enter the number of the item purchased and the order quantity. The item description and unit price are displayed by the order entry program. The single default value on this screen is the subject to tax field. Here, the operator can change the Y (signifying yes to the question, Is this purchase subject to tax?) to N. In this example, the default value was accepted. After entering all the data, the operator can press the Enter key to return to the main menu (Figure 4-38) and enter another order.

This example is a composite of many different order entry systems and illustrates some of the features of these systems.

DATA ENTRY PROCEDURES

The procedures developed for the data entry function are important because accurate data must be entered into a computer to ensure data integrity. In addition, since users are interacting directly with the computer during the data entry function, procedures and documentation must be quite clear. The following issues must be addressed in order to implement a data entry application successfully:

1. Origination of data—Data entered for processing on a computer is generated from many sources throughout a company. It is important to identify which people and operations will generate the data so that appropriate procedures can be written to specify what data is to be gathered, how it is to be gathered, and who is to gather it.

2. Location of the data entry function—Data is generally entered either from the centralized data entry section of the information systems department or from various locations throughout an organization. The hardware, software and personnel needs vary depending upon which of these two locations is used. In a **centralized data entry** operation, the data is keyed by trained operators from source documents. When data is entered in the centralized data entry section, it is usually processed in a batch processing mode.

   Entering data from various locations in an organization is called **distributed data entry**. Quite often the data entry takes place at the site where the data is generated, for example, sales orders being entered by the sales department. Often, data entered using distributed data entry is processed in an interactive processing mode.

3. Timing requirements for acquiring the data—In some applications, the time of day or the day of the week when the data becomes available is important. For example, if all time-cards for employees must be received by Monday at 4 p.m. for employees to be paid Friday, timing is important and must be identified in the documentation for the data entry.

4. Timing requirements for entering the data—The amount of time that can elapse between when the event being reported takes place and when the data about that event must be entered should be specified. In some applications, an event can occur but the data need not be entered until hours or even days later. For example, in the payroll application mentioned above, timecards are retrieved Monday at 4 p.m. These timecards record the workers' time for the previous week. The data may not be entered until Tuesday. Therefore, more than a week might elapse between when the event occurred and when the data about the event was entered.

   In most cases when entry time is not a critical factor, the data is recorded on source documents and given to data entry personnel in either a centralized or distributed location to enter. In other applications, however, the data must be entered as the event or transaction is occurring and at the location where it is occurring. This process is sometimes called **source data collection**. For example, when a retail sale is made using a point of sale terminal, the data must be entered at the moment the sale is made so that the sale can be completed with the customer. Therefore, it is important that the documentation for the data entry system specify the timing requirements for entering data.

5. Flow of the input data—The documentation must specify the flow of the data from the point where it originates to the point where it is entered for processing on the computer. Any handling required, any recording on source documents, and any changes in format from source to data entry must be documented.

6. Transaction volume—The amount of data entered for a given time period and location must be estimated. Any particularly high or low volumes may require special procedures.

7. Manner of entering the data—Based on many of the factors specified in items 1–6, the procedures must specify how the data is to be entered, identifying devices and methods. For example, it could be specified that data is to be entered from source documents using terminals in an online, centralized environment.

8. Editing and error handling—The documentation must specify the editing for the entered data and the steps to take if the data is not valid. Although different applications will have specific criteria for validating input data, there are a number of tests that are performed on input data before the data is processed in a computer. Some of these tests are:

   a. Tests for numeric or alphabetic data (Figure 4-42)—For example, in the United States a zip code must always be numeric. Therefore, the program performing the editing can check the values in the zip code field. If they are not numeric, the data is incorrect.

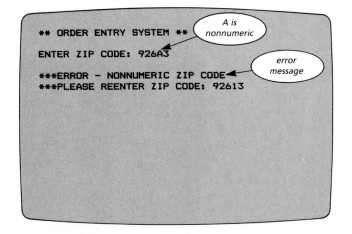

FIGURE 4-42
In this example, a nonnumeric zip code is entered and an error message displays. When a numeric zip code is entered, the data is accepted and no error message displays.

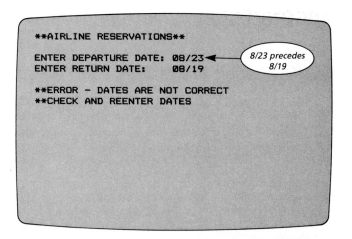

FIGURE 4-43
On this airline reservation screen, the user entered a return date earlier than the departure date and the system displayed an error message.

    b. Tests for data reasonableness—A reasonableness check ensures that the data entered is within normal or accepted boundaries. For example, suppose no employee within a company is authorized to work more than 80 hours per week. If the value entered in the hours worked field is greater than 80, the value in the field would be indicated as a probable error.

    c. Tests for data consistency—In some cases, data entered cannot, by itself, be found to be invalid. If, however, the data is examined in the context of other data entered for the same record or group of fields, discrepancies might be found. For example, in an airline reservation system, round-trip tickets are often purchased (Figure 4-43). If the terminal operator enters the date on which the passenger is leaving, the editing program can only check whether the date entered is valid. Similarly, when the return date is entered, the program can again make sure it is a valid date. In addition, however, the return date can be compared to the departure date. If the return date is earlier than the departure date, it is likely that an error has been made when entering one of the dates.

    d. Tests for transcription and transposition errors—There is always a possibility that an operator will make an error when entering data. A **transcription error** occurs when an error is made in copying the values from a source document. For example, if the operator keys the customer number 7165 when the proper number is 7765, a transcription error has been made. A **transposition error** happens when the operator switches two numbers. Such an error has occurred when the number 7765 is entered as 7756.

  9. Data controls and security—The controls and security that will be applied to the data must be defined. This includes what the controls and security measures are, how they are to be implemented, and what action is to be taken if the security of the data is compromised in any way.

10. Personnel requirements—Specifying personnel requirements includes defining who will gather the data, who will enter it, and how many people will be required to enter the data for the application. Personnel must be educated about gathering and entering the data. They must be trained in using the equipment and software, ensuring reliable data entry, entering the data according to specified procedures, and interpreting any output received from the computer during interactive processing.

ERGONOMICS

To be efficient when you are using a computer, it is important that you be comfortable. Being comfortable results in less fatigue, better accuracy, and higher input rates, factors that are important to all users, but particularly to data entry personnel. **Ergonomics** is the study of the design and arrangement of equipment so that people will interact with the equipment in a healthy, comfortable, and efficient manner. As related to computer equipment, ergonomics is concerned with such factors as the physical design of the keyboard, screens, and related hardware, and the manner in which people interact with these hardware devices.

The first computer terminals contained the keyboard and screen as a single unit. The screen frequently displayed white characters on a black background. Early studies found significant user dissatisfaction with the terminals. One study reported that 90% of the personnel who used these terminals complained of health problems, including eye fatigue, blurred vision, itching and burning eyes, and back problems. As a result of these studies, a number of design recommendations for terminals were made. These recommendations included the following:

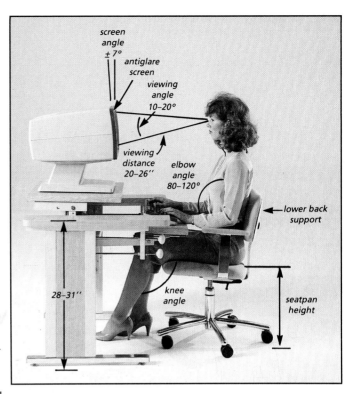

FIGURE 4-44
This illustration shows some of the ergonomic factors that should be considered when using a terminal for a long or repeated length of time.

1. Computer keyboards should be detached from the screen so that they can be positioned on a desk for the convenience and comfort of the user.
2. The screen should be movable, and the angle at which the user views the contents of the screen should be adjustable.
3. Amber or green text on a black background is preferable to black characters on a white background or white characters on a black background.
4. The screen should be of high quality to eliminate any flickering of the image and characters on the screen. The characters displayed on the screen should appear as solid as possible.
5. The images on the screen should be in sharp focus over the entire screen area.
6. The screen should have an antiglare coating. Screen glare has been a common complaint of many terminal users, and it is known that glare can be harmful to eyes. A flat screen, now used on some terminals, can also reduce glare.
7. Screens that will display multiple elements of information should use color to distinguish the different elements, thus cutting down on the strain of looking for and identifying information displayed on the screen.

Figure 4-44 illustrates some of the above recommendations. The keyboard is detachable, the visual display unit is adjustable, and the screen has an antiglare coating. The illustration also shows the use of a lower back support. Note the position of the user's body in relation to the terminal.

As more and more workers use terminals and personal computers, the importance of ergonomically designed equipment increases. Manufacturers are now aware of the importance of ergonomic design and, as a result, are designing and building terminals and personal computers that incorporate ergonomic design for the health and comfort of users.

SUMMARY OF INPUT TO THE COMPUTER

*T*his chapter covered various aspects of input to the computer. We discussed the four types of input and how they are used, input devices, user interfaces, and data entry. After reading this chapter you should have a better overall understanding of computer input.

CHAPTER SUMMARY

1. **Input** refers to the process of entering programs, commands, user responses, and data into the computer memory.
2. The **keyboard** is the most commonly used input device. Special keys may include the **numeric keypads, cursor control keys,** and **function keys.**
3. **Video display terminals** fall into two basic categories: **dumb terminals** and **intelligent terminals.**
4. A **mouse** is a small input device used to control the movement of the cursor and to select options displayed on the screen.
5. **Touch screens** allow the user to interact with a computer by merely touching the screen.
6. **Light pens, digitizers,** and **graphics tablets** are graphic input devices used to translate graphic input data into a form that can be processed by the computer.
7. **Voice input** allows the user to enter data and issue commands to a computer with spoken words.
8. **Magnetic ink character recognition (MICR)** is a type of machine-readable data used almost exclusively in the banking industry.
9. **Scanners** are devices that read printed codes, characters, or images and convert them into a form that can be processed by the computer.
10. **Optical character recognition (OCR)** devices are scanners that read typewritten, computer-printed, and in some cases hand-printed characters from ordinary documents.
11. An **Optical mark reader** is a scanning device that can read carefully placed pencil marks on a specially designed form.
12. **Data collection devices** are designed and used for obtaining data at the site where the transaction or event being reported takes place.
13. A **user interface** is the combination of hardware and software that allows a user to communicate with a computer system.
14. User interfaces have evolved from technical commands to techniques such as prompts and menus.
15. A **prompt** is a message to the user that is displayed on the screen and provides information or instructions regarding some entry to be made or action to be taken.
16. **Data editing** is used to check input data for proper format and acceptable values. It helps to ensure that valid data is entered by the user.
17. A **menu** is a display on a screen that allows the user to select from multiple alternatives. There are several types of menu selection techniques including sequential and alphabetic selection, cursor positioning, reverse video, and icon selection.
18. An **icon** is a pictorial representation of a function to be performed on the computer.
19. Graphics can play an important role in aiding the user to interact effectively with a computer.
20. Features that relate to good interfaces include: system responses, screen design, user responses, error recovery, and control and security.
21. When a user enters data into a computer, the messages and action taken by the computer are referred to as **system responses.**
22. The elapsed time between the instant a user enters data and the instant the computer responds is called the **response time.**
23. Screen design should provide messages and pictures in an uncluttered, simple format.
24. All messages, menus, and prompts within a system should follow a consistent format.
25. Input will be faster and fewer errors will be made if the operator response or input from users is as simple as possible.
26. When user input errors occur, a good interface will tell the user, identify the error, and explain how to correct it.
27. **Passwords** are unique user identification codes that are used on multiuser systems to allow only authorized users access to the computer.

28. Data entry for interactive processing is said to be **online**, meaning that the device from which the data is being entered is connected directly to the computer.

29. Data entry for batch processing is said to be **offline**, meaning that the device from which the data is being entered is not connected to the computer that will process it.

30. In many applications, controls are established to ensure that the data entered is processed accurately. For example, balancing to a predetermined total is called a **batch control**.

31. The procedures developed for the data entry function are important because accurate data must be entered into a computer to ensure data integrity.

32. Within an organization, it is important to identify which people and operations will generate the data.

33. **Centralized data entry** is performed by trained operators from **source documents**.

34. **Distributed data entry** often takes place at the site where the data is generated and is input to the computer by a variety of users.

35. In most applications, timing requirements for acquiring and entering data are important and should be identified.

36. Data documentation should specify the flow of the data from the point where it originates to the point where it is entered for processing.

37. Transaction volume refers to the amount of data that must be entered for a given time period and a given location.

38. Data entry procedures should identify the devices and the methods for entering data.

39. Data editing and error handling procedures include a number of distinct tests that can be performed on the data prior to processing. Some of these are numeric and alphabetic testing, tests for reasonableness and consistency, and transcription and transposition tests.

40. **Transcription errors** refer to operator errors made at the time of input, such as entering 7165 instead of 7665.

41. **Transposition errors** refer to operator errors where two characters are switched, such as entering 7756 instead of 7765.

42. Data controls and security procedures should be defined.

43. Data entry procedures should specify the personnel requirements for both gathering and entering input data.

44. **Ergonomics** is the study of the design and arrangement of equipment so that people will interact with the equipment in a healthy, comfortable, and efficient manner.

45. Manufacturers are now designing equipment that incorporates ergonomic design features.

KEY TERMS

Arrow keys *4.5*
Batch control *4.24*
Centralized data entry *4.29*
Commands *4.3*
Cursor *4.5*
Cursor control keys *4.5*
Data *4.3*
Data collection devices *4.14*
Data editing *4.17*
Default values *4.26*
Digitizer *4.9*
Display terminals *4.5*
Distributed data entry *4.29*
Dumb terminals *4.6*
Ergonomics *4.31*
Function keys *4.5*
Graphic input devices *4.9*
Graphics tablet *4.9*
Icon *4.19*
Image processing system *4.13*

Input *4.3*
Intelligent terminals *4.6*
Keyboards *4.4*
Laser scanner *4.13*
Light pen *4.9*
Magnetic ink character recognition (MICR) *4.10*
Menu *4.18*
MICR readers *4.10*
Mouse *4.7*
Numeric keypad *4.4*
Offline data entry *4.24*
Online data entry *4.22*
Optical character recognition (OCR) *4.11*
Optical mark reader (OMR) *4.12*
Page scanner *4.13*
Password *4.21*
Point of sale terminal *4.7*
Production data entry *4.23*
Programmable terminals *4.6*

Programs *4.3*
Prompt *4.17*
Response time *4.21*
Reverse video *4.18*
Scanners *4.11*
Source data collection *4.29*
Submenus *4.20*
System responses *4.21*
Touch screens *4.8*
Transcription error *4.30*
Transposition error *4.30*
Turn-around document *4.12*
Uploading *4.6*
User interface *4.15*
User responses *4.3*
Video display terminals (VDTs) *4.5*
Voice input *4.10*
Wraparound *4.18*

REVIEW QUESTIONS

1. What are the four types of input and how are they used?
2. Describe the features available on a computer keyboard.
3. Name two types of display terminals. Describe each type.
4. Describe a mouse and list its advantages and disadvantages.
5. Describe three different types of graphic input devices.
6. What are data collection devices? How do they differ from other input devices?
7. What is a user interface? Why is it important?
8. Describe the evolution of user interface software.
9. What is a prompt? What are the attributes of a good prompt?
10. What is a menu? Describe the five types of menu selection.
11. What is an icon? Why is an icon used?
12. Name and briefly describe the five features that apply to good user interfaces.
13. What are the differences between data entry for interactive and for batch processing?
14. List ten procedures associated with data entry.
15. What is ergonomics? List and describe six ergonomic features that a terminal should have.

CONTROVERSIAL ISSUES

1. Manufacturers of computer hardware and software that use the mouse as an input device and icons on the screen claim that the majority of people who use computers will prefer this method. They claim that most people are not familiar with computers and the easier computers are to use, the more people who will use them. Some of their competitors claim that these devices are useful when people are learning to use a computer but that users quickly tire of the "cuteness" and prefer a device on which more productive work can be done. Which argument do you think is correct? Could they both be correct?
2. Proponents of touch screen technology claim that the touch screen is the answer to user interface problems because all a user must do is touch the screen to input data. Opponents claim it is much too limited as an input device. Take a position in this dispute.
3. The use of display terminals has increased significantly in recent years. With the increased use has come claims that using terminals is harmful to health. It has been claimed that long use of video display terminals has caused such problems as miscarriages and back ailments. Some unions have questioned the advisability of sitting in front of a terminal for eight hours. Terminal manufacturers have argued that ergonomically designed terminals present no danger to health. Research the arguments and take a position on this controversy.

RESEARCH PROJECTS

1. Visit a local computer store that sells a computer that uses a mouse and icons. Use the machine for a period of time and report back to your class concerning its good points and bad points.
2. Visit a retail or grocery store in your area and prepare a report on the point of sale terminals in use. Be sure to identify the type of terminal used, the manner in which data is entered, the computer to which the terminal is connected, and any problems or difficulties employees have had using the terminals.
3. Visit a local bank or retail store that has terminals communicating with a large computer. Ask a person at the establishment to show you how they interface with the computer. Pay particular attention to the screen formats, the data that the user must enter, and the response times. Prepare a report on your experiences for your class.
4. Bring a turn-around document that you have received in the mail and explain it to the class.
5. The data entry function has changed significantly during the history of business data processing. Research the history of the data entry function and prepare an oral or written report. Include in your report the hardware devices used, the manner in which data was entered, the location from which data was entered, and the different procedures used for data entry over the years.

CHAPTER 5

The Processor Unit

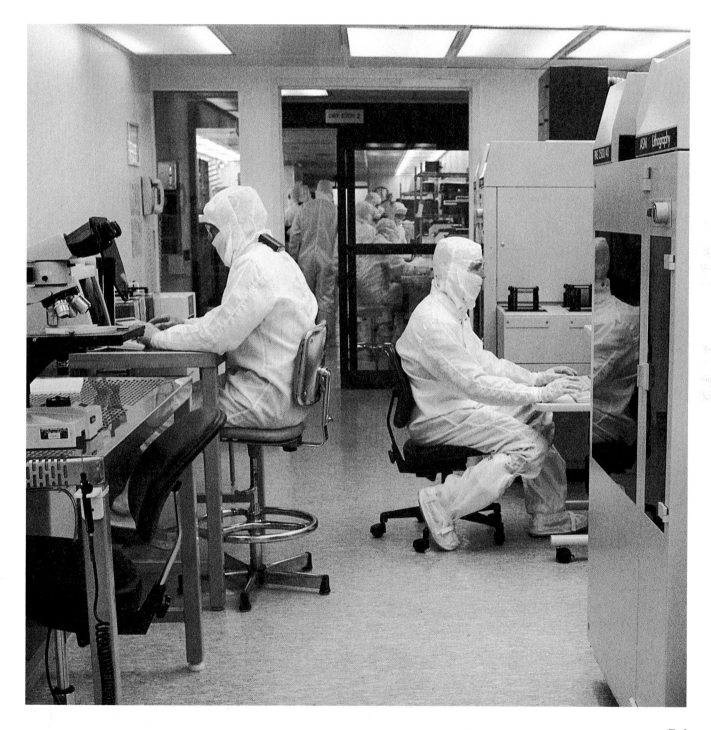

The Processor Unit

OBJECTIVES

- Identify the components of the processor unit and describe their use.
- Define a bit and describe how a series of bits in a byte is used to represent characters.
- Discuss how the ASCII and EBCDIC codes represent characters.
- Describe why the binary and hexadecimal numbering systems are used with computer systems.
- List and describe the four steps in a machine cycle.
- Discuss the three primary factors that affect the speed of the processor unit.
- Describe the characteristics of RAM and ROM memory. List several other types of memory.
- Describe the process of manufacturing integrated circuits.

*T*he information processing cycle consists of input, processing, output, and storage operations. When an input operation is completed and both a program and data are stored in main memory, processing operations can begin. During these operations, the processor unit executes, or performs, the program instructions and processes the data into information.

This chapter examines the components of the processor unit, describes how main memory stores programs and data, and discusses the sequence of operations that occurs when instructions are executed on a computer.

✳ WHAT IS THE PROCESSOR UNIT?

*W*hile the term computer is used to describe the collection of devices that perform the information processing cycle, it is sometimes used more specifically to describe the processor unit. It is in the processor unit that the execution of computer programs and the manipulation of data takes place. The main components of the processor unit are the central processing unit or CPU and the main memory of the computer (Figure 5-1).

✳The Central Processing Unit

The central processing unit (CPU) contains the control unit and the arithmetic/logic unit. These two components work together using the program and data stored in main memory to perform the processing operations.

The control unit can be thought of as the "brain" of the computer. Just as the human brain controls the body, the control unit "controls" the computer. The **control unit** operates by repeating the following four operations: fetching, decoding, executing, and storing. **Fetching** means obtaining the next program instruction from main memory. **Decoding** is translating the program instruction into the commands that the computer can process. **Executing** refers to the actual processing of the computer commands, and **storing** takes place when the result of the instruction is written to main memory.

The second part of the CPU is the **arithmetic/logic unit**. This unit contains the electronic circuitry necessary to perform arithmetic and logical operations on data. Arithmetic operations include addition, subtraction, multiplication, and division. Logical operations consist of comparing one data item to another to determine if the first data item is greater than, equal to, or less than the other.

THE PROCESSOR UNIT

FIGURE 5-1
The processor unit of a computer contains two main components: the central processing unit (CPU), which includes the control unit and the arithmetic/logic unit, and main memory.

Main Memory

In addition to the CPU, **main memory** or **primary storage** is also contained in the processor unit of the computer. (Figure 5-2) Main memory stores three items: (1) the *operating system* or software that directs and coordinates the computer equipment; (2) an *application program* containing the instructions that will direct the work to be done; and (3) the *data* currently being processed by the application program. Data is stored in areas of main memory referred to as input and output areas. These areas receive and send data to the input and output devices. Another area of main memory called working storage is used to store any other data that is needed for processing.

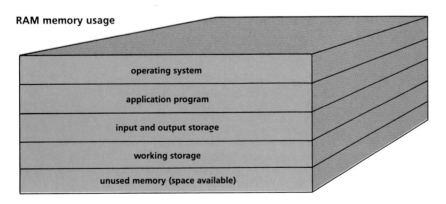

RAM memory usage

operating system

application program

input and output storage

working storage

unused memory (space available)

FIGURE 5-2
Main memory is used to store several types of data and programs. As program instructions are executed and new data and programs are input and output, the allocation of memory space changes.

Within main memory, each storage location is called a **byte**. Just as a house on a street has a unique address that indicates its location on the street, each byte in the main memory of a computer has an address that indicates its location in memory (Figure 5-3). The number that indicates the location of a byte in memory is called a **memory address**. Whenever the computer references a byte, it does so by using the memory address of that location.

FIGURE 5-3
Just as each house on a street has its own address, each byte in main memory is identified by a unique address.

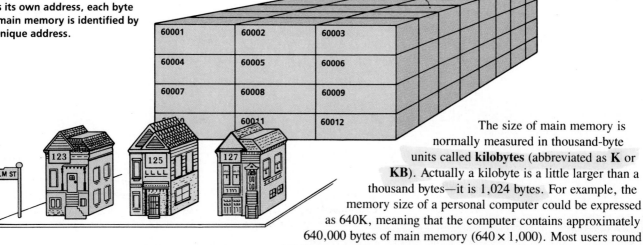

The size of main memory is normally measured in thousand-byte units called **kilobytes** (abbreviated as **K** or **KB**). Actually a kilobyte is a little larger than a thousand bytes—it is 1,024 bytes. For example, the memory size of a personal computer could be expressed as 640K, meaning that the computer contains approximately 640,000 bytes of main memory (640 × 1,000). Most users round kilobyte to 1,000 and measure memory in this manner. If the exact size of memory is needed, it can be calculated by using the value 1,024. The exact size of 640K is 655,360 bytes (640 × 1,024) of main memory. Several other terms are used to describe memory size. When memory exceeds 1,000K or one million bytes, it is measured in **megabytes**, abbreviated **MB**. A billion bytes of memory, available on some large computers, is called a **gigabyte** or **GB**.

HOW PROGRAMS AND DATA ARE REPRESENTED IN MEMORY

Program instructions and data are made up of a combination of the three types of characters: alphabetic (A through Z), numeric (0 through 9) and special (all other characters). To understand how program instructions and data are stored in main memory, it is sometimes helpful to think of them as being stored character by character. Generally speaking, when we think of characters being stored in main memory, we think of one character being stored in one memory location or byte. Thus, the name TOM would take three memory locations or bytes because there are three letters in that name. The number $157.50 would take seven memory locations or bytes because there are seven characters (including the $ and .) in the number (Figure 5-4).

FIGURE 5-4
Each character (alphabetic, numeric, or special) usually requires one memory location (byte) for storage.

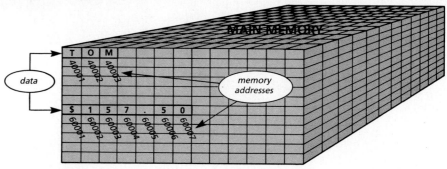

A byte contains eight bits. A **bit** is an element of a byte that can represent only two values. It can either be "off," represented in Figure 5-5 by an open circle, or "on," represented by a filled-in circle. Each alphabetic, numeric, and special character stored in the memory of the computer is represented by a combination of on and off bits. The computer can distinguish between characters because the combination of off and on bits assigned to each character is unique.

A mathematical way of representing the off and on conditions of a bit is to use 0 to represent off and 1 to represent on. The **binary** number system (base 2) represents quantities by using only the two symbols, 0 and 1. For this reason, binary is used to represent the electronic status of the bits inside the processing unit (Figure 5-5). The term bit was derived from the words *bi*nary dig*it*.

Two popular codes that use combinations of zeros and ones for representing characters in memory are the ASCII and EBCDIC codes. A chart summarizing these codes is shown in Figure 5-6. Notice how the combination of bits, represented in binary, is unique for each character.

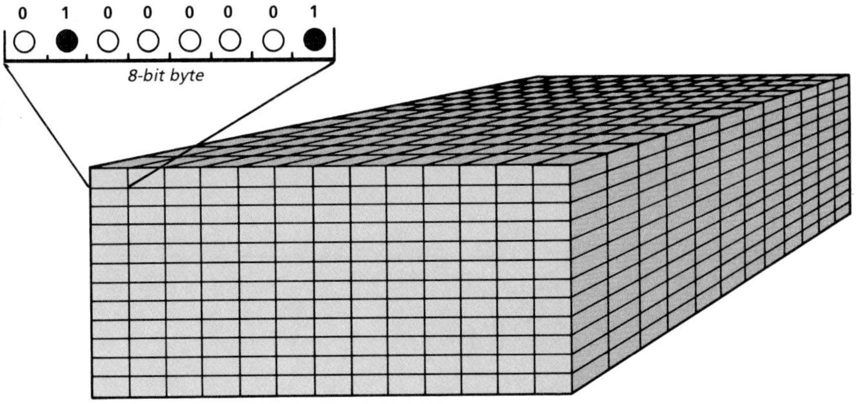

FIGURE 5-5
A graphic example of an eight-bit byte with two bits on and six bits off. The on bits (filled-in circles) are represented by the binary number 1 and the off bits (open circles) are represented by binary 0. (This combination of bits represents the letter A in ASCII code).

FIGURE 5-6
This chart shows alphabetic, numeric, and special characters as they are represented in the ASCII and EBCDIC codes. Note how each character is represented in binary using zeros and ones.

SYMBOL	ASCII	EBCDIC	SYMBOL	ASCII	EBCDIC	SYMBOL	ASCII	EBCDIC
(space)	0100000	01000000	?	0111111	01101111	^	1011110	
!	0100001	01011010	@	1000000	01111100	_	1011111	
"	0100010	01111111	A	1000001	11000001	a	1100001	10000001
#	0100011	01111011	B	1000010	11000010	b	1100010	10000010
$	0100100	01011011	C	1000011	11000011	c	1100011	10000011
%	0100101	01101100	D	1000100	11000100	d	1100100	10000100
&	0100110	01010000	E	1000101	11000101	e	1100101	10000101
'	0100111	01111101	F	1000110	11000110	f	1100110	10000110
(	0101000	01001101	G	1000111	11000111	g	1100111	10000111
)	0101001	01011101	H	1001000	11001000	h	1101000	10001000
*	0101010	01011100	I	1001001	11001001	i	1101001	10001001
+	0101011	01001110	J	1001010	11010001	j	1101010	10010001
,	0101100	01101011	K	1001011	11010010	k	1101011	10010010
–	0101101	01100000	L	1001100	11010011	l	1101100	10010011
.	0101110	01001011	M	1001101	11010100	m	1101101	10010100
/	0101111	01100001	N	1001110	11010101	n	1101110	10010101
0	0110000	11110000	O	1001111	11010110	o	1101111	10010110
1	0110001	11110001	P	1010000	11010111	p	1110000	10010111
2	0110010	11110010	Q	1010001	11011000	q	1110001	10011000
3	0110011	11110011	R	1010010	11011001	r	1110010	10011001
4	0110100	11110100	S	1010011	11100010	s	1110011	10100010
5	0110101	11110101	T	1010100	11100011	t	1110100	10100011
6	0110110	11110110	U	1010101	11100100	u	1110101	10100100
7	0110111	11110111	V	1010110	11100101	v	1110110	10100101
8	0111000	11111000	W	1010111	11100110	w	1110111	10100110
9	0111001	11111001	X	1011000	11100111	x	1111000	10100111
:	0111010	01111010	Y	1011001	11101000	y	1111001	10101000
;	0111011	01011110	Z	1011010	11101001	z	1111010	10101001
<	0111100	01001100	[	1011011	01001010	{	1111011	
=	0111101	01111110	\	1011100		}	1111101	
>	0111110	01101110	]	1011101	01011010			

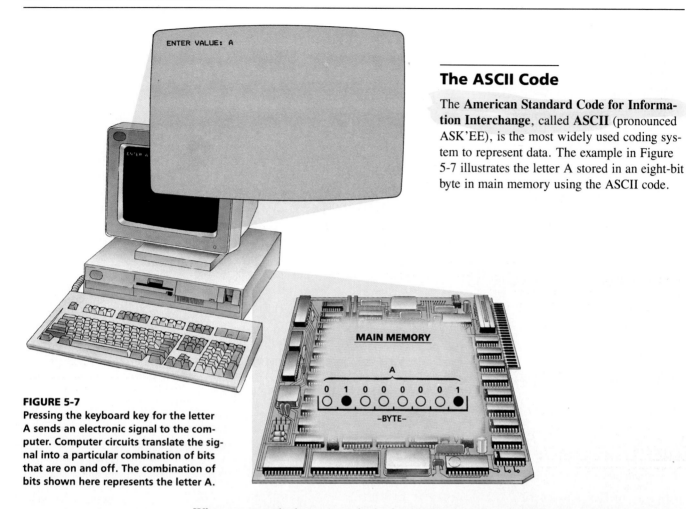

The ASCII Code

The **American Standard Code for Information Interchange**, called **ASCII** (pronounced ASK'EE), is the most widely used coding system to represent data. The example in Figure 5-7 illustrates the letter A stored in an eight-bit byte in main memory using the ASCII code.

FIGURE 5-7
Pressing the keyboard key for the letter A sends an electronic signal to the computer. Computer circuits translate the signal into a particular combination of bits that are on and off. The combination of bits shown here represents the letter A.

When you type the letter A on the keyboard, the electronic circuitry of the computer interprets the character and stores it in main memory as a series of on and off bits. In the example, the combination of bits that are on and off represent the letter A in the ASCII code. When the character is displayed on the screen or printed, the ASCII code is translated back into the alphabetic symbol A.

As you can see by looking at the chart in Figure 5-6, the ASCII code uses only the rightmost seven bits of the eight bits in a byte to represent characters. These seven bits provide 128 combinations, enough to represent all the standard characters including numeric, uppercase and lowercase alphabetic, and special.

The EBCDIC Code

The ASCII code is widely used on personal computers and many minicomputers. Another common coding scheme used primarily on mainframes is called the **Extended Binary Coded Decimal Interchange Code** or **EBCDIC** (pronounced "EB-SEE-DICK").

Binary Representation of Numbers

When the ASCII or EBCDIC codes are used, each character that is represented is stored in one byte of memory. Note, however, that there are other binary formats of data representation that allow multiple digits to be stored in one byte or memory location.

PARITY

Regardless of whether ASCII, EBCDIC, or other binary methods are used to represent characters in main memory, it is important that the characters be stored accurately. For each byte of memory, most computers have at least one extra bit, called a **parity bit**, that is used by the computer for error checking. A parity bit can detect if one of the bits in a byte has been inadvertently changed. Such an error could occur because of voltage fluctuations, static electricity, or a memory chip failure.

Computers are either odd or even parity machines. In computers with **odd parity**, the total number of "on" bits in the byte (including the parity bit) must be an odd number (Figure 5-8). In computers with **even parity**, the total number of on bits must be an even number. Parity is checked each time a memory location is used. When data is moved from one location to another in main memory, the parity bits of both the sending and receiving locations are compared to see if they are the same. If the system detects a difference or if the wrong number of bits is on (e.g., an even number in a system with odd parity), an error message displays. Some computers use multiple parity bits that enable them to detect and correct a single bit error and detect multiple bit errors.

FIGURE 5-8
In a computer with odd parity, the parity bit is turned on or off in order to make the total number of on bits (including the parity bit) an odd number. Here, the letters T and O have an odd number of bits and the parity bit is left off. However, the number of bits for the letter M is even, so in order to achieve odd parity, the parity bit is turned on. Turning on the parity bit makes the total number of bits in the byte an odd number (five).

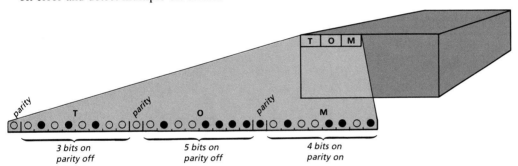

3 bits on
parity off

5 bits on
parity off

4 bits on
parity on

NUMBER SYSTEMS

This section describes the number systems that are used with computers. While thorough knowledge of this subject is required for technical computer personnel, a general understanding of number systems and how they relate to computers is all most users need.

As you have seen, the binary (base 2) number system is used to represent the electronic status of the bits in main memory. It is also used for other purposes, such as addressing the memory locations. Another number system that is commonly used with computers is **hexadecimal** (base 16). Figure 5-9 shows how the decimal values 0 through 15 are represented in binary and hexadecimal.

DECIMAL	BINARY	HEXADECIMAL
0	0000	0
1	0001	1
2	0010	2
3	0011	3
4	0100	4
5	0101	5
6	0110	6
7	0111	7
8	1000	8
9	1001	9
10	1010	A
11	1011	B
12	1100	C
13	1101	D
14	1110	E
15	1111	F

FIGURE 5-9
The chart shows the binary and hexadecimal representation of decimal numbers 0 through 15. Note how letters represent the numbers 10 through 15.

The mathematical principles that apply to the binary and hexadecimal number systems are the same as those that apply to the decimal number system. To help you better understand these principles we will start with the familiar decimal system, then progress to the binary and hexadecimal number systems.

The Decimal Number System

The decimal number system is a base 10 number system (note that "deci" means 10). The *base* of a number system indicates how many symbols are used in it. Decimal uses the 10 symbols 0 through 9. Each of the symbols in the number system has a value associated with it. For example, you know that 3 represents a quantity of three and 5 represents a quantity of five. The decimal number system is also a positional number system. This means that in a number such as 143, each position in the number has a value associated with it. When you look at the decimal number 143, you know that the 3 is in the ones, or units, position and represents three ones or (3 × 1); the 4 is in the tens position and represents four tens or (4 × 10); and the 1 is in the hundreds position and represents one hundred or (1 × 100). The number 143 is the sum of the values in each position of the number (100 + 40 + 3 = 143). Figure 5-10 is a power chart showing how the positional values (hundreds, tens, and units) for a number system can be calculated. Starting on the right and working to the left, we raise the base of the number system, in this case 10, to consecutive powers (10^2 10^1 10^0). These calculations are a mathematical way of computing the place values in a number system.

FIGURE 5-10
This chart shows the positional values in the decimal number 143.

power of 10	10^2	10^1	10^0
positional value	100	10	1
number	1	4	3

$(1 \times 100) + (4 \times 10) + (3 \times 1) =$
$100 \quad + \quad 40 \quad + \quad 3 \quad = 143$

When you use number systems other than decimal, the same principles apply. The base of the number system indicates the number of symbols that are used and each position in a number system has a value associated with it. The positional value can be calculated by raising the base of the number system to consecutive powers.

The Binary Number System

As we have discussed, binary is a base 2 number system ("bi" means two), and the symbols that are used are 0 and 1. Just as each position in a decimal number has a place value associated with it, so does each position in a binary number. In binary, the place values are successive powers of two (such as 2^3 2^2 2^1 2^0) or (8 4 2 1). To construct a binary number, ones are placed in the positions where the corresponding values add up to the quantity that is to be represented and zeros are placed in the other positions. For example, the binary place values are (8 4 2 1) and the binary number 1001 has ones in the positions for the values 8 and 1 and zeros in the positions for 4 and 2. Therefore, the quantity represented by 1001 is 9 (8 + 0 + 0 + 1) (Figure 5-11).

power of 2	2^3	2^2	2^1	2^0
positional value	8	4	2	1
binary	1	0	0	1

$(1 \times 8) + (0 \times 4) + (0 \times 2) + (1 \times 1) =$
$8 + 0 + 0 + 1 = 9$

FIGURE 5-11
This chart shows how to convert the binary number 1001 to the decimal number 9. Each place in the binary number represents a successive power of 2.

The Hexadecimal Number System

Many computers use a base 16 number system called hexadecimal. The hexadecimal number system uses 16 symbols to represent values. These include the symbols 0 through 9 and A through F (Figure 5-9). The mathematical principles previously discussed also apply to hexadecimal (Figure 5-12).

power of 16	16^1	16^0
positional value	16	1
hexadecimal	A(10)	5

$(10 \times 16) + (5 \times 1) =$
$160 + 5 = 165$

FIGURE 5-12
This chart shows how the hexadecimal number A5 is converted into the decimal number 165. Note that the value 10 is substituted for the A during computations.

The primary reason why the hexadecimal number system is used with computers is because it can represent binary values in a more compact form and because the conversion between the binary and the hexadecimal number systems is very efficient. An eight-digit binary number can be represented by a two-digit hexadecimal number. For example, in the EBCDIC code (used by some computers to represent data), the decimal number 5 is represented as 11110101. This value can be represented in hexadecimal as F5.

One way to convert a binary number to a hexadecimal number is to divide the binary number (from right to left) into groups of four digits; calculate the value of each group; and then change any two-digit values (10 through 15) into the symbols A through F that are used in hexadecimal (Figure 5-13).

Summary of Number Systems

As mentioned at the beginning of the section on number systems, binary and hexadecimal are used primarily by technical computer personnel. For the general user, a complete understanding of numbering systems is not required. The concepts that you should remember about number systems are that binary is used for purposes such as representing the electronic status of the bits in main memory and also for memory addresses. Hexadecimal is used to represent binary in a more compact form.

positional value	8421	8421
binary	1111	0101
decimal	15	5
hexadecimal	F	5

FIGURE 5-13
This chart shows how the EBCDIC code 11110101 for the value 5 is converted into the hexadecimal value F5.

HOW THE PROCESSOR UNIT EXECUTES PROGRAMS AND MANIPULATES DATA

The program instructions that users write are usually in a form similar to English. Before these instructions can be executed, they must be translated by the computer into a form called machine language instructions. A **machine language instruction** is one that the electronic circuits in the CPU can interpret and convert into one or more of the commands in the computer's instruction set. The **instruction set** contains the commands such as add or move that the computer's circuits can directly perform. To help you understand how the processor unit works, let's look at an example of a machine language instruction.

Machine Language Instructions

FIGURE 5-14
A machine language instruction consists of an operation code, the lengths of the fields to be processed, and the main memory addresses of the fields.

A machine language instruction is usually composed of three parts: an operation code; values indicating the number of characters to be processed by the instruction; and the addresses in main memory of the data to be used in the execution of the instruction (Figure 5-14).

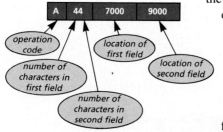

The **operation code** is a unique value that is typically stored in the first byte in the instruction. This unique value indicates what operation is to be performed. For example, the letter A stored as the operation code might indicate that an *add*ition operation is to occur. The letter M might mean that a *move* operation is to take place.

The number of characters to be processed is included in the machine language instruction so that the CPU will manipulate the proper number of bytes. For example, if a four-digit field were to be added to another four-digit field, the number of characters specified in the instruction for each field would be four.

The main memory addresses of the fields involved in the operation are also specified in the instruction. This specification of the main memory address enables the CPU to locate where in main memory the data to be processed is stored.

The illustration in Figure 5-15 shows the steps involved in executing a computer instruction. The instruction A44 7000 9000 indicates that the four-digit fields that begin in locations 7000 and 9000 are to be added together. When this instruction is executed, the following steps occur:

FIGURE 5-15
Executing a program instruction

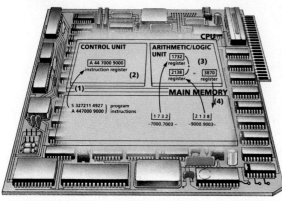

1. The instruction is fetched from main memory and placed in an instruction register. An **instruction register** is an area of memory within the control unit of the CPU that can store a single instruction at a time.

2. After the control unit decodes the instruction, it fetches the data specified at the two addresses in the instruction from main memory.

3. The arithmetic/logic unit executes the instruction by adding the two numbers.

4. The control unit then stores the result of the processing by moving the sum to main memory.

This basic sequence of fetch the instruction, decode the instruction, execute the instruction, and store the results is the way most computers process instructions.

The Machine Cycle

The four steps illustrated above, fetch, decode, execute, and store, are called the **machine cycle**. As shown in Figure 5-16, the machine cycle is made up of the instruction cycle and the execution cycle. The **instruction cycle** refers to the fetching of the next program instruction and the decoding of that instruction. The **execution cycle** includes the execution of the instruction and the storage of the processing results. When the computer is again ready to fetch the next program instruction, one machine cycle is completed.

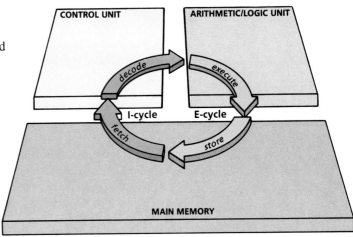

PROCESSOR SPEEDS

Although the machine cycle may appear to be cumbersome and time consuming, computers can perform millions of machine cycles in one second. In fact, the processing speed of computers is often compared in **MIPS**—million instructions per second. A computer with a rating of 1 MIPS could process one million instructions per second. The most powerful personal computers today are rated at between 3 and 4 MIPS. Larger computers can process 75 to 100 MIPS and supercomputers are capable of over 200 MIPS.

The speed in which a computer can execute the machine cycle is influenced by three factors: the system clock, the buses, and the word size (Figure 5-17).

FIGURE 5-16
The machine cycle consists of four steps: fetching the next instruction, decoding the instruction, executing the instruction, and storing the result. Fetching and decoding are considered part of the instruction or I cycle. Executing and storing are considered part of the execution or E cycle.

FACTOR	AFFECT ON SPEED
System clock	The clock generates electronic pulses used to synchronize processing. Faster clock speed results in more operations in a given amount of time.
Bus width	Bus width determines how much data can be transferred at any one time. A 32-bit bus can transfer twice as much data at one time as a 16-bit bus.
Word size	Word size is the number of bits that can be manipulated at any one time. A computer with a 32-bit word size can manipulate twice as much data at one time as a system with a 16-bit word size.

FIGURE 5-17
Factors affecting computer speed.

System Clock

The control unit utilizes the **system clock** to synchronize, or control the timing, of all computer operations. The system clock generates electronic pulses at a fixed rate, measured in **megahertz**. One megahertz equals one million pulses, or cycles, per second. The speed of the system clock varies among computers. Some personal computers can operate at speeds in excess of 30 megahertz.

Buses

As we explained, computers store and process data as a series of electronic bits. These bits are transferred internally within the circuitry of the computer along paths capable of transmitting electrical impulses. The bits must be transferred from input devices to memory, from memory to the CPU, from the CPU to memory, and from memory to output devices. Any path along which bits are transmitted is called a **bus** or **data bus**. Buses can transfer eight, 16, or 32 bits at a time. An eight-bit bus has eight lines and can transmit eight bits at a time. On a 16-bit bus, bits can be moved from place to place 16 bits at a time and on a 32-bit bus, bits are moved 32 bits at a time.

The larger the number of bits that are handled by a bus, the faster the computer can transfer data. For example, assume a number in memory occupies four eight-bit bytes. With an eight-bit bus four steps would be required to transfer the data from memory to the CPU because on the eight-bit data bus, the data in each eight-bit byte would be transferred in an individual step. A 16-bit bus has 16 lines in the data bus, so only two transfers would be necessary to move the data in four bytes. And on a 32-bit bus, the entire four bytes could be transferred at one time. The fewer number of transfer steps required, the faster the transfer of the data occurs.

Word Size

Another factor that affects the speed of a computer is the word size. The **word size** is the number of bits that the CPU can process at one time, as opposed to the bus size, which is the number of bits the computer can transmit at one time. Like data buses, the word size of a machine is measured in bit sizes. Processors can have eight-, 16-, 32-, or 64-bit word sizes. A processor with an eight-bit word size can manipulate eight bits at a time. If two four-digit numbers are to be added in the ALU of an eight-bit processor, it will take four operations because a separate operation will be required to add each of the four digits. With a 16-bit processor, the addition will take two operations and with a 32-bit processor, only one operation would be required to add the numbers together. Sometimes the word size of a computer is given in bytes instead of bits. For example, a word size of 16 bits may be expressed as a word size of two bytes because there are eight bits in a byte. The larger the word size of the processor, the faster the computer is able to process data.

In summary, the speed of a computer is influenced by the system clock, the size of the buses, and the word size. When you purchase a computer, the speed requirements you want should be based on your intended use of the computer. Eight-bit computers may be useful and fast enough for personal and educational applications. Sixteen-bit computers are widely used today for applications such as word processing, electronic spreadsheets, or database. Thirty-two-bit computers are considered very powerful and are useful for multiuser systems and applications that require complex and time-consuming calculations, such as graphics. A few personal computers, many minicomputers, and most mainframes are 32-bit computers. Most supercomputers are 64-bit computers.

ARCHITECTURE OF PROCESSOR UNITS

*T*he processor unit of a computer can be designed and built in many different ways. For example, the processor for a personal computer may be housed on a single printed circuit board while a larger machine may require a number of circuit boards for the CPU, main memory, and the related electronic circuitry.

Microprocessors

The smallest processor, called a **microprocessor** (Figure 5-18), is a single integrated circuit that contains the CPU and sometimes memory. An **integrated circuit**, also called an **IC**, **chip**, or **microchip**, is a complete electronic circuit that has been etched on a small chip of nonconducting material such as silicon. Microcomputers are built using microprocessors for their CPU. Figure 5-19 lists some of the microprocessors commonly used in personal computers today.

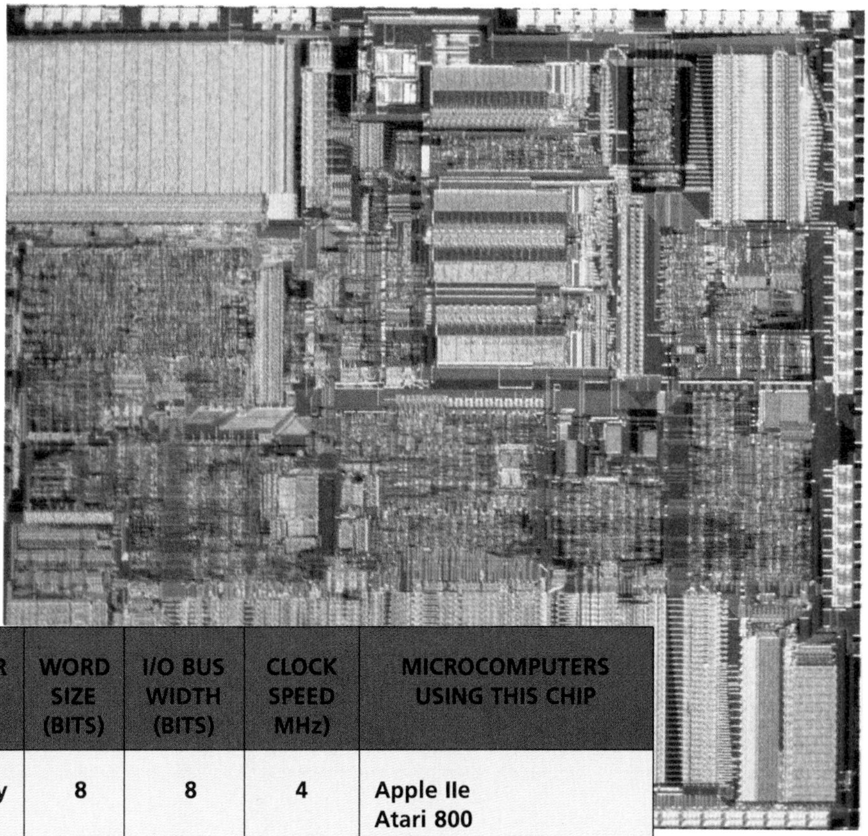

FIGURE 5-18 ▶
The Intel 80386 microprocessor has a word size and bus width of 32 bits and can operate at between 16 and 32 megahertz.

FIGURE 5-19
A comparison of some of the more widely used microprocessor chips. ▼

MICROPROCESSOR	MANUFACTURER	WORD SIZE (BITS)	I/O BUS WIDTH (BITS)	CLOCK SPEED MHz	MICROCOMPUTERS USING THIS CHIP
6502	MOS Technology	8	8	4	Apple IIe Atari 800
8088	Intel	16	8	8	IBM PC and XT HP 150 Compaq Portable
8086	Intel	16	16	8	Compaq Deskpro Many IBM compatibles
80286	Intel	16	16	8–12	IBM PC/AT IBM PS/2 model 50 Compaq Deskpro 286
68000	Motorola	32	16	12.5	Apple Macintosh SE and Commodore Amiga
68020	Motorola	32	32	12.5–32	Apple Macintosh II
80386	Intel	32	32	16–32	Compaq Deskpro 386 IBM PS/2 model 80

Coprocessors

Math

One way computers can increase their productivity is through the use of a **coprocessor**, a special microprocessor chip or circuit board designed to perform a specific task. For example, math coprocessors are commonly added to computers to greatly speed up the processing of numeric calculations. Other types of coprocessors extend the capability of a computer by increasing the amount of software that will run on the computer.

Parallel Processing

1 instruction at a time

Most computers contain one central processing unit (CPU) that processes a single instruction at a time. When one instruction is finished, the CPU begins execution of the next instruction, and so on until the program is completed. This method is known as **serial processing**. **Parallel processing** involves the use of multiple CPUs, each with their own memory. Parallel processors divide up a problem so that multiple CPUs can work on their assigned portion of the problem simultaneously. As you might expect, parallel processors require special software that can recognize how to divide up problems and bring the results back together again.

RISC Technology

As computers have evolved, more and more commands have been added to hardware instruction sets. In recent years, however, computer designers have reevaluated the need for so many instructions and have developed systems based on RISC technology. **RISC**, which stands for reduced instruction set computing (or computers), involves reducing the instructions to only those that are most frequently used. Without the burden of the occasionally used instructions, the most frequently used instructions operate faster and overall processing capability or *throughput* of the system is increased.

In summary, you can see that there are many different types of processor architecture that are used on computers. Regardless of the architecture used, the important concept to remember is that the processor units on all computers perform essentially the same functions.

FIGURE 5-20
This photograph illustrates 32 transistors on an NCR semiconductor chip that is used for computer memory. The transistors are enlarged 600 times their actual size.

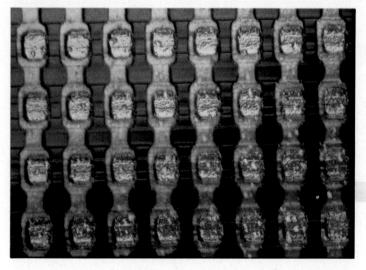

TYPES OF MEMORY

As we noted, electronic components are used to store data in computer memory. The actual materials and devices used for memory have changed throughout the years. The first device used for storing data was the vacuum tube. After the vacuum tube, core memory was used. **Core memory** consisted of small, ring-shaped pieces of material that could be magnetized, or polarized, in one of two directions. The polarity indicated whether the core was on or off. Today, semiconductor memory is used in virtually all computers (Figure 5-20). **Semiconductor memory** is an integrated circuit containing thousands of transistors. A **transistor** is an electronic component that can be either on or off and represents a bit in memory.

When core memory was used as main memory, the time required to access data stored in the memory was measured in **microseconds** (millionths of a second). Access to data stored in semiconductor memory is measured in **nanoseconds** (billionths of a second). In addition, the cost of semiconductor memory is just a fraction of the cost for core memory. Today you can buy 64K of semiconductor memory for about $30, whereas 64K of core memory once cost as much as $15,000. Figure 5-21 shows how the storage capacity of semiconductor memory has increased over recent years, while the cost of semiconductor memory has decreased. The trend is expected to continue. It has been predicted that by the end of the century it will be possible to store over a billion components on a chip.

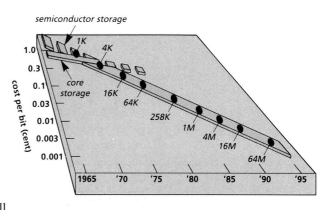

FIGURE 5-21
The chart shows the declining cost and increased storage capacity of semiconductor storage.

As you can see, semiconductor memory is compact, fast, and inexpensive. Several different types of semiconductor memory chips are used in computers. They are RAM, ROM, PROM, EPROM, and EEPROM chips.

RAM Memory

Random access memory, or **RAM**, is the name given to the integrated circuits or chips that are used for main memory. It is the type of memory that we have discussed so far in this chapter. Data and programs are transferred into and out of RAM and data stored in RAM is manipulated by computer program instructions.

There are two types of RAM memory chips: dynamic RAM and static RAM. **Dynamic RAM** chips are smaller and simpler in design than static RAM chips. With dynamic RAM the current or charge on the chip is periodically refreshed or regenerated by special regenerator circuits in order for the chip to retain the stored data. **Static RAM** chips are larger and more complicated than dynamic RAM and do not require the current to be periodically regenerated. The main memory of most computers uses dynamic RAM chips.

The example in Figure 5-22 illustrates the processing that could occur as a series of area codes are entered into RAM (computer memory) from a terminal. The first area code, 212, is entered from the keyboard and stored at memory locations 66000, 66001, and 66002. Once in memory, this field can be processed as required.

FIGURE 5-22
The instruction in the program specifies that the area code is to be read into adjacent memory locations beginning with location 66000. After the data is placed in these locations, it can be processed by the program. When the same instruction is executed the second time, the value 714 entered by the terminal operator is stored in locations 66000, 66001, and 66002, where it can be processed by the same instructions that processed area code 212.

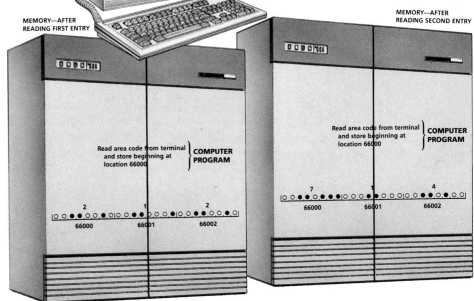

When the instruction to read (input) data into memory from the keyboard is executed again, the second area code entered from the keyboard, area code 714, would replace the previous value (212) at locations 66000, 66001, and 66002 in memory. Area code 714 could then be processed by the same instructions that processed area code 212.

When data is moved from one location to another in main memory, the data at the receiving location is replaced by the new data. The data in the sending location remains intact. Data is not removed from one location and placed in another location. Instead, the data remains in the sending location and a copy of the data is transferred to and stored in the new location.

Another aspect of RAM memory is that it is said to be **volatile** because the programs and data stored in RAM are erased when the power to the computer is turned off. Auxiliary storage is used to store programs or data that may be needed for future use.

ROM Memory

ROM stands for **read only memory**. With ROM, data is permanently recorded in the memory when it is manufactured. ROM memory retains its contents even when the power is off. The data or programs that are stored in ROM can be read and used, but cannot be altered, hence the name "read only." ROM is used to store items such as the instruction set of the computer. In addition, many of the special purpose computers used in automobiles, appliances, and so on use small amounts of ROM to store instructions that will be executed repeatedly. Instructions that are stored in ROM memory are called **firmware** or **microcode**.

Other Types of Memory

PROM means **programmable read only memory**. PROM acts the same as ROM when it is part of the computer; that is, it can only be read and its contents cannot be altered. With PROM, however, the data or programs are not stored in the memory when they are manufactured. Instead, PROM can be loaded with specially selected data or programs prior to installing it in a computer. A variation of PROM is **EPROM** (pronounced "EE-PROM"), which means **erasable programmable read only memory**. In addition to being used in the same way as PROM, EPROM allows the user to erase the data stored in the memory and to store new data or programs in the memory. EPROM is erased through the use of special ultraviolet light devices that destroy the bit settings within the memory.

EEPROM (pronounced "double-E-PROM"), or **electronically erasable programmable read only memory**, allows the stored data or programs to be erased electrically. The advantage of EEPROM is that it does not have to be removed from the computer to be changed.

SUMMARY

*I*n this chapter we examined various aspects of the processor unit including its components, how programs and data are stored, and how the processor executes program instructions to process data into information. While a detailed understanding of this material is not a prerequisite for computer literacy, understanding these principles will increase your overall comprehension of how processing occurs on a computer.

Making a Chip

A chip is made by building layers of electronic pathways and connections by using conducting and nonconducting materials on a surface of silicon. The combination of these materials into specific patterns forms microscopic electronic components such as transistors, diodes, and capacitors that make up the integrated chip circuit. The application of the materials to the silicon is done through a series of technically sophisticated chemical and photographic processes. The following photographs illustrate some of the manufacturing steps.

A chip begins with a design developed by an engineer using a computer aided circuit design program. Some circuits only take a month or two to design whereas others may take a year or more. The computer aided design system (1) allows the engineer to rearrange the design of the circuit pathways and then see them displayed on the screen. Most chips have at least four to six layers but some have up to fifteen. A separate design is required for each layer of the chip circuit. To better review the design, greatly enlarged printouts are prepared (2). After the design is finalized, a glass photo mask is prepared for each layer (3). To provide for mass production of the chips, the design is reduced to the actual size of the circuit, approximately 1/4-inch square, and duplicated over one hundred times on the surface of the photo mask. In a process similar to printing a picture from a negative, the photo mask will be used to project the circuit design onto the material used to make the chips.

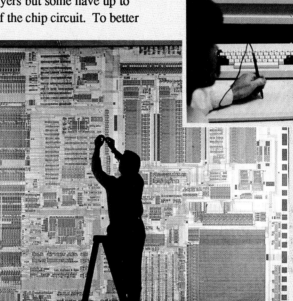

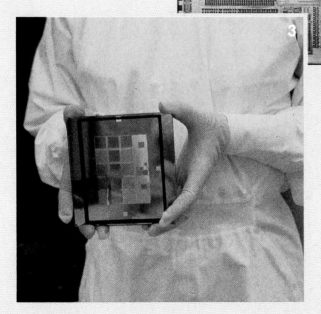

Although other materials can be used, the most common raw material used to make chips is silicon crystals (4) that have been refined from quartz rocks. The silicon crystals are melted and "grown" into a cylinder, called an ingot, two to three feet long and six inches in diameter (5). After being smoothed, the silicon ingot is sliced into wafers four to six inches in diameter and 4/1000 of an inch thick. Much of the chip manufacturing process is performed in special laboratories called "clean rooms." Because even the smallest particle of dust can ruin a chip, rooms are kept 1000 times cleaner than a hospital operating room. People who work in these facilities must wear special protective clothing called "bunny suits" (6). After the wafer has been polished and sterilized, it is placed in a diffusion oven where the first layer of material is added to the wafer surface (7). These layers of materials will be etched away to form the circuits. Before etching, a soft, gelatin-like emulsion called photoresist is added to the wafer. During lithography (8), the photoresist is covered by a photo mask and exposed to ultraviolet light. The exposed photoresist becomes hard and the covered photoresist remains soft. The soft photoresist and some of the surface materials are etched away with chemicals or hot gases leaving what will become the circuit pathways. In some facilities, the etching process is done by a robot (9).

The process of adding material and photoresist to the wafer, exposing it to ultraviolet light, and etching away the unexposed surface, is repeated using a different photo mask for each layer of the circuit. After the circuits are tested on the wafer, they are cut into individual die by the use of a diamond saw (10) or a laser. The individual chip die (11), approximately 1/4-inch square, are packaged in a hard plastic case (12) that contains pins that connect the chip to a socket on a circuit board (13).

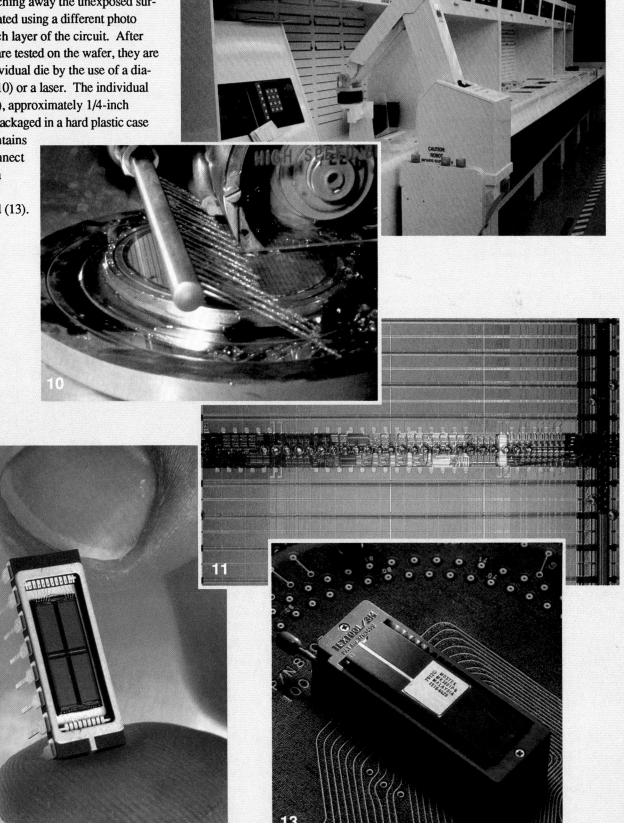

CHAPTER SUMMARY

1. The central processing unit and the main memory are contained in the processor unit.
2. The central processing unit or CPU contains the **control unit** and the **arithmetic/logic unit**. The control unit directs and coordinates all the activities on the computer. The arithmetic/logic unit performs arithmetic and logic operations.
3. The **main memory**, also called **primary storage** stores programs and data.
4. Each storage location in main memory is called a **byte** and is identified by a **memory address**.
5. The size of main memory is normally expressed in terms of **kilobytes** (approximately 1,000 bytes) of storage. A machine with 640K has approximately 640,000 memory locations.
6. A byte consists of eight **bits**. A bit can represent only two values—off and on.
7. When a letter is entered into main memory from a keyboard, the electronic circuitry interprets the character and stores the character in memory as a series of on and off bits. The computer can distinguish between characters because the combination of off and on bits assigned to each character is unique.
8. One of the most widely used codes to represent characters is the **American Standard Code for Information Interchange**, called the **ASCII code**.
9. A code used for mainframes is the **Extended Binary Coded Decimal Interchange Code (EBCDIC)**.
10. Most computers use **parity bits** for error checking.
11. The **binary** (base 2) number system is used by the computer for purposes such as memory addresses and representing the electronic status of the bits in main memory. **Hexadecimal** (base 16) is used to represent binary in a more compact form.
12. A **machine language instruction** can be decoded and executed by the CPU.
13. A machine language instruction is usually composed of an **operation code**; values indicating the number of characters to be processed; and main memory addresses of the data to be processed.
14. Steps in the **machine cycle** consist of: fetch the next instruction; decode the instruction; execute the instruction; store the results.
15. The speed of a computer is influenced by the system clock, the bus size, and the word size.
16. The **system clock** is used by the control unit to synchronize all computer operations.
17. A **bus** is any line that transmits bits between memory and the input/output devices, and between memory and the CPU.
18. The number of bits that the CPU can process at one time is called the **word size**.
19. Computers can be eight-bit, 16-bit, 32-bit, or 64-bit machines.
20. **Microprocessors** are used for the CPU in microcomputers.
21. **Coprocessors** can be used to enhance and expand the capabilities of a computer.
22. Parallel processors divide up a problem so that multiple CPUs can work on their assigned portion of the problem simultaneously.
23. **RISC** technology involves reducing a computer's instruction set to only those instructions that are most frequently used.
24. **Core memory** consisted of small, ring-shaped pieces of material that could be magnetized, or polarized, in one of two directions.
25. **Semiconductor memory** is now used in most computers. It consists of transistors etched into a semiconductor material such as silicon.
26. A **microsecond** is a millionth of a second. A **nanosecond** is a billionth of a second. Access to data stored in semiconductor memory is measured in nanoseconds.
27. **RAM**, which stands for **random access memory**, is used for main memory.
28. Once a character is stored at a location in RAM memory, it will remain there until another character is placed into the same location. When the electrical power supply is turned off, all programs and data in RAM are erased.
29. **ROM** stands for **read only memory**. Data or programs are stored in ROM when the memory is manufactured, and they cannot be altered.
30. **PROM** means **programmable read only memory**. PROM acts the same as ROM except data can be stored into the PROM memory prior to being installed in the computer.
31. **EPROM**, or **erasable programmable read only memory**, can be erased through the use of special ultraviolet devices.
32. **EEPROM** or **electronically erasable programmable read only memory**, can be electronically erased without being removed from the computer.

KEY TERMS

American Standard Code for
  Information Interchange (ASCII) *5.6*
Arithmetic/logic unit *5.3*
ASCII code *5.6*
Binary *5.5*
Bit *5.5*
Bus *5.12*
Byte *5.4*
Chip *5.13*
Control unit *5.3*
Coprocessor *5.14*
Core memory *5.14*
Data bus *5.12*
Decoding *5.3*
Dynamic RAM *5.15*
EBCDIC *5.6*
EEPROM *5.16*
Electronically erasable programmable
  read only memory (EEPROM) *5.16*
EPROM *5.16*
Erasable programmable read only
  memory (EPROM) *5.16*
Even parity *5.7*
Executing *5.3*
Execution cycle *5.11*

Extended Binary Coded Decimal
  Interchange Code (EBCDIC) *5.6*
Fetching *5.3*
Firmware *5.16*
GB *5.4*
Gigabyte (GB) *5.4*
Hexadecimal *5.7*
IC *5.13*
Instruction cycle *5.11*
Instruction register *5.10*
Instruction set *5.10*
Integrated circuit (IC) *5.13*
K *5.4*
KB *5.4*
Kilobyte (K or KB) *5.4*
Machine cycle *5.11*
Machine language instruction *5.10*
Main memory *5.3*
MB *5.4*
Megabyte (MB) *5.4*
Megahertz *5.11*
Memory address *5.4*
Microchip *5.13*
Microcode *5.16*
Microprocessor *5.13*

Microsecond *5.15*
MIPS *5.11*
Nanoseconds *5.15*
Odd parity *5.7*
Operation code *5.10*
Parallel processing *5.14*
Parity bit *5.7*
Primary storage *5.3*
Programmable read only memory
  (PROM) *5.16*
PROM *5.16*
RAM *5.15*
Random access memory (RAM) *5.15*
Read only memory (ROM) *5.16*
RISC (reduced instruction set
  computing) *5.14*
ROM *5.16*
Semiconductor memory *5.14*
Serial processing *5.14*
Static RAM *5.15*
Storing *5.3*
System clock *5.11*
Transistor *5.14*
Volatile *5.16*
Word size *5.12*

REVIEW QUESTIONS

1. Identify the two components of the central processing unit and describe the functions of each.
2. Define the terms bit and byte. Illustrate how the number 14 is represented in binary, hexadecimal, ASCII, and EBCDIC.
3. What does the letter K stand for when referring to main memory?
4. Describe how a group of characters entered into the computer as a field are stored in main memory. Draw a diagram to illustrate how the letters in your first name would be stored using the ASCII code. Begin at main memory address 45663.
5. What is parity and how is it used?
6. What are the two number systems that are used with computers? Why are they used?
7. What are the components of a machine language instruction? Describe the steps that occur in main memory and the CPU when two numbers are added together.
8. What are the three factors that influence the speed of a processor?
9. What is a microprocessor and how is it used?
10. Define each of the following terms: RAM, ROM, PROM, EPROM, EEPROM.
11. Describe the process of manufacturing integrated circuits.

CONTROVERSIAL ISSUES

1. The lower cost of producing electronic components outside the United States has caused many U.S. companies to become involved in offshore manufacturing. In addition, the importation of computer goods from foreign manufacturers has affected the computer industry in this country. Discuss whether restrictions should be placed on integrated circuits and other computer goods that are imported or manufactured offshore.

2. All microcomputers are not compatible. For example, unless special enhancements are made, software that is written for an IBM personal computer system will not run on an Apple Macintosh computer. Some people feel that industry standards should be set to eliminate the problems caused by incompatibility. Others feel that standards would restrict competition and product development. Write a paper to discuss your opinions on this topic.

RESEARCH PROJECTS

1. Many different types of devices and methods have been used for main memory. Research the history of main computer memory and prepare a report. Include information on the way the data was stored, the speed of the memory, any limitations of the method, the amount of memory that could be used, and the cost of the memory.

2. The semiconductor industry is very competitive. It develops both the microprocessors and the memory chips used in most computers today. Not only is the industry competitive in the United States, but significant competition is also generated by foreign manufacturers. Prepare a report on the industry as it is today, and include an analysis of its stance with respect to foreign competition.

# CHAPTER 6

Output from the Computer

Output from the Computer

OBJECTIVES

- Define the term output.
- List the common types of reports and graphs that are used for output.
- Describe the classifications of printers.
- List the types of printers used with personal computers and describe how they work.
- Discuss the quality of output obtainable from various types of printers.
- Describe printers used for large computers.
- Describe the types of screens available and list common screen features.
- List and describe other types of output devices used with computers.

*O*utput is the way the computer communicates with the user; therefore it is important to know the many ways this communication can take place. This chapter discusses the types of output and the devices computers use to produce output.

WHAT IS OUTPUT?

*O***utput** is data that has been processed into a useful form called information that can be used by a person or a machine. Output that is used by a machine, such as a disk or tape file, is usually an intermediate result that eventually will be processed into output that can be used by people. Computer output exists in a variety of forms.

COMMON TYPES OF OUTPUT

*T*he type of output generated from the computer depends on the needs of the user and the hardware and software that are used. The two most common types of output are reports and graphics. These types of output may be printed on a printer or displayed on a screen. Output that is printed is called **hard copy** and output that is displayed is called **soft copy** (Figure 6-1).

Reports

A **report** is data or information presented in an organized form. Most people think of reports as items printed on paper or displayed on a screen. But information printed on forms such as invoices or payroll checks can also be considered types of reports. One way to classify reports is by who uses them. An **internal report** is used by individuals in the performance of their jobs. For example, a daily sales report that is distributed to sales personnel is an internal report because it is used only by personnel *within* the organization. An **external report** is used outside the organization. Payroll checks that are printed and distributed to employees each week are external reports.

Reports may be classified by the way they present information. Three types of reports are common: detail reports, summary reports, and exception reports.

In a **detail report**, each line on the report usually corresponds to one input record that has been read and processed. Detail reports contain a great deal of information and can be quite lengthy. They are usually required by individuals who need access to the day-to-day information that reflects the operating status of the organization. For example, people in the sales department of a retail store should have access to the number of units sold of each product. The units sold report in Figure 6-2 contains a line for each item, which corresponds to each input record.

As the name implies, a **summary report** summarizes data. It contains totals for certain values found in the input records. The report illustrated in Figure 6-3 contains a summary of the units sold for each department. The information on the summary report consists of totals from the information contained in the detail report in Figure 6-2. Summary reports are most useful for individuals who do not require a detailed knowledge of each transaction. For example, detail reports contain more information than most managers have time to review. With a summary report, however, a manager can quickly review information in summarized form.

FIGURE 6-1
This photograph shows the same output in hard copy and soft copy form. An advantage of hard copy is that the user can write comments on it and route it to other users.

```
            UNITS SOLD REPORT

                                          QTY
   DEPT.   DEPT NAME      ITEM  DESCRIPTION  SOLD

     10    MENS FURNISHINGS  105   T-SHIRT      3
     10    MENS FURNISHINGS  109   SOCKS      127
     12    SLEEPWEAR         199   ROBE         6
     14    MENS ACCESSORIES  266   HAT          4
```

FIGURE 6-2
The data for this detail report was obtained from each input record that was read and processed. A line was printed for each record.

```
                SALES BY DEPARTMENT

   DEPT.          DEPT.         UNITS    SALES
    NO.           NAME          SOLD       $

     10     MENS FURNISHINGS    130     653.35
     12     SLEEPWEAR             6     189.70
     14     MENS ACCESSORIES      4      98.00
```

FIGURE 6-3
This summary report contains the sales for each department. The report can be prepared from the same data that prepared the report in Figure 6-2.

```
INVENTORY EXCEPTION REPORT

ITEM      ITEM            QUANTITY
NO.       DESCRIPTION     ON HAND

105       T-SHIRT         24
125       SCARF            3
126       BELT            17
```

FIGURE 6-4
This exception report lists inventory items with a quantity of less than 25. They could have been selected from thousands of inventory records. Only these items met the user's "exception criteria."

An **exception report** contains information that is outside of "normal" user-specified values or conditions and thus is an "exception" to the majority of the data. For example, if an organization with an inventory wanted to have an on-hand quantity of more than 25 of every inventory item at all times, it would design an exception report to tell them if the amount of any inventory items fell below this level. An example of such a report is shown in Figure 6-4.

Exception reports help users to focus on situations that may require immediate decisions or specific actions. The advantage of exception reports is that they save time and money. In a large department store, for example, there may be over 100,000 inventory items. A detail report containing all inventory items could be longer than 2,000 pages. To search through the report to determine the items whose on-hand quantity was less than 25 would be a difficult and time-consuming task. The exception report, however, could extract these items, which might number 100–200, and place them on a two- to four-page report that could be prepared in just a few minutes.

Graphics

Another common type of output is computer graphics. In business, **computer graphics** are often used to assist in analyzing data. Computer graphics display information in the form of charts, graphs, or pictures so that the information can be understood easily and quickly (Figure 6-5). Facts contained in a lengthy report and data relationships that are difficult to understand in words can often be summarized in a single chart or graph.

In the past, graphics were not widely used in business because each time data was revised, a graphic artist would have to redraw the chart or graph. Today, relatively inexpensive graphics software makes it possible to redraw a chart, graph, or picture within seconds rather than the hours or days that were previously required. Many application software packages, such as spreadsheets, include graphics capabilities. As we discussed in Chapter 2, the three most popular types of charts and graphs are pie charts, bar charts, and line charts.

A **pie chart** is normally used to depict data that may be expressed as a percentage of a whole (Figure 6-6). Pie charts show easy visual comparisons of the relative size of each component within a whole, where the whole represents 100 percent. If used with a color output device, most graphics software allows each component to be displayed in a different color, lets text material be placed on the screen in various colors, and provides shading. Some graphics software even allows certain segments of the chart to be shown with a three-dimensional effect for emphasis.

Bar charts are among the most versatile and popular types of display charts used for comparing data (Figure 6-7). Bar charts represent data by vertical or horizontal bars. They are useful for comparing data in which sizes or quantities vary and the amount of variance needs to be made clear. Graphics software can display bars of different colors, vertical or horizontal bars, and text material where required.

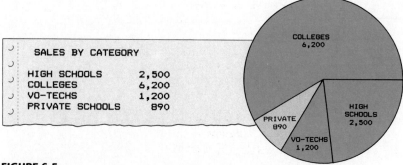

```
SALES BY CATEGORY

HIGH SCHOOLS     2,500
COLLEGES         6,200
VO-TECHS         1,200
PRIVATE SCHOOLS    890
```

FIGURE 6-5
This small report lists sales of magazines by school category. With the addition of the pie chart graphic, however, the manager can easily see that colleges account for more than half the sales and that private schools represent a small percentage of the sales. Both the report and the graphic use the same information, but the graphic helps the manager to understand the information more quickly.

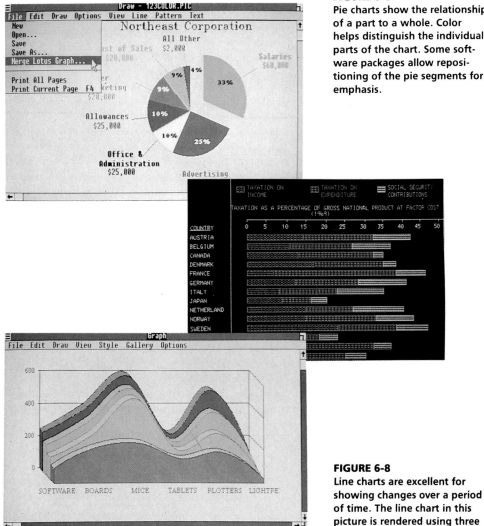

FIGURE 6-6
Pie charts show the relationship of a part to a whole. Color helps distinguish the individual parts of the chart. Some software packages allow repositioning of the pie segments for emphasis.

FIGURE 6-7
A bar chart (left) can have vertical or horizontal bars. The horizontal bars in this picture depict taxation as a percentage of the gross national product for different countries. The length of the bars represents the total taxation. The colors within the bars represent the different parts of the whole taxation amount.

FIGURE 6-8
Line charts are excellent for showing changes over a period of time. The line chart in this picture is rendered using three dimensions and color to enhance the data's presentation.

Line charts may also be generated by graphics software. These charts represent data relationships by a continuous line across the chart (Figure 6-8). Line charts are particularly useful for showing a change in a value or quantity over a period of time.

From the examples of the various types of graphs and charts, you can see how computer graphics offers a powerful tool for the business user who must present data in a meaningful manner or for the manager who must review, analyze, and make decisions based on data relationships.

A variety of devices are used to produce the output created in the information processing cycle. The following paragraphs describe the most commonly used output devices.

PRINTERS

Printing requirements vary greatly among computer users. For example, the user of a personal computer generally uses a printer capable of printing 100 to 200 lines per minute. Users of mainframe computers, such as utility companies that send printed bills to hundreds of thousands of customers each month, need printers that are capable of printing thousands of lines per minute. These different needs have resulted in the development of printers with varying capabilities. Due to the many choices available and because printed output is so widely used, users must be familiar with the factors to consider when choosing a printer (Figure 6-9).

FIGURE 6-9
Factors that affect the choice of a printer

QUESTION	EXPLANATION
How much output will be produced?	Desktop printers are not designed for continuous use. High volume (more than several hundred pages a day) requires a heavy-duty printer.
Who will use the output?	Most organizations want external reports to be prepared on a high-quality printer.
Where will the output be produced?	If the output will be produced at the user's desk, a sound enclosure may be required to reduce the noise of some printers to an acceptable level.
Are multiple copies required?	Some printers cannot use multipart paper.

How Are Printers Classified?

Printers can be classified by how they transfer characters from the printer to the paper, either by impact or nonimpact, and by printer speed.

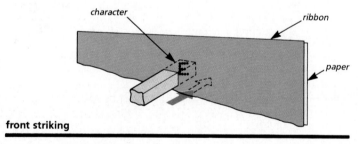
front striking

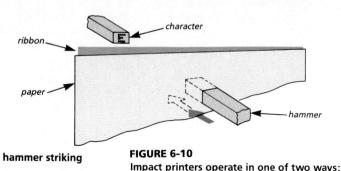
hammer striking

FIGURE 6-10
Impact printers operate in one of two ways: front striking or hammer striking.

Impact and Nonimpact   **Impact printers** transfer the image onto paper by some type of printing mechanism striking the paper, ribbon, and character together. One technique is **front striking** in which the printing mechanism that forms the character strikes a ribbon against the paper from the front to form an image. This is similar to the method used on typewriters. The second technique utilizes a **hammer striking** device. The ribbon and paper are struck against the character from the back by a hammer to form the image on the paper (Figure 6-10).

A number of technologies are used to accomplish nonimpact printing. **Nonimpact printing** means that printing occurs without having a mechanism striking against a sheet of paper. For example, ink is sprayed against the paper or heat is used to transfer the character.

Each of these two methods of printing has its advantages and disadvantages. Impact printing can be noisy because the paper is struck when printing occurs. But because the paper is struck, carbon paper can be used to create multiple copies of a report, such as an invoice, that go to different people. Although nonimpact printers cannot create carbon copies, they are very quiet and are ideal for desktop applications where the normal requirements only call for a single printed copy.

Speed Another way to classify printers is by the speed at which they print. Printers can be classified as low speed, medium speed, high speed, and very high speed.

Low-speed printers print one character at a time. The rate of printing for low-speed printers is expressed in the number of characters that can be printed in one second. Low-speed printers can print from 15 to 600 characters per second.

Medium-speed and high-speed printers are called **line printers** because they can print multiple characters on a line at the same time. The rate of printing for these machines is stated in terms of the number of lines per minute that can be printed. **Medium-speed printers** can print from 300 to 600 lines per minute. Printers that can print from 600 to 3,000 lines per minute are classified as **high-speed printers**.

Very high-speed printers can print in excess of 3,000 lines per minute; some, more than 20,000 lines per minute. Very high-speed printers are often called **page printers** because they print an entire page at one time.

Printer Features

To decide which printer to choose for a particular job, it is important to know the different features that a printer might have. Common feature choices include carriage size, type of paper feed mechanism, and bidirectional printing capability.

Carriage Size Most printers are built with either a standard or wide carriage. A **standard carriage** printer can accommodate paper up to 8 1/2 inches wide. A **wide carriage** printer can accommodate paper up to 14 inches wide. Using a normal character size, most printers can print 80 characters per line on a standard carriage and 132 characters per line on a wide carriage.

Feed Mechanism The feed mechanism determines how the paper is moved through the printer. Two types of feed mechanisms are found on printers, tractor feed and friction feed. **Tractor feed mechanisms** transport continuous form paper through the printer by using sprockets, small protruding prongs of plastic or metal, which fit into holes on each side of the paper. The pages of **continuous form paper** are connected for continuous flow through the printer (Figure 6-11). Where it is necessary to feed single sheets of paper into the printer, **friction feed mechanisms** are used. As the name implies, paper is moved through friction feed printers by pressure on the paper and the carriage, as it is on a typewriter. As the carriage rotates, the paper is transported through the printer.

FIGURE 6-11
Each sheet of continuous form paper is connected with the next. A feed mechanism pulls the paper through the printer using the holes on each side of the form. Perforations between each page allow a printed report to be folded and may be used to separate each page.

Bidirectional Printing   Some printers are designed to print in a **bidirectional** manner. That is, the print head, the device that contains the mechanism for transferring the character to the paper, can print as it moves from left to right, and from right to left. The printer does this by storing the next line to be printed in its memory and then printing the line forward or backward as needed. Bidirectional printing can almost double the number of characters that can be printed in a given period of time.

PRINTERS FOR SMALL AND MEDIUM COMPUTERS

*T*he increased popularity and use of personal computers has resulted in the development of a large number of printers that vary significantly in speed, quality, and price. Some of these printers are also used on larger systems. The following paragraphs describe the print devices most commonly used on small and medium-size computers.

Dot Matrix Printers

Dot matrix printers are used extensively because they are versatile and relatively inexpensive. The Epson printer shown in Figure 6-12 is a well-known dot matrix printer that is used with personal computers. Figure 6-13 shows a popular Printronix printer that is frequently used with many medium-size computers.

A **dot matrix printer** is an impact printer. Its print head consists of a series of small tubes containing pins that, when pressed against a ribbon and paper, print small dots. The

FIGURE 6-12
The Epson FX-86e printer is a dot matrix printer.

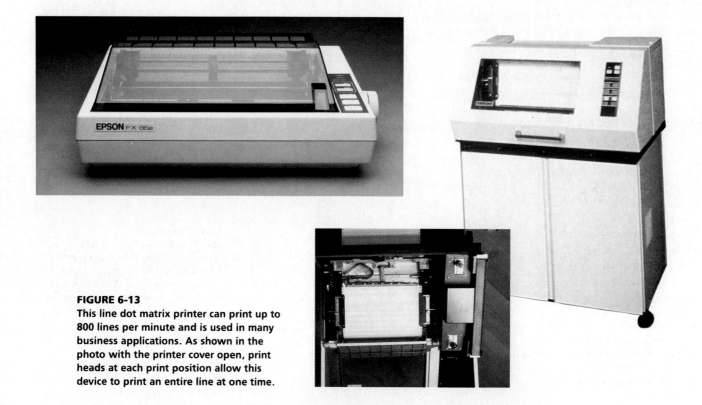

FIGURE 6-13
This line dot matrix printer can print up to 800 lines per minute and is used in many business applications. As shown in the photo with the printer cover open, print heads at each print position allow this device to print an entire line at one time.

combination of small dots printed closely together forms the character (Figure 6-14).

To print a character using a dot matrix printer, the character stored in main memory is sent to the printer's electronic circuitry. The printer circuitry activates the pins in the print head that correspond to the pattern of the character to be printed. The selected pins strike the ribbon and paper and print the character. Low-speed dot matrix printers utilize a movable print head that prints one character at a time. Medium- and high-speed dot matrix printers have print mechanisms at each print position and are able to print an entire line at one time.

Dot matrix printers can contain a varying number of pins, depending on the manufacturer and the printer model. Print heads consisting of nine and 24 pins are most common. Figure 6-15 illustrates the formation of the letter E using a nine-pin dot matrix printer.

A character produced by a dot matrix printer is made up of a series of dots. The quality of print produced is partly dependent on the number of pins used to form the character. A 24-pin print head produces better-looking characters than a nine-pin print head because the dots are closer together.

Several methods are used to improve the quality of dot matrix printers. On a nine-pin printer, one method is to print a line twice. Using this technique a line is printed, and then the print head is shifted very slightly and the line is printed again. This results in overlapping dots, which give the appearance of solid characters (Figure 6-16). The disadvantage, of course, is that the printing takes longer since each character is printed twice. Twenty-four-pin printers can produce the same print quality in a single pass.

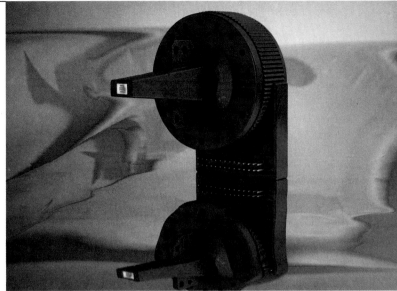

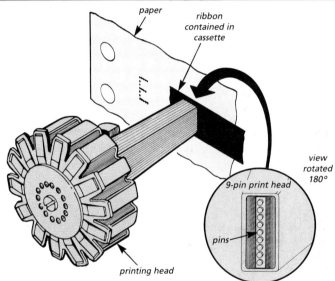

paper

ribbon contained in cassette

view rotated 180°

9-pin print head

pins

printing head

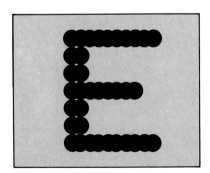

FIGURE 6-16
The letter E in this example is formed by overprinting, or printing the character twice. When it is printed the second time, the print head is slightly offset so that much of the space between the dots is filled in. This gives the character a better appearance and makes it easier to read.

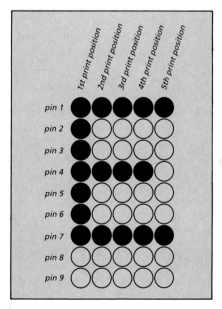

1st print position
2nd print position
3rd print position
4th print position
5th print position

pin 1
pin 2
pin 3
pin 4
pin 5
pin 6
pin 7
pin 8
pin 9

FIGURE 6-14
The print head for a dot matrix printer consists of a series of pins. When activated, the pins strike the ribbon that strikes the paper, creating a dot on the paper.

FIGURE 6-15
The letter E is formed with seven vertical and five horizontal dots. As the nine-pin print head moves from left to right, it fires one or more pins into the ribbon, which makes a dot on the paper. At print position 1, it fires pins 1 through 7. At print positions 2 through 4, it fires pins 1, 4, and 7. At print position 5, it fires pins 1 and 7. Pins 8 and 9 are used for lowercase characters such as p, q, y, g, and j that extend below the line.

CONDENSED PRINT - NORMAL CHARACTERS
CONDENSED PRINT - EMPHASIZED CHARACTERS

STANDARD PRINT - NORMAL CHARACTERS
STANDARD PRINT - EMPHASIZED CHARACTERS

ENLARGED PRINT — NORMAL CHARACTERS
ENLARGED PRINT — EMPHASIZED CHARACTERS

FIGURE 6-17
Three type sizes are shown in this example—condensed, standard, and enlarged. All three are printed using normal and emphasized (also called "bold") print density.

Many dot matrix printers can also print characters in two or more sizes and densities. Typical sizes include condensed print, standard print, and enlarged print. In addition, each of the three print sizes can be printed with increased density or darkness, called bold print. Figure 6-17 illustrates condensed, condensed bold, standard, standard bold, enlarged, and enlarged bold print.

Most dot matrix printers have a graphics mode that enables them to print pictures and graphs (Figure 6-18). In graphics mode, the individual print head pins can be activated separately or in combination to form unique shapes or continuous lines. When special software packages are used, dot matrix printers can print in many different type styles and sizes (Figure 6-19). The flexibility of the dot matrix printer has resulted in widespread use of this type of printer by all types of computer users.

Some dot matrix printers can print in multiple colors using ribbons that contain the colors red, green, and blue. Color output is obtained by repeated printing and repositioning of the paper, print head, and ribbon. Such printers can be useful in printing graphs and charts, but output quality is not comparable to color produced by other types of printers.

FIGURE 6-18
Many dot matrix printers are capable of producing colored output using special ribbons.

Monaco	**Chicago**	*Los Angeles*
Venice	Geneva	Helvetica
Athens	**London**	**San Francisco**
Σψμβολ	Courier	New York

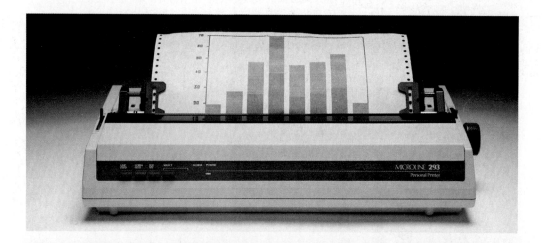

FIGURE 6-19
These letter styles illustrate the abilities of dot matrix printers to print graphics, depending on the software directing the printer.

Daisy Wheel Printers

When users require printed output of high quality, such as for business or legal correspondence, a letter-quality printer is often used. The term **letter quality** refers to the quality of the printed character that is suitable for formal or professional business letters. A letter-quality printed character is a fully formed, solid character like those made by typewriters. It is not made up of a combination of dots, as by a dot matrix printer.

The letter-quality printer most often used with personal computers is the daisy wheel printer (Figure 6-20). The **daisy wheel printer** is an impact printer. It consists of a type element containing raised characters that strike the paper through an inked ribbon.

The daisy wheel element somewhat resembles the structure of a flower, with many long, thin petals (Figure 6-21). Each "petal" has a raised character at the tip. When printing occurs, the type element (daisy wheel) rotates so that the character to be printed is in printing position. A hammer extends, striking the selected character against the ribbon and paper, printing the character. Because of the time required to rotate the daisy wheel, the daisy wheel printer is normally slower than a dot matrix printer; however, the print quality is higher. Printing speeds vary from 20 to 80 characters per second.

An additional feature of the daisy wheel printer is that the daisy wheel can be easily replaced. Daisy wheels come in a variety of sizes and fonts. A font, or typeface as they are sometimes called, is a complete set of characters in a particular style such as script, gothic, or roman. Therefore, whenever the user wishes to change fonts, he or she can remove one daisy wheel and put another wheel on the printer.

The disadvantage of a daisy wheel printer is that it is capable of printing only the characters that are on the wheel. It cannot, therefore, print graphic output.

FIGURE 6-20
A daisy wheel printer produces letter-quality output comparable to that produced by a typewriter. Either continuous form or single-sheet paper can be used with most daisy wheel printers.

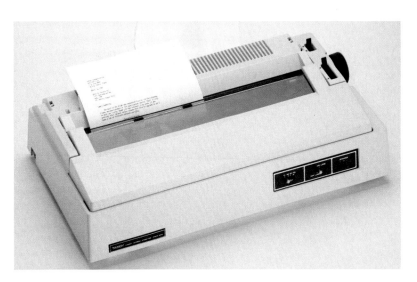

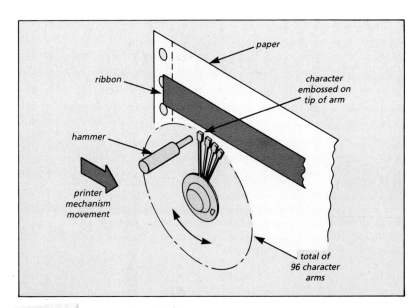

FIGURE 6-21
The daisy wheel print element consists of a number of arms, each with a character at the end. When the printer is running the wheel spins until the desired character is lined up with the hammer. The hammer then strikes against the ribbon and paper, printing the character.

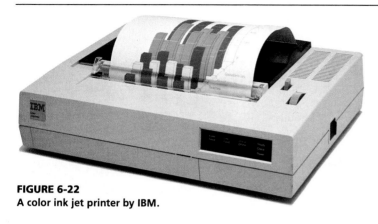

FIGURE 6-22
A color ink jet printer by IBM.

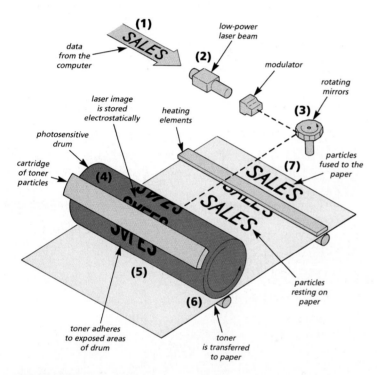

FIGURE 6-23
Laser printers use a process similar to a copying machine. Data from the computer (1), such as the word SALES, is converted into a laser beam (2) that is directed by a mirror (3) to a photo-sensitive drum (4). The sensitized drum attracts toner particles (5) that are transferred to the paper (6). The toner is fused to the paper with heat and pressure (7).

FIGURE 6-24
The output illustrated in this picture was produced by a laser printer. Note that the output contains a mixture of different sizes and styles of print.

Thermal Printers

Thermal printers use heat to produce fully formed characters, usually on special chemically treated paper. An advantage of thermal printers is that they are very quiet. Disadvantages are their need for special paper and their relatively slow printing speed. Thermal printers are not as commonly used as they once were.

Ink Jet Printers

A popular type of nonimpact printer is an **ink jet printer**. To form a character, an ink jet printer uses nozzles that spray ink onto the page. Ink jet printers produce relatively high-quality print and are very quiet because the paper is not struck as it is by dot matrix or daisy wheel printers. Disadvantages are that ink jet printers cannot produce multiple copies, and the ink sometimes smears on soft, porous paper. The ink jet printer in Figure 6-22 is designed for use with personal computers.

Laser Printers

The **laser printer** is a nonimpact printer that operates in a manner similar to a copying machine (Figure 6-23). The laser printer converts data from the computer into a laser beam that is directed by a mirror to a positively charged revolving drum. Each position on the drum touched by the laser beam becomes negatively charged and attracts the toner (powdered ink). The toner is transferred onto the paper and then fused to the paper by heat and pressure. The end result is a high-quality printed image. As shown in Figure 6-24, laser printers can produce a variety of output.

PRINTERS FOR LARGE COMPUTERS

Minicomputers and mainframes are frequently used to process and print large volumes of data. As the demand for printing information from a computer increases, the use of higher speed printers is required. The three types of printers often used on large computers are chain printers, band printers, and high-speed laser printers.

Chain Printers

The **chain printer** is a widely used high-speed printer. It contains numbers, letters of the alphabet, and selected special characters on a rotating chain (Figure 6-25). The chain consists of a series of type slugs that contain the character set. The character set on the type slugs is repeated two or more times on the chain mechanism. The chain rotates at a very high speed. Each possible print position has a hammer that can fire against the back of the paper, forcing the paper and ribbon against the character on the chain. As the chain rotates, the hammer fires when the character to be printed is in the proper position.

The chain printer has proven to be very reliable. It produces good print quality at up to 3,000 lines per minute. The printers in the large computer installation in Figure 6-26 are chain printers.

Band Printers

Band printers, similar to chain printers, utilize a horizontal, rotating band containing characters. The characters are struck by hammers located behind the paper and a ribbon to create a line of print on the paper (Figure 6-27).

Interchangeable type bands can be used on band printers. The different type bands contain many different fonts or print styles. A band printer can produce up to six carbon copies, has good print quality, high reliability, and depending on the manufacturer and model of the printer, can print in the range of 300 to 2,000 lines per minute.

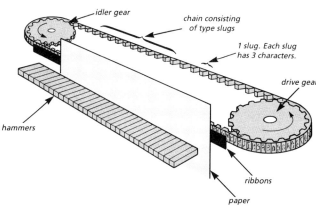

FIGURE 6-25
The chain printer contains a complete set of characters on several sections of a chain that rotates at a high, constant rate of speed. Print hammers are located at each horizontal print position. The paper and ribbon are placed between the hammers and the chain. As the chain rotates, the hammers fire when the proper characters are in front of their print positions.

FIGURE 6-26
These high-speed chain printers are used in a large computer installation to produce thousands of lines of printed output per minute.

FIGURE 6-27
A band printer uses a metal band that contains solid characters. Print hammers (shown inside the band) at each print location strike the paper and the ribbon, forcing them into the band to print the character.

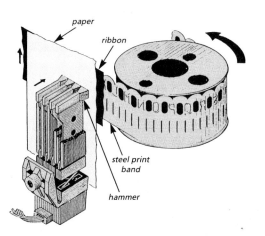

High-Speed Laser Printers

High-speed laser printers, also called **page printers**, can produce printed output at the rate of over 20,000 lines per minute, the equivalent of over 400 pages of 50 lines per page. As shown in Figure 6-28, these high-speed printers usually consist of a dedicated computer and tape drive to maximize the printing speed. When the device is printing, the paper moves so fast that it must be folded and stacked mechanically.

SCREENS

*T*he **screen**, also called the monitor, CRT (cathode ray tube), or VDT (video display terminal), is another important output device. Screens are used on both personal computers and terminals to display many different types of output. For example, responses obtained from user inquiries to a database are frequently displayed on a screen. A screen can also be used to display electronic spreadsheets, electronic mail, and graphs of various types.

Screen Features

Size   The most widely used screens are equivalent in size to a 12- to 15-inch television screen. Although there is no standard number of displayed characters, screens are usually designed to display 80 characters on a line with a maximum of 25 lines displayed at one time. The 25th line is often reserved for messages or system status reports, not for data. This provides for a maximum of 2,000 characters on the screen at once. Some terminals can display up to 132 characters on a single horizontal line. The more characters that are displayed on a line, the smaller the size of the characters. Therefore, an important consideration when selecting a terminal is the number of characters displayed on the screen at one time and the *resolution* (clarity) of the characters displayed.

Color   Most of the early screens displayed white characters on a black background. Research has indicated, however, that other color combinations are easier on the eyes. Today, many screens display either green or amber characters on a black background (Figure 6-29).

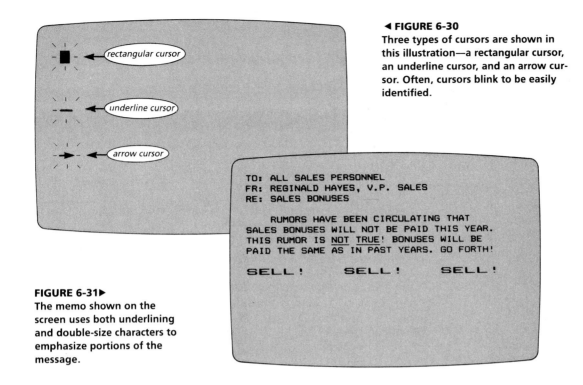

Cursor A **cursor** is a symbol that indicates where on the screen the next character entered will be displayed. It can also be used as a marker on a screen to identify the choices a user can make. Some of the symbols used to represent cursors are shown in Figure 6-30. Most cursors blink when they are displayed on the screen so the user can quickly find their location.

Scrolling **Scrolling** is a method of moving lines displayed on the screen up or down one line at a time. As a new line is added, for example, to the bottom of the screen, an existing one, from the top of the screen, is removed. The line removed from the screen remains in the computer's memory even though it is no longer displayed. When the screen is scrolled in the opposite direction (in this example, down), the line from the top that was removed reappears on the screen and the line at the bottom is removed.

Paging When **paging** is used, an entirely new "page" or screen of data can be displayed. This feature is useful in applications such as word processing when a user wants to use the screen to move quickly through pages of a long document.

Other Screen Features Screen features also include several options that can be used to emphasize displayed characters: reverse video, underlining, bold, blinking, and double size. **Reverse video** refers to the process of reversing the normal display on the screen. For example, it is possible to display a dark background with light characters or a light background with dark characters. Thus, if the normal screen had amber characters on a black background, reverse video shows black characters on an amber background. This feature permits single characters, whole words or lines, and even the entire screen to be reversed. The **underlining** feature allows characters, words, lines, or paragraphs to be underlined. Another feature used for emphasis is the ability to display some characters or words as bold. **Bold** means that characters are displayed at a greater brightness level than the surrounding text. The **blinking** feature makes characters or words on a screen blink, thus drawing attention to them. The **double size** feature means that certain characters or words are displayed at twice the size of normal characters and words. Figure 6-31 illustrates how underlining and double-size characters highlight data on the screen.

FIGURE 6-32
The high resolution of this plasma display allows the screen to display any combination of character fonts, line drawings, charts, sketches and letters.

FIGURE 6-33
The liquid crystal display (LCD) screen used with this portable computer can display numbers, letters, and special characters, and even has some graphics capabilities.

Types of Screens

Several types of screens are used with computers. The most common types are monochrome screens, color screens, plasma screens, and LCD screens. Plasma and LCD screens, which do not use the conventional cathode ray tube technology, are sometimes called **flat panel display screens** because of their relatively flat screens.

Monochrome screens specially designed for use with personal computers or for use as computer terminals usually display a single color, such as white, green, or amber characters on a black background. The characters are displayed without flicker and with very good resolution. Some monochrome screens have graphics capabilities.

The use of **color screens** is increasing in business and science applications, because numerous studies have found that color enables the user to more easily read and understand the information displayed on the screen.

A **plasma screen** produces a bright, clear image with no flicker (Figure 6-32). The screens are flat, so that they can be installed on desks or walls, taking up very little space.

With the development of truly portable computers that could be conveniently carried by hand or in a briefcase came a need for an output display that was equally as portable. Although several technologies have been developed, **liquid crystal displays (LCD)** are used as the output display for a number of laptop computers (Figure 6-33). LCD displays are also used in watches, calculators, and other electronic devices.

How Characters Are Displayed on a Screen

Most screens used with personal computers and terminals utilize cathode ray tube (CRT) technology. When these screens produce an image, the following steps occur (Figure 6-34):

1. The image to be displayed on the screen is sent electronically from the CPU to the cathode ray tube.
2. An electron gun generates an electron beam of varying intensity, depending on the electronic data received from the CPU.
3. The yoke, which generates an electromagnetic field, moves the electron beam horizontally across the **phosphor-coated screen**.
4. The electron beam causes the desired phosphors to emit light. The higher the intensity of the beam, the brighter the phosphor glows. It is the phosphor-emitted light that produces an image on the screen.

On most screens, the phosphors that emit the light causing the image on the screen do not stay lit very long. They must be *refreshed* by having the electron beam light them again. If the screen is not scanned enough times per second, the phosphors will begin to lose their light. When this occurs, it appears that the characters on the screen are flickering. To eliminate flicker, a scan rate of 60 times per second is normal when the screen is used for alphanumeric display.

electron beam

electron gun

2 3 4

yoke

phosphor-coated
screen

FIGURE 6-34
When an image is formed on a screen, the information to be displayed is sent to the screen (1). Then the electron gun (2) generates an electron beam. The yoke (3) directs the beam to a specific spot on the screen (4), where the phosphors struck by the electron beam begin to glow and form an image on the screen.

The brightness of the image on the screen depends on the intensity of the electron beam striking the phosphor, which in turn depends on the voltage applied to the beam. As the beam scans each phosphor dot, the intensity is varied precisely to turn each dot on or off.

Computer screens are divided into addressable locations. The manner of indicating the number of addressable locations varies with the type of screen. On a screen used primarily for characters and alphanumeric displays, the number of locations is usually identified by specifying the number of lines and the number of characters per line that can be displayed (sometimes called the character display addressing scheme).

Screens used for graphics are called **dot-addressable displays**, or sometimes **bit-mapped displays**. On these monitors, the number of addressable locations corresponds to the number of dots that can be illuminated. Each addressable dot that can be illuminated is called a **picture element** or **pixel** (Figure 6-35).

With dot-addressable displays, the resolution or clarity of the characters depends to a great extent on the number of pixels on the screen. The greater the number of pixels, the better the screen resolution. The number of pixels on a screen is determined through a combination of the software in the computer, the connection between the computer and the screen, and the screen itself. Some screens and computers operate in two or more resolution modes. For example, the IBM PS/2 series of personal computers, when operating in graphics mode, can use either medium or high resolution. In medium resolution, the screen contains 64,000 individual pixels arranged in 200 rows, each row containing 320 pixels. When high resolution is used, 480 rows can contain 640 pixels for a total of 307,200 distinct points.

Devices are currently available that offer very high-resolution graphics. The resolution of these devices is high enough to provide

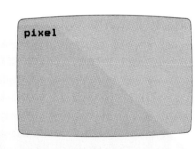

pixel

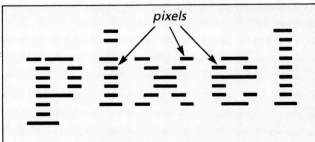

pixels

FIGURE 6-35
The word pixel shown in this drawing is made up of pixels as they would be displayed on a dot-addressable or bit-mapped screen. Each pixel is a small rectangular spot of light that appears on the screen at the point where it is activated by an electron beam. These pixels must be reactivated about 60 times per second to appear as a solid character without screen flicker.

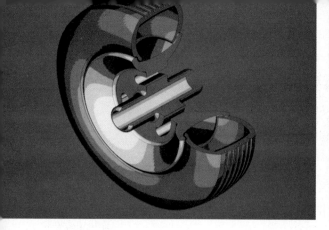

FIGURE 6-36
The picture on the left shows how very high-resolution graphics can depict features such as shading, reflections, and highlights. The picture on the right shows how very high-resolution graphics can be used for simulation exercises; in this case, a flying situation. Through the use of the computer, this picture could be changed quickly to show the plane taking off and landing.

an image that is almost equivalent to the quality of a photograph (Figure 6-36). High-resolution graphics requires a great deal of storage, and it is more difficult electronically to maintain a steady image on the screen. In the past few years, however, there have been great improvements in picture resolutions. In addition, costs have been reduced so that high-resolution graphics are now widely used. Several graphics standards have been developed, including CGA (Color Graphics Adapter), EGA (Enhanced Graphics Adapter), and the latest standard from IBM called VGA (Video Graphics Array). Each standard provides for different numbers of pixels and colors.

How Color Is Produced Color is produced on a screen in several ways. Remember that on a monochrome screen, a single electron beam strikes the phosphor-coated screen, causing the chosen phosphor dot to light. If the characters are green on a black background, the phosphors emit a green light when activated. Similarly, if the characters are amber on black, the phosphors emit an amber light.

To show color on a screen, three phosphor dots are required for each pixel. These dots are red, blue, and green (Figure 6-37). The electron beam must turn on the desired color phosphors within the pixel to generate an image. In the simplest configuration, eight colors can be generated—no color (black), red only, blue only, green only, red and blue (magenta), red and green (yellow), blue and green (blue-green), and red, blue, and green together (white). By varying the intensity of the electron beam striking the phosphors, many more colors can be generated.

Two common types of color screens are composite video monitors and RGB monitors. Both monitors produce color images, and both monitors can be used for color graphics. A **composite video monitor** uses a single electron signal to turn on the color phosphors within the pixel. An **RGB monitor** uses three signals, one for each color, red, green, and blue, to turn on the required phosphors. The difference is that the RGB monitor produces a much clearer display with much better color and character resolution.

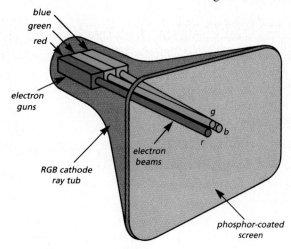

FIGURE 6-37
On color monitors, each pixel contains three phosphor dots: one red, one green, and one blue. These dots can be turned on individually or in combinations to display a wide range of colors.

How Flat Panel Displays Work Plasma screens use a relatively new display technology. A plasma screen consists of a grid of conductors sealed between two flat plates of glass. The space between the glass is filled with neon/argon gas. When the gas at an intersection in the grid is electronically excited, it creates an image. Each intersection of the grid of wires in a plasma screen is addressable. Therefore, characters in a variety of type styles, line drawings, charts, or even pictures can be displayed. Pictures displayed look almost like photographs.

In an LCD display, a liquid crystal material is deposited between two sheets of polarizing material. When a current is passed between crossing wires, the liquid crystals are aligned so that light cannot shine through, producing an image on the screen.

OTHER OUTPUT DEVICES

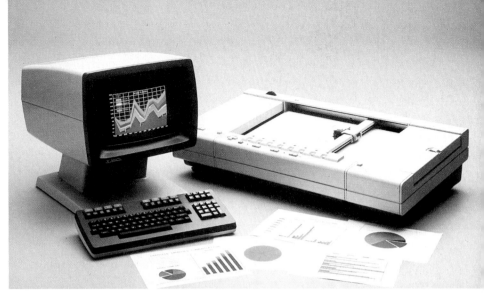

Although printers and display devices provide the large majority of computer output, other devices are available for particular uses and applications. These include plotters, computer output microfilm devices, and voice output devices.

Plotters

A **plotter** is an output device used to produce high-quality line drawings, such as building plans, charts, or circuit diagrams. These drawings can be quite large; some plotters are designed to handle paper up to 40 inches by 48 inches, much larger than would fit in a standard printer. The plotter can also draw numbers and letters to add text to the output. Plotters can be classified by the way they create the drawing. The two types are pen plotters and electrostatic plotters.

As the name implies, **pen plotters** create images on a sheet of paper by moving one or more pens over the surface of the paper or by moving the paper under the tip of the pens.

Two different kinds of pen plotters are flatbed plotters and drum plotters. When a **flatbed plotter** is used to plot or draw, the pen or pens are instructed by the software to move to the down position so the pen contacts the flat surface of the paper. Further instructions then direct the movement of the pens to create the image. Most flatbed plotters have one or more pens of varying colors or widths. The plotter illustrated in Figure 6-38 is a flatbed plotter that can create color drawings. Another kind of flatbed plotter holds the pen stationary and moves the paper under the pen.

A **drum plotter** uses a rotating drum or cylinder over which drawing pens are mounted. The pens can move to the left and right as the drum rotates, creating an image (Figure 6-39). An advantage of the drum plotter is that the length of the plot is virtually unlimited, since roll paper can be used. The width of the plot is limited by the width of the drum.

With an **electrostatic plotter**, the paper moves under a row of wires (called styli) that can be turned on to create an electrostatic charge on the paper. The paper then passes through a developer and the drawing emerges where the charged wires touched the

FIGURE 6-38
An example of a flatbed plotter.

FIGURE 6-39
This drum plotter utilizes eight pens of different colors to create diagrams. As the paper moves forward and back, the pens move left and right and, under software control, draw where instructed.

paper. The electrostatic printer image is composed of a series of very small dots, resulting in relatively high-quality output. In addition, the speed of plotting is faster than with pen plotters.

Factors affecting the cost of a plotter are based on the resolution of the drawing and the speed of the plotting. Resolution is determined by the smallest movement a pen can make on the paper. Typical plotter movements may vary from .001 to .0005 inch. Plotting speeds of up to 36 inches per second are possible. Costs range from under $1,000 to over $100,000 for very high-speed plotters with extremely fine resolution.

Computer Output Microfilm

Computer output microfilm (COM) is an output technique that records output from a computer as microscopic images on roll or sheet film. The images stored on COM are the same as the images that would be printed on paper. The COM recording process reduces characters 24, 42, or 48 times smaller than would be produced on a printer. The information is then recorded on sheet film called **microfiche** or on 16mm, 35mm, or 105mm roll film.

The data to be recorded by the device can come directly from the computer (online) or from a magnetic tape that was previously produced by the computer (offline) (Figure 6-40). After the COM film is processed, the user can view it.

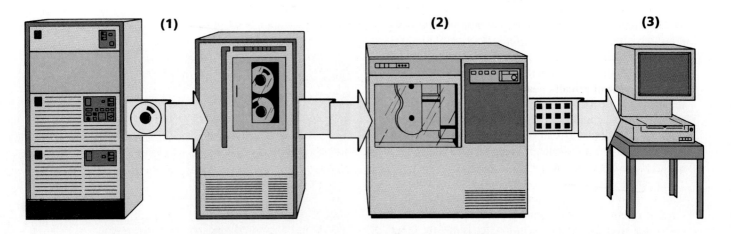

(1)   **(2)**   **(3)**

FIGURE 6-40
This drawing illustrates the computer output microfilm (COM) process. The computer generates printed images on an output tape that is transferred to the tape drive attached to the COM machine (1). The COM machine reads the tape and produces reduced images of the printed output on film (2); in this example, microfiche sheet film. Then the film can be viewed using special microfilm reader devices (3).

Microfilm has several advantages over printed reports or other storage media for certain applications. Some of these advantages are:

1. Data can be recorded on the film at up to 30,000 lines per minute—faster than all except very high-speed printers.
2. Costs for recording the data are lower. The cost of printing a three-part, 1,000-page report is approximately $28, whereas the cost of producing the same report on microfilm is approximately $3.

3. Less space is required to store microfilm than printed materials. A microfiche that weighs one ounce can store the equivalent of 10 pounds of paper.
4. Microfiche provides a less expensive way to store data. For example, the cost per million characters (megabyte) on a disk is approximately $20, while the cost per megabyte on microfilm is approximately $.65.

To access data stored on microfilm, a variety of readers are available. They utilize indexing techniques to provide a quick reference to the data. Some microfilm readers can perform automatic data lookup, called **computer-assisted retrieval**, under the control of an attached minicomputer. With the powerful indexing software and hardware now available for microfilm, a user can usually locate any piece of data in a 200,000,000-character database in less than 10 seconds, at a far lower cost per inquiry than using an online inquiry system consisting of a computer system that stores the data on a hard disk.

Voice Output

The other important means of generating output from a computer is voice output. **Voice output** consists of spoken words that are conveyed to the user from the computer. Thus, instead of reading words on a printed report or monitor, the user hears the words over earphones, the telephone, or other devices from which sound can be generated.

The data that produces voice output is usually created in one of two ways. First, a person can talk into a device that will encode the words in a digital pattern. For example, the words "The number is" can be spoken into a microphone, and the computer software can assign a digital pattern to the words. The digital data is then stored on a disk. At a later time, the data can be retrieved from the disk and translated back from digital data into voice, so that the person listening will actually hear the words.

A second type of voice generation is new but holds great promise. Called a **voice synthesizer**, it can transform words stored in main memory into speech. The words are analyzed by a program that examines the letters stored in memory and generates sounds for the letter combinations. The software can apply rules of intonation and stress to make it sound as though a person were speaking. The speech is then projected over speakers attached to the computer. computer.

You may have heard voice output used by the telephone company for giving number information. Automobile and vending machine manufacturers are also incorporating voice output into their products. The potential for this type of output is great and it will undoubtedly be used in many products and services in the future.

SUMMARY OF OUTPUT TO THE COMPUTER

he output step of the information processing cycle uses a variety of devices to provide users with information. Some of the devices that were discussed in this chapter, including printers and screens, are summarized in Figure 6-41.

FIGURE 6-41
This table summarizes some of the more common output devices

OUTPUT DEVICE	DESCRIPTION
Printers—Impact	
Dot matrix	Prints text and graphics using small dots.
Daisy wheel	Prints letter-quality documents—no graphics.
Chain	High-speed printer to 3,000 lines per minute—designed to print text.
Band	High-speed printer to 2,000 lines per minute—designed to print text.
Printers—Nonimpact	
Thermal	Uses heat to produce fully formed characters.
Ink jet	Sprays ink onto page to form text and graphic output—prints quietly.
Laser	Produces high-quality text and graphics.
High-speed laser	Can exceed 20,000 lines per minute.
Screens	
Monochrome	Displays white, green, or amber images on a black background.
Color	Uses multiple colors to enhance displayed information.
Plasma	A flat screen that produces bright, clear images with no flicker.
LCD	A flat screen used on many laptop computers.
Plotters	Produces hard copy graphic output.
COM	Records reduced-size information on sheet film called microfiche or on roll film.
Voice	Conveys information to the user from the computer in the form of speech.

CHAPTER SUMMARY

1. **Output** is data that has been processed into a useful form called information that can be used by a person or a machine.
2. An **external report** is used outside the organization.
3. An **internal report** is used within an organization by people performing their jobs.
4. The major consideration for internal reports is that they be clear and easy to use. For external reports, the quality of the printed output may be important.
5. In a **detail report**, each line on the report usually corresponds to one input record.
6. A **summary report** contains summarized data, consisting of totals from detailed input data.
7. An **exception report** contains information that will help users to focus on situations that may require immediate decisions or specific actions.
8. **Computer graphics** are used to present information so it can be quickly and easily understood.
9. A **pie chart** is normally used to depict data that can be expressed as a percentage of a whole.

10. A **bar chart** is best used for comparing sizes or quantities.
11. **Line charts** are particularly useful when showing changes over a period of time.
12. Computer printers fall into two broad categories: impact printers and nonimpact printers.
13. **Impact printing** devices transfer the image onto paper by some type of printing mechanism striking the paper, ribbon, and character together.
14. Impact printers can be **front striking** or **hammer striking**.
15. A **nonimpact printer** creates an image without having characters strike against a sheet of paper.
16. Impact printing is noisy but multiple copies can be made.
17. Nonimpact printers are quiet and some print very fast.
18. Computer printers may be classified by the speed at which they print: low, medium, high, and very high speed.
19. The printing rate of **low-speed printers** is expressed as the number of characters that can be printed in one second.
20. The printing rate for **medium-speed printers** and **high-speed printers** is stated as the number of lines printed per minute.
21. Medium- and high-speed printers are sometimes called **line printers**.
22. **Very high-speed printers** are sometimes called **page printers**.
23. Features of printers include carriage size, type of paper feed mechanism, and bidirectional printing.
24. The pages of **continuous form paper** are connected for continuous flow through the printer.
25. **Tractor feed mechanisms** transport continuous form paper by using sprokets inserted into holes on the sides of the paper.
26. **Friction feed** mechanisms move paper through a printer by pressure between the paper and the carriage.
27. **Dot matrix printers** can print text and graphics and are used with more personal computers than any other type of printer.
28. Dot matrix printers have small pins that are contained in a print head. The pins strike the paper and ribbon to print a character.
29. Most dot matrix printers print **bidirectionally**, meaning the print head can print while moving in either direction.
30. The quality of a dot matrix printer is partly dependent on the number of pins used to form the character.
31. Most dot matrix printers can print condensed print, standard print, and enlarged print.
32. Some dot matrix printers can print in color.
33. A **letter-quality** printed character is a fully formed character that is easy to read.
34. The most widely used letter-quality printer for personal computers is the **daisy wheel printer**.
35. Speeds of a daisy wheel printer vary from 20 to 60 characters per second.
36. **Thermal printers** use heat to produce fully formed characters, usually on chemically treated paper.
37. An **ink jet printer** uses a nozzle to spray liquid ink drops onto the page. Some ink jet printers print in color.
38. **Chain printers** print up to 3,000 lines per minute.
39. **Band printers** have interchangeable bands with many different styles of fonts.
40. **Laser printer** are nonimpact printers that operate in a manner similar to a copying machine.
41. Types of screens include monochrome screens, color screens, plasma screens, and LCD screens.
42. **Monochrome** monitors usually display green, white, or amber characters on a black background.
43. **Color screens** are being used more because color enables the user to more easily read and understand the information displayed on the screen.
44. A **plasma** display can produce all kinds and sizes of type styles, charts, and drawings.
45. **Liquid crystal displays** use a polarizing material and liquid crystal to form images.
46. Most screens utilize cathode ray tube (CRT) technology.
47. To display color on a color monitor, three separate dots (red, blue, green) are turned on by an electron beam.
48. The two types of color monitors are: **composite video monitors** and **RGB monitors**.
49. A **computer plotter** is an output device that can create drawings, diagrams, and similar types of output.
50. **Computer output microfilm (COM)** is an output technique that records output from a computer as microscopic images on roll or sheet film.
51. COM offers the advantages of faster recording speed, lower costs of recording the data, less space required for storing the data, and lower costs of storing the data.
52. **Voice output** consists of spoken words that are conveyed to the computer user from the computer.
53. A **voice synthesizer** can transform words stored in main memory into human speech.

KEY TERMS

Band printers 6.13
Bar charts 6.4
Bidirectional 6.8
Bit-mapped displays 6.17
Blinking 6.15
Bold 6.15
Chain printer 6.13
Color screens 6.16
COM 6.20
Composite video monitor 6.18
Computer-assisted retrieval 6.21
Computer graphics 6.4
Computer output microfilm (COM) 6.20
Continuous form paper 6.7
Cursor 6.15
Daisy wheel printer 6.11
Detail report 6.3
Dot-addressable displays 6.17
Dot matrix printer 6.8
Double size 6.15
Drum plotter 6.19
Electrostatic plotter 6.19
Exception report 6.4
External report 6.3

Flatbed plotters 6.19
Flat panel display screens 6.16
Friction feed mechanisms 6.7
Front striking 6.6
Hammer striking 6.6
Hard copy 6.2
High-speed laser printers 6.14
High-speed printers 6.7
Impact printers 6.6
Ink jet printer 6.12
Internal report 6.3
Laser printers 6.12
LCD 6.16
Letter quality 6.11
Line charts 6.5
Line printers 6.7
Liquid crystal displays (LCD) 6.16
Low-speed printers 6.7
Medium-speed printers 6.7
Microfiche 6.20
Monochrome screens 6.16
Nonimpact printing 6.6
Output 6.2
Page printers 6.7

Paging 6.15
Pen plotters 6.19
Phosphor-coated screen 6.16
Picture element 6.17
Pie charts 6.4
Pixel 6.17
Plasma screen 6.16
Plotter 6.19
Report 6.3
Reverse video 6.15
RGB monitor 6.18
Screen 6.14
Scrolling 6.15
Soft copy 6.2
Standard carriage 6.7
Summary report 6.3
Thermal printers 6.12
Tractor feed mechanisms 6.7
Underlining 6.15
Very high-speed printers 6.7
Voice output 6.21
Voice synthesizer 6.21
Wide carriage 6.7

REVIEW QUESTIONS

1. Name and describe three types of commonly used reports.
2. What are the advantages of displaying information in a graphic form? What are the disadvantages? What are the three most commonly used types of charts?
3. What are the two major categories of printers? What are the differences between the two?
4. How does a dot matrix printer produce an image? What effect on the quality of print does this method have? What techniques are used on dot matrix printers to improve the print quality?
5. What does the term "letter quality" mean? What types of printers print with letter quality?
6. Describe some of the print capabilities of dot matrix printers with respect to graphics and character size and style.
7. How does an ink jet printer produce images? What are some advantages of ink jet printers?
8. Explain how a laser printer works. What are some advantages of laser printers?
9. What are the three major types of high-speed printers? List the characteristics such as speed and manner of printing for each one.
10. What types of screens are used with computers? List some screen features.
11. List the steps involved in displaying an image on a CRT screen.
12. Describe some of the different types of plotters and the manner in which they produce drawings.
13. List several advantages of microfilm over printed reports.
14. Describe the two ways of creating voice output.

CONTROVERSIAL ISSUES

1. Some experts in business management have pointed out that much of the paperwork generated within a business organization is not used. Further, they have noted that managers do not have time to examine the reams of paper they receive in order to gain the information they need to make decisions. These experts have argued that very high-speed printers contribute to the paperwork explosion and, therefore, contribute to rather than help solve the problem. Others argue that in their right place, these printers are invaluable. Take a side in this dispute and prepare an argument.
2. "Automation—The Curse of Modern Society" was the title of a speech given at a meeting of union leaders. The speaker stated that the ability of the computer to develop drawings that are equal to or better than those prepared by graphic artists directly threatens the skilled worker. Others have said that having the computer perform these jobs frees people to do more creative work. What do you think?

RESEARCH PROJECTS

1. The speed, quality, and prices of printers are constantly changing as new innovations appear. Examine a current issue of a personal computer magazine and clip out four advertisements for printers. Write to the printer manufacturers and obtain detailed information about the printers. Then make a presentation to your class concerning what you found.
2. Visit an installation in your area that uses plotters. Bring back and share with your class the drawings that are produced on the plotters.

CHAPTER 7

Auxiliary Storage

Auxiliary Storage

OBJECTIVES

- Define auxiliary storage.
- Identify the primary devices used for personal computer auxiliary storage.
- Describe the manner in which data is stored on disks.
- Describe the methods used to back up data stored on floppy and hard disks.
- Identify the types of disk storage used with large computers.
- Explain how tape storage is used with large computers.
- List and describe three other forms of auxiliary storage: optical, solid state, and mass storage.

*S*torage, performed by all computers, is the fourth and final operation in the information processing cycle. Upon completion of this chapter you will be able to add the knowledge you acquire about storage operations to what you have learned in previous chapters about input, processing, and output operations. In addition, you will be familiar with the various types and capabilities of auxiliary storage devices that are used with computers.

WHAT IS AUXILIARY STORAGE?

*C*omputer storage can be classified into two types: main memory and auxiliary storage. As you have seen, main memory temporarily stores programs and data that are being processed. **Auxiliary storage**, or **secondary storage**, stores programs and data when they are not being processed, just as a filing cabinet is used in an office to store records. Records that are not being used are kept in the file cabinet until they are needed. In the same way, data and programs that are not being used on a computer are kept in auxiliary storage until they are needed. Auxiliary storage devices that are used with computers include devices such as magnetic disk and tape (Figure 7-1).

Auxiliary storage devices provide a more permanent form of storage than main memory because they are **nonvolatile**, that is, data and programs that have been placed on auxiliary storage devices are retained when the power is turned off. Main memory is volatile, which means that when power is turned off, whatever is stored in main memory is erased.

Auxiliary storage devices can be used as both input and output devices. When they are used to receive data that has been processed by the computer they are functioning as output devices. When data that they stored is transferred to the computer for processing, they are functioning as input devices.

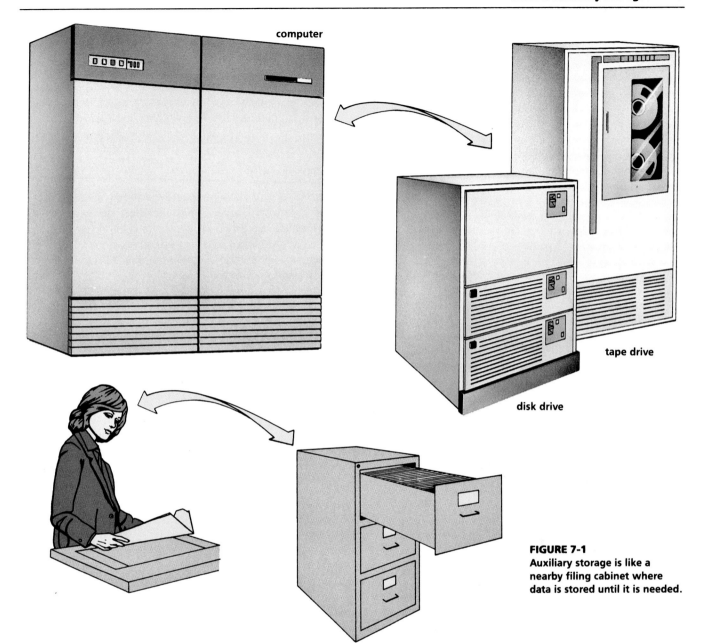

computer

tape drive

disk drive

FIGURE 7-1
Auxiliary storage is like a nearby filing cabinet where data is stored until it is needed.

The auxiliary storage needs of users can vary greatly. Those who use personal computers, may find the amount of data to be stored to be relatively small. For example, the names, addresses, and telephone numbers of several hundred friends or customers of a small business might require only 20,000 bytes of auxiliary storage (200 records × 100 characters per record). Users of large computers such as banks or insurance companies, however, may need auxiliary storage devices that can store billions of characters. To meet the different needs of users, a variety of storage devices are available. In the next section we explain the devices that are designed for users with personal computers. Later in the chapter, we discuss the devices that are used with larger computer systems.

AUXILIARY STORAGE FOR PERSONAL COMPUTERS

*P*ersonal computer users have several categories of auxiliary storage from which to choose. These include floppy disks, hard disks, and removable disk cartridges.

FIGURE 7-2
In this picture, a user is inserting a diskette into the disk drive of an IBM microcomputer.

Floppy Disks

In the early 1970s IBM introduced the floppy disk and the floppy disk drive as a new type of auxiliary storage. Today, **floppy disks**, also called **diskettes**, **floppies**, or just **disks**, are used as a principal auxiliary storage medium for personal computers (Figure 7-2). This type of storage is convenient, reliable, and relatively low in cost.

Floppy disks are available in a number of different sizes. Many personal computers take disks that are 5 1/4 inches in diameter. Smaller disks, 3 1/2 inches in diameter, are also commonly used and are increasing in popularity (Figure 7-3).

A floppy disk consists of a circular piece of thin mylar plastic (the actual disk), which is coated with an oxide material similar to that used on magnetic tape. On a 5 1/4 inch disk, the circular piece of plastic is enclosed in a flexible square protective jacket. The jacket has an opening so that a portion of the disk's surface is exposed for reading and recording (Figure 7-4). On a 3 1/2 inch disk, the circular piece of plastic is enclosed in a rigid plastic cover and a piece of metal called the shutter covers the reading and recording area. When the 3 1/2 inch disk is inserted into a disk drive, the drive slides the shutter to the side to expose the disk surface (Figure 7-5).

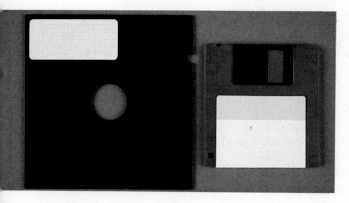

FIGURE 7-3
The most commonly used disks for personal computers are 5 1/4 and 3 1/2 inch disks.

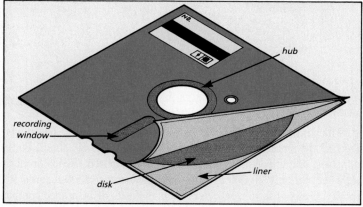

FIGURE 7-4
A 5 1/4 inch floppy disk, or diskette, consists of the disk itself enclosed within a protective jacket, usually made of a vinyl material. The liner of the diskette is essentially friction-free so that the disk can turn freely, but the liner does contact the disk and keep it clean. The magnetic surface of the diskette, which is exposed through the window in the jacket, allows data to be read and stored. The large hole (hub) in the diskette is used to mount the diskette in the disk drive. The small hole is used by some disk drives as an indicator for where to store data.

shutter

shell

liner

metal hub

magnetic coating

base film

FIGURE 7-5
In a 3 1/2 inch diskette the flexible plastic disk is enclosed between two liners that clean the disk surface of any microscopic debris and help to disperse static electricity. The outside cover is made of a rigid plastic material and the recording window is covered by a metal shutter that slides to the side when the disk is inserted into the disk drive.

How Is a Floppy Disk Formatted? Before a floppy disk can be used on a microcomputer for auxiliary storage, it must be formatted. The **formatting** process includes defining the tracks and sectors on the surface of a disk (Figure 7-6). A **track** is a narrow recording band forming a full circle around the disk. Each track on the disk is divided into sectors. A **sector** is a section of a track. It is the basic storage unit of floppy disks. When data is read from a disk, a minimum of one full sector is read. When data is stored on a disk, at least one full sector is written. The number of tracks and sectors that are placed on a disk when it is formatted varies based on the capacity of the disk, the capabilities of the disk drive being used, and the specifications in the software that does the formatting. Many 5 1/4 inch disks are formatted with 40 tracks and 9 sectors on the surface of the disk. The 3 1/2 inch disks are usually formatted with 80 tracks and 9 sectors on each side. A 3 1/2 inch disk has more tracks than a 5 1/4 inch disk because even though it is smaller in size it has a larger storage capacity. When 40 tracks are recorded on a diskette, the tracks are numbered from 0 to 39. When 80 tracks are used, the tracks are numbered from 0 to 79.

FIGURE 7-6
Each track on a diskette is a narrow, circular band. On a diskette containing 40 tracks, the outside track is called track 0 and the inside track is called track 39. The distance between track 0 and track 39 on a 5 1/4 inch diskette is less than one inch. The disk surface is divided into sectors. This example shows a diskette with nine sectors.

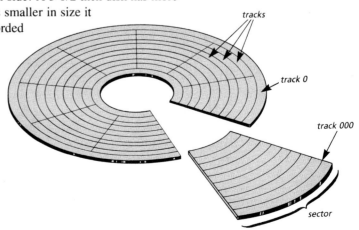

tracks

track 0

track 000

sector

Hard- and Soft-Sectored Diskettes Disks and disk drives are classified as either hard-sectored or soft-sectored. A **hard-sectored disk** has a hole in front of each sector, normally near the center of the disk (Figure 7-7). These holes provide timing information to the drive. Hard-sectored disks will always contain the same number and size of sectors because the sectors are defined by the sector holes. Therefore, the exact storage capacity of a hard-sectored disk can always be determined. For example, a hard-sectored disk that contains 16 sectors with 256 bytes per sector will always be able to store a maximum of 4,096 bytes per track (16 × 256). When the disk is two-sided and contains 40 tracks per side, the total storage capacity of the disk is 327,680 bytes (4,096 × 40 × 2).

FIGURE 7-7
Within its protective jacket this hard-sectored diskette contains 16 holes, evenly spaced around a circle on the disk. The holes indicate exactly where a sector begins.

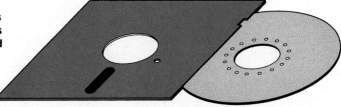

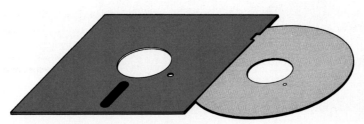

FIGURE 7-8
A soft-sectored disk has only a single index hole. The drive can use the hole to find the beginning of any track. The number of sectors on a track and the number of bytes in each sector are determined by the software that formats the disk.

A **soft-sectored disk** has a single index hole that indicates the beginning of the track (Figure 7-8). The number of sectors per track and the number of characters that can be stored in each sector are defined by the software when the disk is formatted. For example, a soft-sectored disk can be formatted with 40 tracks on each side, nine sectors per track, and 512 bytes per sector, for a total of 368,640 bytes (characters) stored on the disk.

What Is the Storage Capacity of a Floppy Disk? Knowing the storage capacity of a disk gives a user an idea of how much data or how many programs can be stored on the disk. The number of characters that can be stored on a disk depends on three basic factors: (1) the number of sides of the disk used; (2) the recording density of the bits on a track; and (3) the number of tracks on the diskette.

Some disks and drives are designed so that data can be recorded on only one side of the disk. These drives are called **single-sided drives**. Similarly, disks on which data can be recorded on one side only are called **single-sided disks**. Today, most disk drives are designed to record and read data on both sides of the disk. Drives that can read and write data on both sides of the disk are called **double-sided drives** and the disks are called **double-sided disks**. The use of double-sided drives and disks doubles the number of characters that can be stored on the disk. The term cylinder is sometimes used with double-sided disks. A **cylinder** is defined as all tracks of the same number. For example, track 0 on side 1 of the disk and track 0 on side 2 of the disk is called cylinder 0.

Another factor in determining the storage capacity of a disk is the recording density provided by the drive. The **recording density** is the number of bits that can be recorded on one inch of the innermost track on the disk. This measurement is referred to as **bits per inch (bpi)**. The higher the recording density, the higher the storage capacity of the disk.

The third factor that influences the number of characters that can be stored on a disk is the number of tracks onto which data can be recorded. This measurement is referred to as **tracks per inch (tpi)**. As we saw earlier in this chapter, the number of tracks depends on the size of the disk, the drive being used, and how the disk was formatted.

While the capacity of floppy disks can vary, a common capacity for a 5 1/4 inch disk is approximately 360K and for a 3 1/2 inch disk, 720K. On some computers floppy disks can store 2 megabytes (million characters) of data.

How Is Data Stored on a Floppy Disk? Regardless of the type of floppy disk or the formatting scheme that is used, the method of storing data on a disk is essentially the same. When a disk is inserted in a disk drive, the center hole fits over a hub mechanism that positions the disk in the unit (Figure 7-9). The circular plastic disk rotates within its cover at approximately 300 revolutions per minute. Data is stored on tracks character by character, using the same code, such as ASCII (American Standard Code for Information Interchange), that is used to store characters in main memory. Electronic impulses are placed along a track to represent the bit pattern for each character. To do this, a recording mechanism in the drive called the **read/write head** rests on the surface of the rotating disk, generating electronic impulses representing the bits to be recorded (Figure 7-10). To access different tracks on the disk, the drive moves the read/write head from track to track.

FIGURE 7-9
When a floppy disk is inserted in a drive, the center hole is positioned between the collet and the hub. After the door to the disk drive is closed and the disk is engaged, it begins rotating within the protective jacket at approximately 300 RPM.

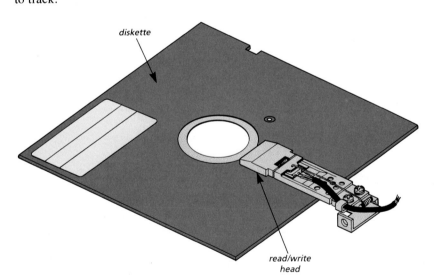

FIGURE 7-10
The read/write head moves back and forth over the opening in the protective jacket to read or write data on the disk.

What Is Access Time? Data stored in sectors on a floppy disk must be retrieved and placed in main memory to be processed. The time required to access and retrieve the data is called the **access time**.

The access time for a floppy disk drive depends on four factors:

1. **Seek time**, the time it takes to position the read/write head over the proper track.
2. **Latency**, the time it takes for the sector containing the data to rotate under the read/write head.

3. **Settling time**, the time required for the read/write head to be placed in contact with the disk.
4. **Data transfer rate**, the time required to transfer the data from the disk to main memory.

The access time for floppy disks varies from about 175 milliseconds (one millisecond equals 1/1000 of a second) to approximately 300 milliseconds. What this means to the user is that, on the average, data stored in a single sector on a diskette can be retrieved in approximately 1/5 to 1/3 of a second.

The Care of Floppy Disks With reasonable care, floppy disks provide an inexpensive and reliable form of storage. In handling floppy disks, take care to avoid exposing them to heat, magnetic fields, and contaminated environments. One advantage of the 3 1/2 inch disk is that it has a rigid plastic cover that provides more protection for the data stored on the plastic disk inside than the flexible cover on a 5 1/4 inch disk. Figure 7-11 shows ways to care for floppy disks properly.

FIGURE 7-11
Guidelines for the proper care of floppy disks.

Hard Disks

Hard disks provide larger and faster auxiliary storage capabilities for personal computers. **Hard disks** consist of one or more rigid metal **platters** coated with a metal oxide material that allows data to be magnetically recorded on the surface of the platters (Figure 7-12). In this section we discuss the two types of hard disks used on personal computers, fixed disks and hard cards.

FIGURE 7-12
A hard disk consists of one or more disk platters. Each side of the platter is coated with a metal oxide substance that allows data to be magnetically stored.

FIGURE 7-13
A hard card is a hard disk on a circuit board that can be mounted in a computer's expansion slot. In the picture below, the protective cover for the disk has been removed.

What Is a Fixed Disk? Hard disks used on personal computers are sometimes called **fixed disks** because the platters used to store the data are permanently mounted inside the computer and are not removable like floppy disks. On fixed disks, the metal disks, the read/write heads, and the mechanism for moving the heads across the surface of the disk are enclosed in a sealed case. This helps to ensure a clean environment for the disk.

The **hard card** is a circuit board that has a hard disk built onto it. Hard cards provide an easy way to expand the storage capacity of a personal computer because the board can be installed into an expansion slot of the computer (Figure 7-13).

FIGURE 7-14
This picture of a hard disk drive illustrates the access arm and the read/write heads, which are over the surface of the disks. These heads are extremely stable. They can read and write tracks very close together on the surface of the disk.
▼

How Is Data Stored on a Hard Disk? Storing data on hard disks is similar to storing data on floppy disks. Hard drives contain a spindle on which one or more disk platters are mounted. The spindle rotates the disk platters at a high rate of speed, usually 3,600 revolutions per minute. In order to read or write data on the surface of the spinning disk platter, the disk drives are designed with **access arms**, or **actuators**. The access arms or actuators contain one or more read/write heads per disk surface (Figure 7-14). These read/write heads "float" on a cushion of air and do not actually touch the surface of the disk. The distance between the head and the surface varies from approximately one-millionth of an inch to 1/2 millionth of an inch. As shown in Figure 7-15, the close tolerance leaves no room for any type of contamination. If some form of contamination is introduced or if the alignment of the read/write heads is altered by something accidentally jarring the computer, the disk head can collide with and damage the disk surface, causing a loss of data. This event is known as a **head crash**. Because of the time needed to repair the disk and to reconstruct the data that was lost, head crashes can be extremely costly for users.

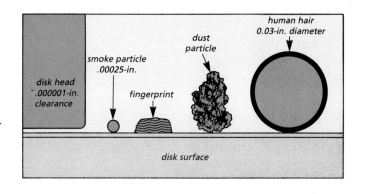

◄ **FIGURE 7-15**
The clearance between a disk head and the disk surface is about 1 millionth of an inch. With these tolerances, contamination such as a smoke particle, fingerprint, dust particle, or human hair could render the drive unusable. Sealed disk drives are designed to minimize contamination.

When reading data from the disk, the read/write head senses the magnetic spots that are recorded on the disk along the various tracks and transfers the data to main memory. When writing, the read/write head transfers data from main memory and stores it as magnetic spots on the tracks on the recording surface of one or more of the disks. As the disk rotates at a high rate of speed, the read/write heads move across its surface.

The number of platters permanently mounted on the spindle in the drive can vary. For 5 1/4 inch drives, the number varies between one and four platters. On many drives, each surface of a platter can be used to store data. Thus, if one platter is used in the drive, two surfaces are available for data. If two platters are used, four surfaces are available for data, and so on. Naturally, the more platters, the more data that can be stored on the drive.

The storage capacity of hard drives is measured in megabytes or millions of bytes (characters) of storage. Common sizes for personal computers range from 10MB to 100MB of storage and even larger sizes are available. As an idea of how much data these storage capacities represent, 10MB of storage is equivalent to approximately 5,000 double-spaced typewritten pages.

In addition to a larger storage capacity, hard disks provide faster access time than floppy disks. The typical access time of a hard disk for a personal computer is between 25 and 80 milliseconds.

The use of a hard disk drive on a personal computer provides many advantages for users. Because of its large storage capacity, a hard disk can store many software application programs and data files. When a user wants to run a particular application or access a particular data file on a hard disk, it is always available. The user does not have to find the appropriate floppy disk and insert it into the drive. In addition, the faster access time of a hard disk reduces the time needed to load programs and access data.

Disk Cartridges   Another variation of disk storage available for use with personal computers is the removable **disk cartridge**. Disk cartridges, which can be inserted and removed from a computer (Figure 7-16), offer the storage and fast access features of hard disks and the portability of floppy disks. Disk cartridges are often used when data security is an issue. At the end of a work session, the disk cartridge can be removed and locked up, leaving no data on the computer.

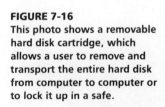

FIGURE 7-16
This photo shows a removable hard disk cartridge, which allows a user to remove and transport the entire hard disk from computer to computer or to lock it up in a safe.

Protecting Data Stored on a Disk

Regardless of whether you are using floppy disks, hard disks, or removable disk cartridges on a personal computer, you must protect the data you store on the disk from being lost. Disk storage is reusable and data that is stored on a disk may be overwritten and replaced with new data. This is a desirable feature allowing users to remove or replace unwanted files. However, it also raises the possibility of accidentally removing or replacing a file that you really wanted to keep. To protect programs and data stored on disks, there are several things you can do.

How Is the Write-Protect Notch Used? One way to protect the data and programs stored on a floppy disk is to use the write-protect notch. On the 5 1/4 inch disks, this notch is located on the side of the disk. To prevent writing to a disk, a user covers this notch with a small piece of removable tape. Before writing data onto a disk, the disk drive checks the notch. If the notch is open the drive will proceed to write on the disk. If the notch is covered the disk drive will not write on the disk (Figure 7-17).

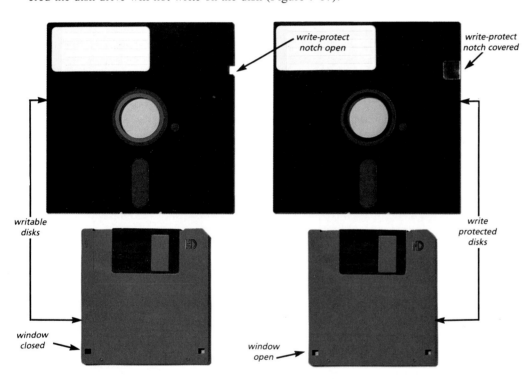

writable disks

write-protect notch open

window closed

window open

write-protect notch covered

write protected disks

FIGURE 7-17
The write-protect notch of the 5 1/4 inch disk on the left is open and therefore data could be written to the disk. The notch of the 5 1/4 inch disk on the right, however, is covered. Data could not be written to this disk. The reverse situation is true for the 3 1/2 inch disk. Data cannot be written on the 3 1/2 inch disk on the right because the small black piece of plastic is not covering the window in the lower left corner. Plastic covers the window of the 3 1/2 inch disk on the left, so data can be written on this disk.

On 3 1/2 inch disks, the situation is reversed. The write-protect notch is a small window in the corner of the disk. A piece of plastic in the window can be moved to open and close the window. If the write-protect window is closed, the drive can write on the disk. If the window is open, the drive will not write on the disk.

Backup Storage Another way to protect programs and data stored on disks is by creating backup storage. As discussed in Chapter 3, backup storage means creating a duplicate copy of important programs and data on a separate disk. To back up floppy disks, simply copy the data on one disk to another floppy disk. When using hard disks, however, the user is faced with a more difficult problem. The amount of data that can be stored on a hard disk can fill many floppy disks. For example, to back up a hard disk containing 10 million characters, approximately thirty 5 1/4 inch diskettes that could each store 360,000 characters would be required. For this reason, cartridge tape is sometimes used to back up hard disk storage.

Cartridge Tape A device commonly used to back up hard disks on personal computers is the **cartridge tape drive** (Figure 7-18). When these devices are available on a personal computer, the data and programs that are stored on a hard disk can be copied onto the tape cartridge for backup storage.

Some cartridge tape drives can operate in a **streaming mode**, without the normal stopping and starting usually associated with tape operations. Tape streaming results in more data being recorded in less time. Using the streaming method, a cartridge tape unit can completely copy a 20 million byte hard disk in approximately four minutes.

FIGURE 7-18
Cartridge tape drives are an effective way to back up and store data that would otherwise require numerous diskettes.

AUXILIARY STORAGE FOR MEDIUM AND LARGE COMPUTERS

A wide variety of devices are available for use as auxiliary storage on medium and large computers. Most of these devices use storage techniques that are similar, if not identical, to the devices that we discussed for personal computers. As you would expect, however, storage devices used for medium and large computers provide greater storage capacity and faster retrieval rates than devices used with small systems. For discussion purposes, we group storage devices for medium and large computers into three categories: magnetic disk, magnetic tape, and other storage devices.

Magnetic Disk

Magnetic disk is the most common type of auxiliary storage device for medium and large computers. Disks for medium and large computers are similar to devices used on personal computers but have larger capacities, usually as a result of having more recording surfaces. Some disk devices used on large computers can store billions of characters of information. Because of their ability to retrieve data directly from a specific location on the disk, disk devices for medium and large computers are sometimes referred to as **direct-access storage devices (DASD)**.

One difference between auxiliary storage for a personal computer and for larger computers is that many more disk devices can be attached to larger computers. While most personal computers are limited to two to four disks, medium computers can support 8 to 16 disk devices and large computers can support over 100 high-speed disk devices. Figure 7-19 shows a large number of disk units attached to a single mainframe computer.

FIGURE 7-19
A mainframe computer can have dozens of fixed disk storage devices attached to it.

Disk devices for medium and large computers fall into two categories: fixed disks and removable disks.

Fixed Disks   Fixed disks, the most commonly used disks for medium and large computers, can be either mounted in the same cabinet as the computer or enclosed in their own stand-alone cabinet. As with fixed disks in personal computers, fixed disks on medium and large computers contain nonremovable platters that are enclosed in airtight cases to prevent contamination (Figure 7-20).

Removable Disks   Removable disk units were introduced in the early 1960s and were the most prevalent type of disk storage for nearly 20 years. During the 1980s, however, removable disks began to be replaced by fixed disks that offered larger storage capacities and higher reliability.

Removable disk devices consist of the drive unit, which is usually in its own cabinet, and the removable recording media, called a **disk pack**. Removable disk packs consist of 5 to 11 metal platters that are used on both sides for recording data. The recording capacity of these packs varies from 10 to 300 megabytes of data. One advantage of removable disk packs is that the data on a disk drive can be quickly changed by removing one pack and replacing it with another. This can be accomplished in minutes. When removable disk packs are not mounted in a disk drive they are stored in a protective plastic case. When the packs are being used, the plastic case is usually placed on top of the drive unit. Figure 7-21 shows a large installation of removable disk devices with the empty protective disk pack cases on top of the drives.

FIGURE 7-20
A high-speed, high-capacity fixed disk drive in a stand-alone cabinet.

FIGURE 7-21
A large installation of removable disk drives showing the protective disk pack cases on top of the drive units.

How Is Data Physically Organized on a Disk?   Depending on the type of disk drive, data is physically organized in one of two ways on disks used with medium and large computers. One way is the sector method and the other is the cylinder method.

As with the floppy disks and hard disks used with personal computers, the **sector method** for physically organizing data on disks divides each track on the disk surface into individual storage areas called sectors (Figure 7-22). Each sector can contain a specified number of bytes. Data is referenced by indicating the surface, track, and sector where the data is stored.

FIGURE 7-22
The sector method of disk addressing divides each track into a number of sectors. To locate data, the surface, track, and sector where the data is stored are specified.

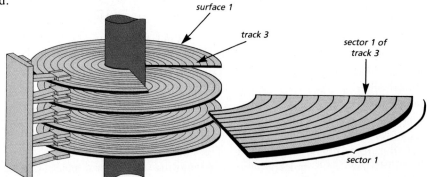

With the **cylinder method**, all tracks of the same number on each recording surface are considered part of the same cylinder (Figure 7-23). For example, if each platter contained 200 tracks, the tenth track on all surfaces would be considered part of the tenth cylinder. All twentieth tracks would be part of the twentieth cylinder, and so on. When the computer requests data from a disk using the cylinder method, it must specify the cylinder, recording surface, and record number. Because the access arms containing the read/write heads all move together, they are always over the same track on all surfaces. Thus, using the cylinder method to record data "down" the disk surfaces reduces the movement of the read/write head during both reading and writing of data.

FIGURE 7-23
The cylinder method reduces the movement of the read/write head (thereby saving time) by writing information "down" the disk on the same track of successive surfaces.

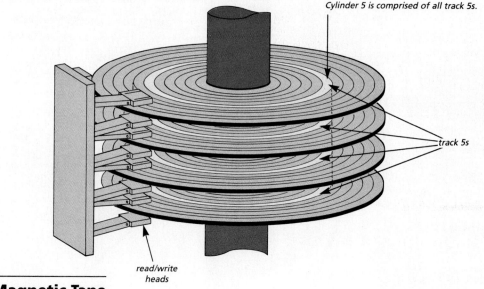

Magnetic Tape

During the 1950s and early 1960s, prior to the introduction of removable disk pack drives, magnetic tape was the primary method of storing large amounts of data. Today, even though tape is no longer used by medium and large computers as the primary method of auxiliary storage, it still functions as a cost-effective way to store data that does not have to be accessed

immediately. In addition, tape serves as the primary means of backup for most medium and large systems and is often used when data is transferred from one system to another.

Magnetic tape consists of a thin ribbon of plastic. The tape is coated on one side with a material that can be magnetized to record the bit patterns that represent data. The most common types of magnetic tape devices are reel-to-reel and cartridge. Reel-to-reel tape is usually 1/2 inch wide and cartridge tape is 1/4 inch wide (Figure 7-24).

Reel-to-Reel Tape Devices Reel-to-reel tape devices use two reels: a supply reel to hold the tape that will be read or written on, and the take-up reel to temporarily hold portions of the supply reel tape as it is being processed. At the completion of processing, tape on the take-up reel is wound back onto the supply reel. As the tape moves from one reel to another, it passes over a read/write head (Figure 7-25), an electromagnetic device that can read or write data on the tape.

Older style tape units (Figure 7-26) are vertical cabinets with vacuum columns that hold five or six feet of slack tape to prevent breaking during sudden start or stop operations.

Newer style tape units (Figure 7-27) allow a tape to be inserted through a slot opening similar to the way videotapes are loaded in a videocassette recorder. This front-loading tape drive takes less space and can be cabinet mounted. The drive automatically threads the end of the tape onto an internal take-up reel.

FIGURE 7-24 ▲
In the top picture a computer operator is positioning a reel of magnetic tape on a tape device. Below is a standard 10 1/2-inch reel of magnetic tape.

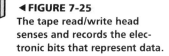

◄ FIGURE 7-25
The tape read/write head senses and records the electronic bits that represent data.

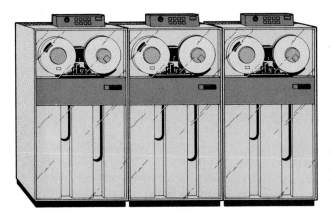

FIGURE 7-26 ▲
Older style reel-to-reel magnetic tape storage devices.

FIGURE 7-27 ▶
Newer style tape drives allow the user to slide the tape into a slot at the front of the unit. The drive automatically threads the tape.

Reels of tape usually come in lengths of 300, 1,200, 2,400 and 3,600 feet and can store up to 100 megabytes of data.

Cartridge Tape Devices Cartridge tape devices for medium and large computers are identical to units previously discussed for personal computers. They are becoming increasingly popular because they can store more data and take less space than the traditional 10 1/2 inch diameter reels of tape (Figure 7-28).

How Is Data Stored on Magnetic Tape? Data is recorded on magnetic tape in the form of magnetic spots that can be read and transferred to main memory. The magnetic spots on the tape are organized into a series of horizontal rows called channels. The presence or absence of magnetic spots representing bits is used to represent a given character on the tape.

Several different coding structures are used with magnetic tape, including both ASCII and EBCDIC. The coding structure for EBCDIC divides half-inch tape into nine horizontal channels. A combination of bits in a vertical column that consists of the nine horizontal channels is used to represent characters and the error-checking parity bit on the tape (Figure 7-29).

FIGURE 7-28
The four inch by five inch tape cartridge can hold 20% more data than the 10 1/2 inch reel of tape.

FIGURE 7-29
One of the most common coding structures found on magnetic tape is the EBCDIC code, which is stored in nine channels on the tape. Eight channels are used to store the bits representing a character. The ninth channel is a parity error-checking channel.

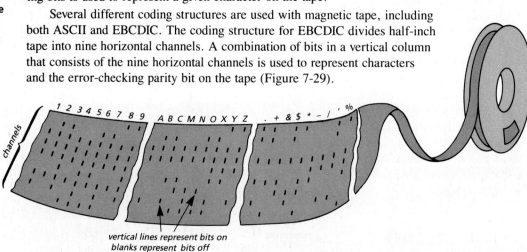

vertical lines represent bits on
blanks represent bits off

Tape density is the number of characters or bytes that can be stored on an inch of tape. As on disk drives, tape density is expressed in bytes per inch or bpi. Commonly used tape densities are 800, 1,600, 3,200 and 6,250 bpi. Some of the newer cartridge tape devices can record at densities of over 38,000 bpi. The higher the density, the more data that can be stored on a tape.

Tape is considered a **sequential storage** media because the computer must read tape records one after another until it finds the one it wants. Tapes do not have fixed data storage location addresses like disk drives that allow direct access of a record.

In order to allow some room for starting and stopping, tapes use **interblock gaps (IBG)**, also called **interrecord gaps (IRG)** (Figure 7-30). These spaces are usually about .6 inch long. To increase recording efficiency, **blocked records** are normally used. Blocking refers to placing two or more individual records, called **logical records**, into a block to form a **physical record** (Figure 7-31). A logical record refers to the amount of data that a program uses when it processes one record. A physical record refers to the amount of data that is physically transferred into memory from the tape. For example, there could be three employee payroll (logical) records contained within one block or (physical) record on a tape. Using blocking has two advantages. First, the tape is used more efficiently. More data can be stored because the gap between each logical record is eliminated. Second, because an entire physical record is read into memory each time data is read from the tape, reading data takes place faster. Two or more logical records are read each time data is transferred from the tape to main memory.

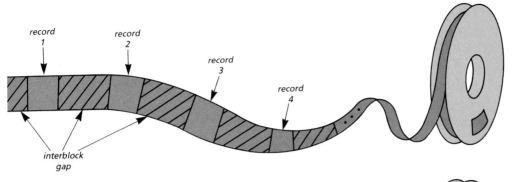

FIGURE 7-30
Records stored on tape are stored sequentially, separated by an interblock gap that allows for the starting and stopping of the tape drive. The interblock gap is typically .6 inch wide.

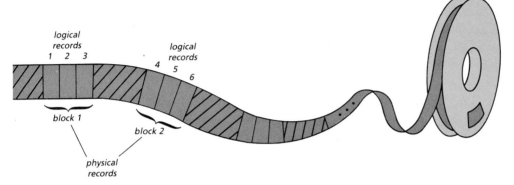

FIGURE 7-31
Three logical records are stored in each block or physical record in this diagram. An entire block of records is brought into main memory each time the tape file is read.

OTHER FORMS OF AUXILIARY STORAGE

W hile the conventional disk and tape devices described above comprise the majority of auxiliary storage devices and media, several other means for storing data are used. These include optical storage technology, solid-state devices, and mass storage devices.

Optical Storage Technology

Optical storage technology is one of the newest and most promising methods of data storage. Enormous quantities of information can be stored on **optical disks** by using a laser to burn microscopic holes on the surface of a hard plastic disk (Figure 7-32). A lower power laser reads the disk by reflecting light off the disk surface. The reflected light is converted into a series of bits that the computer can process.

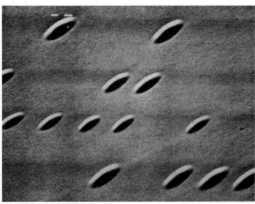

FIGURE 7-32
To record data on an optical disk (left), a laser burns microscopic holes on the surface (right).

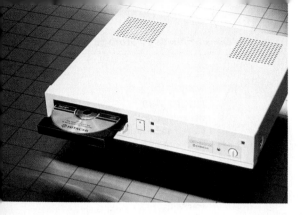

A full-size 12 inch optical disk can store several billion characters of information. The smaller disks, just under five inches in diameter, can store over 800 million characters or approximately 800 times the data that can be stored on a 5 1/4 inch floppy diskette. That's enough space to store approximately 400,000 pages of typed data. The smaller optical disks are called **CDROM**, for compact disk read-only memory (Figure 7-33). They use the same laser technology that is used for the CDROM disks that have become popular for recorded music.

The disadvantage of optical disks now available is that they cannot be modified once the data is recorded. Most optical disks are prerecorded but some devices provide for one-time recording. These units are called **WORM** devices, for write once, read many. Recently announced optical disk devices will be able to erase and rerecord disks.

Even as read-only devices, optical disks have great potential. Because of their tremendous storage capacities, entire catalogs or reference materials can be stored on a single disk. Some people predict that optical disks will soon replace data now stored on film such as microfiche.

FIGURE 7-33
An optical compact disk can store hundreds of times the data as on a comparable-size floppy disk.

Solid-State Devices

To the computer, solid-state storage devices look and act just like disk drives, only faster. But as their name suggests, they contain no moving parts, only electronic circuits. **Solid-state storage devices** use the latest in random-access memory (RAM) technology to provide high-speed data access and retrieval. Rows of RAM chips (Figure 7-34) provide megabytes of memory that can be accessed much faster than the fastest conventional disk drives. Solid-state storage devices are significantly more expensive than conventional disk drives offering the same storage capacity.

Mass Storage Devices

Mass storage devices provide for the automated retrieval of data from a "library" of storage media such as cartridge tapes or floppy disks. Mass storage is ideal for extremely large databases that require all information to be readily accessible even though any one portion of the database may be infrequently required. Mass storage systems take less room than conventional tape storage and can retrieve and begin accessing records within seconds. Figure 7-35 shows a mass storage system that uses tape cartridges.

FIGURE 7-34
Solid-state storage devices use megabytes of RAM chips to simulate a conventional disk drive. ▼

FIGURE 7-35▶
This mass storage system can access any one of thousands of tape cartridges in an average of 11 seconds. Each cartridge is a 4 × 4 inch square and about 1 inch thick.

SUMMARY OF AUXILIARY STORAGE

Auxiliary storage is used to store programs and data that are not currently being processed by the computer. This chapter discussed the various types of auxiliary storage used with computers. The chart in Figure 7-36 provides a summary of the auxiliary storage devices. What you have learned about these devices and storage operations in general can now be added to what you have learned about the input, processing, and output operations of the information processing cycle.

FIGURE 7-36
A summary of some of the more common auxiliary storage devices.

DEVICE	DESCRIPTION
Personal Computers	
Floppy disk	Plastic storage media that is reliable and low in cost.
Hard disk	Fixed metal storage media that provides large storage capacity and fast access.
Hard card	Fixed disk that is built on a circuit board and installed in an expansion slot of a personal computer.
Disk cartridge	Combines storage and access features of hard disk and portability of floppy disks.
Tape cartridge	Used to back up hard disks on personal computers.
Medium and Large Computers	
Fixed disk	Large multiplatter fixed disk with high storage capacity and fast access.
Removable disk	Disk drives with removable disk packs.
Reel tape	Magnetic tape device using the reel-to-reel method of moving tape.
Tape cartridge	Magnetic tape device using cartridge method of holding tape.
Other Storage Devices	
Optical storage	Uses lasers to record and read data on a hard plastic disk. High quality and large storage capacity.
Solid state	Uses RAM chips to provide high-speed data access and retrieval.
Mass storage	Automated retrieval of storage media such as tape cartridges and floppy disks.

CHAPTER SUMMARY

1. **Auxiliary storage** is used to store data that is not being processed on the computer.
2. The **floppy disk** or **diskette** is used as a primary auxiliary storage medium with personal computers.
3. Most personal computers use a diskette 5 1/4 inches in diameter. Smaller diskettes (approximately 3 1/2 inches in diameter) are also available and are increasing in popularity.
4. A floppy disk consists of a plastic disk enclosed within a square protective jacket. A portion of the surface of the disk is exposed so data can be stored on it.
5. Data is stored on a disk in tracks. A **track** is a narrow recording band forming a full circle around the diskette.
6. The number of tracks most often found are 40 tracks or 80 tracks per diskette.
7. Each track on a disk is divided into **sectors**, the basic unit of disk storage. A minimum of one full sector of data is read from a diskette: a minimum of one sector is written on a diskette.
8. A **hard-sectored disk** contains holes in the diskette indicating where each sector begins.
9. A **soft-sectored disk** contains one hole indicating where the tracks begin. The number of sectors and the number of characters in each sector are determined by the software that formats the disk.

10. The factors affecting disk storage capacity are the number of sides of the disk used; the recording density of the bits; and the number of tracks on the disk.
11. **Single-sided drives** read and record data on only one side of a diskette. **Double-sided drives** read and record data on both sides of the disk.
12. The **recording density** is stated as the number of bits that can be recorded on one inch of the innermost track on a disk. The measurement is referred to as **bits per inch (bpi)**.
13. To read or write data on a disk, the disk is placed in the disk drive. Within its protective covering the disk rotates at about 300 revolutions per minute. The **read/write head** rests on the disk and senses or generates electronic impulses representing bits.
14. The time required to access and retrieve data stored on a diskette is called the **access time**.
15. Access time depends on four factors: (1) **seek time**, the time it takes to position the read/write head on the correct track; (2) **latency time**, the time it takes for the data to rotate under the read/write head; (3) **settling time**, the time required for the head to be placed in contact with the disk; and (4) **data transfer rate**, the amount of data that can be transferred from the disk to main memory.
16. Floppy disks should not be exposed to heat or magnetic fields. With proper care, floppy disks provide an inexpensive and reliable form of storage.
17. A **hard disk** consists of one or more rigid metal **platters** coated with a metal oxide material.
18. On **fixed disks**, the metal disks, read/write heads, and access arm are enclosed in a sealed case. These disks provide high storage capabilities and fast access times.
19. To read and write data on a hard disk, an **access arm** moves read/write heads in and out. The heads float very close to the surface of the disk, generating or sensing electronic impulses that represent bits.
20. The number of platters in a hard disk for a microcomputer can vary from one to four. On many disks, both sides of the platters can be used for storing data.
21. The typical access time for a microcomputer hard disk is between 25 and 85 milliseconds.
22. **Removable disk cartridges** offer the storage and access features of hard disks with the portability of floppy disks.
23. The write-protect notch on floppy disks can be used to protect the data stored on a disk from being overwritten.
24. To backup storage means to create a duplicate copy of important programs and data on a separate disk or tape.
25. The normal method for floppy disk backup is to copy the data onto another disk. For hard disk, the disk is often copied to a **cartridge tape**.
26. Disk drives used with large computers can be categorized as either fixed disks or removable disks.
27. **Fixed disks** are sealed in an enclosure and permanently mounted in the disk drive.
28. **Disk packs** contain between 5 and 11 platters that can be mounted and removed from the disk drive.
29. The **sector method** (identifying the surface, track, and sector number) or the **cylinder method** (identifying the cylinder, recording surface, and record number) can be used to physically organize and address data stored on disk.
30. The tracks that can be referenced at one position of the access arm are called a **cylinder**.
31. **Magnetic tape** is used primarily for backup purposes in large computer installations.
32. Data is recorded on **magnetic tape** as a series of magnetic spots along a horizontal channel. Each spot represents a bit in a coding scheme. Large computers commonly use the EBCDIC coding scheme on nine-track tape.
33. **Tape density** is the number of characters or bytes that can be stored on one inch of tape. Common densities are 800, 1,600, 3,200, and 6,520 bytes per inch.
34. **Sequential organization** means records are stored one after the other on the tape.
35. An **interblock gap** separates records stored on tape.
36. **Blocked records** mean two or more **logical records** are stored in a **physical record** on the tape.
37. **Optical disks** use a laser beam recording and reading method and can store enormous quantities of data.
38. RAM chips are used in **solid-state storage devices**. These devices act just like disk drives but provide faster data access and retrieval.
39. Automated retrieval of storage media is provided by **mass storage devices**.

KEY TERMS

Access arms *7.9*
Access time *7.7*
Actuators *7.9*
Auxiliary storage *7.2*
Bits per inch (bpi) *7.7*
Blocked records *7.16*
Cartridge tape drive *7.12*
CDROM *7.18*
Cylinder *7.6*
Cylinder method *7.14*
Data transfer rate *7.8*
Direct-access storage devices
　(DASD) *7.12*
Disk cartridge *7.10*
Diskette *7.4*
Disk pack *7.13*
Disks *7.4*
Double-sided disk *7.6*
Double-sided drive *7.6*

Fixed disk *7.9*
Floppies *7.4*
Floppy disk *7.4*
Formatting *7.5*
Hard card *7.9*
Hard disk *7.8*
Hard-sectored disk *7.6*
Head crash *7.9*
Interblock gap (IBG) *7.16*
Interrecord gap (IRG) *7.16*
Latency *7.7*
Logical records *7.16*
Magnetic tape *7.15*
Mass storage devices *7.18*
Nonvolatile *7.2*
Optical disks *7.17*
Physical record *7.16*
Platters *7.8*

Read/write head *7.7*
Recording density *7.7*
Reel-to-reel *7.15*
Secondary storage *7.2*
Sector *7.5*
Sector method *7.14*
Seek time *7.7*
Sequential storage *7.16*
Settling time *7.8*
Single-sided disk *7.6*
Single-sided drive *7.6*
Soft-sectored disk *7.6*
Solid-state storage devices *7.18*
Streaming mode *7.12*
Tape density *7.16*
Track *7.5*
Tracks per inch (TPI) *7.7*
WORM *7.18*

REVIEW QUESTIONS

1. Differentiate between the uses of main memory and auxiliary storage.
2. Draw a diagram of a diskette and label the main parts.
3. What does formatting a disk mean?
4. What are the three factors influencing the storage capacity of a disk? Briefly describe each of them.
5. Describe the care and handling of floppy disks.
6. Identify the factors that influence the access time of a disk drive.
7. Describe the characteristics of a fixed disk drive. What sizes are commonly used with personal computers?
8. What is disk backup? How are floppy disks normally backed up? How are hard disks backed up?
9. Describe the differences between fixed disks and removable disks on large computers.
10. Describe the sector method of disk organization and the cylinder method of disk organization.
11. How is data stored on magnetic tape? What are typical tape densities?
12. Describe optical storage technology. Why is it one of the most promising methods of data storage?

CONTROVERSIAL ISSUES

1. A study of personal computer owners found that less than 10 percent regularly backup the files and databases they use. The consensus of these users was that new auxiliary storage devices, particularly the hard disk drives, are so reliable and error free that backup is a waste of time and storage. Experts who reviewed this study commented that these users were inviting disaster because even a few failures are enough to justify full file and database backup. Who is right? Take a position on this issue.
2. The cost of semiconductor memory has decreased significantly in recent years. In addition, research is being done constantly to find new ways for storing data. As a result, some experts believe magnetic memory such as disk and tape will be obsolete in a few years. Others say this will never happen. What is your opinion?

RESEARCH PROJECTS

1. The storage capacities of hard disks vary considerably. Obtain the names of five different manufacturers of hard disk drives used with personal computers. Write to each of the manufacturers to obtain literature concerning their drives. Prepare a report summarizing the information you have collected.
2. The storage capacities of optical disks allow complete reference works to be stored on a single compact disk. Write a paper on possible applications of this technology.
3. Data storage requirements vary based on the type of organization. Write a paper on the storage requirements of a bank, a retailer with online cash registers, and the government agency that issues passports. Consider the amount and type of storage required and the necessity of having immediate access to the stored data.

File Organization and Databases

File Organization and Databases

OBJECTIVES

- Describe sequential files, indexed files, and direct (or relative) files.
- Explain the difference between sequential retrieval and random retrieval of records from a file.
- Describe the data maintenance procedures for updating files, including adding, changing, and deleting data in a file or database.
- Discuss the advantages of a database management system (DBMS).
- Describe a relational database system.
- Describe a hierarchical database system.
- Describe a network database system.
- Explain the use of a query language.
- Describe the responsibilities of a database administrator.

---

*T*he data and information that a company has accumulated is usually considered a valuable asset. For data and information to provide maximum benefit to a company, they must be carefully organized, used, and managed. While you are now familiar with the auxiliary storage devices used to store data and information, it is equally important that you understand the various ways in which the data and information stored on these devices is organized, used, and managed. The purpose of this chapter is to explain (1) how files on auxiliary storage are organized, retrieved and maintained (kept current); and (2) the advantages, organization, use, and management of databases.

As you read this chapter, you will notice that several of the file and database concepts that are discussed were introduced earlier in the text. With the computer knowledge that you now have, especially about auxiliary storage devices, you are ready for a more in-depth look at these topics. The first part of this chapter concentrates on how files are organized and used. The second part of this chapter discusses the advantages, organization, and use of databases. Learning this information will help you to better understand how data and information is stored and managed on a computer.

WHAT IS A FILE?

A file is a collection of related records that is usually stored on an auxiliary storage device. A *record* is a collection of related fields and a *field*, also called a *data item* or *data element*, is a fact (Figure 8-1). Files contain data that pertains to one topic. For example, a business can have separate files that contain data related to personnel, inventory, customers, vendors, and so forth. Most companies have hundreds, sometimes thousands of files that store the data pertaining to their business. Files that are stored on auxiliary storage devices can be organized in several different ways and there are advantages and disadvantages to each of these types of file organization.

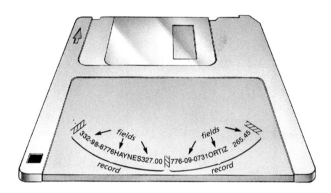

FIGURE 8-1
This payroll file stored on a diskette contains payroll records. Each payroll record contains a social security field, a name field, and a paycheck amount field.

TYPES OF FILE ORGANIZATION

*T*hree types of file organization are used on auxiliary storage devices. These are sequential, indexed, and direct, or relative, file organization.

Sequential File Organization

Sequential file organization means that records are stored one after the other, normally in ascending or descending order, based on a value in each record called the key. The **key** is a field that contains data, such as a social security number, that is used to sequence the records in a file (Figure 8-2). Files that are stored on tape are always sequential files. Files on disk may be sequential, indexed, or direct.

FIGURE 8-2
The student records in this file are stored sequentially in ascending order using the social security number as the key field. The records in this file will be retrieved sequentially.

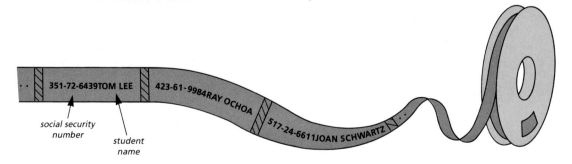

social security number

student name

Records that are stored using sequential file organization are also retrieved sequentially. **Sequential retrieval**, also called **sequential access**, means that the records in a file are retrieved one record after another in the same order that the records are stored. For example, in Figure 8-2, the file contains student records stored in sequence by social security number. The data in the file is retrieved one record after another in the same sequence that it is stored in the file.

Sequential retrieval has a major disadvantage—since records must be retrieved one after another in the same sequence as they are stored, the only way to retrieve a record is to read all preceding records first. Therefore, in Figure 8-2, if the record for Joan Schwartz must be retrieved, the records for Tom Lee and for Ray Ochoa must be read before retrieving the Joan Schwartz record. Because of this, sequential retrieval is not used when fast access to a particular record is required. However, sequential retrieval is appropriate when records are processed one after another.

A common use of sequential files in a computer center is as backup files, where data from a disk is copied onto a tape or another disk so that if the original data becomes unusable, the original file can be restored from the backup file.

Indexed File Organization

A second type of file organization is called **indexed file organization**. Just as in a sequential file, records are stored in an indexed file in an ascending or descending sequence based on the value in the key field of the record.

An indexed file, however, also contains an index. An **index** consists of a list containing the values of the key field and the corresponding disk address for each record in a file (Figure 8-3). In the same way that an index for a book points to the page where a particular topic is covered, the index for a file points to the place on a disk where a particular record is located. The index is usually stored with a file when the file is created. The index is retrieved from the disk and placed in main memory when the file is to be processed.

FIGURE 8-3
The index in an indexed file contains the record key value and the corresponding disk address for each record in the file. In this example, the index contains the employee number, which is the key for the employee file, and the disk address for the corresponding employee record.

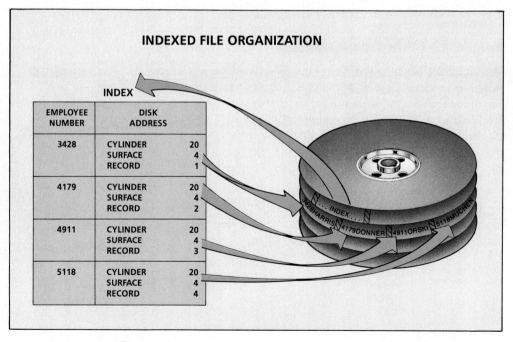

INDEXED FILE ORGANIZATION

INDEX

EMPLOYEE NUMBER	DISK ADDRESS	
3428	CYLINDER	20
	SURFACE	4
	RECORD	1
4179	CYLINDER	20
	SURFACE	4
	RECORD	2
4911	CYLINDER	20
	SURFACE	4
	RECORD	3
5118	CYLINDER	20
	SURFACE	4
	RECORD	4

Records can be accessed in an indexed file both sequentially and randomly. As previously discussed, sequential retrieval means that the records in a file are retrieved one record after another in the same order that the records are stored. **Random retrieval**, also called **random access**, means any record in a file can be directly accessed (retrieved) regardless of where it is stored in the file. For example, the 50th record in a file can be retrieved first, followed by the 3rd record, and then the 20th record. Random retrieval is used when fast access to a record is required, as in a reservation system. For random retrieval to be used, files must be stored on disk.

To randomly access a record in an indexed file, the index is searched until the key of the record to be retrieved is found. The address of the record (also stored in the index) is then used to retrieve the record directly from the file without reading any other records. For example, if an inquiry was received from the personnel office asking the name of employee number 5118, the index could be searched until key 5118 was found (Figure 8-4). The corresponding disk address (cylinder 20, surface 4, record 4) would then be used to read the record directly from the disk into main memory.

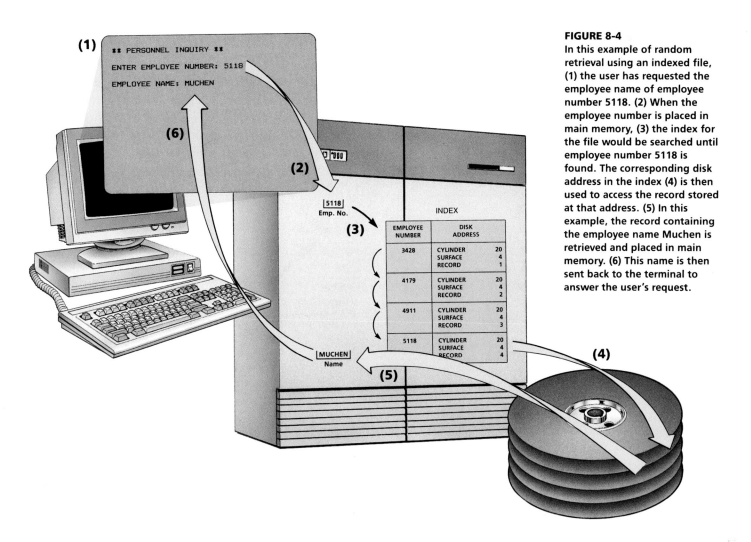

FIGURE 8-4
In this example of random retrieval using an indexed file, (1) the user has requested the employee name of employee number 5118. (2) When the employee number is placed in main memory, (3) the index for the file would be searched until employee number 5118 is found. The corresponding disk address in the index (4) is then used to access the record stored at that address. (5) In this example, the record containing the employee name Muchen is retrieved and placed in main memory. (6) This name is then sent back to the terminal to answer the user's request.

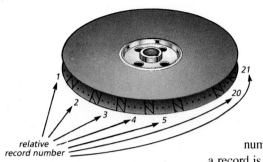

FIGURE 8-5
The relative address of a record is the same as the numeric position of the record in the file. The fifth record has a relative address of 5.

Direct or Relative File Organization

A **direct file** or **relative file** (occasionally called a random file) contains records that are stored and retrieved according to either their disk address or their position within a file. This means that the program that stores and accesses records in a direct file must specify either the exact physical address of a record in the file (for example, cylinder, surface and track number, or track and sector number), or the relative location (position) where a record is stored in the file, such as the first, tenth, or fiftieth record (Figure 8-5).

The location where a record is stored is based on a key value found in the record. For example, a program could establish a file that has nine locations where records can be stored. These locations are sometimes called **buckets**. A bucket can contain multiple records. If the key in the record is a one-digit value (1–9), then the value in the key would specify the relative location within the file where the record was stored. For example, the record with key 3 would be placed in relative location or bucket 3; the record with key 6 would be placed in relative location 6, and so on.

Usually the storage of records in a file is not so simple. For instance, what if the maximum number of records to be stored in a direct file is 100 and the key for the record is a four-digit number? In this case, the key of the record could not be used to specify the relative or actual location of the record because the four-digit key could result in up to 9,999 records. In cases such as these, an arithmetic formula must be used to calculate the relative or actual location in the file where the record is stored. The process of using a formula and performing the calculation to determine the location of a record is called **hashing**.

One hashing method is the division/remainder method. Using this method, a prime number close to but not greater than the number of records to be stored in the file is chosen. A **prime number** is a number divisible by only itself and 1. For example, suppose you have 100 records. The number 97 is the closest prime number to 100 without being greater than 100. The key of the record is then divided by 97 and the remainder from the division operation is the relative location where the record is stored. For example, if the record key is 3428, the relative location where the record will be stored in the file is location 33 (Figure 8-6).

FIGURE 8-6
When the value 3428 is divided by the prime number 97, the remainder is 33. This remainder is used as the bucket where the record with key 3428 is stored in the direct file.

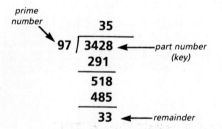

Direct files present one problem not encountered with sequential or indexed files. In all three file organization methods, the key in the record must be unique so that it can uniquely identify the record. For example, the employee number, when acting as the key in an employee file, must be unique. When a hashing technique is used to calculate a disk address, however, it is possible that two different keys could identify the same location on disk. For example, employee number 3331 generates the same relative location (33) as employee number 3428. When the locations generated from the different keys are the same they are called **synonyms**. The occurrence of this event is called a **collision**. A method that is often used to resolve collisions is to place the record that caused the collision in the next available storage location. This location may be in the same bucket (if multiple records are stored in a bucket) or in the next bucket (Figure 8-7).

Once a record is stored in its relative location within a direct file, it can be retrieved either sequentially or randomly. The method normally used with direct files is random retrieval. In order to randomly retrieve a record from a direct file three steps are performed:

1. The program must obtain the key of the record to be retrieved. The value of the key is entered into the computer by a user or as data from an input device.
2. The program determines the location of the record by performing the same hashing process as when the record was initially stored. Thus, to retrieve the record with key 3428, the key value would be divided by the prime number 97. The remainder, 33, specifies the location of the bucket where the record will be found.
3. The software then directs the computer to bucket 33 to retrieve the record.

Sequential retrieval from a direct file can be accomplished by indicating that the record from the first relative location is to be retrieved, followed by the record from the second relative location, and so on. All the records in the file are retrieved based on their relative location in the file.

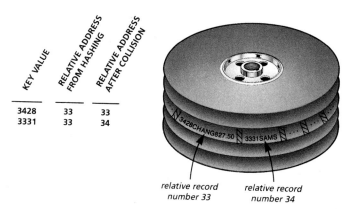

FIGURE 8-7
Sometimes the hashing computation produces synonyms, or records that have the same relative address. In this example, both records have a relative address of 33. When the computer tries to store the second record and finds that location 33 is already full, it stores the second record at the next available location. In this example, record 3331 would be stored in location 34.

Summary of File Organization Concepts

Files are organized as either sequential, indexed, or direct files. Sequential file organization can be used on tape or disk and requires that the records in the file be retrieved sequentially. Indexed files must be stored on disk and the records can be accessed either sequentially or randomly. Direct files are stored on disk and are usually accessed randomly (Figure 8-8).

FILE TYPE	TYPE OF STORAGE	ACCESS METHOD
Sequential	Tape or Disk	Sequential
Indexed	Disk	Random* or Sequential
Direct (Relative)	Disk	Random* or Sequential

* *Primarily accessed as random files*

FIGURE 8-8
The chart shows the type of storage and the access methods that can be used with each of the three file types.

HOW IS DATA IN FILES MAINTAINED?

Data stored on auxiliary storage must be kept current to produce accurate results when it is processed. To keep the data current, the records in the files must be updated. **Updating** records within a file consists of adding records to the file, changing records within the file, and deleting records from the file.

Adding Records

Records are added to a file when additional data is needed to make the file current. For example, if a customer opens a new account at a bank, a record containing the data for the new account must be added to the bank's account file. The process that would take place to *add* this record to the file is shown in Figure 8-9.

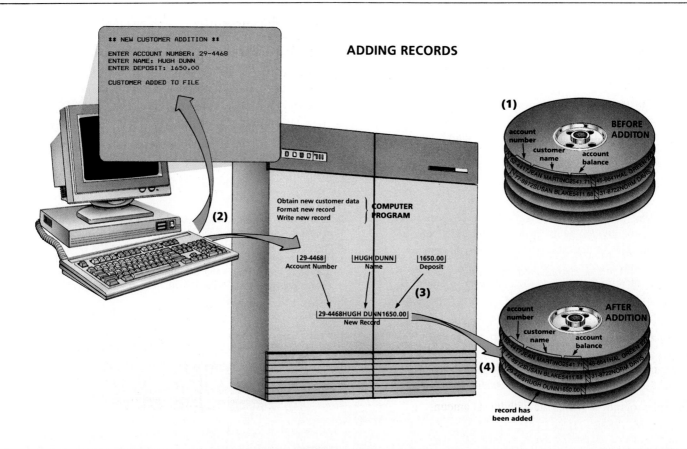

ADDING RECORDS

FIGURE 8-9
In this example of adding records, (1) the file first exists without the new account. (2) The teller enters the account number, customer name, and deposit. (3) This data is used to create a record that is then (4) added to the file.

1. A bank teller enters the new customer data into the computer through a terminal. The data includes the account number, the customer name, and the deposit that will become the account balance.

2. The update program moves the data entered by the user into the new record area in main memory.

3. The update program writes the new record to the file. The location on the disk where the record is written is determined by the program. In some cases, a new record will be written between other records in the file. In other cases, such as illustrated in this example, the added record is added to the end of the file.

Whenever data is stored on auxiliary storage for subsequent use, the ability to add records must be present in order to keep the data current.

Changing Records

The second task that must be accomplished when updating data is to *change* data that is currently stored in a record. Changes to data stored on auxiliary storage take place for two primary reasons: (1) to correct data that is known to be incorrect, and (2) to update data when new data becomes available.

As an example of the first type of change, assume in Figure 8-9 that instead of entering HUGH DUNN as the name for the customer, the teller enters HUGH DONE. The error is not noticed and the customer leaves the bank. Later in the day, when the customer returns to question the transaction, the name stored in the file must be changed so that it contains the correct spelling. Therefore, the teller would enter HUGH DUNN as a change to the name field in the record. This change is made to replace data known to be incorrect with data known to be correct.

The bank account example also illustrates the second reason for change—to update data when new data becomes available. This type of change is made when a customer deposits or withdraws money. In Figure 8-10, Jean Martino has withdrawn $500.00. The record for Jean Martino must be changed to reflect her withdrawal. The following steps occur:

1. The teller enters Jean Martino's account number 52-4417 and the amount 500.00.
2. The update program retrieves the record for account number 52-4417 and stores the record in main memory.
3. The program subtracts the withdrawal amount from the account balance in the record. This changes the account balance to reflect the correct balance in the account.
4. After the balance has been changed in memory, the record is written back onto the disk. After the change, the account balance has been updated, and the record stored on auxiliary storage contains the correct account balance.

Changing data stored on auxiliary storage to reflect the correct and current data is an important part of the updating process that is required for data.

FIGURE 8-10
When Jean Martino withdraws $500.00, the bank's records must be changed to reflect her new account balance. In this example, (1) the teller enters Jean Martino's account number and withdrawal amount, (2) the account number is used to retrieve Jean's account balance record; and (3) the account balance is reduced by the amount of the withdrawal ($500.00). The record is then rewritten back onto the disk (4).

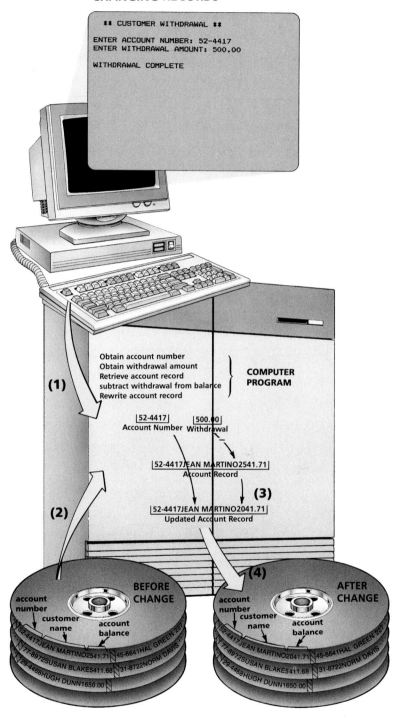

CHANGING RECORDS

Deleting Records

The third major type of activity that must occur when updating data is to delete records stored in a file or database. Records are deleted when they are no longer needed as data. Figure 8-11 shows the updating procedures to *delete* a record for Hal Gruen who has closed his account. The following steps occur:

1. The teller enters Hal Gruen's account number (45-6641).
2. The update program retrieves the record from the disk using the account number as the key. The record is placed in main memory.
3. The actual processing that occurs to delete a record from a file depends on the type of file organization being used and the processing requirements of the application. Sometimes the record is removed from the file. Other times, as in this example, the record is not removed from the file. Instead, the record is *flagged*, or marked, in some manner so that it will not be processed again. In this example, the first three characters of the account number are changed from the actual number to the letters DEL (short for delete).
4. After the letters DEL have been placed in the first three characters of the account number, the record is written back to the file. The application program will not process the record again because it begins with DEL instead of a valid account number. Even though the record is still physically stored on the disk, it is effectively deleted because it will not be retrieved for processing.

FIGURE 8-11
In this example, (1) the account number entered by the teller is used to (2) retrieve Hal Green's account record. (3) The account record is marked as deleted by placing the letters DEL In the first three positions of the account number. The record is then rewritten (4) back to the file. With DEL in the account number, the record will not be retrieved by the application program because it does not have a valid key value.

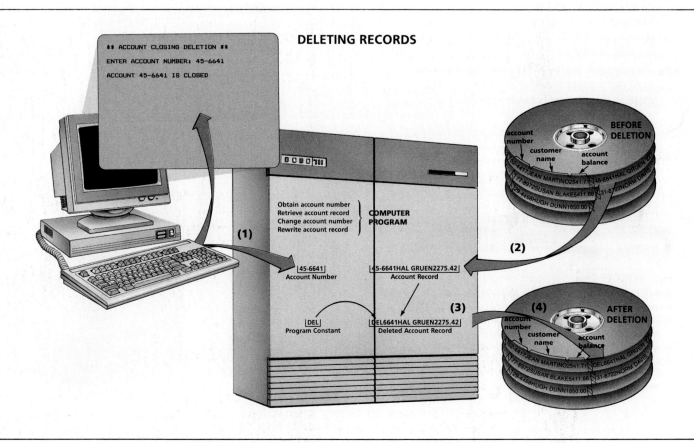

Deleting records from auxiliary storage is important because it provides a way of either removing or flagging records that are no longer needed for processing. This is necessary to keep data accurate.

Summary of How Data Is Maintained

Data maintenance is updating or adding, changing, and deleting data stored on auxiliary storage. The maintenance of data is critical if information derived from the processing of that data is to be reliable. When updating data, it does not matter if the data is stored as a single file or if it is part of a series of files organized into a database. The concept of adding, changing, and deleting data to keep it current remains the same.

DATABASES: A BETTER WAY TO MANAGE DATA AND INFORMATION

As stated at the beginning of this chapter, more and more businesspeople realize that next to the skills of their employees, data (and the information it represents) is one of a company's most valuable assets. They recognize that the information that has been accumulated on sales trends, competitors' products and services, employee skills, and production processes is a valuable resource that would be difficult if not impossible to replace.

Unfortunately, in many cases this resource is located in different files in different departments throughout the organization, often known only to the individuals who work with their specific portion of the total information. In these cases, the potential value of the information goes unrealized because it is not known to people in other departments who may need it or it cannot be accessed efficiently. In an attempt to organize their information resources and provide for timely and efficient access, many companies have implemented databases.

WHAT IS A DATABASE?

Previously in this chapter, we've discussed how data elements (characters, fields, and records) can be organized in files. In file-oriented systems, each file is independent. In a **database**, the data is organized in multiple related files. These related files are not independent of one another and it is possible for them to obtain data from one another. A **database management system (DBMS)** is the software that allows the user to create, maintain, and report the data and file relationships. Note that a **file management system**, sometimes mistakenly referred to as a database management system, is software that only allows the user to create, maintain, and access a single file at a time.

WHY USE A DATABASE?

The following example (Figure 8-12) illustrates some of the advantages of a database system as compared to a file-oriented system. Assume that a business periodically mails catalogs to its customers. If the business is using a file-oriented system, it would probably have a file used for the catalog mailing application that contains information about the catalog plus customer information, such as customer account number, name, and address. Files that are used in a file-oriented system are independent of one another. Therefore, other applications, such as the sales application, that also need to have customer information would each have files that contain the same customer information stored in the catalog mailing file. Thus in a file-oriented system, the customer data would be duplicated several times in different files. This duplication of data wastes auxiliary storage space. In addition, it makes maintaining the data difficult because when a customer record must be updated, all files containing that data must be individually updated.

FIGURE 8-12
In a file-oriented system, each file contains the customer name and address. In the database system, only the customer file contains the name and address. Other files, such as the catalog file, use the customer number to retrieve the customer name and address when it is needed for processing.

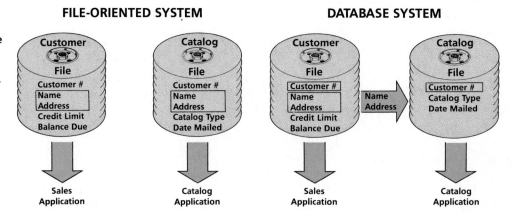

In a database system, however, only one of the applications would have a file containing the customer name and address data. That is because in a database system, files are integrated; related files are linked together by the database software either through predefined relationships or through common data fields. In this example, the link could be the customer account number. If the sales file contained the customer account number, name, and address, the catalog mailing file would only need to contain the customer's account number plus the other catalog information. When the catalog application software is executed, the customer's name and address would be obtained from the sales file. The advantage of the database is that because the files are integrated, the customer name and address would only be stored once. This saves auxiliary storage space. It also allows data to be maintained more easily because update information only needs to be entered once.

As the previous example illustrates, a database system offers a number of advantages over a file-oriented system. These advantages and several others are summarized in the following list:

1. **Reduced data redundancy.** Redundant or duplicate data is greatly reduced in a database system. Frequently used data elements such as names, addresses, and descriptions are stored in one location. Having such items in one instead of many locations lowers the cost of maintaining the data.
2. **Improved data integrity.** Closely related to reduced data redundancy is the database advantage of improved data integrity. Because data is only stored in one place, it is more likely to be accurate. When it is updated, all applications that use the data will be using the most current version.
3. **Integrated files.** As demonstrated by the catalog mailing example (Figure 8-12), a key advantage of a database management system is its ability to "integrate" or join together data from more than one file for inquiry or reporting purposes.
4. **Improved data security.** Most database management systems allow the user to establish different levels of security over information in the database. For example, a department manager may have "read only" privileges on certain payroll data: the manager could inquire about the data but not change it. The payroll supervisor would have "full update"

privileges: the supervisor could not only inquire about the data but could also make changes. A nonmanagement employee would probably have no access privileges to the payroll data and could neither inquire about nor change the data.

Now that we've discussed some of their advantages, let's discuss the different types of databases.

TYPES OF DATABASE ORGANIZATION

*T*here are three major types of database organization: relational, hierarchical, and network. The relational database structure is the most recent of the three methods and is considered a trend for the future. The relational database structure takes advantage of large-capacity direct-access storage devices that were not available when the hierarchical and network methods were developed.

Relational Database

In a **relational database**, data is organized in tables that in database terminology are called **relations**. The tables are further divided into rows (called **tuples**) and fields (called **attributes**). The tables can be thought of as files and the rows as records. The description or name of a particular attribute is called a **domain**. Figure 8-13 illustrates these terms with a student name and address file.

RELATIONAL DATABASE STRUCTURE

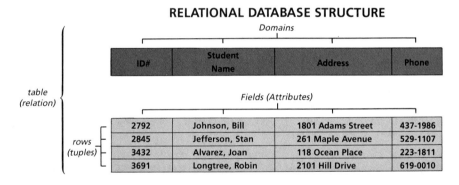

FIGURE 8-13
This example illustrates the terms used to identify the data in a relational database. A relational database is made up of multiple tables that can be thought of as files. In this example, other tables would probably exist for student grades, courses, faculty, and other logical groups of data.

As previously mentioned, a key advantage of a database is its ability to link multiple files together. A relational database accomplishes this by using a common field, sometimes called a **link**, that exists in each file. For example, in a database for a college, the link between files containing student information could be the student identification number. Hierarchical and network databases can also extract data from multiple files, but in these database structures, the data relationships that will enable the multiple file combination must be defined *when the database is created*. The advantage of a relational database is that the data relationships do not have to be predefined. The relational database only needs a common field in both data files to make a relationship between them. Because it is sometimes difficult to know ahead of time how data will be used, the flexibility provided by a relational database is an important advantage.

Another advantage of a relational database is its ability to add new fields. All that needs to be done is to define the fields in the appropriate table. With hierarchical and network database systems, the entire database has to be "redefined": existing relationships have to be reestablished to include the new fields.

Hierarchical Database

In a **hierarchical database** (Figure 8-14), data is organized in a series like a family tree or organization chart (the term hierarchy means an organized series). Like a family tree, the hierarchical database has branches made up of parent and child records. Each **parent record** can have multiple child records. However, each **child record** can only have one parent. The parent record at the top of the database is referred to as the **root** record.

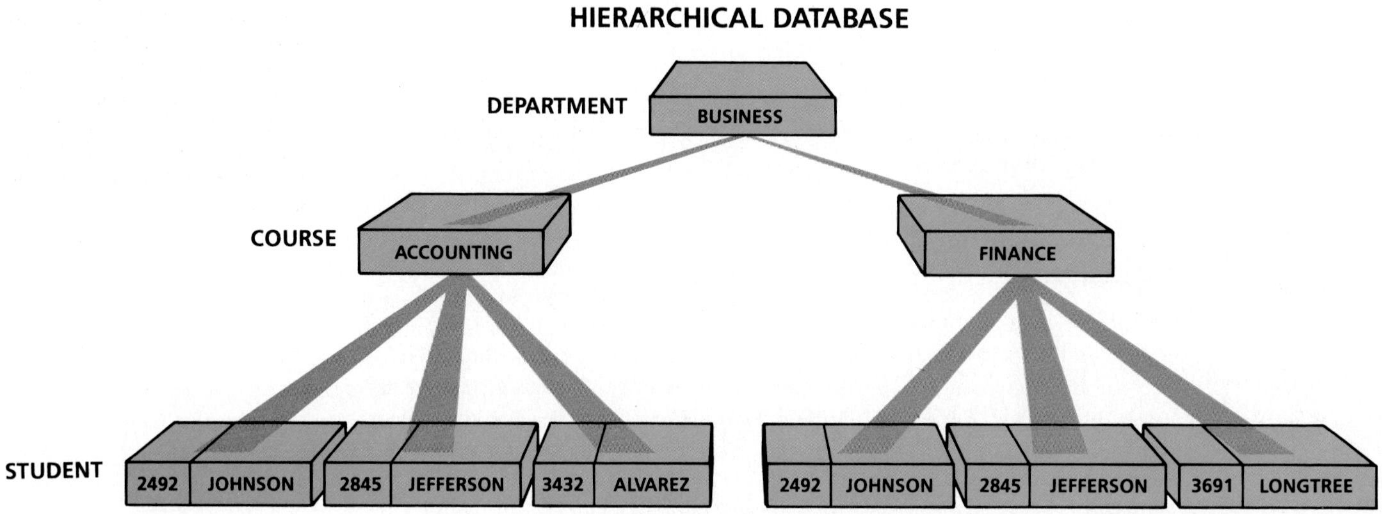

HIERARCHICAL DATABASE

FIGURE 8-14
In this hierarchical database, Johnson, Jefferson, and Longtree are the children of Finance and Finance is their parent. Finance and Accounting are the children of Business and Business is their parent. These relationships must be established before the database can be used.

Hierarchical databases are the oldest form of database organization and reflect the fact that they were developed when the disk and memory capacity of computers was limited and most processing was done in batch mode. Data access is sequential in the sense that an inquiry begins at the root record and proceeds down the branch until the requested data is found. All parent-child relationships must be established before the user can access the database. These relationships are defined by the person who is responsible for designing the database and are established when the database is created in a separate process that is sometimes called "generating the database."

After the database is created, access must be made through the established relationships. This points out two disadvantages of hierarchical databases. First, records located in separate branches of the database cannot be accessed easily at the same time. Second, adding new fields to database records or modifying existing fields, such as adding the four-digit zip code extension, requires the redefinition of the entire database. Depending on the size of the database, this redefinition process can take a considerable amount of time. The advantage of a hierarchical database is that because the data relationships are predefined, access to and updating of data is very fast.

Network Database

A **network database** (Figure 8-15) is similar to a hierarchical database except that each child record can have more than one parent. In network database terminology, a child record is referred to as a **member** and a parent record is referred to as an **owner**. Unlike the hierarchical database, the network database is able to establish relationships between different branches of the data and thus offers increased access capability for the user. However, like the hierarchical database, these data relationships must be established prior to the use of the database and must be redefined if fields are added or modified.

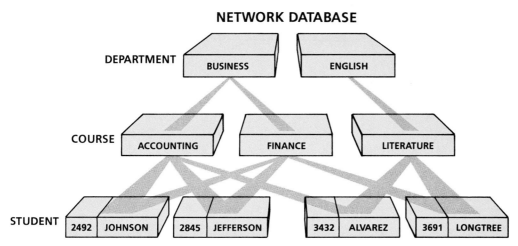

NETWORK DATABASE

FIGURE 8-15
In a network database, lower level (member) records can be related to more than one higher level (owner) record. For example, Longtree's owners are Finance and Literature. Accounting has three members, Johnson, Jefferson, and Alvarez. As in a hierarchical database, these relationships must be established before the database can be used.

DATABASE MANAGEMENT SYSTEMS

atabase management systems, the software that manage the creation, maintenance and reporting of database data, have a number of common features. These features include:

1. **Data dictionary.** The **data dictionary** defines each data field that will be contained in the database files. The dictionary is used to record the field name, size, description, type of data (e.g., text, numeric, or date), and relationship to other data elements.
2. **Utilities.** Database management system utility programs provide for a number of maintenance tasks including creating files and dictionaries, monitoring performance, copying data, and deleting unwanted records.
3. **Security.** Most database management systems allow the user to specify different levels of user access privileges. The privileges can be established for each user for each type of access (retrieve, update, and delete) to each data field. Note that without some type of access security, the data in a database is more subject to unauthorized access than in a decentralized system of individual files.
4. **Query language.** The query language is one of the most valuable features of a database management system. It allows the user to retrieve information from the database based on the criteria and in the format specified by the user.

QUERY LANGUAGES: ACCESS TO THE DATABASE

A **query language** is a simple English-like language that allows users to specify what data they want to see on a report or screen display. Although each query language has its own grammar, syntax, and vocabulary, these languages can generally be learned in a short time by persons without a programming background.

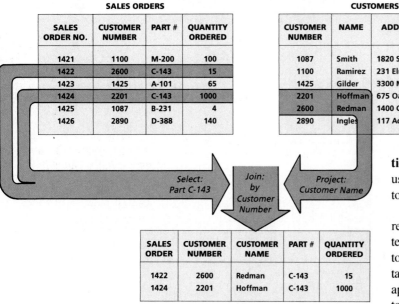

Query: Display customer name and quantity
ordered for all sales orders for Part C-143

A Query Example

Figure 8-16 shows how a user might query a relational database. This example illustrates the relational operations that may be performed when a relational database inquiry is made. These three **relational operations** are select, project, and join. They allow the user to manipulate the data from one or more files to create a unique "view" or subset of the total data.

The **select relational operation** selects certain records (rows or tuples) based on user-supplied criteria. In the example, the user queries the database to select records from the sales order file that contain part number C-143. Selection criteria can be applied to more than one field and can include tests to determine if a field is greater than, less than, equal to, or not equal to a value specified by the user. Connectors such as AND and OR can also be used.

FIGURE 8-16
This example illustrates the three relational operations (select, project, and join) that would be used to produce a response to the query.

The **project relational operation** specifies the fields (attributes) that appear on the query output. In the example, the user wants to see the names of the customers who placed orders for part number C-143.

The **join relational operation** is used to combine two files (relations or tables). In the example, the link used to join the two files is the customer number, a field contained in each file.

After the query is executed, most query languages allow the user to give the query a unique name and save it for future use.

Structured Query Language: An Emerging Standard

One of the most widely used query languages is **Structured Query Language**, often referred to as **SQL**. Originally developed during the 1970s by IBM, SQL has been incorporated into a number of relational database software packages including ORACLE by Oracle Corporation and INGRES by Relational Technology. IBM actively supports SQL and incorporates it into their two major relational database system products, SQL/DS and DB2. SQL received increased support as the emerging relational database management system query language when, in 1985, the American National Standards Institute formed a committee to develop industry standards for SQL. The standards were issued in 1987. Today, it is difficult to pick up a computer industry publication and not read about at least one database software vendor announcing plans to incorporate SQL into its product. The standardization of SQL will further accelerate its implementation on a wide range of computer systems from micros to supercomputers. This fact, coupled with the increasing dominance of relational databases, will mean that SQL will be used by many computer users.

DATABASE ADMINISTRATION

*T*he centralization of an organization's data into a database requires a great deal of cooperation and coordination on the part of the database users. In file-oriented systems, if a user wanted to keep track of some data he or she would just create another file, often duplicating some data that was already being tracked by someone else. In a database system, the user must first check to see if some or all of the data is already on file and if not, how it can be added to the system. The role of coordinating the use of the database belongs to the database administrator.

The Database Administrator

The **database administrator**, or **DBA**, is the person responsible for coordinating all database activities (Figure 8-17). In small organizations, this person usually has other responsibilities such as the overall management of the computer resources. In medium and large organizations, the role of DBA is a full-time job for one or more people. The job of DBA usually includes the following responsibilities:

1. **Database design.** The DBA determines the initial design of the database and specifies where to add additional data files and records when they are needed.
2. **User coordination.** The DBA is responsible for letting users know what data is available in the database and how the users can retrieve it. The DBA also reviews user requests for additions to the database and helps establish priorities for their implementation.
3. **Backup and recovery.** The centralization of data in a database makes an organization particularly vulnerable to a computer system failure. It is often the responsibility of the DBA to minimize this risk, making sure that all data is regularly backed up and that contingency plans are prepared (and periodically tested) for a prolonged equipment or software malfunction.
4. **System security.** It is the DBA's responsibility to establish and monitor system access privileges to prevent the unauthorized use of an organization's data.
5. **Performance monitoring.** The performance of the database, usually measured in terms of response time to a user request, can be affected by a number of factors such as file sizes and the types and frequency of inquiries during the day. Most database management systems have utility programs that enable the DBA to monitor these factors and make adjustments to provide for more efficient database use.

In addition to the DBA, the user also has a role in a database management system.

The Responsibility of the User in a Database Management System

One of the user's first responsibilities is to become familiar with the data in the existing database. First-time database users are often amazed at the wealth of information available to help them perform their jobs more effectively.

Another responsibility of the user, in organizations of any size, is to play an active part in the specification of additions to the database. The maintenance of an organization's database is an ongoing task that must be constantly measured against the overall goals of the organization. Therefore users must participate in designing the database that will be used to help them achieve those goals and measure their progress.

MANAGING DATA ON A PERSONAL COMPUTER

variety of data management systems are available for personal computers, ranging from simple file management programs to full relational database management systems. As with large system packages, many personal computer software vendors are developing or modifying existing packages to support Structured Query Language (SQL). The advantage of SQL packages for personal computers is that they can directly query mainframe databases that support SQL.

The increased computing power of the latest personal computers has also allowed database management packages originally written for mainframe computers to be modified to run on the smaller systems. ORACLE (Oracle Corporation) and INGRES (Relational Technology) are two SQL-based packages that have been adapted to personal computers.

Perhaps the best known and most widely used personal computer-based database management system is the dBASE series from Ashton-Tate Corporation. dBASE III PLUS offers a relational database manager, a programming language, and application development tools. dBASE IV includes a complete implementation of SQL.

With so many data management packages available (a recent survey included 43), it's difficult to decide which one to choose. For those with simple needs, a file management package is probably all that is necessary. For larger databases with multiple files, one of the more popular database management systems will offer increased capability and growth potential. For complex database requirements, the packages originally developed on mainframes should provide all the database resources required. If you need to select a database software package for your personal computer, you may want to refer to the section in Chapter 2 that discusses how to choose software packages for a personal computer.

SUMMARY OF DATABASES

*D*atabases provide a better way of organizing data by relating items in multiple files. With databases, redundant data is minimized and data integrity improved. Database query languages allow data to be retrieved according to the criteria and in the format specified by the user.

Understanding the database and file concepts that have been presented in this chapter will help you to have a better understanding of how data and information are organized and managed on the auxiliary storage of a computer. Whether you are a home computer user who wants to store personal data on floppy disks or a hard drive, or a mainframe user accessing the database of the company where you are employed, a fundamental knowledge of how data is organized and managed will be useful to you.

CHAPTER SUMMARY

1. A file is a collection of related records that is usually stored on an auxiliary storage device. The three types of file organization are sequential, indexed, and direct or relative.
2. When **sequential file organization** is used, records are stored one after the other, normally in ascending or descending order by the value in the **key** field.
3. **Sequential retrieval** means that the records on a tape or disk file are retrieved (accessed) one after another in the same order that the records are stored on the tape or disk.

4. With **indexed file organization**, the records are stored on the disk in an indexed file in ascending or descending sequence based on a key field. An index is used to retrieve records.

5. An **index** consists of entries containing the key to the records and the disk addresses of the records.

6. **Random retrieval**, or access, allows the records in a disk file to be accessed in any order based on the value in a key field or on the location of a record in a file. Random retrieval is used when fast access to a record is required.

7. Random access and sequential access can be used with indexed files.

8. A **direct file** or **relative file** contains records that are stored and retrieved according to their disk address or their physical location within the file.

9. The locations on a disk where records in a direct file can be stored are called **buckets**.

10. **Hashing** means using a formula or performing a calculation to determine the location (position) where a record will be placed on a disk.

11. A **collision** occurs when the hashing operation generates the same disk location (called **synonyms**) for records with different key values.

12. Data maintenance refers to the process of **updating** files and databases by adding, changing, or deleting data from a file.

13. A **database** uses multiple related files to organize data.

14. A **database management system (DBMS)** is the software that allows the user to create, maintain, and report the data and file relationships used in a database.

15. By contrast, a **file management system** allows a user to access only one file at a time.

16. **Reduced data redundancy** (data that is duplicated in several different files), **improved data integrity** (data accuracy), **integrated files** (joining data from more than one file), and **improved data security** (ensuring that the data is accessible only to those with the proper authorization) are the major advantages of using a database.

17. A **relational database** is organized into tables called **relations**. The relations are divided into **tuples** (rows) and **attributes** (fields). Each attribute is given a unique name, called the **domain**.

18. In a relational database, a common attribute or **link** is used to connect multiple files.

19. The advantage of a relational database is that the data relationships do not need to be predefined.

20. A **hierarchical database** is organized in a top to bottom series of parent-child relationships. Each **parent record** can have multiple child records. However, each **child record** can have only one parent. The parent record at the top of the hierarchy is called the **root** record.

21. A **network database** is organized similar to a hierarchical database except each child record (called a **member**) may have more than one parent record (called an **owner**).

22. Data relationships in both the hierarchical database and the network database must be established prior to the use of the database.

23. The database management system consists of a **data dictionary** that defines each data field to be used in the database; utility programs (usually referred to as utilities) that provide a number of special functions (such as copying data, creating files, and deleting records); security levels that control access to the data; and a **query language** that allows users to specify what data they wish to view.

24. The **relational operations** of a relational database include the select relational operation, the project relational operation, and the join relational operation.

25. The **select relational operation** selects specific records based on the specifications provided by the user.

26. The **project relational operation** specifies the fields to be displayed.

27. The **join relational operation** is used to combine two files.

28. A widely used query language is **Structured Query Language (SQL)**.

29. The **database administrator (DBA)** is the person who coordinates all use of the database.

30. The database administrator is responsible for database design, user coordination, backup and recovery, database security, and database performance monitoring.

31. Users should become familiar with the data in their organization's database and should actively participate in the specification of additions to the database that will affect their jobs.

KEY TERMS

Attributes *8.13*	Hashing *8.6*	Performance monitoring *8.17*	Select relational
Backup and recovery *8.17*	Hierarchical database *8.14*	Prime number *8.6*	operation *8.16*
Buckets *8.6*	Improved data integrity *8.12*	Project relational	Sequential access *8.4*
Child record *8.14*	Improved data security *8.12*	operation *8.16*	Sequential file
Collision *8.6*	Index *8.4*	Query language *8.16*	organization *8.3*
Database *8.11*	Indexed file organization *8.4*	Random access *8.5*	Sequential retrieval *8.4*
Database administrator	Integrated files *8.12*	Random retrieval *8.5*	Structured Query Language
(DBA) *8.17*	Join relational operation *8.16*	Reduced data redundancy *8.12*	(SQL) *8.16*
Database design *8.17*	Key *8.3*	Relational database *8.13*	Synonyms *8.6*
Database management system	Link *8.13*	Relational operations *8.16*	System security *8.17*
(DBMS) *8.11*	Member *8.15*	Relations *8.13*	Tuples *8.13*
Data dictionary *8.15*	Network database *8.15*	Relative file *8.6*	Updating *8.7*
Direct file *8.6*	Owner *8.15*	Root *8.14*	User coordination *8.17*
Domain *8.13*	Parent record *8.14*	Security *8.15*	Utilities *8.15*
File management system *8.11*			

REVIEW QUESTIONS

1. Describe sequential file organization. How are records in sequential files retrieved?
2. What is an indexed file? Describe how the index is used to retrieve records from an indexed file.
3. How is the location where a record is stored in a direct file determined?
4. What is a collision? What are synonyms?
5. List the three data maintenance procedures that are used to update files. Give an example of each.
6. Write a definition for the term database.
7. What is the difference between a database management system and a file management system?
8. What are the advantages of a database management system over a file-oriented system?
9. In a relational database, how are different files related to one another?
10. What is the difference between the structures of a hierarchical and a network database?
11. How is a data dictionary used?   12. Why is access security important in a database system?
13. How is a database query used?   14. What are the responsibilities of a database administrator?
15. What are the responsibilities of the user in a database management system?

CONTROVERSIAL ISSUES

1. Security experts have said that the risk of computer crime increases when a database is used in a company as opposed to when application-related files are used. They theorize that since all the data is accessible in one place, it would be easier to manipulate the data for illegal purposes. Database management system developers maintain that with proper security measures, databases are just as secure as files, if not more secure. What do you think?
2. Government attempts to establish a database on all citizens have been opposed by people who claim that it would be an invasion of privacy. Discuss the possible advantages and possible misuse of such a database.

RESEARCH PROJECTS

1. Find articles on relational databases in recent journals and magazines. Report on the performance characteristics of relational databases, particularly with respect to the time required to retrieve and display information from more than one file (a joint operation).
2. Prepare a report on various databases available for use on personal computers.
3. Prepare a report on a database management system that supports Structured Query Language (SQL).

CHAPTER 9

Data Communications

Data Communications

OBJECTIVES

- Define data communications.
- Describe the basic components of a data communications system.
- Describe the various transmission media that are used for communication channels.
- Describe the different types of line configurations.
- Describe how data is transmitted.
- Identify and explain the communications equipment that can be used in a data communications system.
- Describe the functions that communications software can perform.
- Explain the two major categories of networks and describe the common network configurations.
- Discuss how personal computers can use data communications.

*C*omputers are well recognized as important computing devices. They should also be recognized as important communication devices. It is now possible for a computer to communicate with other computers anywhere in the world. This capability allows users to quickly and directly access data and information that otherwise would have been unavailable or that probably would have taken considerable time to acquire. Banks, retail stores, airlines, hotels, and many others businesses use computers for communication purposes. Personal computer users communicate with other personal computer users and also access special databases available on larger machines to quickly and conveniently obtain information such as weather reports, stock market data, airline schedules, news stories, or even theater and movie reviews.

This chapter provides an overview of data communications and explains some of the terminology, equipment, procedures, and applications that relate to computers and their use as communication devices.

WHAT IS DATA COMMUNICATIONS?

 Data communications is the transmission of data over a communication channel, such as a standard telephone line, between one computer (or a terminal) and another computer.

Figure 9-1 shows the basic components of a data communications system. These components include:

1. A computer or a terminal.
2. Data communication equipment that sends (and can usually receive) data.
3. The communication channel over which the data is sent.
4. Data communications equipment that receives (and can usually send) data.
5. Another computer.

As you will see, the basic model of a data communications system illustrated in Figure 9-1 can be applied to virtually all data communications systems.

FIGURE 9-1
A basic model of a data communications system.

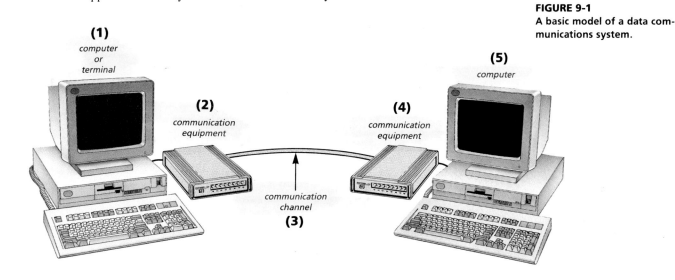

(1)
computer
or
terminal

(2)
communication
equipment

(3)
communication
channel

(4)
communication
equipment

(5)
computer

COMMUNICATION CHANNELS

 communication channel is the link or path that the data follows as it is transmitted from the sending equipment to the receiving equipment in a data communications system. These channels are made up of one or more **transmission media**, including twisted pair wire, coaxial cable, fiber optics, microwaves, and communication satellites.

Twisted Pair Wire

Twisted pair wire (Figure 9-2) consists of pairs of copper wires that are twisted together. To insulate and identify the wires, each wire is covered with a thin layer of colored plastic. Twisted pair wire is commonly used for telephone lines. It is an inexpensive transmission medium, and it can be easily strung from one location to another. The disadvantage of twisted pair wire is that it is susceptible to outside electrical interference generated by fans or air conditioners. This interference can garble the data as it is sent over the line, causing transmission errors to occur.

FIGURE 9-2
Twisted pair wire is most commonly used as telephone wire. It is inexpensive but susceptible to electrical interference that can cause errors in data transmission.

FIGURE 9-3
This photograph shows several types of coaxial cable that can be used to transmit data.

Coaxial Cable

A **coaxial cable** is a high-quality communication line that is used in offices, laid under the ground and under the ocean. Coaxial cable consists of a wire or central conductor surrounded by a nonconducting insulator that is in turn surrounded by a woven metal shielding layer, and finally a plastic outer coating (Figure 9-3). Because of its more heavily insulated construction, coaxial cable is not susceptible to electrical interference and can transmit data at higher data rates over longer distances than twisted pair telephone wire.

There are two types of coaxial cable, named for the transmission techniques they support: baseband and broadband. **Baseband** coaxial cable carries one signal at a time. The signal, however, can travel very fast—in the area of ten million bits per second for the first 1,000 feet. The speed drops off significantly as the length of cable increases and special equipment is needed to amplify (boost) the signal if it is transmitted more than approximately one mile.

Broadband coaxial cable can carry multiple signals at one time. It is similar to cable TV where a single cable offers a number of channels to the user. A particular advantage of broadband channels is that data, audio, and video transmission can take place over the same line.

Fiber Optics

Fiber optics (Figure 9-4) is a technology that may eventually replace conventional wire and cable in communication systems. This technology is based on the ability of smooth hair-thin strands of material to conduct light with high efficiency. The major advantages of fiber optics over wire cables include substantial weight and size savings and increased speed of transmission. A single fiber-optic cable can carry several hundred thousand voice communications simultaneously. Although fiber optics is not yet used on a large scale, it is frequently being used in new installations and promises to dramatically increase data communication capabilities.

FIGURE 9-4
The two-strand fiber-optic cable can transmit as much information as the 1500-pair copper cable.

Microwaves

Microwaves are a type of radio waves that can be used to provide high-speed transmission of both voice and data. Data is transmitted through the air from one microwave station to another in a manner similar to the way radio signals are transmitted. A disadvantage of microwaves is that they are limited to line-of-sight transmission. This means that microwaves must be transmitted in a straight line and that there can be no obstructions, such as buildings or mountains, between microwave stations. For this reason, microwave stations are characterized by antennas positioned on tops of buildings, towers, or mountains (Figure 9-5). Because of the curvature of the earth, the maximum distance between microwave stations is about thirty miles.

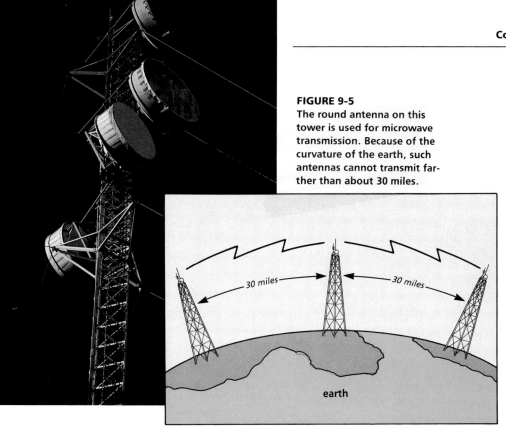

FIGURE 9-5
The round antenna on this tower is used for microwave transmission. Because of the curvature of the earth, such antennas cannot transmit farther than about 30 miles.

FIGURE 9-6
Earth stations use large dish antennas to communicate with satellites and microwave antennas. ▼

Communication Satellites

Communication satellites have the ability to receive signals from earth, amplify the signals, and retransmit the signals back to the earth. **Earth stations** (Figure 9-6) are communication facilities that use large dish-shaped antennas to transmit and receive data from satellites. The transmission to the satellite is called an **uplink** and the transmission from the satellite to a receiving earth station is called a **downlink**. Communication satellites are normally placed about 22,000 miles above the earth in a geosynchronous orbit (Figure 9-7). This means that the satellite rotates with the earth, so that the same dish antennas on earth that are used to send and receive signals can remain fixed on the satellite at all times.

◄ FIGURE 9-7
Communication satellites are placed in geosynchronous orbits approximately 22,000 miles above the earth. This satellite is shown emerging from the cargo bay of a space shuttle.

An Example of a Communication Channel

When data is transmitted over long distances, it is likely that a number of different types of transmission media will be used to make a complete communication channel. The diagram in Figure 9-8 illustrates some of the various transmission media that could be used to transmit data from a personal computer on the west coast of the United States to a large computer on the east coast. The steps that could occur are:

1. An entry is made on the personal computer. The data is sent over telephone lines from the computer to a microwave station.
2. The data is then transmitted between microwave stations that are usually located no more than thirty miles apart.
3. The data is transmitted from the last microwave station to an earth station.
4. The earth station transmits the data to the communications satellite.
5. The satellite relays the data to another earth station on the other side of the country.
6. The data received at the earth station is transmitted to microwave stations.
7. The data is sent by the telephone lines to the large computer.

FIGURE 9-8
This diagram illustrates the use of telephone wires, microwave transmission, and a communication satellite to allow a personal computer to communicate with a large host computer.

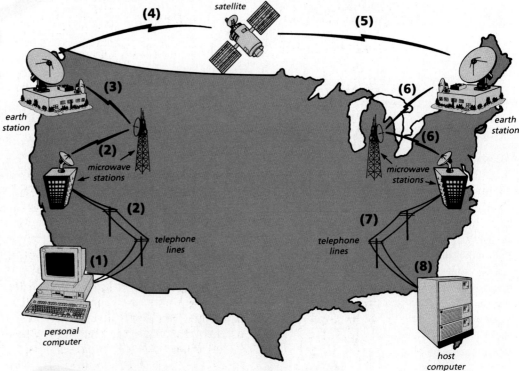

The entire transmission process just described would take less than one second.

Not all data transmission is as complex as this example, but such sophisticated communication systems do exist to satisfy the needs of some users.

LINE CONFIGURATIONS

*T*here are two major **line configurations** (types of line connections) that are commonly used in data communications: point-to-point lines and multidrop or multipoint lines.

Point-to-Point Lines

A **point-to-point line** is a direct line between a sending and a receiving device. It may be one of two types: a switched line or a dedicated line (Figure 9-9).

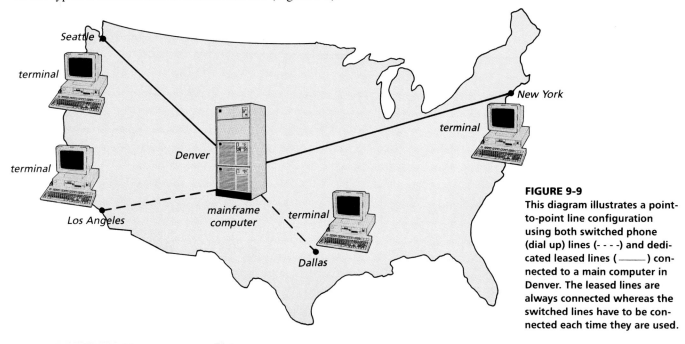

FIGURE 9-9
This diagram illustrates a point-to-point line configuration using both switched phone (dial up) lines (- - - -) and dedicated leased lines (———) connected to a main computer in Denver. The leased lines are always connected whereas the switched lines have to be connected each time they are used.

Switched Line   A **switched line** uses a regular telephone line to establish a communication connection. Each time a connection is made, the line to be used for the call is selected by the telephone company switching stations (hence the name switched line). Using a switched line is the same as one person using a phone to call another person. The communication equipment at the sending end dials the phone number of the communication equipment at the other end. When the communication equipment at the receiving end answers the call, a connection is established and data can be transmitted. When the transmission of data is complete, the communication equipment at either end terminates the call by "hanging up" and the line is disconnected.

An advantage of using switched lines is that a connection can be made between any two locations that have phone service and communication equipment. For example, a personal computer could dial one computer to get information about the weather and then hang up and place a second call to another computer to get information about the stock market. A disadvantage of a switched line is that the quality of the line cannot be controlled because the line is chosen at random by the telephone company switching equipment. A switched line used for data communication is charged the same rate as a regular phone call.

Dedicated Line   A **dedicated line** is a line connection that is always established (unlike the switched line where the line connection is reestablished each time it is used). The communication device at one end is always connected to the device at the other end. A user can create a dedicated line connection by running a wire or cable between two points, such as between two offices or buildings, or the dedicated line can be provided by an outside organization such as the phone company or some other communication service company. If the dedicated line is provided by an outside organization, it is sometimes called a **leased line** or a **private line**. Because a dedicated line is always established, the quality and consistency of the connection is better than on a switched line. Dedicated lines provided by outside organizations are usually charged on a flat fee basis: a fixed amount each month regardless of how much time the line is actually used to transmit data. The cost of dedicated lines varies based on the distance between the two connected points and, sometimes, the speed at which data will be transmitted.

Multidrop Lines

The second major line configuration is called a **multidrop line** or **multipoint line**. This type of line configuration is commonly used to connect multiple devices, such as terminals or personal computers, on a single line to a main computer, sometimes called a **host computer** (Figure 9-10). For example, a ticket agent could use a terminal to enter an inquiry requesting flight information from a database stored on a main computer (Figure 9-11). While the request is being transmitted to the main computer, other terminals on the line are not able to transmit data. The time required for the data to be transmitted to the main computer, however, is short—most likely less than one second. As soon as the inquiry is received by the computer, a second terminal can send an inquiry. With such short delays, it appears to the users that no other terminals are using the line, even though multiple terminals may be sharing the same line.

FIGURE 9-10
This diagram illustrates two multidrop lines connecting several cities with a computer in Denver. Each line is shared by terminals at several locations. Multidrop line configurations are less expensive than individual lines to each remote location.

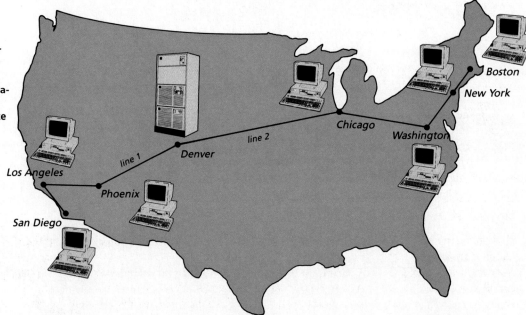

The number of terminals to be placed on one line is a decision made by the designer of the system based on the amount of traffic that will be found on the line. For example, 100 or more terminals could be contained on a single line, provided each of them was only going to be sending short messages, such as inquiries, and each terminal was going to use the communication line only a few hours per day. But if longer messages such as reports were required and the terminals were to be used almost continuously, the number of terminals on one line would have to be smaller.

A leased line is almost always used for multidrop line configurations. The use of multidrop lines can decrease line costs considerably because one line is used by many terminals.

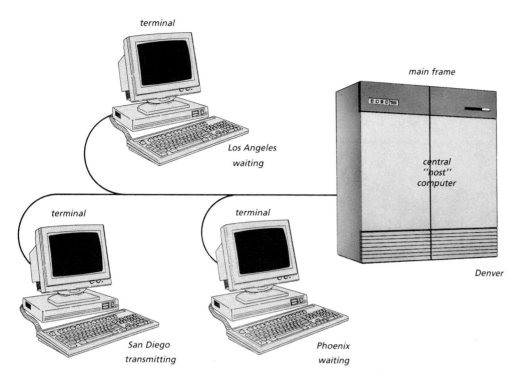

FIGURE 9-11
On a multidrop line, several terminals share the same line. Only one terminal at a time can transmit data to the host computer.

CHARACTERISTICS OF COMMUNICATION CHANNELS

he communication channels we have discussed can be categorized by a number of characteristics, including the type of signal, transmission mode, transmission direction, and transmission rate.

Types of Signals: Digital and Analog

Computer equipment is designed to process data as **digital signals**, individual electrical pulses that can represent the bits that are grouped together to form characters. However, telephone equipment was originally designed to carry only voice transmission, which is comprised of a continuous electrical wave called an **analog signal** (Figure 9-12). Therefore, in order to use voice phone lines to carry data, a special piece of equipment called a **modem** is used to convert the digital signals into analog signals. We discuss modems in more detail later in this chapter.

FIGURE 9-12
Individual electrical pulses of the digital signal are converted into analog (electrical wave) signals for transmission over voice phone lines. At the main computer receiving end, another modem converts the analog signals back into digital signals that can be processed by the computer.

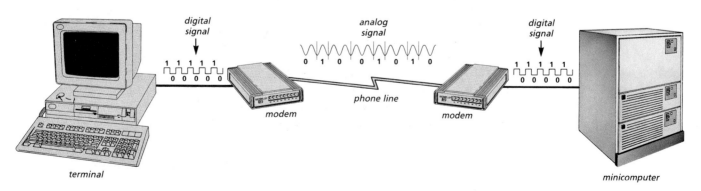

Transmission Modes: Asynchronous and Synchronous

FIGURE 9-13
In asynchronous transmission mode, individual characters are transmitted. In synchronous transmission mode, multiple characters are sent in a block. Synchronous transmission is faster and more accurate.

In **asynchronous transmission mode** (Figure 9-13), individual characters (made up of bits) are transmitted at irregular intervals, for example, as they are entered by a user. To distinguish where one character stops and another starts, the asynchronous communication mode uses a start and a stop bit. An additional bit called a **parity bit** is sometimes included at the end of each character to provide a way of checking against data loss. The parity bit is turned on or off depending on the error detection method being used. As you recall from the discussion on memory in Chapter 5, parity bits are used to detect if one of the data bits has been changed during transmission. The asynchronous transmission mode is used for lower speed data transmission and is used with most communication equipment designed for personal computers.

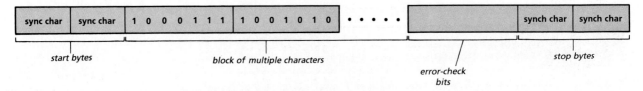

In the **synchronous transmission mode** (also shown in Figure 9-13), large blocks of data are transmitted at regular intervals. Timing signals synchronize the communication equipment at both the sending and receiving ends and eliminate the need for start and stop bits for each character. Error-checking bits and start and end indicators called sync bytes are also transmitted. Synchronous transmission requires more sophisticated and expensive equipment but does give much higher speeds and accuracy than asynchronous transmission.

Direction of Transmission: Simplex, Half-Duplex, and Full-Duplex

The direction of data transmission is classified as either simplex, half-duplex, or full-duplex (Figure 9-14). In **simplex transmission**, data flows in only one direction. Simplex is used only when the sending device, such as a temperature sensor, never requires a response from the computer. For example, if a computer is used to control the temperature of a building, numerous sensors are placed throughout it. Each sensor is connected to the computer with a simplex transmission line because the computer only needs to receive data from the temperature sensors and does not need to send data back to the sensors.

In **half-duplex transmission**, data can flow in both directions but in only one direction at a time. An example is a citizens band radio. The user can talk or listen but not do both at the same time. Half-duplex is often used between terminals and a central computer.

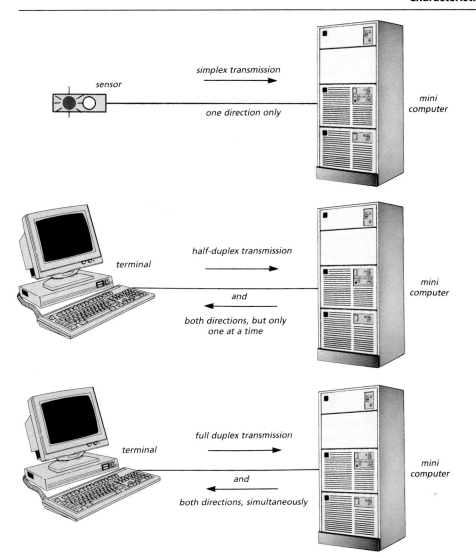

FIGURE 9-14
Simplex transmission allows data to flow in only one direction. Half-duplex allows data to flow in both directions but not at the same time. Full-duplex allows data to flow in both directions simultaneously.

FIGURE 9-14
Simplex transmission allows data to flow in only one direction. Half-duplex allows data to flow in both directions but not at the same time. Full-duplex allows data to flow in both directions simultaneously.

FIGURE 9-15
Bandwidth and relative carrying capacity of communication channels. Bandwidth is measured in Hertz or cycles per second. A megahertz is one million cycles per second; a gigahertz is one billion cycles per second; and a terahertz is one trillion cycles per second.

In **full-duplex transmission**, data can be sent in both directions at the same time. A normal phone line is an example of full-duplex transmission. Both parties can talk at the same time. Full-duplex transmission is used for most interactive computer applications and for computer-to-computer data transmission.

Transmission Rate

The transmission rate of a communication channel is determined by its bandwidth and its speed. The **bandwidth** is the range of frequencies that a channel can carry. Since transmitted data can be assigned to different frequencies, the wider the bandwidth, the more frequencies, and the more data that can be transmitted at the same time. Figure 9-15 summarizes the bandwidths of the communication channels we have discussed.

The speed at which data is transmitted is usually expressed as bits per second or as a baud rate.

TRANSMISSION CHANNEL	BANDWIDTH (HERTZ)	RELATIVE CARRYING CAPACITY
Twisted pair	10–100,000	1
Coaxial cable	1–1000 megahertz	1000
Microwave	1–10 gigahertz	10,000
Satellite	2–40 gigahertz	40,000
Fiber optics	100–1000 terahertz	1,000,000,000

Bits per second (bps) is the number of bits that can be transmitted in one second. Using a 10-bit byte to represent a character (7 data bits, 1 start, 1 stop, and 1 parity bit), a 2,400 bps transmission would transmit 240 characters per second. At this rate, a 20-page single-spaced report would be transmitted in approximately five minutes.

The **baud rate** is the number of times per second that the signal being transmitted changes. With each change, one or more bits can be transmitted. At speeds up to 2,400 bps, usually only one bit is transmitted per signal change and thus the bits per second and the baud rate are the same. To achieve speeds in excess of 2,400 bps, more than one bit is transmitted with each signal change and thus the bps will exceed the baud rate.

FIGURE 9-16
An external modem is connected to a terminal or computer and to a phone outlet.

COMMUNICATION EQUIPMENT

If a terminal or a personal computer is within approximately 1,000 feet of another computer, the two devices can usually be directly connected by a cable. Over 1,000 feet, however, the electrical signal weakens to the point that some type of special communication equipment is required to increase or change the signal to transmit it farther. A variety of complex communication equipment exists to perform this task, but the equipment that a user is most likely to encounter is a modem, a multiplexor, and a front-end processor.

Modems

A **modem** converts the digital signals of a terminal or computer to analog signals that can be transmitted over phone equipment. The word modem comes from a combination of the words *mo*dulate, which means to change into a sound or analog signal, and *de*modulate, which means to convert an analog signal into a digital signal. A modem must be present at both the sending and receiving ends of a communication channel.

An **external modem** (Figure 9-16) is a separate or stand-alone device that is attached to the computer or terminal by a cable and to the phone outlet by a standard phone cord. An advantage of an external modem is that it may be moved from one terminal or computer to another.

FIGURE 9-17
An internal modem is mounted inside a personal computer.

An **internal modem** (Figure 9-17) is a circuit board that is installed inside a computer or terminal. Internal modems are generally less expensive than comparable external modems but once installed, they are not as easy to move.

An **acoustic modem**, also called an **acoustic coupler**, is designed to be used with a phone handset (Figure 9-18). The acoustic coupler converts the digital signals generated by the terminal or personal computer into a series of audible tones, which are picked up by the mouthpiece in the headset in the same manner that a telephone picks up a person's voice. The analog signals are then transmitted over the

FIGURE 9-18
The acoustic coupler in the lower left corner of this picture allows a portable computer user to communicate with another computer over telephone lines. Note that the telephone handset is placed in the molded rubber cups on the acoustic coupler.

communication channel. An acoustic coupler provides portability but is generally less reliable than an internal or external modem, because small outside sounds can be picked up by the acoustic coupler and cause transmission errors. Acoustic couplers are not common and are primarily used for special applications, such as with portable computers.

Modems can transmit data at rates from 300 to 38,400 bits per second (bps). Most personal computers would use either a 1,200 or 2,400 bps modem. Business or heavier volume users would use faster and more expensive modems.

Multiplexors

A **multiplexor** combines more than one input signal into a single stream of data that can be transmitted over a communication channel (Figure 9-19). The multiplexor at the sending end codes each character it receives with an identifier that is used by the multiplexor at the receiving end to separate the combined data stream into its original parts. A multiplexor may be connected to a separate modem or may have a modem built in. By combining the individual data streams into one, a multiplexor increases the efficiency of communications and saves the cost of individual communication channels.

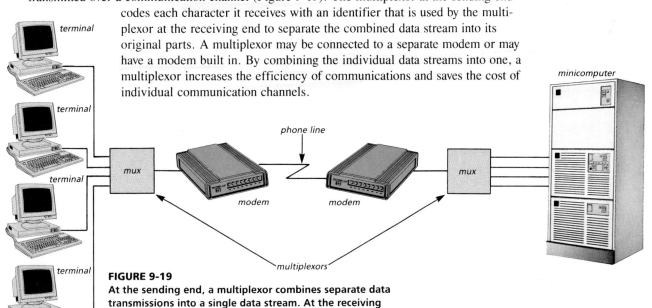

FIGURE 9-19
At the sending end, a multiplexor combines separate data transmissions into a single data stream. At the receiving end, the multiplexor separates the single stream into its original parts.

FIGURE 9-20
This IBM Series 1 minicomputer is often used as a front-end processor to relieve the main computer of data communication tasks.

Front-End Processors

A **front-end processor** (Figure 9-20) is a computer that is dedicated to handling the data communication requirements of a larger computer. Relieved of these tasks, the activity of the large computer is dedicated to processing data, while the front-end processor communicates the data. Tasks that the front-end processor would handle include **polling** (checking the connected terminals or computers to see if they have data to send), error checking and correction, and access security to make sure that a connected device or the user of the connected device is authorized to access the computer.

FIGURE 9-21
Communication software performs a variety of tasks that assist the user in using data communications equipment.

COMMUNICATION SOFTWARE

Sometimes communications equipment is preprogrammed to accomplish its designed communication tasks. In other cases, the user must load a program before beginning data transmission. These programs, referred to as **communications software**, can perform a number of tasks including dialing (if a switched phone line is used), terminal emulation, and data encryption (Figure 9-21).

Dialing software allows the user to store, review, select and dial phone numbers of computers that can be called. The software provides a variety of meaningful messages to assist the user in establishing a connection before transmitting data. For example, a person who uses a personal computer at home to communicate with a computer at the office could use dialing software to establish the communication connection. The software would display the office computer's phone number on the user's personal computer screen. The user would enter the appropriate command for the dialing software, working with a modem, to begin dialing the office computer and to establish a connection. During the 10 or 15 seconds that this process takes, the software would display messages to indicate specifically what was happening, such as "DIALING," "CARRIER DETECT" (which means that the office computer has "answered"), and "CONNECTED" (to indicate that the communication connection has been established and data transmission can begin).

Terminal emulation software allows a personal computer to imitate or appear to be a specific type of terminal so that the personal computer can connect to another computer. Most mini and mainframe computers are designed to work with a limited number of terminals that have specific characteristics such as speed and parity. Terminal emulation software performs the necessary speed and parity conversion.

Data encryption is used to protect confidential data during transmission. **Data encryption** is the conversion of data at the sending end into an unrecognizable string of characters or bits and the reconversion of the data at the receiving end. Without knowing how the data was encrypted, someone who intercepted the transmitted data would have a difficult time determining what the data meant.

COMMUNICATION NETWORKS

A communication **network** is a collection of terminals, computers, and other equipment that use communication channels to share data. Networks can be classified as either local area networks or wide area networks.

Local Area Networks (LANs)

A **local area network** or **LAN** is a communications network that is privately owned and that covers a limited geographic area, such as an office, a building, or a group of buildings.

The LAN consists of a communication channel that connects either a series of computer terminals together with a minicomputer or, more commonly, a group of personal computers to one another. Very sophisticated LANs may connect a variety of office devices, such as word processing equipment, computer terminals, video equipment, and personal computers.

Two common applications of local area networks are hardware resource sharing and information resource sharing. **Hardware resource sharing** allows each personal computer in the network to access and use devices that would be too expensive to provide for each user or would not be justified for each user because of only occasional use. For example, when a number of personal computers are used on the network, each may need to use a laser printer. Using a LAN, a laser printer could be purchased and made a part of the network. Whenever a user of a personal computer on the network needed the laser printer, it could be accessed over the network.

To illustrate, the drawing in Figure 9-22 depicts a simple local area network consisting of four personal computers linked together by a cable. Three of the personal computers (computer 1 in the sales and marketing department, computer 2 in the accounting department, and computer 3 in the personnel department) are available for use at all times. Computer 4 is used as a **network control unit**, sometimes called a **server**, which is dedicated to handling the communication needs of the other computers in the network. The users of this LAN have connected the laser printer to the network control unit. Using the LAN, all computers and the network control unit can use the printer.

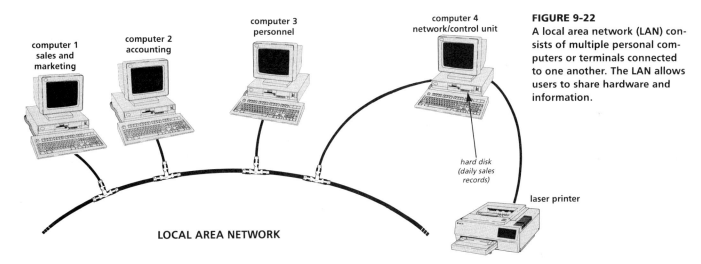

FIGURE 9-22
A local area network (LAN) consists of multiple personal computers or terminals connected to one another. The LAN allows users to share hardware and information.

Information resource sharing allows anyone using a personal computer on the local area network to access data stored on any other computer in the network. In actual practice, hardware resource sharing and information resource sharing are often combined. For example, in Figure 9-22, the daily sales records could be stored on the hard disk associated with the control unit personal computer. Anyone needing access to the sales records could use this information resource. The ability to access and store data on common auxiliary storage is an important feature of many local area networks.

Frequently used software is another type of resource that is often shared on a local area network. For example, if all users need access to word processing software, the software can be stored on the hard disk and accessed by all users as needed. This is much more convenient and faster than having the software stored on a floppy disk and available at each computer. For software written in-house, this is a common approach. Note, however, that the licensing agreement from many software companies does not permit the purchase of a single software package for use by all the computers in a network; therefore, it may be necessary to obtain a special agreement, called a **site license**, if a commercial software package is to be stored on hard disk and accessed by many users. Many software vendors now sell a network version of their packages.

Wide Area Networks (WANs)

A **wide area network** or **WAN** is one that is geographic in scope (as opposed to local) and uses phone lines, microwaves, satellites, or a combination of communication channels. Public wide area network companies include so-called "common carriers" such as the telephone companies. In recent years, telephone company deregulation has encouraged a number of companies to build their own wide area networks and others, such as MCI, to build WANs to compete with the telephone companies. Some common carriers are now offering **Integrated Services Digital Network (ISDN)** services. ISDN establishes an international standard for the digital transmission of data using different channels and communication companies.

NETWORK CONFIGURATIONS

*C*ommunication networks are usually configured or arranged in one or a combination of three patterns, sometimes called a **topology**. These configurations are star, bus, and ring networks. Although these configurations can also be used with wide area networks, we illustrate them with local area networks.

Star Network

A **star network** (Figure 9-23) contains a central computer and one or more terminals or personal computers connected to it, forming a star. A pure star network consists of only point-to-point lines between the terminals and the computer, but most star networks, such as the one shown in Figure 9-23, include both point-to-point lines and multidrop lines. A star network configuration is often used when the central computer contains all the data required to process the input from the terminals, such as an airline reservation system. For example, if inquiries are being processed in the star network, all the data to answer the inquiry would be contained in the database stored on the central computer.

FIGURE 9-23
A star network contains a single, centralized host computer with which all the terminals or personal computers in the network communicate. Both point-to-point and multidrop lines can be used in a star network.

A star network can be relatively efficient and close control can be kept over the data processed on the network. Its major disadvantage is that the entire network is dependent on the central computer and the associated hardware and software. If any of these elements fail, the entire network is disabled. Therefore, in most large star networks, backup systems are available in case the primary system fails.

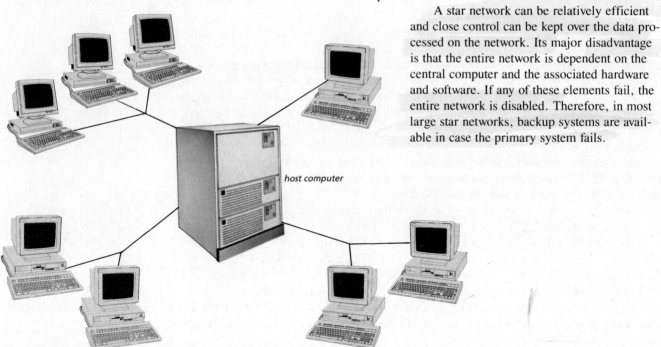

host computer

Bus Network

When a **bus network** is used, all devices in the network are connected to and share a single cable. Information is transmitted in either direction from any one personal computer to another. Any message can be directed to a specific device. An advantage of the bus network is that devices can be attached or detached from the network at any point without disturbing the rest of the network. In addition, if one computer on the network fails, this does not affect the other users of the network. Figure 9-22 illustrates a simple bus network.

FIGURE 9-24
In a ring network, all computers are connected in a continuous loop. Data flows around the ring in only one direction.

Ring Network

A **ring network** does not utilize a centralized host computer. Rather, a series of computers communicate with one another (Figure 9-24). A ring network can be useful when all the processing is not done at a central site, but at local sites. For example, computers could be located in three departments: the accounting department, the personnel department, and the shipping and receiving department. The computers in each of these departments could perform the processing required for each of the departments. On occasion, however, the computer in the shipping and receiving department could communicate with the computer in the accounting department to update certain data stored on the accounting department computer. Ring networks have not been extensively implemented for data communications systems that are used for long-distance communication; they are used more for local communications.

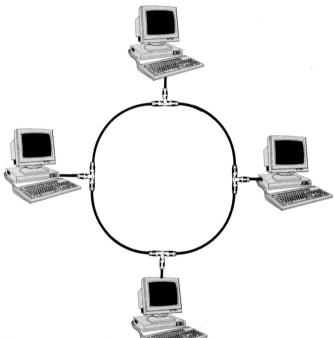

THE PERSONAL COMPUTER AND DATA COMMUNICATIONS

*T*he increased use of personal computers and the decreasing cost of communications equipment has resulted in a number of services that are now available to the individual personal computer user. To use these services, all that is required is a personal computer, a modem, communications software, and a phone line (Figure 9-25). These services include home banking, electronic shopping, commercial databases, and electronic bulletin boards.

Home banking, sometimes called electronic banking, allows a user to schedule payments to creditors, make transfers from one account to another, review bank statements and cleared checks, and inquire about current account balances.

Electronic shopping allows a user to select from a catalog of merchandise that the service offers for sale. The catalog is displayed on the user's screen. Theoretically, these items cost no more or cost less than comparable items found in stores because the electronic shopping seller doesn't have to operate a showroom. In addition, an electronic shopper has the added convenience of not having to go out to make the purchase.

Commercial databases offer a wealth of information in hundreds of subject areas. These services are literally electronic libraries containing information on such topics as economics, education, science, law, and a variety of business subjects. One service, NEXIS, offers access

FIGURE 9-25
This person is using a personal computer to schedule checking account payments with a home banking service. This is one of many services that are now available to individual personal computer users.

to the complete text of the *Encyclopaedia Britannica*. CompuServe offers a variety of databases that include information on world and business news, travel, and weather. Dow Jones provides business and financial information including access to the full text of the *Wall Street Journal*. To access commercial databases, users generally pay an initial subscription fee and additional charges based on the amount of use.

Electronic bulletin boards, like their physical counterparts, allow users to post messages on virtually any subject. These bulletin boards are usually maintained by computer clubs or vendors for local users although some have been established for wider use. Some bulletin boards offer members access to public domain software, programs that are available free to anyone who wants to use them. These programs can be **downloaded** or transferred to the user's own personal computer. If the user wants to contribute a program to the public domain software, it is **uploaded** or transferred to the bulletin board system.

SUMMARY OF DATA COMMUNICATIONS

Data communications will continue to have an increasing impact on the way people work and the way they use computers. Individuals and organizations are no longer limited to local data resources but instead, with communication capabilities, can obtain information from anywhere in the world at electronic speed. With data communications technology rapidly changing, today's businesses are challenged to find ways to adapt the technology to provide better products and services for their customers and make their operations more efficient. For individuals, the new technology offers increased access to worldwide information and services, and provides new opportunities for education.

CHAPTER SUMMARY

1. The transmission of data from one computer (or terminal) to another computer over communication channels is called **data communications**.
2. The basic components of a data communications system are: (1) a personal computer or terminal; (2) data communications equipment that sends (and can usually receive) data; (3) the communication channel over which data is sent; (4) data communications equipment that receives (and can usually send) data; and (5) a computer.
3. A **communication channel** is the link or path that the data follows as it is transmitted from the sending device to the receiving device in a data communications system.
4. A communication channel can consist of various **transmission media** including twisted pair wire, coaxial cable, fiber optics, microwaves, and communication satellites.
5. **Twisted pair wire** is the color-coded copper wires that are twisted together and commonly used as telephone wire.
6. **Coaxial cable** is high-quality underground or suboceanic communication lines consisting of a central conductor or wire that is surrounded by a nonconducting insulator and encased in a woven metal shield.
7. Coaxial cable can be either **baseband**, carrying one signal at a time at very high rates of speed, or **broadband**, carrying multiple signals at a time.
8. **Fiber optics** uses technology based on the ability of smooth, hair-thin strands of material that conduct light waves to rapidly and efficiently transmit data.
9. **Microwaves** are high-speed radio transmissions sent through the air between microwave stations.

10. **Communication satellites** are man-made space devices that receive, amplify, and retransmit signals from earth.
11. **Earth stations** are communication facilities that contain large dish-shaped antennas used to transmit data to and receive data from communication satellites.
12. **Line configurations** can be either point-to-point lines or multidrop lines.
13. A **point-to-point line** is a direct line between a sending and receiving device. It may be either a **switched line** (a connection established through regular telephone lines) or a **dedicated line** (a line whose connection between devices is always established).
14. A **multidrop line**, also known as a **multipoint line**, uses a single line to connect multiple devices to a main computer.
15. Computer equipment processes data as **digital signals**, which are individual electrical pulses representing the bits that are grouped together to form characters.
16. **Analog signals** are continuous electrical waves that are used to transmit data over standard telephone lines.
17. A **modem** is a special piece of equipment that converts the digital signals used by computer equipment into analog signals that are used by telephone equipment.
18. There are two modes of transmitting data: **asynchronous transmission mode**, which transmits one character at a time at irregular intervals using start and stop bits, and **synchronous transmission mode**, which transmits blocks of data at regular intervals using timing signals to synchronize the sending and receiving equipment.
19. Transmissions may be classified according to the direction in which the data can flow on a line: sending only (**simplex transmission**); sending or receiving, but in only one direction at a time (**half-duplex transmission**); and sending and receiving at the same time (**full-duplex transmission**).
20. The transmission rate of a communication channel depends on the **bandwidth** and its speed. The wider the bandwidth, the greater the number of signals that can be carried on the channel at one time, and the more data that can be transmitted.
21. **Bits per second (bps)** is the number of bits that can be transmitted in one second.
22. There are three basic types of modems: an **external modem**, which is a separate stand-alone device attached to the computer or terminal by a cable and to the phone outlet by a standard phone cable; an **internal modem**, which is a circuit board installed inside a computer or terminal; and an **acoustic modem** or **acoustic coupler**, which is a device used with a phone handset.
23. A **multiplexor** combines more than one input signal into a single stream of data that can be transmitted over a communications channel.
24. A **front-end processor** is a computer dedicated to handling the data communications requirements of a larger computer.
25. **Communication software** consists of programs that perform tasks such as dialing (software that stores, selects, and dials phone numbers); **terminal emulation** (software that allows the personal computer to imitate or appear to be a specific type of terminal so that the personal computer can connect to specific types of computers); and **data encryption** (software that can code and decode transmitted data for security purposes).
26. A **network** is a collection of terminals, computers, and other equipment that use communication channels to share data.
27. A **local area network (LAN)** is a communications network that covers a limited geographic area and is privately owned.
28. Two common uses of local area networks are **hardware resource sharing**, which allows all network users to access a single piece of equipment rather than each user having to be connected to his or her own device, and **information resource sharing**, which allows the network users to access data stored on other computers in the network.
29. A **wide area network** or **WAN** is a network that covers a large geographical area.
30. Network **topology** describes the pathways by which devices in a network are connected to each other.
31. A **star network** contains a central computer and one or more terminals or computers connected to it, forming a star.
32. In a **bus network** all devices in the network are connected to and share a single cable.
33. A **ring network** has a series of computers connected to each other in a ring.
34. For a personal computer to access other computers through data communications, it must have a modem, communications software, and a phone line.
35. Some of the data communication services available to personal computer users are home banking, electronic shopping, commercial databases, and electronic bulletin boards.

KEY TERMS

Acoustic coupler *9.12*
Acoustic modem *9.12*
Analog signal *9.9*
Asynchronous transmission
    mode *9.10*
Bandwidth *9.11*
Baseband *9.4*
Baud rate *9.12*
Bits per second (bps) *9.12*
Broadband *9.4*
Bus network *9.17*
Coaxial cable *9.4*
Communication channel *9.3*
Communication satellites *9.5*
Communications software *9.14*
Data communications *9.2*
Data encryption *9.14*
Dedicated line *9.7*
Digital signal *9.8*
Downlink *9.5*
Downloaded *9.18*

Earth stations *9.5*
External modems *9.12*
Fiber optics *9.4*
Front-end processors *9.13*
Full-duplex transmission *9.11*
Half-duplex transmission *9.11*
Hardware resource sharing *9.14*
Host computer *9.8*
Information resource sharing *9.15*
Integrated Services Digital
    Network (ISDN) *9.16*
Internal modem *9.12*
Leased line *9.7*
Line configuration *9.6*
Local area network (LAN) *9.14*
Microwaves *9.4*
Modem *9.9*
Multidrop line *9.8*
Multiplexor *9.13*
Multipoint line *9.8*
Network *9.14*

Network control unit *9.15*
Parity bit *9.10*
Point-to-point line *9.7*
Polling *9.13*
Private line *9.7*
Ring network *9.17*
Server *9.15*
Simplex transmission *9.10*
Site license *9.15*
Star network *9.16*
Switched line *9.7*
Synchronous transmission mode *9.10*
Terminal emulation *9.14*
Topology *9.16*
Transmission media *9.3*
Twisted pair wire *9.3*
Uplink *9.5*
Uploaded *9.18*
Wide area network (WAN) *9.16*

REVIEW QUESTIONS

1. Define data communications. What are the basic components of a data communications system?
2. List five kinds of transmission media used for communication channels.
3. Describe the two major types of line configurations. What are the advantages and disadvantages of each?
4. List and describe the three types of data transmission (direction) that are used.
5. Why is a modem used? Describe some of the types of modems available.
6. Describe some of the tasks that communications software can perform.
7. Compare and contrast a local area network and a wide area network.
8. Discuss the reasons for using a local area network.
9. Name three topologies or configurations that are used with networks. Draw a diagram of each.
10. Describe several data communications services that are available to personal computer users.

CONTROVERSIAL ISSUES

1. Some personal computer users have used communication equipment and software to illegally gain access to private databases. These individuals, known as "hackers," often claim that their illegal access was only a harmless prank. Do you think this type of computer usage is harmless? Explain your position.
2. The use of data communications equipment now allows some individuals to work for their company from their homes. These individuals "commute" electronically and do their work via a computer terminal or personal computer connected by a communication channel to their company's main computer. Discuss the advantages and disadvantages of such a working relationship.

CHAPTER 10

Operating Systems and System Software

Operating Systems and System Software

OBJECTIVES

- Define the terms operating system and system software.
- Describe the various types of operating systems and explain the differences in their capabilities.
- Describe the functions of an operating system, including allocating system resources, monitoring system activities, and using utilities.
- Explain the difference between proprietary and portable operating systems.
- Name and briefly describe the major operating systems that are being used today.

W hen most people think of software they think of applications software such as the word processing, spreadsheet, and database software that we discuss in this text. However, for application software to run on a computer, another type of software is needed to interface between the user, the applications software, and the equipment. This software consists of programs that are referred to as the operating system. The operating system is part of what is called the system software.

WHAT IS SYSTEM SOFTWARE?

S ystem software consists of all the programs including the operating system that are related to controlling the operations of the computer equipment. System software differs from applications software. Applications software tells the computer how to produce information, such as how to calculate the correct amount to print on a paycheck. In contrast, some of the functions that system software perform are: starting up the computer; loading, executing, and storing application programs; storing and retrieving files; and performing a variety of utility functions such as formatting disks, sorting data files, and translating program instructions into machine language. The most important part of the system software is the operating system.

WHAT IS AN OPERATING SYSTEM?

All computers utilize an operating system. An **operating system (OS)** consists of one or more programs that manage the operations of a computer. These programs function as an interface between the user, the application programs, and the computer equipment (Figure 10-1).

For a computer to operate, the essential and most frequently used instructions in the operating system must be stored in main memory. This portion of the operating system is called by many different names: the **supervisor, monitor, executive, master program, control program** and **kernel.** The remaining part of the operating system is usually stored on disk and can be loaded into main memory whenever it is needed.

LOADING AN OPERATING SYSTEM

The process of loading an operating system into the main memory of the computer is called **booting** the system. Figure 10-2 shows the steps that occur when an operating system is loaded on a personal computer. While this process is not identical to that used on large computers, the functions performed are similar:

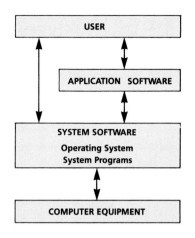

FIGURE 10-1
The operating system and other system programs act as an interface between the user, the application software, and the computer equipment.

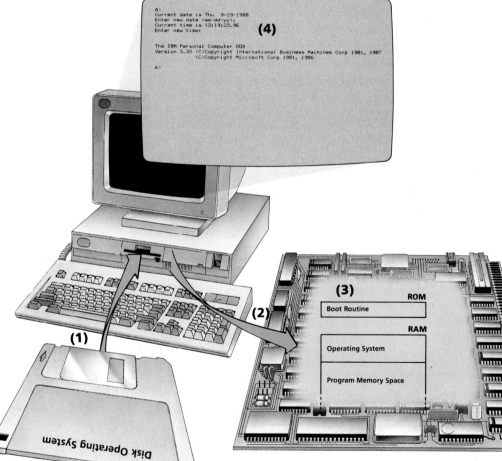

FIGURE 10-2
To load the operating system into a personal computer (1), a copy of the operating system is transferred from the disk (2) and stored in main memory (3). After the user enters the date and time (4), the system prompt (A>) is displayed.

1) multi - tasking -

2) Multi - Programing

1. A floppy disk that contains the operating system is placed in the disk drive. Note that if the operating system was stored on a hard disk, the floppy disk would not be used.
2. When the computer is turned on, the boot routine, which is stored in ROM, issues the commands to load the operating system into main memory. To do this, a copy of the operating system is transferred from the floppy disk or hard disk into main memory.
3. The boot instructions that loaded the operating system transfer control of the computer to the operating system. In many cases, the operating system requests that the user enter the correct date and time, after which the **operating system prompt** is displayed. The prompt indicates to the user that the operating system is ready to accept a command such as to run an application program.

Once the operating system is loaded into main memory, it usually remains in memory until the computer is turned off. The operating system controls the loading and manages the execution of each application program that is requested by the user. When an application program completes its task, the operating system queries the user by displaying the system prompt. The prompt indicates that the operating system is ready to receive a command specifying the next program or operation that is to be performed.

TYPES OF OPERATING SYSTEMS

*T*he various types of operating systems include single program, multiprogramming, multiprocessing, and virtual machine operating systems. These operating systems can be classified by two criteria: (1) whether or not they allow more than one user to use the computer at the same time and (2) whether or not they allow more than one program to run at the same time (Figure 10-3).

	SINGLE PROGRAM	MULTIPROGRAMMING	MULTIPROCESSING	VIRTUAL MACHINE
NUMBER OF PROGRAMS RUNNING	One	More than one	More than one on each CPU	More than one on each operating system
NUMBER OF USERS	One	One or more than one (Multiuser)	More than one on each CPU	More than one on each operating system

FIGURE 10-3
Operating systems can be classified by whether they allow more than one user and more than one program to be operating at one time.

Single Program

Single program operating systems allow only a single user to run a single program at one time. This was the first type of operating system developed. Today, many personal computers use this type of operating system.

Multiprogramming

Multiprogramming operating systems, also called **multitasking** operating systems, allow more than one program to be run at the same time. Even though the CPU is only able to work on one program instruction at a time, its ability to switch back and forth between programs makes it appear that all programs are running at the same time. For example, with a multiprogramming operating system the computer could be performing a complex spreadsheet calculation and at the same time be downloading a file from another computer while the user is writing a memo with the word processing program.

Multiprogramming operating systems on personal computers can usually support a single user running multiple programs. Multiprogramming operating systems on some personal computers and most mini and mainframe computers can support more than one user running more than one program. This version of a multiprogramming operating system is sometimes called a **multiuser-multiprogramming** operating system. Most of these operating systems also allow more than one user to be running the same program. For example, a wholesale distributor may have dozens of terminal operators entering sales orders using the same order entry program.

Multiprocessing

Computers that have more than one CPU are called **multiprocessors**. A **multiprocessing** operating system coordinates the operations of multiprocessor computers. Because each CPU in a multiprocessor computer can be executing one program instruction, more than one instruction can be executed simultaneously. Besides providing an increase in performance, most multiprocessors offer another advantage. If one CPU fails, work can be shifted to the remaining CPUs. The ability to continue processing when a major component fails is called **fault tolerance**.

Virtual Machine

A **virtual machine (VM)** operating system, available on some large computers, allows a single computer to run two or more different operating systems. The VM operating system allocates system resources to each operating system. To users it appears that they are working on separate systems. The advantage of this approach is that an organization can concurrently (at the same time) run different operating systems that are best suited to different tasks. For example, some operating systems are best for interactive processing and others are best for batch processing. With a VM operating system both types of operating systems can be run at the same time.

FUNCTIONS OF OPERATING SYSTEMS

*T*he operating system performs a number of functions that allow the user and the application software to interact with the computer. These functions apply to all operating systems but become more complex for operating systems that allow more than one program run at a time. The functions can be grouped into three areas: allocating system resources, monitoring system activities, and utilities (Figure 10-4).

ALLOCATING RESOURCES	MONITORING ACTIVITIES	UTILITIES
CPU management Memory management Input/output management	System performance System security	File management Sorting

FIGURE 10-4
Operating system functions.

Allocating System Resources

The primary function of the operating system is to allocate the resources of the computer system. These resources include the CPU, main memory, and the input and output devices such as disk and tape drives and printers. Like a police officer directing traffic, the operating system decides what resource will currently be used and for how long.

CPU Management   Because a CPU can only work on one program instruction at a time, a multiprogramming operating system must keep switching the CPU among the different instructions of the programs that are waiting to be performed. A common way of allocating CPU processing is time slicing. A **time slice** is a fixed amount of CPU processing time, usually measured in milliseconds (thousandths of a second). With this technique, each user in turn receives a time slice. Since some instructions take longer to execute than others, some users may have more instructions completed in their time slice than other users. When a user's time slice has expired, the operating system directs the CPU to work on another user's program instructions and the most recent user moves to the "end of the line" to await the next time slice (Figure 10-5). Unless the system has a heavy workload, however, users may not even be aware that their program has been temporarily set aside. Before they notice a delay, the operating system has allocated them another time slice and their processing continues.

APPLICATIONS WAITING TO BE PROCESSED

FIGURE 10-5
With the time slice method of CPU management, each application is allocated one or more fixed amounts of time called slices. Higher priority applications receive more consecutive slices than lower priority applications. When its processing time has expired, an application goes to the end of the line until all other applications have received at least one time slice.

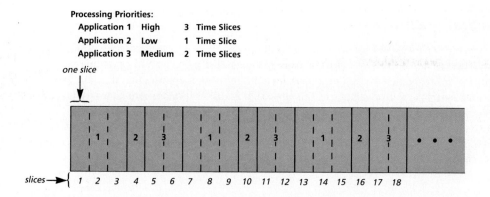

Because some work is more important than other work, most operating systems have ways to adjust the amount of time slices a user receives, either automatically or based on user-specified criteria. One technique for modifying time slices is to have different priorities assigned to each user. The highest priority would receive several consecutive time slices for each time slice received by the lowest priority. For example, it would be logical to assign a higher priority to a program that processes orders and records sales than to an accounting program that could be run at a later time. Another way of allocating time slices is based on the type of work being performed. For example, some operating systems automatically allocate more time slices to interactive processes such as keyboard entry than they do to CPU-only processes such as calculations or batch processing.

Memory Management   During processing, memory is used to store a variety of items including the operating system, application program instructions for one or more programs, data waiting to be processed, and workspace used for calculations, sorting, and other temporary tasks. Data that has just been read or is waiting to be sent to an output device is stored in reserved areas of memory called **buffers**. It is the operating system's job to keep track of all this data by allocating memory.

All operating systems allocate at least some portion of memory into fixed areas called partitions (Figure 10-6). Some operating systems allocate all memory on this basis while others use partitions only for the operating system instructions and buffers. Another way of allocating memory is called virtual memory management or virtual storage.

Virtual memory management increases the effective (or "virtual") limits of memory by expanding the amount of main memory to include disk space (Figure 10-7). Without virtual memory management, an entire program must be loaded into main memory during execution. With virtual memory management, only a portion of the program that is currently being used is required to be in main memory. Virtual memory management is used with multiprogramming operating systems to maximize the number of programs that can be using memory at the same time. The operating system performs virtual memory management by transferring data and instructions to and from memory and the disk by using one or both of the following methods: segmentation and paging.

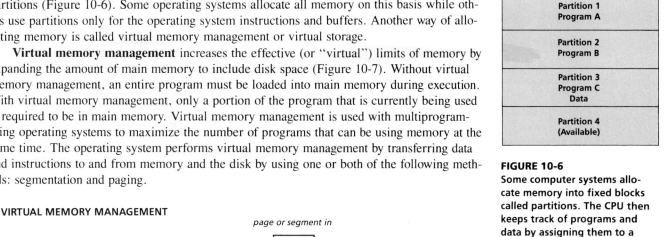

FIGURE 10-6
Some computer systems allocate memory into fixed blocks called partitions. The CPU then keeps track of programs and data by assigning them to a specific partition.

VIRTUAL MEMORY MANAGEMENT

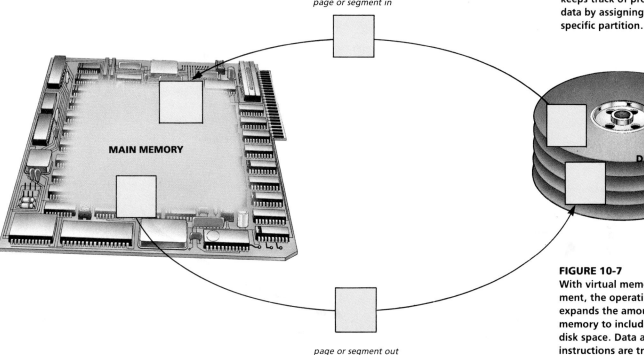

page or segment in

page or segment out

MAIN MEMORY

DISK

FIGURE 10-7
With virtual memory management, the operating system expands the amount of main memory to include available disk space. Data and program instructions are transferred to and from memory and disk as required. The segmentation technique transfers logical portions of programs that may be of different sizes. The paging technique transfers pages of the same size. To make room for the new page or segment, the least recently used page or segment is "swapped," or written back to the disk.

In **segmentation**, programs are divided into logical portions called **segments**. Because the segments are based on logical portions of a program, some segments are larger than others. When a particular program instruction is required, the segment containing that instruction is transferred from the disk into main memory.

In **paging**, a fixed amount of space, generally from 512 to 4K bytes, is transferred from the disk each time data is required. This fixed amount of data is called a **page** or a **frame**. Because a page is a fixed amount of space, it may not correspond to a logical division of a program.

In both segmentation and paging, a time comes when memory is full but another page or segment needs to be read into memory. When this occurs, the operating system makes room for the new data by writing back to disk one or more of the pages or segments currently in memory. This process is referred to as **swapping**. The operating system usually chooses the least recently used page or segment to transfer back to disk.

Input and Output Management   At any one time, a number of different input devices can be trying to send data to the computer. At the same time, the CPU could be ready to send data to an output device such as a terminal or printer or a storage device such as a disk. It is the operating system's responsibility to manage these input and output processes.

Some devices, such as a tape drive, are usually allocated to a specific user or application program. This is because tape is a sequential storage medium and generally it would not make sense to have more than one application writing records to a single tape. Disk drives are usually allocated to all users because the programs and data files that users need are stored on these devices. The operating system keeps track of disk read and write requests, stores these requests in buffers along with the associated data for write requests, and usually processes them sequentially. A printer may be allocated to all users or restricted to a specific user. A printer would be restricted to a specific user, for example, if the printer was going to be used with preprinted forms such as payroll checks.

Because the printer is a relatively slow device compared to other computer system devices, the technique of spooling is used to increase printer efficiency and reduce the number of printers required. With **spooling** (Figure 10-8), a report is first written (saved) to the disk before being printed. Writing to the disk is much faster than writing to the printer. For example, a report that may take half an hour to print (depending on the speed of the printer) may only take one minute to write to the disk. After the report is written to the disk, the CPU is available to process other programs. The report saved on the disk can be printed at a later time or, on a multiprogramming operating system, a print program can be run (at the same time other programs are running) to process the **print spool** (the reports on the disk waiting to be printed).

FIGURE 10-8
Spooling increases both CPU and printer efficiency by writing reports to the disk before they are printed. After the reports are written to disk, the CPU is able to begin processing other programs. Writing to the disk is much faster than writing directly to the printer.

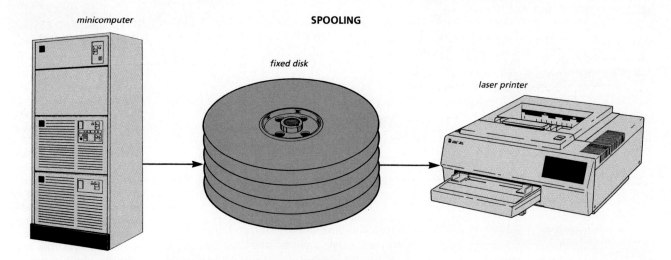

minicomputer   **SPOOLING**

fixed disk

laser printer

Monitoring System Activities

Another function of the operating system is monitoring the system activity. This includes monitoring system performance and system security.

System Performance   System performance can be measured in a number of ways but is usually gauged by the user in terms of response time. **Response time** is the amount of time from the moment a user enters data until the computer responds. Response time can vary based on what the user has entered. If the user is simply entering data into a file, the response time is usually within a second or two. However, if the user has just completed a request for a display of sorted data from several files, the response time could be minutes.

A more precise way of measuring performance is to run a program that is designed to record and report system activity. Among other information, these programs usually report **CPU utilization**, the amount of time that the CPU is working and not idle, waiting for data to process. Figure 10-9 shows a CPU performance measurement report.

Another measure of performance is to compare the CPU utilization with the disk input and output rate, referred to as disk I/O. We previously discussed how a virtual memory management operating system swaps pages or segments from disk to memory as they are needed. Systems with heavy workloads and insufficient memory or CPU power can get into a situation called **thrashing**, where the system is spending more time moving pages to and from the disk than processing the data. System performance reporting can indicate this problem.

System Security   Most multiuser operating systems provide for a logon code, a user ID, and a password that must all be entered correctly before a user is allowed to use an application program (Figure 10-10). Each is a word or series of characters. A **logon code** usually identifies the application that will be used, such as accounting, sales or manufacturing. A **user ID** identifies the user, such as Jeffrey Ryan or Mary Gonzales. The **password** is usually confidential; often it is known only to the user and the data processing manager. The logon code, user ID, and password must match entries in an authorization file. If they don't match, the user is denied access to the system. Both successful and unsuccessful logon attempts are often recorded in a file so that managers can review who is using or attempting to use the system. These logs can also be used to allocate data processing expenses based on the percentage of system use by an organization's various departments.

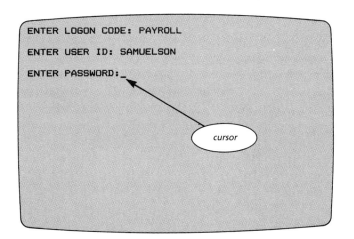

FIGURE 10-9
System performance measurement programs report the amount of time the CPU is actually working and not waiting to process data.

FIGURE 10-10
The logon code, user ID, and password must all be entered correctly before the user is allowed to use the computer. Because the password is confidential, it is usually not displayed on the screen when the user types it in.

Utilities

In addition to allocating system resources and monitoring system activities, most operating systems contain programs called **utilities** that can perform functions such as file management, sorting, and editing. Some of the functions that the file management utility programs can perform include formatting disks and diskettes, deleting files from a disk, copying files from one auxiliary storage device to another, and renaming stored files. Sort utilities are used to place the data stored in files into ascending or descending order based on a value stored in the key field of each record in a file. For example, a sort utility program could be used to sort the records in a personnel file in alphabetical order by the employees' last names. **Editors** allow users to make direct changes to programs and data. An editor would be used by a programmer to change a program instruction that was incorrect or had to be modified.

POPULAR OPERATING SYSTEMS

*T*he first operating systems were developed by manufacturers for the computers in their product line. When the manufacturers came out with another computer or model, they often produced an "improved" and different operating system. Since programs are designed to be used with a particular operating system, this meant that users who wanted to switch computers, either from one vendor to another or to a different model from the same vendor, would have to convert their existing programs to run under the new operating system. Today, however, the trend is away from operating systems limited to a specific model and toward operating systems that will run on any model by a particular manufacturer. For example, part of Digital Equipment Corporation's success in recent years has been attributed to the fact that their VMS operating system is used on all their computer systems. Going even further, many computer users are supporting the move away from **proprietary operating systems** (meaning privately owned) and toward **portable operating systems** that will run on many manufacturers' computers. The advantage of portable operating systems is that the user is not tied to a particular manufacturer. Using a portable operating system, a user could change computer systems, yet retain existing software and data files, which usually represents a sizable investment in time and money. One of the most popular portable operating systems is UNIX, which we will discuss along with the popular personal computer operating system, MS-DOS, and IBM's latest personal computer operating system, O/S 2.

UNIX

The **UNIX** operating system was developed in the early 1970s by scientists at Bell Laboratories. It was specifically designed to provide a way to manage a variety of scientific and specialized computer applications. Because of federal regulations, Bell Labs (a subsidiary of AT&T) was prohibited from actively promoting UNIX in the commercial marketplace. Instead, for a low fee Bell Labs licensed UNIX to numerous colleges and universities where it obtained a wide following. With the deregulation of the telephone companies in the 1980s, AT&T was allowed to enter the computer system marketplace. With AT&T's increased promotion and the trend toward portable operating systems, UNIX has aroused tremendous interest. One of the advantages of UNIX is its extensive library of over 400 instruction modules that can be linked together to perform almost any programming task. Today, most major computer manufacturers offer a multiuser version of the UNIX operating system to run on their computers.

With all its strengths, however, UNIX has not yet obtained success in the commercial business systems marketplace. Some people attribute this to the fact that UNIX has never been considered "user friendly." For example, most of the UNIX program modules are identified by obscure names such as MAUS, SHMOP, and BRK. Other critics contend that UNIX lacks the file management capabilities to support the online interactive databases that more and more businesses are implementing. With the support of most major computer manufacturers, however, these problems are being worked on and UNIX has a good chance of becoming one of the major operating systems of the coming years.

MS-DOS

The Microsoft Disk Operating System or **MS-DOS** was released by Microsoft Corporation in 1981. MS-DOS was originally developed for IBM for their first personal computer system.

IBM calls their equivalent version of the operating system **PC-DOS**. Because so many personal computer manufacturers followed IBM's lead and chose MS-DOS for their computers, MS-DOS quickly became an industry standard. Other personal computer operating systems exist, but by far the majority of personal computer software is written for MS-DOS. This single-user operating system is so widely used that it is often referred to simply as DOS.

OS/2

In 1988, IBM released the **OS/2** operating system for its new family of PS/2 personal computers (Figure 10-11). Microsoft Corporation, which developed OS/2 for IBM, also released their equivalent version, called MS-OS/2. OS/2 is designed to take advantage of the increased computing power of the 80286 and 80386 microprocessors and will only run on systems that use these chips. OS/2 also requires a lot more computing power to operate. For example, OS/2 requires 5MB of hard disk and a minimum of 2MB of main memory just to run the operating system. Additional features offered by OS/2 include the ability to run larger and more complex programs and the ability to do multiprogramming (OS/2 can have up to 12 programs running at the same time).

There are two versions and two editions of OS/2. One of the versions includes the *Presentation Manager*, a graphic windowing environment similar to that available on the Apple Macintosh. The difference between the Standard Edition and the Extended Edition of OS/2 is that the Extended Edition includes database management and communications capabilities.

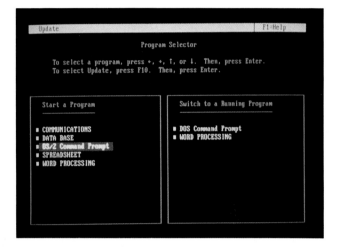

FIGURE 10-11
IBM's OS/2 operating system takes advantage of the increased processing power of the latest personal computer systems.

Other Operating Systems

A number of other popular operating systems exist in addition to the ones just discussed. The Apple Macintosh multiprogramming operating system, currently available only on Apple systems, provides a unique graphic interface that uses icons (figures) and windows (Figure 10-12) that many people find easy to learn and use. The ProDos operating system is used on many of Apple's other computer systems. The PICK operating system is another portable operating system that runs on personal, mini, and mainframe computers. The PICK operating system incorporates a relational database manager and has had much success in the business data processing marketplace. Most mainframe operating systems are unique to a particular make of computer or are designed to be compatible with one of IBM's operating systems such as DOS/VS, MVS, or VM, IBM's virtual machine operating system.

FIGURE 10-12
The Macintosh operating system offers a unique graphic interface and the ability to display information in separate "windows."

SUMMARY OF OPERATING SYSTEMS AND SYSTEM SOFTWARE

S ystem software and the operating system are essential parts of any computer system and should be understood by users who want to obtain the maximum benefits from their computer. This is especially true for the latest personal computer operating systems that include features such as virtual memory management and multiprogramming. Understanding and being able to use these and other features will give users even more control over their computer resources.

CHAPTER SUMMARY

1. **System software** consists of all the programs including the operating system that are related to managing the operations of the computer.
2. An **operating system** consists of one or more programs that manage the operations of a computer.
3. Operating systems function as an interface between the user, the application programs, and the computer equipment.
4. The essential and most frequently used instructions in an operating system are sometimes called the **supervisor** and must be stored in the main memory of a computer for the computer to operate.
5. **Booting** the system is the process of loading the operating system into the main memory of a computer.
6. **Single program** operating systems allow a single user to run a single program at one time.
7. **Multiprogramming** operating systems, also called **multitasking** operating systems, allow more than one program to be run at the same time.
8. A multiprogramming operating system that allows multiple users is called a **multiuser–multiprogramming** operating system.
9. A **multiprocessor** computer has more than one CPU. **Multiprocessor** operating systems coordinate the operations of these computers.
10. A **virtual machine (VM)** operating system allows a single computer to run two or more different operating systems.
11. The functions of an operating system include allocating system resources, monitoring system activities, and utilities.
12. The system resources that the operating system allocates include the CPU, main memory, and the input/output devices.
13. **Time slicing** is a common way for an operating system to allocate the CPU.
14. **Virtual memory management** expands the main memory by using portions of the disk space. With virtual memory management, the operating system transfers data between main memory and the disks by **segmentation** or **paging**.
15. The operating system is responsible for managing the input and output processes of the computer.
16. **Response time** is the amount of time from the moment a user enters data until the computer responds.
17. System performance can be measured by the response time and by comparing the **CPU utilization** with the disk I/O to determine if the system is **thrashing**.
18. System security is monitored by the operating system through the use of **passwords**.
19. Most operating systems contain programs called **utilities** that can perform functions such as file management and sorting.
20. Many computer users are supporting the move away from **proprietary operating systems** and toward **portable operating systems**.
21. Some of the popular operating systems being used today include UNIX, MS-DOS, and OS/2.

KEY TERMS

Booting *10.3*
Buffers *10.7*
Control program *10.3*
CPU utilization *10.9*
Editors *10.9*
Executive *10.3*
Fault tolerance *10.5*
Frame *10.7*
Kernel *10.3*
Logon code *10.9*
Master program *10.3*
Monitor *10.3*
MS-DOS *10.11*
Multiprocessing *10.5*
Multiprocessors *10.5*

Multiprogramming *10.4*
Multitasking *10.4*
Multiuser-multiprogramming *10.5*
Operating system (OS) *10.3*
Operating system prompt *10.4*
OS/2 *10.11*
Page *10.7*
Paging *10.7*
Password *10.9*
Portable operating system *10.10*
Print spool *10.8*
Proprietary operating system *10.10*
PC-DOS *10.11*
Response time *10.8*

Segments *10.7*
Segmentation *10.7*
Single program *10.4*
Spooling *10.8*
Supervisor *10.3*
Swapping *10.8*
System software *10.2*
Time slice *10.6*
Thrashing *10.9*
UNIX *10.10*
User ID *10.9*
Utilities *10.9*
Virtual machine (VM) *10.5*
Virtual memory management *10.7*

REVIEW QUESTIONS

1. Define system software. List some of the functions of system software.
2. Describe how to boot an operating system on a personal computer.
3. List the various types of operating systems and briefly describe their capabilities.
4. The functions of an operating system can be grouped into three areas. What are they?
5. How does an operating system use time slicing?
6. What is virtual memory management?
7. Describe how system performance can be measured.
8. What are three types of authorizations that an operating system uses to provide system security?
9. List several functions that the utilities of an operating system provide.
10. Explain the difference between proprietary and portable operating systems. Name and briefly describe three popular operating systems.

CONTROVERSIAL ISSUE

1. Some users argue that portable operating systems should be avoided because they do not take full advantage of the unique capabilities of a computer. Other users feel that the advantages of using portable operating systems make them a better choice than proprietary operating systems. How do you feel? Be prepared to present your reasons in a class discussion.

RESEARCH PROJECT

1. Visit a computer store and obtain information about the operating systems that are available for personal computers. Prepare a paper on the information you obtained.

CHAPTER 11

Commercial Application Software

Commercial Application Software

OBJECTIVES

- Define commercial application software.
- Describe the difference between general applications and functional applications.
- Describe the difference between horizontal and vertical applications.
- Discuss the factors to be considered in developing or buying application software.
- Discuss each of the five steps of acquiring commercial application software.
- Discuss the information that should be included on a request for proposal (RFP) for application software.
- Identify several sources for commercial application software.

*T*he first computer users had few if any choices when it came to software. If users wanted the computer to perform a specific task, they usually had to develop and write their own computer programs to do the job. Today, however, users have several options when acquiring software. In addition to developing their own software, users may purchase prewritten software packages. Prewritten software is available for computers of all sizes. Most users know about the numerous application packages available for microcomputers. In addition, users should be aware that numerous packages are available for larger machines. This chapter discusses the type of prewritten application software that is available, how to determine your software requirements, and how to acquire the software you need. This information is important to know because it is very likely that some day you will either acquire application software for yourself or participate in software selection for your organization.

WHAT IS COMMERCIAL APPLICATION SOFTWARE?

*C*ommercial application software is software that has already been written and is available for purchase. It may be designed to perform either general or specific tasks. An example of software that performs a general task is word processing. Word processing is considered a "general" task because it can be performed by individuals throughout an organization to create documents. An example of a specific task is medical insurance claim processing. Software that performs this task would only be useful to a company that processes medical insurance claims. Software designed to perform general tasks is called general application software. Software designed to perform specific tasks is called functional application software. In the following sections, we discuss both of these categories in more detail.

general task

GENERAL APPLICATION SOFTWARE

*G*eneral application software provides a way for tasks that are commonly performed in all types of businesses to be done on a computer. These applications are sometimes referred to as **productivity tools** because when they are used, they provide users with a more efficient way to do their work so that they become more productive. There are many popular types of general application software (Figure 11-1). The most common include word processing, spreadsheets, database, and graphics applications. In addition, three others that are commonly used include desktop publishing, electronic mail, and project management.

TYPE	PURPOSE	POPULAR PACKAGES
Word processing	Creates documents	WordPerfect Microsoft Word
Spreadsheet	Manipulates rows and columns of numbers	Lotus 1-2-3 Excel
Database	Stores, organizes, and retrieves data	dBASE III, RBASE
Graphics	Pictorial representation of data	Chart-Master Harvard Graphics
Electronic mail	Transmits electronic messages	Microsoft Mail In Box
Desktop Publishing	Lay out and create documents containing text and graphics	Ventura PageMaker
Project Management	Schedule and track a project's events and resources	Timeline Super Project Expert

FIGURE 11-1
A list of general application software packages. These packages can be used by most organizations and are not limited to a specific type of business.

Review of the Four User Tools

The four user tools described in Chapter 2, word processing, electronic spreadsheets, database, and graphics software, are all examples of general applications software. To review, word processors are used to create documents; spreadsheets are used to manipulate rows and columns of numbers; databases allow data to be stored, organized, and retrieved efficiently; and graphics provide a way of representing data pictorially.

Desktop Publishing

Desktop publishing (DTP) software allows users to design and produce professional-looking documents that contain both text and graphics (Figure 11-2). In business, this software is used to produce documents, such as newsletters, marketing literature, technical manuals, and annual reports, that were previously created by more traditional publishing methods. By using desktop publishing both the cost and time of producing quality documents is significantly decreased.

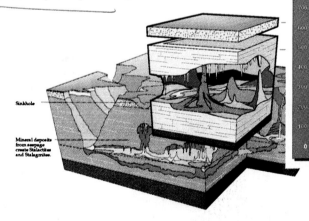

FIGURE 11-2
Desktop publishing software can combine text and graphics to produce documents that previously would have required the work of professional artists and printers. These two illustrations were produced using the Adobe Illustrator™ software programs.

An important feature of desktop publishing is page composition. This means that a user is able to design on the screen an exact image of what a printed page will look like. This capability is called **WYSIWYG**—an acronym for "What You See Is What You Get." Some of the page composition or layout features that are available include the use of columns for text, the choice of different font (type) styles, and the placement and size of art on the page.

The art used in the documents created with desktop publishing usually comes from one of three sources:

1. It can be created on the computer with software that has graphics capabilities, such as software packages that are specifically designed to create graphics, or software such as spreadsheet packages that can create pie, line, and bar charts.
2. A scanner can be used to digitize pictures, photographs, and drawings and store them as files on auxiliary storage for use with desktop publishing software.
3. Art can be selected from "clip art" collections. These are collections of art that are stored on disks and are designed to integrate with popular desktop publishing packages (Figure 11-3).

FIGURE 11-3
Clip art consists of previously created figures, shapes, and symbols that can be added to documents. Users specify the numbers of the piece they want to use.

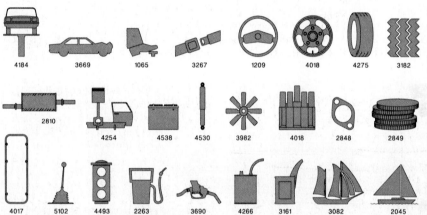

While the text for a document can be created with desktop publishing software, the word processing features of many desktop publishing packages are not as complete as those offered by word processing packages. Therefore, text is usually created with a word processor and then transferred into the desktop publishing package. As new versions of word processing and desktop publishing software are introduced, the capabilities of both applications will increase and the differences between the two applications will decrease. A number of word processing packages now offer desktop publishing features and the word processing features of desktop publishing packages continue to improve (Figure 11-4).

Desktop publishing software is usually executed on a microcomputer with graphics capabilities. Remember from the chapter on Output that graphics capability means that the computer can individually turn on or off the thousands of phosphor dots that make up the display screen. This ability is necessary in DTP to create different sizes and styles of letters and to produce other special DTP effects. Dot matrix and laser printers are used to print the letters and special graphic effects.

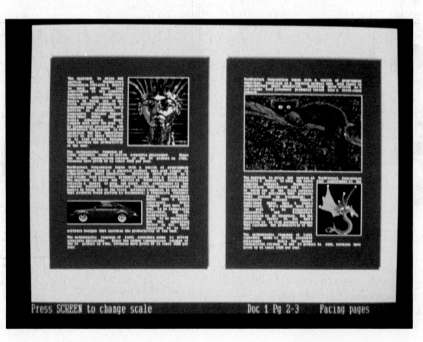

FIGURE 11-4
This document was created using WordPerfect 5.0, which allows graphics to be imported into text.

simple enough to use for anybody in the company

Electronic Mail

Another type of general application software is electronic mail. **Electronic mail** software provides the ability for users to communicate directly with other users by sending text messages electronically over communication channels (Figure 11-5). For example, if the sales manager, Florence Bolduc, wants to send a message congratulating Terry Willis and Sue Rodriguez for closing a recent sale, she would use the electronic mail software to (1) enter the message on her computer, (2) specify that Terry and Sue are to receive the message, and (3) enter a command to send the message. The software places the message in a file referred to as an electronic mailbox. When Terry and Sue use their computers to check for electronic mail, the message from Florence is displayed on their screens. This method of communication is much more efficient than the traditional method of creating and physically delivering a printed document. Correspondence that once took days to reach an individual can now be electronically transmitted from one user to another in seconds.

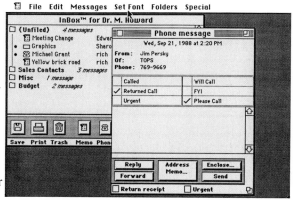

FIGURE 11-5
Electronic mail software allows a user to transmit and receive messages without paperwork. Messages can be saved for future reference or sent back to the sender with a reply.

Project Management

Project management software allows users to plan, schedule, track, and analyze the events, resources, and costs of a project (Figure 11-6). For example, a construction company might use this type of software to manage the building of an apartment complex or a campaign manager might use it to coordinate the many activities of a politician running for office. The value of project management software is that it provides a method for managers to control and manage the variables of a project to help ensure that the project will be completed on time and within budget.

Task ID	Heading/Task	Dur	Actl Dur	Schd Start	Actual Start	Schd Finish	Actual Finish	Oct 88	Nov	Dec	Jan 89	Feb	Mar	Apr
P2	ELM_HIGH.PJ	77	13	10-01-88<	10-01-88	01-18-89								
015	Award	17	13	10-01-88	10-01-88	10-25-88								
001	± Proposal	15	8	10-01-88	10-01-88	10-19-88	10-19-88							
002	± Interview Client	5	0	10-19-88	10-19-88	10-25-88								
003	± Visit Site	1	0	10-19-88	10-19-88	10-19-88								
014	Feasibility	6	0	10-25-88		11-01-88								
004	± Survey Site	1	0	10-25-88		10-26-88								
005	± Concept Meeting	1	0	10-26-88		10-27-88								
006	± Prelim. Design	3	0	10-27-88		11-01-88								
007	± Scale Model	3	0	10-27-88		11-01-88								
012	Design	5	0	11-01-88		11-07-88								
009	± Structure BluePr	2	0	11-01-88		11-03-88								
008	± Interior Design	2	0	11-01-88		11-03-88								
010	± Electrical BlueP	2	0	11-03-88		11-07-88								
011	± Plumb...		0	11-03-88		11-07-88								
013						01-18-89								
						11-18-88								
						11-14-88								

special Tasks

FUNCTIONAL APPLICATION SOFTWARE

Now that we've covered general applications, we'll discuss **functional application software**, software developed to perform a specific task or function.

   With the increasing use of computers, a list of all functional applications might be as long as this book. It's probably safe to say that at least some part of every type of busi-

FIGURE 11-6
This output was prepared using project management software. It shows the individual tasks that make up the project and the elapsed time that each task is scheduled to take.

The following table is a topical list of industry-specific and cross-industry categories of software included in this section. For a [complete list] of software packages, see the Subject/Category Index immediately following this table.

NON-INDUSTRY SPECIFIC

Accounting
Accounting (Basic) N-6
Accounting (Integrated) N-8
Accounts Payable N-24
Accounts Receivable N-42
Billing/Invoicing N-137
Costing N-201
Fixed Assets N-308
General Ledger N-59
Payroll N-572
Tax Preparation & Reporting N-731

Business Administration
Electronic Mail N-247
Office Automation N-548
Personnel Management N-590
Purchasing N-642
Word Processing/Text Editing N-769

Facilities Management
Building Security N-143
Energy Management N-265

Management/Financial A[nalysis]
Decision Support Systems
Financial Planning & Analysis
Financial Planning & Analysis
Financial Planning & Analysis
(Includes standalone spreadsheet
software products with a sp...)
Project Management

Manufacturing
Integrated Systems
Bill of Materials
Computer-Aided Manufactu[ring]
Material Requirements ...
Numerical Control
Process Control
Production Control
Shop Floor Control
Equipment Maintenance &
Other ...

Miscellaneous
Barcode Software N-135
Computer-Based Training N-171
Graphics—Business Applications N-342
Graphics—Utilities & Subroutines N-361
Videotex N-761

INDUSTRY-SPECIFIC

Agriculture N-61

Arts & Humanities N-94

Associations/Membership Organizations
Fund Raising N-327
Political/Non-Profit Organizations N-611
Religious Organizations N-672

Banking/Finance
General N-98
Integrated Banking Systems N-113
Credit Union Management N-115
Deposits & Accounts N-116
Electronic Funds Transfer
Loans & Mortgages
[Credit & Collections]

Legal Services
Docket Scheduling
Practice Management

Manufacturing/Processing
Automotive
Chemicals
Food & Beverage Production/Distribution
Fuel Dealers/Distributors
Lumber & Wood Industries
Metal Industries
Petroleum & Gas
Printing & Typesetting
Textiles & Clothing

Mining & Minerals

Professional Services
Advertising & Public Relations
CPA Services
Professional Time Accounting

Real Estate/Property Management

[Service] Industries

FIGURE 11-7
This is a category listing from an application software catalog that contains information on over 20,000 individual software packages.

ness, government branch, or recreational pastime has been computerized. Figure 11-7 is a category listing from an applications software catalog. Within each category, there are numerous programs available to perform different types of tasks. This catalog contains listings for over 20,000 individual software packages. Notice that this list is divided into two parts: non–industry specific and industry specific. More commonly used terms are horizontal and vertical applications.

Horizontal application software is software that can be used by many different types of organizations. Accounting packages are a good example of horizontal applications because they apply to most organizations. If, however, an organization has a unique way of doing business, then it requires a package that has been developed specifically for that job. Software developed for a unique way of doing business, usually within a specific industry, is called **vertical application software**. Examples of specific industries that utilize vertical software include food service, construction, and real estate. Each of these industries has unique information processing requirements.

The difference between horizontal and vertical application software is important to understand. If you become involved in selecting software, one of the first things you will have to decide is how unique is the task for which you are trying to obtain software. If the task is not unique to your business, you will probably be able to use a horizontal application package. Horizontal application packages tend to be more widely available (because they can be used by a greater number of organizations) and less expensive. If your task is unique to your type of organization, you will probably have to look for a vertical software solution. Often an organization's total software requirements are made up of a combination of unique and common requirements. But before we discuss how to acquire application software, let's discuss if you should consider developing it yourself.

THE DECISION TO MAKE OR BUY APPLICATION SOFTWARE

Each year, the number of application software packages increases. With all that software available, why would an organization choose to develop its own applications? There could be several reasons. The most common reason is that the organization's software requirements are so unique that it is unable to find a package that will meet its needs. In such a case, the organization would choose to develop the software itself or have it developed specifically for them. Application software that is developed by the user or at the user's request is called **custom software**. An example of a requirement for custom software might be a government agency that is implementing a new medical assistance service. If the service has new forms and procedures and is different from previous services, it is unlikely that any appropriate software exists. Another reason to develop rather than buy software is that the new software must work with existing custom software. This is an important point to keep in mind; once an organization chooses to use custom software, it will usually choose custom software for future applications as well. This is because it is often difficult to make custom software work with purchased software. The following example illustrates this point.

Let's say a company that has previously developed a custom inventory control software system now wants to computerize their order entry function. Order entry software packages allow the user to sell merchandise from stock and therefore must work closely with the inventory files. In fact, many order entry systems are sold together with inventory control systems. If the company wants to retain its existing inventory control application, it would probably have a hard time finding a commercial order entry package that would be able to work with its custom inventory files. This is because the software and the file structures used in the commercial package will not be the same as the existing software. For this reason, the company would probably decide to develop a custom order entry application.

Both custom and commercial software have their advantages and disadvantages. The advantage of custom software is that if it is correctly done, it will match an organization's exact requirements. The disadvantages of custom software are that it is "one of a kind," difficult to change, often poorly documented, and usually more expensive than commercial software. In addition, custom software projects are often difficult to manage and complete on time.

The advantage of commercial software is that it's ready to install immediately. After sufficient training, usually provided by the vendor who developed or sold the software, people can begin using the software for productive work. The disadvantage of commercial software is that an organization will probably have to change some of its methods and procedures to adapt to the way the commercial software functions.

A good guideline for evaluating your need for custom or commercial software is to look for a package with an 80% or better "fit" with your requirements. If there is less than an 80% fit, an organization should either consider custom software or reevaluate its requirements. Figure 11-8 shows the most likely software solutions for different application requirements.

APPLICATION CHARACTERISTICS	APPLICATION EXAMPLE	MOST LIKELY SOFTWARE SOLUTION
Applicable to many different types or organizations	Accounts receivable	Horizontal application package
Specific to a particular type of business or organization	Hotel room reservations	Vertical application package
Unique to a specific organization or business	Space shuttle launch program	Custom software

FIGURE 11-8
A guide to the types of functional software applications.

HOW TO ACQUIRE COMMERCIAL APPLICATION SOFTWARE

*T*he first companies to develop commercial application software were the computer manufacturers. Having software to solve specific problems made it easier for them to sell computers. Today, most mini and mainframe computer manufacturers still sell application software, but numerous other sources are available as well. The process of acquiring software involves five steps: (1) evaluating the application requirements, (2) identifying potential software vendors, (3) evaluating software alternatives, (4) making the purchase, and (5) installing the software.

Evaluating the Application Requirements

Evaluating the application requirements is the first and probably the most important step in acquiring commercial application software. Decisions made during this step can determine the eventual success or failure of the software package implementation. The actual evaluation process can and should vary depending on the type of application, how many people will be using it, and how critical it is to the organization. For example, an application to keep track of office supplies is not as critical to an organization as one for processing the payroll. All evaluations should include at least the following steps:

FIGURE 11-9
A transaction volume summary should be prepared to avoid acquiring software that won't handle the projected growth.

1. **Identify the key features of the application.** If the application is an important one, you should prepare a key features list with features that are considered essential to the application. For example, if an organization is a wholesale distributor that makes (or loses) sales based on whether or not it has an item in stock, it would want current inventory status to be part of any order entry program it acquires. Software that only updates the inventory once a day probably would not be acceptable. Therefore, current inventory status should be listed as a key feature.

2. **Determine your current transaction volumes and estimate their growth over the next one to three years.** Figure 11-9 shows a transaction volume summary for an organization's accounts payable application. The figure shows that projected growth over the next year is moderate but increases significantly during the second and third years. This information needs to be considered for both the application software and the equipment that the software will run on. The user would want to be assured that the software and equipment could handle the increased volume of transactions and the corresponding increase in file storage requirements.

MONTHLY VOLUME			
	CURRENT	**1 YEAR**	**3 YEARS**
# of Vendors	50	60	200
# of Invoices	100	120	400
# of Debit Memos	20	25	80
# of Checks	75	100	300

3. **Decide if the software for the new application needs to work with any existing software or equipment.** It may be important that the new application transfer data to or receive data from an existing application. An example would be an accounts payable package that passes data to the general ledger, where all accounting transactions are summarized. In addition, if you already have a particular type of computer, you'll probably want to find software for that system first. On the other hand, if you don't have any equipment, make the decision about the software *first*. It's the software that is the most important element in any system. Choosing the software first is especially important with mini and mainframe systems. Application software for these systems is usually written for a specific manufacturer's computer.

FIGURE 11-10
A request for proposal (RFP) documents the key features that a user wants in a software package.

```
                    REQUEST FOR PROPOSAL
                      ACCOUNTS PAYABLE

                               Standard
Features                       Feature    Comments
--------                       --------   --------

 1.  Interface to general ledger    ✓
 2.  Matching to receiving documents ✓
 3.  Matching to purchasing documents ✓
 4.  Automatic check printing       ✓
 5.  Recurring payments                    PLANNING FOR
                                           NEXT RELEASE
 6.  Flexible payment selection     ✓
 7.  Checking statement reconciliation     WILL DO ON
                                           CUSTOM BASIS
 8.  Consolidated check preparation  ✓
 9.  Duplicate invoice check               NO PLANS FOR
                                           THIS FEATURE
10.  Manual check processing         ✓

Reports

 1.  Vendor listing                  ✓     BY NAME, BUYER
 2.  Invoice register                ✓
 3.  Check register                  ✓
                                           WEEKLY
 4.  Cash requirements               ✓     & MONTHLY
                                           30,60,90,
 5.  Detail aging                    ✓     120 + DAYS
                                           PLANNED FOR
 6.  Form 1099 reports                     NEXT RELEASE
 7.  Account distribution            ✓
 8.  Bank statement reconciliation         WILL DO ON
                                           CUSTOM BASIS
```

One way organizations summarize their software requirements is in a request for proposal. A **request for proposal** or **RFP** is a written list of an organization's software requirements that is given to prospective software vendors to help the vendors determine if they have a product that is a possible software solution. Just as the depth of application evaluations varies, so too do RFPs. RFPs for simple applications may be only a single page consisting of the key features and a transaction volume summary. Other RFPs for large systems may consist of over a hundred pages that identify both key and secondary desired features. An example of a page from an RFP is shown in Figure 11-10.

Identifying Potential Software Vendors

After you have an idea of the software features you want, the next step is to locate potential vendors that sell the type of software you are interested in buying. If the software will be implemented on a personal computer, a good place to start looking for software is a local computer store. Most computer stores have a wide selection of application software and can suggest several alternatives to consider. If you have prepared an RFP, even a simple one, it will help the store representative to narrow the choices. If software is required for a mini or mainframe computer, however, you won't find it at the local personal computer store. For this type of software, which can cost tens to hundreds of thousands of dollars, the best place to start is the computer manufacturer. In addition to having some software themselves, most manufacturers have a list of software companies that they work with—companies that specialize in developing software for the manufacturer's equipment. **Software houses** are businesses that specialize in developing software for sale. **System houses** not only sell software but sell the equipment as well. System houses usually take full responsibility for equipment, software, installation, and training. Sometimes they even provide equipment maintenance, although this is usually left to the equipment manufacturer. The advantage of dealing with a system house is that the user only has to deal with a single company for the entire system.

Another place to find software suppliers, especially for vertical applications, is to look in trade publications, magazines written for specific businesses or industries. Companies and individuals who have written software for these industries often advertise in the trade publications. Some industry trade groups also maintain lists of companies that provide specific software solutions.

For horizontal applications, most computer magazines publish regular reviews of individual packages and often have annual reviews of several packages of the same type. Figure 11-11 shows a software review of an accounting package.

Another way to identify software suppliers is to hire a knowledgeable consultant. Although the fees paid to a consultant will increase the overall software investment, it may be worth it, considering the real cost of making a bad decision. Many consultants specialize in assisting organizations of all sizes identify and implement software packages. A good place to start looking for a consultant would be to contact professional organizations in your industry. Your accountant may also be able to recommend a possible software solution or a consultant.

INFO WORLD THE PC NEWS WEEKLY

REPORT CARD

ACCOUNTING SOFTWARE

PEACHTREE COMPLETE II

VERSION 4.21

Criterion	(Weighting)	Score
Performance	(400)	Good
Documentation	(80)	Excellent
Ease of learning	(40)	Very Good
Ease of use	(120)	Very Good
Error handling	(80)	Very Good
Support		
Policies	(40)	Satisfactory
Technical Support	(40)	Satisfactory
Value	(200)	Excellent
Final score		7.5

PRODUCT SUMMARY

Company: Peachtree Software, 4355 Shackleford Road, Norcross, GA 30093; (800) 247-3224 or (404) 564-5800.
List Price: $199.
Requires: IBM PC or compatible, PS/2 or compatible; 384K of RAM; hard disk; DOS 2.0 or later.
Support: No cost-free support from vendor. Charge: $1 per minute, $20 minimum, with toll-free number; useability warranty; 30-day money-back guarantee (minus $20 charge) if purchased direct from Peachtree.
Pros: Superb value; great manuals; easy to use.
Cons: Reporting capabilities rather inflexible; broad range of modules but shallow in depth; no cost-free support.
Summary: An entry-level accounting package with functions for general ledger, accounts receivable, accounts payable, inventory, job costing, fixed assets, and payroll.

FIGURE 11-11
Many publications regularly evaluate application software. This review also included a narrative discussion of this accounting package.

Evaluating Software Alternatives

After you've identified several possible software solutions, you have to sort them out and choose one. First, match each choice against your original requirements list. Be as objective as possible—try not to be influenced by the salesperson or representative demonstrating the software or the appeal of the marketing literature. Match each package against your list or RFP and give each package a score. If some key features are more important than others, take that into consideration. Try to complete this rating either during or immediately after a demonstration of the package while the features are still fresh in your mind (Figure 11-12).

FIGURE 11-12
You should ask to see a demonstration of any program you are considering purchasing. During or after the demonstration, you should rate how well the package meets your requirements.

The next step is to talk to existing users of the software. For mini and mainframe software packages, software vendors routinely provide user references. For personal computer packages, if the computer store can't provide references, call the software manufacturer directly. User references are important because if a software package does (or doesn't) work for some organization like yours, it probably will (or won't) work for you.

Finally, try the software yourself. For a small application, this may be as simple as entering a few simple transactions using a demonstration copy of the software at the computer store. For large applications, it may require one or more days of testing at the vendor's office or on your existing computer to be sure that the software meets your needs.

If you are concerned about the ability of the software to handle a certain transaction volume efficiently, you may want to perform a benchmark test. A **benchmark test** involves measuring the time it takes to process a set number of transactions. For example, a benchmark might consist of measuring the time it takes a particular software package to produce a sales summary report using 1,000 sales transactions. Comparing the time it takes different packages to perform the same task using the same data and the same equipment is one way of measuring the packages' relative performance.

FIGURE 11-13
A software license grants the purchaser the right to use the software but does not include ownership rights.

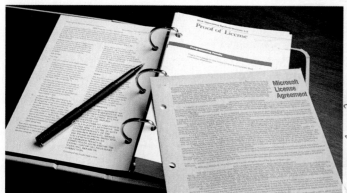

FIGURE 11-14
Most application software comes with detailed installation instructions. Some packages include toll-free telephone numbers in case the user needs to call for assistance. The software seller will also usually offer support.

Making the Purchase

When you purchase software you usually don't own it. What you are actually purchasing is a **software license** (Figure 11-13), the right to use the software under certain terms and conditions. One of the usual terms and conditions is that you can use the software on a single computer only. In fact, some software is licensed to a specific computer and the serial number of the system is recorded in the license agreement. Other license restrictions include prohibitions against making the software available to others (for example, renting it or leasing it) and modifying or translating the software into another language. These restrictions are designed to protect the rights of the software developer who doesn't want someone else to benefit unfairly from the developer's work. For personal computer users, software license terms and conditions usually cannot be modified. But for mini and mainframe users, terms of the license agreements can be modified and therefore should be carefully reviewed and considered a part of the overall software selection process. Modifications to the software license are generally easier to obtain before the sale is made than after.

Installing the Software

After you've acquired the software, the next step is to install it. On small applications this could be a ten-minute task. On large systems, installation of a complete business system could be scheduled over a period of a year or more. Installation includes loading the software on the computer system, training the users, and testing to make sure the software is functioning correctly. Personal computer software can usually be installed by following the instructions in the user manual (Figure 11-14). Mini and mainframe computer software, however, usually requires a written installation plan tailored to the individual organization.

SUMMARY OF COMMERCIAL APPLICATIONS SOFTWARE

This chapter discussed various aspects of commercial applications software including the types of software applications that are available, how to determine your software needs, and how to acquire applications software packages. Whether you need software for personal use or are involved in selecting software for your organization, a knowledge of commercial applications software and how to acquire it is useful.

CHAPTER SUMMARY

1. **Commercial application software** is software that has already been written and is available for purchase.
2. Two categories of commercial application software are general application software and functional application software.
3. **General application software** provides a way for tasks that are commonly performed in all types of businesses to be done on a computer.
4. Software that allows a user to create professional-looking documents that include both text and graphics is called **desktop publishing** software.
5. Page composition, or the ability to design on the screen an exact image of what a printed page will look like, is an important feature of desktop publishing. This capability is called **WYSIWYG**, an acronym for "What You See Is What You Get."
6. **Electronic mail** software provides the ability for users to directly communicate with other users by sending text messages electronically over communication channels.
7. **Project management software** allows users to plan, schedule, track, and analyze the events, resources, and costs of a project.
8. **Functional application software**, developed to perform a specific task or function, can be classified as either horizontal or vertical applications.
9. Software packages that can be used by many different types of organizations, such as accounting packages, are called **horizontal applications**.
10. Software developed for a unique way of doing business, usually within a specific industry, is called **vertical application software**.
11. Application software that is developed by a user, or at the user's request, is called **custom software**.
12. The process of acquiring software involves five steps: evaluating the application requirements, identifying potential software vendors, evaluating software alternatives, making the purchase, and installing the software.
13. Evaluating the application requirements includes: identifying the key features of the application; determining your current transaction volumes and estimating their growth over the next three years; and deciding if the software for the new application needs to work with any existing software or equipment.
14. A **request for proposal** is a written list of an organization's software requirements that is given to prospective software vendors.
15. Identifying potential software vendors for personal computers can usually be done at a local computer store. For larger applications sources include computer manufacturers, **software houses**, **system houses**, trade publications, computer periodicals, and consultants.
16. To evaluate software alternatives, match the features of each possible solution against the original requirements list or RFP.
17. A **benchmark test** involves measuring the time it takes to process a set number of transactions.
18. A **software license** is the right to use software under certain terms and conditions.
19. Installation of the software includes loading the software on the computer system, training the users, and testing to make sure the software is functioning correctly.

KEY TERMS

Benchmark test *11.10*
Commercial application software *11.2*
Custom software *11.6*
Desktop publishing (DTP) *11.3*
Electronic mail *11.5*
Functional application software *11.5*

General application software *11.3*
Horizontal application software *11.6*
Productivity tools *11.3*
Project management software *11.5*
Request for proposal (RFP) *11.8*

Software houses *11.9*
Software license *11.10*
System houses *11.9*
Vertical application software *11.6*
WYSIWYG *11.4*

REVIEW QUESTIONS

1. What is commercial application software? Describe the difference between software that performs a general task and software that performs a specific task.
2. List several types of general applications software. Why are these applications called productivity tools?
3. What does the page composition feature of desktop publishing allow a user to do? What is WYSIWYG?
4. Explain the difference between horizontal and vertical applications.
5. What is custom software and why is it appropriate for some applications?
6. List the five steps in acquiring commercial applications software.
7. Describe the information that an RFP should contain and how the RFP is used.
8. List several ways to find sources for commercial applications software.
9. Describe several things that a user can do to evaluate a software package before purchasing it. What is a benchmark test?
10. What is a software license? Describe some of the terms and conditions that are included in a software license.

CONTROVERSIAL ISSUES

1. Some personal computer users who have purchased application software off the shelf in a computer store have found that learning to use the software has been difficult and time consuming. Many of these users claim that the store that sold the software should provide training on how to use it. While some computer stores do provide limited training, other stores say that training is not their responsibility and explain that they cannot afford to provide training services for customers on all the various software packages that they sell. Do you think that software stores should provide training to customers?
2. Some organizations claim that consultants have saved them considerable sums of money when acquiring application software? Others say that they would have been better off not using a consultant. What role, if any, do you feel a consultant should play in helping an organization to select application software?

RESEARCH PROJECTS

1. Compare the license agreements for three different microcomputer software packages. Prepare a report that discusses the terms and conditions of each license.
2. Visit a store that sells microcomputer software. Select three accounting packages and prepare a report that discusses the features of each package. In the conclusion of your report, state which package you would buy and give the reasons for your selection.

CHAPTER 12

The Information System Development Life Cycle

The Information System Development Life Cycle

OBJECTIVES

- Describe the six elements of an information system: equipment, software, data, personnel, users, and procedures.
- Define the term information system and describe the different types of information systems.
- Explain the five phases of the information system development life cycle: analysis, design, development, implementation, and maintenance.
- Explain the importance of documentation and project management in the information system development life cycle.
- Describe how various analysis and design tools, such as data flow diagrams, are used.
- Explain how program development is part of the information system development life cycle.
- Explain several methods that can be used for a conversion to a new system.
- Discuss the maintenance of an information system.

*E*very day, factors such as competition and government regulations cause people to face new challenges in obtaining the information they need to perform their jobs. A new product, a new sales commission plan, or a change in tax rates are just three examples of events that require a change in the way an organization processes information. Sometimes these challenges can be met by existing methods but other times, meeting the challenge requires an entirely new way of processing data. In these cases, a new or modified information system is needed. As a computer user, either as an individual or within your organization, it is very likely that someday you will participate in the development or modification of such a system. This chapter discusses information systems and how they are developed. To better explain the chapter material, we illustrate each phase of the system development cycle with a case study about the wholesale auto parts division of the Sutherland Company.

WHAT IS AN INFORMATION SYSTEM?

*A*n **information system** is a collection of elements that provide accurate, timely, and useful information. As discussed in Chapter 1, an information system is comprised of six elements: equipment, software, data, personnel, users, and procedures. Each element is important in order to obtain quality information from an information system.

The term information system is frequently used to describe the entire computer operation of an organization, as in a computer information system or the information system(s) department. The term is also used to mean an individual application or "system" that is processed on the computer. For example, an accounting system or an inventory control system can each be thought of as an information system.

Regardless of the scope implied by the use of the term information system, all information systems that are implemented on a computer are comprised of the six elements previously listed. Each element—equipment, software, data, personnel, users, and procedures—contributes to a successful information system and conversely, a weakness in any of these elements can cause an information system to fail. To help ensure success, all six elements should be considered by the people responsible for creating or changing any type of information system.

FIGURE 12-1
Operational systems process the day-to-day transactions of an organization, such as the tax forms that are shown being entered into an IRS computer.

TYPES OF INFORMATION SYSTEMS

*T*he types of information systems that use a computer fall into four broad categories: (1) operational systems; (2) management information systems; (3) decision support systems; and (4) expert systems.

Operational Systems

An **operational system** is designed to process data generated by the day-to-day business transactions of a company. Examples of operational systems are accounting systems, billing systems, inventory control systems, and order entry systems (Figure 12-1).

Management Information Systems

When computers were first used for processing business applications, the information systems developed were primarily operational systems. Usually, the purpose was to "computerize" an existing manual system. This approach often resulted in faster processing, reduced clerical costs, and improved customer service.

Managers soon realized, however, that computer processing could be used for more than just day-to-day transaction processing. The computer's ability to perform rapid calculations and compare data could be used to produce meaningful information for management. This led to the concept of management information systems.

Although the term management information system has been defined in a number of ways, today a **management information system (MIS)** refers to a computer-based system that generates timely and accurate information for the top, middle, and lower levels of management. For example, to process a sales order, the operational system would record the sale, update the customer's accounts receivable balance, and make a deduction from the inventory. In the related management information system, reports would be produced that show slow or fast moving items, customers with past due accounts receivable balances, and inventory items that need reordering. In the management information system, the focus is on the information that management needs to do its job (Figure 12-2).

FIGURE 12-2
Management information systems focus on the summary information and exceptions that managers use to perform their jobs.

Decision Support Systems

FIGURE 12-3
Decision support systems often use graphics to help the user evaluate decision data.

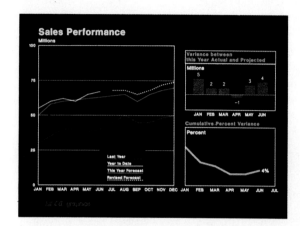

Frequently management needs information that is not routinely provided by operational and management information systems. For example, a vice president of finance may want to know the effect on company profits if sales increase by 10% and costs increase by 5%. This type of information is not usually provided by operational or management information systems. To provide this information, decision support systems have been developed.

A **decision support system** is a system designed to help someone reach a decision by summarizing or comparing data from either or both internal and external sources. Internal sources include data from an organization's database such as sales, manufacturing, or financial data. Data from external sources could include information on interest rates, population trends, or new housing construction. Decision support systems often include query languages, statistical analysis capabilities, spreadsheets, and graphics to help the user evaluate the decision data (Figure 12-3). More advanced decision support systems also include capabilities that allow users to create a model of the factors affecting a decision. A simple model for determining the best product price would include factors for the expected sales volume at each price level. With a model, users can ask "what if" questions by changing one or more of the factors and seeing what the projected results would be. Many people use electronic spreadsheets for simple modeling tasks.

Expert Systems

Expert systems combine the knowledge on a given subject of one or more human experts into a computerized system that simulates the human experts' reasoning and decision making processes (Figure 12-4). Thus, the computer also becomes an "expert" on the subject. Expert systems are made up of the combined subject knowledge of the human experts, called the **knowledge base** and the **inference rules** that determine how the knowledge is used to reach decisions. Although they may appear to "think," the current expert systems actually operate within narrow preprogrammed limits and cannot make decisions based on "common sense" or on information outside of their knowledge base. Expert systems have been successfully applied to problems as diverse as diagnosing illnesses, searching for oil, and making soup. These systems are part of an exciting branch of computer science called **artificial intelligence**, the application of human intelligence to computer systems.

FIGURE 12-4
NEXpert Object is a powerful software tool that allows relatively unsophisticated users to create their own expert system.

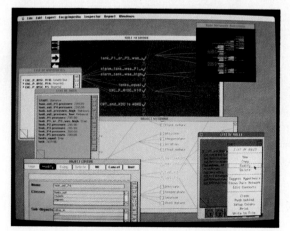

The Integration of Information Systems

With today's sophisticated software, it can be difficult to classify a system as belonging uniquely to one of the four types of information systems. For example, much of today's application software provides both operational and management information system information and some of the more advanced software even includes some decision support capabilities. Although expert systems still operate primarily as separate systems, the trend is clear: to combine all of an organization's information needs into a single integrated information system.

To develop the information systems they need, many organizations use the information system development life cycle.

WHAT IS THE INFORMATION SYSTEM DEVELOPMENT LIFE CYCLE?

*T*he **information system development life cycle (SDLC)** is an organized approach to developing an information system.

Regardless of the type or complexity of an information system, the structured process of the information system development life cycle should be followed whenever an information system is developed. Although some experts group them differently, this chapter divides the activities of the information system development life cycle into five phases.

The Five Phases of the Information System Development Life Cycle

Each of the five phases of the information system development life cycle includes important activities that relate to the development of an information system. The five phases are (Figure 12-5):

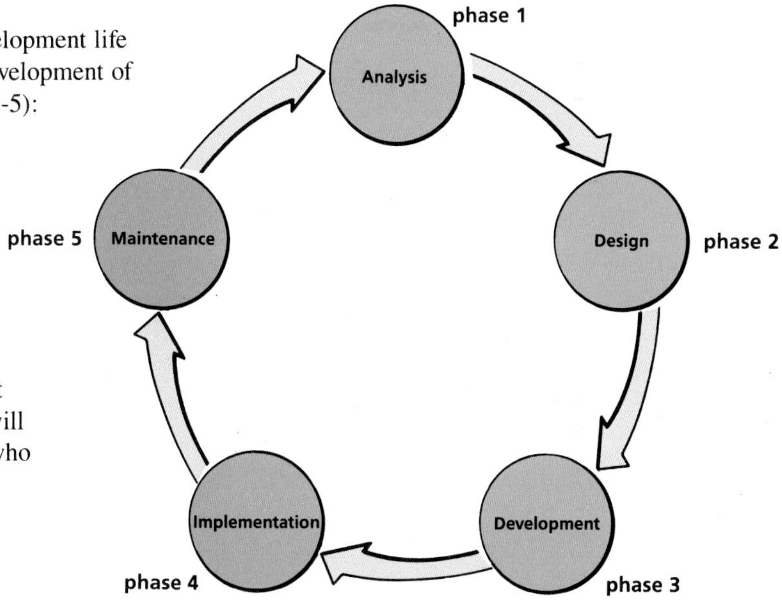

Phase 1 Analysis
Phase 2 Design
Phase 3 Development
Phase 4 Implementation
Phase 5 Maintenance

Before explaining each of the phases, we will discuss project management and documentation because these two activities are ongoing processes that are performed throughout the cycle. In addition, we will identify the information system specialists and users who participate in the various phases of the SDLC.

Project Management

Project management involves planning, scheduling, reporting, and controlling the individual activities that make up the information system development life cycle. These activities are usually recorded in a **project plan** on a week-by-week basis that includes an estimate of the time to complete the activity and the start and finish dates. As you might expect, the start of many activities depends on the successful completion of other activities. For example, implementation (Phase 4) activities can't begin until you have completed at least some, if not all, of the development activities (Phase 3). An effective way of showing the relationship of project activities is with a Gantt chart (Figure 12-6).

FIGURE 12-5
The five phases of the information system development life cycle.

FIGURE 12-6
A Gantt chart is often used in project management to show the time relationships of the project activities.

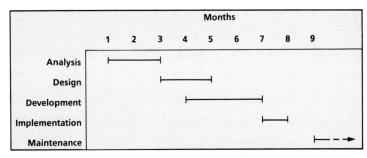

The importance of maintaining a realistic schedule for project management cannot be overstated. Without a realistic schedule, the success of a development project is in jeopardy from the start. If project members don't believe the schedule is realistic, they may not participate to the full extent of their abilities. Project management is a place for realistic and not wishful thinking.

Project management is a task that should be done *throughout* the development process. In most projects, activities need frequent rescheduling. Some activities will take less time than originally planned and others will take longer. To measure the impact of the actual results and revised estimates, they should be recorded regularly and a revised project plan issued. A number of project management software packages are available to assist in this task.

Documentation

Documentation refers to written materials that are produced as part of the information system development life cycle, such as a report describing the overall purpose of the system or layout sheets that are used to design reports and screens. Documentation should be identified and agreed on prior to beginning the project. Well-written, thorough documentation makes it easier for users and others to understand why particular decisions are made. Too often, documentation is put off until the completion of a project and is never adequately finished. Documentation should be an ongoing part of the entire development process and should not be thought of as a separate phase.

Who Participates in the Information System Development Life Cycle?

Every person who will be affected by the new system should have the opportunity to participate in its development. The participants fall into two categories: users and information system personnel such as systems analysts and computer programmers. As discussed in Chapter 1, the systems analyst works closely with both the users and the programmers. The systems analyst's job is challenging, requiring good communication, analytical, and diplomatic skills to keep the development process on track and on schedule. Good communication skills are especially important during analysis, the first phase of the information system development life cycle.

PHASE 1—ANALYSIS

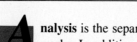 **A**nalysis is the separation of a system into its parts to determine how the system works. In addition, the analysis phase of a development project also includes the identification of a proposed solution to the problems identified in the current system.

A system project can originate in several ways, but a common way is for the manager of a user department, such as accounting or personnel, to contact the information systems department with a request for assistance. The initial request may be oral, but it is eventually written on a standard form that becomes the first item of documentation (Figure 12-7). In most organizations, requests for new system projects exceed the capacity of the information systems department to implement them. Therefore, the manager of the systems department must review each request and make a preliminary determination as to the potential benefit for the company. Requests for large development projects, such as an entirely new system, are often reviewed by committees made up of both user and information systems personnel and representatives of top management. When the managers of both the user and information systems departments determine that a request warrants further review, one or more systems analysts will be assigned to begin a preliminary investigation, the first step in the analysis phase.

The Preliminary Investigation

The purpose of the **preliminary investigation** is to determine if a request justifies further detailed investigation and analysis. The most important aspect of the preliminary investigation is **problem definition**, the identification of the true nature of the problem. Often the stated problem and the real problem are not the same. For example, the investigation of a request for a new accounts receivable report may reveal that the real problem is that customer payments are not being recorded in a timely manner. The existing accounts receivable reports may be fine if the payments are recorded when received instead of once a week. The purpose of the preliminary investigation is to determine the real source of the problem.

The preliminary investigation begins with an interview of the manager who submitted the request. Depending on the scope of the request, other users may be interviewed as well.

The duration of the preliminary investigation is usually quite short when compared to the remainder of the project. At the conclusion of the investigation, the analyst presents the findings to both user and information system management and recommends the next course of action. Sometimes the results of a preliminary investigation indicate an obvious solution that can be implemented at minimal cost. Other times, however, the only thing the preliminary investigation does is confirm that there is a problem that needs further study. In these cases, detailed system analysis is recommended.

```
            REQUEST FOR SYSTEM SERVICES

                                 ISD CONTROL #:  2143

I.  To Be Completed By Person Requesting Services
SUBMITTED BY: MIKE CHARLES    DEPT AUTO PARTS SALES  DATE: 1-22-90
REQUEST TYPE:    [ ] MODIFICATION    [✓] NEW SYSTEM
NEED:         [ ] ASAP   [✓] IMMEDIATE   [ ] LONG RANGE
BRIEF STATEMENT OF REQUEST (attach additional material, if
necessary)
    NEED AUTOMATED ORDER ENTRY AND INVOICING CAPABILITY.
    MANUAL PROCEDURES CAN NO LONGER KEEP UP WITH
    INCREASED SALES VOLUME.

    [ ] ADDITIONAL MATERIAL ATTACHED
===================================================================
II.  To Be Completed By Information Systems Department
REQUEST INVESTIGATED BY: FRANK PEACOCK      DATE: 2-4-90
COMMENTS: MANUAL INVOICING RUNNING 3 DAYS BEHIND
    SHIPMENTS. RECOMMEND DETAILED SYSTEM ANALYSIS FOR
    DEVELOPMENT OF COMPUTERIZED SYSTEM

===================================================================
III.  Disposition
    [✓] REQUEST APPROVED FOR IMMEDIATE IMPLEMENTATION
    [ ] Analyst assigned: MARY RUIZ
    [ ] REQUEST APPROVED FOR IMPLEMENTATION AS SOON AS POSSIBLE
    [ ] REQUEST REJECTED
COMMENTS:

SIGNED: _____      DATE: 2-15-90
```

Detailed System Analysis

Detailed system analysis involves both a thorough study of the current system and at least one proposed solution to any problems found.

The study of the current system is important for two reasons. First, it helps increase the analyst's understanding of the activities that the new system will perform. Second, and perhaps most important, studying the current system builds a relationship with the user. The analyst will have much more credibility with users if the analyst understands how the users currently do their job. This may seem an obvious point, but surprisingly, many systems are created or modified without studying the current system or without adequately involving the users.

The basic fact-gathering techniques used during the detailed system analysis are: (1) interviews; (2) questionnaires; (3) reviewing current system documentation; (4) observing current procedures. During this phase of the system study, the analyst must develop a critical, questioning approach to each procedure within the current system to determine what is actually taking place. Often it is found that operations are being performed not because they are efficient or effective, but because "they have always been done this way."

Information gathered during this phase includes: (1) the output of the current system; (2) the procedures used to produce the output; (3) the input to the current system.

An increasingly popular method for documenting this information is called structured analysis. **Structured analysis** is the use of analysis and design tools such as data flow diagrams, data dictionaries, structured English, and decision tables and trees to document the specifications of an information system.

FIGURE 12-7
The system development project usually starts with a request from a user. The request should be documented on a form such as the one shown here to provide a record of the action taken.

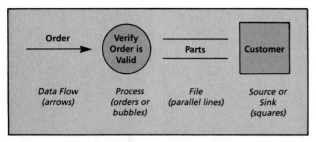

FIGURE 12-8
The symbols used to create data flow diagrams.

Data Flow Diagrams One of the difficulties with the analysis of any system is documenting the results in a way that others can understand. Structured analysis addresses this problem by using graphics to represent the flow of data between processes and files. These graphics are represented by data flow diagrams.

Data flow diagrams (DFD) graphically show the flow of data through a system. The key elements of a DFD (Figure 12-8) are arrows or vectors called data flows, representing data; circles (also called "bubbles") representing processes, such as verifying an order or creating an invoice; parallel lines representing data files; and squares, called sources or sinks, that represent either or both an originator or a receiver of data, such as a customer. Because they are visual, DFDs are particularly useful for reviewing the existing or proposed system with the user. (See Figure 12-9).

FIGURE 12-9
Data flow diagrams (DFD) are used to graphically illustrate the flow of information through a system. The customer (box) both originates and receives data (arrows). The circles indicate where actions take place on the data. Files are shown as parallel lines.

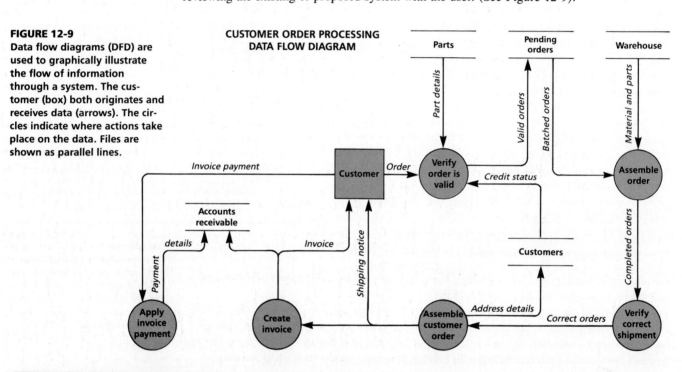

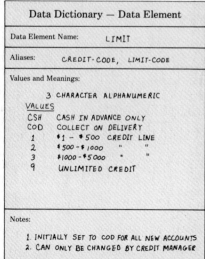

Data Dictionaries The **data dictionary** describes the elements that make up the data flow. Elements can be thought of as equivalent to fields in a record. The data dictionary (Figure 12-10) includes information about the attributes of an element, such as length; where the element is used (what files and data flows include the element); and any values or ranges the element might have, such as a value of 2 for a credit limit code to indicate a purchase limit of $1,000.00. The data dictionary is created in the analysis phase and is used in all subsequent phases.

FIGURE 12-10
The data dictionary is used to document the elements that are included in the data flows. This illustration shows the information on length, type of data, and possible values that is recorded for each data element in the dictionary.

Structured English   Process specifications document what action is taken on the data flows. Referring to the DFD in Figure 12-9, process specifications will describe what goes on in each of the circles. One way of writing process specifications is to use **structured English**, a style of writing and presentation that highlights the alternatives and actions that are part of the process. Figure 12-11 shows an example of a structured English process specification describing a policy for order processing.

```
If the order amount exceeds $1,000,
      If customer has any unpaid invoices over 90 days old,
         Do not issue order confirmation,
         Write message on order reject report.
      Otherwise (account is in good standing),
         Issue order confirmation.
Otherwise (order is $1,000 or less),
      If customer has any unpaid invoices over 90 days old,
         Issue order confirmation,
         Write message on credit follow-up report.
      Otherwise (account is in good standing),
         Issue order confirmation.
```

Decision Tables and Decision Trees   Another way of documenting the system during the analysis phase is with a decision table or decision tree. A **decision table** or **decision tree** identifies the actions that should be taken under different conditions. Figures 12-12 and 12-13 show a decision table and decision tree for the order processing policy described with structured English in Figure 12-11. Decision tables and trees are an excellent way of showing the desired action when the action depends on multiple conditions.

	Rules			
	1	2	3	4
Conditions				
1. Order > $1,000	Y	Y	N	N
2. Unpaid invoices over 90 days old	Y	N	Y	N
Actions				
1. Issue confirmation	N	Y	Y	Y
2. Reject order	Y	N	N	N
3. Credit follow-up	N	N	Y	N

FIGURE 12-11▲
Structured English is an organized way of describing what actions are taken on data. This structured English example describes an order processing policy.

◄FIGURE 12-12
Decision tables help a user quickly determine the course of action based on two or more conditions. This decision table is based on the order processing policy described in Figure 12-11. For example, if an order is $1,000 or less and the customer has an unpaid invoice over 90 days old, the policy is to issue an order confirmation but to perform a credit follow-up on the past due invoice.

Making the Decision on How To Proceed

Just as at the completion of the preliminary investigation, at the completion of the analysis phase, the user, systems analyst, and management face another decision on how to proceed. At this point the analyst should have completed a study of the current system and, using the same tools and methods, developed one or more proposed solutions to the current system's identified problems. Sometimes the systems analyst is asked to prepare a feasibility study and a cost/benefit analysis. These two reports are often used together. The **feasibility study** discusses whether the proposed solution is practical and capable of being accomplished. The **cost/benefit analysis** identifies the estimated costs of the proposed solution and the benefits (including potential cost savings) that are expected. If there are strong indications at the beginning of the project that some type of new system will be developed, the feasibility study and cost/benefit analysis are sometimes performed as part of the preliminary investigation.

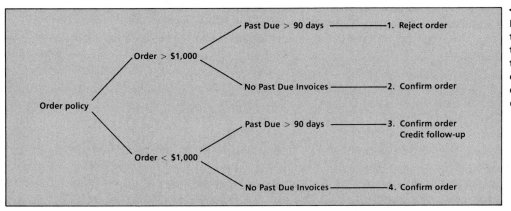

◄FIGURE 12-13
Like a decision table, a decision tree illustrates the action to be taken based on the given conditions, but presents it graphically. This decision tree is based on the order processing policy described in Figure 12-11.

DATE: April 1
TO: Management Review Committee
FROM: George Lacey, Corporate Systems Manager
SUBJECT: Detailed Investigation and Analysis of Order Entry System

Introduction

A detailed system investigation and analysis of the order entry system
was conducted as a result of approval given by the Management Review
Committee on March 1. The findings of the investigation are presented
below.

Objectives of Detailed Investigation and Analysis

The study was conducted to investigate two major complaints of the
wholesale auto parts order entry system. Complaints have been received
that orders were not being shipped promptly, and customers were not
notified of out-of-stock conditions for many days after sending in
orders. In addition, billing invoices are running several days behind
shipments. The objective of this study was to determine where the
problems existed and to develop alternative solutions.

Findings of the Detailed Investigation and Analysis

The following problems appear to exist within the order entry system:

2. Place the order entry and invoicing systems on the computer. Computer
   terminals would be installed in the sales department for order entry
   clerks. As orders are received, they would be entered into the
   computer. Orders could be immediately edited for proper customer and
   part numbers and a check could be made to determine if stock is
   available. Billing invoices could be mailed the same day as
   shipments. Estimated costs: (1) Systems analysis and
   design–$26,000; (2) Programming and implementation–$40,000; (3)
   Training, new forms, and maintenance–$7,000; (4) Equipment (four
   terminals)–$6,000.

Recommended Action

The systems department recommends the design of a computerized order
entry and invoicing system utilizing alternative 2, which is believed to
offer the most effective solution.

George Lacey

FIGURE 12-14
Written reports summarizing the analyst's work are an important part of the development project. This report was prepared at the end of the analysis phase and recommends the development of a computerized order entry and invoicing system.

The results of the analyst's work are presented in a written report (Figure 12-14) to both user and information systems management who consider the alternatives and the resources, such as time, people, and money, of the organization. The end of the analysis phase is usually where organizations decide either to acquire commercial software from an outside source, contract outside the organization for system development, or develop the system internally. If a decision is made to proceed, the project enters the design phase.

PHASE 1—ANALYSIS AT SUTHERLAND

*T*he Sutherland Company is a large corporation with separate divisions that sell tools, electric motors, and auto parts, respectively. Although the tool and electric motor divisions have been computerized for some time, the low sales volume of the auto parts division, started just two years ago, enabled it to rely on manual procedures. In the last six months, however, auto parts sales doubled and the manual order entry and invoicing systems were unable to keep up with the increased workload.

Because he believed the increased sales volume would continue, Mike Charles, the auto parts sales manager, turned in a request for system services to the information systems department that provided computer services for all three Sutherland divisions. Frank Peacock, a systems analyst, was assigned to investigate the request.

As part of the preliminary investigation, Frank interviewed Mike to try to determine the problem. During his interview with Mike and a subsequent tour of the auto parts sales department, Frank discovered that invoices were not being sent to customers until three days after their parts orders had shipped. In addition, Frank found that customers were complaining about shipments being late and about not being notified when parts they ordered were not available. As a result of his preliminary investigation, Frank recommended a detailed system analysis. George Lacey, the corporate systems manager, agreed with Frank's recommendation and assigned systems analyst Mary Ruiz.

Mary reviewed Frank's notes and began to perform a detailed analysis of the auto parts order entry and invoicing systems. As part of her study, Mary interviewed several people in the auto parts division and prepared several documents including a data flow diagram (Figure 12-9), a data dictionary definition for the different credit limits assigned to customers (Figure 12-10), and a structured English statement of the order processing policy (Figure 12-11).

After studying the manual procedures for a week, Mary discussed her findings with her supervisor, George Lacey. Based on Mary's work, George wrote a report to the management review committee recommending that the order entry and invoicing systems be computerized. The report contained two alternative solutions, one utilizing a separate minicomputer system and the other, considered the most effective solution, utilizing terminals connected to the company's central computer. The management review committee meets every month to review requests for additional computer equipment and software. The committee is made up of top management representatives from each division, the finance department, and the information systems department. Based on George's report, the management review committee authorized the corporate systems department to design a computerized order entry and invoicing system.

PHASE 2—DESIGN

*T*he proposed solution developed as part of the analysis phase usually consists of what is called a **logical design**, which means that the design was deliberately developed without regard to a specific computer or programming language and no attempt was made to identify which procedures should be automated and which procedures should be manual. This approach avoids early assumptions that may limit the possible solutions. During the **design** phase the logical design will be transformed into a **physical design** that will identify the procedures to be automated, choose the programming language, and specify the equipment needed for the system.

Structured Design Methods

The system design usually follows one of two methods, top-down design or bottom-up design.

Top-Down Design   **Top-down design**, also called **structured design**, focuses on the major functions of the system, such as recording a sale or generating an invoice, and keeps breaking those functions down into smaller and smaller activities, sometimes called modules, that can eventually be programmed. Top-down design is an increasingly popular method because it focuses on the "big picture" and helps users and systems analysts reach an early agreement on what the major functions of the new system are.

Bottom-Up Design   **Bottom-up design** focuses on the data, particularly the output of the system. The approach used is to determine what output is needed and move "up" to the processes needed to produce the output.

In practice, most system analysts use a combination of the two methods. Some information requirements like payroll checks, for example, have data elements that lend themselves to bottom-up design. Other requirements, such as management-oriented exception reports, are better suited to a top-down design.

Regardless of the structured design method used, the system analyst will eventually need to complete the design activities.

Design Activities

Design activities include a number of individual tasks that a system analyst performs to design an information system. These include designs for the output, input, database, processes, system controls, and testing.

Output Design   The design of the output is critical to the successful implementation of the system because it is the output that provides the information to the users and that is the basis for the justification of most computerized systems. For example, most users don't know (or necessarily care) how the data will be processed, but they usually do have clear ideas on how they want the information output to look. Often requests for new or modified systems begin with a user-prepared draft of a report that the current system doesn't produce. During **output design**, the system analyst and the user document specific screen and report layouts that will be used for output to display or report information from the new system. The example in Figure 12-15 illustrates a report layout sheet.

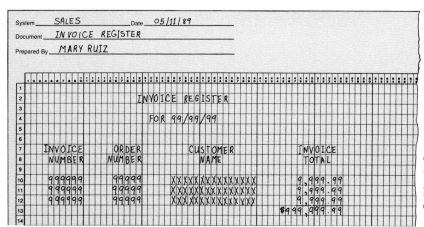

FIGURE 12-15
The report layout form is used to design printed output. Column titles, data width, and report totals are shown on the layout form.

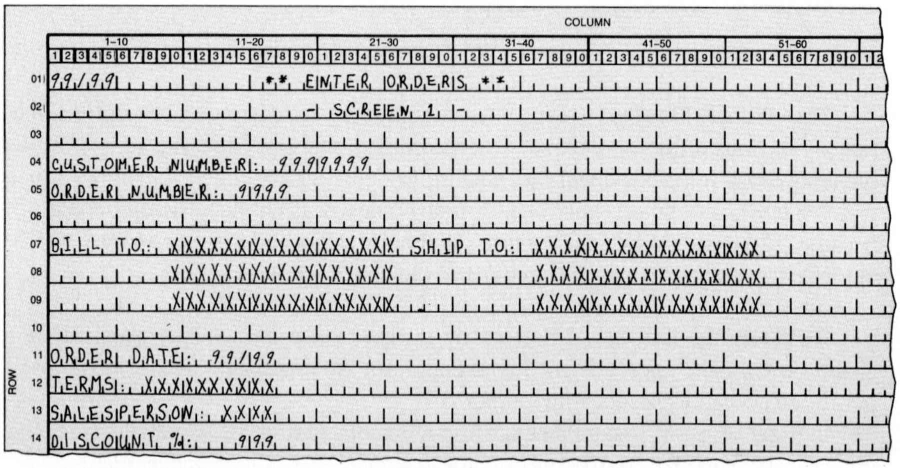

FIGURE 12-16
The display screen layout sheet is similar to the report layout form. Each row and column correspond to a row and column on the screen.

Input Design During **input design** the analyst and user identify what information needs to be entered into the system to produce the desired output and where and how the data will be entered. With interactive systems, the systems analyst and user must determine the sequence of inputs and computer responses, called a **dialogue**, that the user will encounter when entering data. Figure 12-16 shows a display screen layout sheet commonly used to document the format of a screen display.

Database Design During **database design** the systems analyst uses the data dictionary information developed during the analysis phase and merges it into new or existing system files. During this phase of the design, the analyst works closely with the database administrator to identify existing database elements that can be used to satisfy design requirements.

Efficient file design can be a challenging task, especially with relational database systems that stress minimum data redundancy (duplicate data). The volume of database activity must also be considered at this point. For example, large files that will be frequently accessed may need a separate index file (discussed in Chapter 8) to allow inquiries to be processed in an amount of time acceptable to the user.

Process Design During **process design** the system analyst specifies exactly what actions will be taken on the input data to create output information. Decisions on the timing of actions are added to the logical processes identified in the analysis phase. For example, the analysis phase might have found that an exception report should be produced if inventory balances fall below a certain level. During the process design phase, the frequency of the report would be determined.

One way to document the relationship of different processes is with a **system flowchart** (Figure 12-17). The system flowchart shows the major processes (each of which may require one or more programs), reports (including their distribution), data files, and the types of input devices such as terminals or tape drives, that will provide data to the system. The special symbols used in a system flowchart are shown in Figure 12-18.

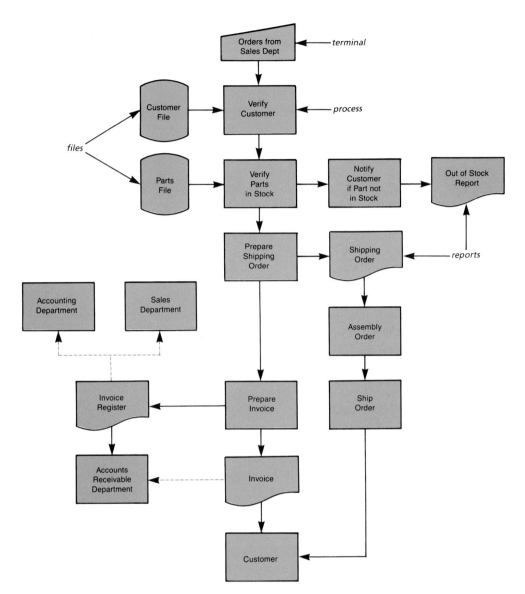

FIGURE 12-17
The system flowchart documents the equipment used to enter data, such as the terminals for the salespeople and the order department, the processes that will take place, such as ''Verify Customer,'' the files that will be used, such as the Parts and Customer files, and the reports that will be produced, such as the shipping order. Dotted lines indicate additional copies of reports, such as the copy of the invoice that is sent to the accounts receivable department.

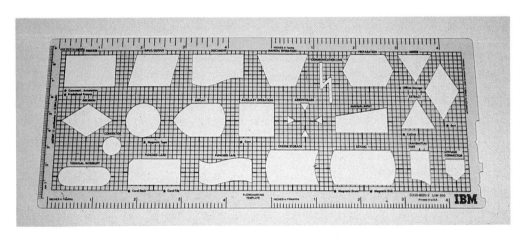

FIGURE 12-18
Symbols used for preparing a system flowchart.

During process design the system analyst, the user, and other members of the development project sometimes meet to conduct a **structured walkthrough**, a step-by-step review of the process design. The purpose of these sessions is to identify any design logic errors and to continue the communication between the systems analyst and the user.

System Controls   An important aspect of the design phase is the establishment of a comprehensive set of system controls. **System controls** ensure that only valid data is accepted and processed. Adequate controls must be established for two basic reasons: (1) to ensure the accuracy of the processing and the information generated from the system; (2) to prevent computer-related fraud.

There are four basic types of controls that must be considered by the systems analyst. These controls are: (1) source document controls; (2) input controls; (3) processing controls; (4) accounting controls.

Source document controls include serial numbering of input documents such as invoices and paychecks, document registers in which each input document is recorded and time-stamped as it is received, and batch totaling and balancing to predetermined totals to assure the accuracy of processing.

Input controls are established to assure the complete and accurate conversion of data from the source documents or other sources to a machine-processable form. Editing data as it enters the system is the most important form of input controls.

Processing controls refer to procedures that are established to determine the accuracy of information after it has been input to the system. For example, the accuracy of the total accounts receivable could be verified by taking the prior day's total, adding the current day's sales invoices, and subtracting the current day's payments.

Accounting controls provide assurance that the dollar amounts recorded in the accounting records are correct. An important accounting control is an audit trail. An **audit trail** is one or more reports that provide a history of how transactions have been summarized before they are recorded in the general ledger. For example, an audit trail for sales would include a daily sales register that shows each individual sale transaction, a monthly sales journal that shows the total sales for each day, and the general ledger that has an entry for total sales for the month. With an audit trail, a user can trace any summary entry in the general ledger back to the individual transactions that make it up.

Testing Design   During the design phase, test specifications are developed. The exact tests to be performed should be specified by someone other than the user or the systems analyst, although both should be consulted. Users and systems analysts have a tendency to test only what has been designed. An impartial third party, who has not been actively involved in the design, is more likely to design a test for, and therefore discover, a procedure or type of data that may have been overlooked in the design. Sometimes organizations avoid test design and test their systems with actual transactions. While such "live" testing is valuable, it might not test all conditions that the system is designed to process. This is especially true of error or exception conditions that do not occur regularly. For example, payroll systems are usually designed to reject input for hours worked over some limit, say 60 hours in a week. If only actual data are used to test the system, this limit may not be tested. Thus it is important to design testing specifications that will test each system control that is part of the system.

Design Review

At the end of the design phase, management performs a **design review** and evaluates the work completed so far to determine whether or not to proceed (Figure 12-19). This is a critical point in any development project and all parties must take equal responsibility for the decision.

Usually the design review will result only in requests for clarification of a few items. But sometimes an entire project may be terminated. Although canceling or restarting a project from the beginning is a difficult decision, in the long run it is less costly than implementing the wrong or an inadequate solution. If the decision is made to proceed, the project enters the development phase. Before discussing the development phase, we describe prototyping, a development method that can be used in several phases of a system development project.

Prototyping

Prototyping is building a working model of the new system. The advantage of prototyping is that it lets the user actually experience the system before it is completed. Some organizations use prototyping during the analysis phase, others use it during the design phase. Still other companies use prototyping to go directly from preliminary investigation to an implemented system. These companies just keep refining the prototype until the user says that it is acceptable. The disadvantage of such an accelerated approach is that key features of a new system, especially exception conditions, may be overlooked. Another disadvantage is that documentation, an important part of any system development effort, is usually not as well or as thoroughly prepared. When used as a tool to show the user how the system will operate, however, prototyping can be an important system development tool.

FIGURE 12-19
The design review is a critical point in the development process. Representatives from the user and information systems departments and top management meet to determine if the system should be developed as designed or if additional design work is necessary.

PHASE 2—DESIGN AT SUTHERLAND

*U*pon approval by the management review committee, Mary Ruiz began designing the order entry and invoicing system. After studying existing manually prepared documents and talking to users, Mary designed printed reports and screen displays. According to Mike Charles, one of the most important reports is the daily invoice register. Using a report layout form (Figure 12-15), Mary showed Mike what the report would look like after it was programmed. Using a similar form for screen displays (Figure 12-16), Mary also showed Mike what the order clerks would see when they enter auto parts orders. To graphically show how the overall system would work, Mary prepared a system flowchart (Figure 12-17). The system flowchart showed that auto parts orders would be entered on terminals in the sales department and would use data in the Parts and Customer files to verify that the orders were valid. Shipping orders and invoices were two of the reports produced. An important part of Mary's design time involved specifying the system controls used during processing. These controls included verifying the customer number before processing the order and checking to see if the ordered part is in stock. If the ordered part is not in stock, the customer is notified immediately.

After completing her design work, Mary met with representatives from the user and information systems departments and top management to review her design. After Mary explained the design, the committee agreed to develop the system.

PHASE 3—DEVELOPMENT

*O*nce the system design phase has been completed, the project enters the system development phase. There are two parts to **development**: program development and equipment acquisition.

Program Development

The process of developing the software, or programs, required for a system is called **program development** and includes the following steps: (1) reviewing the program specifications; (2) designing the program; (3) coding the program; (4) testing the program; and (5) finalizing the program documentation. The primary responsibility for completing these tasks is assumed by computer programmers who work closely with the system analyst who designed the system. Chapter 13 explains program development in depth. The important concepts to understand now are that this process is a part of the development phase of the information system life cycle and that its purpose is to develop the software required by the system.

Equipment Acquisition

During the development phase, final decisions will be made on what additional equipment, if any, will be required for the new system. A preliminary review of the equipment requirements would have been done during the analysis phase and included in the written report prepared by the systems analyst. Making the equipment acquisition prior to the development phase would be premature because any equipment selected should be based on the requirements of the approved design from Phase 2. Equipment selection is affected by factors such as the number of users who will require terminals and the disk storage that will be required for new files and data elements. In some cases, even a new or upgraded CPU is required.

PHASE 3—DEVELOPMENT AT SUTHERLAND

*D*uring the development phase, Mary worked closely with the two programmers who were assigned to the project. She regularly met with the programmers to answer questions about the design and to check on the progress of their work. Prior to starting the programming, Mary arranged for the programmers to meet with the auto parts sales employees so that the programmers would have a better understanding of the purpose of the new system.

When the programming was close to completion, Mary arranged for the terminals to be installed in the sales department.

PHASE 4—IMPLEMENTATION

*I*mplementation is the phase of the system development process when people actually begin using the new system. This is a critical phase of the project that usually requires careful timing and the coordination of all project participants. Important parts of this phase that will contribute to the success of the new system are training and education, conversion, and postimplementation evaluation.

Training and Education

Someone once said, "If you think education is expensive, you should consider the cost without it." The point is that untrained users can prevent the estimated benefits of a new system from ever being obtained or worse, contribute to less efficiency and more costs than when the old system was operational. Training consists of showing people exactly how they will use the new system (Figure 12-20). This may include classroom-style lectures but should definitely include hands-on sessions with the equipment they will be using, such as terminals, and realistic sample data. Education consists of learning new principles or theories that help people to understand and use the system. For example, before implementing a modern manufacturing system, many companies now require their manufacturing personnel to attend classes on material requirements planning (MRP), shop floor control, and other essential manufacturing topics.

Conversion

Conversion refers to the process of changing from the old system to the new system. A number of different methods of conversion may be used including direct, parallel, phased, and pilot.

With **direct conversion**, the user stops using the old system one day and begins using the new system the next. The advantage of this approach is that it is fast and efficient. The disadvantage is that it is risky and can seriously disrupt operations if the new system does not work correctly the first time.

Parallel conversion consists of continuing to process data on the old system while some or all of the data is also processed on the new system. Results from both systems are compared, and if they agree, all data is switched to the new system (Figure 12-21).

Phased conversion is used with larger systems that can be broken down into individual modules that can be implemented separately at different times. An example would be a complete business system that could have the accounts receivable, inventory, and accounts payable modules implemented separately in phases. Phased conversions can be direct, parallel, or a combination of both.

Pilot conversion means that the new system will be used first by only a portion of the organization, often at a separate location such as a plant or office.

Postimplementation Evaluation

After a system is implemented, it is important to conduct a **postimplementation evaluation** to determine if the system is performing as designed, if operating costs are as anticipated, and if any modifications are necessary to make the system operate more effectively.

PHASE 4—IMPLEMENTATION AT SUTHERLAND

*B*efore they began using the new system to enter real transactions, the users participated in several training sessions about the equipment and the software. Because this was the first application in the auto parts division to be computerized, Mary began the training sessions with an overview of how the central computer system processes data. She conducted a basic data entry class to teach the employees how to use the terminals (Figure 12-20).

FIGURE 12-20
All users should be trained on the system before they have to use it to process actual transactions. Training could include both classroom and hands-on sessions.

FIGURE 12-21
During parallel conversion, the user compares results from both the old and the new system to determine if the new system is operating properly.

Before the system could be used, the Parts and Customer files had to be created from existing manual records. Temporary employees trained in data entry skills were hired for this task. Their work was carefully reviewed each day by Mike Charles and other permanent department employees.

Although he knew it would mean extra work, Mike decided that a parallel conversion would be the safest way to implement the new system. Using this method, Mike could verify the results of the new system with those of the existing manual system. Actual use of the system began on the first business day of the month so that transaction totals could be balanced to accounting reports.

Because they were thoroughly trained, the order clerks felt comfortable when they began entering real orders. A few minor problems were encountered, such as orders for special parts that were not on the Parts file. These errors became less frequent and at the end of the month, after comparing manual and computerized report totals, Mike decided to discontinue the use of the manual system.

During the postimplementation review, Mike and Mary discovered that nine out of ten customer orders were now shipped the same day as the order was received. Before the new system was implemented, less than half the orders were shipped within two days of receipt. Invoices, which once lagged three days behind shipments, were now mailed on the same day. Perhaps the most positive benefit of the new system was that customer complaints about order processing were practically eliminated.

PHASE 5—MAINTENANCE

Maintenance is the process of supporting the system after it is implemented. Maintenance consists of three activities: performance monitoring, change management, and error correction.

Performance Monitoring

Performance monitoring is the ongoing process of comparing response times, file sizes, and other system performance measures against the estimates that were prepared during the analysis, design, and implementation phases. Variances from these estimates may indicate that the system requires additional equipment resources, such as more memory or faster disk drives.

Change Management

Change is an inevitable part of any system and should be provided for with methods and procedures that are made known to all users of the system. Sometimes changes are required because existing requirements were overlooked. Other times, new information requirements caused by external sources such as government regulations will force change. A key part of change management is documentation. The same documentation standards that were followed during the analysis and design phases should also be used to record changes. In fact, in many organizations, the same document that is used to request new systems (Figure 12-7) is used to request changes to an existing system (Figure 12-22). Thus the information system development cycle continues as Phase 1 (analysis) begins on the change request.

Error Correction

Error correction deals with problems that are caused by programming and design errors that are discovered after the system is implemented. Often these errors are minor problems, such as the zip code not appearing on a name and address report, that can be quickly fixed by a programmer. Other times, however, the error requires some level of investigation by the systems analyst before a correction can be determined.

PHASE 5—MAINTENANCE AT SUTHERLAND

During the months following the system implementation, a number of minor programming errors were discovered. Most of these errors were quickly corrected by the programming staff but in one case involving special credit terms for a large customer, Mary Ruiz had to become involved and had to prepare specifications for the necessary program changes.

Approximately one year after Mike Charles submitted his original request for a computerized order entry and invoicing system, he submitted another request (Figure 12-22) for a change to the system to provide for a new county sales tax. This type of request does not require a preliminary investigation and will be assigned to Mary Ruiz as soon as she is available. Mike submitted his request five months before the tax was scheduled to go into effect, which should allow ample time for the necessary program changes to be implemented.

```
                    REQUEST FOR SYSTEM SERVICES

                                        ISD CONTROL #: 4703

  I.  To Be Completed By Person Requesting Services

  SUBMITTED BY: MIKE CHARLES DEPT AUTO PARTS SALES DATE: 2-1-91

  REQUEST TYPE:  ☑ MODIFICATION      ☐ NEW SYSTEM

  NEED:          ☑ ASAP     ☐ IMMEDIATE    ☐ LONG RANGE

  BRIEF STATEMENT OF REQUEST (attach additional material, if
  necessary)
     SALES INVOICE PROGRAM NEEDS TO PROVIDE FOR 1%
     COUNTY TAX THAT WILL GO INTO EFFECT JULY 1, 1991.



     ☑ ADDITIONAL MATERIAL ATTACHED COUNTY TAX RATE SCHEDULE
  ==========================================================
  II.  To Be Completed By Information Systems Department

  REQUEST INVESTIGATED BY:_____ DATE:_____

  COMMENTS:_____
  _____
  _____
  _____

  ==========================================================
  III.  Disposition

     ☐ REQUEST APPROVED FOR IMMEDIATE IMPLEMENTATION

     ☐ Analyst assigned:_____

     ☐ REQUEST APPROVED FOR IMPLEMENTATION AS SOON AS POSSIBLE

     ☐ REQUEST REJECTED

  COMMENTS:_____
  _____
  _____

  SIGNED:_____ DATE:_____
```

FIGURE 12-22
The same form that was used to request a new system (see Figure 12-7) is also used to request a modification to an existing system.

SUMMARY OF THE INFORMATION SYSTEM DEVELOPMENT LIFE CYCLE

Although the information system development process may appear to be a straightforward series of steps, in practice it is a challenging activity that calls for the skills and cooperation of all involved. New development tools have made the process more efficient but the success of any project always depends on the commitment of the project participants. The understanding you have gained from this chapter will help you participate in information system development projects and give you an appreciation for the importance of each phase.

CHAPTER SUMMARY

1. An **information system** is a collection of six elements, equipment, software, data, personnel, users, and procedures, that provide accurate, timely and useful information.
2. There are four types of information systems: (1) **operational systems**; (2) **management information systems**; (3) **decision support systems**; and (4) **expert systems**.
3. The trend is to combine all of an organization's information needs into a single integrated information system.
4. The **information system development life cycle** is an organized approach to developing an information system and consists of five phases: analysis, design, development, implementation, and maintenance.
5. Planning, scheduling, reporting, and controlling the individual activities that make up the information system development life cycle is called **project management**. These activities are usually recorded in a **project plan**.
6. **Documentation** refers to written materials that are produced throughout the information system development life cycle.
7. All users and information system personnel who will be affected by the new system should have the opportunity to participate in its development.
8. The systems analyst's job is a challenging one requiring good communication, analytical, and diplomatic skills to keep the development process on track and on schedule.
9. The **analysis** phase is the separation of a system into its parts in order to determine how the system works. This phase consists of the preliminary investigation, detailed system analysis, and making the decision to proceed.
10. The purpose of the **preliminary investigation** is to determine if a request warrants further detailed investigation. The most important aspect of this investigation is **problem definition**.
11. **Detailed system analysis** involves both a thorough study of the current system and as least one proposed solution to any problems found.
12. **Data flow diagrams** are a **structured analysis** tool that graphically show the flow of data through a system.
13. Other tools that are used in the analysis phase include **data dictionaries**, **process specifications**, **structured English**, **decision tables**, and **decision trees**.
14. A **feasibility study** and **cost/benefit analysis** are often prepared to show whether the proposed solution is practical and to show the estimated costs and benefits that are expected.
15. During the **design** phase the **logical design** that was created in the analysis phase is transformed into a **physical design**.
16. There are two major structured design methods: **top-down design** (or **structured design**) and **bottom-up design**.
17. **Output design**, **input design**, and **database design** all occur during the design phase.
18. When designing interactive systems, the systems analyst and user determine the sequence of inputs and computer responses, called a **dialogue**.
19. During the **process design** the systems analyst specifies exactly what actions will be taken on the input data to create output information.
20. One method of documenting the relationship of different processes is with a **system flowchart**.
21. A **structured walkthrough**, or a step-by-step review, is sometimes performed on the process design.
22. **System controls** ensure that only valid data is accepted and processed. Types of system controls include **source document controls**, **input controls**, **processing controls**, and **accounting controls**, including an **audit trail**.
23. At the end of the design phase, a **design review** is performed to evaluate the work completed so far.
24. **Prototyping** is building a working model of the new system.
25. The **development** phase consists of program development and equipment acquisition.
26. **Program development** includes: (1) reviewing the program specifications; (2) designing the program; (3) coding the program; (4) testing the program; and (5) finalizing the program documentation.
27. The **implementation** phase is when people actually begin using the new system. This phase includes training and education, conversion, and the **postimplementation evaluation**.
28. The process of changing from the old system to the new system is called a **conversion**. The conversion methods that may be used are **direct**, **parallel**, **phased**, and **pilot**.
29. The **maintenance** phase is the process of supporting the information system after it is implemented. It consists of three activities: **performance monitoring**, change management, and error correction.

KEY TERMS

Accounting controls *12.14*
Analysis *12.6*
Artificial intelligence *12.4*
Audit trail *12.14*
Bottom-up design *12.11*
Conversion *12.17*
Cost/benefit analysis *12.9*
Database design *12.12*
Data dictionary *12.8*
Data flow diagram (DFD) *12.8*
Decision support systems *12.4*
Decision table *12.9*
Decision tree *12.9*
Design *12.11*
Design review *12.14*
Detailed system analysis *12.7*
Development *12.16*
Dialogue *12.12*
Direct conversion *12.17*
Documentation *12.6*

Expert systems *12.4*
Feasibility study *12.9*
Implementation *12.16*
Inference rules *12.4*
Information system *12.2*
Information system development
    life cycle (SDLC) *12.5*
Input controls *12.14*
Input design *12.12*
Knowledge base *12.4*
Logical design *12.11*
Maintenance *12.18*
Management information system
    (MIS) *12.3*
Operational system *12.3*
Output design *12.11*
Parallel conversion *12.17*
Performance monitoring *12.18*
Phased conversion *12.17*
Physical design *12.11*

Pilot conversion *12.17*
Postimplementation evaluation *12.17*
Preliminary investigation *12.7*
Problem definition *12.7*
Process design *12.12*
Processing controls *12.14*
Process specifications *12.9*
Program development *12.16*
Project management *12.5*
Project plan *12.5*
Prototyping *12.15*
Source document controls *12.14*
Structured analysis *12.8*
Structured design *12.11*
Structured English *12.9*
Structured walkthrough *12.14*
System controls *12.14*
System flowchart *12.12*
Top-down design *12.11*

REVIEW QUESTIONS

1. List the six elements of an information system.
2. What are the four types of information systems? What is meant by integrated information systems?
3. List the five phases of the information system development life cycle.
4. Describe project management and when it should be performed.
5. What is the preliminary investigation? What is the most important aspect of the preliminary investigation?
6. Briefly describe detailed system analysis. What are the fact-finding techniques used during detailed system analysis?
7. What are the symbols used in data flow diagrams? Why are data flow diagram useful?
8. Explain the difference between the logical and physical design of an information system.
9. What are the two methods of structured design? Briefly describe each method.
10. List and describe four basic types of system controls.
11. What is prototyping?
12. What are the steps in program development?
13. Write a description of the four types of conversion methods.
14. Describe the three major activities of system maintenance.

CONTROVERSIAL ISSUES

1. Large systems may take several years to design and implement. Some experts argue that undertaking such a task is ridiculous because the needs of the users and the technology will change so much during the time it takes to implement the system that it will be obsolete before it is implemented. Others point out that there are really no alternatives. What do you think?
2. "The difficulty in developing and implementing an information processing system is the user," proclaimed a systems analyst. "Users never know what they want. When they are shown what the system will do, they give their approval, but when the system is implemented they are never happy. They always want changes. It's impossible to satisfy them." How do you feel about these comments? Are the systems analyst's comments about users correct?

RESEARCH PROJECTS

1. Today there are many software packages available for personal computers to help systems analysts with the tasks they perform during the information system development life cycle. Write a report on one of these packages and be prepared to discuss it in class.
2. Prepare a data flow diagram of how you registered for class. Document your work by obtaining copies of any forms that were used during the registration process.

Program Development

Program Development

OBJECTIVES

- Define the term computer program.
- Describe the five steps in program development: review of program specifications, program design, program coding, program testing, and finalizing program documentation.
- Explain the concepts of structured program design including modules, control structures, and single entry/single exit.
- Explain and illustrate the sequence, selection, and iteration control structures used in structured programming.
- Define the term programming language and discuss the various categories of programming languages.
- Briefly discuss the programming languages that are commonly used today, including BASIC, COBOL, C, FORTRAN, Pascal, Ada, and RPG.
- Explain and discuss application generators.
- Explain the factors that should be considered when choosing a programming language.

As we discussed in Chapter 12, the information system development life cycle covers the entire process of taking a plan for processing information through various phases until it becomes a functioning information system. During the development phase of this cycle, computer programs are written. The purpose of these programs is to process data and produce output as specified in the information system design. This chapter focuses on the steps taken to write a program and the available tools that make the program development process more efficient. In addition, this chapter discusses the different languages used to write programs.

Although you may never write a program yourself, it is likely that you will someday request information that will require a program to be written or modified. Therefore it is important for you to understand the process that takes place when a computer program is developed.

WHAT IS A COMPUTER PROGRAM?

A **computer program** is a detailed set of instructions that directs a computer to perform the tasks necessary to process data into information. These instructions, usually written by a computer programmer, can be coded (written) in a variety of programming languages that will be discussed later in this chapter. To create programs that are correct (produce accurate information) and maintainable (easy to modify), programmers follow a process called program development.

WHAT IS PROGRAM DEVELOPMENT?

*I*n the early days of computing, programming was considered an "art" and the programming process was left to the "interpretation" of the programmer. While there is still room for creativity, **program development**, the process of producing one or more programs to perform one or more specific tasks on a computer, has evolved into a series of five steps that most experts agree should take place when any program is developed. These five steps (Figure 13-1) are:

1. Review of program specifications. The programmer reviews the specifications created by the system analyst during the system design phase.
2. Program design. The programmer determines the specific actions the program will take to accomplish the desired tasks.
3. Coding. The programmer writes the actual program instructions.
4. Testing. The written programs are tested to make sure they perform as intended.
5. Finalizing documentation. The documentation produced during the program development process is brought together and organized.

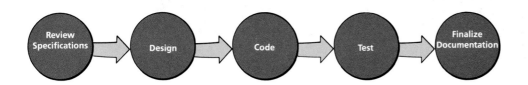

FIGURE 13-1
The five steps of program development.

STEP 1—REVIEW OF PROGRAM SPECIFICATIONS

*T*he first step in the program development cycle is a review of the program specifications. **Program specifications** can consists of data flow diagrams, system flowcharts, process specifications that indicate the action to be taken on the data, a data dictionary identifying the data elements that will be used, screen formats, and report layouts. These documents help the programmer understand the work that needs to be done by the program. Because it is important that the programmer understands the purpose of the program from the user's point of view, one or more meetings are usually held between the programmer, the user, and the systems analyst who designed the system.

If the programmer believes some aspect of the design should be changed, such as a screen layout, it is discussed with the analyst and the user. If the change is agreed on, the design specification is changed. However, the programmer should not change the specified system without the agreement of the analyst and user. If a change is authorized, it should be recorded in the system design. The analyst and user, through the system design, have specified *what* is to be done. It is the programmer's job to determine *how* to do it.

Large programming jobs are usually assigned to more than one programmer. In these situations, a good system design is essential so that each programmer can be given a logical portion of the system to be programmed.

STEP 2—PROGRAM DESIGN

*A*fter the program specifications have been carefully reviewed, program design begins. During **program design** a logical solution to the programming task is developed and documented. The logical solution or **logic** for a program is a step-by-step solution to a programming problem. Determining the logic for a computer program can be an extremely complex task. To aid in program design and development, a method called structured program design is commonly used.

Structured Program Design

Structured program design is a methodology that emphasizes three main program design concepts: modules, control structures, and single entry/single exit. Use of these concepts helps to create programs that are easy to write, read, understand, check for errors, and modify.

Modules   With structured design, programming problems are "decomposed" (separated) into smaller parts called modules. Each **module**, sometimes referred to as a **subroutine** in programming, performs a given task within the program. The major benefit of this technique is that it simplifies program development because each module of a program can be developed individually. When the modules are combined, they form a complete program that accomplishes the desired result.

Structure charts, also called **hierarchy charts**, are often used to decompose and represent the modules of a program. When the program decomposition is completed, the entire structure of a program is illustrated by the hierarchy chart and the relationship of the modules within the program is shown (Figure 13-2).

FIGURE 13-2
A structure chart graphically illustrates the relationship of individual program modules.

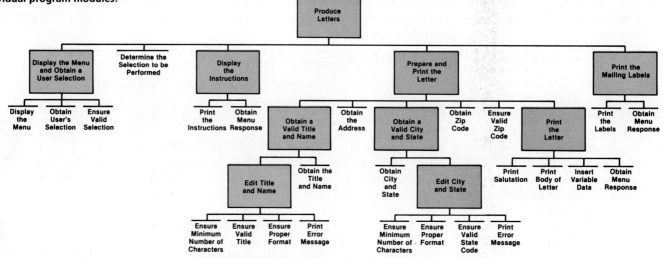

Control Structures   In structured program design three basic **control structures** are used to form the logic of a program. All logic problems can be solved by a combination of these structures. The three basic control structures are: sequence, selection, and iteration.

In the **sequence structure**, one process occurs immediately after another. In Figure 13-3, each rectangular box represents a particular process that is to take place. For example, a process could be a computer instruction to move data from one location in main memory to another location. Each process takes place in the exact sequence specified, one process followed by the next.

The second control structure, called the **selection** or **if-then-else structure**, gives programmers a way to represent conditional program logic (Figure 13-4). Conditional program logic can be expressed in the following way: *If* the condition is true, *then* perform the true condition processing, *else* perform the false condition processing. When the if-then-else control structure is used, the "if" portion of the structure tests a given condition. The true portion of the statement is executed if the condition tested is true and the false portion of the statement is executed if the condition is false. For example, in a payroll program the number of hours worked might be tested to determine if an employee worked overtime. If the person did work overtime, the true portion of the statement would be executed and overtime would be calculated. If the employee did not work overtime, then the false portion of the statement would be executed and overtime would not be calculated. The selection or if-then-else structure is used by programmers to represent conditional logic problems.

The third control structure, called **iteration** or **looping**, means that one or more processes continue to occur so long as a given condition remains true. There are two forms of this control structure: the **do-while structure** and the **do-until structure** (Figure 13-5). In the do-while structure a condition is tested. If the condition is true, the process is performed. The program then "loops" back and tests the condition again. If the condition is still true, the process is performed again. This looping continues until the condition being tested is false. At that time, the program exits the loop and performs some other processing. An example of this type of testing would be a check to see if all records have been processed. The do-until control structure is similar to the do-while except that the conditional test is at the end instead of the beginning of the loop. Processing continues "until" the condition is met.

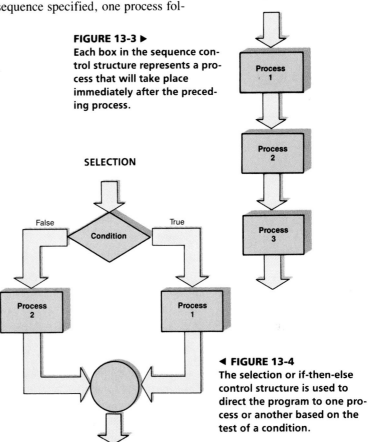

FIGURE 13-3 ▶
Each box in the sequence control structure represents a process that will take place immediately after the preceding process.

◀ FIGURE 13-4
The selection or if-then-else control structure is used to direct the program to one process or another based on the test of a condition.

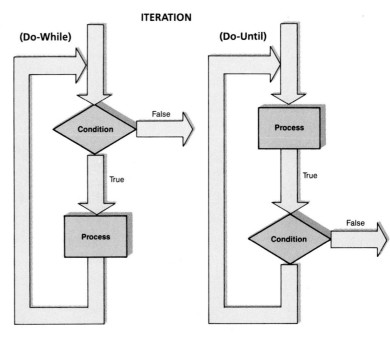

FIGURE 13-5 ▶
The iteration control structure has two forms, do-while and do-until. In the do-while structure, the condition is tested before the process. In the do-until structure, the condition is tested after the process.

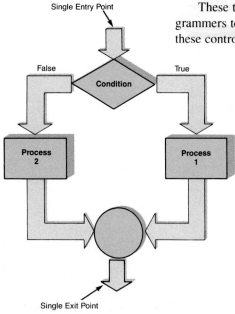

Single Entry Point

False | Condition | True

Process 2 | Process 1

Single Exit Point

FIGURE 13-6 ▲
Structured programming concepts require that all control structures have a single entry point and a single exit point. This contributes to programming logic that is easier to understand.

These three control structures, sequence, selection, and iteration, are combined by programmers to create program logic solutions. A structured program design rule that applies to these control structures and how they are combined is the single entry/single exit rule.

Single Entry/Single Exit An important concept in structured programming is **single entry/single exit**, meaning that there is only one entry point and one exit point for each of the three control structures. An **entry point** is the point where a control structure is entered. An **exit point** is the point where the control structure is exited. For example, in Figure 13-6, when the if-then-else structure is used, the control structure is entered at the point where the condition is tested. When the condition is tested, one set of instructions will be executed if the condition is true and another set will be executed if the condition is false. Regardless of the result of the test, however, the structure is exited at the single exit point.

This feature substantially improves the understanding of a program because, when reading the program, the programmer can be assured that whatever happens within the if-then-else structure, the control structure will always be exited at a common point. Prior to the use of structured programming, many programmers would transfer control to other parts of a program without following the single entry/single exit rule. This practice led to poorly designed programs that were extremely difficult to read, check for errors, and modify.

Program Design Tools

There are several popular program design tools through which structured program design concepts can be applied. These design tools are used by computer programmers to develop and document the logical solutions to the problems they are programming. Three of these design tools are program flowcharts, pseudocode, and Warnier-Orr.

Program Flowcharts Program flowcharts were one of the first program design tools. Figure 13-7 shows a flowchart drawn in the late 1940s by Dr. John von Neumann, a computer scientist and one of the first computer programmers. In a **program flowchart** all the logical steps of a program are represented by a combination of symbols and text.

A set of standards for program flowcharts was published in the early 1960s by the American National Standards Institute (ANSI). These standards, which are still used today, specify symbols, such as rectangles and diamonds, that are used to represent the various operations that can be performed on a computer (Figure 13-8 on the opposite page).

Program flowcharts were used as the primary means of program design for many years prior to the introduction of structured program design. During these years, programmers designed programs by focusing on the detailed steps required for a program and creating logical solutions for each new combination of conditions as it was encountered. Developing programs in this manner led to programs that were poorly designed. Today, programmers are taught to apply the structured design concepts when preparing program flowcharts (Figure 13-9). When the basic control structures are utilized, program flowcharts are a valuable program design tool.

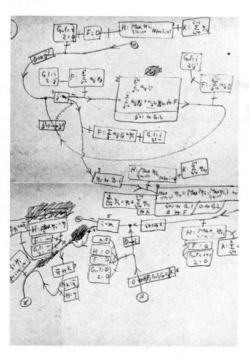

◀ **FIGURE 13-7**
An example of an early flowchart developed by computer scientist Dr. John von Neumann in the 1940s to solve a problem involving game theory.

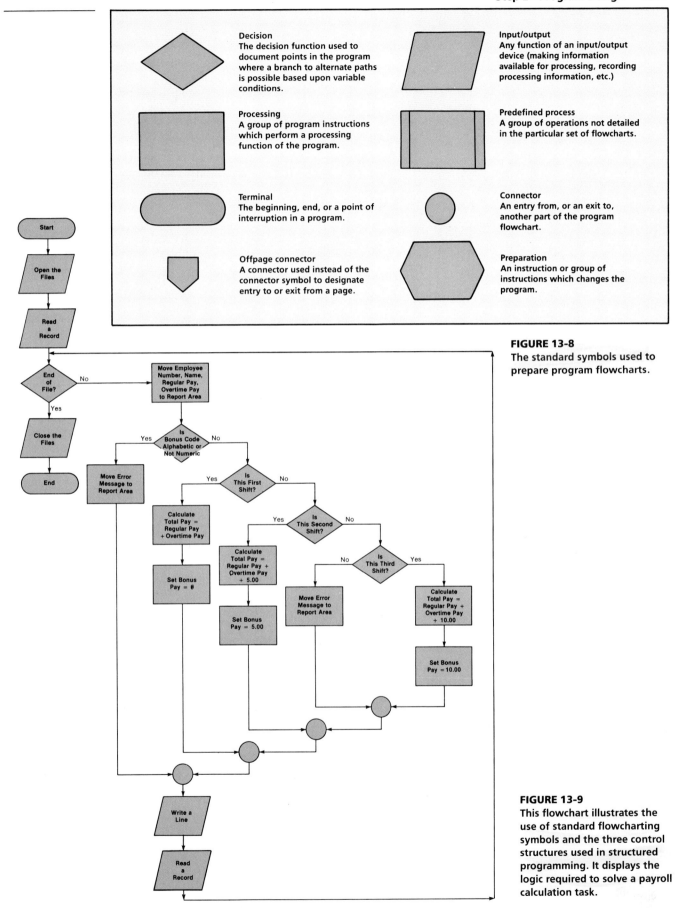

FIGURE 13-8
The standard symbols used to prepare program flowcharts.

FIGURE 13-9
This flowchart illustrates the use of standard flowcharting symbols and the three control structures used in structured programming. It displays the logic required to solve a payroll calculation task.

```
Open the files
Read a record
PERFORM UNTIL end of file
    Move employee number, name, regular pay, and
        overtime pay to the report area
    IF bonus code is alphabetic or not numeric
        Move error message to report area
    ELSE
        IF first shift
            Calculate total pay = regular pay +
                overtime pay
            Set bonus pay to zero
        ELSE
            IF second shift
                Calculate total pay = regular pay +
                    overtime pay + 5.00
                Set bonus pay to 5.00
            ELSE
                IF third shift
                    Calculate total pay = regular pay +
                        overtime pay + 10.00
                    Set bonus pay to 10.00
                ELSE
                    Move error message to report area
                ENDIF
            ENDIF
        ENDIF
    ENDIF
    Write a line
    Read a record
ENDPERFORM
Close the files
End the program
```

FIGURE 13-10
This pseudocode is another way of documenting the logic shown in the flowchart in Figure 13-9.

Pseudocode   Some experts in program design advocate the use of pseudocode when designing the logic for a program. In **pseudocode** the logical steps in the solution of a problem are written as English statements and indentations are used to represent the control structures (Figure 13-10). An advantage of pseudocode is that it eliminates the time spent with flowcharting to draw and arrange symbols while attempting to determine the program logic. The major disadvantage is that unlike flowcharting, pseudocode does not provide a graphic representation, which many people find useful and easier to interpret when examining programming logic.

Warnier-Orr   In the **Warnier-Orr** technique (named after Jean-Dominique Warnier and Kenneth Orr), the programmer analyzes output to be produced from an application and develops processing modules that are needed to produce the output. The example in Figure 13-11 illustrates a completed Warnier-Orr diagram for a checkbook-balancing report program. Each bracket ({) represents a module in the program. The statements within the brackets identify the processing that is to occur within the modules.

Regardless of the design tool used, it is important that the program design is efficient and correct. To help ensure this, many organizations use structured walkthroughs.

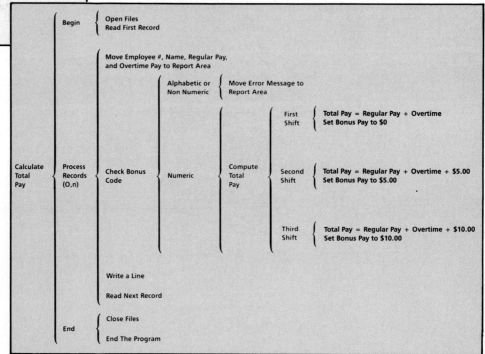

FIGURE 13-11
This Warnier-Orr diagram illustrates the logic for the payroll calculation problem also used for Figures 13-9 and 13-10.

Structured Walkthroughs

After a program has been designed, the programmer schedules a structured walkthrough of the program. The programmer, other programmers in the department, and the systems analyst attend. During the walkthrough, the programmer who designs the program explains the program logic. The purpose of the design walkthrough is to review the logic of the program for errors, and if possible, improve program design. It is much better to find errors and make needed changes to the program during the design step than to make them later in the program development process.

Once the program design is complete, the coding of the program begins.

STEP 3—PROGRAM CODING

*C*oding the program refers to the process of writing the program instructions that will process the data and produce the output specified in the program design. As previously mentioned, programs are written in different languages that each have particular rules on how to instruct the computer to perform specific tasks, such as read a record or multiply two numbers. The differences in these languages will be discussed later in this chapter.

If a thorough program design has been produced, the coding process is greatly simplified and can sometimes be a one-for-one translation of a design step into a program step. Today, program code, or instructions, are usually entered directly into the computer via a terminal and stored on a disk drive. Using this approach, the programmer can partially enter a program at one time and finish entering it at a later time. Program instructions are added, deleted, and changed until the programmer believes the program design has been fully translated into program instructions and the program is ready for testing.

STEP 4—PROGRAM TESTING

*B*efore a program is used to process "real" data and produce information that people rely on, it should be thoroughly tested to make sure it is functioning correctly. Several different types of tests can be performed.

Desk checking is the process of reading the program and mentally reviewing its logic. This is a simple process that can be performed by the programmer who wrote the program or by another programmer. This process can be compared with proofreading a letter before you put it in the mail. The disadvantage of this method is that it is difficult to detect other than obvious errors.

Another type of testing identifies program **syntax errors**, violations of the grammar rules of the language in which the program was written. An example of a syntax error would be the program command READ being misspelled REED. Syntax errors missed by the programmer are discovered by the computer when it decodes the program instructions.

Logic testing is what most programmers think of when the term testing is used. During **logic testing**, the sequence of program instructions is tested to make sure they provide the correct result. Logic errors may be the result of a programming oversight, such as using the wrong data to perform a calculation, or a design error, such as forgetting to specify that some customers do not have to pay sales tax when they purchase merchandise.

Logic testing is performed with **test data**, data that simulates the type of input that the program will process when it is implemented. In order to obtain an independent and unbiased test of the program, test data and the review of test results should be the responsibility of someone other than the programmer who wrote the program. The test data should be developed by referring to the system design but should also try to "break" the program by including data outside the range of data that will be input during normal operations. For example, even though a payroll program should never have more than 60 hours per week input, the program should be designed, coded, and tested to properly process transactions in excess of 60 hours by displaying an error message or in some other way indicating that an invalid number

FIGURE 13-12
In 1945, the cause of the temporary failure of the world's first electromechanical computer, the Mark I, was traced to a dead moth caught in the electrical components. The term "bug," meaning a computer error, has been part of computer jargon ever since.

of hours has been entered. Other similar tests should include alphabetic data when only numeric data is expected, and negative numbers when only positive numbers are normally input.

One of the more colorful terms of the computer industry is **debugging**, which refers to the process of locating and correcting program errors or **bugs** found during testing. The term was coined when the failure of one of the first computers was traced to a moth that had become lodged in the electronic components (Figure 13-12).

STEP 5—FINALIZING PROGRAM DOCUMENTATION

Documentation is an essential but sometimes neglected part of the programming process. As reflected in the title of this section, documentation should be an ongoing part of developing a program and should only be finalized, meaning organized and brought together, after the program is successfully tested and ready for implementation. The difficulty in sometimes obtaining adequate documentation is that many programmers can and do develop programs without it; when the program is completed, they have little incentive to go back and complete the documentation "after the fact." In addition to helping programmers develop programs, documentation is valuable because it helps the next programmer who, six months or one year later, is asked to make a change to the program. Proper documentation can substantially reduce the amount of time the new programmer will have to spend learning enough about the program to know how best to make the change.

Documentation developed during the programming process should include a narrative description of the program, program flowcharts, pseudocode, program listings, and test results. Comments in the program itself are also an important part of program documentation (Figure 13-13).

FIGURE 13-13
Most programming languages allow explanatory comments to be placed directly in the program. This is an effective way of documenting the program.

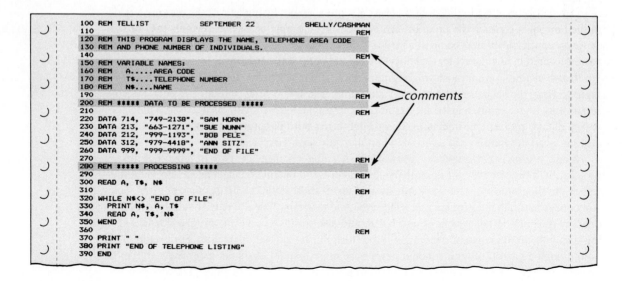

PROGRAM MAINTENANCE

Program **maintenance** includes all changes to a program once it is implemented and processing real transactions. Sometimes maintenance is required to correct errors that were not found during the testing step. Other times, maintenance is required to make changes that are the result of the user's new information requirements. It may surprise you to learn that the majority of all business programming today consists of maintaining existing programs, not writing new programs.

Because so much time is spent on maintenance programming, it should be subject to the same policies and procedures, such as design, testing, and documentation, that are required for new programs. Unfortunately, this is not always the case. Because maintenance tasks are usually shorter than new programming efforts, they often aren't held to the same standards. The result is that over time, programs can become unrecognizable when compared with their original documentation. Maintaining high standards for program maintenance can not only lower overall programming costs, but also lengthen the useful life of a program.

SUMMARY OF PROGRAM DEVELOPMENT

The key to developing quality programs for an information system is to follow the steps of the program development process. Program specifications must be carefully reviewed and understood. Structured concepts should be used to design programs that are modular, use the three control structures, and follow the single entry/single exit rule. The program should be carefully coded and tested. Documentation should be finalized. If each of these steps is followed, quality programs will be developed that are correct and that can be easily read, understood, and maintained.

WHAT IS A PROGRAMMING LANGUAGE?

As mentioned at the beginning of this chapter, computer programs can be written in a variety of programming languages. People communicate with one another through language, established patterns of words and sounds. A similar definition can also be applied to a **programming language**, which is a set of written words and symbols that allow the programmer or user to communicate with the computer. Just like English, Spanish, Chinese, or other spoken languages, programming languages have rules, called syntax, that govern their use.

CATEGORIES OF PROGRAMMING LANGUAGES

There are hundreds of programming languages, each with its own syntax. Some languages were developed for specific computers and others, because of their success, have been standardized and adapted to a wide range of computers. Programming languages can be classified into one of four categories: machine language, assembly language, high-level languages, and fourth-generation languages.

Machine Language

A **machine language** is the fundamental language of the computer's processor. Programs written in all other categories of languages are eventually converted into machine language before they are executed. Individual machine language instructions exist for each of the commands in the computer's instruction set, the operations such as add, move, or read that are specific to each computer. Because the instruction set is unique for a particular processor, machine languages are different for computers that have different processors. The advantage of writing a program in machine language is that the programmer can control the computer directly and accomplish exactly what needs to be done. Therefore, well-written machine language programs are very efficient. The disadvantages of machine language programs are that they take a long time to write and they are difficult to review if the programmer is trying to find an error. In addition, because they are written using the instruction set of a particular processor, the programs will only run on computers with the same type of processor. Because they are written for specific processors, machine languages are also called **low-level languages**. Figure 13-14a shows an example of machine language instructions.

FIGURE 13-14

This chart shows program instructions for: (a) machine language (printed in a hexadecimal form); (b) assembly language; and (c) a high-level language called C. The machine language and assembly language instructions shown in this example correspond to the high-level instructions and were generated when the high-level language statements were translated into machine language.

(a) Machine Language	(b) Assembly Language	(c) High-level Language
9b df 46 0c 9b d9 c0 9b db 7e f2 9b d9 46 04 9b d8 c9 9b d9 5e fc	fild WORD PTR [bp+12];qty fld ST(0) fstp TBYTE PTR [bp-14] fld DWORD PTR [bp+4];price fmul ST(0),ST(1) fstp DWORD PTR [bp-4];gross	gross = qty * price;
9b d9 c0 9b dc 16 ac 00 9b dd d8 9b dd 7e f0 90 9b 8a 66 f1 9e 9b dd c0 76 19	fld ST(0) fcom QWORD PTR $T20002 fstp ST(0) fstsw WORD PTR [bp-16] fwait mov ah,BYTE PTR [bp-15] sahf ffreeST(0) jbe $I193	if (qty > ceiling)
9b d9 46 fc 9b d9 46 fc 9b dc 0e b4 00 9b de e9 9b d9 5e 08 90 9b	fld DWORD PTR [bp-4];gross fld DWORD PTR [bp-4];gross fmul QWORD PTR $T20003 fsub fstp DWORD PTR [bp+8];net fwait	net = gross - (gross * discount_rate);
eb 0d 90	jmp SHORT $I194 nop $I193:	else
8b 46 fc 8b 56 fe 89 46 08 89 56 0a	mov ax,WORD PTR [bp-4];gross mov dx,WORD PTR [bp-2] mov WORD PTR [bp+8],ax ;net mov WORD PTR [bp+10],dx $I194:	net = gross;

Assembly Language

To make it easier for programmers to remember the specific machine instruction codes, assembly languages were developed. An **assembly language** is similar to a machine language, but uses abbreviations called **mnemonics** or **symbolic operation code** to represent the machine operation code. Another difference is that assembly languages usually allow **symbolic addressing**, which means that a specific computer memory location can be referenced by a name or symbol, such as TOTAL, instead of by its actual address as it would have to be referenced in machine language. Assembly language programs can also include **macroinstructions** that generate more than one machine language instruction. Assembly language programs are converted into machine language instructions by a special program called an **assembler**. Even though assembly languages are easier to use than machine languages, they are still considered a low-level language because they are so closely related to the specific design of the computer. Figure 13-14b shows an example of assembly language instructions.

High-Level Languages

The evolution of computer languages continued with the development of high-level languages in the late 1950s and 1960s. **High-level languages** more closely resemble what most people would think of as a language in that they contain nouns, verbs, and mathematical, relational, and logical operators that can be grouped together to form what appear to be sentences (Figure 13-14c). These sentences are called **program statements**. Because of these characteristics, high-level languages can be "read" by programmers and are thus easier to learn and use than machine or assembly languages. Another important advantage over low-level languages is that high-level languages are usually machine independent, which means they can run on different types of computers.

As mentioned previously, all languages must be translated into machine language before they can instruct the computer to perform processing. High-level languages are translated in one of two ways: with a compiler or an interpreter.

A **compiler** converts an entire program into machine language that is usually stored on a disk for later execution. The program to be converted is called the **source program** and the machine language produced is called the **object program** or **object code**. Compilers check the program syntax, perform limited logic checking, and make sure that data that is going to be used in comparisons or calculations, such as a discount rate, is properly defined somewhere in the program. An important feature of compilers is that they produce an error listing of all program statements that do not meet the program language rules. This listing helps the programmer make the necessary changes to correct the program. Figure 13-15 illustrates the process of compiling a program.

FIGURE 13-15
When a compiler is used, a source language program is compiled into a machine language object program. Usually, both the source and object programs are stored on disk. When the user wants to run the program, the object program is loaded into the main memory of the CPU and the program instructions begin executing. Errors in the source program identified during compilation are shown on an error listing that can be used to make the necessary corrections.

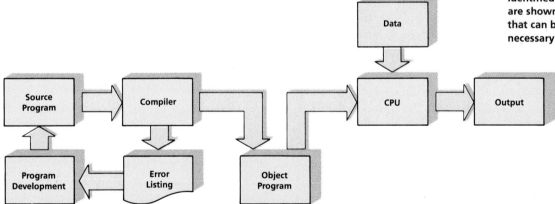

Because machine language is unique to each processor, different computers require different compilers for the same language. For example, a mainframe, minicomputer, and personal computer would each have different compilers that would translate the same source language program into the specific machine language for each computer.

While a compiler translates an entire program, an **interpreter** translates one program statement at a time and then executes the resulting machine language before translating the next program statement. When using an interpreter, each time the program is run, the source program is interpreted into machine language and executed. No object program is produced. Figure 13-16 illustrates this process.

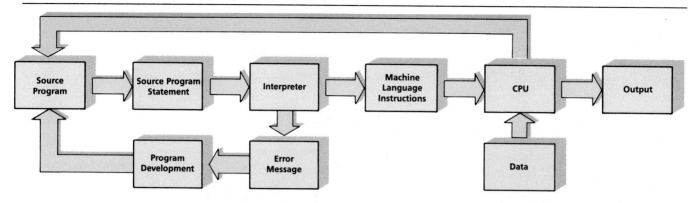

FIGURE 13-16
When an interpreter is used, one source language statement at a time is interpreted into machine language instructions that are executed immediately. Error messages indicating an invalid source language statement are produced as each source program statement is interpreted.

Interpreters are often used with personal computers that do not have the memory or computing power required by compilers. The advantage of interpreters is that the compiling process is not necessary before program changes can be tested. The disadvantage of interpreters is that interpreted programs do not run as fast as compiled programs because the translation to machine language occurs each time the program is run. Compilers for most high-level languages are now available for the newer and more powerful personal computers.

Fourth-Generation Languages

The evolution of computer languages is sometimes described in terms of "generations" with machine, assembly, and high-level languages considered the first, second, and third generations, respectively. Each generation offered significant improvements in ease of use and programming flexibility over the previous generation. Although a clear definition doesn't yet exist, **fourth-generation languages (4GLs)**, sometimes called **very high-level languages**, continue the programming language evolution by being even easier to use than high-level languages for both the programmer and the nonprogramming user.

A common term used to describe fourth-generation languages is **nonprocedural**, which means that the programmer does not specify the procedures to be used to accomplish a task as is done with lower "procedural" language generations. Instead of telling the computer *how* to do the task, the programmer tells the computer *what* is to be done, usually by describing the desired output. A database query language (Figure 13-17) is an example of a nonprocedural fourth-generation language.

FIGURE 13-17
This database query is considered an example of a fourth-generation language because it tells the computer what the user wants, not how to perform the processing.

```
LIST CUSTOMERS CUSTOMER.NAME WITH BALANCE.DUE > '1000'
```

The advantage of fourth-generation languages is that they are "results" oriented ("what" is to be done, not "how") and they can be used by nonprogramming personnel such as users. The disadvantage of fourth-generation languages is that they do not provide as many processing options to the programmer nor are they as efficient as other language generations. Most experts, however, believe that their ease of use far outweighs these disadvantages and predict that fourth-generation languages will continue to be more widely used.

An extension of fourth-generation languages, sometimes called the fifth generation, is a natural language. A **natural language** is a type of query language that allows the user to enter a question as if the user were speaking to another person. For example, a fourth-generation query might be stated as LIST SALESPERSON TOTAL-SALES BY REGION. A natural language version of that same query might be TELL ME THE NAME OF EACH SALESPERSON AND THE TOTAL SALES FOR EACH REGION. The natural language allows the user more flexibility in the structure of the query and can even ask the user a question if it does not understand what is meant by the initial query statement.

PROGRAMMING LANGUAGES USED TODAY

Although there are hundreds of programming languages, only a few are used extensively enough to be recognized as industry standards. Most of these are high-level programming languages that can be used on a variety of computers. This section discusses the popular programming languages that are commonly used, their origins, and their primary purpose.

To help you understand the differences, we show program code for each of the most popular languages. The code is from programs that solve the same problem, the computation of the net sale price using a discount if the gross sale is over $100.00.

BASIC

BASIC, which stands for **B**eginner's **A**ll-purpose **S**ymbolic **I**nstruction **C**ode, was developed by John Kemeny and Thomas Kurtz in 1964 at Dartmouth College (Figure 13-18). Originally designed to be a simple, interactive programming language for college students to learn and use, BASIC has become one of the most commonly used programming languages on microcomputers and minicomputers.

FIGURE 13-18
An excerpt from a BASIC program.

```
5010 REM ****************P R O C E S S    A N D    D I S P L A Y********
5040 GROSS = QTY * SLSPR
5050 IF QTY > CEILING THEN NET = GROSS - (GROSS * DISC) ELSE NET = GROSS
5070 PRINT "THE NET SALES IS $";
5080 PRINT USING "$$#,###.##"; NET
5090 RETURN
```

COBOL

COBOL (**CO**mmon **B**usiness **O**riented **L**anguage) was introduced in 1960. Backed by the Department of Defense, COBOL was developed by a committee of representatives from both government and industry. Rear Admiral Grace M. Hopper was a key person on the committee and is recognized as one of the prime developers of the COBOL language. COBOL is one of the most widely used programming languages for business applications (Figure 13-19). Using an English-like format, COBOL instructions are arranged in "sentences" and grouped into "paragraphs." The English format makes COBOL easy to write and read, but also makes it a wordy language that produces lengthy program code. COBOL is very good for processing large files and performing relatively simple business computations. Other languages are stronger at performing complex mathematical formulas and functions.

FIGURE 13-19
An excerpt from a COBOL program.

```
00100    016200 C010-PROCESS-AND-DISPLAY.
00101    016400*****************************************************************
00102    016600* FUNCTION:              CALCULATE NET SALES AMOUNT   *
00103    016700*                        AND DISPLAY RESULTS          *
00104    016800* ENTRY/EXIT:            B000-LOOP-CONTROL            *
00105    016900* CALLS:                 NONE                        *
00106    017100*****************************************************************
00107    017300    COMPUTE GROSS-SALES-WRK = QUANTITY-SOLD-WRK * SALES-PRICE-WRK.
00108    017500    IF QUANTITY-SOLD-WRK IS GREATER THAN CEILING
00109    017600        COMPUTE NET-SALES-WRK = GROSS-SALES-WRK -
00110    017700            (GROSS-SALES-WRK * DISCOUNT-RATE)
00111    017800    ELSE
00112    017900        MOVE GROSS-SALES-WRK TO NET-SALES-WRK.
00113    018100    MOVE NET-SALES-WRK TO NET-SALES-OUTPUT.
00114    018300    DISPLAY CLEAR-SCREEN.
00115    018500    WRITE PRINT-LINE FROM DETAIL-LINE
00116    018600        AFTER ADVANCING 2.
```

C̄

The **C** programming language was developed at Bell Laboratories in 1972 by Dennis Ritchie (Figure 13-20). Originally designed as a programming language for writing systems software, it is now considered a general-purpose programming language. C is a powerful programming language that requires professional programming skills to be used effectively. The use of C to develop various types of software on microcomputers and minicomputers is increasing.

FIGURE 13-20
An excerpt from a C program.

```
float gross;
gross = qty * price;
if (qty > ceiling)
    net = gross - (gross * discount_rate);
else
    net = gross;
return(net);
```

FORTRAN

FORTRAN (**FOR**mula **TRAN**slator), developed by IBM and released in 1957, was designed as a programming language to be used by scientists, engineers, and mathematicians (Figure 13-21). The language is noted for its ability to easily express and efficiently calculate mathematical equations.

FIGURE 13-21
An excerpt from a FORTRAN program.

```
BEGIN                               (* Begin procedure *)
    GROSS := SALES * QTY;
    IF QTY > CEILING
        THEN NET := GROSS - (GROSS * DISCOUNT_RATE)
        ELSE NET := GROSS;
    WRITELN('THE NET SALES IS $',NET:6:2);
END;                                (* End of procedure *)
```

Pascal

The **Pascal** language was developed by Niklaus Wirth, a computer scientist at the Institut fur Informatik in Zurich, Switzerland, in 1968. The name Pascal is not an abbreviation or acronym, but rather the name of a mathematician, Blaise Pascal (1623–1662), who developed one of the earliest calculating machines. Pascal, available for use on both personal and large computers, was one of the first programming languages that provided statements to encourage the use of structured program design (Figure 13-22).

FIGURE 13-22
An excerpt from a Pascal program.

```
 1   67.000        SUBROUTINE CALC(QTY,SALES,DISC,MAX,GROSS,NET)
 2   68.000        REAL SALES, DISC, MAX, GROSS, NET
 3   69.000        INTEGER QTY
 4   70.000        GROSS = QTY * SALES
 5   71.000        IF(QTY .GT. MAX) THEN
 6   72.000  1         NET = GROSS - (GROSS * DISC)
 7   73.000  1      ELSE
 8   74.000  1         NET = GROSS
 9   75.000  1      ENDIF
10   76.000        PRINT *, "    "
11   77.000        RETURN
```

Ada

The programming language **Ada** is named for Augusta Ada Byron, Countess of Lovelace, a mathematician in the 1800s, who is thought to have written the first program. Introduced in 1980, the development of Ada was supported by the Department of Defense. Ada was designed to facilitate the writing and maintenance of large programs that would be used over a long period of time. The language encourages coding of readable programs that are also portable, allowing them to be transferred from computer to computer (Figure 13-23).

```
31     GROSS_SALES_PRICE := FLOAT(QUANTITY * SALES_PRICE);
32     if GROSS_SALES_PRICE > 100.0 then
33         GROSS_SALES_PRICE := GROSS_SALES_PRICE - (GROSS_SALES_PRICE * 0.05);
34     end if;
```

FIGURE 13-23
An excerpt from an Ada program.

RPG

RPG, which stands for **R**eport **P**rogram **G**enerator, was developed by IBM and introduced in 1964. As the name indicates, this language was primarily designed to allow reports to be generated quickly and easily. Instead of writing a set of instructions as in other languages, in RPG special forms are filled out that describe the desired report (Figure 13-24). With a minimum of training, a user can be taught to fill out the forms, enter the information into the computer, and produce the desired reports without having to design and develop a computer program.

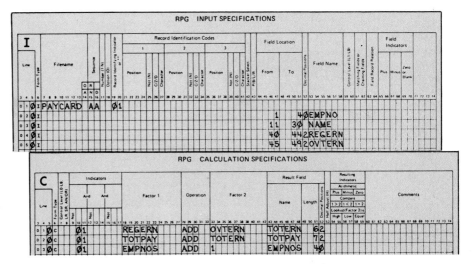

FIGURE 13-24
Special forms help the RPG programmer to quickly specify the input, calculation, and output requirements of a program. The input and calculation forms are shown in this illustration.

Other Popular Programming Languages

In addition to the commonly used programming languages just discussed, there are several other popular languages. Figure 13-25 lists some of these languages and their primary uses.

ALGOL	**ALGO**rithmetic Language. Structured programming language used for scientific and mathematical applications.
APL	**A** **P**rogramming **L**anguage. A powerful, easy to learn language that is good for processing data stored in a table (matrix) format.
FORTH	Similar to C. Creates fast and efficient program code. Originally developed to control astronomical telescopes.
LISP	**LIS**t **P**rocessing. Popular artificial intelligence language.
LOGO	Primarily known as an educational tool to teach problem-solving skills.
MODULA-2	Similar to Pascal. Used primarily for developing systems software.
PILOT	**P**rogrammed **I**nquiry **L**earning **O**r **T**eaching. Used by educators to write computer-aided instruction programs.
PL/1	**P**rogramming **L**anguage/One. Business and scientific language that combines many of the features of FORTRAN and COBOL.
PROLOG	**PRO**gramming in **LOG**ic. Used for artificial intelligence.

FIGURE 13-25
Other popular computer languages.

APPLICATION GENERATORS

Application generators, also called **program generators**, are programs that produce source language programs, such as BASIC or COBOL, based on input, output, and processing specifications entered by the user. Application generators can greatly reduce the amount of time required to develop a program. They are based on the fact that most programs are comprised of standard processing modules, such as routines to read, write, or compare records, that can be combined together to create unique programs. These standard processing modules are stored in a library and are selected and grouped together based on user specifications. Application generators often use menu and screen generators to assist in developing an application.

A **menu generator** lets the user specify a menu (list) of processing options that can be selected. The resulting menu is automatically formatted with heading, footing, and prompt line text (Figure 13-26).

FIGURE 13-26
The screen on the left is part of a menu generator from Oracle Corporation that can be used to quickly create professional-looking menus, as shown in the screen on the right.

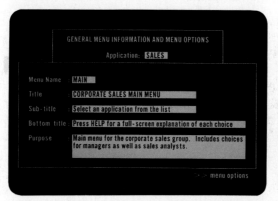
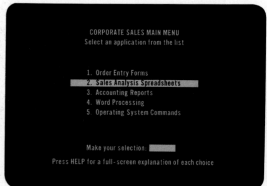

A **screen generator**, sometimes called a **screen painter**, allows the user to design an input or output screen by entering the names and descriptions of the input and output data directly on the screen. The advantage is that the user enters the data exactly as it will appear after the program is created. As each data name, such as Order No., is entered, the screen generator asks the user to specify the length and type of data that will be entered and what processing, if any, should take place before or after the data is entered. The order entry screen shown in Figure 13-27 was created in just one hour using SQL*FORMS, a screen generator product from ORACLE Corporation.

FIGURE 13-27
This order entry screen and the program to process the data were created in just one hour using a screen generator from Oracle Corporation. Using the traditional programming technique of writing individual program instructions would have taken considerably longer.

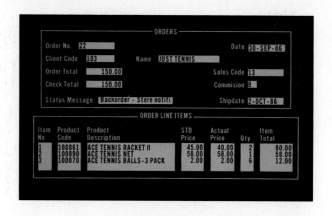

HOW TO CHOOSE A PROGRAMMING LANGUAGE

lthough each programming language has its own unique characteristics, selecting a language for a programming task can be a difficult decision. Following are some of the factors that should be considered in making a choice:

- The programming standards of the organization. Many organizations have programming standards that specify that a particular language is used for all applications.
- The need to interface with other programs. If a program is going to work with other existing or future programs, ideally it should be programmed in the same language as the other programs.
- The suitability of a language to the application to be programmed. As we discussed, most languages are best suited to a particular type of application. For example, FORTRAN works well with applications requiring many calculations.
- The expertise of the available programmers. Unless another language is far superior, the language used by the existing programmers probably should be chosen.
- The availability of the language. Not all languages are available on all machines.
- The need for the application to be portable. If the application will have to run on different machines, a common language should be chosen so the program only has to be written once.
- The anticipated maintenance requirements. If the user anticipates that the application will have to be modified frequently, a language that can be maintained easily and that supports structured programming concepts should be considered.

SUMMARY OF PROGRAMMING LANGUAGES

lthough procedural languages such as COBOL and BASIC will continue to be used for many years, there is a clear trend toward the creation of programs using nonprocedural tools, such as fourth-generation and natural languages, that allow users to specify what they want accomplished. Your knowledge of programming languages will help you to better understand the process that takes place when the computer converts data into information and to obtain better results if you directly participate in the programming process.

CHAPTER SUMMARY

1. A **computer program** is a detailed set of instructions that directs a computer to perform the tasks necessary to process data into information.
2. **Program development** is a series of five steps that take place when a computer program is developed.
3. The five steps in program development are: (1) review of the program specifications; (2) program design; (3) program coding; (4) program testing; and (5) finalizing the documentation.
4. **Program specifications** can include many documents such as data flow diagrams, system flowcharts, process specifications, a data dictionary, screen formats, and report layouts.
5. During **program design** a logical solution or **logic** for a program is developed and documented.
6. **Structured program design** is methodology that emphasizes three main program design concepts: modules, control structures, and single entry/single exit.
7. **Modules** or **subroutines**, which perform a given task within a program, can be developed individually and then combined to form a complete program.
8. **Structure charts** or **hierarchy charts** are used to decompose the modules of a program.
9. The three **control structures** are: **sequence** where one process occurs immediately after another; **selection** or **if-then-else**, which is used for conditional program logic; and **iteration** which is used for **looping**.
10. The two forms of iteration are the **do-while structure** and the **do-until structure**.
11. **Single entry/single exit** means that there is only one **entry point** and one **exit point** from each of the control structures.
12. Three commonly used program design tools are **program flowcharts**, **pseudocode**, and **Warnier-Orr**.
13. Structured walkthroughs are used to review the design and logic of a program.
14. **Coding** is the process of writing the program instructions.
15. Before a program is used to process "real" data it should be thoroughly tested to make sure it is functioning correctly. A simple type of testing is **desk checking**.
16. Programs can be tested for **syntax errors** (grammar). **Logic testing** checks for incorrect results using **test data**.
17. **Debugging** refers to the process of locating and correcting program errors or **bugs** found during testing.
18. **Program maintenance** includes all changes to a program once it is implemented and processing real transactions.
19. A **programming language** is a set of written words and symbols that allow a programmer or user to communicate with the computer.
20. Programming languages fit into one of four categories: machine language; assembly language; high-level languages; and fourth-generation languages.
21. Before they can be executed, all programs are converted into **machine language**, the fundamental language of computers, also called **low-level language**.
22. **Assembly language** is a low-level language that is closely related to machine language. It uses **mnemonics** or **symbolic operation code**.
23. Assembly languages use **symbolic addressing** and include **macroinstructions**. Assembly language programs are converted into machine language instructions by an **assembler**.
24. **High-level languages** are easier to learn and use than low-level languages. They use sentences called **program statements**.
25. **Compilers** and **interpreters** are used to translate high-level **source programs** into machine language **object code** or **object programs**.
26. **Fourth-generation languages**, also called **very high-level languages**, are **nonprocedural**, which means that the user tells the computer "what" is to be done, not "how" to do it.
27. A **natural language** allows the user to enter a question as if the user were speaking to another person.
28. Commonly used programming languages include **BASIC**, **COBOL**, **C**, **FORTRAN**, **Pascal**, **Ada**, and **RPG**.
29. **BASIC** is one of the most commonly used programming languages on microcomputers and minicomputers.
30. **COBOL** is the most widely used programming language for business applications.
31. **C** is an increasingly popular programming language that requires professional programming skills to be used effectively.
32. **FORTRAN** is noted for its ability to easily express and efficiently calculate mathematical equations.

33. **Pascal** contains programming statements that encourage the use of structured program design.
34. **Ada**, developed and supported by the Department of Defense, was designed to facilitate the writing and maintenance of large programs that would be used over a long period of time.
35. **RPG** was primarily designed to generate reports quickly and easily.
36. **Application generators** or **program generators** produce source language programs based on input, output, and processing specifications entered by the user.
37. A **menu generator** lets the user specify a menu of options.
38. A **screen generator** or **screen printer** allows the user to design an input or output screen.
39. Some of the factors that should be considered when choosing a programming language are: the programming standards of the organization; the need to interface with other programs; the suitability of a language to the application to be programmed; the expertise of the available programmers; the availability of the language; the need for the application to be portable; and the anticipated maintenance requirements.

KEY TERMS

Ada *13.17*
Application generators *13.18*
Assembler *13.12*
Assembly language *13.12*
BASIC *13.15*
Bugs *13.10*
C *13.16*
COBOL *13.15*
Coding *13.9*
Compiler *13.13*
Computer program *13.2*
Control structures *13.4*
Debugging *13.10*
Desk checking *13.9*
Do-until structure *13.5*
Do-while structure *13.5*
Entry point *13.6*
Exit point *13.6*
FORTRAN *13.16*
Fourth-generation language (4GL) *13.14*
Hierarchy charts *13.4*

High-level languages *13.13*
If-then-else structure *13.5*
Interpreter *13.13*
Iteration *13.5*
Logic *13.4*
Logic testing *13.9*
Looping *13.5*
Low-level language *13.12*
Machine language *13.12*
Macroinstruction *13.12*
Menu generator *13.18*
Mnemonics *13.12*
Module *13.4*
Natural language *13.14*
Nonprocedural *13.14*
Object code *13.13*
Object program *13.13*
Pascal *13.16*
Program design *13.4*
Program development *13.3*
Program flowchart *13.6*
Program generators *13.18*

Program maintenance *13.11*
Programming language *13.11*
Program specifications *13.3*
Program statements *13.13*
Pseudocode *13.8*
RPG (Report Program Generator) *13.17*
Screen generator *13.18*
Screen painter *13.18*
Selection structure *13.5*
Sequence structure *13.4*
Single entry/single exit *13.6*
Source program *13.13*
Structure charts *13.4*
Structured program design *13.4*
Subroutine *13.4*
Symbolic addressing *13.12*
Symbolic operation code *13.12*
Syntax errors *13.9*
Test data *13.9*
Very high-level languages *13.14*
Warnier-Orr *13.8*

REVIEW QUESTIONS

1. What is a computer program?
2. List the five steps in program development and give a brief description of each step.
3. What is the purpose of reviewing the program specifications? List at least four types of documents that may be included in the program specifications.
4. Draw the three control structures used in structured program design.

5. Briefly describe three types of program design tools that are used by programmers.
6. What is the difference between a syntax error and a logic error?
7. Describe the four categories of programming languages.
8. Explain how a compiler and an interpreter work. What is a source program? What is an object program?
9. Why are high-level languages referred to as machine-independent languages?
10. List five commonly used programming languages and explain their primary uses.
11. How do application generators reduce the amount of time required to program?
12. List seven factors that should be considered when choosing a programming language.

CONTROVERSIAL ISSUE

1. Computer literacy is defined in different ways. Some people believe that to be computer literate a person should learn a programming language and have experience programming a computer. Other people believe that programming knowledge is inappropriate for the general user and should be reserved for those who plan to become computer professionals. What do you think?

RESEARCH PROJECT

1. Review the employment advertisements in your local newspaper for computer programming positions. Prepare a report discussing which programming languages are in demand.

Career Opportunities in the Age of Information Processing

Career Opportunities in the Age of Information Processing

OBJECTIVES

- Discuss the three areas that provide the majority of computer related jobs.
- Describe the career positions available in an information systems department.
- Describe information processing career opportunities in sales, service and repair, consulting, and education and training.
- Discuss the compensation and growth trends for information processing careers.
- Discuss the three fields in the information processing industry.
- Discuss career development, including professional organizations, certification, and professional growth and continuing education.

*I*n discussing career opportunities and computers, it's difficult to decide what to exclude. As society becomes more information oriented, computers are becoming an integral part of most jobs. For this reason, the knowledge you have gained from this text will apply in some way to any career you choose. Some of you, however, may want to consider a career in the information processing industry itself. The purpose of this chapter is to show you the opportunities that exist in the industry, present computer industry career trends, and discuss how to prepare for a career in information systems. Even if you don't choose a computer industry career, it is important to have an understanding of them, as it is likely that any job you choose will at some time provide contact with one or more computer industry representatives.

THE INFORMATION PROCESSING INDUSTRY

*T*he information processing industry is one of the largest industries in the world with annual sales of well over $100 billion. Job opportunities in the industry come primarily from three areas: the companies that provide the computer equipment; the companies that develop computer software; and the companies that hire information processing professionals to work with these products. As in any major industry, there is also a large group of service companies that support each of these three areas. An example would be a company that sells computer supplies such as printer paper and disks.

The Computer Equipment Industry

The computer equipment or hardware industry includes all manufacturers and distributors of computers and computer-related equipment such as disk and tape drives, terminals, printers, and communication equipment (Figure 14-1). The five largest mini and mainframe computer manufacturers in the United States, IBM, Digital Equipment Corporation, UNISYS, Hewlett-Packard, and NCR, are huge organizations with tens of thousands of employees worldwide. Major microcomputer manufacturers include IBM, Apple, Compaq, and Tandy. The largest company, IBM, has had annual sales of over $54 billion. In addition to the major companies, the computer equipment industry is also known for the many new "start-up" companies that appear each year. These new companies take advantage of rapid changes in equipment technology, such as laser printers, video disks, and fiber optics, to create new products and new job opportunities. Besides the companies that make end user equipment, thousands of companies make components that most users never see. These companies manufacture chips (processor, memory, etc.), power supplies, wiring, and the hundreds of other parts that go into computer equipment.

FIGURE 14-1
This photo shows newly manufactured computer keyboards being tested before shipping.

The Computer Software Industry

The computer software industry includes all developers and distributors of application and system software. In the early days, computer software was almost exclusively produced by the computer manufacturers. However, during the 1960s, numerous companies began producing software to compete with that offered by manufacturers. Today, thousands of companies provide a wide range of software from operating systems to complete business systems. The personal computer boom in the early 1980s provided numerous opportunities in the software industry. Thousands of individuals went into business for themselves by creating useful programs for the new microcomputers. Many of these people started by working out of their homes, developing their first software products on their own time while holding other jobs.

Today, software alone is a huge industry whose leaders include companies such as MSA, ASK, Microsoft, Lotus, and Ashton-Tate, with annual sales in the hundreds of millions of dollars. Most of these companies specialize in one particular type of software product such as business application software or productivity tools like word processing or spreadsheets.

Information Processing Professionals

Information processing professionals are the people that put the equipment and software to work to produce information for the end user (Figure 14-2). This includes people such as programmers and systems analysts who are hired by companies to work in an information systems department. These and other positions available in the information processing industry will be discussed in the next section.

FIGURE 14-2
Computer professionals must be able to understand the end user's point of view and often meet with the user to review information processing requirements.

WHAT ARE THE CAREER OPPORTUNITIES IN INFORMATION PROCESSING?

*T*he use of computers in so many aspects of life has created thousands of new jobs. Some of these occupations, such as personal computer software sales representative, didn't even exist ten years ago. The following section describes some of the career opportunities that currently exist.

Working in an Information Systems Department

In Chapter 1 we discussed the various types of career positions that exist within an information systems department. These positions include: data entry personnel, computer operators, computer programmers, systems analysts, database administrator, manager of information systems, and vice president of information systems.

The people in these positions work together as a team to meet the information demands of their organizations. Throughout this book, the responsibilities associated with many of these positions were discussed, including the role of the systems analysts in the information system development life cycle (Chapter 12) and the steps programmers perform in program development (Chapter 13). Another way to visualize the positions and their relationships is to look at an organization chart such as the one shown in Figure 14-3. In addition to management, the jobs in an information systems department can be classified into five categories:

1. Operations
2. Data administration
3. Systems analysis and design
4. Programming
5. Information center

Operations personnel are responsible for carrying out tasks such as operating the computer equipment that is located in the computer center. The primary responsibility of data administration is the maintenance and control of an organization's database. In systems analysis and design the various information systems needed by an organization are created and maintained. Programming develops the programs needed for the information systems, and the information center provides teaching and consulting services within an organization to help users meet their departmental and individual information processing needs. As you can see, an information systems department provides career opportunities for people with a variety of skills and talents.

FIGURE 14-3
This organization chart shows some of the positions available in an information systems department.

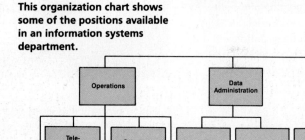
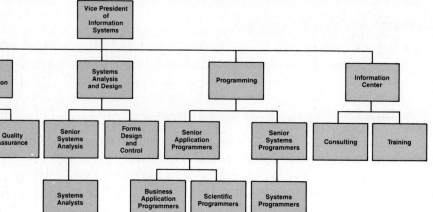

Sales

Sales representatives must have a general knowledge of computers and a specific understanding of the product they are selling. Strong interpersonal or "people" skills are important, including the ability to listen and the ability to communicate effectively both verbally and in writing. Sales representatives are usually paid based on the amount of product they sell, and top sales representatives are often the most highly compensated employees in a computer company.

Some sales representatives work directly for equipment and software manufacturers and others work for resellers. Most personal computer products are sold through dealers such as Computerland or Businessland (Figure 14-4). Some dealers, such as Egghead Discount Software, specialize in selling the most popular software products.

FIGURE 14-4
Computer retailers, such as Computerland, need salespeople who understand personal computers and have good "people" skills.

Service and Repair

Being a **service and repair technician** is a challenging job for persons who like to troubleshoot and solve problems and who have a strong background in electronics (Figure 14-5). In the early days of computers, repairs were often made at the site of the computer equipment. Today, however, malfunctioning components, such as circuit boards, are usually replaced and taken back to the service technician's office or sent to a special facility for repair. Many equipment manufacturers are now including special diagnostic software with their computer equipment that helps the service technician identify the problem. Using a modem, some advanced computer systems can automatically telephone a computer at the service technician's office and leave a message that a malfunction has been detected.

FIGURE 14-5
Computer service and repair is one of the fastest growing computer-related professions. A knowledge of electronics is essential for this occupation.

Consulting

After building experience in one or more areas, some individuals become **consultants**, people who draw upon their experience to give advice to others. Consultants must not only have strong technical skills in their area of expertise, but must also have the people skills to convince their clients to follow their advice. Qualified consultants are in high demand for such tasks as computer system selection, system design, and communication network design and installation.

Education and Training

The increased sophistication and complexity of today's computer products has opened wide opportunities in computer education and training (Figure 14-6). Qualified instructors are needed in schools, colleges, and universities and in private industry as well. In fact, the high demand for teachers has created a shortage at the university level, where many instructors have been lured into private industry because of higher pay. This shortage probably will not be filled in the near future; the supply of Ph.D.s, usually required at the university level, is not keeping up with the demand.

FIGURE 14-6
There is a high demand in schools and industry for qualified instructors who can teach information processing subjects.

COMPENSATION AND GROWTH TRENDS FOR INFORMATION PROCESSING CAREERS

ompensation is a function of experience and demand for a particular skill. Demand is influenced by geographic location, with metropolitan areas usually having higher pay than rural areas where, presumably, the cost of living is lower. Figure 14-7 shows the result of a salary survey of over 70,000 computer professionals across the United States and Canada. These amounts represent an average increase of approximately 7% over the prior year. As shown in Figure 14-8, some industries pay higher than others for the same job position. According to the survey, the communications, utility, and aerospace industries paid the highest salaries. These industries have many challenging applications and are willing to pay the highest rate to obtain the best qualified employees. According to the U.S. Bureau of Labor Statistics, the fastest growing computer career positions between 1982 and 1995 will be systems analyst, applications programmer, machine operator, and computer repair technician (Figure 14-9).

FIGURE 14-7
This table shows salary levels for various computer industry positions based on the number of years of experience. (Source: Source Edp, The Going Rate: 1988 Salaries.)

PROGRAMMING:	YRS. EXP.	20%	MEDIAN	80%
Commercial	<2	19.9	24.3	28.7
	2–3	23.5	28.0	32.5
	4–6	25.8	30.4	35.0
	>6	30.6	36.0	42.5
Engineering/Scientific	<2	23.4	30.0	34.2
	2–3	24.5	30.6	35.5
	4–6	29.6	34.8	40.7
	<6	32.8	40.0	48.4
Microcomputer	<2	18.0	22.0	27.1
	2–3	20.0	25.0	29.8
	4–6	26.1	33.0	38.9
	>6	34.8	43.0	51.6
Minicomputer	<2	19.3	23.2	28.8
	2–3	22.4	27.0	32.9
	4–6	25.4	31.0	37.2
	>6	30.3	37.0	45.9
Software Engineer	<2	23.2	28.6	31.7
	2–3	24.9	29.0	33.6
	4–6	29.1	35.0	40.6
	>6	33.6	41.5	50.2
Systems Software	<2	23.7	27.6	31.5
	2–3	23.5	28.0	31.9
	4–6	26.9	32.0	37.8
	>6	36.1	42.0	50.0
MANAGEMENT:				
Data Center Operations		33.2	40.0	52.0
Programming Development		39.8	48.0	58.1
Software Development		44.0	53.0	64.1
Systems Development		44.8	54.0	65.3
Technical Services		42.5	50.0	61.5
MIS Director		49.2	60.0	76.8
BUSINESS SYSTEMS:				
Consultant	<4	25.4	31.0	37.2
	4–6	30.1	35.0	41.3
	>6	38.7	45.0	53.6
Project Leader	<4	25.8	31.5	37.8
	4–6	30.1	35.0	41.3
	>6	36.1	42.0	50.0

BUSINESS SYSTEMS (Cont.):	YRS. EXP.	20%	MEDIAN	80%
System Analyst	<4	24.0	29.3	35.2
	4–6	28.4	33.0	38.9
	>6	32.7	38.0	45.2
SPECIALISTS:				
Communications Analyst	<4	27.6	32.5	37.4
	4–6	27.3	35.0	44.5
	>6	32.0	41.0	48.8
Database/Management Analyst	<4	20.7	28.0	33.6
	4–6	28.5	33.5	40.5
	>6	34.9	41.5	49.4
Information Center Analyst	<4	20.0	26.0	29.1
	4–6	23.4	30.0	36.0
	>6	30.2	38.2	45.8
Office Automation Analyst	<4	20.0	26.0	29.1
	4–6	25.7	33.0	39.6
	>6	30.5	38.6	46.3
SALES:				
Hardware		30.4	44.0	63.4
Software		26.7	43.8	62.6
Services		28.9	43.1	62.9
Technical Support	<2	18.6	23.2	27.1
	2–3	23.9	29.5	35.1
	4–6	26.6	32.4	39.9
	>6	36.0	45.0	54.0
Management		45.5	61.5	85.5
OTHER:				
Computer Operator	<2	15.2	19.5	21.6
	2–3	16.0	20.0	22.8
	4–6	23.3	28.8	34.3
	>6	26.3	33.7	41.5
Edp Auditor	<4	30.8	35.0	42.0
	4–6	32.5	38.2	48.9
	>6	34.0	40.0	48.4
Technical Writer or Editor	<4	17.2	21.0	24.8
	4–6	27.3	32.5	40.0
	>6	31.2	39.5	47.8

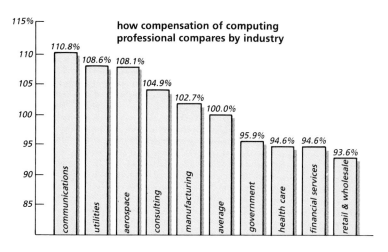

FIGURE 14-8
This chart shows that some industries pay more for the same job position.

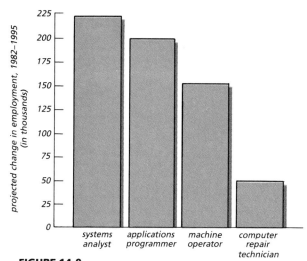

FIGURE 14-9
This chart shows computer careers with the highest projected growth, as compiled by the U.S. Bureau of Labor Statistics.

PREPARING FOR A CAREER IN INFORMATION PROCESSING

To prepare for a career in the information processing industry, individuals must decide what computer field they are interested in and obtain education in the chosen field. This section discusses the three major computer fields and some of the opportunities for obtaining education in those fields.

FIGURE 14-10
There are three broad fields of study in the information processing industry. Each field has specialized study requirements.

What Are the Fields in the Information Processing Industry?

While this book has primarily focused on the use of computers in business, there are actually three broad fields in the information processing industry (Figure 14-10): computer information systems; computer science; and computer engineering. **Computer information systems (CIS)** refers to the use of computers in areas relating to business. The field of **computer science** includes the technical aspects of computers such as hardware operation and systems software. **Computer engineering** deals with the design and manufacturing of electronic computer components and computer hardware. Each field provides unique career opportunities and has specialized study requirements. Several avenues of study are available to persons interested in obtaining formal education in information processing.

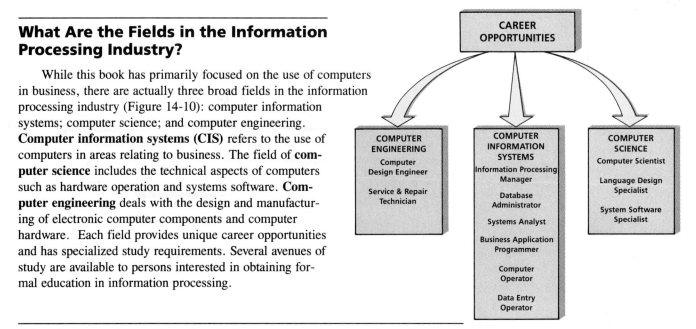

Obtaining Education for Information Processing Careers

The expanded use of computers in today's world has increased the demand for properly trained computer professionals. Educational institutions have responded to this demand by providing a variety of options for students to study information systems. Trade schools, technical schools, community colleges, colleges and universities offer formal education and certification or degree programs in computer-related fields. If you are evaluating a program offered by one of these institutions, it is important that you remember the three areas of information processing: computer information systems, computer science, and computer engineering. Frequently schools will have separate programs for each area. Understanding the differences among the three fields will help you to find the courses you want. For example, in a university, courses relating to computer information systems may be listed with the business courses, computer science courses may be with math, and computer engineering may be with electronic technology or electrical engineering. Because schools list and organize their computer courses in different ways, you should carefully read individual course descriptions whenever you are selecting computer education classes.

With the wide variety of career opportunities that exist in information processing, it is difficult to make anything other than broad general statements when it comes to discussing degree requirements for employment in the industry. As in most other industries, the more advanced degree an individual has in a chosen field, the better that individual's chances are for success. While not having a degree may limit a person's opportunities for securing a top position, it will not prevent entry nor preclude success in information processing.

CAREER DEVELOPMENT IN THE INFORMATION PROCESSING INDUSTRY

*T*here are several ways for persons employed in the information processing industry to develop their skills and increase their recognition among their peers. These include professional organizations, certification, and professional growth and continuing education activities.

Professional Organizations

A number of computer-related organizations have been formed by people who have common interests and a desire to share their knowledge. Some of the organizations that have been influential in the industry include:

- **Association for Computing Machinery (ACM).** An association composed of persons interested in computer science and computer science education. The association has many special interest groups such as computer graphics, database, and business.
- **Association of Information Systems Professionals.** This association was originally aimed at word processing professionals, but now includes a much broader interest area, including office automation.
- **Association of Systems Management (ASM).** A group composed of individuals interested in the improvement of the systems analysis and design field.
- **Data Processing Management Association (DPMA).** A professional association of programmers, systems analysts, and information processing managers.
- **Institute of Electrical and Electronic Engineers (IEEE)** and **IEEE Computer Society**. Organizations primarily composed of computer scientists and engineers.

Each of the above organizations has chapters throughout the United States (several throughout the world), offers monthly meetings, and sponsors periodic workshops, seminars, and conventions. Some organizations have student chapters or offer reduced membership fees for students. Attending professional meetings provide an excellent opportunity for students to learn about the information processing industry and to meet and talk with professionals in the field. In addition to these and other professional organizations, user groups exist for most makes of computers. Most metropolitan areas have one or more local computer societies that meet monthly to discuss topics of common interest about personal computers. For anyone employed or just interested in the computer industry, these groups can be an effective and rewarding way to learn and continue career development.

FIGURE 14-11
The Certificate in Data Processing (CDP) recognizes a high level of knowledge that the recipient has demonstrated by passing a five-part examination. This is a copy of the first CDP ever awarded.

Certification

Many professions offer certification programs as a way of encouraging and recognizing the efforts of their members to attain a level of knowledge about their profession. The best known certification program in the information processing industry is the **Certificate in Data Processing (CDP)**, originated by DPMA but now administered by the **Institute for the Certification of Computer Professionals (ICCP)**. The CDP (Figure 14-11) is awarded to persons who pass an examination that has five parts: (1) computer equipment; (2) computer programming and software; (3) principles of management; (4) accounting and quantitative methods; and (5) systems analysis and design. To be eligible to take the examination, a person must have a minimum of five years of experience in the information processing industry. People who pass the examination are authorized to place the initials CDP after their name.

Professional Growth and Continuing Education

Because of rapid changes in technology, staying aware of new products and services in the information processing industry can be a challenging task. One way of keeping up is by participating in professional growth and continuing education activities. This broad category includes events such as conferences, workshops, conventions, and trade shows that provide both general and specific information on equipment, software, services, and issues affecting the industry, such as computer security. Workshops and seminars usually last a day or two while conferences, conventions, and trade shows often last a week. Some of the larger trade shows, such as **COMDEX** (**COM**puter **D**ealer **EX**position), bring together over a thousand vendors to display their latest products and services (Figure 14-12).

FIGURE 14-12
COMDEX is one of the largest computer product trade shows in the world. Thousands of vendors come together to demonstrate their new equipment, software, and services to prospective customers.

SUMMARY OF COMPUTER CAREER OPPORTUNITIES

With the increased use of computers, the prospects for computer-related career opportunities are excellent. Not only are the numbers of traditional information processing jobs, such as programmer and systems analyst, expected to increase, but the application of the computer to existing occupations will create additional job opportunities. Regardless of an individual's career choice, a basic understanding of computers should be an essential part of any employee's job skills.

CHAPTER SUMMARY

1. As society becomes more information oriented, computers are becoming an integral part of most jobs.
2. Job opportunities in the information processing industry come from three areas: computer equipment companies, computer software companies, and companies that hire information processing professionals.
3. The computer equipment industry includes all manufacturers and distributors of computers and computer-related equipment.
4. The computer software industry includes all developers and distributors of application and system software.
5. Information processing professionals are the people that put the equipment and software to work to produce information for the end user.
6. Career opportunities in information processing include: working in an information systems department; sales; service and repair; consulting; education and training.
7. The jobs in an information systems department can be classified into five categories: (1) operations; (2) data administration; (3) systems analysis and design; (4) programming; and (5) information center.
8. **Sales representatives** are often the most highly compensated employees in a computer company.
9. Being a **service and repair technician** is a challenging job for persons who like to solve problems and who have a strong background in electronics.
10. **Consultants**, people who draw upon their experience to give advice to others, are in high demand for such tasks as computer system selection, system design, and communication network design and installation.
11. According to the U.S. Bureau of Labor and Statistics, the fastest growing computer career positions between 1982 and 1995 will be systems analyst, applications programmer, machine operator, and computer repair technician.
12. The three fields in information processing are computer information systems; computer science; and computer engineering.
13. **Computer information systems** refers to the use of computers in areas relating to business.
14. **Computer science** includes the technical aspects of computers such as hardware operation and systems software.
15. **Computer engineering** deals with the design and manufacturing of electronic computer components and computer hardware.
16. Trade schools, technical schools, community colleges, colleges, and universities offer formal education and certification or degree programs in computer related fields.
17. Computer professionals may continue to develop their skills and increase their recognition among their peers through professional organizations, certification, and professional growth and continuing education activities.
18. Professional organizations, such as the **Data Processing Management Association (DPMA)**, have been formed by people who have common interests and a desire to share their knowledge.
19. The **Certificate in Data Processing (CDP)** is the best known certification program in the information processing industry.
20. Computer professionals stay current by participating in professional growth and continuing education activities such as conferences, workshops, conventions, and trade shows.

KEY TERMS

Association for Computing Machinery
(ACM) *14.8*
Association of Information
Systems Professionals *14.8*
Association of Systems Management
(ASM) *14.8*
Certificate in Data Processing
(CDP) *14.9*

COMDEX *14.9*
Computer engineering *14.7*
Computer information systems
(CIS) *14.7*
Computer science *14.7*
Consultants *14.5*
Data Processing Management
Association (DPMA) *14.8*

Institute for the Certification of
Computer Professionals (ICCP) *14.9*
Institute of Electrical and
Electronic Engineers (IEEE) *14.8*
Sales representatives *14.5*
Service and repair technician *14.5*

REVIEW QUESTIONS

1. Briefly discuss the computer hardware and software industries.
2. The positions in an information systems department can be classified into what five categories?
3. List and discuss four information career opportunities other than working in an information systems department.
4. What are the four fastest growing computer career positions?
5. Describe the three fields in information processing.
6. List five computer-related professional organizations.
7. What are the five parts of the CDP exam?

CONTROVERSIAL ISSUE

1. Some people believe that computer professions such as programming should be subject to mandatory certification or licensing, like certified public accountants. Others believe that because the industry is changing so rapidly, certification programs should be encouraged but remain voluntary. Discuss the advantages and disadvantages of mandatory programs.

RESEARCH PROJECT

1. Contact one of the professional computer organizations listed in the chapter. Either attend a local meeting or write for membership information and prepare a report for your class.

Trends and Issues in the Information Age

Trends and Issues in the Information Age

OBJECTIVES

- Discuss the electronic devices and applications that are part of the automated office.
- Describe the technologies that are developing for the automated factory, including CAD, CAE, CAM, and CIM.
- Discuss the use of personal computers in the home.
- Explain guidelines for purchasing personal computers.
- Discuss social issues related to computers, such as computer crime and privacy.

*A*fter reading the preceding chapters, you know what a computer is, what a computer does, how it does it, and why a computer is so powerful. You have learned about computer equipment and software, and how the system development process is used to combine these elements with data, personnel, users, and procedures to create a working information system. The purpose of this chapter is to talk about current and future trends, including changes taking place in information systems in the workplace. We also discuss the use of personal computers in the home and some of the social issues related to computers, such as security and computer crime, privacy, ethics, and health.

INFORMATION SYSTEMS IN BUSINESS

*T*he largest single user of computers is business. Millions of systems ranging from mainframes to microcomputers are installed and used for applications such as inventory control, billing, and accounting. This section discusses how these traditional applications will be affected by changes in technology and methods. It also discusses two other areas of business applications, the automated office and the automated factory. Although the term automated can be applied to any process or machine that can operate without human intervention, the term is commonly used to describe computer-controlled functions.

How Will Existing Information Systems Change?

Existing business information systems will continue to undergo profound changes as new technology, software, and methods are applied to the huge installed base of traditional business system users. Important overall trends include more online, interactive systems and less batch processing. In addition, the increased use of relational database systems means that users have a wider variety of data and information available for decision making, and more flexibility, presenting information on reports and displays (Figure 15-1).

FIGURE 15-1
Trends that will affect information systems of tomorrow.

SOFTWARE

- Fourth-generation and natural languages that will enable the user to communicate with the computer in a more conversational manner.
- Computer-aided software engineering (CASE) that will shorten the system development time frame.
- Increased use of decision support and artificial intelligence systems to help users make decisions.
- Increased implementation of graphic interfaces using icons and symbols to represent information and processes.

EQUIPMENT

- Increased use of personal computers networked to other personal computers and to central mini or mainframe computers.
- Increased storage capacity of disks using improved and new technologies such as laser disks.
- Terminals that can display 132 or more characters per line, as well as graphics and images.
- Faster, better quality printers.
- Reduced instruction set computers (RISC) and parallel processing that will greatly increase the number of instructions that can be processed at one time.

Profit and Loss Statement					
(in millions)	Actual			Projected	
	1983	1984	1985	1986	1987
Revenues	3.551	5.300	6.170	6.787	7.465
Expenses					
Labor	0.300	0.370	0.550	0.616	0.727
Energy	0.165	0.284	0.350	0.392	0.462
Materials	1.108	1.626	2.513	2.814	3.321
Administration	0.317	0.365	0.388	0.435	0.513
Other	0.447	0.491	0.523	0.586	0.691
Total Expenses	2.337	3.136	4.323	4.842	5.714
Profit (Loss)	1.215	2.163	1.846	1.944	1.751

DATA

- Automatic input of data at the source where it is created.
- Storage and use of non-text data such as voice and image.

INFORMATION SYSTEMS PERSONNEL

- Increased interface with users.
- Emphasis will shift from how to capture and process data to how to use the available data more effectively.

USERS

- Most people will be computer literate, with a basic understanding of how computers work and how they can use them in their jobs.

The Automated Office

The **automated office**, sometimes referred to as the **electronic office**, is the term that describes the use of electronic devices such as computers, facsimile machines, and computerized telephone systems to make office work more productive. As was the case with traditional business applications such as accounting, automated office applications such as word processing, electronic mail, voice mail, desktop publishing, facsimile, image processing, and teleconferencing started out as separate, stand-alone applications. In recent years, however, the trend has been to integrate these applications into a network of devices and services that can share information. A brief review of each of these capabilities follows.

Word Processing   Word processing is the ability to electronically create, store, revise, and print written documents. For many organizations, word processing was the first office application to be automated and among all organizations, word processing still ranks as the most widely used office automation technology. Today, most word processing systems are integrated with other applications. This allows the word processing applications to extract data such as names and addresses or financial data from other application files.

Electronic Mail   Electronic mail is the ability to use computers to transmit messages to and receive messages from other computer users. The other users may be on the same computer network or on a separate computer system reached through the use of a modem or some other communications device. Electronic mail eliminates the need to hand deliver messages or use a delivery service, such as the post office or Federal Express. Electronic mail usage will grow as previously separate personal computers are attached to local area networks.

Voice Mail   **Voice mail** can be considered verbal electronic mail. Made possible by the latest computerized telephone systems, voice mail reduces the problem of "telephone tag," where two people trying to reach each other wind up leaving a series of messages to "please call back." With voice mail, the caller can leave a message, similar to leaving a message on an answering machine. The difference is that with a voice mail system, the caller's message is digitized (converted into binary ones and zeros) so that it can be stored on a disk like other computer data. This allows the party who was called to hear the message later (by reconverting it to an audio form) and also, if desired, add a reply or additional comments and forward the message to someone else who has access to the system.

Desktop Publishing   Desktop publishing involves the use of computers to produce printed documents that can combine different sizes and styles of text and graphics. Desktop publishing allows the user to control the process of creating high quality newsletters, brochures, and other documents that previously would have to have been developed by professional artists. The availability of desktop publishing systems for different computers and levels of user sophistication will increase their use in small as well as large organizations.

Facsimile   **Facsimile** or **Fax** machines are used to transmit a reproduced image of a document over standard phone lines (Figure 15-2). The document can be printed, hand written, or a photograph. Fax machines optically scan the document and convert the image into digitized data that can be transmitted, using a modem, over the phone. A compatible Fax machine at the receiving end converts the digitized data back into its original image. Besides the separate Fax machines, plug-in circuit boards are also available for personal computers. Using a modem, these boards can directly transmit computer-prepared documents or documents that have been digitized with the use of a scanner. Fax machines are having an increasing impact on the way businesses transmit documents. Many documents that were previously sent through the mail are now sent by Fax. With the speed and convenience of a phone call, a document sent by Fax can be transmitted anywhere in the world.

Image Processing   Image processing is the ability to store and retrieve a reproduced image of a document. Image processing is often used when an original document, such as an insurance claim, must be seen to verify data. Image processing and traditional applications will continue to be combined in many areas. For example, in 1988 American Express began sending cardholders copies of the individual charge slips that were related to the charges on their statement. These charge slips were recorded by an image processing system and then merged with the customer statement program.

FIGURE 15-2
This facsimile (Fax) machine can send and receive copies of documents to and from any location where there is phone service and a compatible Fax machine.

Teleconferencing   Teleconferencing once meant three or more people sharing a phone conversation. Today, however, **teleconferencing** usually means **video conferencing**, the use of computers and television cameras to transmit video images and the sound of the conference participants to other participants with similar equipment at a remote location (Figure 15-3). Special software and equipment is used to digitize the video image so that it can be transmitted along with the audio over standard communication channels. Although the video image is not as clear for moving objects as is commercial television, it does contribute to the conference discussion and is adequate for nonmoving objects such as charts and graphs.

FIGURE 15-3
Video conferencing is used to transmit and receive video and audio signals over standard communication channels.

Summary of the Automated Office   The trend toward integrated automated office capabilities will continue. Incompatible devices will be standardized or will be provided with software that will enable them to communicate and transfer data with other devices. The increased productivity provided by automated office devices will encourage more and more organizations to adopt them to help control costs and remain competitive.

The Automated Factory

As in the automated office, the goal of the **automated factory** is to increase productivity through the use of automated, and often computer-controlled, equipment. Technologies used in the automated factory include computer-aided design, computer-aided engineering, computer-aided manufacturing, and computer-integrated manufacturing.

FIGURE 15-4
Computer-aided design (CAD) is an efficient way to develop plans for new products.

Computer-Aided Design (CAD) Computer-aided design (CAD) uses a computer and special graphics software to aid in product design (Figure 15-4). The CAD software eliminates the laborious drafting that used to be required and allows the designer to dynamically change the size of some or all of the product and view the design from different angles. The ability to store the design electronically offers several advantages over traditional manual methods. For one thing, the designs can be changed more easily than before. For another, the design database can be reviewed more easily by other design engineers. This increases the likelihood that an existing part will be used in a product rather than a new part designed. For example, if a support bracket was required for a new product, the design engineer could review the design database to see if any existing products used a support bracket that would be appropriate for the new product. This not only decreases the overall design time but increases the reliability of the new product by using proven parts.

Computer-Aided Engineering (CAE) Computer-aided engineering (CAE) is the use of computers to test product designs. Using CAE, engineers can test the design of an airplane or a bridge before they are built (Figure 15-5). Sophisticated programs are available to simulate the effects of wind, temperature, weight, and stress on product shapes and materials. Before the use of CAE, prototypes of products had to be built and subjected to testing that often destroyed the prototype.

Computer-Aided Manufacturing (CAM) Computer-aided manufacturing (CAM) is the use of computers to control production equipment. CAM production equipment includes software-controlled drilling, lathe, and milling machines as well as robots (Figure 15-6). The use of robots has aroused much interest, partially because of preconceived ideas of robots as intelligent, humanlike machines. In practice, most industrial robots rarely look like a human and can only perform preprogrammed tasks. Robots are often used for repetitive tasks in hazardous or disagreeable environments, such as welding or painting areas.

FIGURE 15-5 Computer-aided engineering (CAE) allows the user to test product designs before they are built and without damaging the product.

FIGURE 15-6 Computer-aided manufacturing (CAM) is used to control production equipment such as these welding robots on an automobile assembly line.

Computer-Integrated Manufacturing (CIM) Computer-integrated manufacturing (CIM) is the total integration of the manufacturing process using computers (Figure 15-7). Using CIM concepts, individual production processes are linked so that the production flow is balanced and optimized, and products flow smoothly through the factory. In a CIM factory, automated design processes are linked to automated machining processes that are linked to automated assembly processes that are linked to automated testing and packaging. Under ideal CIM conditions, a product will move through the entire production process under computer control. Because of its complexity, many companies may never fully implement CIM. But CIM's related concepts of minimum inventory and efficient demand-driven production are valid and will be incorporated into many manufacturers' business plans.

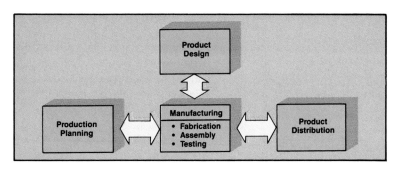

FIGURE 15-7
The concept of computer-integrated manufacturing (CIM) is to use computers to integrate all phases of the manufacturing process from planning and design to manufacturing and distribution.

BRINGING THE INFORMATION AGE HOME

*S*ince personal computers became available in the mid-1970s, millions of personal computers have been purchased for home use. It is expected that the use of personal computers in the home will continue to increase. Just as the use of computers in the workplace will change how we work, the use of computers in our homes will change various aspects of our personal lives. The next two sections discuss how personal computers are used in the home, including some possible new applications, and things you should consider when purchasing a personal computer system.

The Use of Personal Computers in the Home

Personal computers can be used in many different ways in the home. Five general areas of use include: (1) personal services; (2) control of home systems; (3) telecommuting; (4) education; and (5) entertainment.

Personal Services In many ways running a home is similar to running a small business. The productivity tools that are used in the office, such as word processing, spreadsheet, and database, can also be used in the home to aid with creating documents, financial planning and analysis, and filing and organizing data. Personal computer software is also available to assist with home accounting applications such as balancing checkbooks, making household budgets, and preparing tax returns. In addition, using a personal computer to transmit and receive data over telephone lines allows home users to access a wealth of information and services. For example, teleshopping and electronic banking are two services that are becoming more popular, and information such as stock prices and airline schedules is available to home users who subscribe to database services such as CompuServe and The Source. The personal services provided by home computer use allows people to perform personal and business-related tasks quickly and conveniently in the comfort of their own homes. Without a personal computer, completing similar activities would take considerably more time because it would frequently require travel to other locations to conduct business and acquire information.

Control of Home Systems   Another use of computers in the home is to control home systems such as security, environment control, lighting, and landscape sprinkler systems. Personal computers used in this manner are usually linked to special devices such as alarms for security; thermostats for environmental control; and timing devices for lighting and sprinkler systems. When the personal computer system has communication capabilities, a homeowner who is away can use a telephone or another computer to call home and change the operation of one of the control systems. For example, suppose a homeowner is on vacation in Texas and learns that heavy rains have been falling at home in Pennsylvania. It is possible for the homeowner to call home and use the keys of a touch-tone telephone to instruct the computer to turn off the garden sprinkler system. Near Orlando, Florida, an example of the ways that computers may be used in homes of the future is demonstrated in a showcase model called the Xanadu House. In this home computers are used in many ways including controlling home systems.

Telecommuting   **Telecommuting** refers to the ability of individuals to work at home and communicate with their offices by using personal computers and communication lines. With a personal computer, an employee can access the main computer at the office. Electronic mail can be read and answered. Databases can be accessed and completed projects can be transmitted. It has been predicted that by the end of the 1990s 10 percent of the workforce will be telecommuters. Most of these people will probably arrange their business schedules so that they can telecommute two or three days a week. Telecommuting provides flexibility, allowing companies and employees to work out arrangements that can increase productivity and at the same time meet the needs of individual employees. Some of the advantages possible with telecommuting include reducing the time needed to commute to the office each week; eliminating the need to travel during poor weather conditions; providing a convenient and comfortable work environment for disabled employees or workers recovering from injuries or illnesses; and allowing employees to combine work with personal responsibilities such as child care.

Education   The use of personal computers for education, called **computer-aided instruction (CAI)**, is another rapidly growing area. While CAI is frequently used to describe software that is developed and used in schools, much of the same software is available for home users. CAI software can be classified into three main types: drill and practice; tutorials; and simulations.

Drill and practice software uses a "flashcard" approach to teaching by allowing users to practice skills in subjects such as math and language. A problem or word is displayed on the computer screen and the user enters the answer. The computer accepts the answer and responds by telling the student whether or not the answer was correct. Sometimes the user gets second and third chances to select the correct answer before the computer software will display the correct answer. With **tutorial software**, the computer software displays text and graphics and sometimes uses sound to teach a user concepts about subjects such as chemistry, music theory, or computer literacy. Following the instruction, tutorial software may quiz the user with true/false or multiple choice questions to help ensure that the concepts being taught are understood. The increased use of optical disk storage that provides high quality graphics and direct access capability promises to greatly enhance this type of CAI.

The third type of CAI, **simulation software**, is designed to teach a user by creating a model. For example, many simulation packages are available to teach business concepts. One program designed for children simulates running a lemonade stand and another program for adults simulates the stock market. In the lemonade simulation, the user makes decisions about "How many quarts of lemonade to make" and "What price to charge customers for a glass of lemonade." The computer software accepts the user's decisions, performs computations using the software model, and then responds to the user with the amount of profit or loss for the day. Good CAI software is designed to be user friendly and motivate the user to succeed (Figure 15-8).

In addition to CAI software, some trade schools, colleges and universities are now allowing students with personal computers to take electronic correspondence courses from their homes. Lessons and assignments for classes are transmitted between the student and the school over communication lines.

Education in the home through CAI or electronic correspondence courses allow home users to learn at their own pace, in the convenience of their home, and at a time that fits into their personal schedule. Well-written educational software can be so entertaining that it is sometimes difficult to distinguish between it and entertainment software.

FIGURE 15-8
Computer-aided instruction (CAI) software provides a structured yet motivating way to learn. This software package helps the user to develop deductive reasoning, reference, and research skills while learning geography, history, economics, government, and culture.

Entertainment Entertainment software, or game playing, on home computers has always had a large following among the younger members of the family. However, many adults are surprised to find that entertainment software can also provide them with hours of enjoyment. Popular types of entertainment software include arcade games, board games, simulations, and interactive graphics programs. Most people are familiar with the arcade-type games (similar to video games such as Pac-Man) that are available for computers. A popular board game is computer chess. Simulations include games such as baseball and football and a variety of flight simulators that allow users to pretend they are controlling and navigating different types of aircraft (Figure 15-9). Also available are a wide variety of interactive graphic adventure games that range from rescuing a princess from a castle's dungeon to solving a murder mystery. Many of these games can be played either individually or in small groups. The software usually allows players to adjust the level of play to their skill level, that is, beginner through advanced. With entertainment software, the computer becomes a fun, skillful, and challenging game partner.

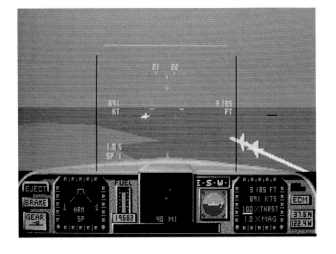

FIGURE 15-9
Flight simulators can be part fun and part educational. Some simulators offer realistic instrument consoles and flight patterns that help teach the user about flying.

A different type of entertainment available to users who have personal computers with communication capabilities is the access and use of electronic **bulletin board systems**, called **BBSs**, that allow users to communicate with one another and share information (Figure 15-10). While some bulletin boards provide specific services such as buying and selling used computer equipment, many bulletin boards function as electronic clubs for special interest groups and are used to share information about hobbies as diverse as stamp collecting, music, genealogy, and astronomy. Some BBSs are strictly social; users meet new friends and conduct conversations by entering messages through their keyboards.

FIGURE 15-10
This is a list of just some of the bulletin boards available in the San Diego, California area. Bulletin board systems are an excellent source for answers to questions about personal computer equipment and software.

300/1200 BPS

A&B Express	447-1009 ✱ Z
Adventure Board	224-2636
The After World	679-7159
Back County PCBBS	789-6377
The BBS	447-8143
The C-64 Exchange	292-9351
The Candy Shoppe	474-5966
Clue Line	566-2562
CMS—Bell Junior High	267-2807
CMS—Kearny Mesa	565-1321
CMS—Patrick Henry	287-2644
CMUG	433-3162
The Commodore Shop	423-7910 ✱
Cougar Country	480-3056 Z
Cuyamaca College	465-3792
Digex—SDCS DIGSIG	454-8078
Disk-Connection	562-1989
Educational Technologies	265-3428
Eight-Bit Tandy	571-6366
Empty V	425-5808 Z
The Evergreen Forest	426-2057 ✱
F&L BBS	670-7462
The Fifth Dimension	670-3969 ✱ Z
Frog's Bible Board	275-0506
The Fun House	282-9124
Guardian's Cavern	563-9004
Heath SIG MS/PC-DOS Support	461-2417
His Majesty's Secret Service	480-8403 Z
JSR Service Net	258-9078
Kit's Hideout	741-0692
The Knight's Realm	746-2029
The Lemonade Stand	941-6158
The Looney Bin	390-9470
Maui's CoCo Hotspot	486-4249
Micro-80 of Oceanside	439-9169
Money Works	579-1403
The Monsoon	259-1507
My Board	743-7194
My House	447-1422
Ocean Beach BBS	224-4878
Outer Limits	941-2424
Paulette's Playhouse	743-3138
The Post Office	479-8558
P.O.C.	437-1911
Private Resort	484-6437
Ramona Country BBS	789-6235
Real-Net BBS	464-4540
Sanyo Users Group BBS	454-8876
SCCG-TIBBS	278-8155
ST—SDACE	284-3821
ST SIG Atari ST & Others	726-4419
SunSplash	297-3230
The 64 & More Store	258-0951
Smart Users Group	480-9686
also	726-4419
Software, Etc.	291-5790 Z
Special Integrated Designs	464-0048
The Surf Shack	567-6017
The Torture Chamber	452-2893
Zeke	755-5675

300/1200/2400 BPS

Adventures In Palancia	222-1785
The Amiga Exchange	223-2734 Z
Apokolips	488-4714
Bear Country	541-7048
Brian Smith's BBS	582-0875
Camelot 3000	462-0542
Classified Connection	566-1745
CMS—El Cajon	444-5442
COM2: Remote BBS	471-8730
Computer Boulevard	589-0565
ComputorEdge On-Line	573-1675
Computer Outlet	282-6815 Z
Computer Outlet, North County	740-0113 ✱ Z
The Computer Room	287-6006
CORE BBS	295-2912
Cornucopia	283-0498
Coronado Wildcat!	435-8070
Dollars and Bytes	483-5477 Z
The Dream Clinic	670-9522
The Enchanted World	692-9518
Enigma—The Next Generation	453-1819
The Fish Express	792-1653
Faultline BBS	481-7340
FSMAO-2	725-6322
The Flare Path	561-2999
The Fun House	282-9124
The Information Center	696-2568
Imperial Beach BBS	575-1562
The Key Of David	479-2104
Kingdom Age BBS	586-7973
The Knowledge Works BBS	528-1058 ✱
Lakeside PC Board	390-7328
MacBonsali	726-1591
The MacConnection	259-8735
Mainstreet Data	439-6624
Mac INFONET	944-3646
Milliway's	268-9614
Morning Star	575-3310
Mouse Trap BBS	462-3975 ✱
Multitech PC	578-9221
Nassau Xpress	433-9777
NEXUS Z-Node #63	486-0735
North San Diego Apple Club	571-9010
Nova	489-8975
PD-SIG	749-2741
also	749-2589
also	566-6329
also	466-3118
also	727-0202
P-Net (pnet01)	444-7006
P-Net (pnet03)	569-9195
P-Net (pnet08)	450-0052
Prides Crossing	464-6271
ProLine [avalon]	271-0131
ProLine [beagle]	452-5565
ProLine [mercury]	697-0261
The Rasta Connection	282-1211
The RPC Library	283-6365
Sabaline	692-1961
San Diego Computer Society	549-3788
San Diego Live	584-1715 $
also	584-4172 $
Scanline	298-2023
Seastalker BBS	581-9379
Sharky's MAChine	747-8719
SomeWares Between Heaven & Hell	436-9861
ST MIDI Connection	452-7535
Star Base 23	560-2996
Surfer's Paradise	724-9520 ✱
Sysport MIDI BBS	698-7155
TeleMac	576-1820 $
Turnkey Technology	563-6688
Z Node #9	270-3148

300/1200/2400/9600
HST STANDARD

Another System	792-0634
Bootcamp I	941-0996
Bytes 'R Us	428-9773
Casino West	470-0771
Dead Zone	755-3350
DOOGER'S PLACE	588-8931
Dworkin's Castle	438-5256
MediaLine BBS	454-1629
The Final Experience	670-4445
Sawyer College of Business BBS	286-8614 Z
Mushin BBS	535-9580
Night Owl, Ham Radio	279-3921
Nuggo's Place	222-3097
ProLine [simasd]	239-1397
ProLine [sol]	670-5379 ✱
PD-SIG	749-6222
also	749-3432
SCANIS	565-0785
Serenity	259-7757
South Bay BBS	421-3189
Starhelm Graystaff	479-3006

300/1200/2400/9600 BPS
Trailblazer

People-Net (pnet12)	259-3704 ✱

300/1200/2400/9600 BPS
Racial Vadic

PD-SIG	749-6384 ✱

LEGEND
✱ New or updated information.
Z After hours or weekends.
$ Requires a one-time donation for access.

ComputorEdge acknowledges this is not a complete listing of all BBSs in San Diego area. We reserve the right to reject or cancel any submission for publication.

In addition to sharing hobby information with other computer users on a BBS, some personal computer users use their home computer as a tool for personal hobbies. Computers are used by hobbyists to design quilt and stained glass patterns, run model trains, organize stamp, doll, and photography collections, and write, transpose, play, and print musical scores.

Summary of the Use of Personal Computers in the Home   As you can see, personal computers are used in homes in a variety of ways. Whether or not you now use a personal computer in your home, it is very probable that you will at some time in the near future. In fact, it is very possible that within the next decade you will have multiple computers in your home. Because computers can be used in so many different ways and also because computer technology is changing so rapidly, it is important that you carefully choose any computer system that you may purchase. Some general guidelines for purchasing personal computers are discussed in the next section.

Guidelines for Buying a Personal Computer

When purchasing a personal computer, make every effort to select a computer system that matches your individual needs as closely as possible. Six general steps recommended for purchasing a personal computer system include:

Step 1. Become computer literate. This is truly the first step and an important step in making a wise purchase. You might be surprised that many people go straight out and buy computer equipment without understanding the capability of a personal computer or the tasks it can and cannot perform. Many times these people buy a computer like the one their neighbor or friend purchased, and expect it to meet their needs. Sometimes it does, but frequently they are disappointed. Hopefully this will not happen to you. You already have an advantage because by reading this book, you now know a great deal about computers and have developed a foundation of knowledge on which you can base your software and equipment decisions. In short, you already are computer literate. Because computer technology is changing rapidly, to stay computer literate you will need to stay current with the changes in the field. You can do this by reading periodicals or attending seminars on "state of the art" computer technology.

Step 2. Define and prioritize the type of tasks you want to perform on your computer. This step will help you to see more clearly exactly what you want to do with your computer and will help you to select software and equipment that will match these needs. Define your needs in writing. Create a numbered list with the most important application at the top and the least important application at the bottom. General applications like word processing, spreadsheets, database, and communications are easy to include on the list. You may, however, have a special application in mind, such as controlling a household security system. Being computer literate will help you to know if a special application is feasible. It will also help you to discuss any special needs you may have with computer professionals who can help you. Once your list is completed you can begin to evaluate the available software.

Step 3. Select the software packages that best meet your needs. Periodicals, computer stores, and user groups are all good resources when it comes to evaluating the available software. For more on evaluating software, review the section in Chapter 2, "Guidelines for Purchasing Microcomputer Applications Software."

In addition to purchasing commercial software, another possibility is to consider selecting shareware and public domain software. **Shareware** is software that users may try out on their own systems before paying a fee. If a user decides to keep and use the software a registration fee is sent to the software publisher (Figure 15-11). **Public domain software** is free software that is not copyrighted and can therefore be distributed among users. While the quality of shareware and public domain software varies greatly, some of the software is quite good. This type of software can be obtained from BBSs and also from public domain software libraries.

FIGURE 15-11
After trying the PC-Write software, users fill out a registration form and mail it with a fee to Quicksoft, the publisher of PC-Write. A user certificate is then sent to the user.

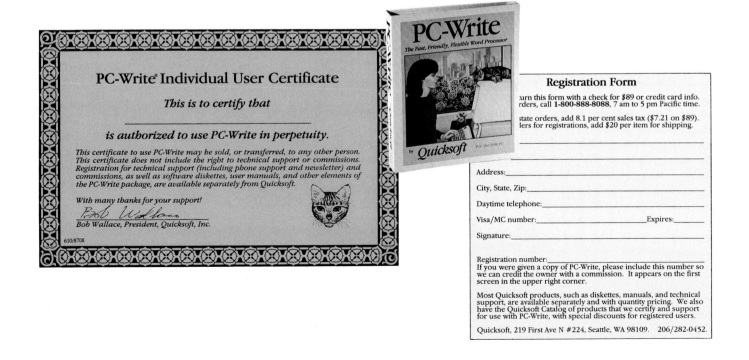

Step 4. Select equipment that will run the software you have selected. The capabilities of the different types of personal computers vary greatly. For example, some personal computers can perform extensive graphics while others cannot. Selecting the software that meets your needs before selecting your equipment guides you in selecting appropriate equipment. Some software only runs on certain types of personal computers. Also, knowing the software you want to run prevents overbuying (purchasing a machine that is more powerful than you need) or underbuying (purchasing a machine that is not powerful enough). Other things to consider when evaluating equipment include: processing speed of the microprocessor, memory size, system expandability, compatibility of the system with other personal computers, monochrome or color display, amount and type of auxiliary storage, printer type and speed, and communications capabilities.

Step 5. Select the suppliers for the software and equipment. Options include used equipment and software, mail order, and computer stores. Price, warranties, training, service, and repair are all things to consider when selecting a supplier. Obtaining the best overall value may not mean paying the lowest price. A store that is willing to provide you with assistance in assembling your system or providing some training may be well worth a slightly higher price.

Step 6. Purchase the software and equipment. If you have followed these guidelines you will probably feel both excited and confident with the decisions you have made. Your efforts to define your computing needs and to select software, equipment, and a supplier that will meet those needs should have helped you to select a personal computer system that is appropriate for you and with which you will be satisfied.

Summary of Bringing the Information Age Home

Personal computers are used in homes to aid in a variety of tasks such as personal services, control of home systems, telecommuting, education, and entertainment. When purchasing a personal computer system for the home, users should first become computer literate and evaluate their computer processing needs, and then purchase software and equipment that meets those needs. The trend is clear. Personal computers will continue to bring the information age into our homes.

The changes that accompany the information age raise several issues that are related to society as a whole. Some of these issues will be discussed in the following section.

SOCIAL ISSUES

Significant inventions such as the automobile and television have always challenged existing values and caused society to think about the right and wrong ways to use the new invention. So too has the computer. This section discusses some of the social issues related to computers, including security and computer crime and privacy.

Computer Security and Crime

Computer security and computer crime are closely related topics. **Computer security** refers to the safeguards established to prevent and detect unauthorized use and deliberate or accidental damage to computer systems and data. **Computer crime** is the use of a computer to commit an illegal act. This section discusses the types of crimes that can be committed and the security measures that can be taken to prevent and detect them.

Software Theft   Software theft, often called **software piracy**, became a major problem with the increased use of personal computers. Some people have a hard time understanding why they should pay hundreds, perhaps thousands of dollars for what appears to be an inexpensive diskette or tape, and instead of paying for an authorized copy of the software they make an illegal copy. This leads software manufacturers to install elaborate copy protection schemes designed to prevent anyone from copying the software. However, the copy protection also prevents authorized users who have paid the license fee from making backup copies of the software for security purposes. Today, software piracy is still an issue. It is estimated that for every authorized copy of a commercial program, there is at least one illegal copy. Although many companies have abandoned copy protection, they still take illegal copying seriously and vigorously prosecute offenders when caught. For large users, the financial incentives for stealing software have been lowered by site licensing and multiple copy discounts. Site licensing allows organizations to pay a single fee for multiple copies of a program used at a single location. Multiple copy discounts reduce the fee of each additional copy of a program license.

Unauthorized Access and Use   **Unauthorized access** can be defined as computer trespassing, in other words, being logged on a system without permission. Many so-called computer hackers boast of the number of systems that they have been able to access by using a modem. These hackers usually don't do any damage and merely "wander around" the accessed system before logging off.

Unauthorized use is the use of a computer system or computer data for unapproved and possibly illegal activities. Unauthorized use may range from an employee using the company computer for keeping his child's soccer league scores to someone gaining access to a bank funds system and creating an unauthorized transfer. Unauthorized use could also include the theft of computerized information such as customer lists or product plans.

The key to preventing both unauthorized access and unauthorized use is an appropriate level of authorization. Authorization techniques range from simple passwords to advanced biometric devices that can identify individuals by their fingerprint, voice, or eye pattern. The level of authorization should match the degree of risk and should be regularly reviewed to determine if the level is still appropriate.

Malicious Damage   Malicious or deliberate damage to the data in a computer system is often difficult to detect because the damaged data may not be used or carefully reviewed on a regular basis. A disgruntled employee or an outsider may gain access to the system and delete or alter individual records or an entire file. One of the most potentially dangerous types of malicious damage is done by a **virus**, a computer program designed to copy itself into other software and spread through multiple computer systems. Figure 15-12 on the following page shows how a virus can spread from one system to another. Although they have been known for a long time, it is only in recent years that viruses have become a serious problem. Besides developing specific programs called "vaccines" to locate and remove viruses, organizations are becoming more aggressive in prosecuting persons suspected of planting viruses. In what was described as the first computer virus trial, in 1988 a former programmer was convicted in Texas of planting a program in his employer's computer system that deleted 168,000 sales commission records.

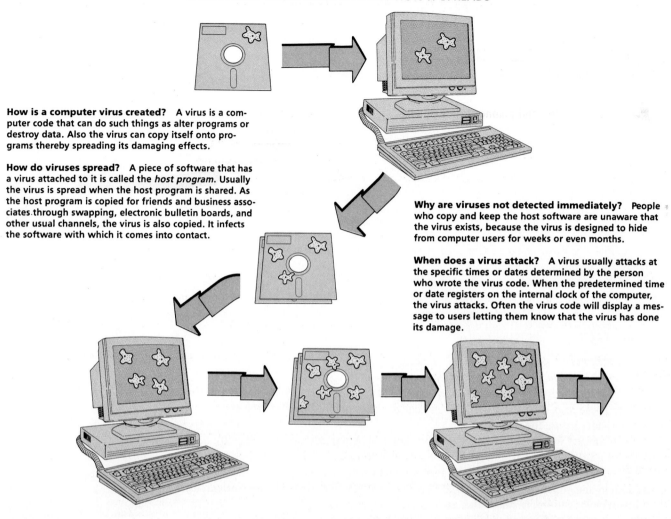

How is a computer virus created? A virus is a computer code that can do such things as alter programs or destroy data. Also the virus can copy itself onto programs thereby spreading its damaging effects.

How do viruses spread? A piece of software that has a virus attached to it is called the *host program*. Usually the virus is spread when the host program is shared. As the host program is copied for friends and business associates through swapping, electronic bulletin boards, and other usual channels, the virus is also copied. It infects the software with which it comes into contact.

Why are viruses not detected immediately? People who copy and keep the host software are unaware that the virus exists, because the virus is designed to hide from computer users for weeks or even months.

When does a virus attack? A virus usually attacks at the specific times or dates determined by the person who wrote the virus code. When the predetermined time or date registers on the internal clock of the computer, the virus attacks. Often the virus code will display a message to users letting them know that the virus has done its damage.

FIGURE 15-12
This illustration shows how a virus program can be transmitted from one computer system to another.

Single acts of malicious damage, especially when performed by employees with authorized access to the computer system, are very difficult to prevent. The best protection against this type of act remains adequate backup files that enable damaged data to be restored.

Privacy

In the past, one way to maintain privacy was to keep information in separate locations—individual stores had their own credit files, government agencies had separate records, doctors had separate files, and so on. However, it is now technically and economically feasible to store large amounts of related data about individuals in one database. Some people believe that the easier access to the data increases the possibility for misuse. Others worry that the increased storage capacity of computers may encourage the storage of unnecessary personal data.

The concern about information privacy has led to federal and state laws regarding the storage and disclosure of personal data. Common points in these laws include: (1) Information collected and stored about individuals should be limited to what is necessary to carry out the function of the business or governmental agency collecting the data. (2) Once collected, provisions should be made to restrict access to the data to those employees within the organization who need access to it to perform their job duties. (3) Personal information should be released outside the organization collecting the data only when the person has agreed to its disclosure. (4) When information is collected about an individual, the individual should know that data is being collected and have the opportunity to determine the accuracy of the data.

SUMMARY OF TRENDS AND ISSUES IN THE INFORMATION AGE

Based on current and planned developments, the impact of computers and the information age will be even greater in the future than it has been to date. However, as a society and as individuals, we have an obligation to use the computer responsibly and not abuse the power it provides. This presents constant challenges that sometimes weigh the rights of the individual against increased efficiency and productivity. The computer must be thought of as a tool whose effectiveness is determined by the skill and experience of the user. As a computer literate member of society, you will be better able to participate in decisions on how to best use computerized information systems.

CHAPTER SUMMARY

1. Existing business information systems will continue to undergo profound changes as new technology, software, and methods become available.
2. Trends will include more online, interactive systems; less batch processing; and increased use of relational database systems.
3. The **automated office**, sometimes referred to as the **electronic office**, is the term that describes the use of electronic devices such as computers, facsimile machines, and computerized telephone systems to make office work more productive.
4. Word processing is the ability to electronically create, store, revise, and print written documents.
5. Electronic mail is the ability to transmit messages to and receive messages from other computer users.
6. **Voice mail** can be considered verbal electronic mail.
7. Desktop publishing involves the use of computers to produce printed documents that can combine different sizes and styles of text and graphics.
8. **Facsimile** or **Fax** machines are used to transmit a reproduced image of a document over standard phone lines.
9. Image processing is the ability to store and retrieve a reproduced image of a document.
10. **Teleconferencing** usually means **video conferencing**, the use of computers and television cameras to transmit video images and the sound of the conference participants to other participants with similar equipment at a remote location.
11. The goal of the **automated factory** is to increase productivity through the use of automated, and often computer-controlled, equipment.
12. **Computer-aided design (CAD)** uses a computer and special graphics software to aid in product design.
13. **Computer-aided engineering (CAE)** is the use of computers to test product designs.
14. **Computer-aided manufacturing (CAM)** is the use of computers to control production equipment.
15. **Computer-integrated manufacturing (CIM)** is the total integration of the manufacturing process using computers.
16. Personal computers are used in the home in many different ways, including: (1) personal services; (2) control of home systems; (3) telecommuting; (4) education; and (5) entertainment.
17. The personal services provided by home computer use allow people to perform personal and business-related tasks quickly and conveniently in the comfort of their own homes.
18. Another use of computers in the home is to control home systems such as security, environment control, lighting, and landscape sprinkler systems.
19. **Telecommuting** refers to the ability of individuals to work at home and communicate with their offices by using personal computers and communication lines.
20. The use of personal computers for education, called **computer-aided instruction (CAI)**, is a rapidly growing area.
21. CAI software can be classified into three main types: **drill and practice software**; **tutorial software**; and **simulation software**.
22. Popular types of entertainment software include arcade games, board games, simulations, and interactive graphics programs.

23. Electronic **bulletin board systems**, called **BBSs**, allow users to communicate with one another and share information.
24. The guidelines for purchasing a personal computer recommend that you: (1) become computer literate; (2) define and prioritize the type of tasks you want to perform on your computer; (3) select the software packages that best meet your needs; (4) select equipment that will run the software you have selected; (5) select the suppliers for the software and equipment; (6) purchase the software and equipment.
25. **Shareware** is software that users may try out on their own systems before paying a fee.
26. **Public domain software** is not copyrighted and can therefore be distributed among users.
27. **Computer security** refers to the safeguards established to prevent and detect unauthorized use and deliberate or accidental damage to computer systems and data.
28. **Computer crime** is the use of a computer to commit an illegal act.
29. Today, **software piracy** is still an issue and it is estimated that for every authorized copy of a commercial program, there is at least one illegal copy.
30. **Unauthorized access** can be defined as computer trespassing, in other words, being logged on a system without permission.
31. **Unauthorized use** is the use of a computer system or computer data for unapproved and possibly illegal activities.
32. The key to preventing both unauthorized access and unauthorized use is an appropriate level of authorization.
33. One of the most potentially dangerous types of malicious damage is done by a **virus**, a computer program designed to copy itself into other software and spread through multiple computer systems.
34. The concern about information privacy has led to federal and state laws regarding the storage and disclosure of personal data.

KEY TERMS

Automated factory *15.6*
Automated office *15.4*
Bulletin board systems (BBSs) *15.10*
Computer-aided design (CAD) *15.6*
Computer-aided engineering (CAE) *15.6*
Computer-aided instruction (CAI) *15.8*
Computer-aided manufacturing (CAM) *15.6*

Computer crime *15.13*
Computer-integrated manufacturing (CIM) *15.7*
Computer security *15.13*
Drill and practice software *15.8*
Electronic office *15.4*
Facsimile (Fax) *15.4*
Public domain software *15.11*
Shareware *15.11*
Simulation software *15.9*

Software piracy *15.13*
Telecommuting *15.8*
Teleconferencing *15.5*
Tutorial software *15.8*
Unauthorized access *15.13*
Unauthorized use *15.13*
Video conferencing *15.5*
Virus *15.13*
Voice mail *15.4*

REVIEW QUESTIONS

1. List three electronic devices that are used in an automated office. What is voice mail? How is a Fax machine used?
2. What is the goal of the automated factory? Briefly explain the four technologies that are used.
3. What are some of the personal services available to home computer users?
4. Describe the three general categories of educational software.
5. List the six guidelines for buying a personal computer. Why is it recommended that you select your software before your equipment?
6. What is software piracy?
7. What is unauthorized access and unauthorized use? How can they be prevented?
8. Explain why computer viruses are malicious. What is a "vaccine" program?
9. Discuss the four common points covered in the state and federal information privacy laws.

Introduction to DOS

Introduction to DOS

OBJECTIVES

You will have mastered the basics of using DOS when you can:

- "Boot" your microcomputer
- Enter the time and date, if required
- Establish the system default disk drive
- List a disk directory
- Cancel commands
- Format diskettes, using /S and /V
- Use file specifications to address files on various disks
- Copy files on the same disk and from one disk to another
- Rename and erase files
- Organize and manage file subdirectories on a hard disk
- Start application programs

INTRODUCTION

An **operating system** is one or more programs that control and manage the operation of the computer. These programs provide an interface among the user, the computer equipment, and the application programs. For instance, to use a computer to print a memo, you'd first use the operating system to start the computer. Next, you would enter a keyboard command that the operating system processes to activate the word processing program. When the word processing program instructs the computer to print the memo, the operating system finds the proper file on the disk, retrieves the data from the disk, and routes the output to the printer. The operating system is not part of the application program itself, but it provides essential services that the application program uses to perform its functions.

Operating Systems for IBM PCs

Microsoft Corporation joined forces with IBM to develop the program known as **DOS**, an acronym for **Disk Operating System**, used since 1981 in IBM PC and IBM-compatible computers. **PC-DOS** is the name for versions of DOS distributed by IBM for its Personal Computer and Personal System/2 lines. All IBM-compatible computers use versions of this operating system distributed by Microsoft as **MS-DOS**. This book uses the term DOS to refer to any of the various editions of PC- or MS-DOS and covers information applicable to all versions of DOS, unless otherwise noted.

DOS Versions

The numbers following the abbreviation DOS indicate the specific version and release of the product (Figure 1). The **version** number is the whole number and signifies a major improvement of the product. The **release** number is the decimal number and identifies minor corrections or changes to a version of the product. For example, DOS 1.1 corrected some minor problems with DOS 1.0.

Software developers try to maintain **upward compatibility**, that is, that all the features of an earlier version remain supported by a later one. However, "downward" compatibility is not common. Programs or equipment that require the features of DOS 3.3, for example, will not function with DOS 3.2 or earlier versions.

DOS VERSION RELEASE	MAJOR FEATURE SUPPORTED	YEAR
3.3	Introduction of PS/2	1987
3.2	Token-Ring Networks, 3.5'' Diskette	
3.1	Addition of Networking, 1.2 mb 5.25 Diskette	
3.0	Introduction of PC/AT	1985
2.1	Enhancements to 2.0	
2.0	Introduction of PC/XT	1983
1.1	Enhancements to 1.0	
1.0	Introduction of IBM/PC	1981

FIGURE 1

USING THE DISK OPERATING SYSTEM (DOS)

Starting the Computer

turn on computer

DOS programs are normally stored on a diskette or on a hard disk. To begin using the operating system, it must be read into main memory, a process known as **booting**. If you are using a system with two diskette drives, insert the diskette containing DOS into drive A of the computer and turn on the computer (Figure 2). If you are using a system with a hard disk, DOS is already available on the hard disk. Turn on the computer (Figure 3) and be certain you do not insert a diskette before the system has completed its startup process. If the computer is already on and your DOS diskette is in drive A (or DOS is on the hard disk and drive A is empty), you can restart the system by pressing the CTRL, ALT, and DEL keys simultaneously (Figure 4).

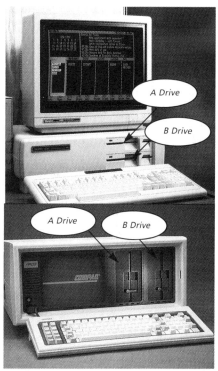

A Drive
B Drive
A Drive
B Drive

FIGURE 2

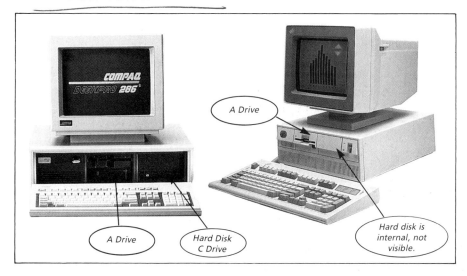

A Drive
A Drive
Hard Disk C Drive
Hard disk is internal, not visible.

FIGURE 3

turn dos on first.

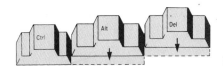

Ctrl   Alt   Del

FIGURE 4

series of test when turn on computer

The Cold Start.
Starting the computer by turning on the power switch is known as a **cold start** or **cold boot**. The computer will first run some tests to diagnose its own circuitry (known on some computers as a **power-on self-test**, or **POST** process). After running this test, the computer will begin to read the DOS diskette.

The Warm Start or Reset.
Restarting the operating system by pressing the CTRL, ALT, and DEL keys simultaneously is called a **warm start**, or **warm boot**, because the computer has already been turned on. This procedure does not repeat the POST process, but it does erase all programs and data from main memory and reloads DOS. Do not worry about losing data from diskettes during this process, however, because data properly stored on diskettes will remain there.

Might ask you

```
Current date is Tue  1-01-1980
Enter new date (mm-dd-yy):
```

FIGURE 5

Loading DOS.
While the system is being booted, the status light on the disk drive flashes on and off, and the disk drive whirls for a few seconds. During this time, the program from the operating system is being loaded into main memory. When DOS has been loaded into main memory, an image similar to Figure 5 appears on the screen. When DOS has been loaded into main memory, the system will perform various activities depending upon how the startup procedure has been tailored for the specific computer.

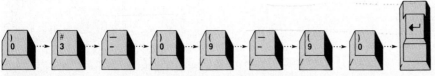

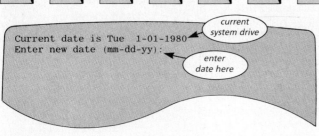

```
Current date is Tue  1-01-1980
Enter new date (mm-dd-yy):
```
current system drive
enter date here

FIGURE 6

```
Current date is Tue  1-01-1980
Enter new date (mm-dd-yy): 03-09-90
Current time is  0:00:32.95
Enter new time:
```
current system time

FIGURE 7

Setting the Date and Time

Although not required, it is a good practice to enter the date and time so that files you create are accurately documented. Enter the current date when the computer screen displays the message shown in Figure 6. To enter the date, always enter the month, day, and year separated by hyphens (-), slashes (/), or, in DOS 3.30 and later versions, periods (.). For example, assume that today is March 9, 1990. Type 03-09-90. Then press the Enter key (Figure 7).

If the date displayed is already correct—which it may be if your computer has an internal clock—you do not need to enter the date. Instead, press the Enter key when the message "Enter new date:" appears on the screen.

You enter the time in the format hh:mm:ss.xx, where hh stands for hours, mm stands for minutes, ss stands for seconds, and xx stands for hundredths of a second. As with the date, you are not required to enter the time, although it is a good practice to do so. For practice, type the time as 11:50 and press the Enter key (Figure 8). (If you do not include seconds and hundredths of seconds, the operating system assumes a value of zero for them.)

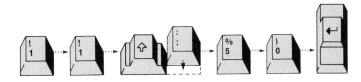

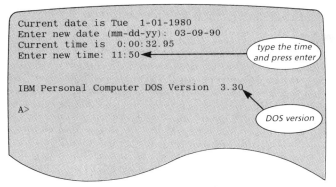

```
Current date is Tue  1-01-1980
Enter new date (mm-dd-yy): 03-09-90
Current time is  0:00:32.95
Enter new time: 11:50
```

type the time and press enter

```
IBM Personal Computer DOS Version  3.30

A>
```

DOS version

FIGURE 8

The DOS Prompt

After the messages are displayed, the **system prompt**, also called the **DOS prompt**, indicates that the operating system is ready to receive your commands (Figures 9 and 10). The letter displayed within the prompt > indicates which drive has been assigned as the default disk drive. The **default drive** is the disk drive in which the operating system assumes the disk or diskette containing the operating system and other programs is located. Another term used for the default drive is **current drive**, because it is the drive that is assumed to be in current use.

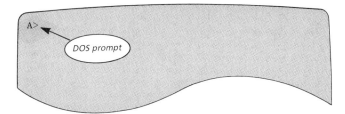

```
A>
```
DOS prompt

FIGURE 9

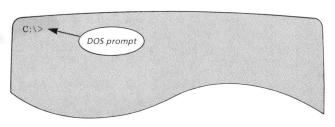

```
C:\>
```
DOS prompt

FIGURE 10

The Default Drive

The default drive assignment will vary depending upon the specific hardware you are using. A two-diskette system typically assigns drive A as the default drive (Figure 9). If your computer has a hard disk, the default drive will initially be drive C, and the prompt will appear as it is shown in Figure 10.

At times you will need to change the default drive assignment. Before you do so, be certain that the new drive is ready. A hard disk is always installed, but in a two-diskette system the disk drive must have a diskette inserted before it can be assigned as the default drive. If the drive does not have a diskette in it, the computer will give you an error message.

To change the drive assignment, type the letter of the new drive to be used, followed by a colon, and then press the Enter key. For example, to change the default to drive B, type the letter B, followed by a colon (:), and then press the Enter key (Figure 11, step 1). The prompt will display drive B as the default drive. Now, change the default drive back to drive A by typing A: ↵ (Figure 11, step 2).

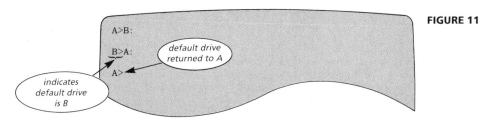

FIGURE 11

```
A>B:

B>A:

A>
```

default drive returned to A

indicates default drive is B

Step 1: Change the default drive from A to B.   **Step 2: Change the default drive from B to A.**

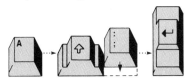

In most of the examples in this text, the default drive will be drive A. You will be told when the procedures for a hard disk are different than those for a diskette system. Figure 12 shows how to change the default drive for a hard disk system from drive C to drive A (step 1) and back to drive C (step 2).

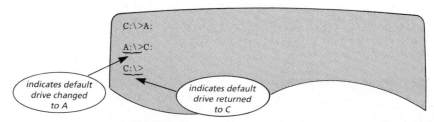

C:\>A:

A:\>C:

C:\>

indicates default drive changed to A

indicates default drive returned to C

Step 1: Change the default drive from C to A.   **Step 2: Change the default drive from A to C.**

   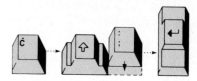

FIGURE 12

ENTERING DISK OPERATING SYSTEM (DOS) COMMANDS

Now that you have booted the DOS system, you are able to enter commands to instruct the computer. DOS includes a variety of commands to assist you in using the computer. Some of the commands might be called "status" or "informative" commands because they instruct DOS to give you information about the system's operation. The directory command, DIR, is one such informative command. It lists the names of files stored on a disk. Other commands support DOS functions, helping you use the computer. FORMAT, for instance, prepares a new disk for use in storing files.

The DOS commands you have entered so far have been typed in capital letters. You can type capital letters either by pressing the Caps Lock key or by holding down one of the two shift keys. However, you do not have to enter all DOS commands in capital letters. Commands, drive specifiers, and other entries to the operating system can be entered in any combination of uppercase and lowercase letters.

Internal and External Commands

An **internal command** is part of the operating system program. Once you have loaded DOS into main memory, an internal command is always started there. You can enter an internal command at any time. It does not matter whether the DOS system diskette is in the default drive. DIR, COPY, CLS, ERASE, RENAME, and DEL are examples of internal commands.

External commands, on the other hand, are stored on the DOS system disk as program files. They must be read from the disk into main memory before they can be executed. This means that the DOS system disk must be in the default drive or the specified drive so that the program can be found on the disk and loaded into main memory for execution. FORMAT and CHKDSK are examples of external commands. Another easy way to identify external commands is to look for the extensions .BAT, .COM, or .EXE following the filename, such as FORMAT.EXE.

DIRECTORY COMMAND (DIR)

One of the functions of the operating system is to store files containing both programs and data on diskettes. To facilitate that storage, the operating system maintains a directory of all the files stored on a diskette. To display the directory of the diskette you have placed in drive A of your computer, use the **DIR command**. At the A> prompt, type DIR and press the Enter key (Figure 13).

The directory of the diskette in the default drive will then be displayed as in Figure 14. Because the default drive is drive A (as specified by the system's A> prompt), the directory of the diskette in drive A is displayed. If you are using a hard disk and your default disk is drive C, the DIR command will display the directory of your hard disk.

The directory itself consists of the names of the files on the diskette, the number of bytes required to store the file on the diskette, the date of the last change of the file, and for some files, the time of the last change of the file. The message at the end of the directory listing indicates the number of files on the diskette (in Figure 14 there are 15 files on the diskette) and the remaining space available on the diskette (181248 unused bytes remain on the diskette in Figure 14). At the end of the directory display, the system prompt reappears on the screen, indicating that the system is ready for your next command.

FIGURE 13

disk drive is confirmed

size of file in bytes

file name and extension

date file was stored

```
A>DIR
  Volume in drive A has no label
  Directory of  A:\

COMMAND   COM    25307   3-17-87   12:00p
ANSI      SYS     1678   3-17-87   12:00p
COUNTRY   SYS    11285   3-17-87   12:00p
AUTOEXEC  BAT       44   1-01-80   12:00a
DRIVER    SYS     1196   3-17-87   12:00p
CONFIG    SYS       18   3-09-90   12:05p
FORMAT    COM    11616   3-18-87   12:00p
DOSNOTES  DOC     2967   3-09-90   12:18a
MODE      COM    15487   3-17-87   12:00p
PRINTER   SYS    13590   3-17-87   12:00p
REPLACE   EXE    11775   3-17-87   12:00p
SELECT    COM     4163   3-17-87   12:00p
SYS       COM     4766   3-17-87   12:00p
VDISK     SYS     3455   3-17-87   12:00p
XCOPY     EXE    11247   3-17-87   12:00p
        15 File(s)    181248 bytes free
A>
```

time file was stored

number of unused bytes of storage on the disk

number of files on the disk

the DOS prompt redisplayed after the command is executed

FIGURE 14

Displaying Directories of Other Disks

The directories of files on diskettes in other disk drives of the computer can be displayed as well. For practice, remove your system diskette from drive A and move it to drive B. To display the directory, type the command DIR B: and press the Enter key, as in Figure 15. You have directed the operating system to display the directory of the diskette located in drive B. The entry B: specifies that drive B is to be used.

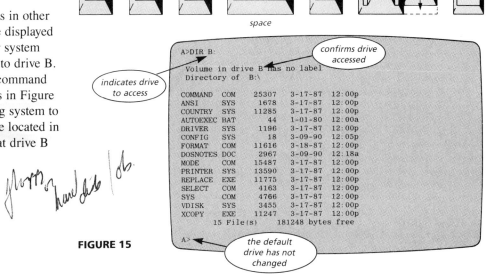

space

indicates drive to access

confirms drive accessed

```
A>DIR B:
  Volume in drive B has no label
  Directory of  B:\

COMMAND   COM    25307   3-17-87   12:00p
ANSI      SYS     1678   3-17-87   12:00p
COUNTRY   SYS    11285   3-17-87   12:00p
AUTOEXEC  BAT       44   1-01-80   12:00a
DRIVER    SYS     1196   3-17-87   12:00p
CONFIG    SYS       18   3-09-90   12:05p
FORMAT    COM    11616   3-18-87   12:00p
DOSNOTES  DOC     2967   3-09-90   12:18a
MODE      COM    15487   3-17-87   12:00p
PRINTER   SYS    13590   3-17-87   12:00p
REPLACE   EXE    11775   3-17-87   12:00p
SELECT    COM     4163   3-17-87   12:00p
SYS       COM     4766   3-17-87   12:00p
VDISK     SYS     3455   3-17-87   12:00p
XCOPY     EXE    11247   3-17-87   12:00p
        15 File(s)    181248 bytes free
A>
```

FIGURE 15

the default drive has not changed

If your computer has a hard disk and you have been using drive C as the default drive, you can insert a diskette into drive A and then list the directory of that diskette drive by typing DIR A: and pressing the Enter key (Figure 16).

FIGURE 16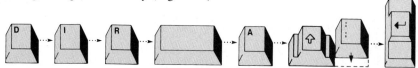

Note the use of the **colon**, :, with the disk drive letter. Whenever you refer to a specific disk drive, type the letter designating the drive followed by the colon, such as A:, B:, or C:.

Pausing Directory Listings

The directory of your diskette will often contain more files than can be displayed on the screen at one time. DOS has two methods of handling this situation: the pause screen option and the DIR command options.

Pause Screen (Control S). To use a **pause screen** function, first make certain that your DOS diskette is in drive A. Type DIR and press the Enter key (Figure 17, step 1). When approximately one screenful of information is displayed, press Control-S. The directory display immediately halts (Figure 17, step 2). You can then examine the screen for any information you require. To continue the display, press any character key on the keyboard. The directory display will continue to scroll as if it had never halted. This pause screen operation can be used with many DOS commands.

Step 1: Display a directory of the default drive.

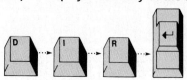

Step 2: Halt the directory listing.

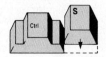

Step 3: Continue the display by pressing any character key.

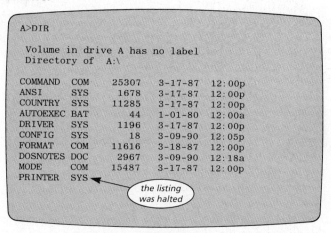

```
A>DIR

   Volume in drive A has no label
   Directory of   A:\

COMMAND   COM    25307    3-17-87   12:00p
ANSI      SYS     1678    3-17-87   12:00p
COUNTRY   SYS    11285    3-17-87   12:00p
AUTOEXEC  BAT       44    1-01-80   12:00a
DRIVER    SYS     1196    3-17-87   12:00p
CONFIG    SYS       18    3-09-90   12:05p
FORMAT    COM    11616    3-18-87   12:00p
DOSNOTES  DOC     2967    3-09-90   12:18a
MODE      COM    15487    3-17-87   12:00p
PRINTER   SYS
```
the listing was halted

FIGURE 17

DIR Command Options. It is not always easy to pause the directory listing where you want it. Therefore, you might want to use two other options with the DIR command. One option, /P, causes the screen to pause. The second option, /W, displays more data on the screen by increasing the **width** of the display area.

/P—the Pause Option. To demonstrate the pause option, type DIR followed by /P and press the Enter key (Figure 18). When the screen is full, the listing stops and the message "Strike a key when ready . . ." appears at the bottom of the screen. When you are ready to continue the listing, press any character key.

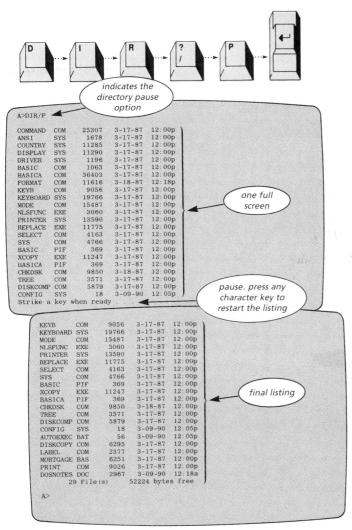

```
A>DIR/P

COMMAND   COM    25307   3-17-87  12:00p
ANSI      SYS     1678   3-17-87  12:00p
COUNTRY   SYS    11285   3-17-87  12:00p
DISPLAY   SYS    11290   3-17-87  12:00p
DRIVER    SYS     1196   3-17-87  12:00p
BASIC     COM     1063   3-17-87  12:00p
BASICA    COM    36403   3-17-87  12:00p
FORMAT    COM    11616   3-18-87  12:18p
KEYB      COM     9056   3-17-87  12:00p
KEYBOARD  SYS    19766   3-17-87  12:00p
MODE      COM    15487   3-17-87  12:00p
NLSFUNC   EXE     3060   3-17-87  12:00p
PRINTER   SYS    13590   3-17-87  12:00p
REPLACE   EXE    11775   3-17-87  12:00p
SELECT    COM     4163   3-17-87  12:00p
SYS       COM     4766   3-17-87  12:00p
BASIC     PIF      369   3-17-87  12:00p
XCOPY     EXE    11247   3-17-87  12:00p
BASICA    PIF      369   3-17-87  12:00p
CHKDSK    COM     9850   3-18-87  12:00p
TREE      COM     3571   3-17-87  12:00p
DISKCOMP  COM     5879   3-17-87  12:00p
CONFIG    SYS       18   3-09-90  12:05p
Strike a key when ready
```

```
KEYB      COM     9056   3-17-87  12:00p
KEYBOARD  SYS    19766   3-17-87  12:00p
MODE      COM    15487   3-17-87  12:00p
NLSFUNC   EXE     3060   3-17-87  12:00p
PRINTER   SYS    13590   3-17-87  12:00p
REPLACE   EXE    11775   3-17-87  12:00p
SELECT    COM     4163   3-17-87  12:00p
SYS       COM     4766   3-17-87  12:00p
BASIC     PIF      369   3-17-87  12:00p
XCOPY     EXE    11247   3-17-87  12:00p
BASICA    PIF      369   3-17-87  12:00p
CHKDSK    COM     9850   3-18-87  12:00p
TREE      COM     3571   3-17-87  12:00p
DISKCOMP  COM     5879   3-17-87  12:00p
CONFIG    SYS       18   3-09-90  12:05p
AUTOEXEC  BAT       56   3-09-90  12:05p
DISKCOPY  COM     6295   3-17-87  12:00p
LABEL     COM     2377   3-17-87  12:00p
MORTGAGE  BAS     6251   3-17-87  12:00p
PRINT     COM     9026   3-17-87  12:00p
DOSNOTES  DOC     2967   3-09-90  12:18a
       29 File(s)    52224 bytes free

A>
```

FIGURE 18

FORMATTING A DISKETTE

You cannot use a brand new diskette to store files. The diskette must first be formatted using the DOS FORMAT program. The **formatting** process establishes sectors on the diskette and performs other functions that allow the diskette to store files. Be careful when selecting disks to be used with the FORMAT command. Formatting a diskette destroys all files previously stored on the diskette. Therefore, you must be extremely careful to place the correct diskette in the drive and to make the correct drive letter designation. With a hard disk, extra precaution is necessary to avoid losing files by formatting the hard disk accidentally. DOS versions 3.0 and later provide some protection against accidental formatting of a hard disk, but your own precautions are still the best insurance.

/W—the Wide Display Option. The second option for displaying a long list of files is the **/W option**, which displays the information in a wide format. To use the /W option, type DIR /W, then press the Enter key (Figure 19). Note that only the file and directory names are listed, not the size, time, or date of the files.

Canceling a Command (Break)

In some cases, you only need to see a portion of the directory and so you might want to cancel the DIR command after you have seen that portion. To cancel a command you use the Break key. Locate this key on your keyboard; on many keyboards it is on the side of a key, often on the Scroll Lock key or the Pause key. When you press Ctrl-Break the characters ^C appear on the screen and the system prompt reappears. You will often hear this keystroke combination referred to as **Control-Break** or the **Break key**. The characters ^C indicate that you canceled the command by using the Break key. In general, you can cancel any DOS command that has been initiated by pressing Control-Break. An alternate method of canceling DOS commands is pressing Control-C (Figure 20).

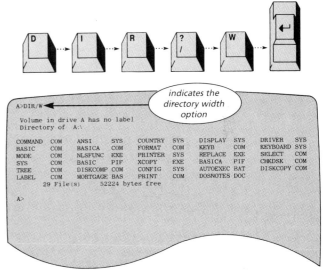

```
A>DIR/W

 Volume in drive A has no label
 Directory of  A:\

COMMAND  COM  ANSI     SYS  COUNTRY  SYS  DISPLAY  SYS  DRIVER   SYS
BASIC    COM  BASICA   COM  FORMAT   COM  KEYB     COM  KEYBOARD SYS
MODE     COM  NLSFUNC  EXE  PRINTER  SYS  REPLACE  EXE  SELECT   COM
SYS      COM  BASIC    PIF  XCOPY    EXE  BASICA   PIF  CHKDSK   COM
TREE     COM  DISKCOMP COM  CONFIG   SYS  AUTOEXEC BAT  DISKCOPY COM
LABEL    COM  MORTGAGE BAS  PRINT    COM  DOSNOTES DOC
      29 File(s)     52224 bytes free

A>
```

FIGURE 19

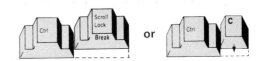

FIGURE 20

The FORMAT Command

To initiate the FORMAT program, select a new diskette, or one that may be erased. (Use the DIR command to check the contents of your diskette if you are not certain it may be erased.) Because FORMAT is an external DOS command, the FORMAT.COM program file must be on the system disk in the computer when you use this command.

To format a diskette on a two-diskette system, place the DOS diskette in drive A. Type the command FORMAT B: and press the Enter key (Figure 21).

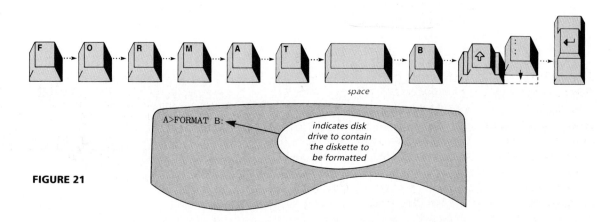

FIGURE 21

When you press the Enter key, the FORMAT program is loaded into main memory and is executed. A message appears on the screen instructing you to "Insert new diskette for drive B: and strike ENTER when ready" (Figure 22). If the disk you want to format is already in drive B, simply press the Enter key.

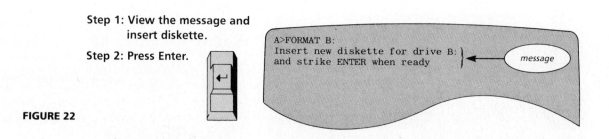

Step 1: View the message and insert diskette.

Step 2: Press Enter.

FIGURE 22

The FORMAT procedure on a hard-disk system is essentially the same as for a two-diskette system, except that the FORMAT program is stored on drive C, the hard disk. Be careful NOT to format drive C accidentally. To format a diskette in drive A at the C> prompt, type FORMAT A: and press the Enter key (Figure 23). The program will instruct you when to place the diskette to be formatted into drive A (Figure 24).

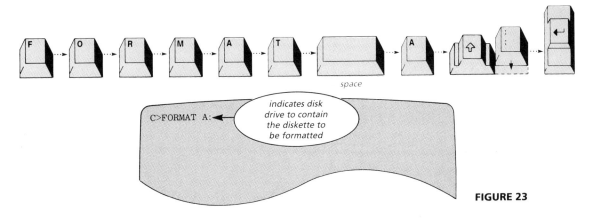

space

C>FORMAT A:◄— *indicates disk drive to contain the diskette to be formatted*

FIGURE 23

To complete the format process, place the diskette to be formatted into the appropriate drive (drive B for a two-diskette system; drive A for a computer with a hard-disk) and press the Enter key. While formatting occurs, a message appears indicating that the process is underway. Figure 25 shows the message from a two diskette system and Figure 26 illustrates the message on a computer with a hard-disk. Messages may differ slightly depending upon the version of DOS you are using. When the formatting process is complete, the messages shown in Figure 27 or 28 appear.

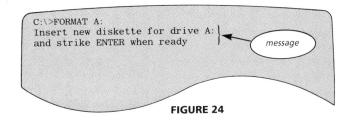

```
C:\>FORMAT A:
Insert new diskette for drive A:
and strike ENTER when ready
```
message

FIGURE 24

```
A>FORMAT B:
Insert new diskette for drive B:
and strike ENTER when ready

Head:  0 Cylinder: 16
```
◄— *indicates area of diskette currently being formatted*

FIGURE 25

```
C:\FORMAT A:
Insert new diskette for drive A:
and strike ENTER when ready
Head:  0 Cylinder: 16
```
◄— *indicates area of diskette being formatted*

FIGURE 26

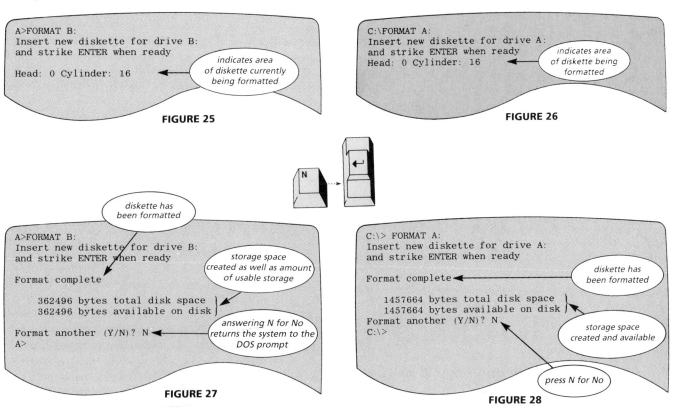

diskette has been formatted

```
A>FORMAT B:
Insert new diskette for drive B:
and strike ENTER when ready

Format complete

     362496 bytes total disk space
     362496 bytes available on disk

Format another (Y/N)? N
A>
```
storage space created as well as amount of usable storage

answering N for No returns the system to the DOS prompt

FIGURE 27

```
C:\> FORMAT A:
Insert new diskette for drive A:
and strike ENTER when ready

Format complete

    1457664 bytes total disk space
    1457664 bytes available on disk
Format another (Y/N)? N
C:\>
```
diskette has been formatted

storage space created and available

press N for No

FIGURE 28

The FORMAT program specifies that the diskette is formatted for a total number of bytes and that all of these bytes are available for storage. Finally, the FORMAT program asks if there are other diskettes to be formatted. If there are, press the letter Y and then the Enter key to continue the formatting process. If there are no more diskettes to be formatted, press the letter N and then the Enter key to end the FORMAT program.

Formatting a System Disk (/S Option)

The FORMAT command shown in Figures 26 and 27 will format a diskette so that it can be used for both data files and program files. However, the diskette cannot be used to boot the system because it does not contain the special system programs that are required for booting. To format a diskette so that it contains these special programs, thus creating what is called a **system disk**, you must use the **/S option**.

Use the same diskette you used in the last exercise. If you are using a two-diskette system, use the following commands. If you are using a hard-disk system, use drive C as the default drive and place the diskette to be formatted in drive A. Be very certain NOT to format drive C accidentally.

To create a system disk on a two-diskette system, type FORMAT B:/S and press the Enter key (Figure 29). On a hard-disk system, type FORMAT A:/S. You will be prompted to insert a new diskette in drive B (or A); if the diskette you formatted earlier is still in the disk drive, simply press the Enter key. After the diskette is formatted, the "System transferred" message appears. In general, if you are formatting a diskette to be used only for storing data files, do not place system programs on the diskette so that more space is available for the data files.

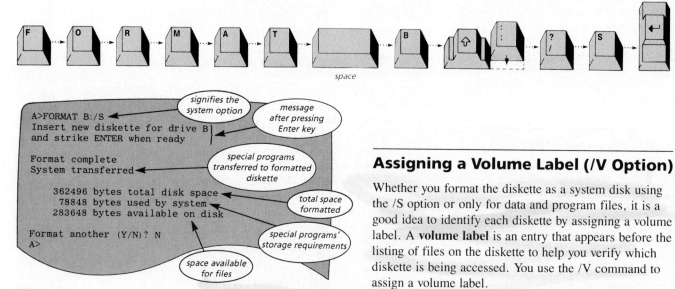

FIGURE 29

Assigning a Volume Label (/V Option)

Whether you format the diskette as a system disk using the /S option or only for data and program files, it is a good idea to identify each diskette by assigning a volume label. A **volume label** is an entry that appears before the listing of files on the diskette to help you verify which diskette is being accessed. You use the /V command to assign a volume label.

To assign a volume label, you would type FORMAT B:/V and press the Enter key (Figure 30). You will again be instructed to insert a diskette into drive B. Insert a new diskette, or press the Enter key if the diskette from the previous exercise is still in drive B. When the format process is complete, you will receive the message "Volume label (11 characters, ENTER for none)?" as a prompt to enter your label. You may use 11 characters—letters, numbers, or spaces—but not punctuation or special characters. After you enter a label and press the Enter key, a message appears asking if you want to format another diskette. You would press N and the Enter key to return to the DOS prompt.

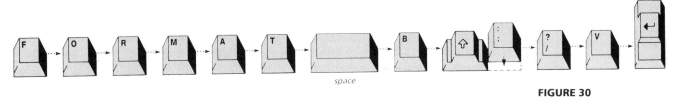

FIGURE 30

CLS COMMAND

Quite often, as you issue several commands or perform lengthy processes, the display screen will become crowded and difficult to read and interpret (Figure 31). To clear the screen and place the system prompt on the first line of the screen, you can use the CLS (Clear Screen) command. Type the letters CLS, then press the Enter key to execute the Clear Screen command.

MANAGING DATA AND PROGRAM FILES ON DISKS

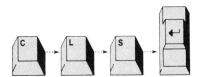

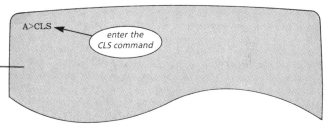

A>CLS

enter the
CLS command

A **data file** is a collection of data created by application or system programs and used by the programs. The data can be the figures used for a spreadsheet showing sales revenues, names and addresses in a database file, or a word processing document announcing the arrival of a new employee. A **program file** contains machine-readable instructions that the computer follows to perform its tasks. The program might be an operating system program or one of the application programs such as word processing that uses data files. Both data files and program files require your attention to be stored on a disk correctly.

FIGURE 31

Assigning File Specifications

DOS identifies the files on a disk by a combination of several specifications (Figure 32). A **file specification** lets DOS know exactly where to search for a file and gives its exact name. There are four parts to a DOS file specification: (1) the drive specifier, which you already know as drive A: or B: or C:, if there is a hard disk; (2) a directory specification (explained later); (3) the filename; (4) the filename extension.

FIGURE 32

LEGEND	DEFINITION
d:	The disk drive letter specifies the drive containing the file you are requesting. For example, A: specifies disk drive A. If you omit the drive letter, DOS assumes the file is located on the default drive. A disk drive letter is always followed by a colon (:).
\path	A path is an optional reference to a subdirectory of files on the specified disk. It is preceded, and sometimes followed, by a backslash (\).
filename	The filename consists of from one to eight characters.
.ext	A filename may contain an optional extension of a period followed by from one to three characters. The extension is used to add further identity to files.

Filenames.   Regardless of the type of data in the file, you must assign a filename to every data file, as well as to every program file. A **filename** consists of one to eight characters and is used by DOS to identify a specific file. You may use any combination of characters except: period (.), quotation mark ("), slash (/), backslash (\), brackets ([ ]), colon (:), less than (<), greater than (>), plus (+), equals (=), semicolon (;), and comma (,).

In general, your filename should reflect the data stored in it. For example, if your file contains employee records, it is more meaningful to use the filename EMPLOYEE than to use the filename FILE1, even though DOS will accept either filename.

Filename Extensions.   A filename can be made more specific by an optional extension. A **filename extension** consists of a period followed by one to three characters. The same characters that are permitted for a filename are permitted for a filename extension. The filename extension can identify a file more specifically or describe its purpose (Figure 33). For example, if you wish to create a copy of the EMPLOYEE file, you could use the filename extension .CPY to identify the file as a copied file. The entire file specification for the file would be EMPLOYEE.CPY.

FIGURE 33

.COM Files		.EXE Files		.BAT Files	
COMMAND	COM	APPEND	EXE	AUTOEXEC	BAT
ASSIGN	COM	ATTRIB	EXE	WP	BAT
BACKUP	COM	FASTOPEN	EXE	INSTALL	BAT
BASIC	COM	FIND	EXE		
BASICA	COM	JOIN	EXE		
CHKDSK	COM	NLSFUNC	EXE		
COMP	COM	REPLACE	EXE		
DEBUG	COM				
DISKCOMP	COM				
DISKCOPY	COM				
FORMAT	COM				
LABEL	COM				

Certain programs associated with the Disk Operating System use special filename extensions. All files with the filename extensions .COM or .EXE are executable programs. Files with the extension .BAT are **DOS batch files** and contain a series of DOS commands to be executed in sequence. Any DOS command with one of these filename extensions is an external command. You can execute any external command simply by typing the filename (the extension is not required) and pressing the Enter key.

COPY COMMAND

O nce you have formatted a diskette and are ready to use it to store data or program files, you will need a method of placing these files on the diskette. Use the **COPY command** to copy one file or a series of files to the same or a different diskette. As a DOS internal command, COPY may be used at any time, with or without the system disk.

Using the COPY Command

The COPY command is often used to make working copies of program and data diskettes. Copying original files from one diskette creates a second diskette that can be used for everyday work to protect the original disk from damage. A similar use for COPY is to make a **backup copy** of a diskette to guard against accidental loss of data. One frequently used technique is to make a backup copy of a file whenever you work on revisions to an existing file. In fact, some application programs will make a backup file automatically, using the filename extension .BAK or .BAC to indicate that it is a backup file.

Copying Files from One Diskette to Another

In the following examples of the COPY command, you will copy files from drive A to drive B. Check to see that you have the Data Diskette provided to instructors in drive A and your formatted diskette in drive B. If you are using a hard disk system, use drive C as the default drive, copying the files to drive A.

For practice, copy the file DOSNOTES.DOC from drive A to drive B. Your instructor will make the DOSNOTES.DOC file available to you or will give you the name of another file to copy. Type COPY DOSNOTES.DOC B: and press the Enter key. Note that after the word COPY you leave one or more spaces, then state the file specification of the file to be copied. In DOS terminology, this file is called the **source file**. In Figure 34, the filename DOSNO-TES.DOC is specified as the source file. Since no drive specification is included, the operating system assumes the file is located on the default drive, drive A.

root by a Back slash.

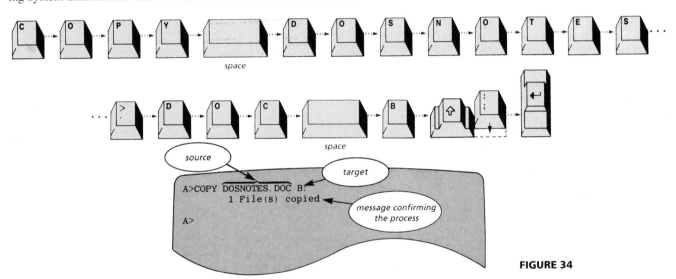

FIGURE 34

Following the source file is one or more blank spaces. Then, the **file specification**, which can include the drive specification, and the name of the **target file**, that is, the filename and filename extension of the source file after it is copied, is specified. In Figure 34, the drive specification B: states that the file is to be copied to a diskette in drive B. Because no filename is specified for the target file on drive B, DOS defaults to the same name as the source file, and so the name of the file on drive B will be DOSNOTES.DOC. The message "1 File(s) copied" signals that the command is completed.

When you copy a file from a diskette in one drive to a diskette in another drive, you can assign a new name to the target file. To copy the file DOSNOTES.DOC from the diskette in drive A to the diskette in drive B, giving the new file the name NOTECOPY on drive B, type COPY DOSNOTES.DOC B:NOTECOPY and press the Enter key (Figure 35). Again, the message "1 File(s) copied" appears when the task is completed, as in Figure 34.

Ren - rename.

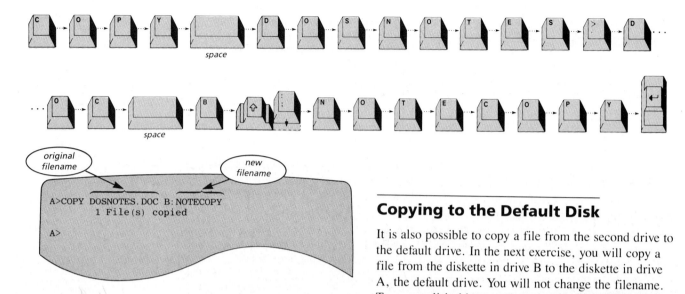

FIGURE 35

Copying to the Default Disk

It is also possible to copy a file from the second drive to the default drive. In the next exercise, you will copy a file from the diskette in drive B to the diskette in drive A, the default drive. You will not change the filename. To accomplish this procedure, type COPY B:NOTE-COPY A: and press the Enter key. This command copies the file named NOTECOPY from the diskette in drive B to the diskette in drive A. When the message "1 File(s) copied" appears, as in Figure 36, the copying process is completed. Because no target filename was given in the command, the file NOTECOPY will be on drive A under the same name as it is on drive B.

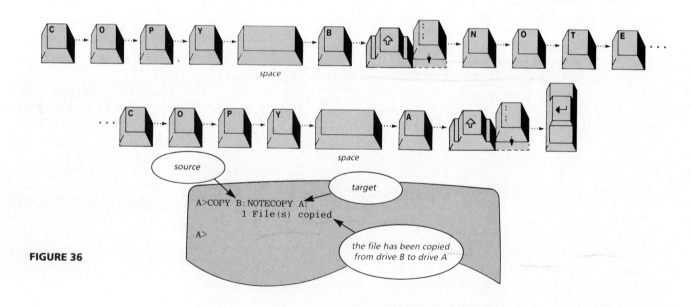

FIGURE 36

Copying a File to the Same Diskette

It is possible to copy a file to the same diskette, but you must use a different filename. For practice, copy the file named DOSNOTES.DOC stored on drive A onto the same diskette. Give the filename DOSNOTES.BAK to the target file. Type the command COPY DOSNO-TES.DOC DOSNOTES.BAK and press the Enter key.

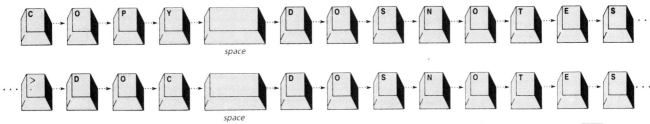

space

space

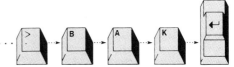

When your COPY command is executed, the file DOSNO-TES.DOC in drive A is copied to the same diskette on drive A as DOSNOTES.BAK (Figure 37). The file extension .BAK is used to distinguish the files. If you had used the same filename to designate both the target and source files on the same diskette, an error message would be displayed, stating that a file cannot be copied onto itself. You would then have to reenter the COPY command using a different name for the target file.

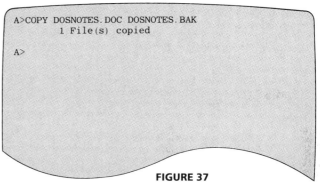

```
A>COPY DOSNOTES.DOC DOSNOTES.BAK
        1 File(s) copied

A>
```

FIGURE 37

Global Filename Characters ("Wildcards")

You can copy more than one file at a time using a single COPY command. To copy more than one file, you use **global characters**, or **wildcards**. These are special characters indicating that any character may occupy that specific location in the filename. The two global characters are the * (asterisk) and the ? (question mark).

To use wildcards, you need to know the files stored on the diskette. Figure 38 shows the directory of the diskette in drive A. (Your directory may look different.) Notice that the files DOSNOTES.BAK and NOTECOPY appear, a result of the COPY commands you used earlier. Notice also that several files have the same filename extensions. It is not uncommon, on any disk with many files, to find several files with similarities in filenames or extensions. These similarities can be exploited by using wildcard characters.

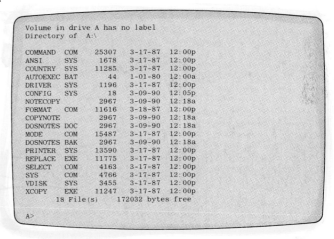

```
Volume in drive A has no label
Directory of  A:\

COMMAND   COM    25307   3-17-87   12:00p
ANSI      SYS     1678   3-17-87   12:00p
COUNTRY   SYS    11285   3-17-87   12:00p
AUTOEXEC  BAT       44   1-01-80   12:00a
DRIVER    SYS     1196   3-17-87   12:00p
CONFIG    SYS       18   3-09-90   12:05p
NOTECOPY          2967   3-09-90   12:18a
FORMAT    COM    11616   3-18-87   12:00p
COPYNOTE          2967   3-09-90   12:18a
DOSNOTES  DOC     2967   3-09-90   12:18a
MODE      COM    15487   3-17-87   12:00p
DOSNOTES  BAK     2967   3-09-90   12:18a
PRINTER   SYS    13590   3-17-87   12:00p
REPLACE   EXE    11775   3-17-87   12:00p
SELECT    COM     4163   3-17-87   12:00p
SYS       COM     4766   3-17-87   12:00p
VDISK     SYS     3455   3-17-87   12:00p
XCOPY     EXE    11247   3-17-87   12:00p
     18 File(s)   172032 bytes free

A>
```

FIGURE 38

The * Character. You can use the global character * (asterisk) to indicate a portion of the filename or extension. When the * global character appears, any character can occupy that position and all the remaining positions in the filename or the filename extension.

For example, let us use the wildcard asterisk (*) to copy files with the filename extension .COM from the diskette in drive A to the diskette in drive B. Type COPY *.COM B: and press the Enter key. In Figure 39, the source files are specified by the entry *.COM. The asterisk (*) in the filename portion of the specification means that any filename can be used. The file extension .COM states that the file specification must include the file extension .COM. In Figure 38, five filenames satisfy this criterion: COMMAND.COM, FORMAT-.COM, MODE.COM, SELECT.COM, and SYS.COM.

FIGURE 39

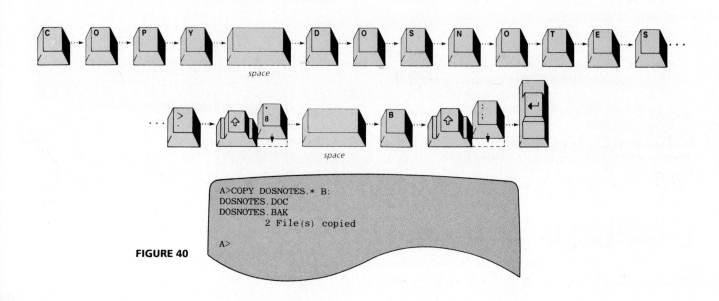

```
A>COPY *.COM B:
COMMAND.COM
FORMAT.COM
MODE.COM
SELECT.COM
SYS.COM
        5 File(s) copied

A>
```

wildcard for filename

specify the extension

lists each file copied

the number of files copied

These files are copied to the diskette in disk drive B. The filenames for the copied files on the diskette in drive B remain the same as the source filenames on the diskette in drive A because you specified no new names in the copy command. When you copy files with a COPY command using the * global character, all files copied are listed by the COPY command. Figure 39 lists the five copied files.

You can also specify the global character * as the filename extension to copy a specific filename with any extension. For example, the diskette contains two files with the name DOSNOTES, DOSNOTES.BAK and DOSNOTES.DOC. Type the command COPY DOSNOTES.* B: as in Figure 40 and press the Enter key to copy both the files with the filename DOSNOTES to drive B.

```
A>COPY DOSNOTES.* B:
DOSNOTES.DOC
DOSNOTES.BAK
        2 File(s) copied

A>
```

FIGURE 40

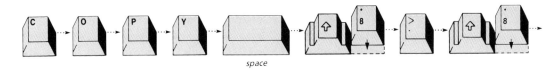

space

Copying All Files from One Diskette to Another.

You can also use the COPY command to copy all of the files on one diskette to another diskette by using the * global character. This technique is useful in making backup or working copies of entire diskettes. You use the * wildcard in both the filename and extension positions to signify "all filenames.all extensions" in the command. Practice by typing COPY *.* B: and pressing the Enter key to copy all files on drive A to drive B (Figure 41).

The ? Character.

The ? (question mark) global character can also be used to represent any character occupying the position in which the wildcard character appears. However, the ? represents only a single character replacement, whereas the * can represent one or more characters. You can use a single ? or several in a command to identify files. Practice this option by typing COPY DOSNOTES.BA? B: and pressing the Enter key to copy DOSNOTES.BAK to drive B (Figure 42).

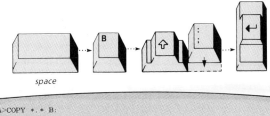

space

```
A>COPY *.* B:
COMMAND.COM
ANSI.SYS
COUNTRY.SYS
AUTOEXEC.BAT
DRIVER.SYS
CONFIG.SYS
NOTECOPY
FORMAT.COM
COPYNOTE
DOSNOTES.DOC
MODE.COM
DOSNOTES.BAK
PRINTER.SYS
REPLACE.EXE
SELECT.COM
SYS.COM
VDISK.SYS
XCOPY.EXE
        18 File(s) copied

A>
```

FIGURE 41

Using Wildcards with DOS Commands

You have learned to use the wildcard characters with the COPY command. Many DOS commands support the use of global replacement characters. For example, you can use the wildcards with the DIR command to look for files of a common type. To look at all DOS batch files on a diskette, you would type the command DIR *.BAT and press the Enter key to display all files with the filename extension .BAT.

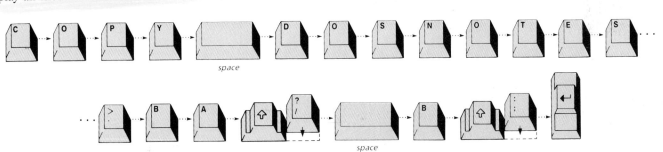

space

space

RENAME COMMAND

```
A>COPY DOSNOTES.BA? B:
DOSNOTES.BAK ◄──── the ? is replaced
        1 File(s) copied    by the letter K

A>
```

FIGURE 42

*U*se the **RENAME command** when you want to rename a file on a diskette. If you assign a filename already used by a file currently on the diskette, DOS creates the new file on the diskette and destroys the previously existing file with that name. You will not receive any warning that this has happened. Thus, you should periodically check the filenames on a diskette to avoid accidental replacement of files. If you discover a filename you might reuse, you can use the RENAME command to change the name of the file.

In the example in Figure 43, the file with the filename NOTECOPY on drive A is to be renamed DOSFILE. Type the command RENAME NOTECOPY DOSFILE immediately after the system prompt and press the Enter key. When you press the Enter key, the filename on the diskette in drive A is changed from NOTECOPY to DOSFILE.

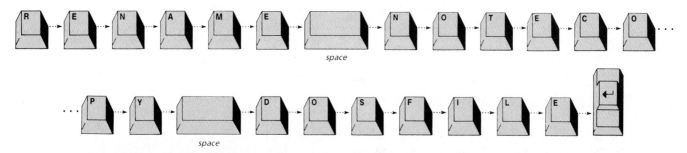

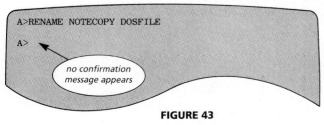

FIGURE 43

You can use the global characters * and ? with the RENAME command. In Figure 44, all files with the file extension .BAK are renamed with a file extension .BAC. Type the wildcard character * with the command RENAME *.BAK *.BAC and press the Enter key. All characters represented by the * will remain the same in the new filename. Thus, in Figure 44, all the filenames in the renamed files will remain the same, but the file extensions will change from .BAK to .BAC. RENAME does not confirm the operation on the screen, so you should use the DIR command before and after you use the RENAME command to assure the command was executed (Figure 45).

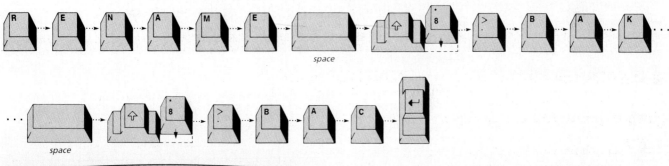

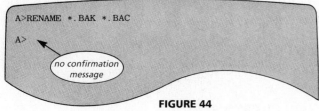

FIGURE 44

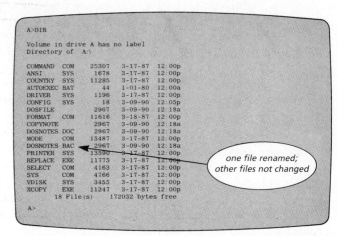

FIGURE 45

ERASE AND DEL COMMANDS

As a part of diskette file management, you should periodically remove unneeded files from your diskette. The **ERASE command** will erase, or remove, a file from a diskette. An alternative command that functions like the erase command is the **DEL** (delete) command. Take care when using the ERASE or DEL commands, because once a file has been erased from the directory, it cannot be easily recovered. Such inadvertent erasing of a file is another reason for keeping backup files.

Removing Files

We will begin by removing a single file, DOSFILE, from drive A. Type ERASE DOSFILE and press the Enter key, as shown in Figure 46. (You could use the DEL command instead, typing DEL DOSFILE and pressing the Enter key.) Use the DIR command to assure that the file has been removed from the diskette.

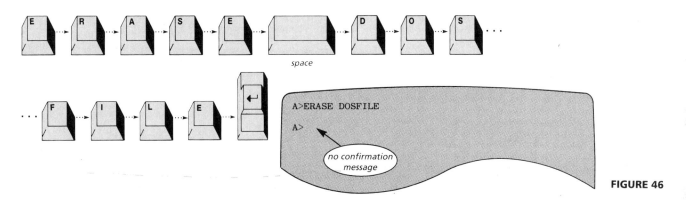

FIGURE 46

USING DIRECTORIES AND SUBDIRECTORIES

Directory Entries and Subdirectories

When you need to view the files on any disk, the computer does not actually read the entire disk looking for the file. Instead, a **file directory** or listing of each of the filenames on the disk is searched. This directory, created when the diskette is formatted, is called the **root directory**. Entries for subdirectories are made in the root directory. The root directory is the highest level directory of a disk (Figure 47).

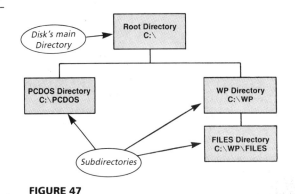

FIGURE 47

You can make three types of entries into a disk directory: (1) the filename and extension, (2) the volume label, (3) a subdirectory entry. We have previously discussed (1) and (2).

You can create a **subdirectory** to group all files of a similar type together (Figure 47). For example, you can create a subdirectory containing all the files related to DOS.

There are at least two good reasons to use subdirectories. First, the operating system provides a limited number of entries in the file directory. A diskette has room for only 112 entries; a hard disk allows up to 512 entries. This capacity may be sufficient on a diskette, but a hard disk with many millions of bytes of storage may have more files than the directory permits.

It is also easier to find files that are organized by related groups than to search randomly through all the files on a disk.

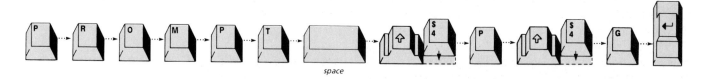

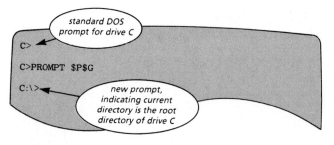

standard DOS prompt for drive C

C>

C>PROMPT PG

C:\>

new prompt, indicating current directory is the root directory of drive C

FIGURE 48

The PROMPT Command

The standard DOS prompt, A>, B>, or C>, does not tell you what subdirectories you are using. DOS provides a way for you to monitor which directory is in use through the **PROMPT command**. To have DOS include the subdirectory information as a part of the DOS prompt, type PROMPT PG and press the Enter key (Figure 48). Whenever you change disk drive addresses, you will see the subdirectory information as a part of the prompt.

Making Subdirectories

To create a subdirectory, use the **MKDIR command**, usually abbreviated as **MD**. If you have a hard disk, and *if your instructor approves*, create a subdirectory on drive C. Otherwise, practice the command on a diskette in drive A. To create a subdirectory called "PCDOS" on your diskette or disk drive, type MD A:\PCDOS and press the Enter key (Figure 49).

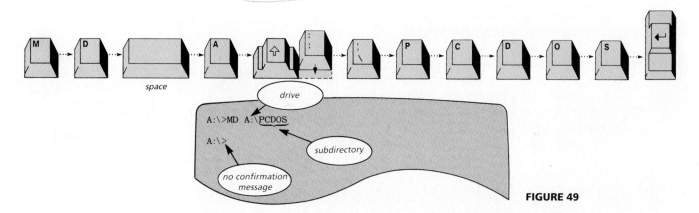

drive

A:\>MD A:\PCDOS

A:\>

subdirectory

no confirmation message

FIGURE 49

There are specific steps to the MD command. (1) Start a subdirectory entry with the drive designation. If the directory is to be on drive C, enter C: immediately after the MD command. Use the command MD A:\PCDOS to use drive A on a diskette. You can omit the drive specification if you are creating the directory on the default drive.

(2) Begin a subdirectory entry with the **backslash** character, \. The root directory for your hard disk is designated by a backslash alone. For example, C:\ designates the root

directory of drive C. The subdirectory made for the DOS files is C:\PCDOS. Notice that because you have issued the PROMPT command, the DOS prompt now includes the root or subdirectory name, C:\> or C:\PCDOS>.

(3) The subdirectory name, like any filename, can contain one to eight characters, followed optionally by a period and one to three characters in an extension. (Generally, subdirectory names do not include extensions.)

(4) You can assign a subdirectory entry to an existing subdirectory. For instance, you can create a subdirectory for a word processing program and a subordinate subdirectory for the data files created by the program. To create the word processing subdirectories shown in Figures 50 and 51, make the word processing subdirectory by typing MD A:\WP and press the Enter key. To make the subordinate subdirectory, type MD A:\WP\FILES and press the Enter key. The program subdirectory is A:\WP, and the word processing files can be stored in a second subdirectory, A:\WP\FILES. These two operations result in a series of related directories. Refer back to Figure 47 to see the relationships among the directories and subdirectories we have created.

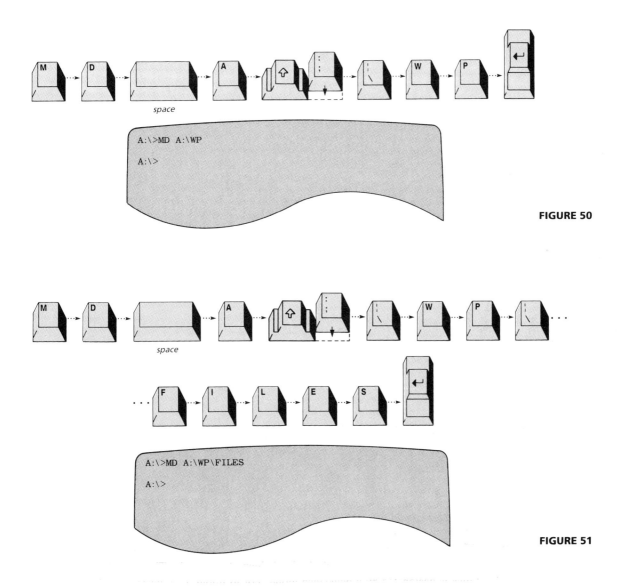

FIGURE 50

FIGURE 51

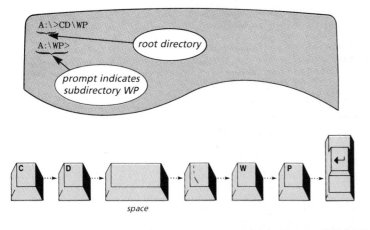

FIGURE 52

Changing Directories

Use the **CHDIR command** to move from one directory to another. Enter the letters CD immediately following the DOS prompt. Then type the backslash character and the subdirectory name and press the Enter key. To change from the root directory to the WP directory, for instance, type the entry CD \WP and press the Enter key. The result shown in Figure 52 should appear on your screen. To move to a lower subdirectory, such as the FILES subdirectory, type CD \WP\FILES and press the Enter key.

If you are moving to a directory that is subordinate to the current subdirectory, you can simply type CD and the subdirectory name. For instance, if your current directory is WP, you can move to the FILES subdirectory by entering CD FILES. Note that the entry omits both the reference to WP (the current directory) and the backslash character.

To return to the root directory simply type CD\ and press the Enter key. The backslash character entered by itself signifies the root directory.

The Current Directory. Just as there is a default or current disk drive, there is a current directory. The **current directory** is the one in which you are currently working. When you first access a disk, the root directory is the current directory. You can, however, direct DOS to a subdirectory, which then becomes the current directory for that disk. If you temporarily set another drive as the default drive, the named directory remains the current directory for the first disk.

FIGURE 53

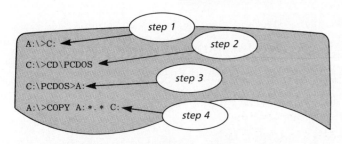

For practice, set your default drive to drive C by entering C: (Figure 53, step 1). Then set PCDOS as the current subdirectory for drive C by entering CD \PCDOS (step 2). Switch to drive A as the default drive (step 3) and copy files from drive A to drive C: type the copy command COPY A:*.* C: (step 4). Files are copied from the A drive to the PCDOS subdirectory on drive C even though the subdirectory is not specified in the copy command.

Step 1: Change default to drive C. **Step 2: Change from root directory of drive C to PCDOS directory.**

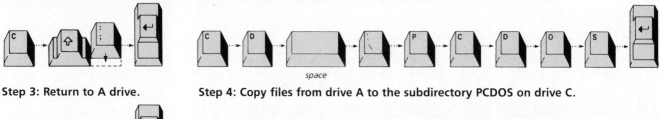

Step 3: Return to A drive. **Step 4: Copy files from drive A to the subdirectory PCDOS on drive C.**

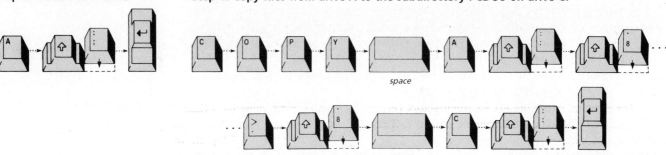

Specifying a Path to Subdirectories and Files

You will find it very convenient to group files in subdirectories. To use the technique you must learn to specify the path to a file. The **path** includes three components: (1) the drive, (2) the name of the subdirectories, (3) the name of the file. The path specifies the route DOS is to take from the root directory through subdirectories leading to a file. Specify the path whenever you wish to access a file for DIR, COPY, or similar commands. Unless you specify a path, DOS may not find the file you desire because it would search only the current directory of the default drive.

Specifying Paths in Commands.   One way to specify the path is to include it in the command you are using. For example, you can make a backup copy on a diskette of a file named DOSNOTES.DOC stored in the FILES subdirectory under the WP subdirectory, by typing the command COPY C:\WP\FILES\DOSNOTES.DOC A:. The COPY command includes the source drive (C:), both directories specified together (\WP\FILES), and the filename preceded by a backslash (\DOSNOTES.DOC). On drive A, the file is stored simply as DOSNOTES.DOC under the root directory, because no subdirectory has been made or referenced on that disk.

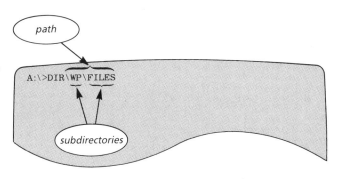

FIGURE 54

You can use this style with other DOS commands and when specifying files in many programs. For example, to display the file contents of the FILES subdirectory, enter DIR \WP\FILES and press the Enter key (Figure 54). Enter DIR \WP to list the program files for the word processing software stored under the WP subdirectory.

Managing Files Within Subdirectories

To copy files or data to subdirectories, you can use the COPY command or any file storage techniques offered by your application program. Some programs may not recognize the subdirectory structure on your diskette, so you may need to set the current directory before you use the program. The RENAME, DIR, ERASE, and other DOS commands work in subdirectories in nearly the same way as they do in the main directory.

Removing Subdirectories

When you no longer need a subdirectory, you can remove it. Use the **RMDIR command**, abbreviated to **RD**, to remove a specified directory from a disk.

Erasing Subdirectory Files.   To remove a subdirectory, you must first remove all files stored within it. You can do so by using the global character * with the ERASE command. You can issue this command from the subdirectory to be removed or from another directory if you give the full path specification. If you issue the command from another directory, make certain to use the correct subdirectory and path information or you might inadvertently erase files from another part of the disk.

For practice, delete the FILES subdirectory (Figure 55, step 1). First, enter the FILES subdirectory by typing the command CD\WP\FILES and pressing the Enter key. Next, empty the subdirectory of files by typing ERASE *.* and pressing the Enter key (step 2). You will receive the message "Are you sure (Y/N)?", to which you must press Y and then the Enter key (step 3).

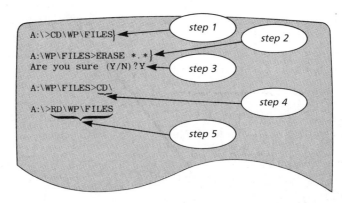

Step 1: Change the directory to WP\FILES.

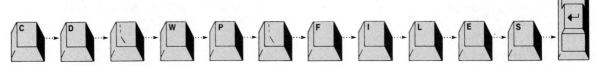

Step 2: Erase all files.

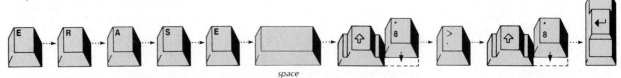

space

Step 3: Respond "Yes" to the prompt.   **Step 4: Change to the root directory.**

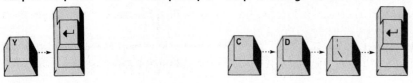

Step 5: Remove the FILES subdirectory.

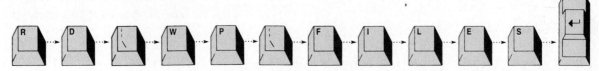

FIGURE 55   **Removing a Subdirectory.**   After you have emptied the subdirectory files, you can remove the subdirectory. Enter the root directory by typing the command CD\ and pressing the Enter key (step 4). To remove the FILES subdirectory, enter RD \WP\FILES and press the Enter key (step 5). Note that you must specify the full path, even though the WP directory is to remain. You must specify the full path so that DOS follows the path from the root directory, where the WP directory entry is stored, through the WP directory to find and remove the FILES entry.

LOADING A PROGRAM

 program is a series of instructions that specifies the steps your computer must perform to accomplish a specific purpose. To execute a program, you must first load the program into main memory from diskette or disk storage. The program must be stored either on a diskette, which you have inserted into one of the disk drives, or on the internal hard disk. If you are using a two-diskette system, place the diskette containing the program to be executed in the default drive, usually drive A. Then type the program name (or name abbreviation) and press the Enter key. (Notice that loading and executing an application program is essentially the same as issuing an external DOS command.)

SUMMARY

1. An **operating system** is one or more programs that control and manage the operation of a computer.
2. The operating system for an IBM Personal Computer is **PC-DOS**. Other compatible computers use a similar program called **MS-DOS**.
3. The **version** number of a program is the whole number and signifies a major improvement of the product. The **release** number is the decimal number and identifies minor corrections or changes to a version of the product.
4. "Booting" the computer refers to loading the operating system from a disk into main memory.
5. The computer can be "booted" by turning it on with the operating system located on a disk in the computer. This is called a "cold start."
6. To reload the operating system when the computer is already switched on, hold down the **Control** and **Alternate** keys and press the **Delete** key. This process is called a "warm start" or "reset."
7. The operating system will **prompt** you for its commands. DOS has two general types of commands: (1) **internal commands** that are executed from the program stored in the main memory; (2) **external commands** that are programs loaded from a disk as the command is executed.
8. After the operating system has been loaded into main memory, you may be prompted to enter the date or time. Some systems have an internal clock that provides this information for you.
9. The **DOS prompt** includes the letter address of the **default disk drive**, the disk that is currently in use for data or program access.
10. The default drive of a two-diskette computer is usually drive A. A computer with a hard disk drive will generally use drive C as its default drive.
11. You can change the default drive by entering a valid drive letter, followed by a colon, and pressing the Enter key.
12. To examine files on a disk, issue the **DIR** (directory) command. Use the /**P** option to pause a long directory listing when the screen is full. Use the /**W** option to list files across the width of the screen.
13. Give the **pause-screen** command by holding down the Control key and pressing the S key.
14. Many commands can be canceled by holding down the **Control** key and pressing the **Break** key or by pressing Control-C.
15. Use the **FORMAT** command to prepare diskettes for storing data or program files. Several options are available for various types of diskettes. Use /**S** to format the diskette as a **system disk**. The /**V** option prompts a **volume label**.
16. Filenames must be created by following specific rules. A **filename** may consist of up to eight letters, numbers, or certain symbols. The filename **extension** is an optional one- to three-character addition, separated from the filename by a period.
17. Files with the extensions **.BAT**, **.COM**, or **.EXE** are external, executable command files.
18. Use the COPY command to transfer a file to another diskette or to create a backup file on the same diskette.
19. **Wildcards**, the * and ? characters, can be used in conjunction with many DOS commands to replace specific characters.
20. A file to be copied is the **source** file. The resulting copy is called the **target** file.
21. You can change a file's name by specifying the target file used during the COPY command or by using the **RENAME** command.
22. To remove a file from a disk, execute the **ERASE** or the **DELETE** command.
23. Disks can be better organized through the use of **subdirectories**. A disk's primary directory is the **root** directory, signified by a **backslash** following the drive letter, such as C:\.
24. Use the **MKDIR** or the **MD** command to create a subdirectory. The entry includes the drive, backslash, and directory name, such as C:\WP.
25. To switch from one directory to another, use the **CHDIR** or **CD** command, for example, CD\WP.
26. A directory can be removed by first erasing all the files in the directory, then using the REMOVE DIRECTORY command, **RD**.
27. To **load a program** for execution, type the name of the program file at the DOS prompt.

STUDENT ASSIGNMENTS

True/False Questions

Instructions: Which of the following statements are true and which are false?

1. PC-DOS and MS-DOS are essentially the same operation system.
2. When DOS is updated for a new version, programs operating in prior versions may not work under the newer edition.
3. The programs comprising an operating system such as PC-DOS can be stored on a diskette.
4. "Booting" the computer refers to the procedure of starting the operating system.
5. DOS commands are divided into two types: internal and external commands.
6. As a part of the system startup procedures, you are requested to enter the computer's serial number.
7. After the operating system has been loaded, you can type the command DIR and press the Enter key to display a directory of the diskette in the default drive.
8. The computer may have a built-in clock that the operating system automatically accesses to input the date and time.
9. The symbol A>, which appears on the computer screen, is called the DOS prompt.
10. A defective disk drive is one that improperly stores data.
11. To change the disk drive assignment to drive C, type C:↵.
12. All DOS commands must be entered in uppercase characters.
13. You can list the directory of the default disk drive by typing DIR and pressing the Enter key.
14. The option /P used with the DIR command will cause the listing to pause when the screen is full.
15. Holding down the Control key and then pressing the Break key will cancel a command function.
16. To format a diskette, put the diskette to be formatted in disk drive A and enter the command FORMAT B:.
17. The command Copy A: can be used to copy all files from one disk drive to another.
18. The ERASE command can be used to remove a file from the file directory.
19. To include the operating system on a formatted disk, use the command FORMAT B:/S.
20. When you use the FORMAT option /V, the system will prompt you to enter a volume label.
21. To cancel a command, hold down the ALT key and press the END key.
22. A DOS filename may contain from 1 to 11 characters plus an optional extension of 1 to 3 characters.
23. The disk containing the file to be copied is known as the source disk.
24. Global replacement characters include *, ?, and \.
25. Hard disk drives are generally addressed as drive C.
26. Subdirectories on disks are used to group filename entries for convenient storage and retrieval.
27. A disk's main file directory is called the root directory.
28. The current directory is the one in which you are currently working.
29. To move from one current directory to another, use the MD command.
30. A file address contains the disk drive letter, the subdirectory path, and the filename.
31. A program cannot be loaded from a disk unless the program disk is in the current drive.

Multiple-Choice Questions

1. "Booting" the computer refers to
   a. loading the operating system
   b. placing covers over the disk drives
   c. using application programs to access disk drives
   d. the system interface

2. "DOS" stands for
   a. Digital Organizing Software
   b. Data Output Stream
   c. Disk Operating System
   d. Dielectric Orthanographic Startup

3. PC-DOS is used on IBM Personal Computers and Personal System/2 systems. IBM-compatible computers generally use
   a. PC-OMD
   b. MS-DOS
   c. XD-DOS
   d. CP/DUZ

4. A term describing your ability to use newer editions of software while retaining features and data used in earlier ones is
   a. software generation
   b. compatibility curve
   c. upward compatibility
   d. version control

5. When you start up the computer, you load the operating system
   a. from a diskette in drive A
   b. from the computer's internal memory
   c. from the fixed disk if the computer is so equipped
   d. both a and c

6. The term for restarting the operating system in a computer already powered on is
   a. warm start
   b. cold start
   c. warm boot
   d. both a and c

7. The symbol A>
   a. is called a DOS prompt
   b. indicates the name of a program
   c. indicates the default disk drive
   d. both a and c

8. Listing the files on a disk is accomplished by
   a. typing DIR and pressing the Enter key
   b. typing LIST and pressing the Enter key
   c. typing CHKDSK and pressing the Enter key
   d. typing RUN FILES and pressing the Enter key

9. To pause a listing on the screen, press
   a. Control and Break
   b. Alternate, Control, and Delete
   c. Control and S
   d. either b or c
10. To cancel a command, press
   a. Control and Break
   b. Alternate, Control, and Delete
   c. Control and S
   d. either c or d
11. The _____ command establishes sectors on a diskette and performs other functions that allow the diskette to store files.
   a. CHKDSK
   b. DIR
   c. REUSE
   d. FORMAT
12. A valid DOS filename specification consists of
   a. 10 alphanumeric characters
   b. a 9-character filename
   c. an 11-character name, separated by a period at any position within the name
   d. an 8-character filename plus an optional extension of a period followed by 3 characters
13. A common use of the COPY command is to make working copies of program and data disks, producing
   a. file disks
   b. backup copies
   c. extension disks
   d. authorized disks
14. To copy the file PROGRAM.EXE from drive A to drive B, type the command
   a. COPY PROGRAM.EXE TO DRIVE B
   b. COPY A:PROGRAM.EXE TO B:PROGRAM.EXE
   c. COPY A:PROGRAM.EXE B:
   d. either b or c
15. To copy all files on drive A to drive C, type the command
   a. COPY DRIVE A TO DRIVE C
   b. COPY ALL FILES TO C
   c. COPY A:*.* C:*.*
   d. COPY A: C:
16. To change the name of a file from FILEX.DOC to FILEA.DOC, enter
   a. ALTER FILEX.DOC TO FILEA.DOC
   b. CHANGE FILEX.DOC TO FILEA.DOC
   c. ASSIGN FILEX.DOC AS FILEA.DOC
   d. RENAME FILEX.DOC FILEA.DOC
17. To remove a file from a disk, type
   a. REMOVE FILE
   b. DELETE FILEX.DOC
   c. ERASE FILEX.DOC
   d. either b or c
18. Filenames are grouped on disks into
   a. index lists
   b. directories and subdirectories
   c. subject and filename entries
   d. internally labeled entries

19. The MKDIR, or MD, command will
    a. manage directory files
    b. make a directory on a disk
    c. create a file copy
    d. either a or b
20. To shift from the root directory to a directory of files under a word processing directory, type the command
    a. CH /FILES
    b. GOTO WP FILES
    c. CD \WP\FILES
    d. C:\WP\FILES*.*

Projects

1. Start your computer without a DOS disk in drive A. What is the display on the screen? Why did this display appear? Insert a DOS disk in drive A and restart the computer by pressing the Ctrl Alt Del keys simultaneously.
2. Start your computer with the DOS disk in the default disk drive. If permitted in your computer lab, prepare a new diskette as a system disk using the proper FORMAT command options for the task at hand and for the specific diskette your computer uses.
3. Prepare a diskette to be a file disk using the FORMAT command. Give the diskette a volume label using your own name. Determine the proper type of diskette to use on the computer and, after formatting, determine the amount of free space remaining on the diskette.
4. If permitted in your computer lab, create a working copy of your application program diskettes.
    a. First, format a new diskette. Will there be enough room on the diskette to contain both the operating system and the program? How can you know?
    b. Using one command, copy all files from the master copy of the disk to your newly prepared diskette.
5. Create a subdirectory named SUB1 on your diskette.
6. Make subdirectory SUB1 the current directory. Copy all .DOC files into SUB1 and display the directory.
7. Remove the subdirectory created in Project 6.

DOS Index

Photo Credits: **Opening Page and Figure 2a**, Radio Shack, a division of Tandy Corp.; **Figures 2b and 3a**, Compaq Computer Corp.; **Figure 3b**, International Business Machines Corp.

Learning to Use Microsoft Works

UNIT I

Introduction to Microsoft Works

What Is Microsoft Works?

OBJECTIVES

- Identify each of the four tools in Microsoft Works.
- Explain the use of each tool.
- Discuss ways in which integration makes software easier to use.
- Explain the purpose of the template disk.
- Describe how to handle floppy disks safely.

INSIDE MICROSOFT WORK

*T*he five major types of application software are word processing, database, spreadsheet, charting or graphics, and communications. Separately, each of these applications can be used on the computer to accomplish tasks and solve problems. In this tutorial, you won't just be reading about a computer—you will be using one. You will use Microsoft Works, a program that integrates all five types of application software in one package. You will learn to use each of these tools on an IBM or IBM-compatible computer. This lesson introduces you to the Works tools and shows how they work together through integration. In this lesson, you will also find out what hardware and software you need to run Works, and how to take care of floppy disks.

In this tutorial, you will be working on files for an imaginary video store, Lugosi's Classic Video, which specializes in thrillers, chillers, comedies, and science fiction movies. Using the Works tools and integration, you will help the store plan for the grand opening of a new location. You will write letters and reports, analyze lists of customers, organize lists of movies, and calculate costs and sales information. And to tie it all together, you will move information from one tool to another, combining data from every tool.

The Word Processor

With the Works Word Processor you can write letters, school papers, brochures, proposals, even poems and novels. Writing always seems to involve some rewriting. If you are like most people, you probably find that your first draft needs a little reworking. Perhaps you start marking changes in pen. After a while, arrows point in all directions, whole paragraphs are circled or crossed out, and insertions are scrawled into the margins. When at last you feel ready to type your final draft, you may have a hard time figuring out what all the lines, arrows, circles, insertions and deletions mean. Even then, you are not secure—if you make a mistake typing the last line of a page, you may have to retype the whole page.

FIGURE 1-1
Lugosi's is an imaginary video store.

A word processor takes the mess out of rewriting. In Unit II of the Works tutorial, you will practice writing with the Works Word Processor. The Word Processor is an electronic tool for writing—much more sophisticated than a pen or typewriter, and in many ways, much easier to use. It turns the computer into a writing machine. You can spend more time thinking about what you want to say, rather than dreaming up ways to avoid reorganizing or reformatting. The computer takes care of the mechanical chores. Do you want wider margins for a cleaner appearance on the page? The computer can readjust all the text so that it fits your new specifications. Do you want to highlight a word with boldface type? The computer can do it for you. Do you want to center a title? The computer can do it automatically, without your having to count spaces. You can even move a paragraph from the end of a report to the front, copy it from one report to another, or erase it entirely—all without having to retype a single word. So in your final, printed draft nothing is crossed out, there are no eraser marks—everything looks as though you had written it correctly the very first time.

It is important to know how word processors operate because you will probably find yourself using a word processor in your work. People use word processors in nearly all businesses, schools, and scientific organizations. Almost every document you read today, from a newspaper or magazine article to a business letter or scientific report, has been prepared with some kind of word processor. The word processor has even spawned a whole new industry called **desktop publishing**. Desktop publishing software can be used with a word processor to create attractive reports and documents that would have required professional production and printing a few years ago.

In Figure 1-3 you see a Works Word Processor document. Along the top of the screen are the names of menus; each menu contains numerous computer commands you can issue to tell the Word Processor what you want done. Below this row of menu names, known as the menu bar, you see the name of the document, a ruler, and the work area. The work area opens a window onto your document. The lines you can see in that window are like an electronic piece of typing paper, where your document appears as you write. Of course, your document may

FIGURE 1-2
These documents were created with word processing software on personal computers, then produced with desktop publishing software.

be much longer than what you can see here. You can bring the rest into view at any time. The lines at the bottom of the screen give you information about your document or about the program. In Unit II of this tutorial, you will use the Works Word Processor to write, correct, change, arrange, and print several different documents for Lugosi's Classic Video Store.

FIGURE 1-3
A Works Word Processor document on screen.

```
 File  Edit  Print  Select  Format  Options  Window  Help

============================ FRANK.WPS ============================
 [········1········2········3········4········5········]········7····=
» Frankenstein's·Stepsister¶
 ¶
 A·wild·comedy·starring·Joan·Calder·about·the·stepsister·of·
 the·evil·genius·who·had·tried·to·create·a·monster,·with·
 disastrous·results.··Ms.·Frankenstein·starts·out·wanting·
 nothing·to·do·with·the·family·heritage.··She·even·changes·
 her·name·to·Frankenstone·to·emphasize·the·point.··On·a·visit·
 to·the·family·castle·in·Transylvania,·things·begin·to·
 change.··She·becomes·obsessed·with·her·predecessor's·work,·
 and·starts·out·to·build·a·creature·of·her·own.¶
 ¶
 Maria·Estefan·costars·as·her·assistant,·Igra,·granddaughter·
 of·the·original·Igor.··Bob·Brown·plays·a·young·detective·
 interested·in·the·new·Dr.·Frankenstein,·and·Park·Chung·her·
 former·assistant.¶
 ¶
 →    STARS:··Joan·Calder,·Maria·Estefan,·Bob·Brown,·Park·
 Chung¶

Pg 1/1                    PIC12                          <F1=HELP>
Press ALT to choose commands.
```

The Database

You probably have a number of lists lying around your house: grocery lists, class lists, lists of things to do. Lists contain **data**, or raw facts which include numbers and words. A **database** is a collection of data. When data that has been put into a form that has meaning and is useful, we call it **information.** In this sense, a telephone book is a database of useful information.

Sometimes you know a person's last name and street address, but you've forgotten the person's first name. To find that person's phone number in the telephone book, you would have to flip back and forth through the entries for everyone with that last name; if the last name is a common one, you'd have to skim through hundreds of entries in tiny type. Even if you live in a small town, that kind of task would be hard. But when you talk to an information operator who has the information stored in a computer database, the computer can find the one person with that last name living at that address in less than a second. Putting a database on a computer automates many tasks that used to be too tedious to attempt. Your access to information is faster and surer.

Businesses find databases most useful for keeping track of their records. In this tutorial, you will use the Works Database to help Lugosi's Classic Video Store with their records. The store has thousands of videotapes. When customers come in with a request, say for movies starring their favorite actor, a clerk can quickly find out whether the movies are in stock or not by using the computer. The records might indicate that only one copy is in stock. When a customer rents the movie, the file is updated to show that the tape is no longer available. Suppose another customer inquires about an old movie: The clerk can search through the database file and find that, sure enough, there is a movie that meets the customer's criteria. What if a customer moves away or a new one joins Lugosi's tape club? The store can remove the old name from the customer list or add the new one. The list is always up to date.

FIGURE 1-4
A telephone book is a simple database.

FIGURE 1-5
A clerk can consult a database to see if an unusual video is in stock.

The Database tool is designed to make **information retrieval** easy. You can look up facts quickly. But not only can the Database find information in the file, it can also help you arrange it, rearrange it, or select a particular group of records all of which match certain criteria that you provide. It can sort your records by customer last name, by date of rental, by dollar amount, and you can print out half a dozen different reports on the same data, then create mailing labels, using the Database tool.

Organizations of all kinds—from businesses to schools—use database programs to manage their records. Businesses keep databases of their inventory, sales, and cost figures, for example. Schools maintain class lists and report cards with the help of databases. Hospitals keep track of patients, operating room schedules, doctors' time, and room availability. Charitable organizations list donations, membership, and volunteer activities. Without databases, many of these functions would be difficult and some would be impossible to perform.

Figure 1-6 shows you a typical Works Database screen. Across the top of the screen you see the names of the menus, each of which contains a group of related computer commands. Below the menus you see the name of this particular file. The center of the screen displays 18 lines of information from the database file. Each line is a record of information about a particular movie. You can look at your records one by one, for full details; or you can collect them all in a list, as you see here. The information in each record has been stored in categories known as fields. The name of the category, or field, appears at the top of each column. There are many more records not shown; you can bring them into view using computer commands. At the bottom of the screen, the lines provide you with messages about your current situation and the program.

FIGURE 1-6
A Works Database file on screen.

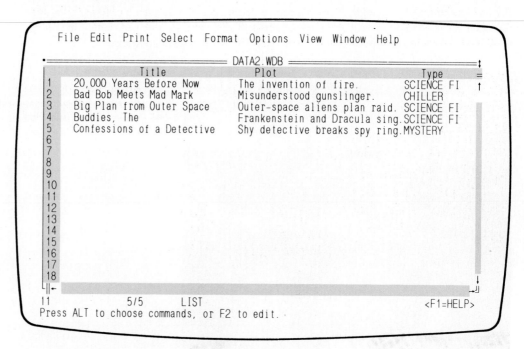

In Unit III of this tutorial, you will use the Works Database to help Lugosi's Classic Video Store organize their records and plan for their new store.

The Spreadsheet with Charting

The Spreadsheet tool helps you create, analyze, and present numbers in rows and columns. Until the advent of computers, accountants used paper spreadsheets to keep track of the income and expenses of a business. All the calculations were done with adding machines, abacuses, or on the fingertips. If a calculation affected numbers upon which other calculations were based, the accountants had to perform additional calculations and all the numbers had to be changed by hand. Imagine having to recalculate dozens of different amounts five or ten times. You avoid all that labor—and many of the incidental mistakes—by using an electronic spreadsheet such as the one in Works, because the program can perform all the recalculations automatically.

A business like Lugosi's Classic Video Store uses a spreadsheet for many purposes. A spreadsheet file helps the store plan budgets in order to determine how much money is available to pay employees, buy merchandise, and cover the cost of operating the store. Another spreadsheet calculates how much money the store needs to pay off their loans. A third spreadsheet even helps the store determine what price to charge for videotape rentals.

The advantage of using an electronic spreadsheet like the one in Works over manual calculations is its ability to recalculate a large set of numbers as many times as necessary. For example, suppose Lugosi's needs a loan to buy supplies for their new store. Before going to the bank to apply for a loan, the store can use the Spreadsheet to figure out the best terms based on what they can afford. Lugosi's can test several alternatives. The store can analyze different loan periods: one year, five years, and ten years. The manager can examine various monthly payment schedules to see how long it would take to pay off the loan at each payment level. Or she can try different percentages for interest payments to calculate how much of the total loan would be taken up by interest. This is what makes the electronic spreadsheet so flexible: the ability to try and see, try and see, try and see—over and over again, until you have seen what will happen for any conceivable alternative. Each alternative is called a **scenario.** By trying different scenarios, businesses can analyze decisions to help determine if they will be great successes, costly mistakes, or somewhere in between.

FIGURE 1-7
Recalculating paper spread-sheets by hand is difficult and time-consuming.

The screen in Figure 1-8 shows you part of a Works Spreadsheet file. At the top of the screen you see the menu bar. The menu names are similar to those in the other tools, but some of the commands on the menus are different. Just below the menu bar you see the formula bar, which displays the contents of the highlighted cell. A cell is just the box formed by the intersection of a row and a column. The 18 lines in the center of the screen contain rows and columns used to organize the numbers in a meaningful way. Some of the cells contain formulas used to calculate the figure that appears on the screen. At the bottom of the screen are the status line and the message line. The status line helps you keep track of where you are in the spreadsheet and what is being done. The message line displays suggestions and brief descriptions of the commands.

FIGURE 1-8
A Works Spreadsheet file on screen.

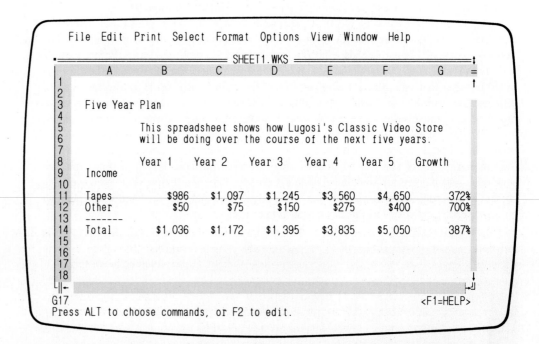

When Sarah Lugosi has to present her figures to the bank in applying for a loan, she needs to make them immediately understandable. Charts help people make sense of the numbers. For instance, a bar chart can show next year's sales projections for different retail outlets. A pie chart can show how much of the operating expenses last year went for rent, salaries, and utilities.

Businesses use charts to demonstrate their financial success, to explain a budget, or to compare possible scenarios. Charts help track monthly income and expense; plot the distribution of data in laboratory experiments; show the distribution of student grades. Many people incorporate charts in their proposals and reports, to show readers the message behind the numbers.

In Unit IV of this tutorial, you will use the Works Spreadsheet and Charting tools to help Lugosi's Classic Video Store prepare a budget for their new location, calculate a loan, and analyze their sales.

Communications

With Works Communications, you can send information from your computer over cables or telephone lines to another computer. The other computer could be down the hall, or across the

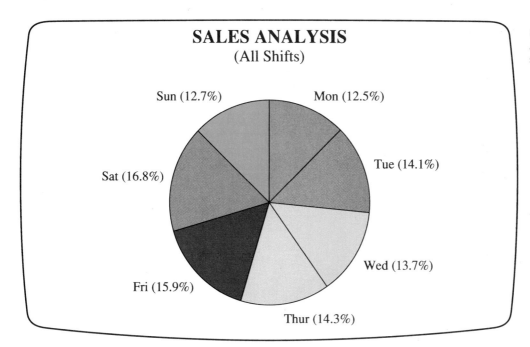

SALES ANALYSIS
(All Shifts)

Sun (12.7%)

Mon (12.5%)

Tue (14.1%)

Sat (16.8%)

Wed (13.7%)

Fri (15.9%)

Thur (14.3%)

FIGURE 1-9
A Works Spreadsheet chart on screen.

country. You can send and receive Works files, files created in other application programs, and short electronic mail messages. You can also look up the latest news, track the progress of your stocks, and order products to be shipped to you.

Many businesses today send reports, letters, memos, budgets, and other **communications** over the telephone lines, rather than through the mail. The message gets through in minutes, rather than days or weeks. At the other end, the recipient can print out the file, or take the file itself and make modifications, then send it back.

You send your messages out through a device known as a modem. Basically, it modifies the signals from your computer so they can be sent through the telephone lines without distortion. At the other end, your recipient's modem translates the signals back from telephone-talk to computerese, so that the other computer can receive and store the message.

The real power of the Communications tool lies in its menus. The commands there allow you to set up your computer so it will dial out automatically, even when you are out to lunch or home asleep, and you can prepare it to send or receive almost any kind of file. In Unit V of this tutorial, you will learn how to use the Communications tool.

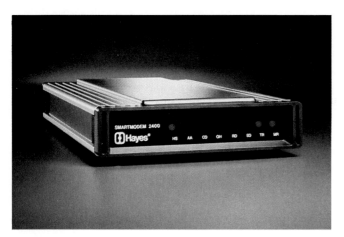

FIGURE 1-10
A modem allows your computer to send and receive information over the telephone lines, communicating with another computer.

Integration

Integrated software combines several applications into one program. For example, Works combines the Word Processor, Database, Spreadsheet with Charting, and Communications tools. Other programs combine spreadsheets and graphics software or desktop publishing with word processing and graphics.

Before integrated software, every application required a separate program, and every program usually worked differently. One program might require you to enter a command like SAVE to store a file on a disk, while another might require you to enter the command STORE to save the file on a disk. Learning all these different programs could be difficult and time-consuming. The way you issued commands, chose options, or moved around in the program—the **user interface**—varied enormously from program to program. Integrated software offers a consistent user interface in every tool. The screen layout in one application is similar to that in the others, and the commands are similar. For example, the *Save* command in all Works tools appears in the same position on the File menu, in the same part of the screen, and it works the same way, too, as shown in Figure 1-11. This kind of consistency means that once you learn how to use one tool, you are well on your way to being able to use the others.

Separate programs also make it hard to switch from one program to another. Imagine you are writing a letter with a word processor program and want to look up an address in a database file. With separate programs, you might have to save your letter, quit the word processor, start the database, open the address file to find the address, save the address file, and quit the database program. Then you would have to start up the word processor program again, and open the file with the letter once more. That is quite a bit of work for what would seem to be a simple task. With an integrated program like Works, you can have several files open at once, from all the application tools, and switch easily among them. For example, in your work for Lugosi's, you might have open a spreadsheet that calculates operating costs of the new store, a database file of customers' addresses, and a word processor file for a memorandum. You could easily combine or transfer information from each of the files to produce a comprehensive report.

Finally, the information you produce with one program cannot easily be transferred into another program because each stores the data in a different way on disk. This means you may have a hard time copying or moving information back and forth; in fact, that may be impossible. The task becomes simple when applications are integrated. In Works, for example, if you want to integrate spreadsheet information into a memo, all you have to do is use the *Copy* command, as in Figure 1-12.

A special form of integration happens when you take names and addresses from a database and apply them to a standard letter, turning out dozens, hundreds, or even thousands of form letters, each customized and addressed to an individual. This merging of database information with the form letters is known as **mail merge.** To create a form letter, you set up a database with the information you want to keep in individual records and collective lists, such as customer names, addresses, and telephone numbers. Then you use the Word Processor tool to make a standard letter you want to personalize for each customer. Wherever you want the person's name to appear, you put a placeholder. The **placeholder** tells Works that when you print the letter, it should look in the database, find the next person's name, and insert it at this point in the letter. Works turns out as many letters as there are records in your database, so everyone gets the letter. Except for addresses and salutations, the letters might be identical.

For this tutorial, you will prepare a plan for the grand opening of Lugosi's new location. It seems that many of their customers live in a neighborhood that is far away from the existing store. Lugosi's could serve these customers better and possibly increase sales by building a new store closer to the customers. When the plan is approved, you will use the *Print Form Letters* command to send out a letter to customers in the area, offering them discounts at the new branch because they have been so loyal.

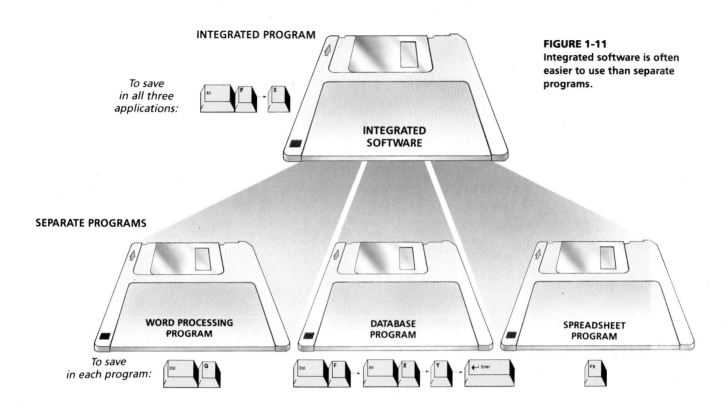

FIGURE 1-11
Integrated software is often easier to use than separate programs.

In Unit VI of this tutorial, you will use the integration features of Works to move Database and Spreadsheet information into a Word Processor document, and you will also produce some form letters to be sent to the customers of Lugosi's Classic Video Store.

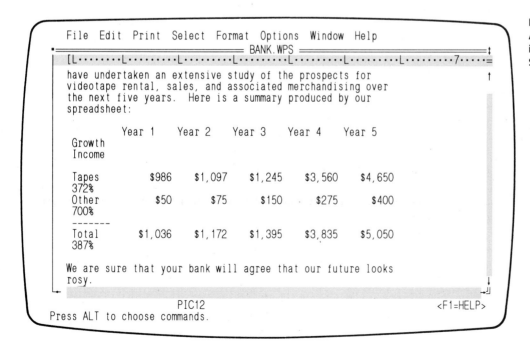

FIGURE 1-12
A Word Processor file integrating information from the Spreadsheet.

WHAT YOU NEED TO GET STARTED

The Works application runs on any MS-DOS computer. To use Works you need hardware—the computer system—and software, which comes on floppy disks.

Hardware

Works runs on almost any IBM or IBM-compatible computer that uses Version 3.01 or later of MS-DOS. You can use almost any monitor, but you need a graphics card in order to display the charts (CGA, EGA, VGA, Monochrome Graphics, or Tandy). Works will work with almost any printer you can attach directly to your computer. And if your computer happens to have a mouse, you'll be able to use that device to issue commands and move around in your documents.

Software

For the computer activities in this part of the tutorial, you need the MS-DOS startup disk, the Works program disk, and the disk that accompanies this book and contains sample files, called a **template** disk.

MS-DOS   You need to load the operating system into your computer before you can load Works. If you have a hard disk with MS-DOS on it, then the operating system will be loaded into the computer automatically when you start up. But if you are using one or two floppy disk drives, you must begin by providing the Microsoft version of the Disk Operating System.

Program Disk   Your instructor has probably provided the Works software for you, using either 5 1/4-inch low-density or high-density floppy disks, a 3.5-inch floppy disk, or a hard disk. The Works **program disk** contains the program and some other files needed occasionally by the program, such as *Help*.

Template Disk   A **data disk** contains files that have been created with an application program. The disk that comes with this tutorial is a type of data disk called a template disk. The files are called templates because they give you an example of a letter, a budget, or an address file; you can modify the sample for your own purposes, if you wish. Templates save you the trouble of making files from scratch. For example, a template disk may contain a spreadsheet file that can be used to compute loan payments. Rather than preparing a complete

FIGURE 1-13
An architect's template makes
drawing shapes easier.

FIGURE 1-14
A template disk contains pre-made files, saving computer users some work.

spreadsheet to compute the payments, you would simply insert a few required numbers, and the spreadsheet would automatically calculate the monthly payments.

The name *template* comes from the small metal or plastic plates with cutout shapes used by architects, engineers, computer programmers, and others as an aid to drawing. These professionals save time and effort using a template rather than drawing shapes freehand.

The template disk you will use with this tutorial contains several sample files. These files are designed to make your work easier. You will be able to spend more time learning how to use the computer and less time simply entering information.

How to Handle Disks   Disks are not fragile, but they are sensitive and must be handled carefully. They can crack in the cold and warp in the heat, becoming unusable. A small amount of dust, oil, dirt, or moisture can damage large amounts of data. The main thing to remember in disk care is to use common sense.

Handle a disk by its jacket only. Never touch the exposed recording surface.

Do not bend or fold a disk.

Never use rubber bands or paper clips on disks.

If possible, write on disk labels *before* attaching them to the disk. If the label is already on a disk, write gently with a felt-tip pen.

Do not use an eraser on the label—the rubber can get into the disk jacket and damage the recording surface.

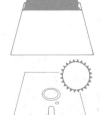 Put the disk back into its protective envelope immediately after using it.

 Store disks upright in a dry area away from direct sunlight and extremes of hot and cold.

Keep disks away from magnets, including those in television sets, telephones, and large motors. Magnets can erase any data stored on a disk. Avoid exposing disks to X-rays such as those found at airport security check points.

 Insert disks gently into disk drives—never force them.

In this lesson, you have learned about the four Works tools, what you need to get started in using Works on the computer, and how to take care of floppy disks. In Lesson 2, you will begin using the Works software.

KEY TERMS

communications   *MSW 11*
data   *MSW 7*
data disk   *MSW 14*
database   *MSW 7*
desktop publishing   *MSW 6*
information   *MSW 7*
information retrieval   *MSW 8*
mail merge   *MSW 12*
placeholder   *MSW 12*
program disk   *MSW 14*
scenario   *MSW 9*
user interface   *MSW 12*
template   *MSW 14*

REVIEW QUESTIONS

1. Why should you keep disks away from magnets?
2. On a hot summer day, should you leave a disk on the sill of a window? Why or why not?

3. What is the main purpose of the Word Processor tool? The Database? The Spreadsheet and Charting? The Communications?
4. Why would you want to integrate information from a database file into a word processor file?
5. What are the three major benefits of integration?
6. What is the worst thing that can happen if you do not take care of your data disk?
7. In brief, how does Works allow you to create form letters?
8. What is data? Give some examples of data that might be produced by a business, a high school, and a research laboratory.
9. Can you think of some tasks that would be made easier through the use of a word processor, database, spreadsheet, and communications? Describe them.

Getting Started

OBJECTIVES

- Start the program.
- Browse through the Works menus.
- Choose commands from the menus.
- Explore the Works screen and window.
- Use the Works calculator.
- Get help.
- Quit the program.

STARTING MICROSOFT WORKS

ow that you've seen what Microsoft Works can do, you are ready to begin using the actual software. In this lesson, you will learn how to start Microsoft Works, explore the menus, choose a command, and use the Help system.

Loading DOS

To provide the computer with an operating system, you need to load DOS from a floppy disk into the computer. You can then use DOS to load the Microsoft Works program from its disk.

When inserting a disk, hold the disk with the label face up and toward you, as demonstrated in Figure 2-1. Make sure that the disk fits all the way into the disk drive, but do not force it. Some disk drives have a small lever or door that you must close after you have inserted the disk. If you forget to close the door, the drive will not be able to read the disk. Instead, the drive will make noises, and after a few seconds, you will see a message on the monitor indicating that the computer cannot read the disk in that drive. Make sure that the disk is inserted snugly in the drive, close the drive door, and try again.

1. Turn on the monitor. The switch may be on the right side of the monitor, in the rear, or on the front, as in Figure 2-2.
2. Insert the MS-DOS Startup disk into drive A.
3. Turn on the computer. As you face the computer, the switch may be on the front, side, or on the back of the computer on the right side, as seen in Figure 2-3.

   If your computer is already on, press and hold the CTRL, ALT, and DEL keys all at once to restart.

FIGURE 2-1
Inserting a disk into a disk
drive.

MS-DOS is now loaded into the computer's memory. After a few seconds, you see the computer's idea of today's date, with a request that you enter a new date if necessary. Usually you don't need to correct the date, but just in case something has gone wrong with the computer's clock, or if your computer does not have an internal clock, you are offered the opportunity to bring it up to date. Whenever you make or change a file, the computer records the date and time along with the file name. When you look at a list of files, you will always know when you last worked on each file.

4. If the computer's date is incorrect, key the current month as a number, a hyphen, the day's date, a hyphen, and the year. For example, if the current date were December 20, 1991, you would key 12-20-1991. (If the computer's date is correct, you do not need to key anything.)

FIGURE 2-2
The monitor switch may be in
front.

FIGURE 2-3
On this computer, the switch is
in the back on the right side.

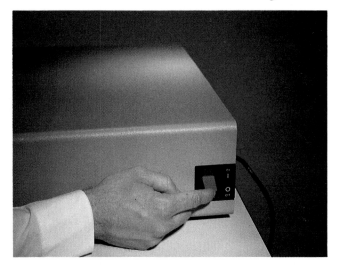

5. Press the Enter key to confirm the date the computer displayed or the date you just keyed, and to enter that date into the computer's memory for future use. The computer now displays its idea of the current time.

   By the way: Some keyboards have two Enter keys. You can use either.

6. If the computer's time is incorrect, key the hour (using the numbers 0 to 23 to indicate the hours from 12:00 AM to 11:00 PM), a colon (:), and the minute. For instance, if the time is twenty minutes past two in the afternoon, you would enter 14:20. You do not need to key the values for seconds and hundredths of a second. (If the computer's time is correct, you do not need to key anything.)

7. Press the Enter key again to accept the current time.

You now see some information about the computer, some copyright messages, and the MS-DOS prompt, A>, on the screen. A **prompt** is a message from the computer, asking you to perform some action or issue a command. The A> prompt means MS-DOS has been loaded into memory, and the computer expects you to tell it what program to look for and start on the disk in drive A.

Starting Microsoft Works

Now that you have loaded the operating system, MS-DOS, into the computer, you can use it to load and run the Microsoft Works program.

1. When you see the A> prompt, remove the MS-DOS Startup disk, and insert your Microsoft Works program disk in drive A. If you have a second disk drive, insert the template disk in drive B. The template disk contains several documents, or files, you will use in this tutorial.

2. At the A> prompt, key works and then press Enter to load Microsoft Works from the disk in drive A into the computer's memory.

   Pressing the Enter key sends the command you have just keyed to the computer to act on. In this case, you have issued a command to read the files on the disk in drive A, find the one named Works, and load that program into the computer's memory.

   In a few moments, the Works **opening screen** appears, as shown in Figure 2-4.

If you do not see the Microsoft Works opening screen, turn off your monitor and computer, and repeat these steps. If you still have trouble, please ask your instructor for help.

EXPLORING THE WORKS SCREEN

Many computer programs use menus as a way of offering choices—like the menus in restaurants, listing choices of food. The opening screen contains three menus next to the copyright notice. One of these menus, the File menu, is open; and the first command, *Create New File*, is highlighted. The names of the other two menus, Options and Help, appear in the top row, known as the **menu bar**. In this part of the tutorial, you will learn how to find out more about a command and how to issue one.

Using a Menu

The three menus on the opening screen are basic to Works. With some variations, they appear in each of the tools to assist you in the Word Processor, Database, Spreadsheet, and Communi-

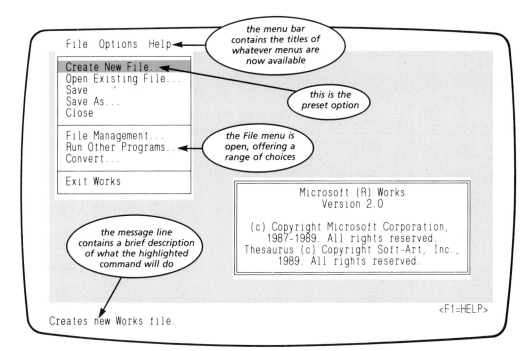

FIGURE 2-4
The Microsoft Works opening screen.

cations. In this section, you'll learn how to find out what a command does and how to choose a command.

Finding Out About a Command   Whenever you start Works, you see the opening screen with the File menu pulled down below its title on the menu bar. A **file** is the electronic form of a document. The commands on the File menu help you store a file on a disk for reuse later, open a file you've previously stored on disk, make a copy of a file, or move a file from one disk to another. Before you can do some work, you need to create a new file or open an existing one. That is why this menu appears in the opening screen.

One of the choices, the *Create New File* command, is highlighted (with a dark background). That is the **preset option;** it has been selected beforehand, because the programmers believe it is the command most people will want to use when they start the program.

At the bottom of the screen, a message explains what the highlighted command does. On the right, another message tells you that by pressing **F1,** the first of your **function keys,** you can get help—a more detailed description of the command. A function key acts like a command; pressing the key tells the program to perform a particular function. Function keys speed up many routine operations because they let you issue the command without going to a menu.

1. Press F1. The program displays a description of what the *Create New File* command does, followed by a step-by-step procedure, as shown in Figure 2-5.

   As you can see from the help window, the *Create New File* command lets you start a brand new file in any of the four Works tools. First you choose the command; then you select the type of file you want to create (Word Processor, Spreadsheet, Database, or Communications).

2. To return to the File menu, press the Esc key. Esc closes the help window and displays the File menu again.

   The **Esc key** offers you a way out—an escape from many parts of the program. If you

FIGURE 2-5
Information about the high-lighted command, *Create New File.*

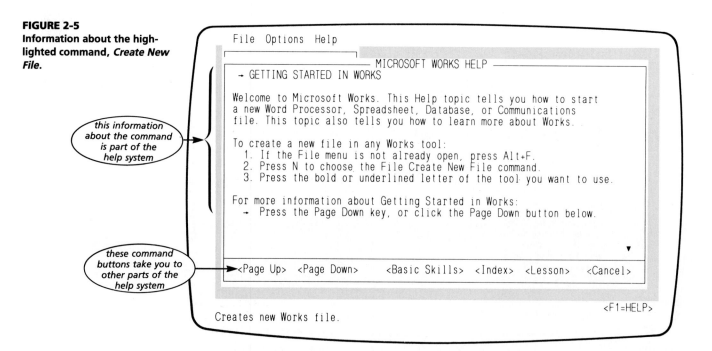

this information about the command is part of the help system

these command buttons take you to other parts of the help system

```
 File  Options  Help

┌──────────────────────── MICROSOFT WORKS HELP ─────────────────────┐
│ → GETTING STARTED IN WORKS                                        │
│                                                                   │
│ Welcome to Microsoft Works. This Help topic tells you how to start│
│ a new Word Processor, Spreadsheet, Database, or Communications    │
│ file. This topic also tells you how to learn more about Works.    │
│                                                                   │
│ To create a new file in any Works tool:                          │
│   1. If the File menu is not already open, press Alt+F.          │
│   2. Press N to choose the File Create New File command.         │
│   3. Press the bold or underlined letter of the tool you want to use.│
│                                                                   │
│ For more information about Getting Started in Works:             │
│   → Press the Page Down key, or click the Page Down button below.│
│                                                                  ▼│
├───────────────────────────────────────────────────────────────────┤
│ <Page Up>  <Page Down>   <Basic Skills>  <Index>  <Lesson>  <Cancel>│
└───────────────────────────────────────────────────────────────────┘
                                                        <F1=HELP>
 Creates new Works file.
```

find you've made a mistake, or if you just want to return to the place you were one step before, pressing Esc cancels the current operation and takes you back to the previous location.

Choosing a Command   One way to choose a command from a menu is to use the Down Arrow or Up Arrow to move the highlighting over the command; then press Enter to signal the computer that you want it to carry out the selected command.

1. Press the Down Arrow to move the highlighting down, one command at a time.

   Brief explanations of each command appear in the message line. Using the Arrow keys is one way to select a command.

2. Use the Down Arrow or the Up Arrow to move the highlighting to the *Create New File* command.

   The **three dots** after the command indicate that when you choose this command, you will be asked for additional information—in this case, the Works tool you'll be using in the new file.

   You have now selected a command, but you have not yet told the computer to carry it out. That is the next step.

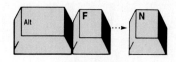

Create New File

3. With the highlighting on the *Create New File* command, press Enter. You see a dialog box asking you what kind of a file you want to create (Figure 2-6).

   A **dialog box** is the way in which Works requests the extra information it needs to carry out the command. In this case, Works needs to know what kind of a file you want to create. Works makes a different kind of file for each tool, so you're being asked to identify which tool you want to use. As you use Works, you'll see several kinds of dialog boxes. Some ask you to key in some text; others offer you a list from which to choose items, check boxes to turn certain features on or off, and option boxes to select. Think of the dialog box as part of an ongoing conversation with the computer, as you explain exactly how you want it to carry out your command.

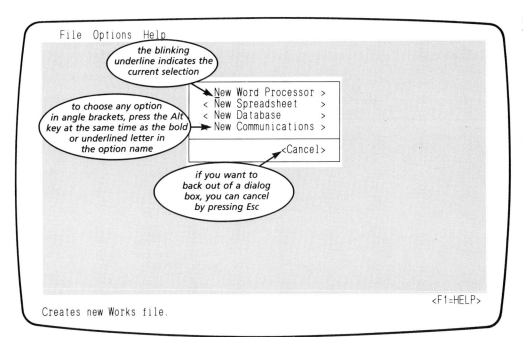

FIGURE 2-6
The Create New File dialog box.

Whenever you see an option or command surrounded by angle brackets, that means you should issue the command by pressing the **Alt key** at the same time as the bold or underlined letter in the command name. Sometimes you can issue the command by pressing just the letter, but if that does not work, remember that you are supposed to be pressing the Alt key at the same time.

Some dialog boxes also display lists in boxes. Each box has a name, often with a bold or underlined letter in the name. To move the cursor into a particular box, you need to press the Alt key at the same time as the letter. (You'll soon become familiar with this process, as you go through the tutorial.)

4. Press the Alt key at the same time as the letter W to have Works create a Word Processor file. In a moment, a new menu bar appears, part of the Works screen for a Word Processor document, shown in Figure 2-7.

Congratulations! You have issued a command, given Works some specifics in the dialog box, and in a blink of an eye, you have the results in front of you.

Exploring the Works Screen

As you saw in the opening screen, the **Works screen** always begins with the menu bar at the top. And at the bottom of the screen, you always see the status line and the message line. Now that you have created a file and started to work in one of the tools, Works adds a window—containing the document itself—and a number of symbols that give you control over the window and tell you where you are in the file.

Looking into the Works Window

The Works screen provides access to the commands, guidance, and help available in the program. You apply that power to the file, which appears inside a special area of the screen known as the file **window.**

FIGURE 2-7
The Works Screen in the Word Processor.

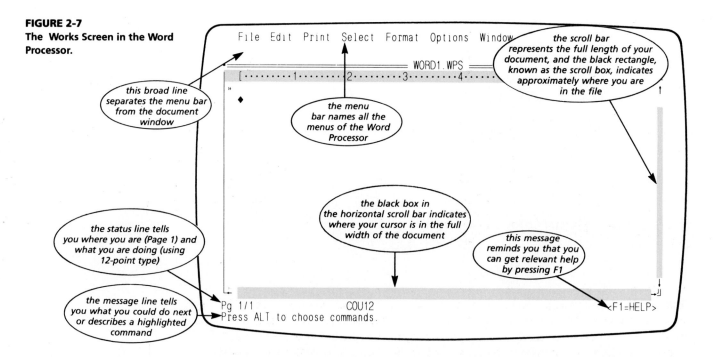

The window gives you a view of part of your document. The window has a name—the name of the file. The window starts below the menu bar and extends down to the horizontal scroll bar at the bottom of the screen. On the left, it starts at the border, extending to the vertical scroll bar on the right.

FIGURE 2-8
The window.

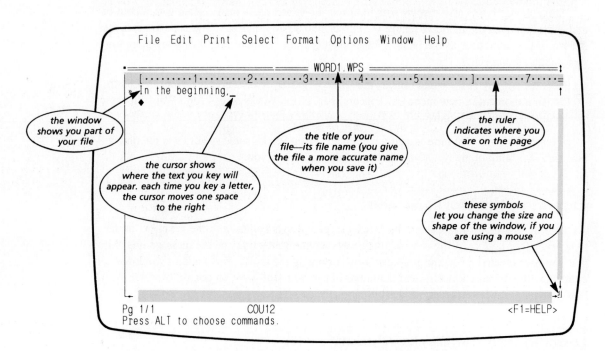

The window is ready for you to key in. The blinking underline, known as **the cursor**, indicates where the text you key will appear.

FIGURE 2-9
The Microsoft Mouse.

Using a Mouse   If you have a **mouse,** a palm-size device that you roll around on your desk to move a pointer on the screen, you can use some of the other symbols in the Works screen, as shown in Figure 2-10. In a long document, for instance, you can point to one of the arrows along the bottom or right-hand side of the screen, click the left mouse button, and move in that direction through your file. You can point to a scroll box, hold down a mouse button, and drag the box through the scroll bar, changing your horizontal or vertical position in the document. You can click the little button in the top left corner of the window to close the file. You can drag the bottom right corner of the window up and down to change the size and shape of the window. And you can click on the double arrow at the top right corner to restore the window to its full size and shape.

The mouse makes possible the **point-and-click interface,** in which you point at an object or a place on the screen, and click to select it or place the cursor in that position. With a mouse, you can point to a menu name, and it opens; point to a command and have it initiated;

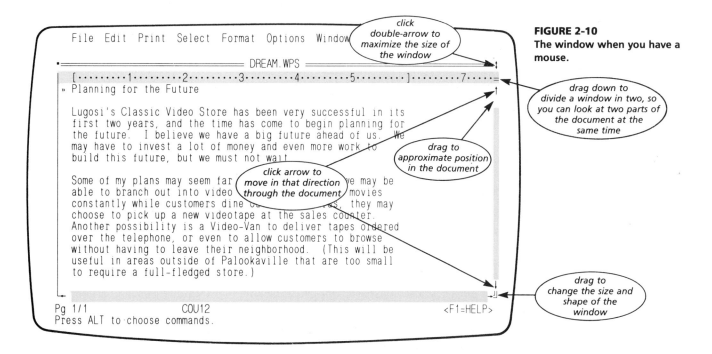

FIGURE 2-10
The window when you have a mouse.

or click directly on an option to select it. Many people find pointing and clicking easier than using the keyboard. On the other hand, accomplished typists often prefer to keep their fingers on the keyboard, issuing every command from there, without stopping to pick up the mouse and move it around.

If you don't have a mouse, don't despair. You can make all these adjustments using commands and the Arrow keys. In this tutorial, we will tell you how to do everything from the keyboard.

Choosing a Command—Another Way   When you chose to create a new file, you used the Arrow keys to highlight the command, then pressed Enter. Now you have seen the Works screen and the window containing your Word Processor document. To return to the opening screen, to continue our exploration of its menus, you must put away this file. That is known as **closing the file.** To close a file, you need a command from the File menu.

1. Press the Alt key. That activates the menu names with a bold or underlined letter.

   Alt stands for Alternate. Whenever you need to activate menu names, press Alt.

   Now that you have activated each menu, you can open a menu by striking the bold or underlined letter. The bold or underlined letter in the name of the File menu is, not too surprisingly, F.

2. To open the File menu, strike F. The menu opens.

   From now on, when you want to open a menu, press Alt and then the bold or underlined letter in the menu name. We will condense this from now on, and say: *Press Alt-F.*

   Now that you have a file open on the screen, the commands *Save, Save As,* and *Close* have become active. Each command you can use contains a bold or underlined letter in the name. To issue one of these commands, you just strike that letter. Closing removes a file from the computer's memory without storing it on a disk. To store the file safely, you must save it. But you do not need to save this file.

3. To close the file, strike C.

   The file disappears from the screen—and from the computer's memory. You return to the opening screen.

   From now on, you can choose a command from any menu in two steps. You press Alt and the bold or underlined letter of the menu name; then you strike the bold or underlined letter of the command. Follow these two steps whenever we say something like, "Choose the X command from Menu Y."

Browsing through the File Menu

The File menu makes it easy to work with a document as a whole, in its electronic form. First you create a file; then you save it on a disk, giving it your own name, and closing the file. Later, you can reopen the file to do more work in it, make a copy of the whole file, rename it, and save it somewhere else, if you wish. You've already explored the first command, *Create New File.* Now you'll get an idea of what the other file commands can do for you.

You use the second command, *Open Existing File,* to bring a file from a disk into the computer so you can work on it again.

1. Choose the *Open Existing File* command. You see a dialog box containing a list of files.

Remember: To choose a command, use the Arrow keys to move the highlighting to the command, then press Enter. Or just strike the bold or underlined letter in the command's name.

If you were really looking for a file, you would now highlight the one you want, and press Enter. But for now, you are just browsing.

2. Press Esc to put away the dialog box.
3. Press Alt-F to open the File menu.

The next three commands do not apply to what you are doing right now; you have no file open, so you cannot close it or save it. That is why these commands have no bold or underlined letters, and they cannot be selected now.

The *File Management* command allows you to do a lot of housekeeping chores with files on disks. With this command, you can copy, rename, or delete a file on disk; create or remove a **directory**—a file specifically designed to hold a group of related files on a disk; format a new disk so it can store files; and copy the contents of one disk onto another. You can even reset the computer's date and time if you need to.

4. Strike F to choose the *File Management* command. A dialog box presents a list of the **options.**

Works lets you do these tasks from inside the program, without having to leave and issue commands in MS-DOS. That is a great convenience.

5. Press Esc to leave the dialog box.
6. Open the File menu again.

Remember: To open the File menu, press Alt then F.

The *Run Other Programs* command lets you switch to another program, use it for a while, and return to Works when you quit that program.

The *Convert* command transforms files you created in other applications so that Microsoft Works can read them, and you can work on them in Works. In addition, you can save a Microsoft Works file in a format that many other applications can read.

The last command, *Exit Works*, lets you quit the program.

After you have used the program for a while, you will come to know the bold or underlined letters for commands you use a lot. The letter often forms the beginning or an important part of the key word in each command, making it a little easier to recall.

Checking Out Your Options

The second menu on the opening screen offers you the chance to tailor the program to your own situation.

1. Press the Right Arrow to move to the Options menu.

Once you are in a menu, the Direction keys let you move up and down through that menu or right and left from one menu to the next.

The first command in the Options menu, *Works Settings*, lets you establish your preferences as to units of measure, screen colors, number of lines on the screen, and local or national conventions for formatting dates and currency. In addition, this command lets you provide the program with information about your phone for purposes of sending and receiving files, using the Communications tool.

2. Choose *Calculator*. You see a screen version of a simple calculator, as shown in Figure 2-11.

FIGURE 2-11
The Works calculator.

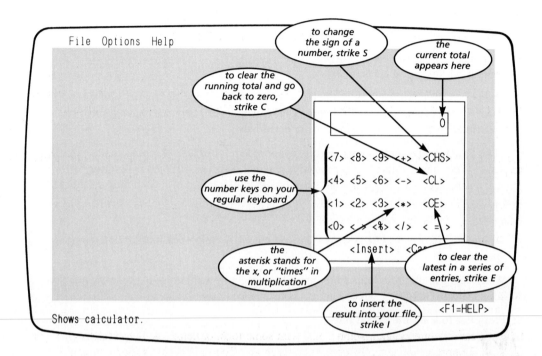

No matter what tool you are in or what file you are working on, you can go to the Options menu and choose the *Calculator* command, bringing up an electronic version of the hand-held calculator. You can do addition, subtraction, multiplication, division, and percentages using the keys on your regular keyboard.

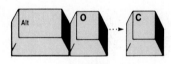

Calculator

3. Using the number keys directly above the letter keys on your regular keyboard, key: 256-64=

   In a moment, the calculator displays the result: 192.

4. Key: +32=

   Remember to hold down the Shift key to make the plus sign. The calculator keeps a running total, so it adds 32 to 192, and when you press the equal sign, displays the result: 224.

   When you've completed your calculations, you can have Works put the number into the file you are working on, at the spot where you left the cursor, by striking I for Insert.

5. Strike C for Clear to erase whatever number is in the total box.

   Clearing wipes out your running total. But what if you've been adding a series of numbers, and you make one mistake in entering a number? Striking E eliminates the last entry, but does not erase the running total from the computer's memory, so you can go on. Here's an example:

6. Key: 5+6+7 E =

   You've added 5 and 6 to get 11, then added 7 more, but changed your mind and pressed E to clear the last entry. The calculator shows the 7 changed to 0. To find out where you are in your calculation, you press the equal sign, and sure enough, you're back to 11. Your running total has been preserved and the last entry thrown away.

7. Press Esc to put away the calculator.
8. Press Alt-O to see the Options menu again.

You can press the Alt key at the same time as the letter O for Options, or you can press the Alt key and then strike O.

The Alarm Clock lets you set a time for an alarm and a message to be delivered.

The last command, *Dial This Number*, has no bold or underlined letter, because you have not yet specified any particular phone number to dial. (You do that in the Communications tool.)

These four commands are available in the Options menu in every Works tool, with one minor exception in Communications. In Communications, you have the first three options (the Works Settings, Calculator, and Alarm Clock), but you do not have the Dial This Number option. That is because Communications has a whole menu for dialing (the Connect menu). In place of the Dial This Number option, the Communications tool offers the Phone option, which allows you to specify the phone number you want dialed.

Each tool also has extra options of its own, added to its Options menu.

GETTING HELP

Most software programs now come with some form of help. The **help system** gives you support as you actually work in the program. The information appears on your screen, so it is handier than the manual. Works provides a lot of help. You have already seen that whenever you select a command, you can press the first function key, F1, to get a detailed explanation of what the command will do and how you can use it. In this section of the tutorial, you will learn how to find the help you need on topics such as basic skills, the tools, the keyboard, and various common tasks people do in Works.

Using the Index

With the highlighting in the Options menu, press the Right Arrow to open the Help menu.

If you do not have the Options menu open, press Alt-H to open the Help menu.

Works provides so much information in the Help system that you need to learn how to move through the various topics to find the one you want. Choosing the *Using Help* command gives you a good overview of the best ways to locate a topic. You've already used the first method, pressing F1 for information about a selected command. Now you'll learn to branch out.

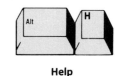

Help

Using the Help Index   To select a Help topic yourself rather than leaving it to Works to decide what information applies to your task, you use the **Help Index.**

1. In the Help menu, choose *Help Index*. You see the index shown in Figure 2-13.

On the left, you see a list of the major categories of information in the Help system. At first, *Basic Skills* is selected. In the box on the right, you see a list of the topics in whatever category has been selected. The first topic, *Backing Up Files*, is highlighted. Let's say you want to know a little more about typing in Works. The first place to look is in the list of basic skills. There are so many skills, though, that they do not all appear in the box at once.

Help Index

FIGURE 2-12
The Help menu.

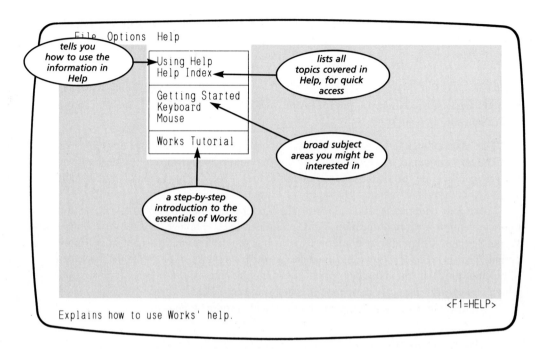

FIGURE 2-13
The Help Index.

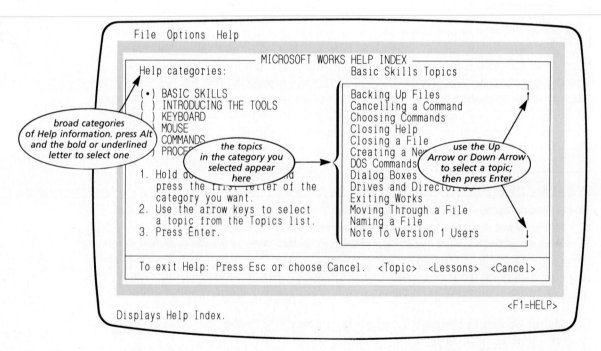

You need to use the Up and Down Arrow keys to move the highlighting up and down the list.

2. Press the Down Arrow to move highlighting down through the topics in the box on the right. Don't stop when you reach the *Notes To Version 1 Users* topic. Keep pressing the Down Arrow. The list itself moves up, allowing the highlighting to go through other topics. Stop when you have highlighted the *Typing* topic.

You have just **scrolled** through the list. The black rectangle in the scroll bar on the right indicates where your highlighting is in relation to the whole list. When the rectangle hits the bottom, you know you've reached the end of the scrollable list.

At the bottom of the Help window, you see the actions you can take. The angle brackets indicate that you should press the Alt key at the same time as the bold or underlined letter. To choose a topic, then, you must select it, then press Alt and T.

3. Press Alt-T to see the information on the topic of typing. In a moment, you see a window with tips on typing in the Word Processor and Communications, shown in Figure 2-15.

   The triangle pointing down indicates that there is more information to follow.

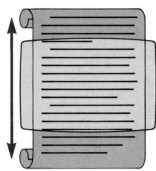

FIGURE 2-14
Scrolling moves text from below the screen into view.

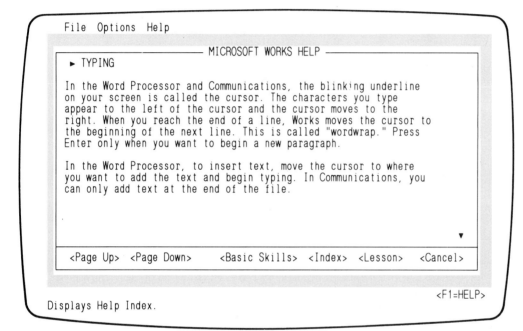

```
 File  Options  Help

                 ─── MICROSOFT WORKS HELP ───
  ▶ TYPING

  In the Word Processor and Communications, the blinking underline
  on your screen is called the cursor. The characters you type
  appear to the left of the cursor and the cursor moves to the
  right. When you reach the end of a line, Works moves the cursor to
  the beginning of the next line. This is called "wordwrap." Press
  Enter only when you want to begin a new paragraph.

  In the Word Processor, to insert text, move the cursor to where
  you want to add the text and begin typing. In Communications, you
  can only add text at the end of the file.

                                                                  ▼
  ─────────────────────────────────────────────────────────────────
  <Page Up>  <Page Down>     <Basic Skills>  <Index>  <Lesson>   <Cancel>

                                                         <F1=HELP>
 Displays Help Index.
```

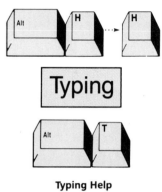

FIGURE 2-15
Help on Typing.

4. Press the Page Down key to see more. You see the second panel of information about typing. Two rectangles replace the triangle, indicating that this is the end of the information about typing.
5. When you have read the information, press Alt-I to return to the Help Index.

   Perhaps you want to know what the various function keys can do for you when you are typing. The information you have seen so far has not answered that question. Perhaps Works provides the answer under the category of Keyboard. You need to change categories.

Changing Categories in the Help Index   The Help Index starts off offering you topics in the Basic Skills category. Sometimes you want to investigate a more specific or complex topic, such as function keys. For that, you need to switch categories. Each category has a bold or underlined letter in its name. To change from one category to another, you must press the Alt key at the same time as the letter in the category you want.

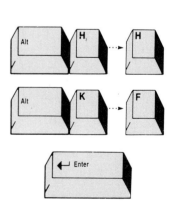

Function Keys Help

1. To change to the Keyboard category, press Alt-K. The dot and underline drop down to that category, and a new list of topics appears on the right.
2. Strike F to move the highlighting to the first topic that begins with F. The highlighting moves to *Function Keys*.

Striking a letter zips you through the topics faster than pressing the Down Arrow.

3. Press Enter to see information about the Function Keys. You see a list of functions in alphabetical order, with the keys to press to execute those functions, as in Figure 2-16.

FIGURE 2-16
Help on Function Keys.

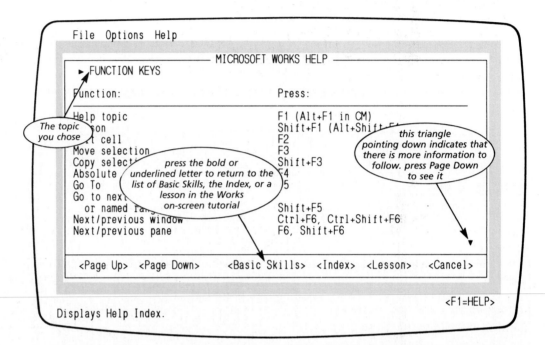

You now have several things you can do next. You can press the Page Down or Page Up key to browse through more help. Or you can issue a command. The commands at the bottom of the window are all surrounded by angle brackets. To issue one of these commands, you need to press the Alt key at the same time as the bold or underlined letter in the command name. If you want to look something else up, you can press Alt-B to return to the index with the Basic Skills category selected and a list of those topics displayed on the right. Or, if you want to return to the index with the Keyboard category selected, you can press Alt-I; that returns you to the index as you left it, to look at other topics in the same category. Or, if you have found the information you sought, you can press Esc to close the Help window and put away the Help system.

4. Press Esc to put away Help.

QUITTING WORKS

he File menu is the first one you see when you start Works, and it is the menu you use to leave Works in an orderly way.

1. Press Alt-F to open the File menu.
2. Strike x to exit the program. The Works screen vanishes, and you return to the DOS prompt.

If you happen to be working in a file and choose to exit the program, Works reminds you to save the file before it closes down. That gives you a chance to preserve your work or to cancel if you decide not to quit after all.

3. Remove the Works program disk from the disk drive.
4. Turn off the monitor and then turn off the computer.
5. Put the program disk in its envelope and store it safely.

Congratulations! You have finished your first session with the Works software. You have started up the program, practiced opening and using menus, chosen commands, explored the Works screen and window, used the calculator, and looked up information in the Help system. In the next lesson of this tutorial, you will begin using the Works Word Processor to make a new file.

KEY TERMS

Alt key *MSW 23*
cursor *MSW 24*
dialog box *MSW 22*
directory *MSW 27*
Esc key *MSW 21*
F1 *MSW 21*
function keys *MSW 21*

Help Index *MSW 29*
menu bar *MSW 20*
mouse *MSW 25*
MS-DOS *MSW 19*
opening screen *MSW 20*
options *MSW 27*

point-and-click interface *MSW 25*
preset option *MSW 21*
prompt *MSW 20*
three dots *MSW 22*
window *MSW 23*
Works screen *MSW 23*

COMMANDS

Alt-O-A (Alarm Clock)
Alt-O-C (Calculator)
Alt-F-N (Create New File)
Enter
Alt-F-F (File Management)
Alt-H (Help)
Alt-H-H (Help Index)
Alt-F-O (Open Existing File)
Alt-O-W (Works Settings)

REVIEW QUESTIONS

1. What is the purpose of a help system in an application program?
2. How do you start up a program like Works? List the steps required.
3. What key do you usually press to send a command to the computer to carry out? Where is the key on the keyboard?
4. What key do you press to cancel an action or escape from a dialog box? Where is the key on the keyboard?
5. What are two ways to choose a command?
6. In what ways can you learn more about a command?
7. When are the first three commands on the Options menu available?

8. How would you look up information about procedures for using the calculator, using the Help Index?
9. How do you quit Works?

APPLICATIONS

1. Start Works. Look up creating a new file in the Help system. Write down the steps.
2. In the Help system, look up the basic skill of cancelling a command. Write down how this is done. Remember to look for additional information by paging up and down, if necessary.
3. Look up the Works screen in the Help system. Write down a list of the elements that make up the screen.

UNIT II

The Word Processor

Getting Started with the Word Processor

OBJECTIVES

- Describe the basic elements of word processing.
- Make a new file.
- Write and correct text.
- Save a file on disk.
- Print a document.
- Remove a file from a disk.

WORD PROCESSOR BASICS

When you write with a pen and paper, you are, in a sense, doing word processing. **Word processing** is just a fancy way of saying "working with words." When you decide what words to put first, how to arrange the information on the page, and how to correct mistakes you may have made, you are functioning as a kind of word processor.

In word processing, what you write—whether it is a letter, short story, report, poem, or something else—is called a **document.** The content of the document—the actual words you put on the page—is called **text.**

Word processing—with a pen or with a computer—involves three main activities. The first activity is writing: transposing thoughts from your head onto paper or onto the computer's screen. The second part is **editing:** modifying what you have written by correcting errors, rearranging the information so that it flows more logically, or just rewriting to make everything sound better. Editing improves the content of a document. The third activity in word processing is **formatting:** arranging the text on the page. Formatting improves the appearance of a document. Of course, these three activities do not always take place in order. Sometimes you will edit as you write. For example, you might cross out a word as you are writing a note. Sometimes you will adjust the format as you write. For example, you may decide to use narrower margins for a quotation, and then return to wider margins when you finish typing the quote. No matter when or how you do your writing, editing, and formatting, you will probably always do some of each on any document.

The three lessons on word processing in this tutorial are organized mainly around these three activities. In this lesson, you will concentrate on writing. Lesson 4, "Working with a Document," emphasizes the process of editing text. Lesson 5, "Formatting a Document," concentrates on formatting documents.

To start with, you will write a letter from Lugosi's Classic Video Store to a distributor of videotapes. The distributor supplies industrial training films about subjects like Bessemer-process steel making that Lugosi's feels may not be appropriate for or interesting to their customers. The store would like to inform the distributor that their specialty is thrillers and chillers rather than industrial training tapes.

MAKING A NEW FILE

*T*he first step in writing with the Word Processor is to make a new file to hold your document. Every time you begin a new document, you need to make a new file. A computer file is the electronic version of the document, and it resembles a manila folder you might store in a file cabinet. One Works file contains one document. You begin the process of making a new Works file at the File menu.

1. Start up Works. Use the startup procedures you learned in Lesson 2.
2. On the opening screen, the *Create New File* command is already selected. Just press Enter to choose it. A dialog box appears listing the four Works tools. The first tool, the Word Processor, has already been selected.
3. Press Enter to have the new file created in the Word Processor tool. You see the Word Processor menu names appear in the menu bar above the window containing the new document, shown in Figure 3-1.

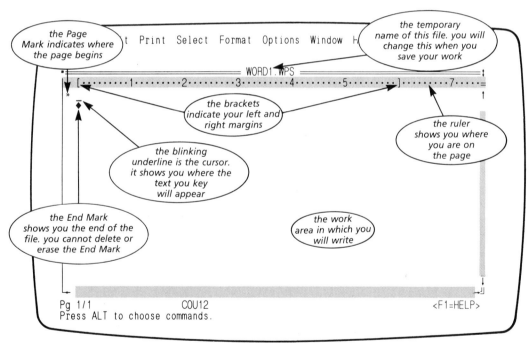

FIGURE 3-1
The new Word Processor document.

WRITING WITH THE WORD PROCESSOR

*W*henever you create a new Word Processor file, you see a document window like the one shown in Figure 3-1. The work area—the blank space in the middle of the document window—has room for 19 lines of text at a time, but you can scroll to see the rest of your document if it is longer than 19 lines. The ruler shows the length of your lines, measured from the left margin in inches. The brackets indicate the left and right margins.

The Keyboard

If you know how to type with a typewriter, you know a lot about writing with a Word Processor. The letters and numbers are laid out on your keyboard in the same positions they have on a standard typewriter, with a few extra keys around them. When you key a letter or number, you see it appear on the screen, just as it would appear on paper in a typewriter. But to speed up some of your work in the Word Processor, Works takes advantage of some keys that do not exist on a typewriter and modifies the way other keys act.

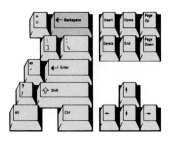

Correcting Keying Errors   If you make a keying error while writing, you can correct your mistake with the Backspace key. This key erases the character to the left of the cursor and also moves characters that follow the cursor back one space. You'll practice this now, as you start writing the letter to Nehemia Sloman, president of Sloman Video.

1. Key this name:

Nathan

2. Oops! That's not his name. Press Backspace to delete all the characters except the *N*; then type the correct name:

Nehemia Slowman, President

Backspacing takes you back over whatever you have just typed. If you make a mistake in the middle of a sentence and notice it only at the end, you can use the Arrow keys to move the cursor back to the character just to the right of the mistake, then Backspace over the error.

3. Use the Left Arrow to move the cursor back to the *m* in *Slowman*. To correct the mistake, press Backspace. That erases the offending *w* without leaving an embarrassing gap in the name.

4. Use the Right Arrow to move the cursor back to the space after *President*.

Some Familiar Keys on the Keyboard   Most of the keys on the keyboard work like ordinary typewriter keys. The Shift key lets you write capital letters or the upper symbol for a particular key (such as the dollar sign over the 4). The Tab key moves the cursor to the next tab stop, pushing any existing characters to the right. The Caps Lock key locks the letter keys so that they produce only capital letters. It is not the same as the Shift key or the Shift Lock key on a typewriter because it affects only the letter keys. The Space Bar is also slightly different. You can use a typewriter space bar to space past letters, as well as to make space between words. On a computer, the Space Bar generates an actual character. You can have Works display spaces and other normally invisible characters.

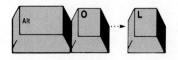

**Show All
Characters**

1. Press Alt-O to open the Options menu.
2. Choose the *Show All Characters* command. A dot appears between *Nehemia* and *Sloman*, and between the comma and *President*. Those dots are the space characters. After the word *President*, there is a Return character. It represents the end of a paragraph.

Pressing Enter   The biggest difference between the Word Processor keyboard and a typewriter keyboard is the way the Enter or Return key works. On an electric typewriter, the Return key ends a line and returns the carriage or typing element to the beginning of the next line. Pressing Enter on the computer keyboard moves the cursor down to the next line, but it also generates a character, which you can now see after the word *President*.

1. Press Enter. A new Return character appears, and the cursor moves to the next line.

2. Key this address:

```
Sloman Video
444 Movieland
Hollywood, NB  68842-1234
```

Remember to press Enter to begin each new line in the address.

3. After the address, press Enter twice to leave a blank line before the salutation.
4. Key the salutation: Dear Mr. Sloman
5. Press Enter twice to move to the first line of the letter.

Great! You have completed the address and salutation, beginning your letter.

Word Wrap   With an electric typewriter you need to press the Return key to move down to the next line. But in the Word Processor, you do not have to press Enter at the end of every line; only at the end of a paragraph or where you want to leave a blank line. That is because the Word Processor knows when a line is getting too long and automatically moves any words that do not fit to the next line. This feature is called **word wrap,** because words that do not fit wrap around to the beginning of the next line. Word wrap is illustrated in Figure 3-2.

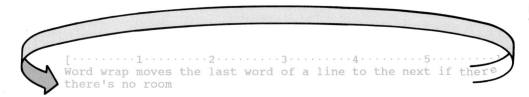

FIGURE 3-2
Word wrap.

```
[· · · · · · · · ·1· · · · · · · · ·2· · · · · · · · ·3· · · · · · · · ·4· · · · · · · · ·5· · · · · · · · ·]
Word wrap moves the last word of a line to the next if there
there's no room
```

You pressed Enter at the end of each line of the address, because you were not typing continuous text. Now that you are going to write the body of the letter, you will get a chance to see word wrap in action. As you write, watch the end of each line on the screen. You will see the Word Processor automatically move extra characters at the end of a line to the beginning of the next line.

1. Key this beginning of a sentence (but do not press Enter):

   Thank you for your offer to supply videotapes of industrial training

   Did you see the last word, training, wrap around to the beginning of the next line? When you key the remaining part of the paragraph, watch for word wrap (you do not have to press Enter).

2. Key the rest of the sentence, followed by the rest of the paragraph.

   films to our store. Although the films may be interesting to those in the field of high-temperature ceramics production, they are not appropriate for our needs. If you should come upon a film in our specialty--thrillers and chillers--we would be happy to consider including it in our lineup.

   Did you see the words wrapping automatically at the end of each line? After you finish writing, your screen should be similar to Figure 3-3.

Moving the Cursor   You can move the cursor around the document with the Arrow keys. Pressing the Left Arrow or Right Arrow moves the cursor forward or back one character

FIGURE 3-3
The document after typing.

```
 File  Edit  Print  Select  Format  Options  Window  Help

══════════════════════════════ WORD1.WPS ═══════════════════════════════
[········1········2·······3········4········5·······]········7···══
» Nehemia·Sloman, ·President¶
  Sloman·Video¶
  444·Movieland¶
  Hollywood, ·NB··68842-1234¶
  ¶
  Dear·Mr.·Sloman¶
  ¶
  Thank·you·for·your·offer·to·supply·videotapes·of·industrial·
  training·films·to·our·store.··Although·the·films·may·be·
  interesting·to·those·in·the·field·of·high-temperature·
  ceramics·production, ·they·are·not·appropriate·for·our·needs.··
  If·you·should·come·upon·a·film·in·our·specialty--thrillers·
  and·chillers--we·would·be·happy·to·consider·including·it·in·
  our·lineup.¶
  ◆


Pg 1/1                        COU12                        <F1=HELP>
Press ALT to choose commands.
```

at a time. Pressing the Up Arrow or Down Arrow moves the cursor up or down one line at a time. But the computer keyboard offers several other keys that allow you to take larger jumps.

1. Press the Left Arrow to move the cursor back through the words *our lineup*.
2. Press the Control key (labeled Ctrl) at the same time as you press the Left Arrow, to jump one word at a time back through the sentence to the *h* in *happy*.
3. Key the word `very` and a space before the word *happy*.

   Just type. Works moves the other text over to make room for your insertion—something even a fancy typewriter couldn't manage.

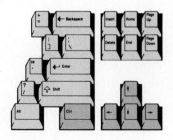

4. Press the Up Arrow once to move up to the next line; then press the Left Arrow to move the cursor to the *f* in *film*.
5. Key: `video or`

   Again, the other text moves over to accommodate your insertion.

   Now you notice that you have not put the date on your letter. Use a **Control Key Sequence** to move the cursor. This means you press the Ctrl key and hold it down while you press another key. You could press Ctrl-Up Arrow to jump up one paragraph at a time. But there is an even faster way.

6. Press Ctrl-Home. The cursor jumps to the *N* in *Nehemia*, at the very beginning of your document.

   The Home key by itself takes the cursor back to the beginning of a line; combined with Ctrl, you get a giant leap to the beginning of your document. (For a complete list of these keystroke shortcuts, see the list of Word Processing keys in the Keyboard category of Help.) Now you are in position to insert the date.

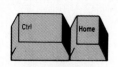

Move Cursor to Beginning of Document

7. Key the current date at the beginning of your letter.
8. Press Enter four times to separate the date from the address.
9. Press Ctrl-End to skip back to the very end of the document. Your completed document should look like the one in Figure 3-4.

```
     File  Edit  Print  Select  Format. Options  Window  Help

  •━━━━━━━━━━━━━━━━━━━━━━ WORD1.WPS ━━━━━━━━━━━━━━━━━━━━━━━━↕
     [·········1·········2·········3·········4·········5·········]·········7·····•=
  »  September·15,·19--¶                                                          ↑
     ¶
     ¶
     ¶
     Nehemia·Sloman,·President¶
     Sloman·Video¶
     444·Movieland¶
     Hollywood,·NB··68842-1234¶
     ¶
     Dear·Mr.·Sloman¶
     ¶
     Thank·you·for·your·offer·to·supply·videotapes·of·industrial·
     training·films·to·our·store.··Although·the·films·may·be·
     interesting·to·those·in·the·field·of·high-temperature·
     ceramics·production,·they·are·not·appropriate·for·our·needs.··
     If·you·should·come·upon·a·video·or·film·in·our·specialty--
     thrillers·and·chillers--we·would·be·very·happy·to·consider·
     including·it·in·our·lineup.¶

  Pg 1/1                 COU12                              <F1=HELP>
  Press ALT to choose commands.
```

FIGURE 3-4
The completed document.

When you have a document that is several pages long, the Ctrl key, in combination with the Arrow keys, Home key, and End key, will let you move through the text in leaps and bounds. Now you know how to use all these cursor controls to move the cursor swiftly from word to word and from beginning to end.

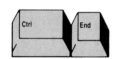

**Move Cursor
to End of
Document**

SAVING A FILE

*T*he file you have spent the last few minutes working on can disappear in a second if the power to the computer fails. The file is currently stored only in memory. Computer memory only lasts as long as the computer is turned on. To make a permanent record of the file, you need to save it on a disk. Once the file is safely stored on a disk, it will always be available when you need to refer to it or modify it.

File names

Every file needs a unique file name so that both you and the computer can tell one file from another. File names should always clearly identify the contents of the file. The rules for naming files vary from program to program, but all names must follow the conventions of the operating system, MS-DOS. Your file name can be up to eight characters long. You can use any characters except the space character. Also, you may not use any of the following marks of punctuation, because each has some special meaning for MS-DOS: * ? / . , ; [ ] + = \ : | < >.

Here are some examples of file names.

OK	Not OK
2Q34B	SecondQuarter (too long)
MyBook	My Book (includes a blank space)
12-20-87	12/20/87 (uses DOS special characters)

Works adds an **extension to a file name** to identify which tool you used to create the file.

For this tool	Works adds this extension	Example
Word Processor	.WPS	Novel.WPS
Spreadsheet	.WKS	Budget.WKS
Database	.WDB	Tapes.WDB
Communications	.WCM	Chat.WCM

Choosing to Save a File

You should save your work every ten or fifteen minutes as a precaution against the computer forgetting it all when the power goes out or when someone trips over the power cable. There are two commands for saving a file. The first time you save a document, you should choose *Save As*, because that command always lets you change the name that Works temporarily assigned to the file. The first Word Processor document you create in a work session gets a temporary name of *Word1.WPS*. In the Save As dialog box, you need to give the file a name that will mean something to you later when you are searching for it.

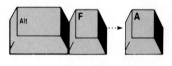

Save As

1. Press Alt-F to open the File menu.
2. Choose the *Save As* command. A dialog box appears allowing you to rename the file, specify where to put it, and decide what format to save it in, as in Figure 3-5.

FIGURE 3-5
The Save As dialog box.

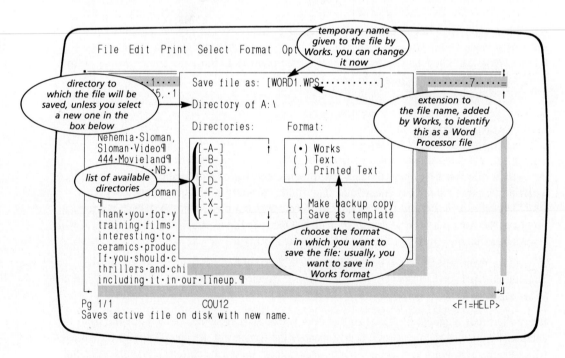

3. Insert the Template disk in a disk drive.

If your computer has only one drive, remove the Works program disk from drive A and replace it with the template disk. The current Directory remains A:\ meaning that your file will be saved on the disk in drive A. You do not need to change the directory.

If your computer has two disk drives, put the template disk in drive B, then press Alt-I to move to the box listing available directories in which you can place the file. Use the Down

Arrow to select the B: directory. Its name appears at the top of the dialog box, followed by a colon, meaning that the file will be placed there. To move the cursor back to the file name box, press Alt-S.

4. Key `Sloman` as your part of the file name.
5. Press Enter. Works quickly adds an extension, *.WPS*, next to your file name, identifying this as a Word Processor file. The dialog box disappears, and in the status line you briefly see the percentage of the file that has been saved so far. When the saving process has been completed, you return to the open file. Saving does not close the file; it just makes a record of the file on the disk.

PRINTING A DOCUMENT

You can print a copy of a Word Processor document whenever necessary. For example, suppose Sarah Lugosi, president of Lugosi's Classic Video Store, has asked to see a copy of your letter, even though you have not written the closing. No problem—just print a copy for her.

Some people refer to a printed document that was prepared with a computer as a hard copy. A **hard copy** is simply the printed form of a document, which can be used without a computer, unlike a copy that exists electronically on a disk or in memory.

Before you print a document, you may need to make sure that Works knows what kind of printer you are using. You'll find out how to do that in the next section.

Setting Up the Printer

On your Works program disk, there are one or more **printer driver files.** A printer driver file translates the codes Works uses into the codes the printer uses, so that your document is printed correctly. Each printer has its own set of codes, so you need to tell Works which printer you are going to be using to print your document. Works then reads that printer's driver file. If you only have one printer, your instructor may already have set the software up to communicate with that printer, so you do not need to do so again. If not, you only need to do this once. But if you regularly switch among several printers, you should confirm that Works knows which printer you want to use each time.

1. Press Alt-P to open the Print menu.
2. Choose *Printer Setup*. You see the Printer Setup dialog box, shown in Figure 3-6.
3. Select the printer you are going to use. (Your instructor will tell you which one you should select.)
4. If several models of that printer appear in the Model box, press Alt-D to move to that box, and select the model you are going to use.
5. If you are using regular fanfold computer paper, leave the Page feed option set to *Continuous*. If you have to feed individual sheets into the printer one at a time by hand, press Alt-A to choose *Manual*.
6. Select the port to which your printer cable is attached, in the back of your computer. (Your instructor will tell you which one to select.)

    You are not printing any graphics, so you can ignore the various dots-per-inch resolutions offered in the Graphics box.

7. Press Enter to confirm this printer is the one you intend to use.

    Works will use this printer's driver file from now on, until you change the Printer Setup.

Printer Setup

FIGURE 3-6
The Printer Setup dialog box.

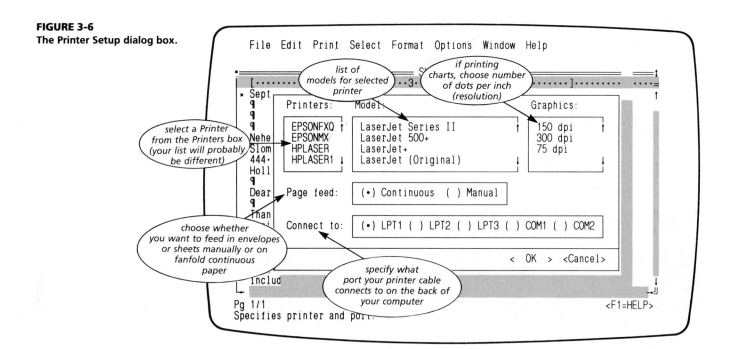

Printing

Print

You can print a document at any time. Check to make sure that your printer has paper loaded, that the printer cable is securely fastened to the printer and the computer, and that the printer is turned on.

1. Choose *Print* from the Print menu. The Print dialog box appears, as shown in Figure 3-7.

FIGURE 3-7
The Print dialog box.

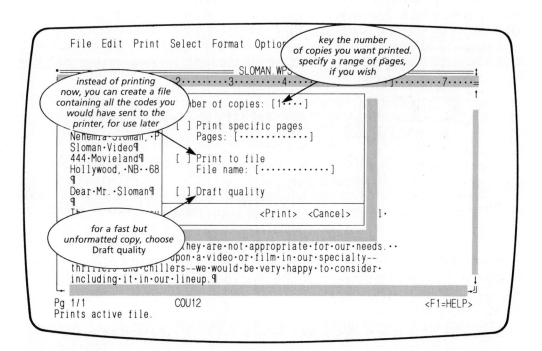

2. Leave the preset options as they are in the dialog box, and press Enter.

Works begins printing your document. You will be getting one copy of the whole document, not just some specified pages. You will get the document formatted as you have seen it on the screen, not just the text, as you would in Draft quality. And instead of sending all the printer codes, along with the text, to a file for future use, you are sending the information directly to a printer. Printing to a file, one of the options in the dialog box, can be useful when you want to send a file to someone who has a similar printer, but does not have Works. The recipient can print the file accurately without Works.

If you need to stop printing at any time, press Esc.

REMOVING A FILE FROM A DISK

Periodically you will find that you have some files on a disk that you no longer need. For example, they may be early drafts of a document. When a disk begins getting full, you may want to remove these files so that you will have more room to store files that you need. Your template disk contains an extra file that needs to be removed. It is called *Leftover.WPS*.

File Management

1. Choose the *File Management* command on the File menu. The File Management dialog box opens, with a list of options, as shown in Figure 3-8.

FIGURE 3-8
The File Management dialog box.

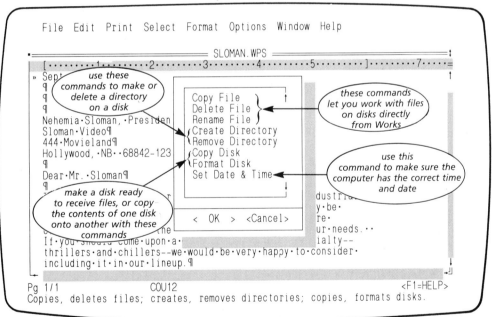

2. Select the *Delete File* command and press Enter. Works presents a dialog box in which you can specify the file to be deleted.
3. Make sure that the directory named at the top of the dialog box is that of the drive containing your Template disk.

If you placed your template disk in drive A, the dialog box should read: *Directory of A:*

If you placed your template disk in drive B, the dialog box should read: *Directory of B:*

To change the directory, press Alt-I to enter the box listing the Directories, use the Arrow keys to select another, then press Enter. The suggested file to delete and the current directory change at the top of the dialog box.

4. Press Alt-F to move to the list of files; then use the Down Arrow and Up Arrow to move through the list. Highlight *Leftover.WPS*.
5. Press Enter to delete Leftover.WPS. Works asks you if it is OK to delete Leftover.WPS. Press Enter again to confirm that you want to delete the file.

Works asks the question at this point to make sure you are not accidentally deleting an important file. You can always press Esc at this point to stop the deletion. But once you have gone through with the deletion, you cannot recover the file from the disk.

6. Press Esc to leave the File Management dialog box and return to your document.

QUITTING WORKS

ou have printed your document and removed the unneeded file from the template disk. Now you can add the closing to your letter and leave Works.

1. Press Ctrl-End to move the cursor to the end of your document.
2. Press Return two times to insert one blank line below the body of the letter.
3. Key: Sincerely
4. Press Enter four times to insert three blank lines below the close.
5. Key your name.

You have now completed your letter.

6. Choose *Exit Works* from the File menu. Works stops you for a moment to ask whether or not you want to save the changes you have just made to the document.

You should always save your work before quitting. But just in case you forget, Works reminds you that you have made changes to the document—changes that you have not saved to disk.

7. Press Enter to have Works save the changes. Works saves the changed file to disk, with the same name, replacing the version that was there before. Then the Works screen disappears, and you return to the DOS prompt.
8. Remove the disks from the disk drives and put them in their envelopes.
9. Turn off the monitor and the computer.

Good job! In this lesson, you have made a new Word Processor document, written a letter, practiced with the keyboard, and saved and printed the document. In the next lesson, you will practice editing a Word Processor document.

KEY TERMS

control key sequence   *MSW 40*
document   *MSW 36*
editing   *MSW 36*
extension to a file name   *MSW 42*
formatting   *MSW 46*
file name   *MSW 41*
hard copy   *MSW 43*
printer driver file   *MSW 43*
text   *MSW 36*
word processing   *MSW 36*
word wrap   *MSW 39*

COMMANDS

Backspace
Ctrl
Ctrl-End
Ctrl-Home
Ctrl-Down Arrow
Ctrl-Left Arrow

Ctrl-Right Arrow
Ctrl-Up Arrow
Alt-F-N (Create New File)
Alt-F-X (Exit Works)
Alt-F-F (File Management)
Home

Alt-P-P (Print)
Alt-P-S (Printer Setup)
Alt-F-A (Save As)
Alt-F-S (Save)
Alt-O-L (Show All Characters)

REVIEW QUESTIONS

1. What is the difference between a document and a file?
2. What are the three major activities in word processing? Briefly explain them.
3. How do you correct keying errors as you enter text?
4. What steps do you take to make a new Word Processor file?
5. What are the rules for file names in Works?
6. What are the extensions to file names? What do they tell you?
7. What is the purpose of a printer driver file?
8. If you try to exit Works before you have saved your work, what happens and why?
9. Can you think of some file names that are acceptable in Works? What about file names that are unacceptable? List five examples of each.

APPLICATIONS

1. Use the Word Processor to prepare a letter asking Lugosi's Classic Video Store for a summer job. To do this, you must make a new file for the Word Processor. Name it *JobXXX* (but use your own initials instead of XXX).
   Note that any time XXX is shown, it means that you are to add your initials to the file name, using your initials in place of the XXX. That way you will be able to keep track of what files you have edited or changed.
   Key the text of the letter as shown on the next page.

```
(Today's date)

Sarah Lugosi
Lugosi's Classic Video Store
10525 Golden Highway
Palookaville, WA  99207-8591

Dear Ms. Lugosi

I am interested in a summer job at your store. My family has purchased many video-
tapes at your store, and we enjoy the atmosphere you have created there.  I will
work very hard for you. The money I earn will go toward my college education.

Thank you for your consideration.

Sincerely


(your name)
```

Key today's date and your name where indicated. Save your file on the template disk. Print a copy of the letter after saving your file.

2. Write a 150-word summary of a news story from today's newspaper with the Word Processor. Name it *ArtclXXX*. Save the file on your template disk and print a copy.

3. Write a short story (no more than 200 words) with the Word Processor. Name it *StoryXXX*. Save the file on your template disk and print a copy of the story.

4. Make a backup copy of your template disk. Use the *File Management* command on the File menu to copy the disk. Prepare a label for the backup disk that includes your name and today's date.

Working with a Document

OBJECTIVES

- Get a file from a disk.
- Find specific text in a file automatically.
- Replace text.
- Use the thesaurus to find a word.
- Delete a block of text.
- Search for specific text and replace it automatically.
- Copy and move blocks of text.
- Set, remove, and use tabs.
- Add a footnote.
- Check the spelling throughout a document.
- Rename a file.

GETTING A FILE FROM A DISK

*I*n the last lesson, you learned how to write a document with the Word Processor. In this lesson, you will edit a document that has already been written. You will see how the power of a Word Processor can help you correct mistakes automatically throughout a document. You will also add a footnote, erase a large block of text, move and copy information, and work with a table of information.

You will be working with a document written by Morris Yu, who is preparing a public relations campaign for the new branch that Lugosi's Classic Video Store is opening. Morris has already made some corrections to his draft press release, but they are on paper. You will make the corrections to the Works file. The marked-up draft is shown in Figure 4-1. You will turn this marked-up draft into a clean, final draft, and print a copy.

You have practiced making a new file and saving it onto a disk. Now you will fetch an existing file from a disk, load it into the computer's memory, and display it on the monitor's screen. Sometimes this process is called loading a file. Your changes to the copy in the computer's memory do not affect the original copy that remains on disk unless you save the changes over the original. See Figure 4-2.

1. Start up Works. Use the startup procedures you learned in Lesson 2.
2. If you have only one disk drive, replace the Works program disk with the template disk. If you have two disk drives, insert the template disk into drive B.

FIGURE 4-1
Document with editing marks.

PRESS RELEASE

CONTACT: Morris Yu
Lugosi's Classic Video Center *(store)*
10525 Golden Highway
Palookaville, WA 99207-8591
(509) 555-7223

copy to bottom

FOR IMMEDIATE RELEASE

FAITHFUL FRIGHT FANS FEASTED FIENDISHLY IN FAIRFAX

FAIRFAX, WA--The faithful fans of Lugosi's Classic Video
Center will be in for a feast next Friday at the Center's
new branch location in Fairfax.

Sarah Lugosi, founder of the videotape sales and rental
center, says the Center will throw a big dinner for 400
tape-club members from Fairfax at a special   *new word*
pre-Grand-Opening celebration. Lugosi says the feast will
feature "a mystery entree, simmering soup, and chiller
vaniller shakes."

The faithful fans have travelled "20 miles each way twice a
week to rent our classic videos," she says, and she wants
"to repay them for their support."

Lugosi's is opening the new Center because their database
has shown a high level of sales from members who live in
Fairfax. They hope that many of the Fairfax members will
become regular customers at the new location.

CITY	Year 1	Year 2
Palookaville	5,382	7,429
Fairfax	237	414
Riverside	111	247 ← *add*

Customers report that Lugosi's is a fun place to go for
thrillers, chillers, comedies, and bad science fiction
movies. "I like the way the clerks dress up like Dracula
and Frankenstein," said Jennifer Marquez, 17, of Fairfax
High. Her friend Oliver Brown, also 17, thinks the barrels
of "boiling oil" are a nice touch.

The database that Lugosi's uses to keep track of their
customers has also led to plans to open a new Center in
Riverside, scheduled for early next year. Their memberships
have been growing steadily in all three areas, as shown in
this chart:
move table here
Anyone interested in finding out more about the feast, or in
becoming a member of Lugosi's tape club, should call Morris
Yu at (509) 555-1232, or call him at home at 555-4239.

incorrect phone number (use no. shown at top of page)

FIGURE 4-2
Opening a file copies the file
from disk to the memory of the
computer. The original file
remains on disk.

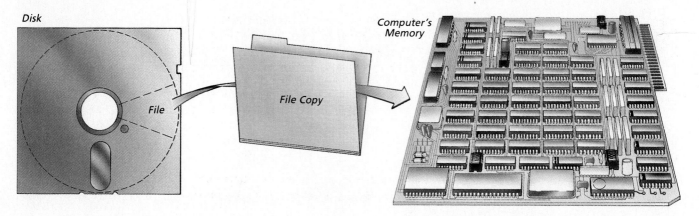

Disk

File

File Copy

Computer's
Memory

3. From the File menu, choose the *Open Existing File* command. A dialog box appears, listing the files in drive A. If the template disk is in drive B, press Alt-I to move to the Directories box, use the Down Arrow to select drive B, and press Enter. The files in the template disk appear in the box on the left, as shown in Figure 4-3.

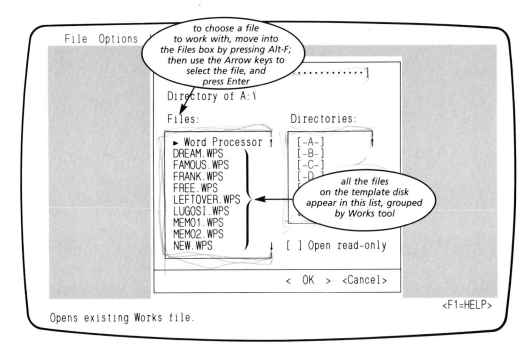

FIGURE 4-3
List of files on the template disk.

The document you will be working with is a press release stored in a Word Processor file named *Release.WPS*. When you open a copy of this file, you will be able to edit the document. After you have edited the document, you can send it out to all the newspapers and broadcasting stations in Palookaville.

4. Press Alt-F to move to the list of files. Use the Down Arrow key to select the file named *Release.WPS*; then press Enter. The document appears in a window on the Works screen, with the Word Processor menu bar above it, as shown in Figure 4-4.

MAKING CORRECTIONS

*E*diting is the process of making corrections and otherwise improving the text of a document. The press release you are working on has some words that need to be replaced, corrected, moved, and deleted. Then there are some inconsistencies. For example, look at the phone number in the address at the top and the phone number at the bottom. Morris Yu has noted that the number at the bottom should be the same as the one at the top.

Finding Text Automatically

Application programs like Works often have features that make it easy for you to locate information in a file. So to correct the phone number at the bottom of the letter, you do not have to

FIGURE 4-4
A Word Processor file opened from disk.

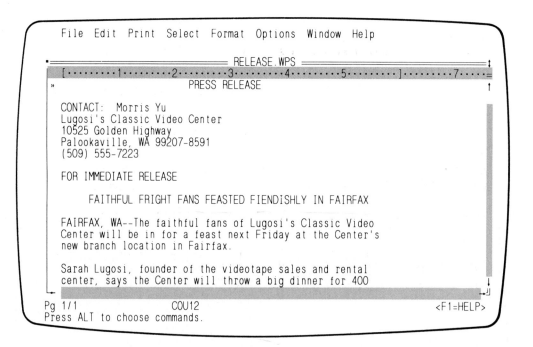

press the Down Arrow key several times—you just tell Works what to look for and let the program find it for you. You tell Works that you want it to find something for you by using the *Search* command from the Select menu. The text you want Works to look for is called the **search text.**

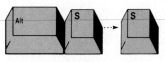

Search

1. Choose *Search* from the Select menu. The Search dialog box opens, as shown in Figure 4-5.

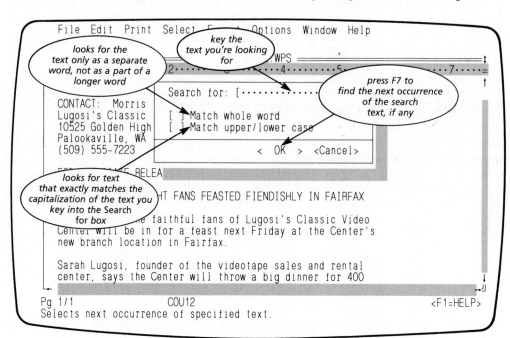

FIGURE 4-5
The Search dialog box.

You are looking for a phone number from Palookaville, where all telephone prefixes are 555. That would be a good choice for the search text.

You don't need to select either of the options from the Search dialog box. You want to find 555 when it is part of a longer phone number, not a separate word, and numbers aren't capitalized, so you don't need to make sure that Works finds only text that exactly matches the capitalization of your search text. You can leave both options unselected.

2. Key 555 and press Enter. Highlighting appears on the *555* in the first phone number. This phone number is correct. You want to change another number at the end of the document to be the same as this one.
3. Choose *Search* from the Select menu again. The dialog box reappears, containing the search text you entered before, *555*.
4. Press Enter to search for *555* again. The text scrolls up and you see the second *555* highlighted at the end of the press release. The screen looks like that in Figure 4-6.

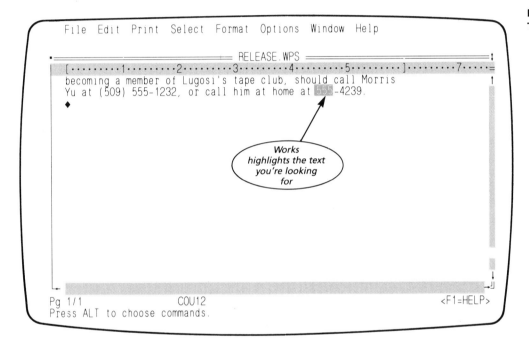

FIGURE 4-6
The search text highlighted.

Replacing Selected Text   The cursor you have been using so far is called the *insert cursor*. With the insert cursor, when you strike a key for a letter, number, or symbol, that character is inserted into the document. If you use the insert cursor to insert information in the middle of a sentence, the rest of the sentence is pushed over to make room. There are times, though, when you do not want to insert new text; you want to replace old text. First you select the old text, then you choose the *Typing Replaces Selection* command on the Options menu, and type away. The new replaces the old.

Typing Replaces Selection

1. Press the Right Arrow key to move the cursor to the number *1* in the second part of the phone number.
2. To select that part of the phone number, hold down Shift, and press the Right Arrow four times. The suffix *1232* is highlighted.
3. Choose *Typing Replaces Selection* from the Options menu.
4. Key 7223. Notice that the old suffix disappears as soon as you type the first digit. As you type the remaining three digits, the rest of the sentence moves over to make room for the numbers you are inserting.
5. Turn off this option by choosing *Typing Replaces Selection* from the Options menu again. Now even if you are typing next to a selected passage of text, the text will move over, rather than disappearing.

Replacing Text Automatically   There are times when you have used the same word repeatedly throughout a document, and then decide that instead of that word, you would rather use another. You could carefully read through the whole document looking for the original word, selecting it, and replacing it. But you can have Works do the job for you, with the *Replace* command from the Select menu.

You are concerned about a mistake in the store's name. You want to replace *Center* with *Store*.

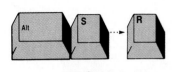

Replace

1. Press Ctrl-Home to move the cursor to the beginning of the document. You want to catch every instance of the word *Center*.
2. Choose *Replace* from the Select menu. A dialog box appears, containing the text you entered in the *Search for* box before. In fact, this dialog box looks a lot like the Search dialog box, with some added lines that tell Works what to do with the text it finds.
3. Key Center (with a capital C) in the *Search for* box. As soon as you strike the capital C, the selected *555* disappears.

   You want to find all instances of the word *Center* when it appears in the store's name. It will always be capitalized there. You aren't interested in any other occurrences of the word *center*, which would probably begin with a lowercase letter. So you want to narrow the search by telling Works to look for instances of *Center* that exactly match the capitalization you have used.

4. Press Alt-U to select the *Match upper/lower case* option.
5. Press Alt-W to move to the *Replace with* box, and key Store there.
6. Press Alt-R to replace the first instance. The word *Center* is highlighted in the address. The dialog box asks whether you want to replace this occurrence.
7. Press Enter to have this occurrence of the word *Center* replaced with *Store*. The highlighting moves to the next occurrence.
8. Press Enter again. Now that you see that Works is finding the word you want and replacing it correctly, you can shift to high gear.
9. Press the Right Arrow twice to highlight the brackets around Cancel.
10. Press Enter.
11. Press Alt-S-R to return to the Replace dialog box.
12. Press Alt-A to have Works replace all further occurrences. Works tells you how many occurrences it has replaced. Press Enter to confirm that is what you want to do. The dialog box disappears, and all the rest of the *Centers* are changed to *Stores*.

You may be unable to complete this lesson in one session. If this should happen, follow the steps in the "SAVING THE FILE UNDER A NEW NAME" section at the end of this lesson. This will preserve the original file and save the file containing all your changes in a new file with a different name. When you return to complete this lesson, use the *Open Existing File* command from the File menu to open the file you have worked on, so you can continue where you left off. Follow this procedure whenever you are interrupted before completing a lesson.

Using the Thesaurus

Sometimes you use one word, but you want a better word. The Works **thesaurus**—literally, a treasure-chest of words—can suggest similar words, from which you can pick the one you like, and have Works put that word into your document in place of the original. In the second paragraph of his press release, Morris circled the word *dinner*. The *Thesaurus* command on the Options menu will help find a better word, preferably one that begins with a *b*, as in *big*.

1. Press Ctrl-Home to move the cursor back to the top of the document. The second paragraph of the press release contains the word *dinner*.
2. Use the Arrow keys to move the cursor just in front of the word *dinner*.
3. Press the Shift-Ctrl-Right Arrow keys to select the entire word *dinner*.
4. Choose the *Thesaurus* command on the Options menu. The Thesaurus dialog box appears, with the word *dinner* at the top, a definition on the left, and suggested synonyms on the right, as shown in Figure 4-7.

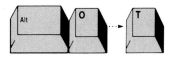

Thesaurus

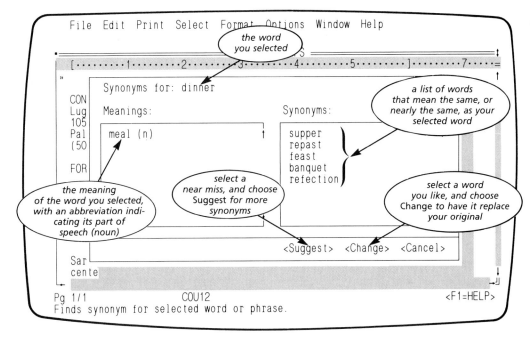

FIGURE 4-7
The Thesaurus dialog box.

5. Press Alt-Y to move the cursor into the Synonyms box.
6. With the Arrow keys, select *banquet*.
7. Press Alt-C to have *dinner* changed to *banquet*. The dialog box disappears, and now you have a big banquet instead of dinner.

Deleting a Block of Text

The Backspace key backs up over characters, deleting them as you go. That is fine for a few typos, but for more than a couple of words, backspacing can be tedious. There is a faster way to delete large blocks of text: the *Delete* command. In this example, you will use the *Delete* command to erase the reference to Morris Yu's home phone number.

1. Press Ctrl-End to go to the end of the document. You want to delete everything after the first phone number in the last line. You will delete the comma and the clause, *or call him at home at 555-4239*.
2. Press Shift-Ctrl and the Left Arrow key eleven times to select the comma and *or call him at home at 555-4239*. Pressing Shift and the Arrow key alone selects one character at a time; adding the Ctrl key moves you along one word at a time.

Delete

3. Choose *Delete* from the Edit menu. That gets rid of the selected text. The text you remove with the *Delete* command is not only gone from the screen, it is gone from the computer's memory. So before you remove a block of text, make sure you have the right text highlighted.
4. Key a period to finish the sentence.

COPYING AND MOVING TEXT

S ometimes while editing a document you will discover that you want to repeat something or make a copy of it. Other times, you will decide that some text might be better placed somewhere else—moved. The *Copy* and *Move* commands in Works make this easy.

Copying Text

Morris Yu wants the contact information from the top of the document to be at the bottom as well. Rather than reentering the text, why not just copy it? The *Copy* command is on the Edit menu.

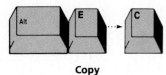

Copy

1. Press Ctrl-Home to move to the top of the document. Your cursor blinks under the *P* in *PRESS RELEASE*, at the beginning of the file.
2. Press Ctrl-Down Arrow twice to move the cursor down to the *C* in *CONTACT*.
3. Press Ctrl-Shift-Down Arrow five times to select all five lines of the contact information.
4. Choose *Copy* on the Edit menu. That puts a copy of this text in the computer's memory, but does not affect the original.
5. Press Ctrl-End to move to the end of the document.
6. Press Enter. The contact information you copied from the beginning of the document appears at the end as well.
7. Press Enter twice more to move the contact information down to its own area.

Moving Text

Now that you know how to copy text, **moving text** should be easy. The *Move* command works in the same way as the *Copy* command, except that the highlighted text is erased from its old position, rather than copied.

The *Move* command comes in handy when something ends up in the wrong place in your document. For example, somehow the table listing the membership figures for Lugosi's tape club for the last two years was placed in the middle of the press release, rather than near the end, where it is supposed to be. With the *Move* command, you can move it to the proper location.

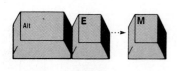

Move

1. Use the Arrow keys to move up to the *C* in *CITY*, at the top of the table.
2. Press Shift-Ctrl-Down Arrow five times to select the table and one extra line.
3. Choose *Move* from the Edit menu.
4. Press the Down Arrow until the cursor is on the *A* in *Anyone* (above the address in the last paragraph).
5. Press Enter. Works inserts the table where it belongs.

USING TABS

he table fits right in there in its new position. Unfortunately, it is missing a line. It should also contain the membership figures for Riverside, the second town where Lugosi's is planning to establish a branch store.

The table is laid out in rows and columns. Although you can make a table by pressing the Space Bar between entries, it is easier to make it using tab stops and the Tab key. Tab stops are locations to which the Tab key jumps the cursor. When you use tabs to make a table, entering a line means simply keying the first entry, pressing Tab, keying the second entry, pressing Tab, keying the third entry, and so on. Without tabs, you would have to press the Space Bar several times to get from one column to the next.

The Tab key inserts a **tab mark.** You can see the tab marks when you choose the *Show All Characters* command on the Options menu.

Works comes with tab stops preset every half inch across the ruler. But you can position tab stops wherever you want, overriding the preset tab stops.

Setting Tab Stops

To finish the last line of the table, you will set up your own tab stops, and then use the Tab key while keying the data.

1. Choose *Show All Characters* from the Options menu. You see the Return characters directly above and below the table.
2. Move the cursor to the Return character above the word *CITY*. Then press Shift-Ctrl-Down Arrow six times to select the entire table and the lines above and below it.
3. Choose *Tabs* from the Format menu. The Tabs dialog box appears, as shown in Figure 4-8.

Tabs

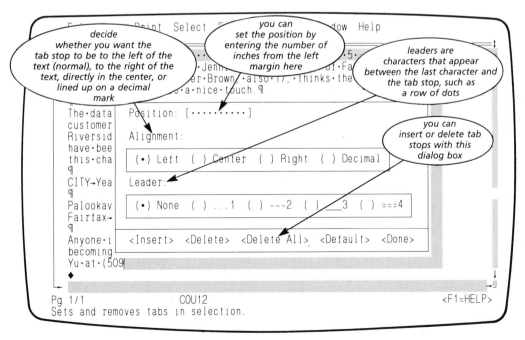

FIGURE 4-8
The Tabs dialog box.

4. Key 2.25 in the Position box, press Alt-R to have it line up just to the right of any text you type after pressing Tab, then press Alt-I to insert it. An R appears on the ruler in that position. All the preset tab stops to its left have been erased. (You couldn't see them before, and you can't see that they have gone, but when you press the Tab key, the cursor will glide past all those positions to the one you just inserted.)
5. Key 3.75 in the Position box, and press Alt-I to insert it.
6. Press Alt-D to say you are done with the dialog box. The numbers in your table line up as they would for addition, as shown in Figure 4-9.

FIGURE 4-9
After setting tab stops.

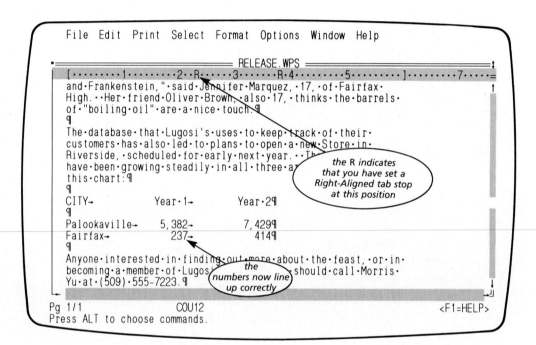

Using Tabs to Key Text

Now that you have set the new tab stops, you can put them to use. The table needs one more line to be complete: the membership figures for the city of Riverside. First you need to key the city name, then tab over for the first amount, and tab again for the second amount. The Tab key works like a giant Arrow key, leaping the cursor across spaces to the next tab stop.

1. Position the cursor under the Return character right under the *F* in *Fairfax*.
2. Key: Riverside
3. Press Tab to move to the next column. The cursor should line up under the tab mark after *237*.
4. Key the number: 111
5. Press Tab to move to the next column.
6. Key the number 247 and then press Enter. Now the table should look like this:

```
CITY          Year 1    Year 2

Palookaville   5,382     7,429
Fairfax          237       414
Riverside        111       247
```

Great! You have set tab stops and then used them to finish the table.

ADDING A NOTE

Works makes it easy to add a footnote. You don't have to worry about whether it will fit at the bottom of the page; you can leave that kind of calculation to Works. Morris Yu wants to give credit to Works for his database. The *Footnote* command on the Edit menu lets you add the note.

1. Use Arrow keys to move the cursor to the space after the word *database*, in the first line of the paragraph before the table.
2. Choose *Footnote* from the Edit menu. The Footnote dialog box appears, as shown in Figure 4-10.

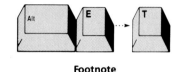

Footnote

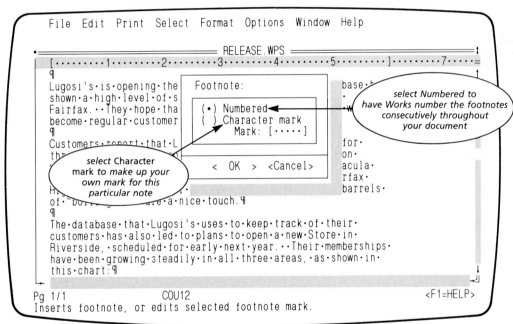

FIGURE 4-10
The Footnote dialog box.

You are not writing a formal essay here, so you do not need to have Works number all your footnotes in order. You just need an asterisk to mark the note.

3. Press Alt-C to select *Character mark*, then press Alt-M to move the cursor to the *Mark box*. Key an asterisk (*) and press Enter.

A Footnote window opens up with its own ruler, and the cursor appears in the work area, as shown in Figure 4-11.

4. Press the Space bar twice, then key the text of your footnote: We use Microsoft Works to track our customers' preferences and addresses.
5. Press F6 to return to the document window. The cursor returns to the space after the footnote character, right after the word *database*.

FIGURE 4-11
The Footnote window.

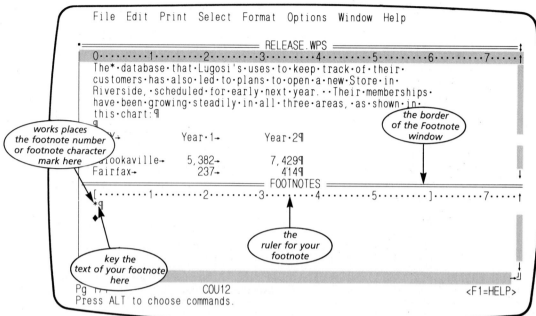

CHECKING YOUR SPELLING

You're almost ready to print the press release. To make sure you haven't made any typos, you can have Works check your spelling. You could have Works read every word and compare it with the entries in its large dictionary. But there is only one word you're suspicious of—*vaniller*. You can have the Works **spelling checker** look up one word, or a selection of text, to see if anything is misspelled.

1. Move the cursor up to the second paragraph, and press Shift-Ctrl-Right Arrow to select the word *vaniller*. You know that Morris Yu wanted a rhyme with *chiller*, but you're not sure if this is a real word.

2. Choose *Check Spelling* from the Options menu. A dialog box appears, announcing that this is a misspelled word, as in Figure 4-12.

3. Press Alt-S to request suggestions—words that Works guesses you might mean. Three words appear, and sure enough, there is *vanilla*.

You decide to sacrifice rhyme for correct spelling. You need Works to change *vaniller* to *vanilla*.

4. Press Alt-C to tell Works to Change the misspelling. The dialog box goes away, and you see a message saying that the spelling check is finished. Press Enter to return to the document.

You have polished and perfected Morris Yu's press release. You are ready to send it off to the news organizations. Lugosi's Classic Video Store can use the publicity for its new location.

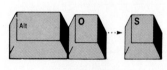

Check Spelling

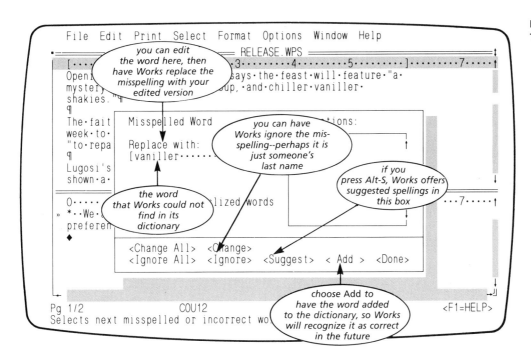

FIGURE 4-12
The Spelling Checker window.

SAVING THE FILE UNDER A NEW NAME

You have made a lot of changes to the Release.WPS file. You should save the file on disk so that you do not lose the changes you have made to it. But rather than save them on top of the old version, you can rename the file before you save it. That allows you to have both the old version and the new one on disk.

Remember that when you work with a file in Works, you are working with a copy of the original file, which remains on the disk. When you save a file, Works erases the old version from the disk and replaces it with the new version. When you change the name of the file and then save it, Works leaves the old file alone, saving the new version on another part of the disk. One reason to save a file with a new name is to keep track of different versions of the same document so you know what part of the document was changed and when.

To indicate that this is a new version of an old document, you should modify the original name, rather than use a completely new name. For this exercise, simply add your initials to the syllable *Rel*.

1. Choose *Save As* from the File menu. The file-handling dialog box appears.
2. Key: RelXXX

   Rel stands for Release. *XXX* should be replaced with your initials.

3. Press Enter.

With the file safely stored on disk, you can exit Works. If you have forgotten the procedure for quitting, go back to the end of the last lesson to review the instructions.

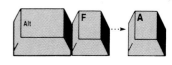

Save As

FIGURE 4-13
Saving a file over the original
file.

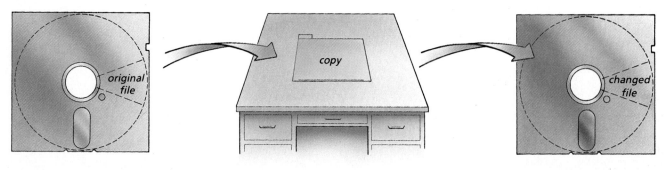

FIGURE 4-14
Saving a file with a new name.

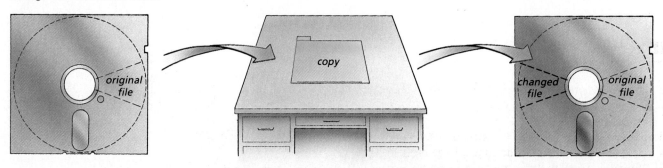

Congratulations! You have finished editing a file: deleting, replacing, copying and moving text, adding a note, polishing a table, and checking the spelling. In the next lesson you will practice formatting a document.

KEY TERMS

copying text *MSW 56*
footnote *MSW 49*
moving text *MSW 56*
replacing text *MSW 54*
search text *MSW 52*
spelling checker *MSW 60*
tab mark *MSW 57*
tab stop *MSW 57*
thesaurus *MSW 54*

COMMANDS

Alt-O-S (Check Spelling)
Alt-E-C (Copy)
Alt-E-D (Delete)
Alt-E-T (Footnote)
Alt-E-M (Move)
Alt-F-O (Open Existing File)
Alt-S-R (Replace)
Alt-F-A (Save As)
Alt-S-S (Search)
Alt-O-L (Show All Characters)
Alt-T-T (Tabs)
Alt-O-T (Thesaurus)
Alt-O-Y (Typing Replaces Selection)

REVIEW QUESTIONS

1. How would you find the word *effervescent* in a large file?
2. How would you find synonyms for the word *effervescent*? How could you have Works place one of those synonyms in the text in place of effervescent?
3. How would you replace the word *effervescent* with *bubbly* throughout a long document?
4. How would you go about deleting a large block of text?
5. You have a word that you just cannot wait to get rid of. Should you use the Delete key? Why or why not?
6. Can you set your own tab stops in a file? Why would you want to set your own tab stops? What command would you use?
7. How can you quickly select large amounts of text?
8. How are the *Copy* and *Move* commands similar? How are they different?
9. You want to have numbered footnotes at the bottom of the pages of your report. How can you manage this with Works?
10. You get a file from disk and make some changes to the file. You want to keep the original file but also save the changes. What can you do?

APPLICATIONS

1. Open *Frank.WPS* from the template disk. It needs a lot of work. You will have to fix the file to make it read more easily. First, use the *Move* command to make the second paragraph first; then use the *Replace* command to change the word Joan to Jean; and, finally, use the *Delete* command to remove the first sentence. Perform the other editing tasks as indicated on the marked-up draft in Figure 4-15.

   Rename the file *FrankXXX*(remember to substitute your initials for XXX) before you save it and print a copy.

2. Open *Dream.WPS* from the template disk. Sarah Lugosi has been dreaming of a videotape empire, described in this file. But she left out a table that belongs in the middle of the file. She has asked you to move the cursor to the middle of the file and insert this table:

TAPE SUPPLIES	BOOKS	SOUVENIRS
VHS tapes	Star biographies	Posters
S-VHS tapes	Scripts	Key chains
8mm tapes	Industry books	Star dolls

FIGURE 4-15
Marked-up draft for
Application 1.

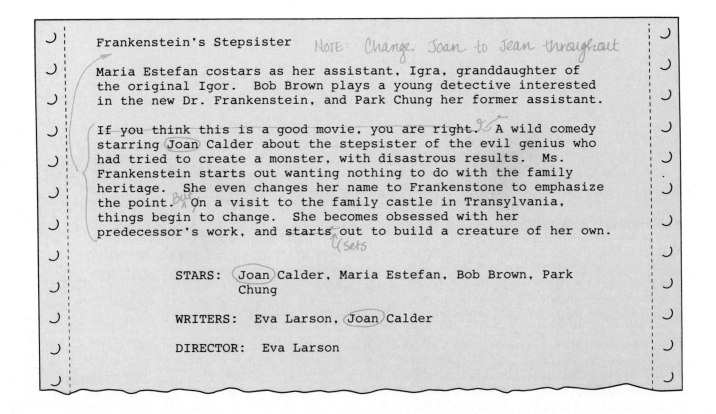

Set the tab stops for the table. Be sure to leave several spaces between columns. The exact position of the columns is not important, but they should line up perfectly. Change the name of the file to *DreamXXX*, and then save the file and print a copy.

3. Sarah Lugosi, the president of Lugosi's Video, has promised to promote your favorite movie. She has purchased five copies to rent out, but they came without descriptions of the movie. She has asked you to come up with a description to put in the box with the movie and to make four copies of the description. Make a new Word Processor file. Write a short paragraph describing your favorite movie. At the end of the paragraph, skip a line, and write Description 1. Make four copies of the whole thing in the same file (using the *Copy* command). Then replace the numbers on the descriptions, so they are Description 1, Description 2, Description 3, and so on. Save the file as *MovieXXX* and print a copy.

Formatting a Document

OBJECTIVES

- Explain the difference between formatting text and formatting a page.
- Align text between the margins.
- Set the size and font of characters.
- Use boldface and underlined text.
- Adjust the line spacing.
- Insert page breaks.
- Adjust the margins.
- Indent a passage.
- Create headers and footers.
- Preview the way a document will look when printed.
- Print the reformatted file.

WHAT IS FORMATTING?

You can transform the appearance of a document in many ways. For example, one version may have wider margins and take up fewer pages. Another may have larger type and take up more pages. Both versions contain exactly the same text, but each has a different format. Their **format** is the way the text appears and the way it is arranged on the page. The format of a document includes the size of the margins, the size of the type (characters), the alignment of text, and other factors that affect the appearance of the document but do not directly affect its content.

This lesson shows you how to format a Word Processor document. First, you format the text, adjusting the words and characters; then, you format the page, adjusting the margins and the information printed at the top and bottom of each page. In this lesson of the tutorial, you will format a memorandum to Sarah Lugosi outlining a promotional campaign for the new branch of Lugosi's Classic Video Store. The memo was written by Mortimer Cranial, her inventive and resourceful assistant. Included with the memo are a title page and a flyer that are finished but not completely formatted. The rest of the formatting is up to you. Figure 5-1 shows what the first page of the printed document looks like now and how it will look when you finish.

FIGURE 5-1
Before and After: the partially formatted and completed versions of a document.

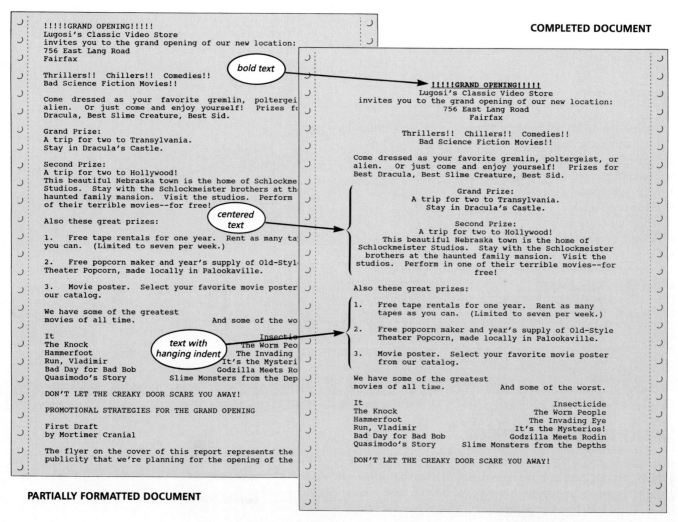

PARTIALLY FORMATTED DOCUMENT

FORMATTING TEXT

With Works, you can adjust the way a whole paragraph or a group of paragraphs lines up against the margins. You can center the text, line it up so the text appears even on either side, or leave one side uneven. You can even put a border around a key headline. Within a paragraph, or a series of paragraphs making up a section of your document, you can change the line spacing, too. Normally Works uses single spacing. But you can quickly change that to double or more. And at the level of individual characters or words, you can format the text by changing its style from plain to italic or bold, switching fonts, or increasing the size at which the text will be printed.

Aligning Paragraphs

Normal paragraphs line up the text evenly along the left **margin** of the page. Along the right margin, the text appears **ragged**; that is, the words do not all end exactly at the margin. The way text lines up is known as **alignment.** Works allows you to adjust the alignment of individual paragraphs or a group of paragraphs. To realign text, you must first select the text, then apply a new alignment.

Centering Paragraphs   When you create a new Word Processor document and start keying, your text appears in a format known as a **normal paragraph.** In a normal paragraph, the text is **aligned left**; that is, lined up against the left margin. The text appears single-spaced, with no extra space before or after the paragraph, and no indentations from the margin. Mortimer Cranial's first draft is a series of normal paragraphs. They are normal enough, but not very dramatic.

Every time Mortimer pressed Enter, Works inserted a paragraph mark, also known as a return mark, and moved the cursor down so he could start writing the next paragraph. The paragraph mark contains all Works' information about the format of the paragraph. If you delete the paragraph mark, the paragraph loses its unique formatting; the text slides down to join the text of the following paragraph, and takes on that paragraph's format.

To change the formatting of some paragraphs, you will issue formatting commands. You won't see these commands anywhere in the document, but they will appear there, hidden in the paragraph mark. Commands like this are often called **embedded commands** to distinguish them from commands that are visible as codes in a document, such as the tab marks and paragraph marks that you can see whenever you choose *Show All Characters* from the Options menu.

1. Start up Works, and choose to open an existing file.

    Use the *Open Existing File* command on the File menu. If you only have one drive, remove the Works program disk, and replace it with the template disk. If you have two disk drives, place the template disk in drive B.

2. Open the *Opening.WPS* file on the template disk. The document appears on the screen as shown in Figure 5-2. It looks very different from the final version you looked at in Figure 5-1, but that will change when you change its formatting and print a new version.

    Notice all the paragraph marks. (If you don't see any, choose *Show All Characters* from the Options menu.) Evidently, Mortimer Cranial pressed Enter after each of the first eight lines, to set each one off. To Works, that means each of these lines is an individual paragraph, with its own format. At the moment, that format is *normal*—the text hugs the left margin and appears in single-spacing.

3. Make sure the cursor is at the beginning of the document on the top line, and press Shift-Down Arrow eight times to select the Grand Opening announcement, the store address, and the types of movies offered. You are going to center all of this crucial information, so it really stands out.

4. Choose *Center* on the Format menu. The highlighted text lines up midway between the left and right margins. It's much more like a headline calling out to the customers now. To deselect the text, move the cursor with an Arrow key. The beginning of the flyer looks like Figure 5-3.

Center

    Perhaps you should also emphasize the prizes you are offering to visitors to the new store.

FIGURE 5-2
The Opening document.

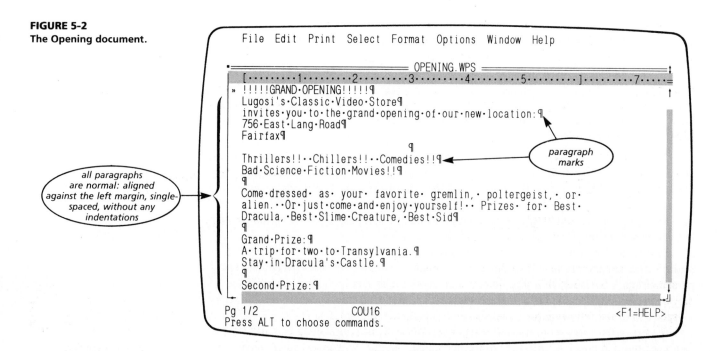

FIGURE 5-3
The announcement of the Grand Opening, centered on the page.

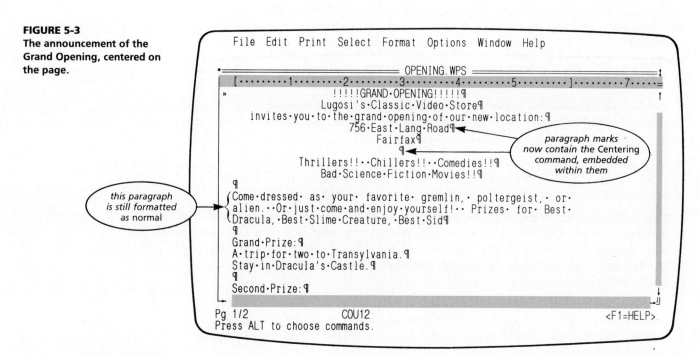

5. Use the Arrow keys to move the cursor to the *G* in *Grand Prize*, then hold down Shift as you use the Arrow keys to select the descriptions of the Grand Prize and the Second Prize.

6. Press Ctrl-C, the shortcut for centering. The description of these two prizes now appears centered.

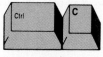

Center

Congratulations! You have centered text between the left and right margins. Centering is appropriate for headlines and announcements. You've reformatted the beginning of the flyer so it's much more appealing.

Indenting   Sometimes you want a particular paragraph to be narrower than the normal paragraph. You need to **indent** it. Indenting puts some distance between the left or right margin and the beginning or end of the lines in a paragraph.

Mortimer Cranial has asked you to format the announcements of the other prizes as **hanging indents.** That means that the first line of the paragraph starts at or near the left margin, but the rest of the paragraph is indented. So the first line appears to be hanging there on the left; or, looked at another way, the rest of the paragraph dangles from the long first line. Figure 5-4 illustrates a hanging indent.

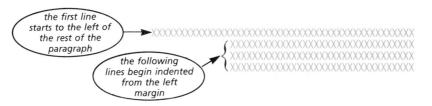

FIGURE 5-4
A hanging indent.

1. Select the paragraphs describing the three additional prizes, from the first one, through the end of the third one, *from our catalog.*
2. Choose *Indents & Spacing* from the Format menu. You see a dialog box in which you can specify exactly how much you want the first line of your paragraph to be indented from the left margin, how much you want the beginning of every following line to be indented from the left margin, and how much you want the ending of every line to be indented from the right margin, as shown in Figure 5-5.

Indents & Spacing

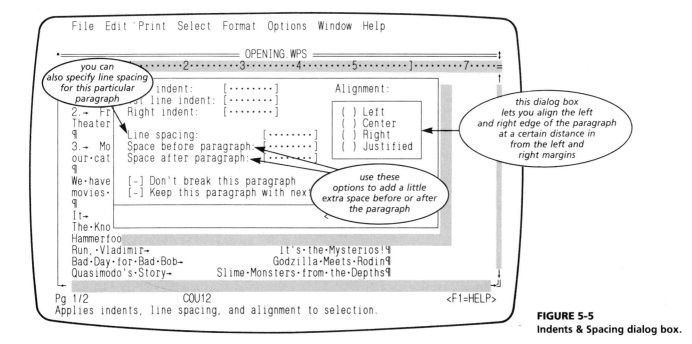

FIGURE 5-5
Indents & Spacing dialog box.

3. To align the left side of these paragraphs an inch in from the left margin, key the number 0.5 into the bracket after Left indent. In essence, for these paragraphs, you're adding a half-inch to the width of the left margin, pushing the text in.
4. To have the number appear to the left of the body of the paragraph, key the number −0.5 in the bracket after *1st line indent.* This means that you want to subtract half an inch from

the basic left indent you just created. The hyphen means *minus*. In effect, you're cancelling the indent for this one line.

5. Press Enter. The dialog box disappears, and your text is rearranged. The first line of each paragraph starts at the left margin of the page, but the second lines are all indented half an inch from the left margin. You have created hanging indents, so that the numbered prizes stand out without seeming to be headlines.

Adding a Border   You have been formatting the flyer that Lugosi's will use to try to get customers to come to their new location. Following the text of the flyer comes a memo from Mortimer Cranial to Sarah Lugosi describing the promotional activities planned for the Grand Opening.

Works lets you set off a paragraph or several paragraphs, by placing lines above, below, and to the sides. You can even have Works draw a box completely around the paragraphs. To set off the beginning of his memo, Mortimer has asked you to create a border outlining its title.

1. Press the Page Down key once to get to the heading *PROMOTIONAL STRATEGIES FOR THE GRAND OPENING*. That is the beginning of Mortimer's memo.
2. Center that heading and the information that this is a first draft by Mortimer Cranial.
3. With those paragraphs still highlighted, choose *Borders* from the Format menu. You see the Borders dialog box, shown in Figure 5-6.

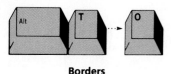

Borders

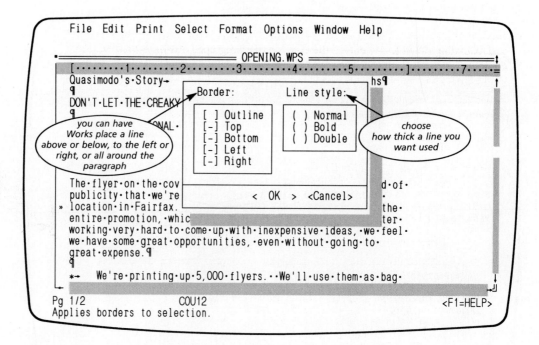

FIGURE 5-6
Borders dialog box.

4. Strike the letter *O* to choose *Outline*.
5. Strike the letter *B* to choose a *Bold* line. Then press Enter. Works puts a box around the title, as shown in Figure 5-7.

Justifying Paragraphs   The text of the memo needs to be justified. **Justified text** lines up smoothly against the left and right margins, as in some magazines and books (although not this one). Justification can give text a certain dignity.

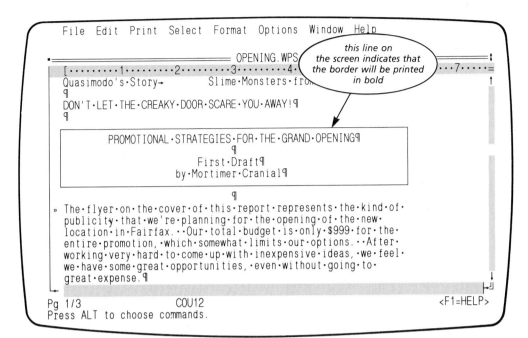

FIGURE 5-7
Border around the title of the memo.

1. Just below the title of the memo, highlight the text beginning *The flyer on the cover* . . . and extending down to the end of the concluding paragraph, *less than $1,000*.
2. Choose *Justified* from the Format menu. The text now spreads out so that it lines up evenly on both the right and left margins. Works inserts spaces between the words in a line, to ensure that the last character of the last word touches the right margin. Press an Arrow key to deselect the text. The end of the memo now looks like Figure 5-8.

Justify

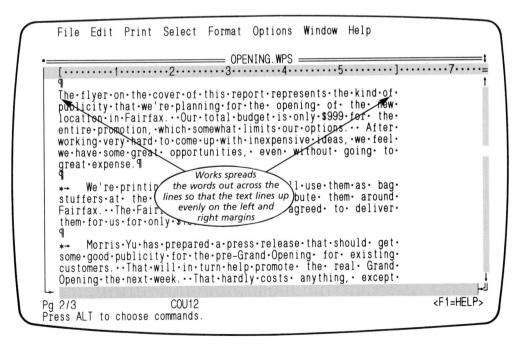

FIGURE 5-8
Justified text in the memo.

Copying a Format   Sometimes you get things lined up just perfectly in one place, and they look so good you want to copy that format for another section of your document. Works provides a quick way to do that. You've noticed the way the hanging indents look on numbered descriptions of the less important prizes. You think that format would look good in the memo, applied to the starred items in the list. You'll use the *Copy Special* command on the Edit menu to make the change.

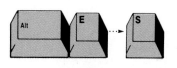

Copy Special

1. Move the cursor to the first paragraph describing another great prize. It begins: *1. Free tape rentals.*
2. Choose *Copy Special* from the Edit menu. Works copies the alignment you have set up in the paragraph your cursor is in.
3. Use the Page Down key twice to move to the first starred item in the list of promotion activities. It begins * *We're printing up. . . .*
4. Hold down Shift, and use the Down Arrow key to select all the starred items, down to the phrase, *paying 100%.*
5. Press Enter to have the format applied to these paragraphs. Another dialog box appears, asking if you intend to apply the paragraph format, and you do, so press Enter again. The paragraphs leap to attention, and become neatly formatted hanging indents, as in Figure 5-9.

You've captured the formatting of one paragraph and applied it to many others. This is a convenient way of making your document look consistent without having to remember each detail of the format.

FIGURE 5-9
Copy Special.

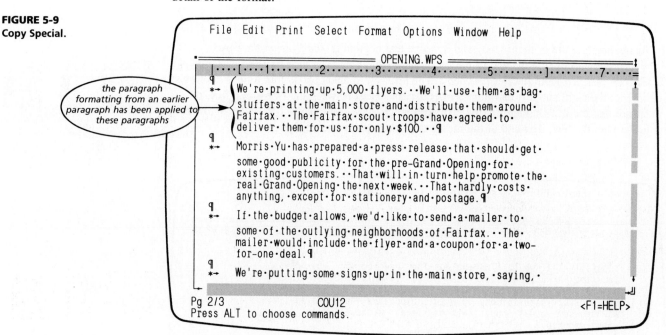

the paragraph formatting from an earlier paragraph has been applied to these paragraphs

Adjusting Line Spacing

With a typewriter, you can set your **line spacing** to single spacing, double spacing, and sometimes triple spacing. With single spacing, there is very little space between the bottom of a descending letter on one line and the top of an ascending letter on the line below. With double spacing, there is a whole blank line in between. With the computer and Works, you can assign almost any line spacing you want. Mortimer Cranial was concerned that the memo appeared a little dense. He has asked you to make the spacing a little more open.

1. Highlight the entire text of the memo. This begins with *The flyer on the cover . . .* , includes the starred items, and concludes with *for less than $1.000.*
2. Choose *Double Space* from the Format menu. Use the Arrow keys to scroll back up to see the results. The text now appears a little too open, so you need to choose a non-standard spacing—something other than single spacing and double spacing.
3. Select the passage again, choose *Indents & Spacing* from the Format menu, and key 1 . 5 into the Line spacing box. You are assigning one-and-one-half line spacing to the core of the memo. Press Enter.
4. Scroll up to view the results, as shown in Figure 5-10. The text is now much more open, with room for Sarah Lugosi to write her comments on the draft.

Double Space

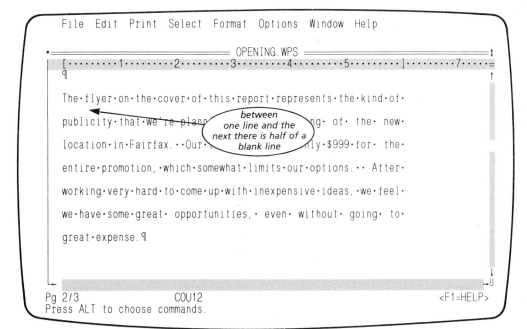

FIGURE 5-10
Text in one-and-one-half spacing.

Changing the Style, Font, and Size of Characters

Works lets you change the formatting of individual characters and words, as well as paragraphs. You want to make the headlines jump off the flyer and memo, so you are going to increase the size of the characters and make the headlines bold.

1. Scroll up to the headlines you put in a border at the beginning of the memo.
2. Select the heading, *PROMOTIONAL STRATEGIES FOR THE GRAND OPENING.*
3. Choose *Bold* from the Format menu. The text changes to a bolder look on the screen, indicating that it will be printed bold.
4. Press Ctrl-Home to leap back to the beginning of the document, to the first line of the flyer.
5. Select the whole first line: *!!!!!GRAND OPENING!!!!!.*
6. Choose *Font & Style* from the Format menu. You see a dialog box similar to the one shown in Figure 5-11.
7. Choose the Bold Style and the Underline Style (you can combine these styles) by striking B and U. In the Fonts box you see the various fonts your printer can create.
8. Pick pica, if that's available; otherwise, pick the first font. When you select a font, you see the sizes that are available on your printer for that font. Select the 16 point size or the largest one closest to that size.

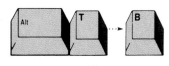

Bold

Font & Style

FIGURE 5-11
The Font & Style dialog box.

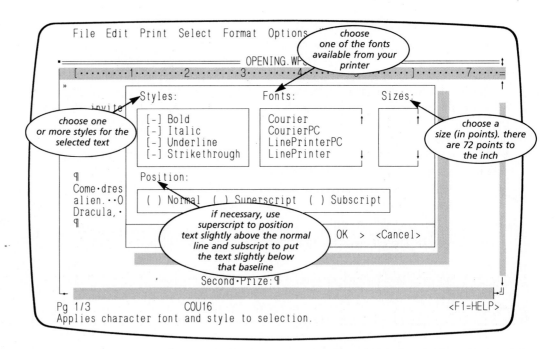

There are 72 points to an inch, so the 16/72 of an inch is 2/9 of an inch—not very tall, but tall enough to tower over the rest of the text, which is 12 point, or a sixth of an inch high. The display of the text changes a little, but the characters do not get any larger. This part of the Works program uses only a text mode on the screen, displaying everything in 12 point characters. When you get a preview of what the printed page will look like, Works switches to a different way of displaying information on the screen—graphic mode. In graphic mode, it can provide you with a somewhat fuzzy picture of what the page will look like printed, including larger size characters for your headline.

You could, of course, have chosen another font. A **font** is a set of characters—the complete alphabet in upper and lowercase, the numbers from 0 through 9, most marks of punctuation, and many standard symbols. All of the characters in a font have been designed to look alike. You can see examples of several fonts in Figure 5-12.

9. Press Enter to accept these settings and return to the document.

You have now reformatted the text in many ways. Mortimer Cranial will scratch his head in wonder at the improvement.

FORMATTING THE PAGE

  n reformatting the text of the flyer and memo, you have worked with individual paragraphs. Now it is time to make a few adjustments at a higher level, using commands that affect one or more pages at a time.

Inserting a Page Break   The text of the flyer runs right into the text of the memo. Mortimer would like you to separate the two, putting the memo on a separate page. You can break the text up like that by inserting an embedded character known as a **page break**.

FIGURE 5-12
Characters in different fonts.

The extra touches at the ends of lines are called serifs. Palatino is a serif font.

Palatino

No serifs. Avant Garde is called a sans-serif font because it has no curlicues at the end of each stroke.

Avant Garde

This font is called Palatino. It is based on the shapes of letters created when someone uses a brush.

This font is called Avant Garde. It is very clean, as if it were stamped out by a metal press.

1. Press the Page Down key twice to move to the end of the flyer, which says, *DON'T LET THE CREAKY DOOR SCARE YOU AWAY!*
2. Use the Arrow keys to place your cursor under the paragraph mark after that line. (If you do not see any paragraph marks, use the *Show All Characters* command on the Options menu to have Works display the paragraph marks.)
3. Choose *Insert Page Break* from the Print menu. You are embedding the *Page Break* command at this point. A string of solid dots crosses the window, marking the end of one page and the beginning of the next. When you print, the *Page Break* command will tell the printer to start a new page after printing, *DON'T LET THE CREAKY DOOR SCARE YOU AWAY!*

Insert Page Break

Adjusting the Margins   The current margins for the opening document appear in the **ruler** at the top of the window, as shown in Figure 5-13. (If you don't see the ruler, choose *Show Ruler* from the Options menu.)

1. Choose *Page Setup & Margins* from the Print menu. You see the dialog box shown in Figure 5-14.
2. Move the left margin in a little farther from the left edge of the paper you'll be printing on. Key 1.5 as the left margin. (You do not need to type the quotation marks that indicate you are using inches as the unit of measurement.)
3. Move the right margin in a little farther from the right-hand side of the paper you will be printing on. Key 1.5 as the right margin.
4. Press Enter. The bracket on the right-hand side of the ruler moves in a little, and the text reflows to fit the new margins.

Page Setup & Margins

Oops! The tabbed list of best and worst movies of all time has been shaken up by the new margins. Inadvertently, you wiped out a tab stop that Mortimer had set up, so Works went back to its standard tab positions, yanking all the bad movies over to the left. You can remedy this with one command, though.

FIGURE 5-13
The Ruler at the top of the
opening document.

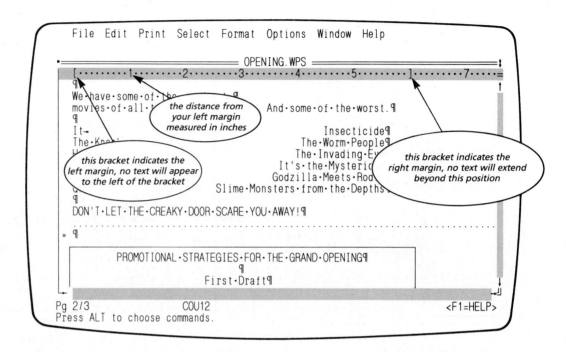

FIGURE 5-14
The Page Setup & Margins
dialog box.

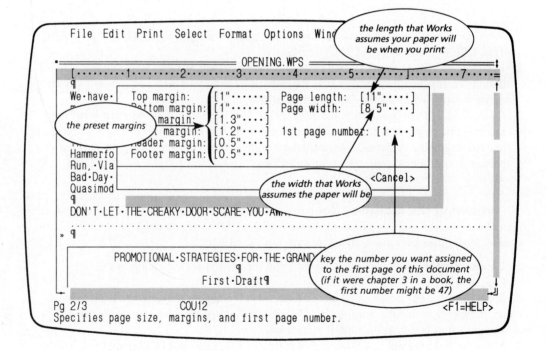

5. Select the text from *We have some of the greatest . . .* through *Slime Monsters from the Depths.*
6. Choose *Tabs* from the Format menu. You see the Tabs dialog box.
7. Key 5.25 into the Position box, to place a tab 5.25 inches from the left margin.
8. Choose to make this a Right Tab, so that any tabbed item will line up with the tab on its right.

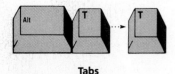

Tabs

FIGURE 5-15
Margins in a standard Word processor document.

9. Choose *Insert* and *Done*. The tabbed list lines up correctly again. But there are some unnecessary tab characters between the phrase *the greatest movies of all time* and the phrase *And some of the worst*.

10. Use the Arrow keys and the Backspace key to delete the three unnecessary tab characters, bringing the phrase *And some of the worst* up to the same line as *movies of all time*. Your list should now look like the one in Figure 5-16.

FIGURE 5-16
The list of the best and the worst.

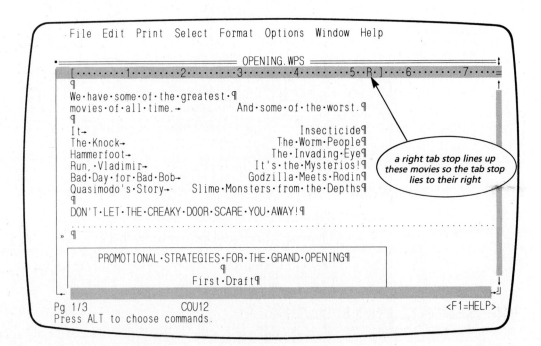

Great! You have narrowed the margins and recovered from the most common problem caused by shrinking margins—a mass of tab characters flung together.

Creating Headers and Footers   A **header** is the text that appears at the top of every page in your document. A **footer** is the text that appears at the bottom of every page. You use the *Headers & Footers* command on the Print menu to set up the text; then Works applies it to every page during printing.

1. Choose *Headers & Footers* from the Print menu. You see the dialog box shown in Figure 5-17.

2. In the Header area, key: `First Draft - &p`

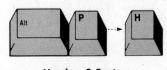

Headers & Footers

The *&p* is a code telling Works to figure out what page number it is printing, and to put that number in the header, right after the name of the document, *First Draft*.

3. Press Tab to move to the Footer area, and key: `&d`

That is the code for the current date. As you begin printing, Works will look up the day's date in the computer, and print that at the bottom of every page.

4. Press Enter to confirm the header and footer.

Now when you print, every page will be identified as a first draft; every page will have the correct page number; and no matter when you print, every page will carry the date of printing at the bottom. Works makes repetitive typing chores a snap.

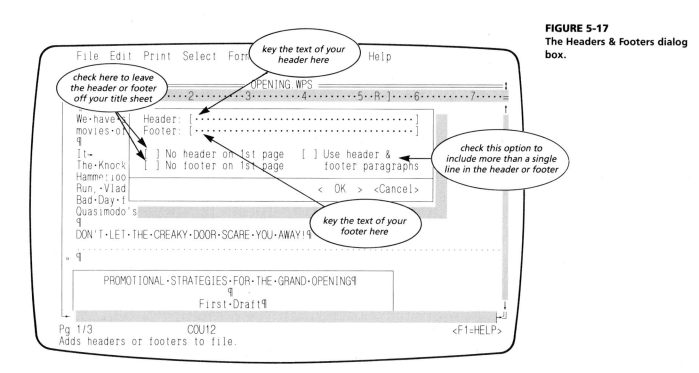

FIGURE 5-17
The Headers & Footers dialog box.

PREVIEWING AND PRINTING

Works lets you see a rough picture of what your printed page will look like, so you can make corrections before you take the time to send the document to the printer. This advance look is known as a **preview**. To display the preview, Works blanks the screen for a moment as it shifts from text display to a graphics display. The graphics display makes it possible for you to get an idea of how different size fonts will look on the printed page.

Previewing   You should always get a preview before printing. You can reassure your-self that all is formatted correctly before you print, rather than after.

1. Choose *Preview* from the Print menu. You see the standard Print dialog box.
2. Ignore the options, and press Enter to proceed directly to your preview. After a moment, the screen goes blank, then you see a representation of your first page. You can make out key words, and you can see how your paragraphs are aligned, as in Figure 5-18.
3. Press Page Down to see the next page; and press it again to see the last page. Press Esc to return to the document. The screen goes blank again as you return to the text display. But you're confident because you've seen how the flyer and memo are laid out.

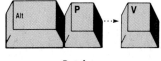

Preview

Printing and Quitting   You have reformatted the text and the pages, and now you've gotten a somewhat fuzzy preview of what the printed pages will look like. Time to print!

1. Make sure your printer is on, securely connected to the back of your computer, and on-line.
2. Choose *Print* from the Print menu. Press Enter.

Printing should begin. Wait until all three pages have been printed before you quit.

Print

FIGURE 5-18
The preview of the opening document.

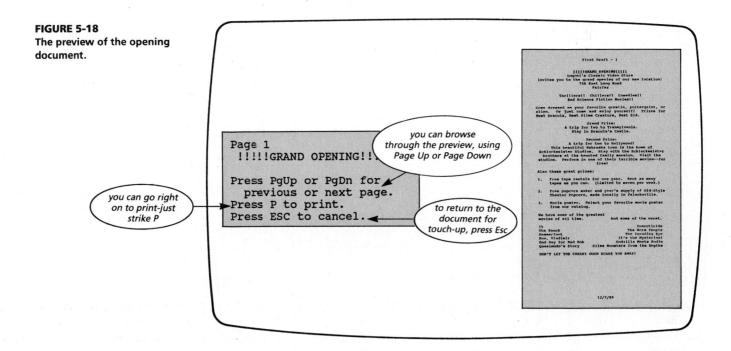

3. Choose *Exit Works* from the File menu. You return to the DOS prompt.
4. Remove your disks and store them in their envelopes.
5. Turn the computer off.

KEY TERMS

aligned left *MSW 67*
alignment *MSW 67*
embedded command *MSW 67*
font *MSW 74*
footer *MSW 78*
format *MSW 65*

indent *MSW 69*
hanging indent *MSW 69*
header *MSW 78*
justified text *MSW 70*
line spacing *MSW 72*
margin *MSW 67*

normal paragraph *MSW 67*
page break *MSW 74*
preview *MSW 79*
ragged *MSW 67*
ruler *MSW 75*

COMMANDS

Alt-T-B (Bold)
Alt-T-O (Borders)
Alt-T-C (Center)
Ctrl-C (Center)
Alt-E-S (Copy Special)
Alt-T-D (Double Space)

Alt-T-F (Font & Style)
Alt-P-H (Headers & Footers)
Alt-T-A (Indents & Spacing)
Alt-P-I (Insert Page Break)
Alt-T-J (Justify)
Alt-T-N (Normal Paragraph)

&p (Page Number in Header or Footer)
Alt-P-M (Page Setup & Margins)
Alt-P-V (Preview)
Alt-P-P (Print)
Alt-T-T (Tabs)
&d (Today's Date in Header or Footer)

REVIEW QUESTIONS

1. What is the difference between formatting text and formatting a page? Can you give two examples of each?
2. What are the preset settings for the left margin, right margin, line spacing, character size, and alignment? What does Works consider a *normal paragraph*?
3. How would you make larger characters for a title page? How do you perform this task?
4. What are embedded commands? Can you give two examples?
5. What are three ways you can align text? Describe them.
6. What is the purpose of a header and a footer? How do you insert a header or footer in a document?
7. How could you copy the format of one paragraph and apply that format to another paragraph?
8. What are two circumstances in which you would insert a page break in a document? How would you perform this task?
9. How do you adjust the margins of a document?

APPLICATIONS

1. Open the file *Special.WPS* from the template disk. The file contains a document offering a special deal to members of the Tape Club from Fairfax. They will receive a discount on their first ten tapes at the new Fairfax location of Lugosi's Classic Video Store. Your job is to format the document so that it looks more exciting. The marked-up copy in Figure 5-19 shows you where to make formatting changes on the document.

   Save the file to disk, then print a copy of the document.

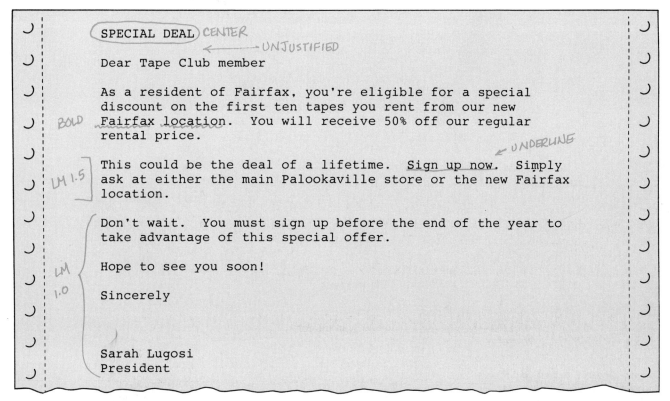

FIGURE 5-19
File named *Special.WPS* marked up for formatting.

2. Open the file *Play.WPS* from the template disk. The document tells employees of Lugosi's how to use their videotape player. You need to add a header and footer and change the line spacing, as indicated on the marked-up copy in Figure 5-20.

   After you finish making the changes, save the changed document under the name *PlayXXX* and then print a copy.

3. Make a new Word Processor file from scratch. Write your own document, making use of at least six formatting commands you learned in this lesson. Try to make the document look as attractive as possible. Suggested ideas: an announcement of a school play, an advertisement for a local business that might want to advertise in the school newspaper, or a flyer for a local charity function. Name the file *IdeasXXX*.

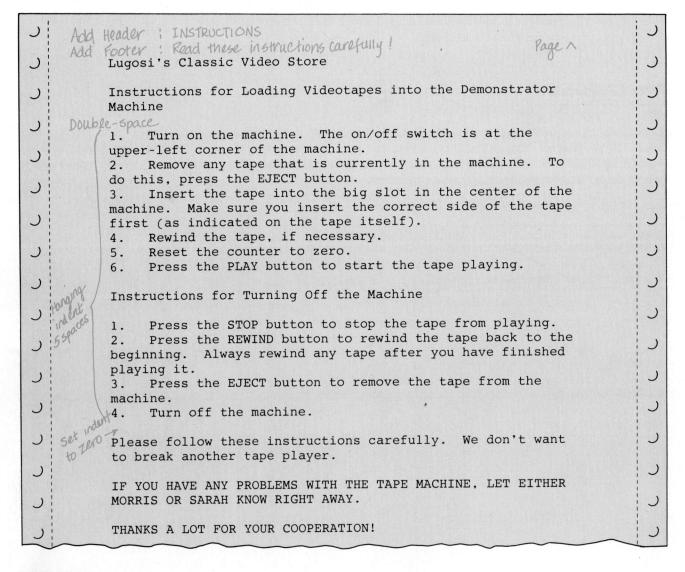

FIGURE 5-20
File named *Play.WPS* marked up
for formatting.

UNIT III

The Database

Getting Started with the Database

OBJECTIVES

- Discuss the basic functions of a database management system.
- Open a Database file.
- Move the cursor around in a Database file and make simple changes to entries.
- Explain the two different ways of looking at records and how to switch between them.
- Arrange records in a file.
- Find records that meet one criterion.
- Select records by searching within categories.
- Print a screen.

DATABASE BASICS

*I*n Lesson 1, you learned that any organized collection of information—from a short grocery list to a large telephone book—is a form of database. A database stored on paper, such as a telephone book, always remains in the same form. The information in the telephone book, for example, always appears in the same order. To find a listing, you have to look for it alphabetically. On the other hand, an electronic database is very flexible. A database application program, or **database management system,** turns the computer into a tool for managing data. A database management system like the Works Database tool can be used to organize information, keep records updated, and produce a variety of reports. For example, if your phone book was stored in a database file, you could locate all the Robinsons on Main Street or list all the people whose phone numbers begin with the numbers 436.

Each list of information used with a database program is stored in a separate file, like a file in a file cabinet. Figure 6-2 shows an example of a file for the Works Database tool that contains a list of the movies available at Lugosi's Classic Video Store. The file is comprised of sets of related information called **records.** In this case, each record in the database contains information about a single movie. Each record is divided into categories of information called **fields.** A field contains space for information about one aspect of a record, like the title of a movie or the year it came out. Each field has a unique **field name** so the database program can identify it. The information listed under each field in a single record is called an **entry.** Figure 6-2 shows you what these terms represent. For example, look under the Type field in the record for the movie *Eternal Flame*: The entry for the Type is Melodrama.

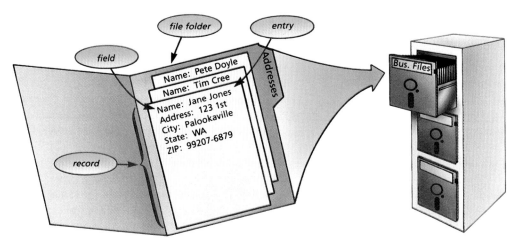

FIGURE 6-1
An electronic database file is similar to a paper file.

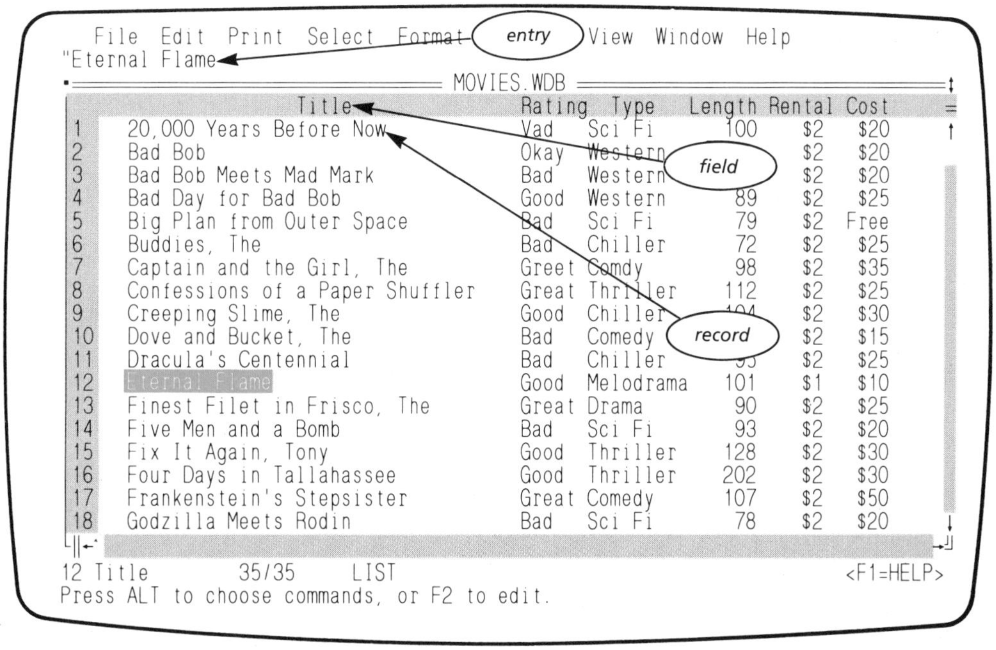

FIGURE 6-2
A Database record.

A database is rarely complete because it becomes inaccurate whenever some of the information it contains changes. Even the telephone book becomes inaccurate as soon as one person changes his or her number or moves away. Unfortunately paper databases like the telephone book are not only hard to rearrange, but are difficult to keep up to date. Coming out with a new telephone book every time someone moves would be impossible. It would also be impossible to print a different telephone book for each of the many different ways that people might want to look up information—one in alphabetical order, another in order by telephone number, and a third listed by street address.

An electronic database is designed to be rearranged and kept up to date easily. With a database program like Works, you can always change records to reflect current data, add new records, or remove out-of-date ones. For example, if Lugosi's Classic Video Store rents out the last copy of *The Knock*, you can readjust the entry for the number of copies in stock to zero, so that the clerks will know that there are none left. When a customer returns the tape, you can change the entry to show that a copy is once again available.

Updating files constantly like this allows an organization to make better decisions. For example, Lugosi's sells blank videotapes. The store manager knows to reorder blank tapes whenever the supply falls below a certain number. Since the clerks record each sale in the database, and the database subtracts each sale from the total number in stock, the manager can quickly determine when to place a new order for blank tapes. Of course, the manager could go out and count the number of blank tapes on the shelf to decide when to reorder, but the store stocks many other items that also need to be counted and reordered. Using the computer is faster, easier, and more fun.

Not only can you look at database information on the screen, you can also print a copy of the information as a **report.** A report contains a chosen arrangement of the information in a selected set of records. For example, from the *Movies.WDB* file you could print one report that lists all the movies in the store in alphabetical order, a second report containing only movies that star Annabelle Lee, and another report listing just those movies written by Forbes W. Rogers, the science fiction genius. You would end up with three completely different reports, all selected from the same set of information. Figure 6-3 shows several different reports made from the list of movies.

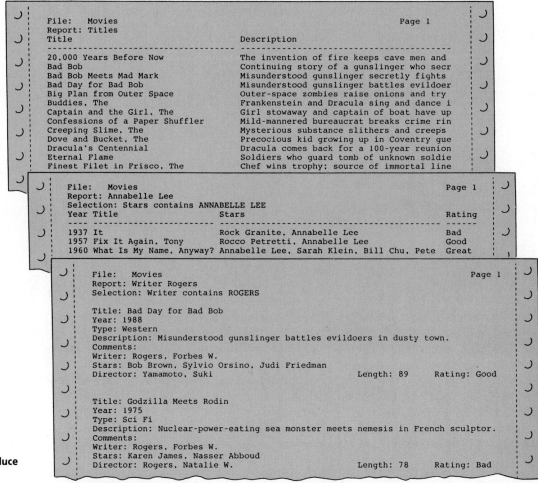

FIGURE 6-3
One database file can produce many different reports.

OPENING A DATABASE FILE

You can find Database files as well as Word Processor files on the template disk. For this lesson you will work with a list of the movies at the new branch of Lugosi's Classic Video Store. The list is stored in a file called, simply enough, *Movies.WDB*. As with any computer file, you need to open the file before you can work on it.

1. Start up Works. Use the startup procedures you learned in Lesson 2. You end up with a regular Microsoft Works window.
2. If you have only one disk drive, replace the Works program disk with the template disk. If you have two disk drives, insert the template disk into drive B.
3. From the File menu, choose the *Open Existing File* command. A dialog box appears, listing the files in drive A and providing a line for keying the name of a file. You have already learned how to select the file you want from a list. If you know the name of the file, typing the name can be faster.
4. If the template disk is in drive B, key B:Movies.WDB. If the template disk is in drive A, key A:Movies.WDB. The A or B tells the computer on which drive to look for the file. The colon tells it that the name of the file follows. *Movies* is, of course, the name of the file, and *.WDB* is the extension Works uses to identify database files.
5. Press Enter. Works displays the first record of the Movies database, as shown in Figure 6-4.

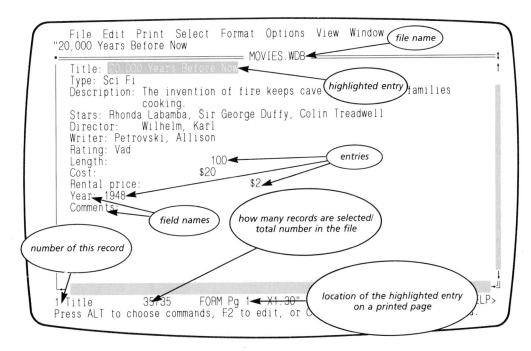

FIGURE 6-4
A database file opened from the disk.

LOOKING AT RECORDS

A database program like Works can display information in different layouts, which Works calls **views.** The layout on your screen, and shown in Figure 6-4, displays a single record—information about one movie. To the left of the screen, you see the field names. Each field name is followed by a colon. To the right of each field name is the entry for this record. The highlight indicates which entry is selected. Information you key or commands you choose will affect the selected entry. The information in the highlighted entry also appears underneath the menu bar in the area called the **formula bar,** which is used for editing entries. Works puts double quotes in front of the entry in the formula bar to indicate that the entry contains text instead of numbers. The quotes alert Works not to try to perform calculations on the 20,000 in the movie title. This layout is called the **Form view** because information is laid out the way it might be in a form.

Database programs can also display multiple records, as shown in Figure 6-2. The layout in Figure 6-2 shows a list of movies and is called the **List view.** Whenever you open an existing file, Works displays the layout that was on the screen when the file was last saved.

Moving Around in the Form View

A customer has just offered a useful comment about the movie *Bad Bob*, and you want to add her opinion to the database. To do so you need to go to the record for *Bad Bob*. If you think of the database as a stack of index cards, moving from record to record in the Form view is like flipping through the stack.

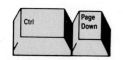

Go Down One Screen's Worth of Records in List View

1. To display the next record in the database, press Ctrl-Page Down. You see the record for the movie *Bad Bob*. It's record 2 in the database. Notice that the entry in the Comments field is blank. You will enter a comment there, as shown in Figure 6-5.
2. To select the Comments entry, press the Tab key several times until the space next to the Comments field name is highlighted. The highlight changes size as it moves because the size of each field is different.

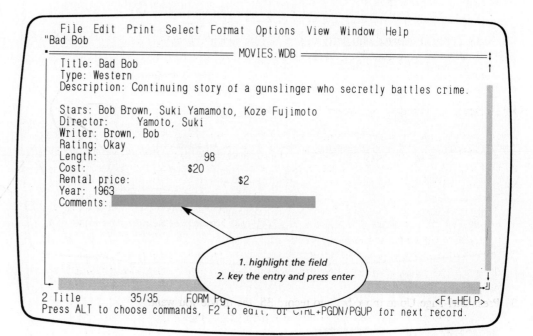

FIGURE 6-5
Keying a comment.

3. Key the following:

   Not violent, okay for young children

   As you key, Works displays the comment in the field and in the formula bar. The formula bar has a cursor, like the cursor in the Word Processor, that shows where the next character you key will appear. If you make a mistake, backspace over it and key the correct entry.

4. Press Enter to add the comment to the database. Works puts quotes in front of the entry in the formula bar. The highlight stays put.
5. Press Shift-Tab several times to move the highlight back to the title of the movie.
6. Press Ctrl-Page Up to flip back to the first record in the file.

Go Up One Screen's Worth of Records in List View

You can also use the Arrow keys to move around in the Form View, and if the record contains too much information for the screen to show at once, you can bring more into view. This chart shows which keys to use in the Form view:

CURSOR MOVEMENT	KEYS
Next record	Ctrl-Page Down
Previous record	Ctrl-Page Up
First entry in the first record	Ctrl-Home
Last entry in the last record	Ctrl-End
Next entry	Tab
Previous entry	Shift-Tab
Left or Right one field or space	Left or Right Arrow
Up or Down one field or space	Up or Down Arrow
Down one screenful	Page Down
Up one screenful	Page Up

In long or complicated databases you can also move among records and fields rapidly with the *Go To* command on the Select menu.

Printing a Single Record

Sometimes you want a quick printout of something in a file. Sarah Lugosi just asked you to bring her the record for *What Is My Name, Anyway?*. The fastest way to get it for her would be to display the record on the screen and then to print a copy of just that record. *What Is My Name, Anyway?* is the last movie in the database.

1. Make sure your computer is hooked up to a printer, and that the printer is turned on and is on-line. Also, make sure it has paper. If you do not have a printer attached to your computer, skip to Step 6.
2. Press Ctrl-End to jump to the end of the file. You see a blank record, number 36. Many database programs, like Works, keep a blank record ready for when you want to add a new record.
3. Press Ctrl-Page Up to move back to record 35, the movie you want.
4. Choose *Print* from the Print menu (you can press Alt-P, then P).
5. Press Enter to accept the standard settings. Works automatically prints a copy of the record on the screen.
6. Press Ctrl-Home to jump back to the first record in the file. Then move the highlight to the movie title (*20,000 Years Before Now*).

Now you know how to move through a file displayed in the Form view and print a record. Next you will explore the List view.

Switching Between Views

To work with the details of a single record, as when you enter new records or look up information contained in one record, you use the Form view. To compare records or group all the records in a particular category, as when you select all the science fiction movies, you use the List View. You can enter data or edit the database in either view.

Some typographical errors in the *Movies.WDB* file need to be corrected. You will switch to the List view to make the changes.

1. To switch to the List view choose the *List* command on the View menu. The screen in Figure 6-6 appears, displaying the *Movies.WDB* file in the new layout.

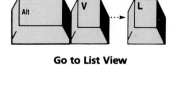

Go to List View

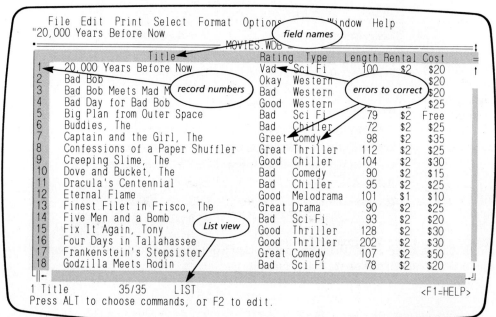

FIGURE 6-6
A database file in List view.

In a database List view, each record takes up one row on the screen. Each field takes up a column. An entry appears where a row and column meet. One entry is highlighted, and it appears in the formula bar. The Works screen displays a maximum of 18 rows of data, so you can see up to 18 records at once. The screen is not wide enough for all the data in a record, so you also see fewer fields than appeared in the Form view. You will see how to bring the rest of the fields into view later. In the movies database, the width of each field has been adjusted to make the entries easier to read. Even so, some entries may be cut off because they are wider than the space available. The information in shortened entries is not actually lost; it is still stored in the database, but is not displayed until the width of the field is expanded to make room for it all. The fields in the List view are arranged in a different order than their order in the Form view. All of these changes affect only how the database is displayed; they do not alter the information contained in the database.

Before you start to work in the List view, practice switching to the Form view and back. You can display the Form view by choosing *Form* from the View menu. A very convenient way to switch views is to press F9. That key takes you to the Form view if the List view is on screen and takes you to the List view if the Form view is on screen.

2. Choose *Form* from the View menu. Works displays the Form view.
3. Press F9. You return to the List view.

Go to Form View

Moving Around Within an Entry

You have learned how to move from entry to entry, from record to record, and from view to view. Sometimes you also need to move within an entry, for example, to be able to correct the keying errors in the Movies database. With Works, the F2 key lets you work within an entry. Pressing F2 puts a cursor at the end of the entry in the formula bar. After you have pressed F2, the Left and Right Arrows, as well as the Home and End keys, let you move the cursor within the entry; the Delete and Backspace keys let you erase characters. Each of these keys performs the same functions as in the Word Processor.

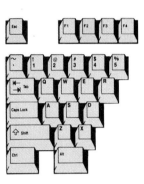

 After you revise an entry, you must confirm the changes before they become part of the record. You can confirm them by pressing Enter or by pressing one of the keys that moves the highlight to a different entry. Alternately, you can cancel the changes you made and restore the original entry by pressing Esc.

 While you are working within an entry, most of the commands listed on the menu bar are unavailable.

Moving Around in the List View

There are a number of entries that need to be corrected. Start by changing the rating for *20,000 Years Before Now* from *Vad* to *Bad*.

1. Press the Right Arrow to highlight the Rating field in row 1.
2. To be able to revise the entry, press the F2 key. Works puts a blinking cursor after the entry in the formula bar. Using the Left Arrow, you can move the cursor within the entry, and you can use the Backspace key to delete the character to the left of the cursor.
3. Use the Left Arrow to move the cursor to the letter *a*. Press Backspace to delete the *V*. Then key B so the entry reads *Bad*.
4. To confirm the change, press Enter. That puts the changes made in the formula bar into the record without moving the highlight. If you need to make more revisions, you can press F2 again.
5. Use the Down Arrow to highlight the Rating field in row 7.
6. Press F2, and then correct the entry to *GREAT*.
7. Press Tab. The Tab key enters your change in the record and also moves the highlight to the next field.
8. Press F2, and then correct the entry to *Comedy*.

 A friend was looking over your shoulder as you made the last correction. He bets you a dollar that *The Captain and the Girl* was directed by Sally Brown. Want to see if he was right? The Director field is off the screen to the right.

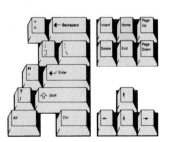

1. To jump to the right by a large block of data, press Ctrl-Right Arrow. You just won a dollar.
2. Press Home to jump to the first field in that record.

FIGURE 6-7
Correcting an error in an entry.

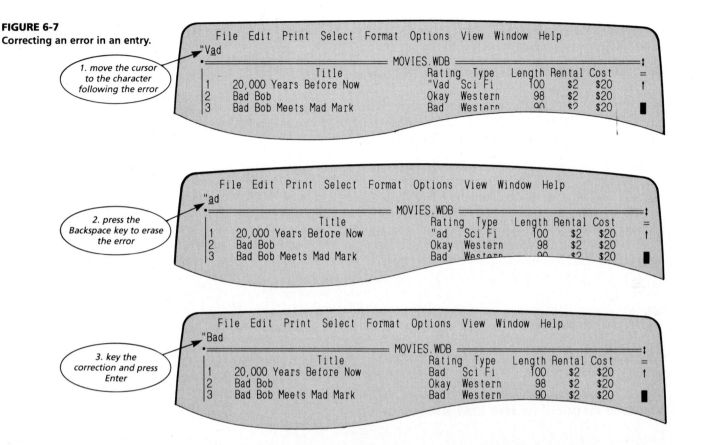

The following chart shows which keys to use when moving around in the List view:

CURSOR MOVEMENT	KEY
Next Row	Down Arrow
Previous Row	Up Arrow
Next field in Row	Tab
Previous field in Row	Shift-Tab
First field in row	Home
Last field in row	End
First field of first record	Ctrl-Home
Last Field of last record	Ctrl-End
Left or Right one field	Left or Right Arrow
Down one screenful	Page Down
Up one screenful	Page Up
Left one screenful	Ctrl-Page Up
Right one screenful	Ctrl-Page Down
Left, right, up, or down by a large block of data	Ctrl-Arrow

In either the Form view or List view, when you want to move back and forth within an entry in the formula bar, press F2, then use the following keys:

ACTION	KEY
Move the cursor left or right	Left or Right Arrow
Erase the character left of the cursor	Backspace
Erase the character at the cursor	Delete

ARRANGING RECORDS

A database program like Works lets you rearrange records in any order you choose and pick out the particular ones you are interested in. All of the records are stored electronically in your computer's memory, so Works can easily organize them, find ones that you specify, or display only records that meet criteria you have set.

The *Movies.WDB* file is currently arranged alphabetically by title. Suppose you want to reverse the order of the file, so that the Z's come first? Or what if you want to arrange the records by year? Ordering the records is called **sorting,** and you do it with the *Sort Records* command on the Select menu. When you sort the database, all the records, including any that are not currently displayed on the screen, are arranged in the new order. Works lets you sort by three fields at once, so you can have arrangements within arrangements.

You are helping a friend who is writing a term paper on film writers. You are going to provide her with a list of films arranged by writer and arranged by year among the films of each writer.

1. Choose *Sort Records* from the Select menu. Works displays a dialog box for specifying how you want the records arranged.

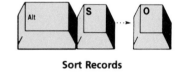

Sort Records

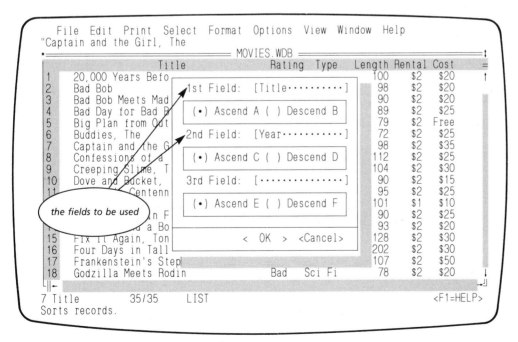

FIGURE 6-8
The Sorting Records dialog box.

2. Key `Writer` in the space for the first field. The field name you key replaces the name already in the field. The preset arrangement, ascending order, is what you want, so you do not need to change it.
3. To move to the second field, press Alt-2. Key `Year` in the space for the second field.
4. Press Enter. In a flash, the screen displays the movies in a new order.
5. To bring the Year and Writer fields into view, press Ctrl-Page Down, and then press the Right Arrow twice (Figure 6-9).

FIGURE 6-9
New arrangement of file by writer and year.

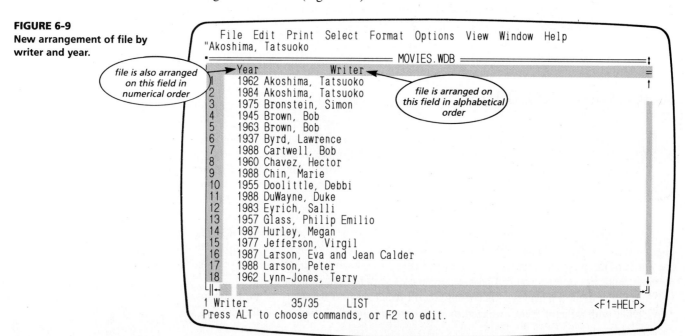

FINDING RECORDS

Sometimes scanning screens in the List view or flipping through records in the Form view is too slow for finding a particular record. Imagine trying to find a record in the full list of 5,000 tapes available at Lugosi's Classic Video Store—it could take all day! With the *Search* command, you can have Works do the hunting for you—you just view the results.

The *Search* command tells the database program that you want to find some records. The program asks you what you want to find, you tell it by providing **comparison information**, and it finds all the records that match. Comparison information can be any combination of words, numbers, or other characters that you want the database program to find. You can use part of a word, one letter, or a whole phrase. Works will look for any characters that match your comparison information, regardless of whether they appear in the middle of a word or use uppercase or lowercase.

A customer comes into the video store and asks for a movie, but he cannot remember the title. All he remembers is that it was written by someone named Bob, or stars Bob, or something like that. Maybe Bob was part of the title. After you enter *Bob* as the comparison information, the *Search* command will quickly find all the records that match your request.

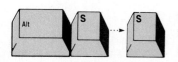

Search

1. Choose *Search* from the Select menu. A Search dialog box appears.

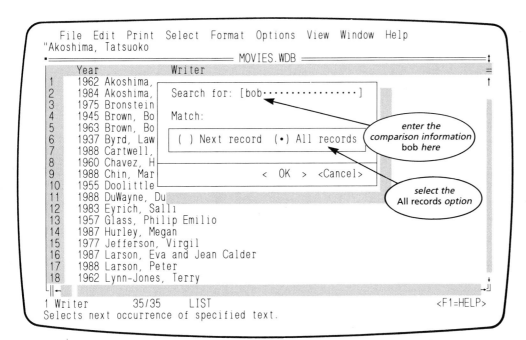

FIGURE 6-10
Search dialog box.

2. Key *bob* as the comparison information. You do not have to key a capital B because when searching, Works does not distinguish between uppercase and lowercase letters.
3. Because you want to find all the records containing *Bob*, select the *All records* option.
4. Press Enter. Works finds all the records in the *Movies.WDB* file that contain *bob* in some form and displays them.

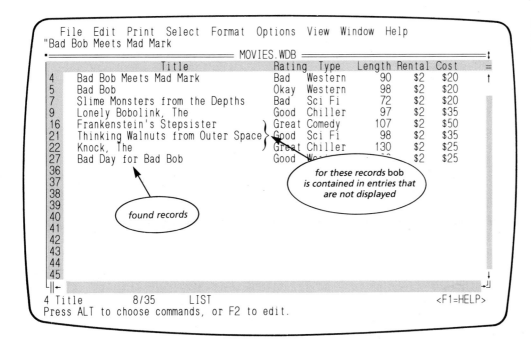

FIGURE 6-11
Records found with the *Search* **command.**

Some of the records are nothing like what you want to find. For example, you can write off *The Lonely Bobolink* immediately. The *Search* command finds every record that contains your comparison information, including what you can see are inappropriate records. A database program like Works sees your comparison information as just a string of characters and looks for those characters wherever they may appear. *Bob* is indeed part of *Bobolink*, but not as a person's name. Other records seem to be displayed by mistake, but they do contain the characters *bob* somewhere in the record, even if that part of the record is not shown on the screen.

If you are dissatisfied with the results of the first search, you can try a narrower approach to reduce the number of records that are found. The more specific you make your comparison information, the more likely it is that a database program will find just the records you are trying to locate. Fortunately, your customer recalls that the movie he is looking for involves the great actor Bob Brown. Try a search using *bob brown* as the comparison information.

1. Choose *Search* from the Select menu again.
2. Key bob brown as the comparison information, select the *All records* option, and then press Enter. Now Works finds just six records with *bob brown* in them. (The records with *Brown, Bob* do not match the comparison information—they were found because *bob brown* appears somewhere in the record.)

FIGURE 6-12
Records found by narrowing a search.

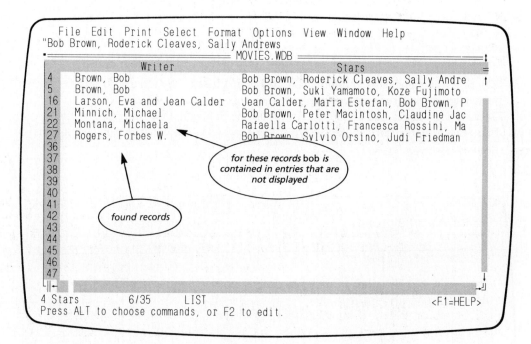

Because the List view does not show all the information in longer entries, one of the records still seems to be there by mistake, but if you highlight the Stars field and scan the formula bar, you will see that they all contain *bob brown*.

Making a Snapshot of the Screen

You want a quick printout of the records Works found, so you can give the list to the customer. Earlier, you printed out a single record in the Form view. In the List view, the fastest way to print a list of movies would be to display them and then print a copy of the screen. The command to print a copy of the screen is *Shift-PrtSc*. The PrtSc (Print Screen) key appears in different locations on different keyboards. You may find it with the F keys or on the numerical and arrow keypad. You can use Shift-PrtSc whenever you want a printed copy of the screen, not just when using Works.

1. Press Home to jump back to the first field in the record. Everything shifts over, so now you can see the movie titles.
2. Make sure your printer is turned on and selected (or on-line). Skip to Step 5 if you do not have a printer attached to your computer.
3. Press Shift-PrtSc. The printer immediately starts printing a copy of whatever is displayed on the screen, including the menu bar and status and message lines. The printer stops at the end of the screen, without moving to the top of the next page as it would with a print-out of a file.
4. To advance the paper to the top of the next page—a courtesy to the next person who uses the printer, press the Select or On-Line button on the printer, so that the Select light (or On-Line light) goes off. Now press the Form Feed button. After the printer advances the paper, press the Select or On-Line button to turn the light back on. Tear off your printout.
5. Choose *Show All Records* from the Select menu to go back to the full database.

Print Screen

Good job—you have found a set of records with the *Search* command, then narrowed the search, and printed a copy of the screen. As you have seen, hunting through the database with the *Search* command sometimes turns up inappropriate records. Even though they contain the comparison information, they are not the records you are looking for. The *Search* command looks anywhere in the file for your comparison information. Another type of search lets you be much more specific in telling the program what fields to look in and what kinds of records to find.

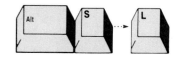

Show All Records

SELECTING RECORDS

Finding records with the *Search* command lets you match one piece of information that can appear anywhere within a record. This method is ideal for quickly scanning an entire database for a particular name or title. For many records you will want to find, however, the *Search* command is too inexact and inflexible. For example, if you were looking for movies made in 1960 and used 1960 as the comparison information, you might turn up a movie whose Description said, *This movie shows the history of Hollywood from 1940 through 1960.* If you were looking for all movies made before 1960, the *Search* command would not let you find them.

Lugosi's Classic Video Store is planning a promotion of older films from its collection. You will use Works to select the records for movies made before 1959. These are the films that Lugosi's will include in its promotion. To select these records, you will need to conduct a more advanced kind of search that Works terms a **query.** A query is a request to display records that match a variety of conditions.

1. Choose *Query* from the View menu. Works displays the Query window. Like the window of the Form view, the Query window contains a list of all the fields in a record. Instead of entering information to create a record, you enter instructions that tell Works which records to find.
2. Use Tab or Shift-Tab to highlight the Year field.
3. Key in < 1959, then press Enter. The left angle is a symbol meaning *less than*. You have instructed Works to select records whose entry in the Year field is less than 1959.

Go to Query View

FIGURE 6-13
The Query window.

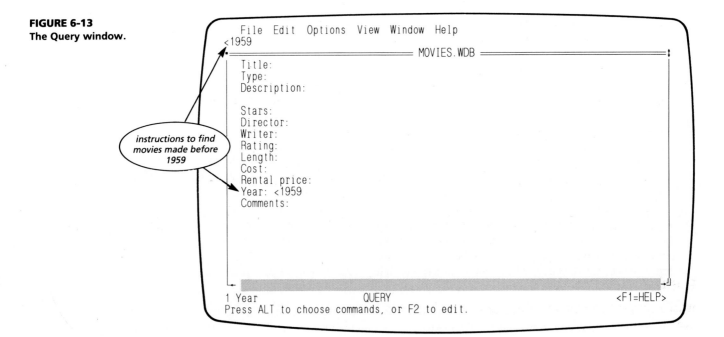

FIGURE 6-14
Selected records.

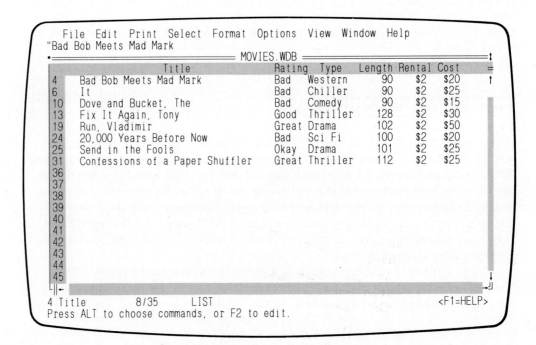

4. Press F10 to return to the List view. Works searches all the records in the database, selects the movies made before 1959, and displays the records on the screen. The other records in the database are hidden. If you wanted to see the records from 1959 and later, you could display the records that are now hidden by choosing *Switch Hidden Records* from the Select menu.

Using the Query window is more specific than using the *Search* command. A query hunts within specific fields for entries that match your comparison information instead of hunting throughout the record. In addition, your comparison information can include more complicated instructions than a string of characters. Database programs refer to your search instructions as **selection rules.** Because you can build complex instructions using symbols and mathematical expressions like *equals* or *greater than*, selection rules sometimes are called **query formulas.**

Each selection rule applies to a specific field in the database, includes a **comparison** like *equals* or *is greater than*, and includes comparison information. Your selection of movies made before 1959 applies to the Year field, includes the comparison *less than* (<), and includes the comparison information *1959*. When you applied the selection rule, Works looked at all the dates in the Year field and then selected only those lower than 1959. By the way, if you added new records to the database and again wanted to select all the movies made before 1959, you could take a shortcut that bypasses the Query window. Choosing *Apply Query* from the Select menu instructs Works to search the database, using the most recent set of selection rules.

Combining Selection Rules

What if Lugosi's wants its promotion to feature movies starring the incomparable Annabelle Lee? Now you need to select records of movies made before 1959 and starring Annabelle Lee. You can have Works find records that meet this combination of criteria by putting comparison information in more than one field. You will key the expression <1959 in the Year field and Annabelle Lee's name in the Stars field.

The Query window lets you perform very specific searches, but your instructions must be precise. If you key just Annabelle Lee in the Stars field, Works will look for films starring Annabelle Lee and no one else. The presence of any additional stars' names in a record will cause Works to decide that the record does not match the selection rule. You want Works to find Annabelle Lee whether her name is alone in the field or embedded among the names of other movie stars. Works lets you do just that with **wildcard characters.** In a query formula that uses text, a question mark (?) stands for *any single character in that position, and an asterisk (*) stands for any character or combination of characters.* For example, the formula *kit?* would find *kit*, *kits*, or *kite*. The formula *kit** would find those entries plus *kitten*, *kittens*, *kittens and puppies*, *kitchen*, and so on. The formula **Annabelle Lee** tells Works to find the actress's name no matter what characters precede or follow it.

1. Choose *Query* from the View menu again. Works displays the Query window. The program has remembered the last selection rule you used, so *<1959* is still shown in the Year field, and you do not need to rekey it.
2. Highlight the Stars field.
3. Key *Annabelle Lee*, and then press Enter, as shown in Figure 6-15.
4. Press F10. Works searches through all the records and lists the movies made before 1959 and in which Annabelle Lee stars.

When you enter selection rules in two fields of the query window, you are instructing Works to find records that meet the first rule and the second rule. To be selected, a record must meet both criteria—as if the word *and* connected the two selection rules. When selection rules are combined, words like *and* are, in fact, called **connectors.**

Database programs like Works let you combine selection rules with a variety of different connectors. Suppose you want to find the movies which Bob Brown wrote or starred in, in other words, records which meet at least one of the criteria. Or, suppose you want to find the movies which Bob Brown starred in but did not write. *And, or,* and *not* are the most common connectors used to combine selection rules.

FIGURE 6-15
Combining selection rules.

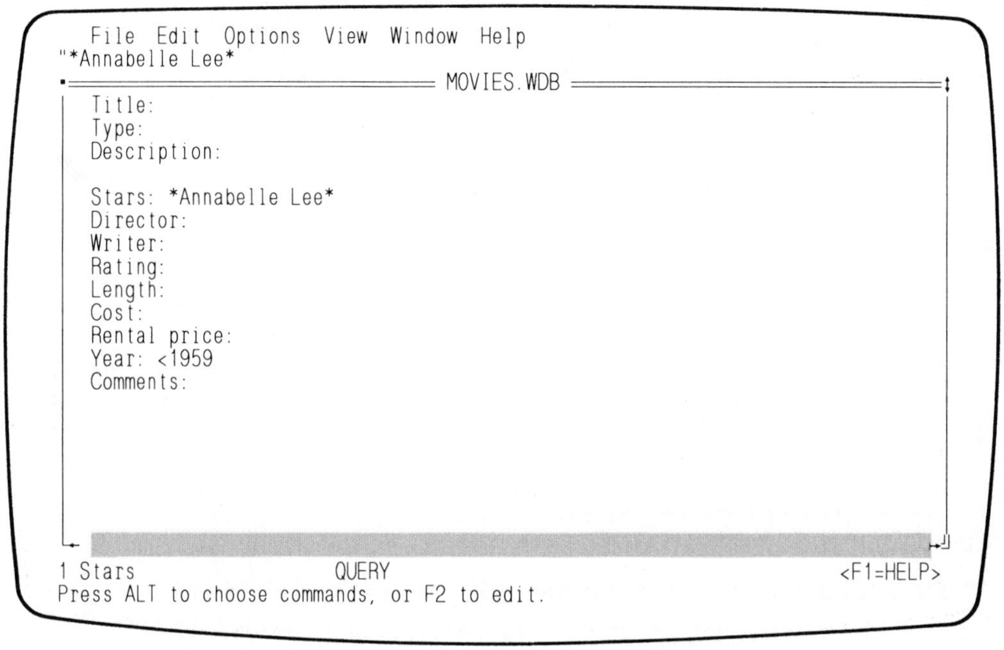

```
   File  Edit  Options  View  Window  Help
"*Annabelle Lee*
                              ═══════ MOVIES.WDB ═══════
  │  Title:
  │  Type:
  │  Description:
  │
  │  Stars: *Annabelle Lee*
  │  Director:
  │  Writer:
  │  Rating:
  │  Length:
  │  Cost:
  │  Rental price:
  │  Year: <1959
  │  Comments:
  │
  │
  └
  1 Stars                     QUERY                              <F1=HELP>
  Press ALT to choose commands, or F2 to edit.
```

Connecting criteria with *or*, and *not* in Works requires you to enter a formula. A formula begins with an equal sign, as in the Spreadsheet. For example, to locate films Bob Brown wrote or starred in, you would enter the following query formula in the Stars field of the Query window:

```
=="*Bob Brown*"|Writer="Brown, Bob"
```

Let's go over this formula step by step. The first equal sign tells Works that what follows is a formula rather than a simple entry. The second equal sign means that the contents of the Stars field must be equal to the contents of the set of quotation marks that follow. The quotes tell Works that the entry is text rather than numbers. (Most formulas involve numerical calculations.) The asterisks are wildcard characters that tell Works to disregard any information in the field that comes before or after the name *Bob Brown*. The symbol (|) stands for the connector *or*. *Writer* is the name of the Writer field, and *Brown, Bob* is the entry Works is to look for in the Writer field. Translated into plain English, the formula reads, *Locate records in which the Stars field contains Bob Brown or the Writer field equals Brown, Bob*. Now you can go ahead and perform the search.

1. Choose *Query* from the View menu. Works displays the Query window. The selection rules you used last time appear in the Year and Stars fields. Before you can enter the new formula, you need to erase the old selection rules.
2. Choose *Delete Query* from the Edit menu. Works erases the old entries.
3. In the Stars field key in the formula:

```
=="*Bob Brown*"|Writer="Brown, Bob"
```

(handwritten annotation: above the Back Slash)

(handwritten annotation: Stands for or connector together)

Be sure to enter the formula exactly the way it is printed here, beginning with two equal signs in a row, with no space between them.

4. Press Enter, and then press F10. If you have keyed the formula correctly, Works displays the six records it found. In each, Bob Brown is either the writer or one of the stars. (In some of the records, he is both.) If you see an error message, press Enter to clear it from the screen, and then go back and repeat Steps 1 through 4.
5. Choose *Show All Records* from the Select menu to return to the complete database.

```
    File  Edit  Options  View  Window  Help
=="*Bob Brown*"|Writer="Brown, Bob"
                                  = MOVIES.WDB =
    Title:
    Type:
    Description:

    Stars: =="*Bob Brown*"|Writer="Brown, Bob"
    Director:
    Writer:
    Rating:
    Length:
    Cost:
    Rental price:
    Year:
    Comments:




1 Stars                QUERY                                <F1=HELP>
Press ALT to choose commands, or F2 to edit.
```

FIGURE 6-16
Using the connector *or* to combine selection rules.

SAVING THE DATABASE FILE AND QUITTING WORKS

*S*ome database programs automatically save changes you make to the file as you work. Others, including Works, have a command for saving changes. Before you quit your work with the movies database, you should save the *Movies.WDB* file, so you do not lose the changes you have made. Rather than save changes in the original file, you should rename the file before you save it. In that way, you will have both the old and new versions on disk. To indicate that this is your version of the file, simply add your initials to the file name.

1. Choose *Save As* from the File menu. You see the file handling dialog box.
2. If the template disk is in drive A, key A:MovieXXX. If the template disk is in drive B, key B:MovieXXX. XXX should be replaced with your initials.
3. Press Enter.

With the file safely stored on disk, you can exit Works.

1. Choose *Exit Works* from the File menu. The Works screen disappears and you see the DOS prompt.
2. Remove the disks from the disk drives and put them in their envelopes.
3. Turn off the monitor and computer.

Good job. In this lesson, you have found your way around a database file, printed a record, arranged records in different ways, found records that met a single criterion, and selected records that met a combination of criteria. In the next lesson, you will practice updating a database and print a report.

Save As

KEY TERMS

comparison *MSW 99*
Comparison information *MSW 94*
connectors *MSW 99*
database management system *MSW 84*
entry *MSW 84*
field name *MSW 84*
fields *MSW 84*
formula bar *MSW 88*
Form view *MSW 88*

List view *MSW 88*
query *MSW 97*
query formulas *MSW 99*
records *MSW 84*
report *MSW 86*
selection rules *MSW 99*
sorting *MSW 93*
views *MSW 87*
wildcard character *MSW 99*

COMMANDS

Alt-V-Q then Alt-E-L (Delete Query)
Tab (Enter change in record)
Alt-V-F (Go to Form View)
Alt-V-Q (Go to Query View
Ctrl-Home (Go to the first entry in the first record)
Home (Go to the first entry in record)
Ctrl-End (Go to the last entry in the last record)
Ctrl-Right Arrow (Go to the last entry in the record)
Ctrl-Page Down (Go down one screen's worth of records in List View)
Alt-V-L (Go to List View)
Ctrl-Page Up (Go up one screen's worth of records in List View)
Alt-P-P (Print)
Shift-Print Screen (Print Screen)
F10 (Return to previous view from Query window)
F2 (Revise an entry)
Alt-F-A (Save As)
Alt-S-S (Search)
Alt-S-L (Show All Records)
Alt-S-O (Sort Records)
Alt-S-W (Switch Hidden Records)

REVIEW QUESTIONS

1. What are the three functions that can be performed with a database management system?
2. When you are looking at a record in the Form view, what command would you use to see the next record? What command would you use to let you revise an entry?
3. When you are looking at a single record in the Form view and want to see several records at once, what command would you use?
4. Are you likely to see the same fields in both Form and List views? Why or why not?
5. Why would you want to arrange a database file using two or more different fields at one time?
6. What are the differences between finding records with the *Search* command and using selection rules in the Query window?
7. What is the difference between combining selection rules with the connector *and* and the connector *or*?

8. How would you print a copy of a single record in a database?
9. What selection rule would you use to find movies that sell at Lugosi's for less than $25?
10. What is another word for selection rule?

APPLICATIONS

1. Open the *Staff.WDB* file from the template disk. The file is currently in order by last name. Perform the following tasks. Print a copy of the screen for each task if you have a printer attached to your computer.

    a. Find the record for Morris Yu, then display it in the Form view. (Hint: use his last name for the comparison information.)
    b. Switch to the List view. Rearrange the file so that it is grouped by city with the ZIP codes in order for each city.
    c. Rearrange the file so that it is in chronological order by hire date.

2. Open the *Staff.WDB* file from the template disk. Sarah Lugosi wants to know which employees have over one week's vacation time saved up, so that she can send them a note reminding them that they have been working hard enough and should take some time off. The Vacation Hrs field lists the number of vacation hours for each employee. One week's vacation is listed as 40 hours, so employees with more than that will be informed that they should take their vacations now.

    Print a copy of the screen after you perform each step.

    a. Use the Query window to select records of employees with more than 40 hours of vacation time.
    b. Arrange the selected records so that they are in alphabetical order by last name.
    c. Select records for employees whose vacation hours are over 40 and who live in Fairfax.

3. Open the file named *PT.WDB* from the template disk. This database is a list of the elements in the periodic table. Perform the following tasks, and make a screen printout of the results of each task.

    a. Rearrange the file so that it is in alphabetical order under the field Element.
    b. Switch to Form view, then use the *Search* command to find praseodymium.
    c. Switch back to List view. Select the records that contain the words *rare earth* in the Notes field.
    d. Select the records for the elements with an atomic weight that is greater than 100.

Working with a Database

OBJECTIVES

- Explain why it is important to keep database files up to date.
- Change an entry in a database file.
- Delete a record.
- Insert a new record.
- Copy an entry.
- Fill entries.
- Explain the purpose of database reports.
- Produce a report.

UPDATING A DATABASE FILE

Organizations thrive on accurate records. For this reason, a database file is almost never complete. Every day something may change that affects the contents of almost any file. In order for database files to remain accurate, they must be changed. At Lugosi's Classic Video Store, a new employee may be hired, a copy of a videotape in stock may be sold, or a supplier may move to a new address. So, to keep their files up to date, the store must add the new employee's record to the employee list, adjust the number of copies for the tape, and change the supplier's address. Even if no new changes are required, the thousands of entries in a file are likely to contain some mistakes that must be corrected. All of these changes require **updating** the file—bringing it up to date.

A database program like the Works Database tool makes adding, changing, and removing information from a file easy. You can update a file at any time to keep your records accurate. After you make changes, the *Sort Records* command lets you arrange the records in the proper order. Once the information has been updated, it is necessary to communicate the information to other people. Having up-to-date files is not very useful if you have no way of showing the information to people who need it but have no access to computers. The solution is to produce a printed version of information in the file—a **report.** Reports provide a printed record of your changes and can be distributed easily to anyone who needs access to the information in the file.

In this lesson of the Works tutorial you will practice updating a file for Lugosi's Classic Video Store. The file is a list of suppliers to the store. You will change entries, copy an entry, fill a column of entries, remove a record, and insert a new record. Then you will produce a report from the updated file.

FIGURE 7-1
Database programs make it easy for organizations to update their files to reflect changing data.

CHANGING AN ENTRY

A database file for a large organization may contain thousands or even millions of records, and some of these records will probably contain mistakes that need to be corrected—perhaps a misspelling, an incorrect date, or an incorrect number. Other records may contain information that is simply out of date and must be deleted or changed to reflect the way things are now. For example, Lugosi's maintains an inventory file to keep track of the products on hand at each store. The entries for the number of products in stock changes every time an item is sold or new items are purchased. So, even if all the data in the file has been entered accurately, some of the data will change, and the records in the file must reflect these changes. A database program must allow for both types of changes: correcting mistakes and keeping track of the latest information. One of the most important features of a database program is that it lets you easily update files, including the ability to change information, correct errors, or completely replace incorrect entries.

In Lesson 6 you learned how to edit an entry to correct typing errors. In this lesson, you will practice some other ways to change an entry.

Deleting an Entry

The information in an entry may be garbage. In that case, the entry can be deleted in its entirety. A new field for listing credit ratings was added to Lugosi's file of suppliers. Although credit rating information has not yet been entered in the database, someone has keyed a stray entry in the field by mistake, and you need to delete it.

1. Start up Works and open the *Vendor.WDB* file from the template disk. Works displays the file in List view, as shown in Figure 7-2.
2. Highlight the Rating field in row 1. Because the width of the field is narrower than the field name, not all of the field name is visible. The entry in the field is *c*.
3. Choose *Clear* from the Edit menu. Works erases the contents of the field, so the entry is blank. You can also erase an entry by pressing Backspace.

Clear

FIGURE 7-2
A database file in need of corrections.

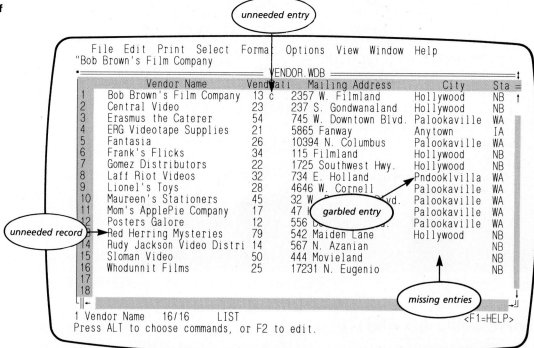

Replacing an Incorrect Entry

When an entry is completely wrong, replacing all the information may be easier than editing the entry. For example, look at the record for Laff Riot Videos. The city listed in the record has an odd-looking name: Pndooklvilla. Sarah Lugosi had written the original vendor record on paper. Whoever entered this record into the database probably misread the name of the city that Ms. Lugosi had written. The city is not *Pndooklvilla*, but *Palookaville*. You will have to correct that error. You can replace the incorrect entry with the correct one, simply by typing in the correct information.

1. Tab over to the City field, and then use the Down Arrow to highlight the entry in row 8.
2. Key `Palookaville` and press Enter. The updated entry completely replaces the incorrect one.

Keying replaces any highlighted entry, so it is easy to wipe out an entry by mistake. Hit a stray key, and you will find that letter occupying the space some valuable data occupied a moment ago. Remember, though, that whatever you key is not entered in the database until you move the highlight—by pressing Enter, Tab, or another key that moves you around the screen. If the field you have replaced by mistake is still highlighted, press Esc and the original entry will reappear. If you have already moved on, you will need to reenter the information.

Congratulations! You have corrected two entries, the first by using the *Clear* command to erase an entry, the second by replacing the entry. Remember that you can also press F2 and edit an entry in the formula bar, as you learned in Lesson 6.

COPYING AN ENTRY

Copy

Sometimes a file has many entries that contain the same information. Rather than making each entry from scratch, you can copy the information with the *Copy* command. The Shift and F7 keys together let you enter the information you copied as many times as you like.

1. Highlight the entry *Hollywood* in the City field in row 13.
2. Choose *Copy* from the Edit menu. The message line instructs you to select a new location and press Enter. That means to highlight the location where you want to insert the information you copied.
3. Highlight the blank City entry in the next row, and then press Enter. Works inserts the name *Hollywood*.
4. Move the highlight down to the next row and press Shift-F7. Works inserts *Hollywood* there, as well. Repeat this step to insert the city name in row 16.

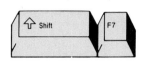

**Repeats Copying
an Entry**

```
     File  Edit  Print  Select  Format  Options  View  Window  Help
  "Hollywood
  •                        ════════ VENDOR.WDB ════════                      ‡
               Vendor Name        VendRati   Mailing Address        City     Sta ═
   1   Bob Brown's Film Company   13    2357 W. Filmland        Hollywood   NB  ↑
   2   Central Video              23    237 S. Gondwanaland     Hollywood   NB
   3   Erasmus the Caterer        54    745 W. Downtown Blvd.   Palookaville WA
   4   ERG Videotape Supplies     21    5865 Fanway             Anytown     IA
   5   Fantasia                   26    10394 N. Columbus       Palookaville WA
   6   Frank's Flicks             34    115 Filmland            Hollywood   NB
   7   Gomez Distributors         22    1725 Southwest Hwy.     Hollywood   NB
   8   Laff Riot Videos           32    734 E. Holland          Palookaville WA
   9   Lionel's Toys              28    4646 W. Cornell         Palookaville WA
  10   Maureen's Stationers       45    32 W. Downtown Blvd.    Palookaville WA
  11   Mom's ApplePie Company     17    47 Homecooked Lane      Palookaville WA
  12   Posters Galore             12    556 Downtown Blvd.      Palookaville WA
  13   Red Herring Mysteries      79    542 Maiden Lane         Hollywood   NB
  14   Rudy Jackson Video Distri  14    5⌐─ entries copied  ──►Hollywood   NB
  15   Sloman Video               50    ( with the Copy      ──►Hollywood   NB
  16   Whodunnit Films            25    ⌐  command           ──►Hollywood   NB
  17
  18
  └‖←                                                                      ─‖
  16 City          16/16      LIST                              <F1=HELP>
  Press ALT to choose commands, or F2 to edit.
```

FIGURE 7-3
Copying entries.

Copying can save you a lot of time when you are creating a database file. You will use it for files that repeat the same entry in many records. You are not limited to copying a single entry. The *Cells* command on the Select menu lets you highlight a range of entries, and you can then copy all of them. But when you need to enter the same information in a whole row or column, filling provides an even faster method.

FILLING AN ENTRY

Filling is a method of copying information into a range of entries in one step. Instead of copying the information, highlighting each entry where you want to insert it, and pressing Shift-F7, you can highlight the entries first and copy the information to all of them automatically. The *Cells* command lets you highlight a series of entries. Then the *Fill* command tells Works to copy the information in the first highlighted entry and insert it in all the other entries.

Sarah Lugosi has asked you to enter information in the Vendor file for the new Ratings field. These are the credit ratings of all the vendors. Looking up the ratings, you find that all the companies are rated A + , so you need to insert A + in the Rating field in each record.

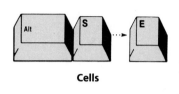

Cells

1. In row 1, highlight the Rating field.
2. Key A+, and then press Enter.
3. Choose *Cells* from the Select menu.

FIGURE 7-4
Selected cells.

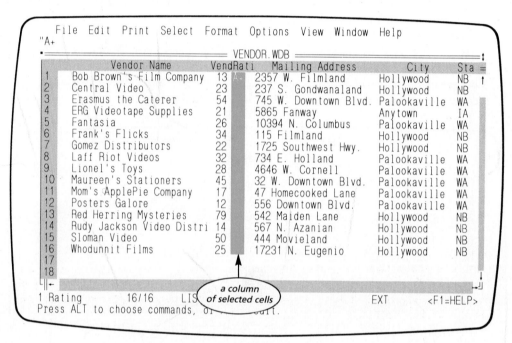

Fill Down

4. Press the Down Arrow until rows 1 through 16 of the Rating column are highlighted, as shown in Figure 7-4.
5. Choose *Fill Down* from the Edit menu. Works automatically copies the first entry and inserts the information in all the entries, so they all contain A + .

Database programs like Works let you Fill Right as well as Fill Down. The feature is particularly useful when long formulas that are complicated to key need to be entered over and over again.

Now the file is almost complete—in fact, a bit too complete, since one of the records is out of date.

REMOVING A RECORD FROM A FILE

*S*ometimes you need to remove a complete record from a file. For instance, Red Herring Mysteries, which used to supply videotapes of classic mystery movies to Lugosi's, has gone out of business. Therefore, the record of it in the list of vendors is no longer required. Rather than remove the record one entry at a time, you can use the *Delete Record/Field* command to remove the record all at once. This command lets you remove any highlighted records, so you could use it to remove a series of more than one record.

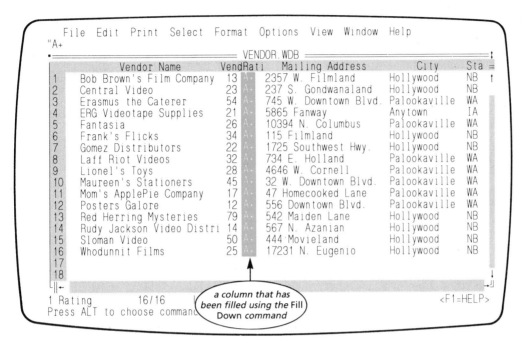

FIGURE 7-5
A filled column.

1. Highlight the record for Red Herring Mysteries. You do not need to select the entire record; you can highlight any entry in row 13.
2. Choose *Delete Record/Field* from the Edit menu. Works displays a dialog box for selecting whether to delete the highlighted record or the highlighted field, as shown in Figure 7-6. The preset option is *Record*, which is what you want to delete.

Delete Record/Field

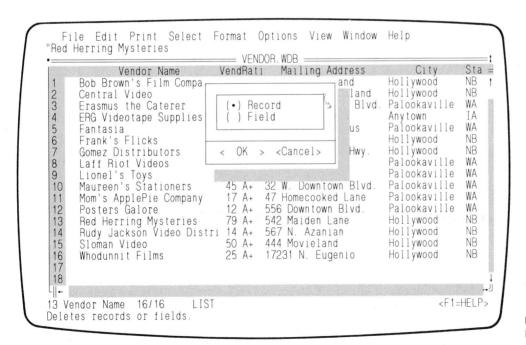

FIGURE 7-6
Delete Record/Field dialog box.

3. Press Enter to delete the record. The record disappears from the screen.

The record is removed from the computer's memory. When you save the file, the record will no longer be included on the disk. Once you have deleted a record and saved the file, the only way to get that record back is by reentering the data. Always double-check before deleting records to make sure that you really want to do so and that you have an entry for the correct record highlighted.

INSERTING A NEW RECORD

Just as some records must be removed to keep a file up to date, other records must be added. For example, Lugosi's has just found a new supplier that specializes in films thought to be lost forever, Packard's Lost Treasures. The record is shown in Figure 7-7, a paper form used by Lugosi's before they automated their records with the database. You need to add the record to the Vendor file.

FIGURE 7-7
Vendor Record Form.

> LUGOSI'S CLASSIC VIDEO STORE
>
> **VENDOR RECORD**
>
> Vendor Name _Packard's Lost Treasures_   Vendor# _83_
>
> Mailing Address _5768 W. Eldorado_ Street Address _____
> _Hollywood, NB_ _____
> _68842-1234_ _____
>
> Phone _(308) 555-8384_
>
> Suppliers of _Lost Films, Classics_
>
> Major Titles _____
> _____
>
> Category _Videos_

You can add records to the database in either view. In the List view, the *Insert Record/Field* command lets you add new records. In the Form view, you can add a new record with the *Insert Record* command. (You can add a new field in the Form view just by typing the field name followed by a colon.) In either view, Works will insert the new record above the selected record. After you finish inserting records, you can rearrange the file to put all the records into proper order. You will add the record and enter information to it in the Form view.

1. Switch to the Form view. (You can use the *Form* command on the View menu or press F9.)
2. Choose *Insert Record* from the edit menu. Works displays a blank record form. Since the form is identical in all the records except that this one is blank, you might think that Works has erased the entries you were just looking at, but that record is still part of the database.
3. If the Vendor Name field is not highlighted, use Shift-Tab to highlight it.

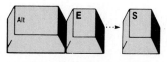

Insert Record—Form View

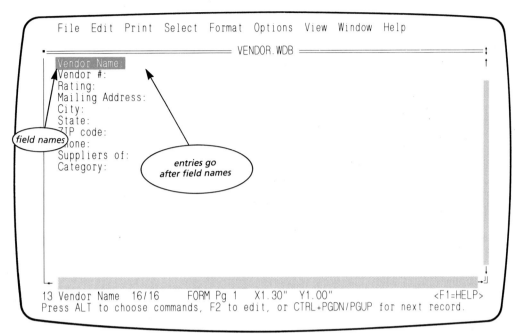

FIGURE 7-8
New record form.

4. Key Packard's Lost Treasures for the first entry. If you make an error, correct it with the Backspace key before accepting your entry. (If you notice an error after accepting the entry, replace the entry as you did earlier in this lesson.)
5. Press Tab. This accepts your entry and highlights the next field.
6. Key the entries for the other categories for this new vendor as shown below, pressing Tab after each entry except the one for the last field. After the last entry, press Enter. That way, Works will not display a new blank record.

After you key the last entry, *Videos*, your screen should look like Figure 7-9.

```
  File  Edit  Print  Select  Format  Options  View  Window  Help
"Videos
▪════════════════════════ VENDOR.WDB ═══════════════════════╤┊
│  Vendor Name: Packard's Lost Treasures                     ↑
│  Vendor #:    83
│  Rating: Bad
│  Mailing Address: 5768 W. Eldorado
│  City: Hollywood
│  State: NB
│  ZIP code: 68842-1234
│  Phone: 308/555-8384
│  Suppliers of: Los films, classics
│  Category: Videos
│
│
│
│
│
│
│
│
│
│
│
│
└                                                            ↲
│▒▒▒▒▒▒▒▒▒▒▒▒▒▒▒▒▒▒▒▒▒▒▒▒▒▒▒▒▒▒▒▒▒▒▒▒▒▒▒▒▒▒▒▒▒▒▒▒▒▒▒▒▒▒▒▒▒▒▒↲
13 Category    16/16    FORM Pg 1   X1.30"  Y2.50"      <F1=HELP>
Press ALT to choose commands, F2 to edit, or CTRL+PGDN/PGUP for next record.
```

FIGURE 7-9
A new record.

7. Switch to the List view. The new record shows up above the row where your highlight had been before you inserted the new record.

When you make a new database file in the next lesson, you will enter all the records using a blank form, as you did for this record. As you finish each record, press Tab. You then move to a new blank form ready for entering the next record. Whenever you finish entering all the new records into a file, you can use the *Sort Records* command to put the file back in order. Try it now, since the new record may be out of order.

8. Move the highlight to the Vendor Name field.
9. Choose *Sort Records* from the Select menu. Works displays the Sort Records dialog box, as shown in Figure 7-10. Since you highlighted the Vendor Name field before choosing the *Sort Records* command, that field name is already entered as the field by which to arrange the records.

FIGURE 7-10
The Sort Records dialog box.

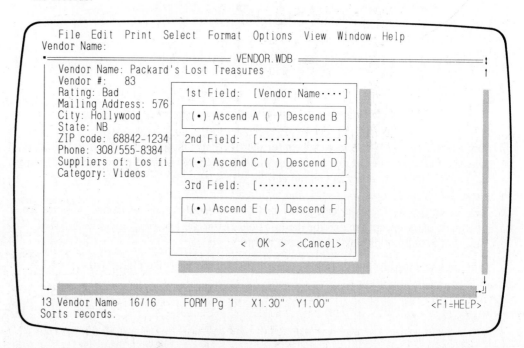

10. Press Enter. The file is now back in alphabetical order.

SAVING THE FILE WITH A NEW NAME

ow that you have finished making changes to the file, save your changes so that they will be stored safely on a disk. Use the *Save As* command, as you did in Lesson 6, and add your initials after the file name.

1. Choose *Save As* from the File menu.
2. Change the name of the file to *VendXXX.WDB* before you press Enter. Replace XXX with your own initials.
3. Press Enter.

With the file safely stored away, you are ready to try printing a report. Saving your work is particularly important before you print, because computer trouble occurs most often when printing. The report you print will give you a printed copy of the changed file.

PRINTING A LIST

Reports give you a printed record of some or all of the contents of a database file. A report can be more than a simple list of all the records in a file. In fact, one file can be used to produce any number of completely different reports. Reports can vary both in content (the records that are included) and the arrangement of data (which categories are included and how they appear on the page). For example, one report produced from the Vendors file may contain only names and addresses, while another could include all the categories in the file. The two reports could also list different sets of records from the same file.

A **report definition** determines what will be printed in a report. Every report, no matter how simple or complex, must have a report definition that tells the computer what information

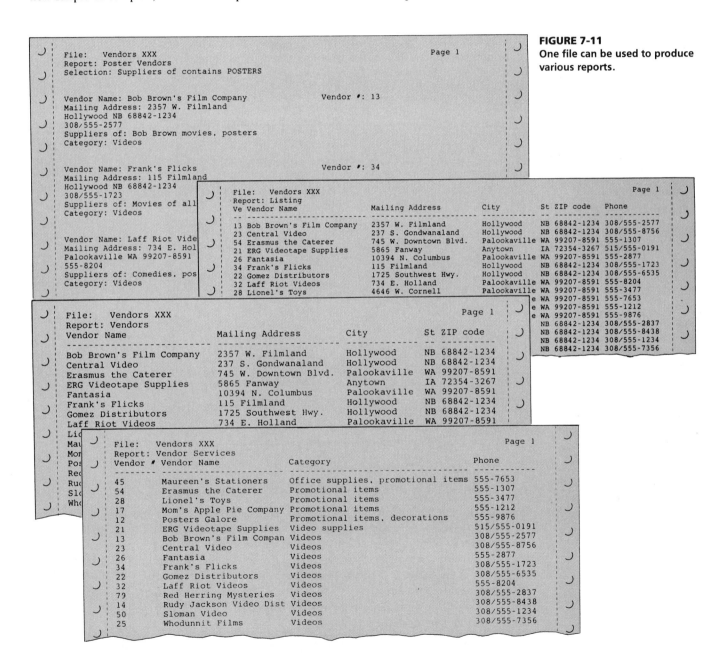

FIGURE 7-11
One file can be used to produce various reports.

to include and how to arrange it. When you choose to print a report, you can make a new report definition or use one that has already been prepared and saved with the file on the disk. Each file can have several report definitions, and you can name them to tell them apart.

Getting a Report Definition

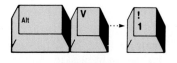

**Listing—A
Report Definition**

For this report you will use a definition named *Listing* that has already been prepared. It prints a list of the entries in the vendor file, arranged in a convenient order for looking up names and addresses. Works displays each report definition in its own separate view, so the report definition is listed on the View menu.

1. Choose *Listing* from the View menu. You see page 1 of the printed report, as shown in Figure 7-12. Works displays the separate pages of the report, and you can flip though them by pressing Enter. This screen version of the report is useful for a last minute check for errors, but it does not show a good likeness of the printed version.

```
LUGOSI'S CLASSIC VIDEO STORE
VENDORS LIST

NAME                        ADDRESS

Bob Brown's Film Company    2357 W. Filmland
Central Video               237 S. Gondwanaland
Erasmus the Caterer         745 W. Downtown Blvd.
ERG Videotape Supplies      5865 Fanway
Fantasia                    10394 N. Columbus
Frank's Flicks              115 Filmland
Gomez Distributors          1725 Southwest Hwy.
Laff Riot Videos            734 E. Holland
Lionel's Toys               4646 W. Cornell
Maureen's Stationers        32 W. Downtown Blvd.
Mom's ApplePie Company      47 Homecooked Lane
Packard's Lost Treasures    5768 W. Eldorado
Page 1                           REPORT
Press ENTER to continue, ESC to cancel.
```

FIGURE 7-12
Page 1 of a Report view.

2. Press Esc to display the report definition itself.

The report definition, as shown in Figure 7-13, displays each of the elements of the report. There are rows for specifying what will appear at the head of the report, such as a title or date; rows for specifying what will appear at the top of each page; a row for specifying what entries from the database to print; and rows for specifying summary information that will appear at the end of the report. This report definition instructs Works to print the store name and the title *Vendors List* at the top of page 1. Underneath column headings, the report prints all the vendor names and all the mailing addresses on page 1. You will learn more about report definitions in the next lesson.

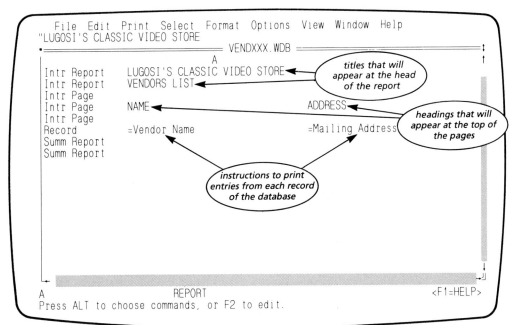

FIGURE 7-13
A Report definition—elements of the report.

Previewing Your Report

You can get an idea of how the printed page will look with the *Preview* command. This command displays a small image of a printed page on the screen. **Previewing** a report before you print it is a good way to check that the report appears the way you want it. In fact, when you create a report definition, you should switch back and forth frequently between previewing and the Report view.

1. Choose *Preview* from the print menu, then press Enter to accept the preset options. The computer churns for a few moments while Works builds an image of the report; then an image of page 1 appears on the screen, as shown in Figure 7-14.
2. To see each of the next two pages, press Page Down.

When previewing, the words are hardly large enough to make out, and you cannot edit anything. You can see, though, that the entries fit on the page without running into one another, and that the overall appearance of the report is pleasing. Now you are ready to print the report.

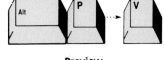

Preview

Printing Your Report

As you preview your report, you can see from the instructions on the screen that you can print the report just by pressing P.

1. Make sure that your computer is connected to a printer and the printer is ready to print.
2. Press P. Works immediately prints one copy of the report.

Since the records contain too many fields to fit across one page, database programs like Works print the first couple of fields for all the records, then print the next set of fields, and so on until all the fields have been printed. Your report is three pages long.

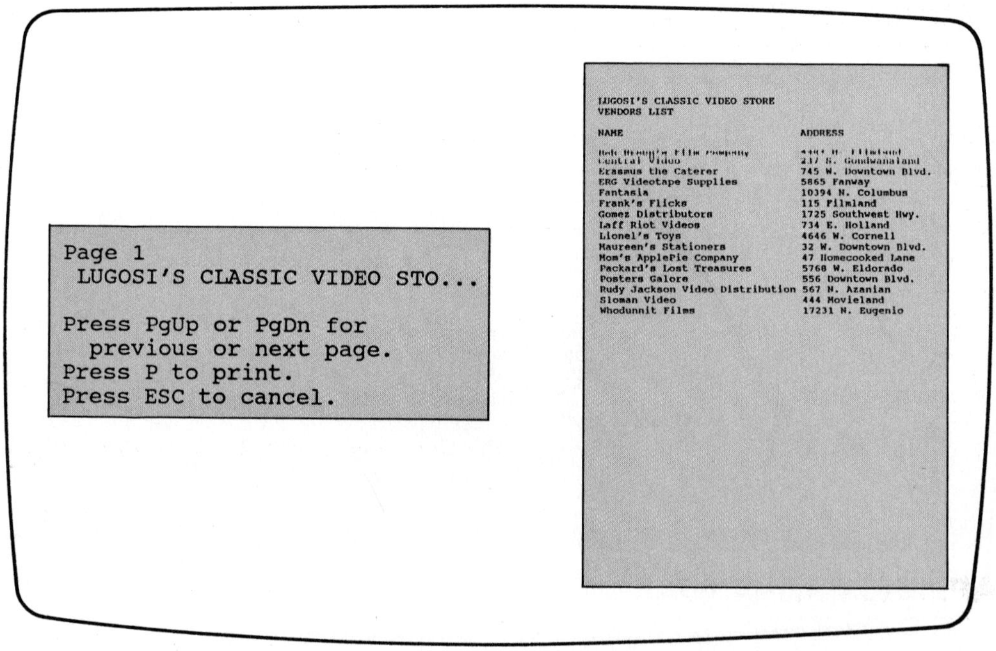

FIGURE 7-14
A Report preview screen.

Good work! You have updated a file, made corrections, deleted a record, and added a new record. You have also printed a report for a permanent copy of the changes. Now you can save the file and quit Works. In the next lesson, "Making a New Database File," you will plan and create a new file from scratch.

KEY TERMS

filling   *MSW 107*
previewing   *MSW 115*
report   *MSW 104*
report definition   *MSW 114*
updating   *MSW 104*

COMMANDS

Alt-S-E (Cells)
Alt-E-E (Clear)
Alt-E-C (Copy)
Alt E-D (Delete Record/Field)
Alt-E-F (Fill Down)
Alt-E-S (Insert Record—Form View)
Alt-V-1 (Listing—a report definition)
Alt-P-V (Preview)
Shift-F7 (Repeats copying an entry)

REVIEW QUESTIONS

1. Why would you need to update a database file?
2. How would you correct a misspelled word in an entry in the Works database?
3. What effect does typing have when an entry is highlighted? How can you recover an entry when you have replaced it by mistake?
4. Why would you want to delete an entire record?
5. Can you do anything about a record that you accidentally inserted in the wrong order?
6. When you add records, do you add them in Form view or in List view?
7. Why copy entries instead of entering them separately for each record? What command do you use to copy a whole column of entries automatically?
8. Suppose you want a list of vendors who supply videos and another list of vendors who supply promotional items? Can you print these as two different lists? How?
9. Why allow different report definitions in a database program? Why not simply print a list of everything in the file?
10. Why should you preview a report before you print it?

APPLICATIONS

1. Open the *Mags.WDB* file from the template disk. It contains a list of Lugosi's Classic Video Store magazine subscriptions. Some of the information in the file is wrong or out of date. Make the following changes to the file:

   a. Lugosi's no longer subscribes to *Time Magazine*. Delete the record.
   b. Correct the misspelling in the record for *Video Store News*.
   c. The correct price for *Movie Guide Magazine* is $24.25 for 12 issues.

   Save your changes with your initials added to the end of the file name, and print a report using the *Listing* report format provided. This report prints the titles, prices, and renewal dates for the store's magazine subscriptions.

2. Open the *Books.WDB* file from the template disk. Switch to the Form view and insert the following record.

   ```
   Title: Art of Bob Brown, The
   Author: Mussorgsky, Modestina
   Publisher: Brainpower Press
   Year: 1989
   Description: Explains how Bob Brown became a great actor.
   Subject: Movies
   ```

   Return to List view and arrange the file so that it is in alphabetical order under the Title field. Using the *Fill Down* command, copy the Subject entry for the first record so that it appears in all the other records.

   When you have finished making all the changes, save the file under a new name with your initials added to the file name. Print the file, using the report format named *Standard*. This report lists the title, authors, and year of each book. Quit Works if you are finished using the program.

3. Open the *Cities.WDB* file from the template disk. This file lists the largest cities in the world, based on the most recent census data or estimates. Unfortunately, it contains several errors. Your job is to correct these errors. Complete the following steps:

   a. The population of Karachi is 5,005,000. Correct the entry.
   b. Peking is now spelled *Beijing*. Correct the entry.
   c. The country listed for New York City should be USA. Correct the entry.
   d. Palookaville is not one of the largest cities in the world. Delete the record.
   e. Save the file with your initials added to the file name.

   After you finish making these corrections, rearrange the file on the Population category so that it is in reverse numerical order (from 9 to 0). Then print the file using the *Pop* report definition. Quit Works when you are finished.

Making a New Database

OBJECTIVES

- Plan the requirements for a new database.
- Determine fields.
- Develop the layout for the Form and List views.
- Make a new Database file.
- Set up fields.
- Add records.
- Change the layout of the screen.
- Print the records.

PLANNING A NEW DATABASE

Sarah Lugosi has asked you to make a new database file so that the computer can be used to take customer orders. Processing orders with the old paper order forms is becoming too cumbersome to accommodate the increase in business at the store. A new, computerized order form could save a lot of storage space and make it faster to serve customers.

FIGURE 8-1
A database file is ideal for keeping track of orders.

So far, you have worked with files that have already been created for you on the template disk. When you opened a database file from a disk, it appeared on the screen with fields set up and records already entered in the file. A new database has none of this information. You must decide for yourself what kind of information should be stored and how people will look for it. You must also decide how to divide the information into different categories—that determines what fields to set up. Doing it correctly, so that the Database can be used most effectively for both storing and retrieving information, takes planning. You already know much about using a database. With the files on the template disk, you have found, arranged, selected, removed, and corrected records. You have also already printed a list. Now you are ready to plan a new Database, developing fields of your own that you will enter into a brand new file.

Planning a database can be fun. You get to experiment with ideas about what to include and how the file will be used. Then you decide on the specific categories to include and their arrangement on the screen. Finally, you can test out your plan by making the file and entering sample records. Sometimes it will work the way you think; other times you may need to make changes to the structure of the Database that make it more usable.

In this lesson, you will make a new Database file for entering customer orders at Lugosi's Classic Video Store. You will plan the Database, make a new file with the Works Database tool, and enter some records and print them.

Figuring Out What to Include in the File

Before you can make a new database file, you need to know what you want to include in the file: the general types of information required, the kind of entries, how the information will eventually be arranged and presented, and how records might be selected. In other words, before you make the file, you should know what it is you want to do with it—the kind of information that people will want to get out of the database and how they will want to look at it.

The form Sarah Lugosi has asked you to create sounds simple enough—something to keep track of customer orders. To start, ask yourself what information is required. Then see if you can break down the information further, being as specific as possible about each type of information to be recorded. In the end, you will have come up with names of categories to include in the file. After you have decided on tentative categories, you can whittle them down to the minimum number of categories that will meet your goals.

Listing the Subjects of the File

What do you need when a customer places an order? A list of topics might look like the following:

- The current date
- The customer's name
- The customer's account number
- The customer's address
- The title of the movie
- The date on which the movie should be returned
- A space for items other than movies (in case customers buy a blank tape or another item)
- The price of the item

You might be able to think of other subjects that could be included, but these will do for a start. Take a look at the subjects. What about them could be broken into more specific subjects? That is the next step in planning a database.

Breaking the Subjects Down into Smaller Components

When you are planning a database, you should try to think of as many tentative fields as possible, so that you are sure that you will not leave any useful and relevant information out of the database. You can always refine the number and names of fields later. Your goal is to determine the exact reasons why people will be using the database. What kind of information will they want to find in it? How will they want to arrange it? What different types of reports would be most useful? What categories must be included to make all of this possible?

Remember that the database is sorted by field and that you also select records by looking in particular fields for the information contained there. So, the fields are the main building blocks of a database. You should divide the file up into fields that are as specific as possible. Take a look at all the subjects in the list and see if they can be made more specific.

Take the date fields, for instance. These are examples of subjects that are as simple as they need to be. The dates could be broken down into smaller components, like the month, day, and year. However, in database programs like the Database tool in Works, you can search for a date by month or year without breaking up the date field into its components. So, each type of date that you need to record can be kept as one field.

Other types of information can be more difficult to deal with. What about the customer's name? It seems simple enough. You might record their names like this:

Sally Baker
Jane Fischer
Roger Smith

You are more likely to want to sort the file by last name than by first name—a very common arrangement. To be able to sort by last name, you could enter the last name first, followed by a comma and the first name, like this:

Baker, Sally
Fischer, Jane
Smith, Roger

However, you may not even want the first and last names in the same field. For example, with integration, you may want to take the names out of the Database file to use in a word processor document. If you were to use the names in form letters addressed to specific customers, you would want to have the last name in a separate field. Then you could begin letters with a salutation like this: *Dear Ms. Baker* or *Dear Mr. Smith*.

Why not split the name into two fields: the first name and last name? That would let you use the names separately in form letters, reports, and selections. Suppose you have a promotion and you want to mail out form letters. With the names in separate fields, you could send formal letters to potential customers using their last names (*Dear Ms. Baker*), and less formal letters to good customers, addressing them by their first name (*Dear Jane*).

So, the date fields should remain as single fields, but the name category should be divided into two separate fields, one for the first name and one for the last name. What about the field for movies that are rented? Many customers will want to rent more than one tape at a time. You have several different possibilities here. You can enter one rental per record or enter many movies in several categories per record. With the latter arrangement, each record could contain all the movies each customer rents at one time. You would need to enter the customer's name and account number only once per transaction. But how many movie fields should you include? If you have room for three movies per record, a customer who rents four movies would require two records to keep track of the transaction. And what if the movies have different prices? That would require a separate price entry for each movie entry. Then there is the issue of keeping track of the other products a customer purchases. Do you have separate price entries for each of these, too?

Testing the two alternatives with some made-up records can help you determine the best one. The following chart illustrates the possibilities and how each would be used to record the rental of four movies and the purchase of one product.

ALTERNATIVE 1: One record per rental or purchase.

Transaction recording four rentals and one purchase	
Record 1 Movie: Bad Bob Other: - Price: $2	**Record 4** Movie: Bad Bob at Black Rock Other: - Price: $1
Record 2 Movie: Big Day for Bad Bob Other: - Price: $3	**Record 5** Movie: - Other: Blank Tape Price: $5
Record 3 Movie: Bad Day for Bad Bob Other: - Price: $2	

ALTERNATIVE 2: One record for up to three movies and one purchase.

Transaction recording four rentals and one purchase	
Record 1 Movie1: Bad Bob Price1: $2 Movie2: Big Day for Bad Bob Price2: $3 Movie3: Bad Bob at Black Rock Price3: $1 Other: Blank Tape Price4: $5	**Record 2** Movie1: Bad Day for Bad Bob Price1: $2 Movie2: - Price2: - Movie3: - Price3: - Other: - Price4: -

You can see that the first alternative has fewer categories per record, since each rental or purchase takes up one record. This alternative may require more records per transaction. The second alternative works well for up to three rentals, since they all fit in one record, but will require additional records for anything over three rentals and one purchase. The second alternative also requires more fields in each record. Both alternatives record the information adequately, and the choice depends on how well each meets the needs of Lugosi's Classic Video Store. The average customer at the store rents only one movie at a time, many rent two, a few three, and a tiny number even more. For now, try the second alternative—having separate fields for up to three movies and an additional field for other products—and see if it works out.

Now take a look at the customer address field. Splitting addresses into four fields would make searching easier: Street Address, City, State, and ZIP Code. This will let you select records by area to analyze what parts of the city or state have high concentrations of customers. You can use information like this in determining where to expand or promote the business. That adds four more fields to the list of subjects.

The list of subjects seems to have expanded significantly:

Date	Movie1
First Name	Price1
Last Name	Movie2
Account Number	Price2
Street Address	Movie3
City	Price3
State	Other
ZIP Code	Price4
	Date Due

Once again, you may be able to think of additional fields, like separate due dates for each movie. However, these seem to be sufficient for now. You are ready for the next step in planning a database.

Simplifying the Fields

Once you have chosen tentative fields for the database, you can start thinking about how they should be arranged in the layouts of both the Form view and the List view. At the same time, you can eliminate or add fields as necessary. As you go through this process, you may change your original plan for the database because you come upon another idea that seems better.

Determining How Information Will Be Entered into the File   First of all, how do you want the clerks to enter the information? They could enter it on forms in Form view, or they could enter it in List view. The easiest way to enter information for a transaction is probably in Form view because it would be very similar to using the paper forms that everyone is already familiar with. Take that approach for this file.

Determining How the Information Will Be Used   You should also consider how you might want to look at the information after it has been entered into the file. In other words, what sort of analysis might you perform on the file and what sort of reports would you need?

How will you use the information in this file? Of course, the database will be used to keep track of all rentals and purchases at the store. The database could also be used to analyze sales. For example, you might want to see what type of movie each customer prefers to rent, like chillers or thrillers, so that you could send them a notice when you promote that type of movie. Or you might want to see which movie of each type rent best—which are most popular. These are two purposes for which you might use the file, and they point out something interesting. You have no field to specify the type of movie rented. You might want to add this as a new field. Since you are currently considering separate entries in the record for each movie and each movie's price, you would also have to include separate entries for each movie's type, increasing the number of fields by three:

Date	Movie1
First Name	Price1
Last Name	Type1
Account Number	Movie2
Street Address	Price2
City	Type2
State	Movie3
ZIP Code	Price3
	Type3
	Other
	Price4
	Date Due

Reviewing Your Field Selections   With all of these fields, each record is going to look rather complicated. You may have trouble analyzing this file with record-selection rules because it is too complicated. For example, to get a list of all customers who rented *Bad Day for Bad Bob*, you would have to search in all three movie fields: Movie1, Movie2, and Movie3. To search for rentals of a particular type of movie, you would also have to search in three different fields: Type1, Type2, and Type3. In addition, with a total now of 20 fields, it would be difficult to include most of the categories in a List view report without making some categories very short, taking others out, or having the report spill over onto several pages. You should consider combining or eliminating some fields.

To decide which fields to change or remove, ask yourself some questions. How will users enter information? If having all of these fields in each record makes the form confusing, maybe it would be better to have one record for each movie that is rented. This step removes six fields from the list: two each for movie names, type, and price. The new plan would easily meet the needs of most customers, who only rent one movie at a time. For additional orders, clerks would simply use an additional record.

A separate record for each movie would also let you copy information between records if you have one customer checking out several movies. For example, if the customer wants to check out five movies, you could enter all the information for the first record in Form view; then skip over duplicate information like the name, address, and date in the other records, entering only the information about each movie. Then you could switch over to List view and copy or fill down the duplicate information, saving time in data entry.

Another thing to consider in planning a new file is whether some of the information is available elsewhere. For example, the current list of fields for this file includes the customer's address, city, state, and ZIP code. Would that be necessary if you also had a separate file only for customers' records that included their addresses? If the information is available elsewhere, you may not need to include it here. Lugosi's has a separate file of customer addresses. So, in this file used for recording orders, only the customer's name and account number are really necessary. Other customer information will be available in the customer file whenever needed. That removes three more categories from the record. The total number of categories is down to nine—much more manageable:

Date
First Name
Last Name
Account Number
Movie
Type
Other
Price
Date Due

This new set of categories will make it easier to enter records and also will make searching and selecting more efficient, allowing for reports that are easier and faster to read and analyze. Because the management of Lugosi's Classic Video Store will be able to use the information better, this well-designed file could also lead to more profits.

Testing Your Assumptions

After you decide on what you want to include in each record, you should test your assumptions with a hypothetical example to make sure that the file will work the way you expect. Of course, you will only know for sure when you make the file on the computer and enter some data. A preliminary test like this will help you prevent major problems before you enter everything into the computer.

For your test case, assume a customer rents two movies and buys a blank tape. What are the steps the clerk would follow?

1. Enter the customer's name.
2. Enter the customer's account number.
3. What happens if the customer has no account number? Open the Database file containing the customer account list, add a new record for the new customer, and assign an account number. Return to the order form and enter the account number.
4. Enter the information for the first movie. After the record is completed, go to the next record.
5. Enter the information for the second movie, skipping over duplicate information like the name, date, and account number. After the record is completed, go to the next record.
6. Enter the information for the blank tape, once again skipping duplicate information.
7. After the transaction is performed, switch to List view and copy all the duplicate entries.

Based on this preliminary test, the file format should work well. You have overcome the first big hurdle—getting something that seems to work effectively. Now you need to determine how everything should be arranged on the screen in both Form and List views.

Arranging the Information

After you have determined what to include, you need to decide how it will appear on the screen. In the Form view, you would probably want to lay out the screen to look like a paper form that is easy to fill out. In List view, you will want the categories arranged in a way that makes it easy to find the information that you are looking for when analyzing the contents of the file. In Works, you can see up to 73 characters of each record on the screen at once, so you will need to see how many fields fit on the screen and how wide to make them. You can do some of this planning on paper and then nudge the fields into their final layouts on the screen.

First lay out the Form view. This is relatively straightforward. Make it look good and easy to use. Many layouts can meet these criteria. For example, you may want to lay it out as shown in the box on the following page.

To see how much of the record will fit on the screen in List view, write out all the categories side-by-side with enough room for all possible responses. Under each category, keep track of the number of characters available for an entry. Most of the data for this particular file should fit in the 73 spaces Works displays at once, but in some fields, the entries will be cut off or run into the next field. After creating the file, you will see the records displayed on the screen. At that point, you may need to decide between squeezing fields together or leaving plenty of room between them. When the fields are squeezed together, you may be able to see more of them at once. When plenty of room is left between them, the entries may be easier to

```
                                    Date: Jan 11, 1999

  First Name: Chris                 Last Name: Jefferson
  Account Number: 1001
  Movie: Bad Day for Bad Bob
  Type: Western
  Other:                            Price: $2.00

                                    Date Due: Jan 12, 1999
```

read, and the information in the Database may be easier to find. However, you may have to scroll to the right to bring some of the fields into view (as you did with the movies database). The plan below keeps all the fields on the screen while leaving a little space between most of the fields.

```
Date       Last Name First Name  Acct# Movie       Type Other    Price

10/21/92 Jefferson  Chris        0001 Bad Day for BadWestBlank Tape  $99.00
123456789123456789012345678901212345123456789012345123412345678901234 5678
```

MAKING THE NEW FILE

fter you have finished planning the Database, you are ready to make the new file. You will create a new file to contain the records, set up the fields and field names, and add the first records.

Creating a New File to Contain the Records

Creating a new database file is similar to creating a new word processor file.

1. Start up Works. Works starts with the File menu open and the *Create New File* command already selected.
2. Press Enter. Works displays the dialog box shown in Figure 8-2 so you can specify what kind of file to create.
3. Choose the *Database* option. Works opens a new Database file.

Create New File

   You see an empty work area with the standard file name *DATA1.WDB*. Later, when you save the file, you will enter a different name. The status line below the work area shows that the file has no records yet. When you create a new Database file, Works starts you out in the Form view, where it is easier to set up fields. That is what you are ready to do next.

Setting Up Fields

In the Database, a form is no more than a list of fields, very much like the paper form you fill out when you order from a catalog, register for school, or apply for a driver's license. In the Form view, you add a field to the Database by keying its name, followed by a colon. Inside the work area, the highlight shows where the text you key will appear. With the Direction Arrows, you could position the highlight anywhere you wanted to locate a field, but for now you will enter fields in a simple list, one above the other.

FIGURE 8-2
Dialog box for creating a new file.

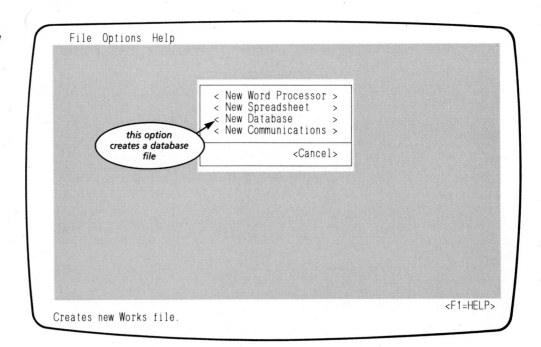

FIGURE 8-3
A new Database file.

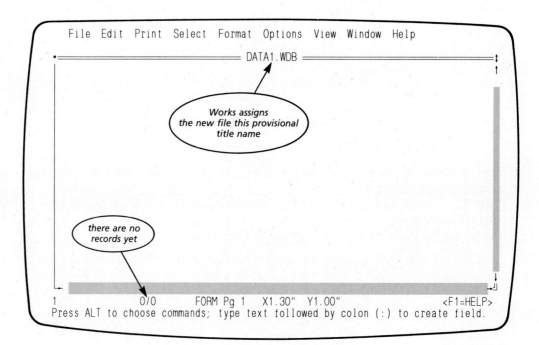

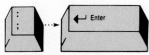

(field name)

Enter Create Field

1. Key Date: for the first field name. Be sure to type the colon. That is how Works knows that what you keyed is the name of a field. The name you key appears in the formula bar with a cursor. If you make a mistake, backspace over it and key the name correctly.
2. Press Enter. Pressing Enter adds the field to the Database and displays a dialog box for setting the size of the field. The standard size Works suggests is 20 characters wide and 1 row high.

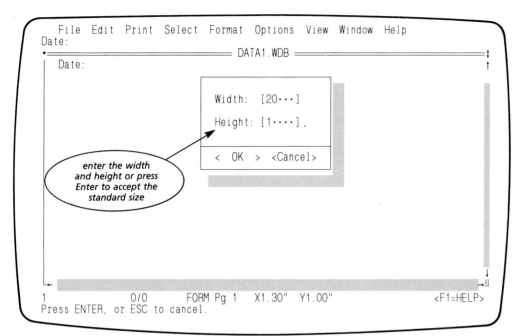

FIGURE 8-4
Field size dialog box.

3. Key 10 to leave plenty of room for the date; then press Enter. Works moves the highlight to the next line, ready for you to create another field. Notice that the field name *Date* has disappeared from the formula bar. Your screen should appear as shown in Figure 8-5.

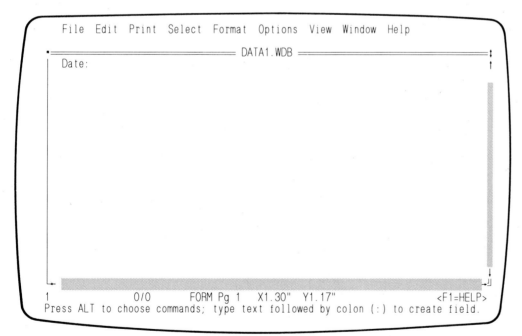

FIGURE 8-5
A new Database with one field.

4. Key First Name: and press Enter. Key 12 for the field size, and press Enter. Remember to key a colon at the end of the field name. If you forget the colon, Works treats the name as other text you want to place on the form, such as titles and instructions. If you do forget, highlight the name and then key it again followed by the colon, to replace the highlighted text.

5. In the same way, enter the next two fields, Last Name: and Acct#:. For now, accept the standard sizes for these.

6. Key Movie: but press Enter only once so the Field Size dialog box is displayed. Some of the movies at Lugosi's have long titles, and you want all of the title to appear on the screen. In the Field Size dialog box, key 40 to make the field 40 characters wide, and then press Enter.

7. Create the rest of the fields for this file. You can press Enter twice after keying each name to accept the standard field width.

   Type:
   Other:
   Price:
   Date Due:

When you finish creating the fields, your screen should look like Figure 8-6. Now you are ready to enter records.

FIGURE 8-6
Fields in a new Database.

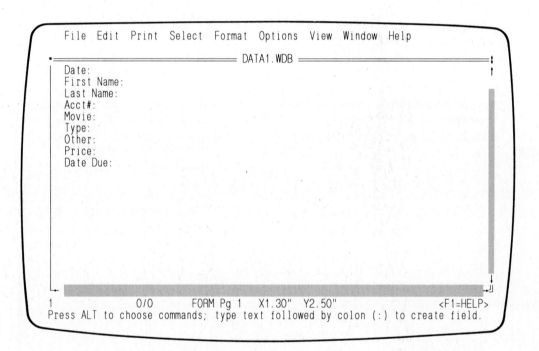

Adding Records

You will create each record by highlighting the field next to each field name and keying an entry. Sarah Lugosi has told you to go ahead and start with the orders already taken today at the store. Since the first field calls for today's date, you can have Works do the work for you: pressing Ctrl and the semicolon (;) key at the same time enters the current date. From now on, this step will be referred to as Ctrl-;.

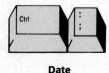

Date

1. Press Shift-Tab. Works highlights the field next to the Date Due field name. Press Shift-Tab several more times until the space to the right of the Date field is highlighted.

2. Press Ctrl-; and then press Tab to highlight the next field. Works displays today's date. When you press Tab, Works puts the date at the right edge of the field. Many database programs, like Works, are preset to move dates and numbers over to the right.

3. Key `Chris` for the first name. After keying the entry, press Tab to highlight the next field. From what you have entered, Works recognizes that the first name field contains text, and so the entry stays at the left side of the field.
4. Key `Jefferson` for the last name.
5. Skip the account number for the time being. Press Tab to highlight the Movie field.
6. Key `Bad Day for Bad Bob` for the movie.
7. Key `Western` for the type.
8. Press Tab to skip over the Other field.
9. Key `2` for the price. Even though you know money is shown in dollars and cents, you do not have to enter a dollar sign or decimals. Later you will learn how to have Works add them automatically.
10. For the date due, key tomorrow's date in numerical format (month/day/year) like this: `10/22/92`. Date Due is the last field. When you press Tab after entering the date due, Works shows you a new blank form for the next record.
11. Enter the two records shown below in the same way you entered the first. Press Tab to skip over the blank fields.

Date: (today's date)	Date: (today's date)
First Name: `Yasmin`	First Name: `Heather`
Last Name: `Abboud`	Last Name: `Huxley`
Acct#:	Acct#:
Movie: `Invasion of the Slime Creatures`	Movie:
Type: `Sci Fi`	Type:
Other:	Other: `Tape Rack`
Price: `2`	Price: `27.95`
Date Due: `(tomorrow's date)`	Date Due:

Press Enter after keying the price. If you keep tabbing away, you will go right into another record.

12. Now that you have finished entering the records, save the file on your template disk. In the dialog box, enter the drive and file name *A:OrderXXX.WDB* or *B:OrderXXX.WDB*, depending on which drive the template disk is in. Replace the X's with your initials.

Congratulations! You have made a new file, set up categories, and entered the first few records. Now you are ready to format the Price field.

Formatting a Field

Formatting a field changes the way a database program like Works displays and prints the entries in the field. When you keyed entries in the Price field, you keyed only numbers. You would like Works to display and print prices with a dollar sign and two decimal places—in what is called **currency format**. Formatting a single entry in a single record changes all the entries for that field throughout the database.

1. Highlight the entry in the Price field of record 3 (27.95). If you pressed Tab after creating this record, your screen probably shows a blank record, and you have to press Ctrl-Page Up to go back to record 3.
2. Choose the *Currency* option from the Format menu. Works displays a dialog box for setting the number of decimal places. Press Enter to accept the standard two decimal places. Works displays a dollar sign in the field to the left of the entry. In the other records, Works also adds two decimal places, so that *27.95* becomes *$27.95* and *2* becomes *$2.00*.

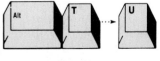

Currency

Next you will arrange the fields on the screen.

CHANGING THE LAYOUT OF THE SCREEN

When you make a new file, a database program like Works has no idea how you want the fields arranged in either the Form view or the List view. In the Form view, the fields are listed down the left side of the screen in the order in which you entered them. In the List view, the fields are listed from left to right in the order in which they were entered. All of the fields are 10 characters wide. This arrangement is especially bad, since some fields are too wide, and others are too narrow. You can correct the arrangement of fields by changing the layout of the screen.

Adjusting the Form View

To make the form easier to use for entering information, arrange it so that it looks like an order form. The fields in the layout need not simply line up along the edge of the screen. You can move them around so that they are more like the categories on a paper form. Figure 8-7 shows the customer order form that Lugosi's has been using. It includes several of the categories that you eliminated from the Database file in order to simplify it, so your computer form will look a little different. But in order to make the transition from paper to computer easier for Lugosi's staff, the Form view should resemble the old form.

FIGURE 8-7
A paper order form.

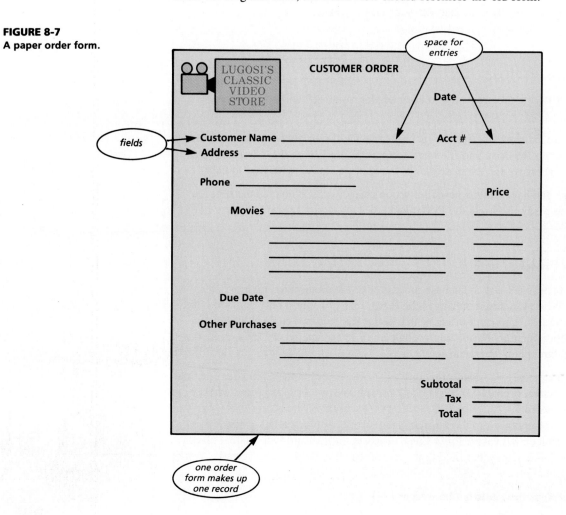

Moving Fields   You can have more than one field on a line (allowing enough room for an entry after each field name), and you can move the fields up and down as well as right and left. You can insert blank lines in the Form view and move fields into them. However, you cannot locate a field on top of another field; fields in a database file do not move over when another field is inserted.

1. Highlight the Date field. You will move this field to the right.
2. From the Edit menu choose *Move Field*. Works highlights both the field name and the field.
3. Press the Right Arrow to move the highlight until it is in the middle of the screen, beginning roughly below the Format menu title.
4. Press Enter. Works displays the field name and entry there.
5. Press Tab twice to highlight the Last Name field.
6. Press F3 to choose the *Move Field* command. That is a shortcut you can use from now on, if you prefer, instead of choosing *Move Field* from the Edit menu.
7. Move the field to the right so that the field name will line up below the field name of the Date field, then press Enter.
8. Press Shift-Tab to highlight the First Name field, and then press F3 to move it.
9. Move the First Name field down one line, so it is on the same line as the Last Name field, then press Enter.
10. In the same way you moved the Date and Last Name fields, move the Price and Date Due fields to the right. Line them up under the Date and Last Name fields. When you are done, the screen should look like Figure 8-8.

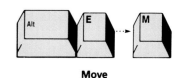

Move

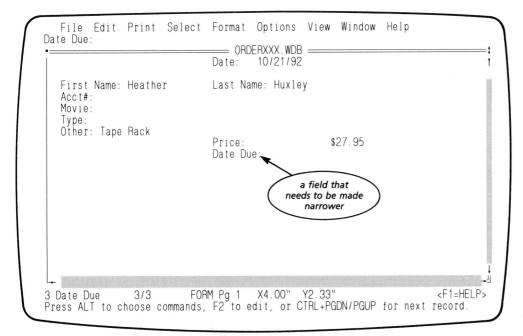

FIGURE 8-8
A rearranged Form view.

Narrowing a Field   Pretty good. One change will make the layout complete. Entries in the Date Due field will appear too far to the right. You can correct that by narrowing the field.

1. Highlight the field to the right of the name Date Due.
2. From the Format menu, choose *Field Size*. You see the same dialog box you used to set the size of the fields when you created them (Figure 8-4).

Field Size

3. On the width line, key 10 and press Enter.
4. Highlight the field to the right of the name Price, choose *Field Size*, and make its width 13.
5. Switch to the List View. Press Home to highlight the first field in the record, and then press Page Up to bring all the records into view.

The changes you made to the Form view have no effect on the way Works displays the Database in the List view. Arranging the List view's layout is the next step.

Adjusting the List Layout

The List view is shown in Figure 8-9. (If you have inadvertently created an extra record when you were entering data, you can get rid of it now by highlighting any cell in it, choosing *Delete record/field*, choosing *Record*, and pressing Enter.)

In List view, each field is a column, and in a new Database file, all the columns are 10 characters wide, even if you have adjusted the widths in the Form View. You can move the fields to the right or left and make them wider or narrower. You want to arrange the screen so all the fields can be displayed at once.

FIGURE 8-9
List view of a new Database file.

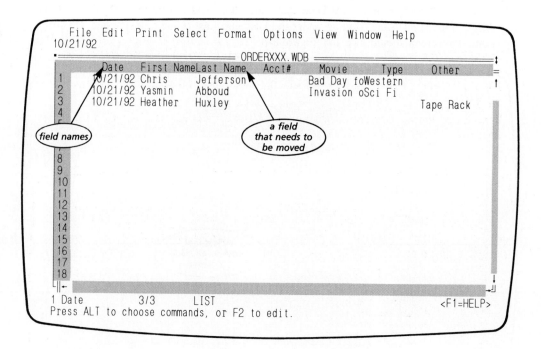

Moving a Field When you move a field in Works' List view, its width changes to the width of its new location. For that reason, changing the order of fields is easiest when they are the same width. You planned to put the Last Name field to the left of the First Name field. To make that change, you first select the entire field, and then move it.

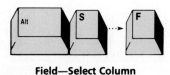

Field—Select Column

1. Highlight an entry in the Last Name column.
2. From the Select menu, choose *Field*. Works highlights the entire Last Name column, as shown in Figure 8-10.

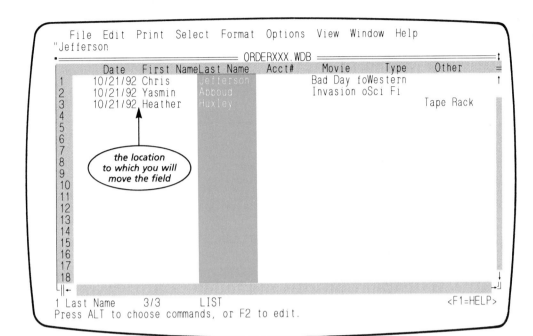

FIGURE 8-10
A selected field.

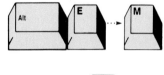

Move

3. Press F3 so that you can move the column. Only the original field is highlighted, but pressing the Right or Left Arrows now moves the entire column.
4. Press the Left Arrow once to highlight a field in the First Name column, as shown in Figure 8-11.
5. Press Enter. Works moves the Last Name field into the location you selected, as shown in Figure 8-12.

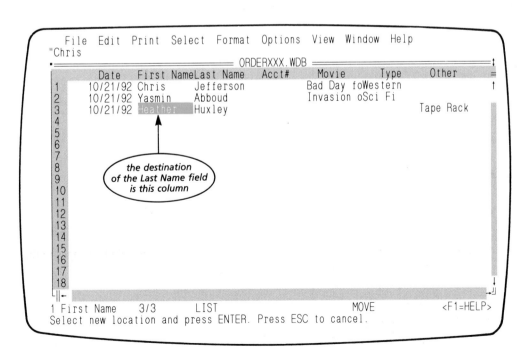

FIGURE 8-11
The new location.

FIGURE 8-12
A new arrangement of fields in
the List view.

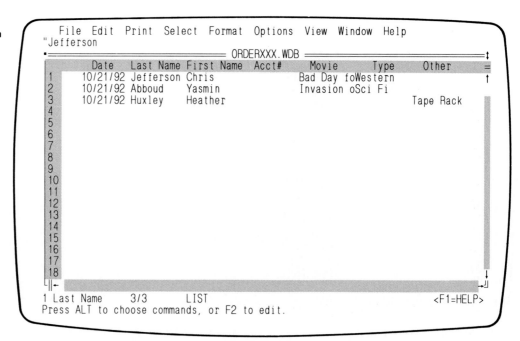

```
  File  Edit  Print  Select  Format  Options  View  Window  Help
 "Jefferson
═══════════════════════ ORDERXXX.WDB ═══════════════════════
          Date   Last Name First Name  Acct#      Movie       Type     Other     =
 1       10/21/92 Jefferson Chris                 Bad Day foWestern              ↑
 2       10/21/92 Abboud    Yasmin                Invasion oSci Fi
 3       10/21/92 Huxley    Heather                                   Tape Rack
 4
 5
 6
 7
 8
 9
10
11
12
13
14
15
16
17
18
1 Last Name      3/3        LIST                                    <F1=HELP>
Press ALT to choose commands, or F2 to edit.
```

Filling a Series of Entries   This is a good time to enter account numbers. Sarah Lugosi has suggested that you inaugurate the store's electronic method of record-keeping by assigning customers new account numbers, starting with 1001. That task is very easy to do in the List view. In Lesson 8, you learned how to copy the same entry repeatedly by filling down. You can also insert a sequence of values by filling in series. **Filling in series** puts a different entry in each record, but the entries form a series that you specify, such as "1...2...3...4.... or 2...4...6...8." In the Orders database, you will use filling in series to assign a sequence of account numbers, starting with 1001.

1. Highlight the Acct# field in row 1, key 1001, and then press Enter.
2. From the Select menu, choose *Cells*.
3. Use the Down Arrow to extend the highlight in the Acct# field to rows 2 and 3, as shown in Figure 8-13.
4. From the Edit menu, choose *Fill Series*. Works displays the dialog box shown in Figure 8-14. The standard options fill the highlighted fields with a series of numbers, each one larger than the last. That is exactly what you need.
5. Press Enter to confirm the standard options. Works fills in the highlighted fields. Yasmin Abboud receives the account number 1002, and Heather Huxley receives the number 1003.

When you need to enter a long series of dates or numbers, filling in series can save you considerable work.

Adjusting Field Widths   The next task is to change the widths of the fields to match the plan. The Date Due field was not included in your original plan, and the current layout does not allow room on the screen for it or for the Price field. You want to adjust column widths to bring all the fields into view.

You do not need to select the entire field when changing its width; changing the width of a field in any record changes the width in all the records.

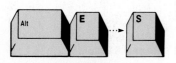

Fill Series

1. Highlight the Last Name field in any row.

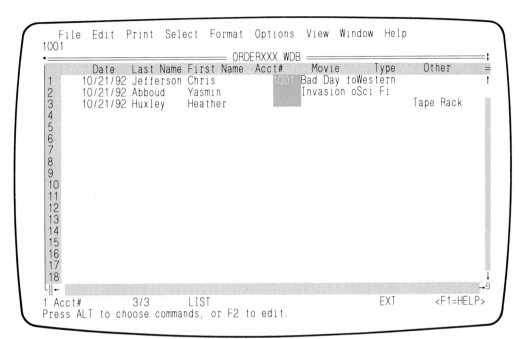

FIGURE 8-13
Selected cells.

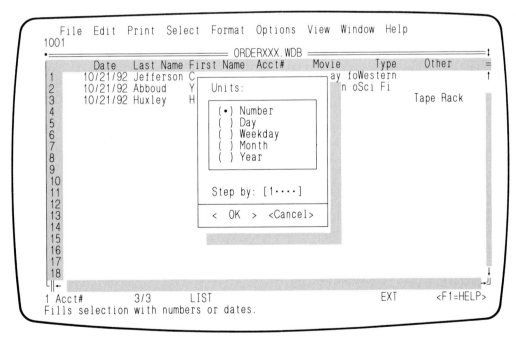

FIGURE 8-14
Fill Series dialog box.

2. From the Format menu, choose *Field Width*. You see a dialog box, as shown in Figure 8-15, similar to the Column Width dialog box.

   If your data is longer than the width of the field, Works remembers the extra information, but does not display it on-screen.

3. To accept the preset 10 in the Width line, press Enter.

Field Width

FIGURE 8-15
Field Width dialog box.

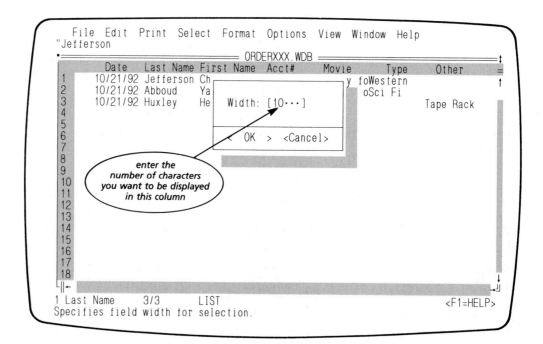

4. Change the width of the other entries as follows:

First Name	1
Acct#	6
Movie	15
Type	3
Other	10
Price	8
Date Due	9

5. Press Home to go back to the first field. Your screen should look like Figure 8-16.

FIGURE 8-16
Layout after changing the field widths.

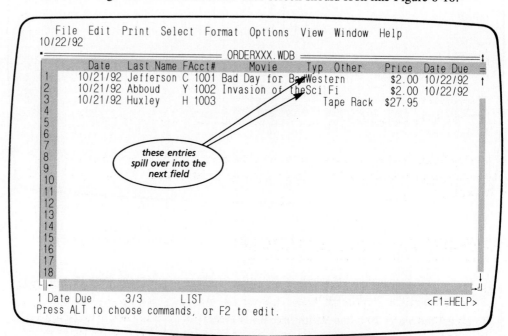

6. To separate the movie names from the types, highlight any entry in the Type field, choose *Field* from the Select menu, and choose *Insert Record/Field* from the Edit menu. That inserts a column between the movies and the types. While the column is still highlighted, choose *Field Width* from the Format menu, and set it to 1. You've created a one-character empty column between the movie title and the type.

You can now see an interesting feature of the Works List view. The Type field is only three characters wide, but you can see the full entries in records 1 and 2. That is because the next field in those records, Other, is blank. When a field is blank, the entry in the previous field can spill over into it. The movie titles, though, cannot spill over because they bump into entries for the type of films. In a sense, the movie titles dive underground at that point. Of course, Works still keeps track of the complete entries, even when not displaying them all, and it still knows in which field the entries belong. You can also see that the Price and Date Due fields now fit on the screen. Your screen should now look like Figure 8-17.

7. Save the file. Since you already saved it during this lesson, you do not see a dialog box, nor do you need to enter a drive and name for the file.

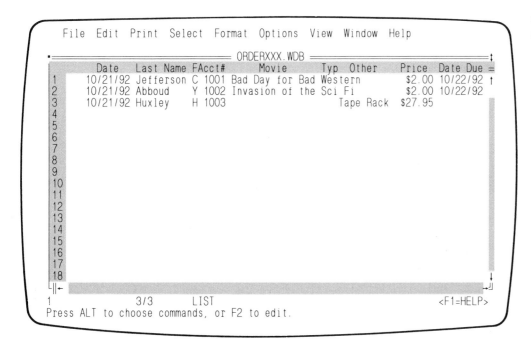

FIGURE 8-17
Adjusted List view.

Good job! The List view is now easy to read and work with. You have moved a column, filled in entries in series, and adjusted column widths. Before you quit Works, you will print the records.

PRINTING THE NEW DATABASE

S arah Lugosi has asked to have a look at the records entered in the new Database. You will print the records in the Form view for her, but with a few changes. On the screen, the field names help a clerk who is entering records to know what information goes where. On a printed record, though, you hardly need to label some fields to recognize the information they contain. Works lets you hide field names. The current date and the person's name can be printed with the field names hidden.

On the screen, the customer's first and last names are entered in separate fields. In printed form, a name would look funny with so much space between the first and last names. Many database programs let you **slide** entries in printing to remove any unused space between them. Sliding is especially useful when some entries may be blank. For example, a database might have a field for a customer's middle initial. Ordinarily, when the program prints a name that does not have a middle initial, it leaves a blank space. When instructed to slide the entries, however, the program closes up the space.

Preparing the Form view

You hide field names with the *Show Field Name* command. This command works like a toggle switch. Normally, the command is turned on, and the highlighted field name is displayed. The command is turned on when you see a bullet next to it on the Format menu, as shown in Figure 8-18. When it is turned on, choosing *Show Field Name* turns it off and hides the field name.

FIGURE 8-18
Format menu.

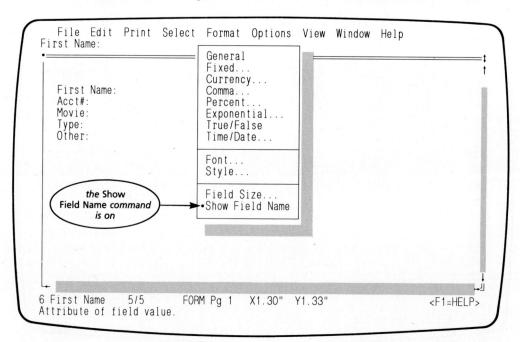

Sliding fields is an option of the *Style* command on the Format menu. The option is normally turned off, as shown in Figure 8-19. When you choose the *Slide to left* option, an *X* appears next to it.

1. Switch to the Form view. If you are looking at a blank record, or something other than the first record, press Ctrl-Page Up to zip to the first record.
2. Select the entry in the Acct# field, choose *Field Size* from the Format menu, key 5, and press Enter. That brings the short account numbers closer to their field name, so the numbers don't float in space. You already made a similar adjustment in List View, but the widths you choose there do not apply to Form View.
3. Highlight the name of the First Name field, then choose *Show Field Name* from the Format menu. That hides the field name.

Show Field Name

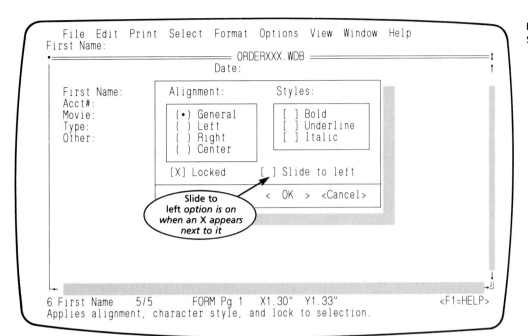

FIGURE 8-19
Style dialog box.

4. Choose *Style* from the Format menu. In the dialog box, select the *Slide to left* option by striking S, and then press Enter.
5. With the field itself highlighted, choose *Move Field*, move the highlighting over to the left margin, and press Enter.
6. Highlight the name of the Last Name field, then choose *Show Field Name* from the Format menu to toggle off the field name.
7. Choose *Style* from the Format menu. In the dialog box, select the *Slide to left* option, and then press Enter.
8. With the field itself still highlighted, choose *Move Field*, and move the highlighting over to the left so there is one blank space after the end of the First Name field. (The First Name field ends where 1001 ends.) Press Enter. Now the last name will begin one space after the first name.

Now you are ready to print the records.

Style

Printing the Records

In Lesson 6 you printed one record in the Form view. Now you will print all the records on one page.

1. Choose *Print* from the Print menu. Works displays the Print dialog box. You will change several options.
2. To print all the records, press Alt-A. Works puts a bullet next to the *All records* option.
3. If an *X* appears next to the Page breaks option, press Alt-B to turn the option off. (If there is no *X* next to the option, skip to Step 4.) You have chosen not to print a single record per page. Since several records will print on each page, Works lets you set the space between them.
4. To separate the records, choose the *Space between records* option (Alt-R).
5. At the cursor, key 1, and then press Enter. Works prints the records.
6. When you are done, quit Works. Choose not to save the changes. You do not want the

FIGURE 8-20
Print dialog box.

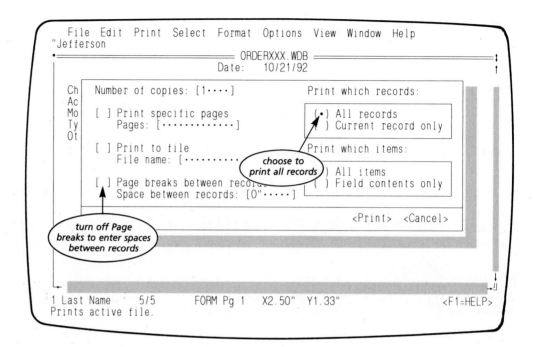

changes you made to the Form view for the purposes of printing the records to be permanent.

Congratulations! You have created a database file from scratch, arranged the layouts of both the Form and List views, and printed a copy of the records. In the next lesson, you will learn how to create more complex reports based on the Orders database.

KEY TERMS

currency format   *MSW 129*
filling in series   *MSW 134*
slide   *MSW 138*

COMMANDS FOR MAKING A NEW DATABASE FILE

Alt-F-N (Create New File)
Ctrl-; (Insert Date)
field name: (Enter Create Field)
Tab Next Field (at end of record selects first field of next record)

COMMANDS FOR ADJUSTING THE FORM VIEW

Alt-T-U (Currency)
Alt-T-Z (Field Size)
Alt-E-M or F3 (Move)
Alt-T-N (Show Field Name)
Alt-T-S (Style)

COMMANDS FOR ADJUSTING THE LIST VIEW

Alt-T-U (Currency)
Alt-T-W (Field Width)
Alt-S-F (Field—select column)
Alt-E-S (Fill Series)
Alt-E-M or F3 (Move)
Alt-T-S (Style)

REVIEW QUESTIONS

1. When the Form view is used to enter data from printed forms, why is it a good idea to make the layout look like the printed form?
2. Why should someone planning a new database file care how people will enter information into the file and how they will use it?
3. How many fields do you need in a database file?
4. Should you review your field selections before you actually make the new file? Why or why not?
5. What is the point of testing a database plan before you make the file?
6. How do you make a new database file on the computer? Explain the steps up to the actual process of entering data.
7. When you arrange the layout of the Form view, must all the fields line up along the left edge of the screen? What changes can you make to the layout?

8. When you arrange the layout of the List view, why would you try to display all the fields at once? How can you make room on the screen for more fields?
9. Why might you want the List view to display fewer fields at once?
10. How does filling in series work?

APPLICATIONS

1. Create a Database file called *CustXXX.WDB* (short for Customer file). Include the fields and enter the data shown in the record in Figure 8-21. Then arrange the layout of the Form view so it matches the paper form.

FIGURE 8-21
Customer Record form for Application 1.

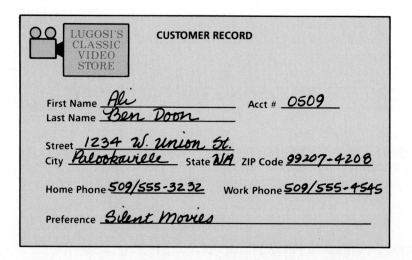

Use Shift-PrintScreen to print a hard copy of the screen showing the layout and the data for this record.

2. Arrange the layout of the *CustXXX.WDB* file in the List view according to the plan shown below. (Some fields are off the screen to the right.)

Field	Width
Acct #	5
First Name	11
Last Name	11
City	12
Home Phone	12
Preference	22
Work Phone	12
Street	15
State	4
ZIP code	12

Add the following two additional records. Save the file and print a hard copy of the screen in List view.

Account Number: 9089
First Name: Peter
Last Name: Pascali
Address: 345 Sunrise Blvd.
            Palookaville, WA 99207-8123

Home Phone: 509/555-3845
Preference: Westerns
Work Phone: 509/555-8769

Account Number: 7475
First Name: Elizabeth
Last Name: Hu
Address: 2746 Homestead Ave.
        Palookaville, WA 99207-6143
Home Phone: 509/555-2939
Preference: Sci Fi
Work Phone: 509/555-3291

3. Make a file that can be used as a personal telephone directory. Use the sample card below to help you design the layout of the Form view. Arrange the fields to reflect the layout in Figure 8-22.

Plan the file completely. Make a list of all the fields that are included in the card shown. Since the card does not include field names for each of the entries, you will have to choose your own. Most are easy to determine: Name, Address, and so on. Be sure to include separate fields for first and last name.

Make the new file (name it *MyAddXXX.WDB*) and enter the field names. Arrange the Form view so that it resembles the sample card.

Enter at least five records. You can use the names of friends and relatives or you can make up the information.

Adjust the List view so that the person's name, address, city, state, ZIP code, and home phone number fit neatly on the screen, if possible. Print a hard copy of the List view screen.

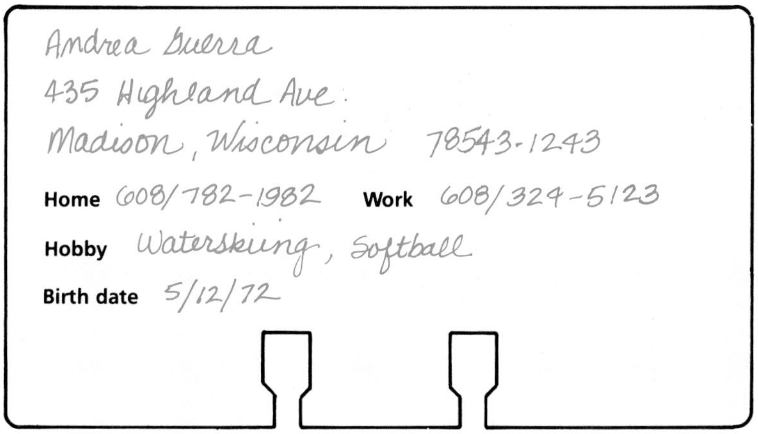

FIGURE 8-22
Sample layout for Application 3.

Arrange the Form view so you can print the file in an arrangement similar to the card—without field names appearing, except for home phone number, work phone number, hobby, and birth date. Slide the fields that will make up the name and address lines of the printed record. Set a space of .5 inches between records. Finally, print your directory.

Working with Calculations and Reports

OBJECTIVES

- Include calculations in a field.
- Make a new field that calculates results from other fields.
- Include subtotals and column totals in a report.
- Prepare a report layout.
- Print multiple reports from one file.
- Use special printer options.

INCLUDING CALCULATIONS IN A DATABASE

Many databases contain numbers, and database programs like Works let you make calculations using fields that contain numbers. Yesterday was such a busy day at Lugosi's Classic Video Store, for example, that Morris Yu forgot to total up some of the day's receipts. Since the records are all stored on disk, he has asked you to print up a report including calculations for sales tax, total purchases per customer, and total sales for the day. To prepare a report for Morris Yu, you will add new fields to the database file for the tax amounts and totals.

Morris Yu wants you to calculate the sales tax for the day's orders. Then he wants you to calculate the total purchase amount for each customer. Finally, he wants a total of all the receipts. That sounds like a lot of work, and it would be if you had to figure it out yourself with a calculator. Fortunately you have the Works database tool to do the work for you. Works lets you create a special field called a **calculated field**, that makes calculations using data from other fields. For sales tax, you can make a calculated field that takes a number from the Price field, multiplies it by the proper amount for the sales tax, and enters the result. Works calls the instructions used for a calculation the **formula**. You provide the formula when you set up a calculated field. On the screen, only the results of the formula appear in the field, not the formula itself.

Making a Simple Calculated Field

You will work with the *New.WDB* file on the template disk. This database file is an expanded version of the orders database you created in Lesson 8, with additional records. Your first step is to create a field to calculate the tax on each transaction.

1. Start up Works and open the *New.WDB* file from the template disk. Works displays the file in List view, as shown in Figure 9-1. Some of the records will look familiar—you entered them in Lesson 8. Additional orders have been added, and the records have been alphabetized by last name.

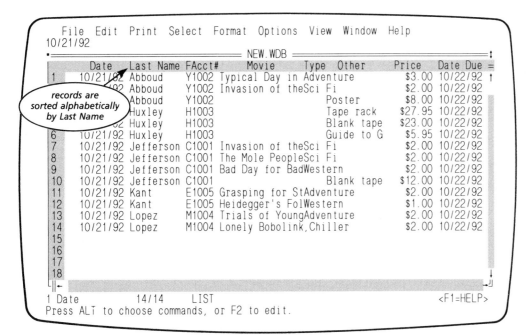

FIGURE 9-1
A database file containing new orders.

The amount of each transaction is listed in the Price field, and the sales tax for Lugosi's Classic Video store is six percent. You want Works to look in the Price field and multiply the amount it finds there by six percent (.06). You have already created one formula—a query formula—in Lesson 6, so you know that formulas in Works must start with an equal sign (=). Most database programs, including Works, use the asterisk symbol (*) to indicate multiplication. The formula for calculating sales tax is therefore = *Price*0.06.* You need to create a new field for the sales tax, and in the List view you can do that by entering information in any blank column.

2. Highlight any empty cell in the column to the right of the Date Due column (pressing End once and then the Right Arrow once is the quickest way).

3. Key `=Price*0.06` and then press Enter. The result is dramatic. Works calculates the sales tax for each record and displays it. In a flash, a column of figures appears. Because you have added the tenth field to the database and not yet named it, Works titles it *Field10.* Your screen now should look like Figure 9-2.

4. To rename the new field, choose *Field Name* from the Edit menu. You see the dialog box shown in Figure 9-3.

5. Key `Tax` on the Name line, then press Enter. Works places the new name at the head of the column. Now you will format the field so all of the entries are displayed to two decimal places.

6. Choose *Currency* from the Format menu, and press Enter to accept the standard two decimal places. Works rounds off the entries.

7. Finally, use the *Field Width* command and narrow the column to seven spaces wide.

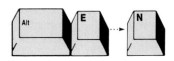

Field Name—List View

FIGURE 9-2
A database with a newly created field.

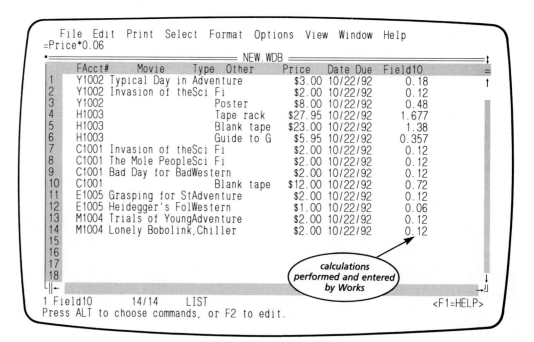

FIGURE 9-3
Field Name dialog box.

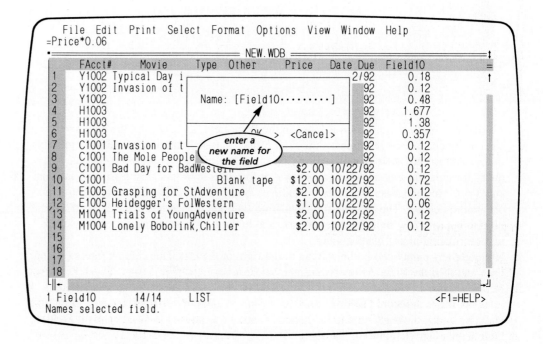

Making a Calculation Using Another Calculated Field

In addition to calculated fields based on data you have entered in a database, you can create a calculated field that uses the results of another calculated field in its formula.

For example, to provide Morris Yu with a total amount for each purchase, you would need to add the price of the item and the tax, which is itself a calculated field. With Works, the formula for this calculation is *= Price + Tax*.

1. Press the Right Arrow once to highlight a cell in the empty column next to the Tax field.
2. Key =Price+Tax and then press Enter. Works creates a new field, names it *Field11*, makes the calculations, and enters the results.
3. Use the *Field Name* command to rename the field *Total*.
4. Format the new field as currency.
5. Change the width of the field to eight spaces. That will leave room for totals above $100. When you are done, your screen should resemble Figure 9-4.
6. Press Home to return to the first field in the record.
7. Save your file on the template disk. Be sure to use the *Save As* command and save the file as *NewXXX.WDB*—replace the X's with your own initials.

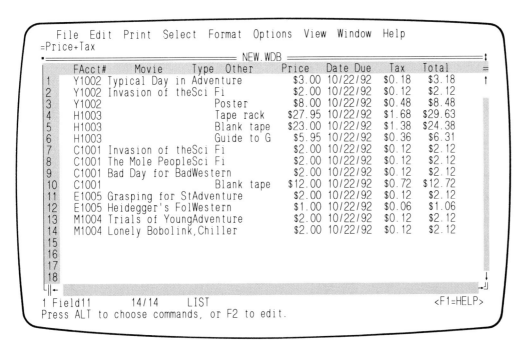

FIGURE 9-4
A database containing two calculated fields.

PREPARING A REPORT

Morris Yu has asked for a printed copy of the tax information. You could just print the database in the List view, but that would not really give Morris Yu the information he needs. He would like the total purchases for each customer as well as a grand total for the day. Much of the information stored in the database, such as the dates movies are due and the types of movies, are not relevant to this task. To provide the information that Morris Yu needs, organized so he does not have to hunt for it, you will prepare a report.

Reports let you organize, summarize, and present the information stored in a database in a meaningful way. You have already printed information for Sarah Lugosi that came from several different database files and was arranged in several different layouts. In the broadest sense, all of these printouts were reports, but Works reserves the term for layouts created in the Report view. These layouts are saved with the database file, and you can save more than one, so you can have different layouts for different purposes, and use them over and over. You will create a new report for Morris Yu. Not only will he receive the information he seeks today, but he will never again need to tally the day's purchases by hand.

Looking at the Report View

The *New Report* command on the View menu lets you create a new report layout. When you choose *New Report*, Works opens an unedited layout that includes all the information in the database. You can change the report to suit your needs.

New Report

1. Choose *New Report* from the View menu. Works displays page 1 of the report, as shown in Figure 9-5.

```
Date      Last Name FAcct#Movie            TypeOther

10/21/92 Abboud     Y1002 Typical Day in Adve
10/21/92 Abboud     Y1002 Invasion of theSci
10/21/92 Abboud     Y1002                    Poster
10/21/92 Huxley     H1003                    Tape rack
10/21/92 Huxley     H1003                    Blank tape
10/21/92 Huxley     H1003                    Guide to G
10/21/92 Jefferson  C1001 Invasion of theSci
10/21/92 Jefferson  C1001 The Mole PeopleSci
10/21/92 Jefferson  C1001 Bad Day for BadWest
10/21/92 Jefferson  C1001                    Blank tape
10/21/92 Kant       E1005 Grasping for StAdve
10/21/92 Kant       E1005 Heidegger's FolWest
10/21/92 Lopez      M1004 Trials of YoungAdve
Page 1                        REPORT
Press ENTER to continue, ESC to cancel.
```

FIGURE 9-5
Page 1 of a new report layout.

The format resembles the layout of the List view, and in fact, reports are based on the List view, since it is best suited for organizing and summarizing information from many records. Fewer fields are visible than were visible in the List view because fewer fit on a printed page. If a database contains too many fields to fit across the width of a single page, Works prints as many columns as will fit. After printing the entries in all the records for those fields, Works goes back and prints the remaining columns on another page.

2. Press Enter until you see page 2. This page contains the remaining fields.

In a database with many records, for example, a file containing a month's worth of orders, Works might need to print many pages containing the first set of fields before printing another set of pages with the rest of the fields.

When you are displaying pages of the report, you cannot make changes to the layout. Works created the page layout you are viewing by following a set of instructions called the **report definition**. You change the layout by revising the report definition.

3. To display the report definition, press Esc. Works displays the screen shown in Figure 9-6.

Looking at the Report Definition The report definition is a very condensed way of telling Works how to print each line of the report. Each row of the report definition defines a different kind of line in the report. A label at the beginning of the row tells Works *where* in the report to print the line. Information entered to the right of each label tells Works *what*

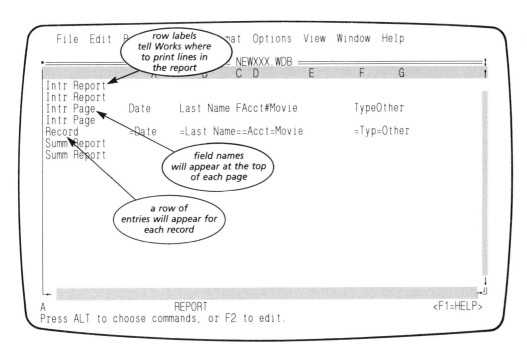

FIGURE 9-6
A report definition.

to put on the line. When you chose *New Report*, Works opened a standard layout containing the elements that Works' programmers thought the average user would want included in a report.

Look at the first row of the report definition. The *Intr Report* label tells Works to print a line only at the very beginning (or "Introduction") of the report. The second row of this report definition is also labeled *Intr Report*, and in this standard layout the area telling Works what to print in both rows is blank. If you printed the file using the report definition as is, Works would dutifully leave two blank lines at the top of the report. But the lines are usually used for the report's title, and if you keyed something on either row in the work area, whatever you entered would appear at the beginning of the printed report.

The third and fourth rows are labeled *Intr Page*, and as you might imagine, each tells Works to print a line at the top of each page of the report. Intr Page lines are often used for column headings. Information entered in an Intr Page row tells Works what to print on these lines. This standard layout includes column headings—the field names for the database—in the first line and leaves the second line blank. You can add to, revise, or delete any of the entries. Because the screen is not wide enough to display the entire row, some of the field names are off the screen to the right.

The fifth row in the report definition is labeled *Record*. Unlike the other rows, which defined single lines of the printed report, a row labeled *Record* tells Works to print one line for each record in the database. This is the row used to define how you want the data stored in the database to be printed. Works has again provided standard entries for the Record row: formulas instructing Works to print the contents of each field in the database. Some of the formulas are off the screen.

The last two rows in the report definition are labeled *Summ Report*. This label instructs Works to print a line at the very end of the report. Summ Report rows are often used for calculations that summarize a column of figures, for example, subtotals or grand totals. Works has left these rows blank.

You will edit the report definition to create exactly the report you need.

Organizing the Report Layout

The new report contains all the fields in the database, but not all of them are necessary. Why not delete the extra fields from the report? Then the report will contain only the information you need. After you delete the non-essential fields, you will need to add titles to the report. You can set the title off from the rest of the report by inserting a blank row below it. The database displays dates in numerical "short" form. Since this report is meant to be read, why not change the format of the dates to "long" form so the names of the months appear instead of just numbers?

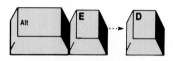

**Delete Row/Column—
Report Definition**

Deleting Fields from the Report Definition   Begin by deleting unnecessary fields.

1. Highlight the cell in column B in the Record row (the Last Name field).
2. Choose *Delete Row/Column* from the Edit menu. You see the dialog box shown in Figure 9-7.

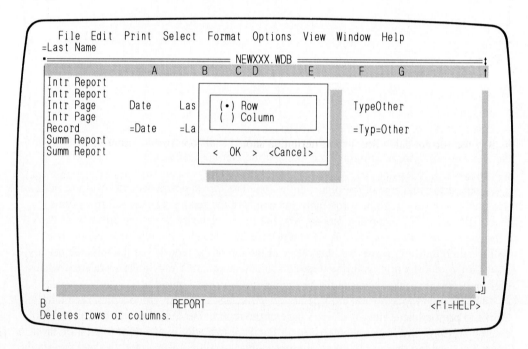

FIGURE 9-7
Delete Record/Field dialog box.

3. In the dialog box, select the *Column* option, and then press Enter. Works removes the column from the report definition, deleting both the field name in the Intr Page row and the formula in the Record row. The remaining entries to the right shift left to occupy the vacant column.
4. In the same way that you deleted the column containing the Last Name field, delete the columns containing the First Name and Date Due fields. (Only the initial *F* of the First Name field is visible.) Figure 9-8 shows what the screen looks like after the three columns are deleted.

Making Titles   Next you will enter a title and the date in the Intr Report rows so that Works will print them at the top of the report.

1. Highlight the first field in the first Intr Report row.
2. Key DAILY TAX AND TOTALS. Use all capital letters to make the title stand out.

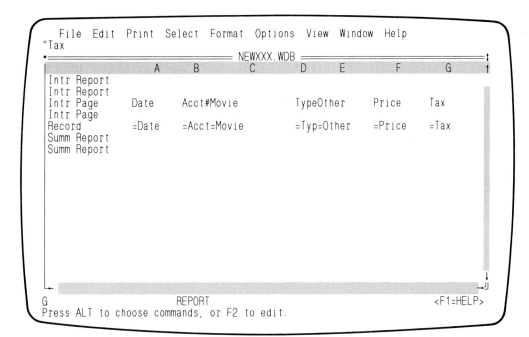

FIGURE 9-8
Report definition after deleting three columns.

3. Press Enter. Because there are no other entries in the row, the entire title is displayed, even though it is much wider than the field in which you entered it.
4. Highlight the first field in the second Intr Report row.
5. Key the current date. Your report definition should now look like Figure 9-9.

Inserting a Row   Inserting a blank row between the report title and the column headings will make the title stand out.

1. Move the highlight to the first Intr Page row.

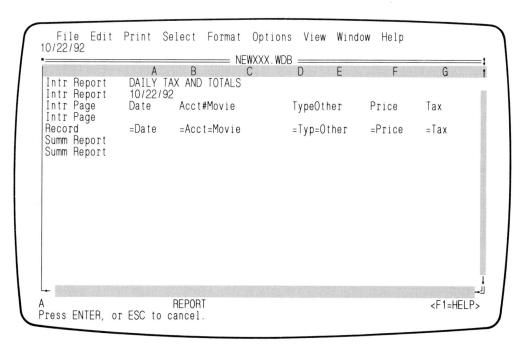

FIGURE 9-9
Titles entered in a report definition.

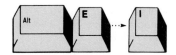

**Insert Row/Column—
Report Definition**

2. Choose *Insert Row/Column* from the Edit menu, and then press Enter to accept the *Row* option. The dialog box shown in Figure 9-10 lets you select the type of row.

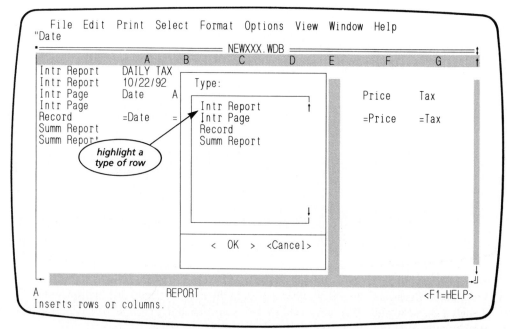

FIGURE 9-10
Dialog box for inserting a row in a report definition.

3. In the dialog box, highlight *Intr Report*, and then press Enter. Works adds a blank Intr Report row to the report definition.

Formatting the Dates The dates are currently formatted in numerical (short) format. They will look better in the report if the name of the month is written out (long format). You will show the month and year in the title of the report. The dates in the record line need show only the month and day.

1. Highlight the date in the second Intr Report row.
2. From the Format menu, choose *Time/Date*. Works displays the dialog box shown in Figure 9-11.
3. Select the *Month, year* option and the *Long* option, and press Enter. In the report definition, the format of the date changes, for example, from *10/22/92* to *Oct 1992*.
4. Highlight the date formula (= Date) in the Record line.
5. Choose *Time/Date* again. In the dialog box, select the *Month, day* and *Long* options, then press Enter. The report definition does not reflect the change you made to the date format, but Works will print the date Oct 22.

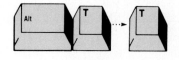

Time/Date

Adding Totals to the Report

Reports let you organize and format the information in a database, but the ability to summarize information is what really makes reports useful. This report will break the database down by customer and provide information about the number and total of each customer's transactions. To set that up, you will first sort the database in order to create groups by customer. Then you will insert calculations that summarize the transactions.

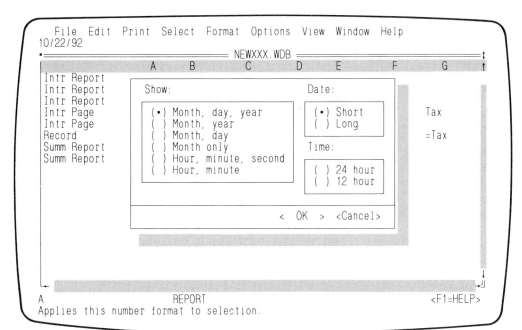

Grouping the Records You need to provide totals for the purchases of each customer. That means breaking the database up into groups defined by the customers' account numbers. Most database programs let you break up the records into groups and perform calculations for each group. With Works, you can further divide the groups into subgroups and those subgroups into yet another set of subgroups. For example, if you were interested in figures on the types of movies customers preferred, you could divide the records into groups according to the type of movie rented: Westerns in one group, Sci Fi in another group, and so on. You could then further divide each type into subgroups according to the movie titles. Calculating total purchases for each customer will require only one set of groups. To create groups, you sort the records and specify that you want to **break** the database up into groups.

1. Choose *Sort Records* from the Select menu. Works displays the dialog box shown in Figure 9-12. The cursor is on the 1st Field line.
2. Key Acct# in the 1st Field line.
3. Press Alt-G to select the *Break* option (an X appears next to the option), and then press Enter. Works sorts the database file so all the records with the same number in the Acct# field are grouped together. To the report definition, Works adds a new line labeled *Summ Acct#*. This line defines what will be printed at the end of each group, and it lets you summarize calculations for the group. You will learn about the unfamiliar formulas on this line in the next section.

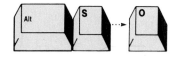

Sort Records

Summary Calculations and Functions The row Works inserted in the report definition when you sorted the database contains unfamiliar calculations that summarize all the records with the same account number. Calculations that summarize the data in a field contained in several records are called **summary calculations**.

These summary calculations use two built-in formulas called **functions**. Programmed into Works are a variety of functions that let you perform calculations that would be complicated or even impossible to key as formulas yourself, for example, finding an angle's cosine or calculating the average of a group of numbers. Two standard functions, COUNT and SUM, appear in summary calculations in the Summ Acct# row. The columns are too narrow to show

FIGURE 9-12
Dialog box for sorting records in a report.

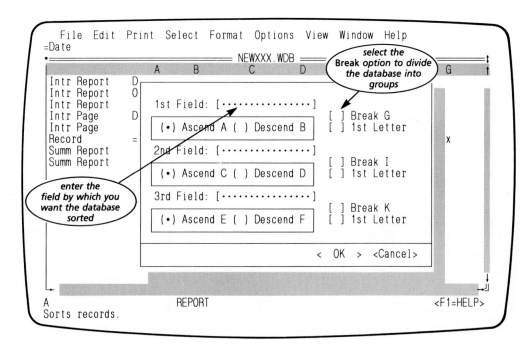

FIGURE 9-13
Report definition after grouping records.

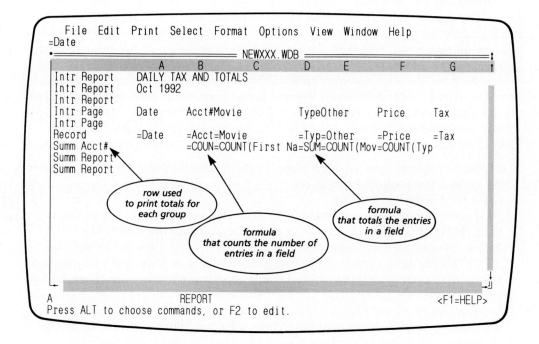

any of the formulas in its entirety, and they are crowded together. If you highlight a field containing one of the formulas, you can view it in the formula bar.

The COUNT function calculates the number of items in a column. When a database field contains text, Works assumes you want to know how many of the records contain an entry in the field, so the program inserts summary calculations for each text field, for example, Movies and Other, that use the COUNT function to count the entries.

The SUM function calculates the total of a group of numbers. When a database field contains numbers, Works assumes you want to know their total, so the program inserts summary calculations for each numerical field, using the SUM function to total the entries.

Adding Group Totals   You want to add formulas to the Summ Acct# row to calculate group totals. The formulas you insert will use the COUNT and SUM functions, but you can insert these formulas more easily by first deleting the summary calculations Works has put there.

1. Highlight the first cell in the Summ Acct# row. Use the Right Arrow key to highlight the first formula in the row, then use the Backspace key to delete it. Continue moving to the right, deleting each formula until you have removed them all. (The last formula, = *SUM(Total)*, may be off the screen in column K.)
2. Move the highlight to the cell in column D on the Summ Acct# row.
3. From the Edit menu, choose *Insert Field Summary*. Works displays the dialog box shown in Figure 9-14.

**Insert Field Summary—
Report Definition**

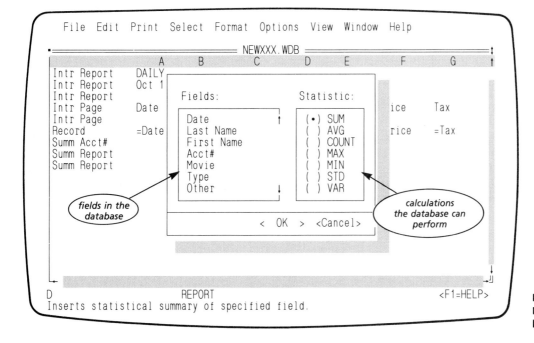

**FIGURE 9-14
Insert Field Summary dialog box.**

The Fields box lists all the fields in the database, including those you deleted from this report definition. (Works takes the information it needs to perform a calculation from your computer's memory, so entries in a field do not need to be included in the report definition in order to perform a calculation based on them.) The Statistic box lists the summary calculations.

4. Use the Down Arrow to highlight the Acct# field. You want to tally the number of account number entries in each group. The formula that performs this calculation is COUNT.
5. Select the *COUNT* option.
6. Press Enter. Works inserts the formula =COUNT(Acct#) in the highlighted cell. (The column is not wide enough to show the entire formula, but it is all visible in the formula bar.) This formula will count the number of entries in the account number field for each group and print the result below each group, etc.

7. Move the highlight to the cell in column H of the Summ Acct# row.
8. Repeat the process described in Steps 3-5, but select the Total field and the SUM statistic, and then press Enter. Works inserts the formula =SUM(Total) in the highlighted cell. This formula will add all the entries in the group and print the result. You can only use SUM with numerical fields.
9. From the Format menu, choose *Currency*, and press Enter. That formats the total as currency, with two decimal places.

Entering a Grand Total

1. Move the highlight to the cell in column H of the last Summ Report row. You can key summary formulas instead of using the Insert Field Summary dialog box.
2. Key =SUM(Total) and press Enter. Although this is the same formula you entered in the Summ Acct# row, the result Works calculates will be different because the formula is located in a different type of row. Entered in a Summ Acct# row, the formula adds the entries in the Total field for each account number group. Entered in a Summ Report row, the formula adds the entries for all the records.
3. Format the formula as currency.

Labeling the Totals

1. Highlight the cell in column F of the Summ Report row, to the left of the formula you just entered.
2. Key GRAND TOTAL and press Enter.
3. Go back to the Summ Acct# row, highlight the cell in column C, and key ITEMS. Press Enter.
4. Highlight the cell in column F in the same row. Key SUBTOTAL and press Enter. Figure 9-15 shows how your screen should look when you are done.

FIGURE 9-15
A report definition with labeled formulas for summary calculations.

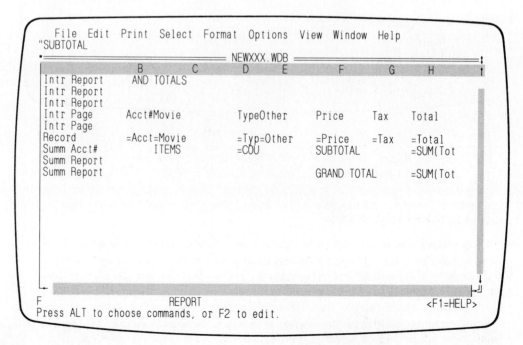

5. To see how the groups you have made change the report, choose *Report1* from the View menu. The screen shown in Figure 9-16 is dramatically different from the screen when you opened the new report. Now the transactions for each account number are grouped together. Below each group of records, a summary line shows the number of transactions and a group total for the Total field. You can see only the SUBTOTAL label since the column containing the Total field is not visible on the screen.

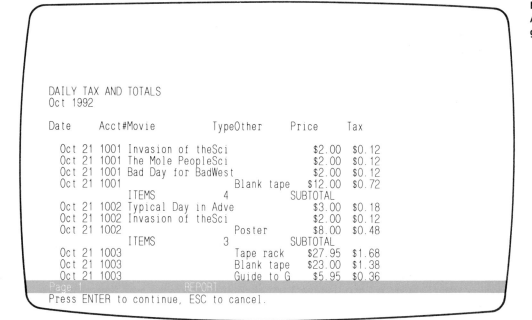

FIGURE 9-16
A Report view with groups and group totals.

6. Press Esc to return to the report definition.
7. For a more accurate idea of how the printed report would look, choose *Preview* from the Print menu, and press Enter to accept the preset options. As shown in Figure 9-17, the preview screen displays the groups clearly. Previewing the report also points out some areas that can use improvement. Why not align the field names so they are not crowded together? You can also insert blank rows between the groups to space them better and emphasize the subtotals that are the focus of the report. The ITEMS and SUBTOTAL labels can be brought closer to their respective calculations. Finally, the Total field does not appear on the page. To print the entire report on one page, you must reduce the left and right margins of the page so the area available for the report is wider. You will make these changes next.

Adding Embellishments

You will complete the report definition by adding some finishing touches that will make your printed report much better looking, focusing attention on the information Morris Yu wants, and fitting the entire report on one page. The additions include changing the alignment and style, and adding blank rows.

Changing Alignment and Style   Alignment refers to the way an entry lines up in relation to the edges of its field. When you create a field and key entries, Works aligns the

FIGURE 9-17
A Report preview.

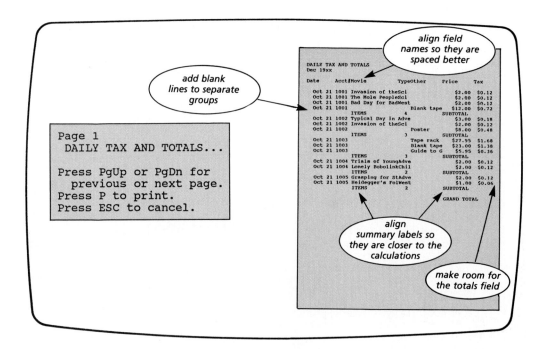

entries according to the program's internal rules: Text is placed to the left, dates and numbers to the right, and when the length of the entry permits, one space is left blank on the right and left so entries do not run into one another in the List view. This is General alignment. Works lets you change the alignment to line entries up at the Left, Right, or Center of the field.

Style refers to the way letters and numbers are printed. Works lets you change the style from plain text, which is standard, to Bold, Underline, or Italic, or any combination of the three. You change both alignment and style in the same dialog box with the *Style* command.

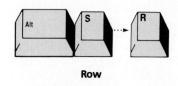

Row

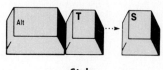

Style

1. Highlight any entry in the Intr Page row. The entries in this row will be column headings in the printed report.
2. From the Select menu, choose *Row*. Works highlights the row, and now the changes you make will affect everything in the row.
3. From the Format menu, choose *Style*. You see the dialog box shown in Figure 9-18.
4. In the Alignment box, select the *Center* option. In the Styles box, select *Underline*. An X appears next to the Underline option. Press Enter. The headings shift so they are centered in their columns. As a result, they are spaced more evenly throughout the row. When Works prints the report, the headings will also be underlined, but this change may not be displayed on your screen.
5. Select the Summ Acct# row the same way you selected the Intr Page row.
6. Choose *Style* from the Format menu, and in the dialog box set the alignment to Right and the style to Bold, and press Enter. Works moves the ITEMS and SUBTOTAL labels and the formulas as far to the right as possible within their fields. Since the fields containing the formulas are narrower, they cannot move as far. When Works prints the labels and the calculations, the labels will be closer to the calculations.
7. Select the row containing the grand total, and change its alignment to Right and its style to Bold.

Inserting Blank Rows The addition of blank rows between the account number groups will make the report look less dense. The group totals will stand out more from the other rows of text and numbers.

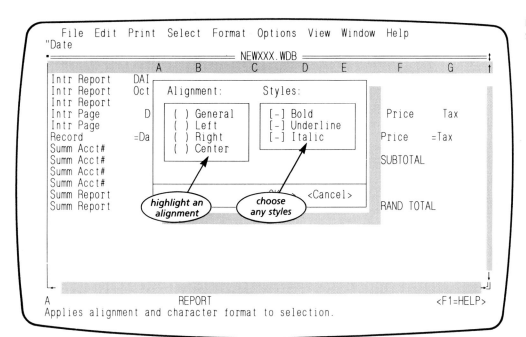

FIGURE 9-18
Style dialog box.

1. Highlight any cell in the Summ Acct# row.
2. From the Edit menu, choose *Insert Row/Column*, and insert a blank Summ Acct# row.
3. Highlight the first Summ Report row and insert two more Summ Acct# rows. You should end up with four Summ Acct# rows, as shown in Figure 9-19. The formulas should be in the second row.

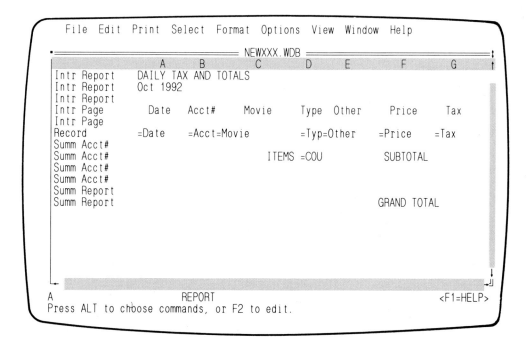

FIGURE 9-19
Report definition after inserting blank rows.

Changing the Margins

When you create a new report, Works uses the standard margin settings. They allow the printer up to six inches per line. Since standard typefaces print 10 characters per inch, that gives your report room for 60 characters per line. If your report has longer lines, as this one does, and you want everything to fit on one page, you can change the margin settings. When you save the file, the new margin settings are saved with the report layout.

1. From the Print menu, choose *Page Setup & Margins*. You see the Page Setup & Margins dialog box, containing Works' standard margin settings, as shown in Figure 9-20.

FIGURE 9-20
Page Setup & Margins dialog box.

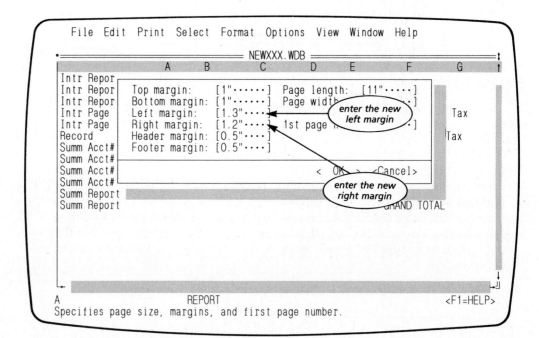

2. Change the left margin to 0.75.
3. Change the right margin to 0.5, and press Enter.
4. Save your file on the template disk by choosing Save from the File menu. Since you already saved it during this lesson with your initials, you do not see a dialog box, nor do you need to enter a drive and name for the file.

Congratulations! You have organized the layout of a report, arranged the records to break the report into groups, added summary calculations to the report, and fine-tuned the layout. Now you can turn on your printer and enjoy the fruits of your work.

Printing the Tax and Totals Report

The report is ready to print.

1. From the Print menu, choose *Preview* and press Enter to accept the standard settings. Check the report preview on your screen. If everything looks right, go on to print the report. If you see places where corrections need to be made, press Esc to return to the report definition, make the necessary changes, then preview the report again.
2. When your printer is ready, press P to print the report.

PRODUCING MULTIPLE REPORTS

One of the greatest advantages of using a database for printing reports is that you are not limited to one type of report. You can print as many different reports for each file as you require. You have printed one arrangement of information from the *NewXXX- .WDB* database. Suppose Morris Yu wants to analyze some other reports, one on sales tax and another showing the rentals of each type of movie, so that he can see which type is most popular. With database programs like Works, you can easily prepare other reports from the same file. They will use exactly the same set of data but look different and serve different purposes. They may even contain completely different information, even though all the information comes from the same file. In this part of the lesson, you will change the report layout to meet the new requirements and print the other reports.

Preparing a Report on Sales Tax

The sales tax report is based directly on the Daily Tax and Totals report that you just printed. One way to prepare the report is to make the changes in this report definition and print the new report. But then you would no longer have a copy of the initial report on disk. You can have both formats, though, by making a copy of this format and then changing the copy.

Renaming and Copying a Report Definition   The Daily Tax and Totals report is listed in the View menu as *Report1*. Since you will be creating an additional report, you want each to have a distinctive name that will remind you of its purpose. Before you make a copy of the Daily Tax and Totals report, you will change its name.

1. From the View menu, choose *Reports*. Works displays the Reports dialog box shown in Figure 9-21. The report layout you just prepared is listed as *Report1*. The dialog box lets you rename, delete, and copy report layouts.

Reports

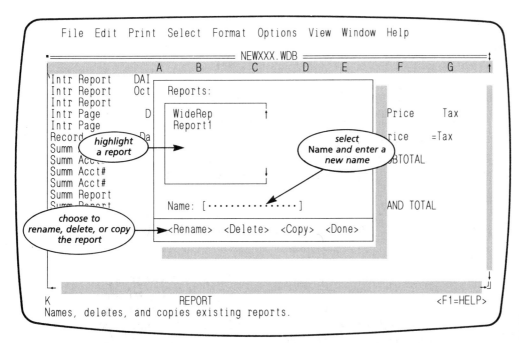

FIGURE 9-21
Reports dialog box.

2. In the list, highlight *Report1*.
3. Select *Name*. Works puts a cursor on the blank Name line.
4. Key Sales and select the *Rename* option. The name of the report layout changes to Sales. When you use the View menu again, you will see the report listed under its new name.
5. Select Copy. Works copies the report and adds it to the list in the dialog box as Report1. (If you had not renamed the original report layout, Works would have named the copy Report2.)
6. Select the new report (Report1, probably), then go to the *Name* box and key Tax as a name for the new report. Choose *Rename* and then choose *Done*. You see the report definition. Because the Sales and the Tax reports are, at this point, identical, you want to make sure you are working with the one named Tax.
7. Open the View menu. You should see a bullet next to *Tax* on the menu, indicating that it is the displayed report definition. If not, choose *Tax* from the menu.

Changing the Report Definition This report should concentrate on sales tax, so you should start by getting rid of the Total column and the Type column, which are no longer needed. Then you can tell the database to print totals in the Tax column. The result will be a report showing the sales tax for each item purchased, the total sales tax paid by each customer, and the total sales tax collected. Finally, since you have eliminated two columns, you can widen the margins of the page.

1. To eliminate the Type column, put the highlight in column D and choose *Delete Row/Column* from the Edit menu.
2. In the dialog box, select the *Column* option and press Enter.
3. Repeat the procedure to delete the Total column.
4. Highlight column A in the first Intr Report row, the cell in which the title of the report is entered. Replace the title with SALES TAX.
5. Highlight the ITEMS label in the Summ Acct# row (the formula that counted the number of items was deleted when you deleted the Type column). Press Backspace to delete the label.
6. Move the highlight to column F in the Summ Acct# row, just to the right of the SUBTOTAL label.
7. Key the formula =SUM(Tax) and press Enter.
8. Format the formula you just entered as currency.
9. From the Edit menu choose *Copy* to copy the formula.
10. Highlight the cell in column F in the Summ Report row, to the right of the GRAND TOTAL label, and press Enter to place a copy of the formula there. Whoops! Inserting the formula in column F cut off part of the label in column E. Column E is not wide enough for the GRAND TOTAL label.
11. Highlight *GRAND TOTA* and widen the column to 13 spaces. Your screen should now look like Figure 9-22.
12. From the Print menu, choose *Page Setup & Margins*. In the dialog box, change the left margin to 1.0 and the right margin to 1.0, and then press Enter. That completes the report layout.

Printing the Report Now the report is ready to be printed. Follow the same procedure as before.

1. From the File menu, choose *Save* to preserve the new report.
2. From the Print menu, choose *Preview*, and press Enter to preview the report as it will be printed.
3. If everything looks good, ready your printer and then press P to print the report. If

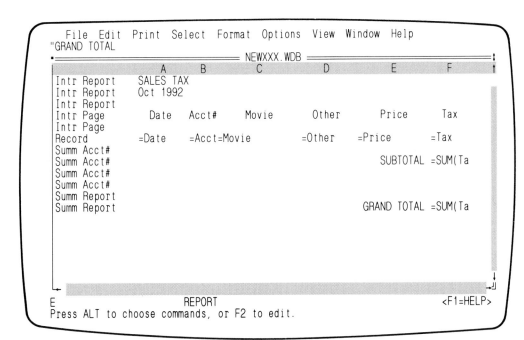

FIGURE 9-22
Sales Tax report definition.

anything needs to be corrected, press Esc to return to the report definition, make the changes, and then repeat step 2.

Printing a Wide Report

To fit the Daily Tax and Totals report on an 8 1/2-inch by 11 1/2-inch page, you needed to narrow the left and right margins. Even then, the layout did not have room for the full movie titles or types. The width of that report was 66 characters—not unusually wide, and sometime you may need to print a much wider report. A wide-carriage printer, which accepts paper up to 15 inches wide, can easily accommodate wide layouts. But if your printer is limited to 8 1/2-inch by 11 1/2-inch paper, you can still print wide reports by using condensed type. Many printers offer a condensed type option, which lets you print in font sizes smaller than standard 12 point Pica. Smaller sizes print more than the standard 10 characters per inch, so your layout can have more characters on each line.

One of the report layouts in the *NewXXX.WDB* database file, WideRep, is set up to print 96 characters per line. If your printer can print condensed type (8 or 10 points), follow these instructions to select a small font size, set the page margins, and print the report. Even if your printer is unable to print condensed type, follow the steps to learn how to change the font size with Works.

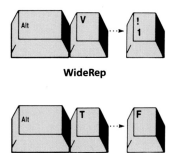

1. From the View menu, choose *WideRep*, and then press Esc to display the report definition.
2. From the Format menu, choose *Font*. You see the dialog box shown in Figure 9-23.

   The dialog box displays two lists, showing the fonts and sizes available on your printer. To change the type size, you highlight a font in the list on the left and then highlight a size in the list on the right.

3. Highlight different fonts with the Up and Down Arrows. When you select each, you see the available sizes in the Size list. If 8-point is available in any font, press Alt-S to select a size, use the Up and Down Arrows to highlight 8, and press Enter. Then skip to step 5. If

FIGURE 9-23
Fonts dialog box.

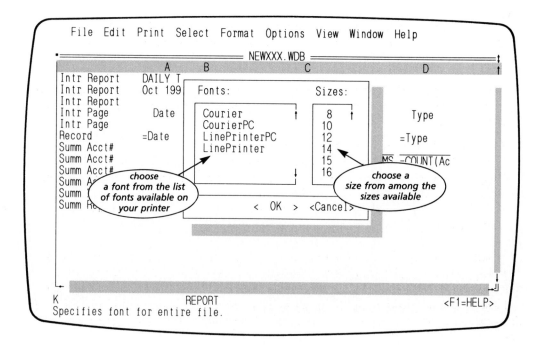

10-point is the smallest available size, select it, press Enter, and continue with step 4. If 12-point is the smallest available size, skip the rest of this procedure—your printer does not allow printing with condensed type.

4. If you selected a 10-point font size in the previous step, choose *Page Setup & Margins* from the Print menu. Change the left and right page margins to 0.0. The report will take up the entire width of the page.

5. Preview the report. You should see the entire report, including the Total column on the right and the Grand Total at the bottom of the report.

6. Press P to print the report.

Condensed printing and wide-carriage printers are especially useful when reports contain more information from each record than can fit in an 80-character line. Printers that only allow up to 10 characters per inch and 8-inch wide lines must print two or more pages to include all the information in the report.

Preparing a Report on Rentals by Type

Your final report from this file should show the total rentals for each type of movie. This is a very simple report. But because it is so different from the earlier reports, it vividly demonstrates the variety of reports that can be produced from a single database file.

Copying and Renaming the Report Layout Once again you can begin by making a copy of an existing report layout and then changing the definition.

1. From the View menu, choose *Reports*.

2. In the dialog box, select the Tax report and choose *Copy*. Works makes a copy and adds it to the list as *Report1*.

3. Highlight *Report1*, choose the *Name* option, and on the Name line key Rentals.

4. Choose *Rename*. Works renames the copy and adds the Rentals layout to the View menu.

5. Choose *Done*. You can safely make changes to the copy without affecting the original.
6. Open the View menu and confirm that you are looking at the Rental report. If you do not see the report definition, press Esc to display the report definition.

Removing Fields from the New Report   This report is concerned only with the types of movies that have been rented and their rental price. So you can eliminate many of the fields from the layout.

1. To delete the Date field, highlight any cell in column A.
2. From the Edit menu, choose *Delete Row/Column*. In the dialog box, select the *Column* option, then press Enter. Works deletes the column containing the Date field. The title of the report was in column A, so it is deleted, too.
3. Follow the same procedure to remove the Acct#, Other, and Tax fields. When you are done, only the Movie and Price fields should remain.

Inserting a Field   Now you need to put the Type field back into the report. This is a three-stage process, as shown in Figure 9-24. First you will create a column for the field. Next, you will insert the field name into the new column, in the Intr Page row. Finally, you will insert the formula for the field contents into the new column in the Records row. You will also need to change the alignment and style of the field name to match the other names in the row.

1. Highlight any cell in the Price column (column B).
2. From the Edit menu, choose *Insert Row/Column*. In the dialog box, select the *Column* option, then press Enter. Works inserts an empty column. To make room for it, the column containing the Price field moves to the right.

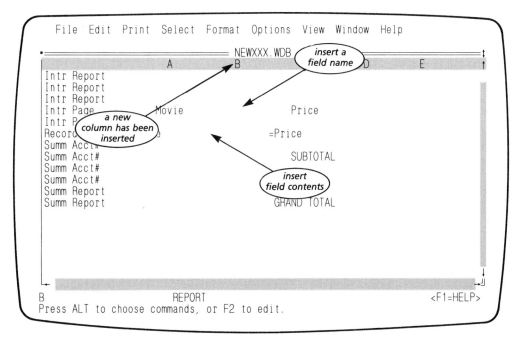

FIGURE 9-24
Rentals report layout.

Insert Field Name—
Report Definition

3. Highlight the cell of the first Intr Page row that is in column B—the row containing field names. You want to insert the name of the Type field.
4. From the Edit menu, choose *Insert Field Name*. Works displays the list of fields shown in Figure 9-25.

FIGURE 9-25
Insert Field Name dialog box.

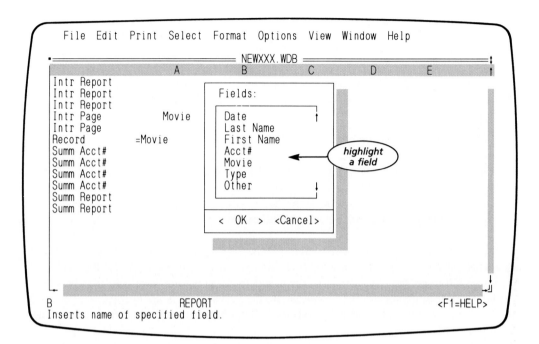

5. Use the Down Arrow to highlight *Type*, then press Enter. Works inserts Type in the highlighted cell.
6. Highlight the cell of the Record row in the same column.
7. This time, choose *Insert Field Contents* from the Edit menu. Works displays a similar dialog box.
8. Highlight *Type*, then press Enter. Works inserts the formula =Type in the highlighted cell. Of course you could key both the formula and the field name instead of using the Edit menu. The menu is useful when you cannot remember the exact name of the field you want to insert.
9. To align and style the field name, highlight the name *Type* in the Intr Page row.
10. From the Format menu, choose *Style*. Works displays a dialog box listing alignments and styles.
11. In the Alignment box, select *Center*; in the Styles box select *Underline*; then press Enter. The field name moves to the center of the field. The name will be centered and underlined when you print the report, but most video monitors do not show underlined characters.

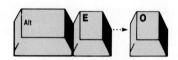

Insert Field Contents—
Report Definition

Changing the Widths of the Fields   You want to see as much of the movie titles and types as possible, and you have room enough to make these fields wider.

1. From the Format menu, choose *Column Width*.
2. In the dialog box key 15 and then press Enter. That broadens the Type field to 15 spaces.
3. Highlight any cell in column A, and then repeat the procedure to widen the column to 35 spaces.

Arranging Records and Adding a New Group Total   You want this report to show total rentals for movies grouped by type. To do that, you need to sort the file on the Type field with a break for group totals. You also need to insert formulas to calculate group totals and a grand total.

1. From the Select menu, choose *Sort Records*. Works displays the dialog box shown in Figure 9-26.

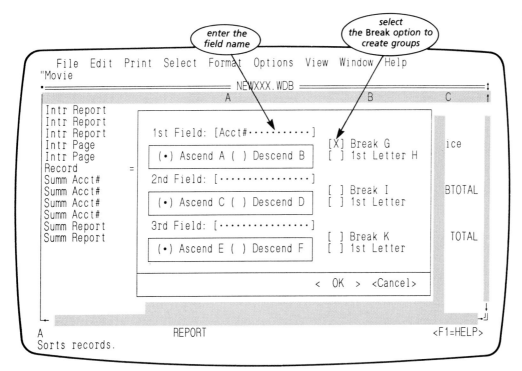

FIGURE 9-26
Sorting Records dialog box.

The field name you entered the last time you sorted the database may still be entered as the 1st Field, and the *Break* option may be checked.

2. Key Type on the 1st Field line.
3. Select the *Break* option. (If the *Break* option is checked already, do not select it again. That would turn it off.)
4. Press Enter.

Works groups the database by Type and replaces the Summ Acct# rows that were copied from the Tax report layout with Summ Type rows. You want to insert summary calculations in the Summ Type and Summ Report rows in column C. But first you need to move the labels.

5. Highlight the SUBTOTAL label in column C.
6. From the Edit menu, choose *Copy*.
7. Press the Left Arrow once to move the highlight to column B, then press Enter. Works copies the label into column B. The right alignment of the label is preserved.
8. Repeat the last 3 steps to copy the GRAND TOTAL label into column B in the Summ Report row.
9. Highlight the original SUBTOTAL label in column C.
10. Key =SUM(Price) and press Enter. That enters the calculation in the Summ Type row. Next, you need to format the calculation as currency.
11. From the Format menu, choose *Currency*, and press Enter to accept the standard two decimal places.
12. To insert a copy of the calculation in the Summ Report row, choose *Copy* from the Edit menu, highlight the original GRAND TOTAL label in column C, and then press Enter.

Adding a Title Your final step in preparing the layout is adding a title.

1. In the first Intr Report row, highlight the cell in column A.
2. Key RENTALS BY TYPE, and then press the Down Arrow once to move the highlight to the second Intr Report Row.
3. Press Ctrl-; to enter today's date, and then press Enter.
4. To align the date, choose *Style* from the Format menu. In the Alignment section of the dialog box, select *Left*, then press Enter.
5. To make this date look like the other dates, choose *Time/Date* from the Format menu, choose the *Long* option, and press Enter. When you are done, the report definition should look like Figure 9-27.

FIGURE 9-27
Rentals by Type report definition.

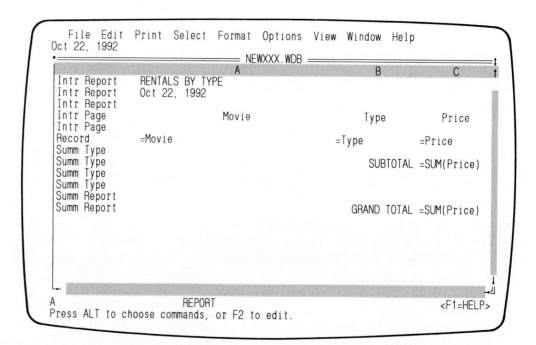

Selecting Records for a Report The other reports you prepared included all the records in the *NewXXX.WDB* database file. This report concerns only movie rentals, not purchases of other items. You can select a set of records to include in a report, and for this report you want only records of movie rentals. Since an entry is always included in the Movie field when a movie is rented, but never for purchases, you can select just those entries where the Movie field contains an entry. The procedure for selecting records in a report is exactly the same as it is to select records for display on the screen.

1. From the View menu, choose *Query*. You see the Query window like the one you worked with in Lesson 6.
2. In the Query window, press Tab or Shift-Tab until the Movie field is highlighted.
3. Key * (asterisk) and press Enter. This wild card character means *anything at all* and selects the record if any entry appears in the field.
4. Choose *Rentals* from the View menu to return to your report, and then press Esc to display the report definition.

That does it. You are ready to print the report.

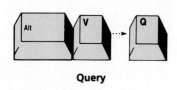

Query

Printing the Report   Follow the same procedure to print this report as you have for the others.

1. Save the changes you have made to the file.
2. Use *Preview* to check the report.
3. If everything looks good, ready your printer and then press P to print the report. If anything needs to be corrected, press Esc to return to the report definition, make the changes, and then repeat Step 2.

Now you have four (or three) different versions of reports on the same file—see how they compare in Figure 9-28. They hardly look as if they use the same data, but you know that they all are made from information in the *NewXXX.WDB* file—and you have created three report layouts yourself. Good Work! In the next lesson you will begin working with spreadsheets.

```
DAILY TAX AND TOTALS                                      Daily Tax and Totals Report.
Dec 19xx

   Date    Acct#     Movie      Type   Other      Price     Tax    Total

   Oct 21 1001 Invasion of theSci                $2.00   $0.12   $2.12
   Oct 21 1001 The Mole PeopleSci                $2.00   $0.12   $2.12
   Oct 21 1001 Bad Day for BadWest               $2.00   $0.12   $2.12
   Oct 21 1001                    Blank tape    $12.00   $0.72  $12.72

                  ITEMS   4              SUBTOTAL          $19.08


   Oct 21 1002 Typical Day in Adve               $3.00   $0.18   $3.18
   Oct 21 1002 Invasion of theSci                $2.00   $0.12   $2.12
   Oct 21 1002                    Poster         $8.00   $0.48   $8.48

                  ITEMS   3              SUBTOTAL          $13.78


   Oct 21 1003                    Tape rack     $27.95   $1.68  $29.63
   Oct 21 1003                    Blank tape    $23.00   $1.38  $24.38
   Oct 21 1003                    Guide to G     $5.95   $0.36   $6.31
```

```
   SALES TAX                                              Sales Tax Report.
   Dec 19xx

   Date    Acct#     Movie          Other       Price     Tax

   Oct 21 1001 Invasion of the                  $2.00   $0.12
   Oct 21 1001 The Mole People                  $2.00   $0.12
   Oct 21 1001 Bad Day for Bad                  $2.00   $0.12
   Oct 21 1001                 Blank tape      $12.00   $0.72

                              SUBTOTAL  $1.08


   Oct 21 1002 Typical Day in                   $3.00   $0.18
   Oct 21 1002 Invasion of the                  $2.00   $0.12
   Oct 21 1002                 Poster           $8.00   $0.48

                              SUBTOTAL  $0.78


   Oct 21 1003                 Tape rack       $27.95   $1.68
   Oct 21 1003                 Blank tape      $23.00   $1.38
   Oct 21 1003                 Guide to G       $5.95   $0.36
```

FIGURE 9-28
Reports from the sale file.

FIGURE 9-28 (continued)
Reports from the sale file.

Wide Report in 8-point type.

```
DAILY TAX AND SALES TOTALS
Oct 1992

Date   Acct#          Movie              Type        Other       Price    Tax     Total

Oct 21 1001 Invasion of the Slime Creatures Sci Fi               $2.00   $0.12   $2.12
Oct 21 1001 The Mole People              Sci Fi                  $2.00   $0.12   $2.12
Oct 21 1001 Bad Day for Bad Bob          Western                 $2.00   $0.12   $2.12
Oct 21 1001                                          Blank tape  $12.00  $0.72   $12.72

                                         ITEMS       4      TOTALS  $18.00  1.08   $19.08


Oct 21 1002 Typical Day in a Typical Life Adventure             $3.00   $0.18   $3.18
Oct 21 1002 Invasion of the Slime Creatures Sci Fi              $2.00   $0.12   $2.12
Oct 21 1002                                          Poster      $8.00   $0.48   $8.48

                                         ITEMS       3      TOTALS  $13.00  0.78   $13.78


Oct 21 1003                                          Tape rack   $27.95  $1.68   $29.63
Oct 21 1003                                          Blank tapes $23.00  $1.38   $24.38
Oct 21 1003                                          Guide to Great $5.95 $0.36  $6.31

                                         ITEMS       3      TOTALS  $56.90  3.41   $60.31
```

Rentals by Type Report.

```
RENTALS BY TYPE
Dec 7, 1989

            Movie                        Type          Price

Typical Day in a Typical Life         Adventure        $3.00
Trials of Young Werther               Adventure        $2.00
Grasping for Straws                   Adventure        $2.00

                                      SUBTOTAL         $7.00


Lonely Bobolink, The                  Chiller          $2.00

                                      SUBTOTAL         $2.00


Invasion of the Slime Creatures       Sci Fi           $2.00
The Mole People                       Sci Fi           $2.00
Invasion of the Slime Creatures       Sci Fi           $2.00
```

KEY TERMS

break   *MSW 153*
calculated field   *MSW 144*
formula   *MSW 144*
function   *MSW 153*
report definition   *MSW 148*
summary calculations   *MSW 153*

COMMANDS

Alt-E-D (Delete Row/Column—Report definition)
Alt-E-N (Field Name—List view)
Alt-T-F (Font)
Alt-E-O (Insert Field Contents—Report definition)
Alt-E-N (Insert Field Name—Report definition)
Alt-E-S (Insert Field Summary—Report definition)
Alt-E-I (Insert Row/Column—Report definition)

Alt-V-N (New Report)
Alt-V-Q (Query)
Alt-V-R (Reports)
Alt-S-R (Row)
Alt-S-O (Sort Records)
Alt-T-S (Style)
Alt-T-T (Time/Date)

REVIEW QUESTIONS

1. What is a calculated field, and how do you set one up?
2. Can you set up a calculated field to include another calculated field?
3. Why would you want to include calculated fields in a report?
4. What is a report definition?
5. Does the row of the report definition in which you enter information matter? What are the different types of rows and what are they used for?
6. How do you divide the records in a database into groups for a report?
7. In what kinds of reports would you want to break the database into groups?
8. In what parts of a report definition are summary calculations used?
9. What are two examples of functions?
10. How are functions used in reports?

APPLICATION

Morris Yu wants a report on the types of products that customers buy rather than the ones they rent. Using the *NewXXX.WDB* file, make a new report layout called Other. Organize the report the following way:

a. Include only three fields: Acct#, Other, and Price.
b. Make sure that there is room in the Other field for long entries.
c. Arrange the records in numerical order on the Acct# field with breaks between groups.
d. Select only records where the Other field has entries.
e. Set up summary calculations that print (1) the number of items each customer has purchased, (2) the number of items purchased by all customers, (3) the total price spent by each customer, and (4) the total purchases for all customers.
f. Format the calculations based on the Price field as currency.
g. Enter labels for the summary calculations, and then apply the Bold style to the labels and calculations in the Summ Acct# and Summ Report rows.
h. Title the report SALES BY ACCOUNT NUMBER.
i. Preview the report and if necessary, change the page margins so the report prints on one page.

Save the changes you have made, then print one copy of the report.

UNIT IV

The Spreadsheet

Getting Started with the Spreadsheet

OBJECTIVES

- Identify and explain the parts of a spreadsheet.
- Move the cursor around a spreadsheet file.
- Enter words and numbers into a spreadsheet.
- Change words and numbers on a spreadsheet.
- Recalculate the results of equations by changing numbers.
- Print a spreadsheet.

SPREADSHEET BASICS

An electronic spreadsheet program like the Works Spreadsheet helps you perform many kinds of calculations. If you were to do some of these calculations with a pencil, paper, and a pocket calculator, you would need to write down page after page of numbers. You might need a big eraser, too, because every time you changed one number, you might have to recalculate, erase the old results, and write down the new ones. With an electronic spreadsheet, the changes are made electronically, so you can try many alternatives without having to go through a lot of work. The numbers are stored in the computer's memory, where they can be easily adjusted as you work.

A glance around your home or classroom will give you a good idea of the kind of calculations you can perform with a spreadsheet program. Even in your daily newspaper, you may see numbers that have been analyzed with a spreadsheet. On the front page, a story about the new government budget may have a table showing how much money the government collects and how much it spends for particular programs. That table is a simple form of a spreadsheet. In the business pages, data on a company's sales, costs, and profits form another kind of spreadsheet. In the sports section, statistics on a baseball team's performance, such as batting averages, are easily calculated with a spreadsheet program.

Whenever you see numbers in rows and columns with the results of some kind of calculation, you are looking at material that may have been developed using a spreadsheet. An annual report, for instance, shows detailed calculations about a company's financial performance. The charts and graphs in social science and math books may have been prepared with spreadsheet programs. A spreadsheet can even convert the amounts of ingredients needed in a recipe to serve different sized groups—for example, converting a recipe that serves four people to amounts that can be used for three people.

FIGURE 10-1
You may find many examples
of simple spreadsheets around
home or school.

The Parts of a Spreadsheet

Most electronic spreadsheet programs display numbers in rows and columns. Figure 10-2
shows an example of a Works Spreadsheet. **Columns** run vertically; they are labeled with letters. **Rows** run horizontally; they are labeled with numbers. A column intersects with a row
to form a **cell**. You identify a cell by its column letter and row number. For example, cell F3
exists at the intersection of column F and row 3. The cell letter and row number form the
coordinates of the cell. Coordinates are also called **cell references** because they refer to the
location of a cell.

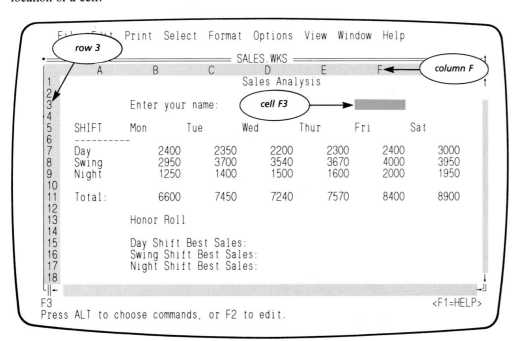

FIGURE 10-2
Column, row, and cell on a
Works spreadsheet screen.

Selecting a Cell

To select a cell, you use the arrow keys to move highlighting onto it. When the highlighting lands on a cell, the cell becomes current, or active, and the coordinates of the cell appear in the status line, at the bottom left-hand corner of the screen. The contents of the cell now appear in the formula bar for you to read or edit, as shown in Figure 10-3.

FIGURE 10-3
You select a cell by moving the highlighting onto the cell.

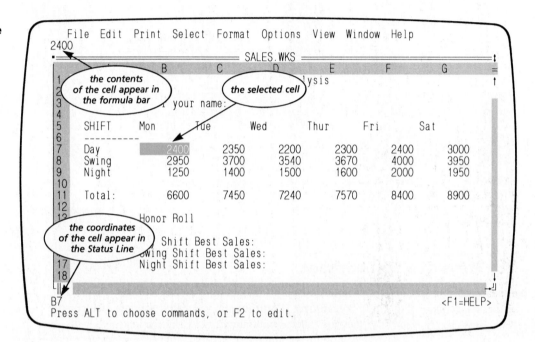

Entering Information in a Cell and Editing

When you have selected a cell, you key your entry in the formula bar at the top of the window, just below the menu bar. The first character you key replaces any information that existed in the cell before. If you decide you prefer the information that existed before, you can always press Esc, to restore the original. Once you are satisfied with your entry, you press Enter to confirm that you want to place that information into the cell itself.

But what if you want to modify, or **edit**, the original entry, rather than replace it completely? You need to press F2 to place a cursor at the end of the formula bar, so you can make precise changes. You can then backspace over individual characters deleting them, use the arrow keys to move through the text without disturbing it, or key new characters. When you complete your editing, you press Enter. The cursor disappears from the formula bar, and any earlier entry in that cell is replaced with this new one. And now, if you press an arrow key, it moves the highlighting to another cell.

What You Can Put in Cells

A spreadsheet cell can contain a number, formula, date, or text. You can, for instance, enter a number in any cell. Or you can enter a **formula** in a cell—an equation that tells the Spreadsheet how to calculate a value to display in this cell. The Spreadsheet will perform the specified calculation, then display the result in the formula's cell. You see the result, but—secretly—the cell also contains the formula. You only see the formula when you select the cell or when you tell Works that you want to see all the formulas displayed for a while, instead of the results. Normally when you select a cell, the formula appears in the formula bar, while the resulting number remains visible in the cell itself. So when you look at a spreadsheet, some of the numbers you see are just numbers, but other numbers are the result of calculations based on formulas.

The heart of the spreadsheet is its numbers. But to describe the numeric information in a row or column, you can also enter some letters or words in a cell; that text is known as a **label**. You can also enter the date of a transaction or your most recent changes. To avoid accidentally including a date in some calculation, the Spreadsheet considers a date as a kind of text, rather than a number. To the Spreadsheet, text is whatever cannot be or should not be included in a calculation. Imagine the confusion if it tried to add the word *Budget* to the number *$1,000*! Figure 10-4 shows a spreadsheet with different kinds of information entered in the cells.

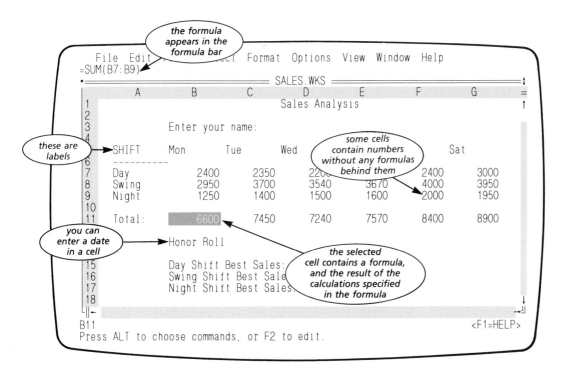

FIGURE 10-4
Contents of a spreadsheet.

EXPLORING A SPREADSHEET

Sarah Lugosi has always figured out for herself how much to charge for different products that Lugosi's Classic Video Store sells. Now that the store is expanding, she needs to delegate this task to others so she has more time for planning. She has begun making a spreadsheet that will calculate prices automatically using a formula she developed, but the spreadsheet still needs some work. After you explore the spreadsheet a little, you will add labels and numbers and use a formula to calculate different prices.

Opening a Spreadsheet File

The file with the pricing spreadsheet is called *Pricing.WKS*. *WKS* is an extension of the file name; it stands for worksheet. The area in which you arrange your numbers in rows and columns is sometimes known as a worksheet.

1. Start up Works. Use the startup procedures you learned in Lesson 2.
2. If you have only one disk drive, replace the Works program disk with the template disk. If you have two disk drives, insert the template disk into drive B.
3. Choose *Open Existing File* from the File menu. In the dialog box that appears, select the drive in which your template disk is located, and then select the file *Pricing.WKS*.

The Pricing spreadsheet document appears on the screen, as shown in Figure 10-5. It has been set up for a user to enter a product name and its wholesale price. The spreadsheet will then follow several formulas to determine the price Lugosi's should charge the customer for the product.

FIGURE 10-5
The pricing spreadsheet.

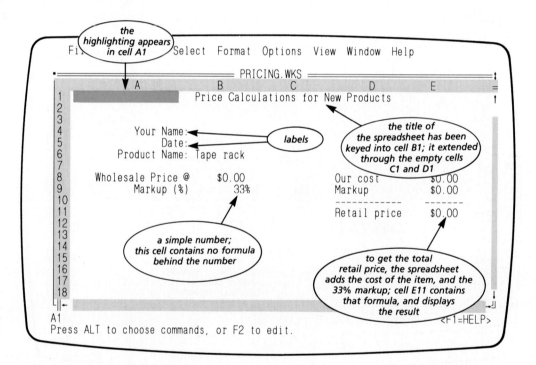

Moving Around the Spreadsheet

The highlighting is currently on cell A1. You can move the highlighting up, down, left, or right, with the arrow keys. As you move the highlighting, selecting one cell after another, you see each cell's coordinates appear in the status line at the bottom of the screen. Try it.

1. Press the Down Arrow key three times to move the highlighting to the *Your Name:* label.

The contents of the cell appear in the formula bar, preceded by quotation marks. The Spreadsheet inserts those in front of any entry that begins with a letter to indicate that the entry contains text, not numbers.

2. Press End to move the highlighting along the same row to either the entry in the last column that contains any data or the last column on that screen—column E in this case. Notice that the width of the highlighting is less than it was in column A. That's because Sarah Lugosi adjusted the column widths as she created the spreadsheet, and the highlighting always fills up the cell in which it lands.

3. Press Home to return along the same row to the cell that appears in column A. You return to the label *Your Name:*.

4. Press Ctrl-End to move down to the last entry in the last row in the last column that contains any data in your spreadsheet. You see *$0.00* in the cell, and the formula used to arrive at that total appears in the formula bar, as shown in Figure 10-6. It's convenient to be able to move around in the area that contains meaningful data.

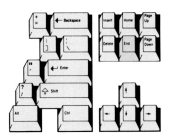

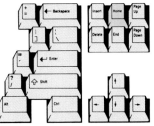

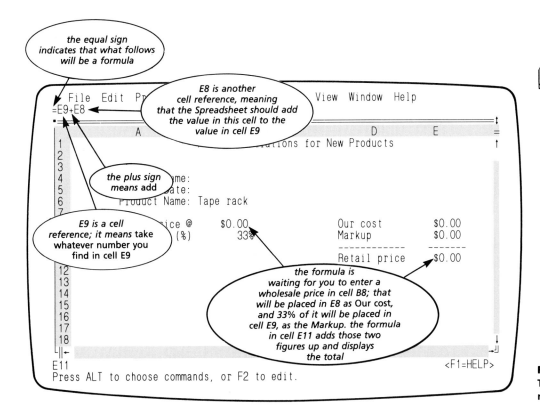

**Move to Last
Entry You Made in
the Spreadsheet**

FIGURE 10-6
The formula for calculating the retail price.

5. Press Ctrl-Down Arrow. The highlighting skips to row 4096. The data you were just looking at is now far above, out of sight.

   Use this keystroke combination to zip down to the next entry—no matter how far away it is—or to the very bottom of the spreadsheet, if there is no other entry. The Works Spreadsheet has 4096 rows and 256 columns.

6. Press the Right Arrow and keep pressing it to move the highlighting to the last possible column in the spreadsheet.

   Watch the column letters change from A through Z, to AA through AZ, BA through BZ, all the way to IV, the last column on the right. At the same time, the scroll box at the bottom of the window moves to the right. The scroll bar itself represents the full extent of the spreadsheet, and the box shows your approximate position as you move from left to right, as shown in Figure 10-7.

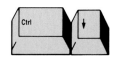

**Move Down to Next
Entry—or Last
Cell in Column**

FIGURE 10-7
The Works horizontal scroll bar represents the entire width of the spreadsheet.

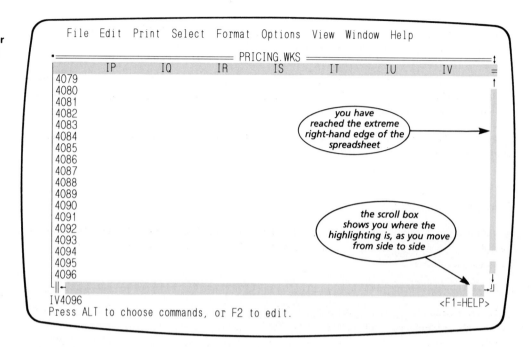

As you lean on the arrow key, reflect on how convenient it is that Works offers you a way to skip and jump, instead of plodding like this.

7. Press Ctrl-Home to return to the home spot—cell A1.

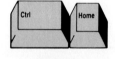

Return to Cell A1

ENTERING INFORMATION

ou enter text and numbers in a spreadsheet in three stages. You highlight the cell, key letters for a label or numbers for a value, and press Enter. When you press Enter, the information is placed in the cell itself, replacing anything that existed there before.

Entering Labels

To begin using this spreadsheet, enter your first name and the current date. That will let other people know who determined the price of the product, and when.

1. Use the arrow keys to move to cell B4. Check the status line to make sure you have in fact arrived.

2. Key your first name—but do not press Enter yet.

Your name appears in the formula bar at the top of the screen and in the cell itself. Notice that the formula bar contains the cursor, the blinking underline that indicates where the text you key will appear.

3. Press Enter.

The cursor disappears from the formula bar, and Works enters your name in the cell. Now if you key something else, it will completely replace your name.

4. Key the first letter of your name, but do not press Enter. Ooops! There goes your name.
5. Press Esc to recapture your original entry.
6. Press the Down Arrow to move to cell B5.
7. Press Ctrl-; to enter the current date. Once you have entered the current date in this way, it does not change, even if you use the spreadsheet on another day. Press Enter to tell Works that the entry is complete.

Congratulations! You have entered your first labels into the Spreadsheet. Now you are ready to enter a number.

Entering a Number

You enter numbers the same way you enter labels. In this section, you will enter the wholesale cost of the tape rack. The Spreadsheet will use that figure to determine the retail price Lugosi's should charge.

1. Move the highlighting to cell B8.

   In the formula bar you see the current dollar amount—zero. But in the cell itself, you see how that amount has been formatted by the Spreadsheet, following Sarah's instructions. Often you will find that you only have to key a number, and you can leave the formatting to the Spreadsheet.

2. Key 10 but do not press Enter yet. In the formula bar, the cursor is waiting for any further numbers.
3. Watch cells E8, E9, and E11 as you press Enter.

   Works takes the contents of your entry in cell B8, puts that into cell E8, figures the markup and puts that figure into cell E9, then adds the cost and the markup to get the resulting Retail price, in cell E11. This calculation takes place automatically. You know immediately what the retail price should be, as shown in Figure 10-8.

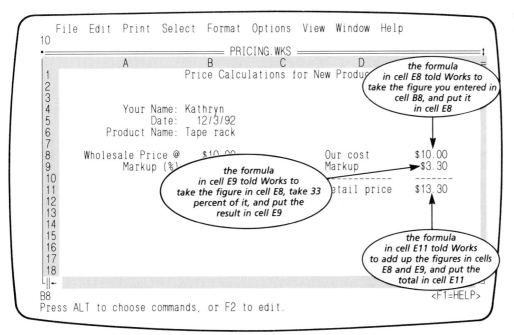

FIGURE 10-8
Entering a number.

CHANGING INFORMATION

The biggest advantage of the electronic spreadsheet over pen, paper, and pocket calculator is its ability to calculate—and recalculate—automatically. Recalculating means changing the results of formulas that use a number whenever you change that number. For instance, suppose Sarah Lugosi wants you to calculate a price for a poster that costs the store $7.65. You can enter the new information on this spreadsheet without having to change anything except the name of the product and the wholesale price.

Replacing a Label

You replace a label the same way you enter one. You highlight the cell whose contents you want to replace, make the new entry, and press Enter.

1. Select cell B6. The cell shows the words *Tape rack* right now. In the formula bar, those words are preceded by quotation marks, inserted by the Spreadsheet to indicate that what follows is a label, not a formula or a number.
2. Key `Poster` but do not press Enter yet.

    Notice that the label you just entered appears in the formula bar and in the current cell, but the cursor is still blinking in the formula bar. This shows you that you have not yet completed your entry. If you were to press Esc, the original entry would reappear in the cell.

3. Press Enter.

    Works removes the cursor from the formula bar and erases the earlier entry from memory. *Poster* is now the entry in cell B6, as shown in Figure 10-9. You can now use the arrow keys to move the highlighting elsewhere.

FIGURE 10-9
Replacing a label.

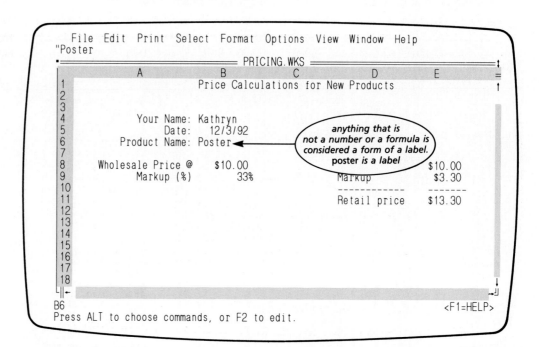

Replacing a Number

You replace a number the same way you enter one. You highlight the cell whose contents you want to replace, make the new entry, and press Enter.

You don't want to replace your formulas. You just need to replace any numbers they use in their calculations, and leave it to the Spreadsheet to recalculate, producing new results, and placing them in the right cells.

1. Select cell B8.
2. Key 7.65 but do not press Enter yet.

Notice that the number you just keyed appears in the formula bar and in the current cell, but the cursor is still blinking in the formula bar. This shows you that you have not yet completed your entry. If you were to press Esc, the original entry would reappear in the cell.

3. Press Enter. In cell B8, the number *7.65* shifts to the right, and a dollar sign pops up in front of it.

Earlier, Sarah selected this cell, and used the *Style* command on the Format menu to tell the Spreadsheet to align its contents—whatever they became—with the right edge of the cell, and to apply currency formatting to the number. These formatting choices continue to apply to the contents of the cell, no matter how the contents change. That's why you were able to leave the dollar sign and arrangement to Works.

In addition, the Spreadsheet recalculates the markup and retail price for the poster. The retail price will be $10.17. The screen looks like Figure 10-10.

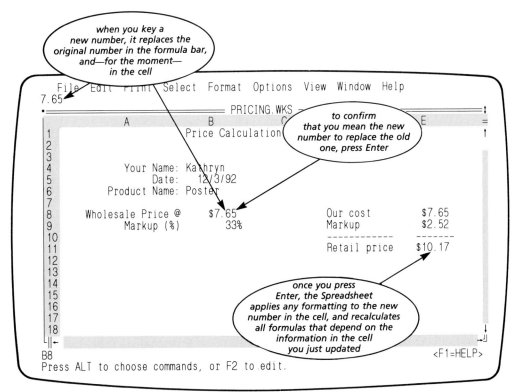

FIGURE 10-10
Replacing a number.

What if it turns out that the poster actually costs the store $6.00 rather than $7.65? Try the new number and watch Works recalculate again.

4. In cell B8, key 6 and press Enter. Watch the retail price in cell E11 as it is recalculated.
5. Enter another number and watch Works recalculate the results. Try as many numbers as you wish, but when you are finished, change the wholesale price back to 7.65. You can also change the markup to see how it will affect the retail price. Try it.
6. Select cell B9, and key 1.25 for the new markup.

When you press Enter, 1.25 is reformatted as 125% because Sarah Lugosi earlier instructed Works to display numbers in this cell as percentages without decimal places. Marking up the price by 125% means your markup will be more than the original cost. Look at the retail price that Works has recalculated, taking the new markup into account, as shown in Figure 10-11.

FIGURE 10-11
A new markup.

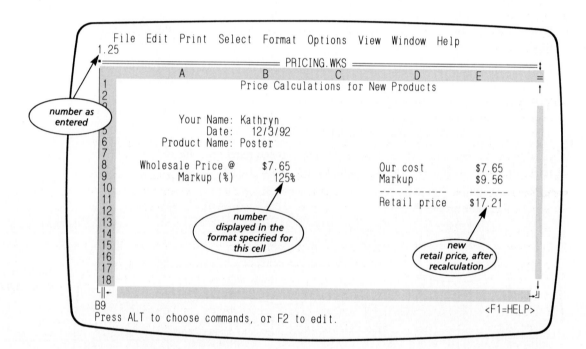

Works can recalculate as often as you change the numbers used in the formulas in a spreadsheet. For example, with the Pricing spreadsheet, you can calculate a price for any product the store carries. You only have to change the name of the product and the store's cost to get a new price.

In the future, you may design more sophisticated spreadsheets with many different values that you can change. These numbers are called **variables** because their amounts can vary. For example, Sarah Lugosi might develop a spreadsheet that will help her determine if her store will be profitable. Variables could include the amount of monthly rent, cost of electricity and gas, number of employees and their salaries, and so forth. While the store might be profitable with a monthly rent of $1,000, she might discover that it would no longer be profitable if the rent doubled to $2,000. However, suppose she increased the price of video rentals by 50%—maybe that would make the store profitable again, even with the higher rent. Each time she tries an alternative, she will be able to see the effects of her decisions. Trying many alternatives will help her make better choices for the future of her business.

SAVING A SPREADSHEET FILE

After you finish making changes to a spreadsheet file, you should save the changes. Sometimes, especially with complicated spreadsheets that have many variables, you will want to save many different versions of the same file so that you can keep track of the alternatives. For this file, you can save your changes once.

Save As

1. Choose *Save As* from the File menu to tell Works that you want to change the name of the file at the same time you save your changes. Make sure that your template disk is in either drive A or drive B. You see the Save As dialog box.
2. Select the Directories box by pressing Alt-I, then use the arrow keys to select the drive in which you have placed the template disk. Works places that drive name into the *Save as* line at the top of the dialog box.
3. Move back to the top of the dialog box by pressing Alt-S.
4. Press the Right Arrow once, so you don't wipe out the selected drive name.
5. Key *PriceXXX* (where XXX are your initials) as the name for your new version of this file, and press Enter.

PRINTING A SPREADSHEET

In the Database unit of this tutorial, you printed many different reports from a single database file. With the Spreadsheet, you can print what you see on the screen directly—without preparing a report. In fact, if you wish, you can print out your spreadsheet every time you make a change, just to keep a record of all the work you've done. Make sure that your printer is turned on, connected to the computer, and on-line.

1. Press Ctrl-Home to move the highlighting to cell A1.
2. Hold down the Shift key at the same time you press the Down Arrow ten times to highlight all the way down to cell A11. Then, while still holding the Shift key down, press the Right Arrow four times to extend the highlighting to row E. You have now selected the meaningful data in your spreadsheet—the material you want to print out.
3. Choose *Set Print Area* from the Print menu. You are telling Works to print only this part of the spreadsheet. (You aren't interested in having Works print all 4096 rows and all 256 columns, because most of those are empty.)
4. Choose *Headers & Footers* from the Print menu. It's usually helpful to identify your spreadsheet in the header or footer, or both. You see the Headers & Footers dialog box, as shown in Figure 10-12.
5. In the Header box, key: `Poster`
6. In the Footer box, key the file name: *PriceXXX*
7. Choose *Page Setup & Margins* from the Print menu, and in the dialog box, set the left margin to 0.5 and the right margin to 0.5, so there will be plenty of room. Press Enter.
8. Choose *Print* from the Print menu. In the dialog box, select the *Print row and column labels* option. These help you identify the exact cell in which information appears, in case you need to make revisions. (If you were printing the spreadsheet out for display to customers or clients, you would not want to print the row and column labels.) Press Enter. The spreadsheet should begin printing.

FIGURE 10-12
The Headers & Footers dialog box.

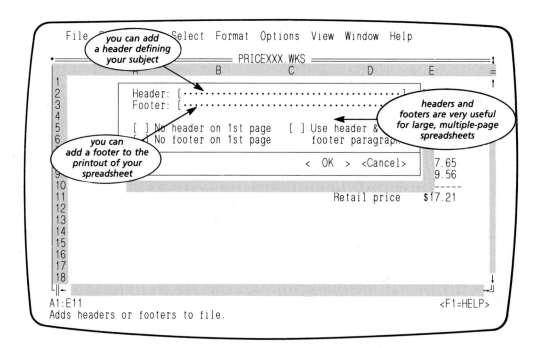

KEY TERMS

cell   *MSW 175*
cell reference   *MSW 175*
column   *MSW 175*
coordinate   *MSW 175*
edit   *MSW 176*
formula   *MSW 176*
label   *MSW 177*
row   *MSW 175*
variable   *MSW 184*

COMMANDS

F2 (Edit contents of formula bar)
Ctrl-semicolon (;) (Enter current date)
End (Move highlighting to last entry in row)
Home (Move highlighting to first entry in row)
Ctrl-Down Arrow (Move down to next entry—or last cell in column)
Ctrl-Right Arrow (Move right to next entry—or last cell in row)
Ctrl-End (Move to last entry you made in the spreadsheet)
Enter (Place contents of formula bar in cell)
Ctrl-Home (Return to cell A1)
Alt-F-A (Save As)
Alt-P-H (Set Headers & Footers)
Alt-P-A (Set Print Area)
Alt-P-M (Page Setup & Margins)

REVIEW QUESTIONS

1. How does the Spreadsheet know you are entering a label?
2. How can you replace the contents of the cell you have just highlighted?
3. What is the fastest way to move to the last row of a spreadsheet? To the last column? To the cell A1?
4. If a highlighted cell contains a formula and displays the result of that calculation, how can you see the formula itself?
5. When you change a number that is used in formulas in other cells, what does the Spreadsheet do automatically in those other cells?
6. How many cells are there in a Works spreadsheet? How can you limit the number of cells you print?
7. Explain what the following formula means: $= E9 + E8$.
8. How many times can you change the numbers in a spreadsheet and cause formulas to recalculate?
9. Why might you want to print more than one version of a spreadsheet?
10. If you highlight a cell that contains a number, then type a new entry, how can you restore the original entry without retyping it?

APPLICATIONS

1. Open the *Fest.WKS* file from the template disk. This file is an expense account form for employees of Lugosi's Video who travel to film festivals and for other purposes. Suppose that you have been sent to the Vail Film Festival in Colorado. The file has already been mostly filled out for you, except for your name and department, your expenses for Saturday, and the day you returned.

    a. Enter your name in cell B3.
    b. Enter Purchasing as your department in cell B4.
    c. Enter 19 in G9 for the cost of your brunch on Saturday morning.
    d. Enter 4 in G10 for the cost of the movie on the flight back.
    e. Enter 21 in G14 for the number of miles you drove from the airport to your home.

    As you enter the information, notice how the Spreadsheet recalculates the totals in column I and row 17. Save the file with a new name, *FestXXX.WKS*, using your initials in place of XXX, then print a spreadsheet report with your changes. After you print the report, go ahead and play with the file, changing numbers here and there and watch it recalculate.

2. Open the *Store.WKS* file from the template disk. This file contains a budget to help Lugosi's plan for a new store location. Amounts listed are in thousands of dollars. You have just been informed that the estimated rental sales for the first month will be half of what appears in the spreadsheet. In addition, the rent will be twice as much, and because of scheduled raises for employees, salaries will increase by $5,000 in both Month 2 and Month 3. Make the changes to see what effect they have on profitability.

    a. Enter your name in cell B2.
    b. Change the Tape Rentals amount in C5 to 50.
    c. Increase the monthly rent to 20 for all months.
    d. Increase salaries to 20 in Month 2 and 25 in Month 3.

    When you finish making the changes, save the file with the new name of *StoreXXX.WKS*. Print a copy of the spreadsheet.

3. Lugosi's has just added two new products to their line, but they have yet to calculate the prices for the items. The products are a book about the history of the VCR, which is incredibly exciting, and a holder that will keep drinks hot or cold, which is printed with the Lugosi label. Use the *PriceXXX.WKS* spreadsheet to calculate the prices. Be sure to enter the name of the product as well as the wholesale cost and markup. The VCR book costs $7.49 plus a 40% markup. The drink holder costs $1.24, with a 124% markup. After making each calculation, print a copy of the spreadsheet.

Working with a Spreadsheet

OBJECTIVES

- Use the *Go To* command to find cells.
- Enter formulas.
- Insert functions in formulas.
- Copy labels, numbers, and formulas.
- Edit cell contents.
- Enter labels that begin with a number or symbol.
- Change the format of labels and numbers.

USING FORMULAS AND FUNCTIONS

In Lesson 10, you learned that the cell forms the basic building block of your spreadsheet. A cell may contain a label, a date, a number, or a formula. As you saw, a formula uses numbers found in other cells to make a calculation. When you change one of those numbers, the Spreadsheet uses the formula to recalculate. In this way, formulas bring your worksheet to life. They also make it easy for you to have the Spreadsheet perform extremely difficult or complicated calculations.

The formulas you have seen so far work like calculation rules in the Database. They perform simple arithmetic operations on information in cells, such as adding the numbers in several cells. To tell the Spreadsheet which cells to go to for numbers, these formulas use cell references, referring to the cell by its coordinates. But many tasks could become tedious to perform if you had to enter every coordinate and every arithmetic operator, such as the plus sign. For example, to add up five numbers, you would have to enter five references and five plus signs, like $+B7+B8+B9+H12+N17$ to get the total. If you wanted to add up thirty numbers, you'd have to enter a separate reference for each number.

Fortunately, there is a much simpler way to do this: using a **function**. A function is a built-in calculation you can use to perform more complicated arithmetic and mathematical operations. For example, one special Spreadsheet function, the $=$**SUM** function, is designed to add up large sets of numbers. To sum, of course, means to add up. The equal sign is used to tell you and the computer that what follows is a function. Every function name begins with an equal sign.

The Works Spreadsheet has functions designed for many different purposes. In this lesson, you will use some of these functions to turn a simple spreadsheet into one that can analyze numbers in a sophisticated way.

In creating a formula that uses one or more functions, you'll find you can also speed up the way you create references. You can just highlight an individual cell and have Works place the correct cell reference in your formula. And when you want to refer to a whole string of cells, you can describe them as a **range**, identifying the first and the last cells, and having Works look up all the cells in between.

You'll be working with the spreadsheet that sums up daily sales totals for Lugosi's Classic Video Store. Its file name is *Sales.WKS*. It's also designed to calculate maximum and minimum daily sales for the week. The spreadsheet is not quite finished, though. It needs several formulas that will help you analyze the store's sales. That is what you will work on in this section. In addition, there are some problems with the way things look on the spreadsheet—its **format**. You will polish the appearance of the spreadsheet in a later section, "Formatting a Spreadsheet."

Looking Through the Spreadsheet

You can find the *Sales.WKS* file on the template disk. Before making new formulas that include functions, you should look at some of the functions already on the spreadsheet to see how they work.

By the way: Remember that you should save your work every ten or fifteen minutes, as a precaution against the computer forgetting it all when the power goes out. Whenever you save a file you have been working on, use *Save As* from the File menu, and add your initials to the first part of the file name, so that you will not accidentally overwrite the original file on your template disk.

Going to a Cell   You will start out by opening the file and entering your name. Then you can jump right to one of the formulas with the *Go To* command from the Select Menu. In the Spreadsheet, the *Go To* command takes you directly to a cell or a range of cells. You provide the cell or range reference, such as B7, or select the name of the range, and let the program do the work.

1. Start up Works.
2. Open the *Sales.WKS* spreadsheet from the template disk.

   Works displays the file, as shown in Figure 11-1. The Spreadsheet highlights cell E3, right after the label that asks you to enter your name. You can see that the file has sales figures for each day of the week, broken down into sales by shift. At the bottom of the spreadsheet, you'll find the honor roll of sales for the week. Using formulas, the Spreadsheet will determine these numbers by reviewing the row of daily totals. You will see how these formulas work in a moment.

3. Key your name in cell E3, then press Enter. Now you are ready to use the *Go To* command to jump to one of the cells on the spreadsheet.
4. Choose *Go To* from the Select menu. The Go To dialog box appears, as shown in Figure 11-2.
5. Key the cell reference F11 on the Go to line, and press Enter. The highlight jumps to cell F11, which contains a formula that sums up the total sales for Friday, as shown in Figure 11-3.

Go To

The = SUM function adds up any numbers that you specify. The parentheses contain the **argument** for this function—the extra information that Works needs to carry out the function. In this case, that information is a list of references telling Works in which cells to look for numbers to be added together. The colon between the two references stands for all the cells that appear between the two references (which could be a very long list). This formula tells Works to calculate the sum of the numbers in cells F7 through F9.

FIGURE 11-1
The Sales spreadsheet.

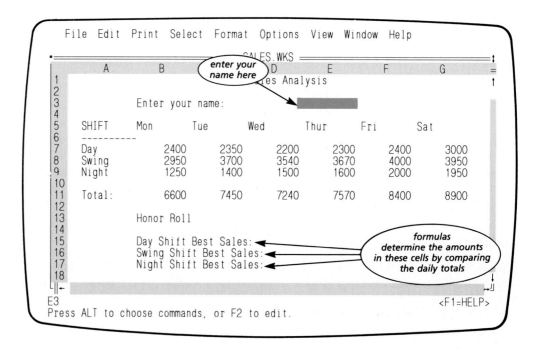

FIGURE 11-2
The Go To dialog box.

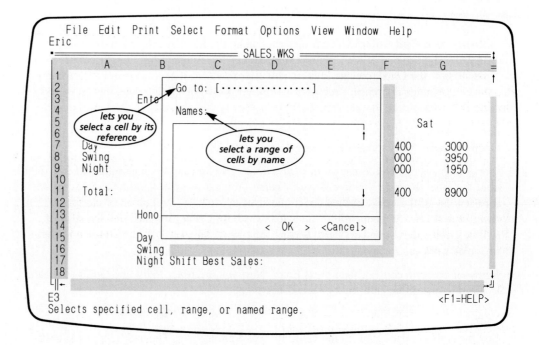

Other cells in row 11 contain formulas. Take a look at them.

6. Use the Down Arrow key to move the highlighting down to cell F19. In the formula bar, you see a formula using a different kind of function:

```
=MAX(B11:H11)
```

This formula uses the = MAX function to get the highest (maximum) number found in cells B11 through H11.

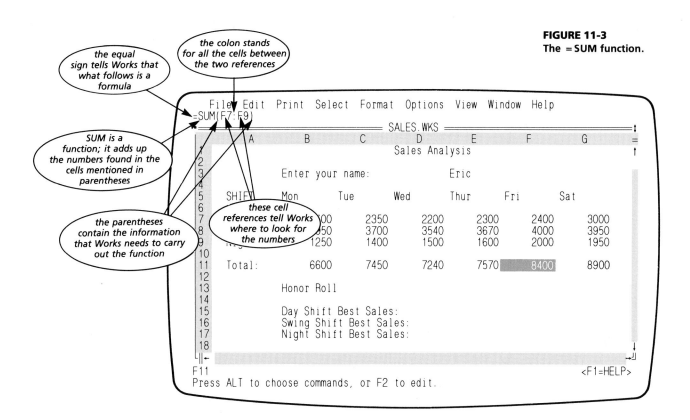

FIGURE 11-3
The = SUM function.

Finding a Cell Off the Screen   This spreadsheet extends beyond the edges of your screen. You will be adding some formulas to an area that is now off the screen, on the right. The *Go To* command lets you go directly to cells that are currently off the screen, as well as cells that you can see right now.

1. Choose *Go To* from the Select menu. The Go To dialog box appears.
2. Key the cell reference J7 on the Go to line, and press Enter. The Spreadsheet jumps right to cell J7, as shown in Figure 11-4.

Good—you have learned how to use the *Go To* command to find cells both on and off the screen. You have also taken a look at two functions already being used in formulas on this spreadsheet. Now that you know how formulas and functions work, you are ready to make some of your own.

Adding a Function

To complete this spreadsheet, you need to add formulas to get total sales, average sales, percent of sales in each shift, and the high and low sales figures for each shift. First you will add some formulas, then you will see how to copy and edit the formulas so that you can complete the spreadsheet.

Here's how you create a formula with a function: You move the highlight to the cell, key = to tell the Spreadsheet that you are entering a formula rather than a number or a label, key the name of the function you are using, provide the cell or range references in parentheses, and press Enter. You are creating your formula in the formula bar, so you can use an arrow key to move the highlighting to a particular cell, and have Works enter that cell reference in the formula for you. You'll learn how to point to the cells like this. Pointing can be faster than keying the cell references one by one. After you enter the formula, the Spreadsheet calculates

FIGURE 11-4
Columns without formulas.

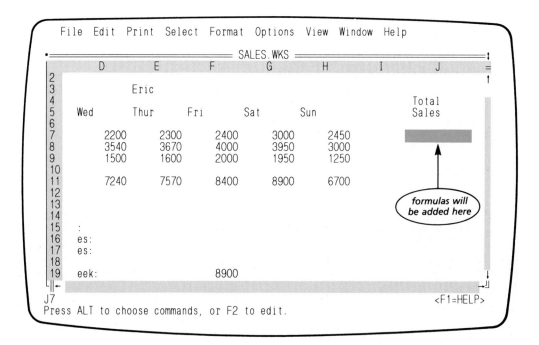

the results and shows you the number in the active (highlighted) cell. The formula itself appears in the formula bar.

The highlight is on cell J7. The label at the top of this column shows that this column will include calculations of total sales for the week, shift by shift. Cells J7, J8, and J9 will include the total weekly sales for each shift at the video store. The daily sales for the day shift, as you saw earlier, appear in row 7, from column B through column H. The = SUM function adds up amounts in a range of cells and displays the result. So the first new function you will add to this spreadsheet will be an = SUM function in cell J7.

1. Key = but do not press Enter yet. (Pressing the Enter key tells the Spreadsheet that you have finished entering the formula, and you haven't reached the end.)
2. Key SUM as the function name, but again, do not press Enter yet. (You do not have to use all uppercase letters when keying the function name. Now you need to tell the Spreadsheet what numbers to add up.)
3. Key (as the opening parenthesis. Within the parentheses, you will key references to the cells whose numbers you want the Spreadsheet to add up.
4. Use the arrow keys to move the highlight to B7.

Notice that as you move the highlight, the name of the currently active cell appears in the formula bar, as shown in Figure 11-5. Because you have already keyed an opening parenthesis, the Spreadsheet knows that when you move the highlight, you are planning to select a cell to be included in the formula. It understands you are just pointing to a cell so it can pick up the coordinates and put them into your formula.

5. Key a colon (:). The colon tells Works that you will be including a range of cells with this function, extending from B7 to another cell. Now you can simply select the last cell of the range, and Works will enter it into the formula for you.
6. Press the Right Arrow key to move the highlight to H7. You have now highlighted the range of cells from B7 through H7. **H7** now appears to the right of the colon.
7. Key) as the closing parenthesis. That completes the argument—your description of the cells from which Works should draw the numbers to be added up.

FIGURE 11-5
Highlighting a cell.

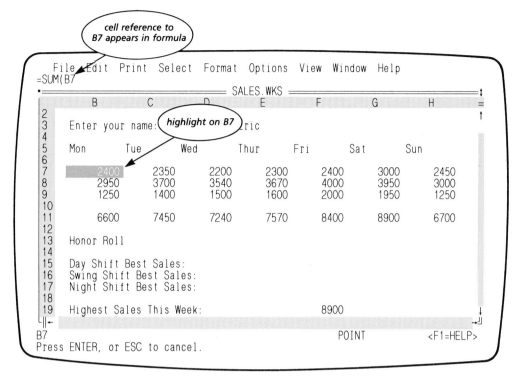

8. Press Enter. Works makes the calculation, puts the result in cell J7, and moves the high-lighting back to that cell.

Congratulations! You have written your first formula.

FIGURE 11-6
The completed formula.

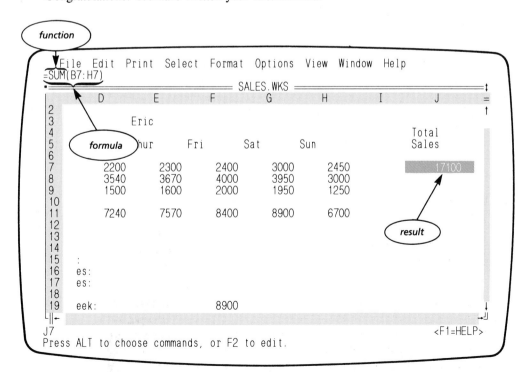

The formula you just entered calculates total sales for the day shift. The total sales for the day shift this week were 17100. The Sales spreadsheet still needs formulas to calculate sales for the swing and night shifts, too. You could enter them the same way you entered this one— but why bother? In a later section called "Editing the Spreadsheet," you will learn how to copy the formula. For now, you need to make another formula using another function.

Calculating an Average

Now that you have calculated the total day-shift sales in cell J7, you can move to the next cell in that row, cell K7, and set up a formula that will calculate the average daily sales for the day shift. One way to do this would be to prepare a formula that divides the total sales by the number of days in the week. To save you the trouble, Works provides a function that automatically calculates averages: **= AVG.**

You enter the = AVG function the way you entered the = SUM function: You key the equal sign and the name of the function, provide the cell or range references in parentheses, and press Enter. Works will add up the numbers in the range of cells and divide the result by the number of cells in the range.

1. Use the Right Arrow key to move the highlight to cell K7. Now you can key the function and an opening parenthesis.
2. Key: =AVG(
3. Use the Left Arrow key to select cell B7, the first cell in the range of cells you need to include in the formula.
4. Key a colon to tell Works that you want to find the average of a range of cells, beginning with B7. Your formula should look like this: =AVG(B7:B7
5. Move to cell H7, the last cell in the range.
6. Key) as the closing parenthesis, and press Enter. Works calculates the average sales for the week's day shift. See Figure 11-7.

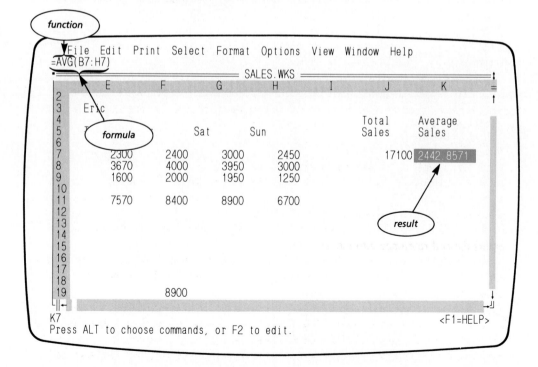

FIGURE 11-7
The = AVG function.

Notice that the amount is displayed to four decimal places. The way a number is displayed is its **format**. The standard format used by Works, known as the General format, does not have a specific number of decimal places; instead, Works chooses the most accurate method of displaying the entire number. So, when you enter a number, the Spreadsheet displays it just as you type it. When the Spreadsheet performs a calculation, though, it displays the result with as many decimal places as are needed for the sake of accuracy, within the limits of the cell. When Works calculated total sales in cell J7 by adding a series of whole numbers, the result did not require any decimal places. The calculation of the average daily sales, though, does require decimal places to show the complete result.

These are all dollar figures. You can choose to change the format of this spreadsheet to display all amounts preceded with dollar signs, using two decimals for cents. You will learn how to format numbers in the section titled "Formatting a Spreadsheet" later in this lesson.

Entering a Formula Without a Function

You can create a formula without using a function. Column L requires a set of formulas to calculate the percentage of total sales contributed by each shift. The percentage of sales that each shift makes will be calculated by dividing the total sales for the shift by the total sales for all shifts. For example, suppose that the sales during the day shift amount to $5,000, and the total sales for all three shifts on that day amount to $10,000. To calculate the day shift's percentage of the total sales on paper, you would use an equation like this:

$$
\begin{aligned}
\text{Day-shift sales divided by Total sales} &= \text{percentage} \\
5{,}000/10{,}000 &= \text{percentage} \\
&= .50 \\
&= 50\%
\end{aligned}
$$

This simple calculation does not require a function, just an arithmetic operator. The slash sign (/) is the operator, or math symbol, meaning *divided by*. It's the same symbol you used for division in the Database.

The total sales for each shift will appear in Column J. To calculate the percentage of total sales that were earned during the day shift, you will need to divide the number from J7 (total sales for the day shift) by the number from J11 (total sales for all shifts).

Remember that when you enter a number, the Spreadsheet takes it as a number; when you enter a letter, the Spreadsheet considers it a label. When you enter the equal sign (=), the Spreadsheet knows you are entering a function—or a formula. You can then select a cell, and the Spreadsheet will enter that into your formula.

1. Move the highlight to cell L7.
2. Key = to tell Works that you are entering a formula.
3. Move the highlight to cell J7. Notice that a cell reference appears in the formula bar, as shown in Figure 11-8, and that it changes as you move into different cells, just as it did when you were selecting references for a function.
4. Key / as the Works symbol for division. The highlight jumps back to cell L7 as Works enters the cell reference into the formula.
5. Move the highlight to cell J11. This cell does not contain a formula or number now, but it will, and when it does, your current formula will be set up to use its number. (You will copy a formula to this cell later.)
6. Press Enter to complete the formula. A notice saying ERR, meaning ERROR, appears in the cell, as you can see in Figure 11-9. Do not worry—you have done nothing wrong. The warning appears because cell J11 contains no formula or number, so Works could not carry out the calculation in your formula. Works looked in cell J11, found nothing, and

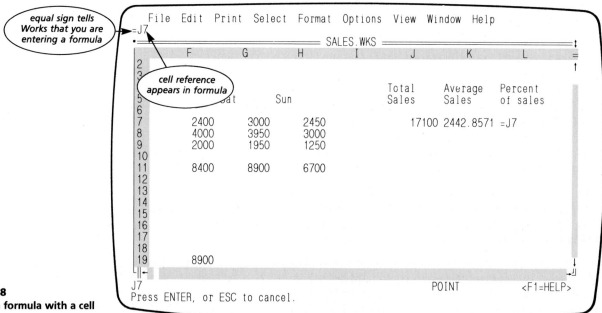

FIGURE 11-8
Beginning a formula with a cell reference.

figured that you were trying to divide by zero. Dividing by zero is impossible, so Works warns you of the error. Later, when you put a formula into cell J11, the error message will disappear, and a number will show up in cell J11.

FIGURE 11-9
Works warns you when it encounters an error.

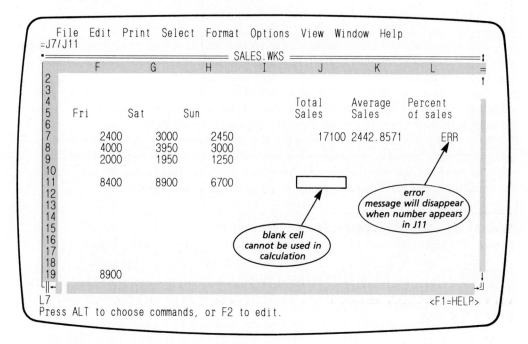

Using the Maximum (=MAX) Function

Column M has been designed to show the highest daily sales for each shift. The **=MAX** function, which you saw used earlier to find the highest daily sales for the week, locates the highest number in a list. The list can include numbers or references to individual cells or to a range of cells. To use = MAX, you follow the same procedure you used to enter the = SUM function: You key the function name and the opening parenthesis, select the range of cells to be used, key the closing parenthesis, and press Enter.

1. Move the highlight to cell M7.
2. Key: =MAX(
3. Use the Left Arrow key to select cell B7.
4. Key a colon to tell Works that you want to include a range of cells in this function. Your formula should now look like this: =MAX(B7:B7
5. Use the Right Arrow key to select cell H7.
6. Key the closing parenthesis, and press Enter. Your formula should now look like this: =MAX(B7:H7)

Once again, Works calculates the result, locating the highest number in the range of numbers in cells B7 through H7, and displaying that in the active cell, M7. The highest sales total for the day shift was 3000, as you can see in cell M7, where you entered the formula (see Figure 11-10).

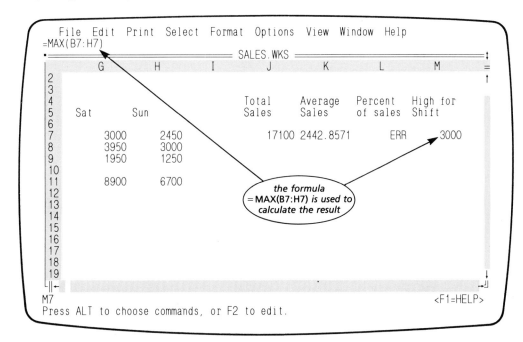

FIGURE 11-10
Entering the = MAX function.

Using the Minimum (= MIN) Function

The last column of this spreadsheet needs a formula to determine the lowest daily sales amount for each shift. The formula is almost the same as the formula you entered to find the highest sales amount for each shift. Both formulas use the same range of cells (B7 to H7). But you will use the = **MIN** function to have Works locate the absolute minimum—the lowest entry in that range.

1. Move the highlight to cell N7.
2. Key: =MIN(
3. Use the Left Arrow key to select cell B7.
4. Key a colon to tell Works that you want to include a range of cells in this function, beginning with cell B7. Your formula should now look like this: =MIN(B7:B7
5. Use the Right Arrow key to select cell H7.

6. Key the closing parenthesis, and press Enter. The formula should now read:
=MIN(B7:H7)

Once again, Works calculates the result, locating the lowest number in the range of numbers in cells B7 through H7, and displaying that in the active cell, N7. The lowest sales total for the day shift was 2200, as you can see in cell N7, where you entered the formula (see Figure 11-11).

FIGURE 11-11
Entering the = MIN function.

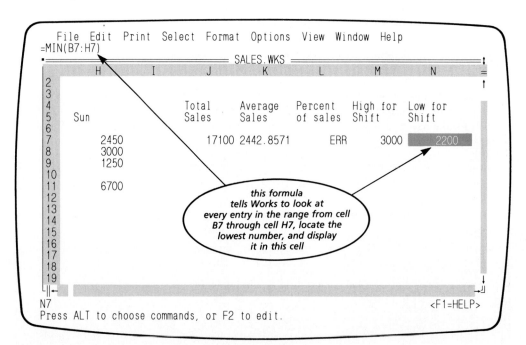

COPYING AND FILLING INFORMATION

You can often save time by copying formulas and other information rather than keying them over and over again. Works lets you copy labels and numbers exactly from one location to another. With formulas, Works offers you a choice. You can have a formula copied without any changes or you can have Works make changes to reflect its new location.

Copying a Label

To copy a label, date, or a number, you just select the information, choose the *Copy* command from the Edit menu, highlight the cell in which you want the Spreadsheet to put the material, and press Enter. You can copy the information from a single cell, a column, a row, or a range of cells.

You can put a copy of the information from one cell into several neighboring cells, too, using the *Fill Right* command to place the material into a series of cells to the right, or the *Fill Down* command to place the material into a series of cells below. For example, the line of dashes at the beginning of row 6 should extend across the whole row. Rather than type an entire row of dashes, you can select cell A6, select the cells you want to contain those dashes, and use *Fill Right* to extend the dashes into those cells, filling them up.

1. Move the highlight to cell A6. That selects the cell, and its contents—the dashes.

2. Press F8 and use the Right Arrow key to extend the selection to cell N6. That shows Works where you want to extend the dashes. Think of F8 as your extender key.
3. Choose *Fill Right* from the Edit menu, then press Enter. The dashes fill up the cells from B6 through N6, as shown in Figure 11-12.

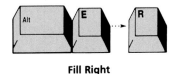

Fill Right

FIGURE 11-12
Filling completed.

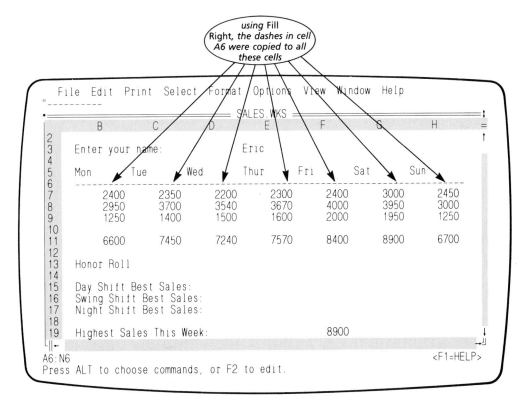

Whenever you use the *Fill Right* or *Fill Down* commands, you copy material from one cell into its immediate neighbors—the cell next to it, and the one next to that, and so on. With the *Copy* command, you can place material in cells near or far, copying to a single cell or a range of cells, even if they are not located right next to the original.

A Word about Special Labels

Take a close look at cell A6. At first it looks like a row of dashes. Now look in the formula bar. Notice the quotation mark (") before the dashes. The quotation mark tells the Spreadsheet that what follows is a label, not a number or formula.

Whenever you key a simple dash at the beginning of a cell, the Spreadsheet takes it as a minus sign, indicating that you want to enter a number. For your protection, the Spreadsheet will then keep you from following the dash with anything other than a number or a formula for calculating a number. You couldn't key another dash. To continue keying dashes as ordinary text, you need to begin the label with a quotation mark ("). The quotation mark will not actually appear in the cell—it just serves as a signal to the Spreadsheet that what follows is text and not a number or formula. Later, in "Editing the Spreadsheet," you'll practice creating these **special labels**.

Copying a Formula

When you copy a formula, you may be copying references to other cells, or ranges of cells. Those references tell Works how to find a cell, so the number displayed there can be used in calculating the formula. For instance, if you enter the formula $= A1 + 3$ in cell A3, Works understands that it should go up two cells to find the cell containing the number, then add 3 to that number, and display the result. The cell reference is relative to its position.

If you were to copy the formula $= A1 + 3$ from cell A3 to cell C3, Works would still look for a number in the cell that is two cells up: cell C1. As part of copying, Works would change the formula to read $= C1 + 3$. Unless you say otherwise, Works takes all your references as relative, so you don't have to go through the tedious process of reconstructing these references.

Occasionally, though, you want a reference to remain unchanged, so it continues to refer to exactly the same location, no matter where you copy the formula to. If so, you need to define the reference in the original formula as an **absolute reference**. You make it absolute by placing a dollar sign before each coordinate, like this: $= \$A\$1 + 3$. An absolute reference is like an exact street address: It describes one location, and only one location, in the spreadsheet. When you copy a formula with an absolute reference, the reference continues to describe the same cell.

For instance, if you made the original reference absolute, your formula at A3 would be $= \$A\$1 + 3$. When you copied that formula to C3, the formula would continue to read $= \$A\$1 + 3$, so Works would know that even here it should draw the number from A1 for the calculation.

If you happen to jostle the cell you refer to absolutely—for example, by adding rows above it or columns next to it—then the absolute reference changes to keep pointing at exactly the same cell as before. It's like a compass arrow swinging always toward the same cell.

FIGURE 11-13
Two ways to copy a formula.

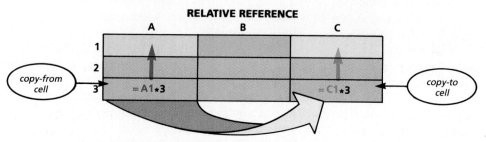

Original formula and copy point to same cell.

Original and copy point to different cells.

Making Relative Copies

In row 11 you see a series of totals. On each day of the week, there is a total of the sales registered by all three shifts. Cells B11 through H11 all have similar formulas. Basically, these formulas tell Works to add up the three figures above and display the total. You need to get some similar totals for Total Sales. In J7, you see the total amount sold by the day shift during the week; in J8 you will see the total amount sold by the swing shift during the week; and in J9 you will see the total amount sold by the night shift. To find out how much the store sold in a week, you need to add up the figures in J7, J8, and J9. That grand total should go into cell J11.

You could create a new formula for cell J11. But it is easier to copy the one you already have in cell H11. That formula adds up the three sales figures for the Sunday shifts. But because copying is relative, the version in cell J11 will apply to cells J7, J8, and J9, and the result will have a different meaning.

For similar reasons, you can copy the formula into cells K11 (to get the sales figure for an average day) and L11 (to make sure that the three shifts' percentages of sales add up to 100%).

1. Highlight cell H11. This contains the formula you want to copy.
2. Choose *Copy* from the Edit menu.
3. Highlight cell J11. Notice that you are not copying to an adjacent cell, so you can't use the *Fill Right* command without filling in the empty column I with a meaningless zero. Copying is cleaner.
4. Press Enter to have Works place a relative copy of the formula from cell H11 into cell J11. Check the formula bar to make sure it reads =SUM(J7:J9). That shows that Works has changed the cell reference to accord with the new position of the formula. You have no figures in cells J8 and J9, so the total displayed in cell J11 is the same as that in cell J7. (You will fill in the empty cells in a minute or two.)

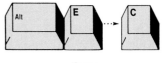

Copy

The formula in cell L7 takes the total sales for the day shift, and divides those by the total sales for the day, to determine what percentage of the day's sales were brought in by the day shift. At the moment, though, there are no totals for the swing and night shifts, so it seems as if all the sales for the day came from the day shift. In cell L7, Works divides $17,100 by $17,100, and gets 1. Expressed as a percentage, that would be 100%.

5. Hold down the Shift key and press the Right Arrow key twice to extend the highlighting to cells K11 and L11.
6. Choose *Fill Right* from the Edit menu. That places a relative copy of the formula into these two neighboring cells, as shown in Figure 11-14.

You do not need a total of the weekly high points and low points; that would not mean much. So, you do not need to fill the formula into cells M11 and N11.

Making a Reference Absolute

Look at column L. It shows how much each shift's weekly sales contributed to the overall sales of the store. The formula you entered divides the shift's total weekly sales into the store's total weekly sales, to find out what percentage the shift made. You will want to put a similar formula into cell L8 for the swing shift and L9 for the night shift. *Filling Down* will make that easy. But if you just filled down, the copying would be relative. So the formula in L8 would look to cell J12 for a total, and the formula in L9 would look even farther down, in cell J13, for a total. Both would be disappointed. The grand total of sales for the week is

FIGURE 11-14
Two ways to copy a formula.

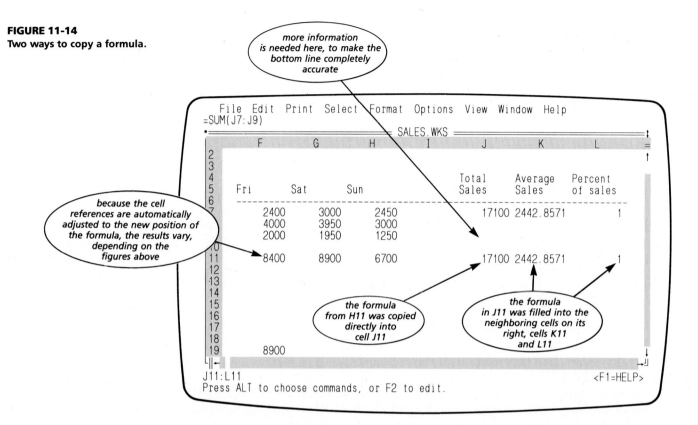

found in only one place: cell J11. So that reference must remain absolute, no matter where the copies of the formula end up.

In this section, you will make that particular reference absolute. The procedure is not difficult, but oddly enough it takes a lot of $.

1. Highlight cell L7.
2. Press F2 to edit the formula in the formula bar. That places the cursor at the end of the entry in the formula bar.
3. Insert a dollar sign (yes, a $) in front of the *J* in *J11*, and another one in front of the *11* in *J11*, so that the formula reads: =J7/$J$11
4. Press Enter.

Now no matter where you copy that formula to, the divisor will always be the figure in cell J11, the grand total of sales for the week. This formula is now ready to be copied. One part of it will adapt to its new surroundings—that is the first part. The other part will remain absolute, unchanged—that is the divisor.

You do not have to copy all the references in a formula in the same way. For example, here you have two cell references in one formula, and you can copy one as an absolute reference and the other as a **relative reference**.

Be cautious about making any reference absolute. Make sure that the information you need is only found in one cell. When the reference is absolute, the formula always goes to the same cell, even if it has been bumped around by you inserting new rows, or deleting columns, or changing the surroundings. If you happen to redefine the cell to which this formula points absolutely, then your formula will be rendered meaningless. Also, remember that you might come back to this formula later, copying it and placing the copy in some new location. If you overlook the fact that the reference is absolute, then you will be surprised to see that the results of the formula are exactly what they were in its original setting.

Using Fill to Copy a Group of Formulas

All the formulas in cells J7 through N7 refer back to information in cells B7 through H7. Using *Fill Down*, you can copy these formulas and have Works adjust all the references to the new position—all except for the one that will remain absolute.

1. Highlight cell J7. That's where you're going to start extending the highlighting.
2. Hold down the Shift key, and use the Right Arrow key to extend the highlighting to cells K7, L7, M7, N7, and then down to N10, creating a large block.
3. Choose *Fill Down* from the Edit menu. Numbers fill the cells. Your grand totals are also updated, so that you can now see exactly how much the store earned that week (in cell J11) and what sales were on an average day (in cell K11). In row 10 you see a few new ERR messages. Ignore those for now.

Fill Down

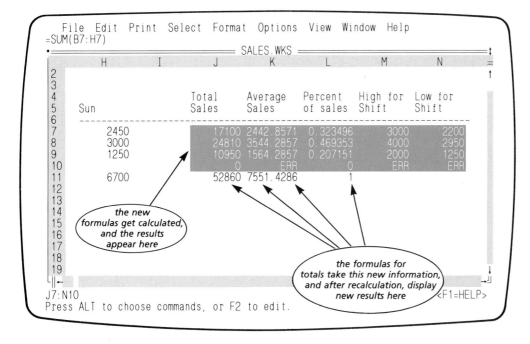

FIGURE 11-15
The effect of using *Fill Down* on five formulas at once, copying them down into three more rows.

Copying a Value Without the Formula

Sometimes you want to borrow the results from a cell without copying the formula. For instance, in the honor roll at the bottom of the spreadsheet, you need to put in the best sales each shift attained this week. Those values are displayed in cells M7, M8, and M9. If you copied the formulas, though, they would refer to completely different cells in their new locations, and that would result in gibberish in the honor roll. Better to copy the values, and leave the formulas behind. There are two ways to copy a value without a formula. The first method involves the *Copy Special* command on the Edit menu.

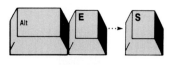

Copy Special

1. Highlight cell M7.
2. Choose *Copy Special* from the Edit menu.
3. Highlight cell F15, and press Enter to place the contents of cell M7 here. You are asked whether to place Values only. That means placing the number, but not the formula. That is the preset option, so press Enter again. The number appears in cell F15, but as you can see from a glance at the formula bar, the formula has not been copied along with it.

This special form of copying brings the number from one place to another, but severs all further ties between the two cells. If you think that the original figure may change—for instance, that late-breaking news might show that Sunday's totals went over 6000, for a new high—you would not want to use *Copy Special*. Instead you would want a very special kind of formula, = M7. That means: *take whatever number you find displayed in M7 and display it here.*

Upon reflection, you decide it will be safer to use this very short formula instead of the special copy.

4. With the highlighting still on cell F15, key =M7 and press Enter.
5. Hold down the Shift key, and press the Down Arrow key twice, to extend the highlighting over cells F16 and F17.
6. Choose *Fill Down* from the Edit menu.

The other two cells pick up the figures from M8 and M9, as shown in Figure 11-16. You have avoided the problems inherent in copying a formula from one area of your spreadsheet to a completely different area, where the cell references would no longer make sense, even relatively speaking. You are telling Works to go look at those other cells every time it recalculates the spreadsheet, returning with the current figure; in a way, you are saying, "Go copy that number for me every time."

FIGURE 11-16
Grabbing a number from another cell: the simplest formula.

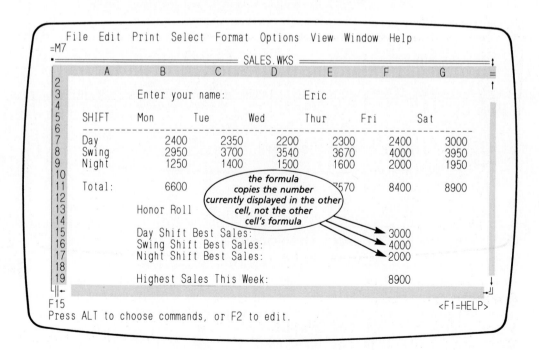

EDITING THE SPREADSHEET

 Sometimes you may make mistakes when you are entering information and formulas into the spreadsheet. At other times, you will want to erase information that you no longer need or that was copied accidentally. Through editing, you can erase or change the contents of cells.

Erasing Large Areas of the Spreadsheet

We've made a mistake. Row 10 should actually be a blank row. In the excitement of *Filling Down*, we copied formulas into cells J10 through N10. But row 10 has no information in the rest of the cells, so the total sales are zero, and no average, high, or low figures are available. Works displays the ERR message as a warning that it could not perform the calculation demanded by the formula. Do not worry about that. You don't need these formulas here; you just need some empty cells to form a clear dividing line between the data above and the grand totals below. In essence, you want to get rid of the contents of cells J10 through N10. You can erase them quickly with the *Clear* command from the Edit menu.

1. Move the highlighting to cell J10.
2. Hold down the Shift key and use the arrow keys to select cells J10 through N10.
3. Choose the *Clear* command from the Edit menu. That erases the contents of the range of cells, without deleting the row.

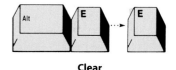

Clear

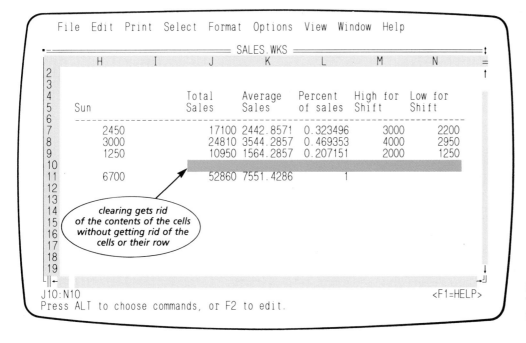

FIGURE 11-17
The garbage has been cleared from row 10.

Correcting a Label

The last item on the Honor Roll is a little ambiguous. It reads, `Highest Sales This Week`. Does that mean highest sales on a given shift on a given day? Or does it mean highest daily total? Sarah Lugosi has told you that she meant the highest daily total. You decide to edit the label to make that clear.

1. Highlight cell B19. That's where this long label begins.
2. Press F2 to edit in the formula bar.
3. Backspace to delete This Week.
4. Replace that with in a Day so that the whole label reads: Highest Sales in a Day.
5. Press Enter. The new label replaces the old. Editing like this allows you to keep most of your original entry intact, while correcting or changing what needs to be fixed.

Entering a Label That Does Not Begin with a Letter

Sometimes you will want to begin a label with a number or symbol. For example, the line of dashes separating the column titles from the numbers is a label that begins with a symbol. Another example would be a label that begins with a percent sign. If you keyed a percent sign alone, Works would interpret that as zero percent, and after you pressed Enter, would display 0%. Here is how to create a label that begins with a symbol or number.

1. Highlight cell L4. It contains the label Percent.
2. Press Backspace to get rid of that text.
3. Key a quotation mark and then the percentage symbol: "%
4. Press Enter.

   The quotation mark tells Works that what follows is a label, and should be treated as ordinary text, not some mathematical phenomenon. So, Works enters it into the cell unchanged.

5. You decide to emphasize the Honor Roll by putting two lines underneath that label. Highlight cell B14, key ten equal signs in a row, and then press Enter.

   If you remembered to place a quotation mark first, you did really well. As a reward, you can skip steps 6-9.

   On the other hand, if you forgot the quotation mark, Works thinks you intended to create a formula, and you see a dialog box warning you that you have a *Missing operand*. Sounds dangerous, but it is just a reminder, in case you forgot to type a formula—which is what Works expects after an equal sign.

6. Press Enter to get rid of the dialog box and automatically enter the Edit mode. A cursor appears in the formula bar.
7. Use the Left Arrow key to move the cursor to the first position.
8. Key a quotation mark. It will not be seen, but it will exist in the cell as an alert to Works, saying, *What follows is a label*.
9. Press Enter.

   The equal signs now underline the label *Honor Roll* as shown in Figure 11-18. Remember the quotation mark. You can use this technique to enter any symbol or number as a label.

Inserting and Deleting Columns or Rows

Sometimes you want to add rows or columns to a spreadsheet or to delete them. For example, in this spreadsheet, the total sales in column J are separated from the daily figures by an empty column, column I. It would be better to have the total figures right next to the daily figures. You can delete the blank column I to solve that problem. In addition, you might want to separate the total sales column from the other columns that analyze sales (K through N) by inserting a new blank column. This will emphasize that the figures in the last set of columns

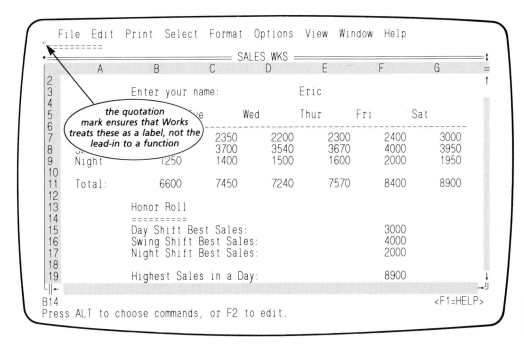

FIGURE 11-18
Equal symbols used to emphasize the Honor Roll.

are not part of the sales figures themselves, but instead, analyze that information.

Works makes it easy to delete and insert columns. On the Edit menu you will find two commands: *Delete Row/Column* and *Insert Row/Column*.

1. Highlight any cell in Column I. That's the column between Sunday's sales figures and the Total Sales figures.
2. Choose *Delete Row/Column* from the Edit menu. You see a dialog box asking if you want to delete the row the cell is in or the column it is in. Press Alt-C to choose *Column*, then press Enter. That's all it takes. The column disappears. Everything else moves closer together. And behind the scenes, all the formulas are readjusted so that the cell references remain correct.

   Now you need to insert a column to the right of column I. But when you insert a column, Works always puts it to the left of the cell you have highlighted. So, you now need to move the highlighting to the right.

3. Move the highlighting one column to the right, so it is in the Average Sales column, column J.
4. Choose *Insert Row/Column* from the Edit menu, select *Column* in the dialog box, and press Enter. The screen opens up to look like Figure 11-19.

   Notice that none of the calculations have gone haywire, because none of the formulas referred to any of the values in the columns you just deleted or inserted. The Spreadsheet also automatically changed all the references in the formulas to reflect their new positions, so that the results would remain the same. (Because the formulas are one column closer to the values they use, the Spreadsheet must take into account their new positions.)

   As you survey your spreadsheet with satisfaction, you decide that the equal signs do emphasize the Honor Roll, but seem to crowd the labels above and below. You need more room there. So, you will use the same *Insert Row/Column* command from the Edit menu. That always inserts a row above the one your highlighting is in.

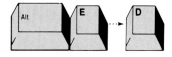

Delete Row/Column

Insert Row/Column

FIGURE 11-19
One column has been deleted, and another inserted.

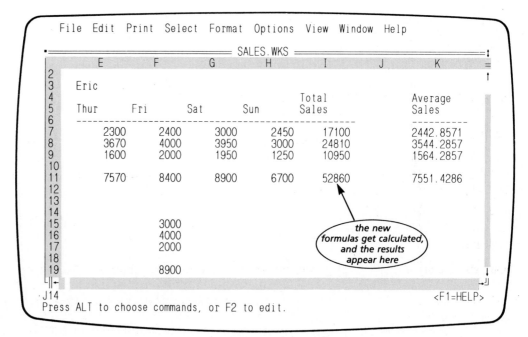

5. Highlight cell B15. That's the cell containing the label, `Day Shift Best Sales:`.
6. Choose *Insert Row/Column* from the Edit menu. Make sure that *Row* is selected this time, then press Enter. An empty row appears between the row of equal signs and the Day Shift Best Sales figure, as shown in Figure 11-20.

FIGURE 11-20
A row has been inserted.

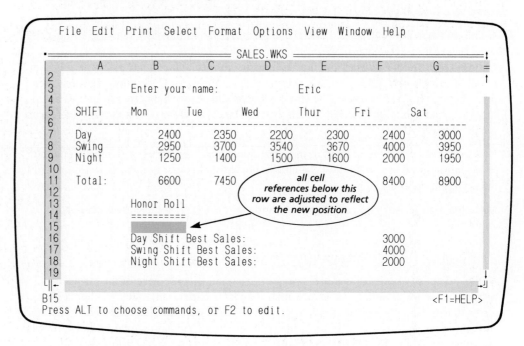

Adding and subtracting rows and columns allows you to group related information for the viewer, and to separate items that do not belong together. In addition, an extra row or column can lend emphasis where needed.

But the spreadsheet still needs some work. The labels above the shift figures should line up with the numbers, and the numbers might look better if they were displayed with dollar signs or as percentages. The next section shows you how to format the spreadsheet to polish up the way it looks.

FORMATTING A SPREADSHEET

*T*he format of a cell in the Works Spreadsheet can be applied automatically by Works. For instance, you can format an empty cell, then come along later and enter information. Works will remember the formatting and apply it to the new data right away. This saves you time and ensures consistency.

Labels

Normally when you enter a label, the Spreadsheet aligns it on the left edge of the cell. Sometimes, though, it makes more sense to align labels in the middle or on the right edge of the cell. For example, in this spreadsheet, the numbers are all lined up on the right side of the columns, but the labels are on the left side. That makes it hard to tell which label belongs with which column of numbers. You can correct that by right-justifying all the column titles.

1. Highlight cell B5, containing the label for Monday.
2. Hold down the Shift key and press the Right Arrow key to extend the highlighting over to cell N5, then press the Up Arrow key once to extend it to include the parts of the labels that are in row 4.
3. Choose *Style* from the Format menu. You see the dialog box shown in Figure 11-21.

Style

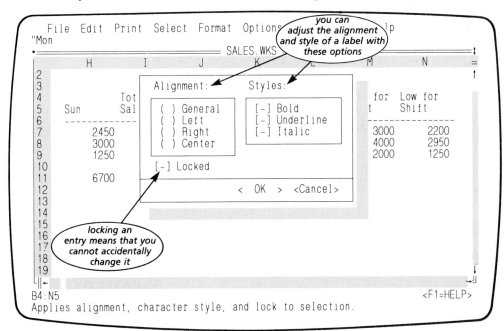

FIGURE 11-21
The Style dialog box.

4. Select *Right Alignment* and *Bold*, then press Enter. The labels move over so they show up right over the numbers, as in Figure 11-22. That is an improvement.

Unfortunately, right-justifying the two-line labels on the far right of the spreadsheet still doesn't make them look good. They need to be centered over the numbers.

FIGURE 11-22
The labels are right-justified now.

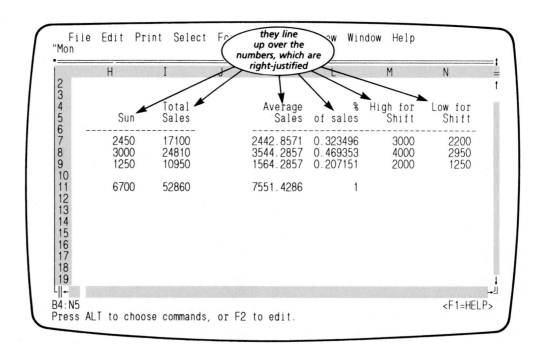

5. Highlight the block of cells from cell K4 to cell N5.
6. Choose *Style* from the Format menu, set the options to *Center* and *Bold*, and then press Enter.

   That looks better. The percent symbol no longer hugs the right margin of its column, and the text seems better organized.

Numbers

Because this is a spreadsheet, you can have Works format numbers in dozens of ways. You can set the format up in an empty cell, then enter raw data, and have Works format it; or you can enter the data, then tell Works how to reformat it so it looks better or makes more sense to an average viewer.

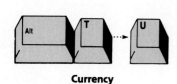

Currency

1. Highlight the range of cells from B7 over and down to I11.
2. Choose *Currency* from the Format menu. You are asked how many decimal places to show.
3. Key 0 because you don't want to show any nickels and dimes in this overview. Then press Enter.

   Instantly all the figures have dollar signs in front of them and commas to distinguish thousands. Each entry takes up more room, of course, and that could mean trouble if your columns were especially narrow. But for now, all goes well, as shown in Figure 11-23.

4. Format the figures in cells F16, F17, F18, and F20 the same way.
5. Format the average sales figures in cells K7 through K11 as *Currency*, with two decimal places.

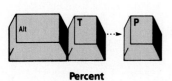

Percent

6. Format the Highs and Lows as *Currency*, but with no decimal places.
7. Format the percentage of sales, including the total, as *Percent*. (Use the *Percent* command on the Format menu, and use no decimal places). That section of your spreadsheet should end up looking like Figure 11-24.

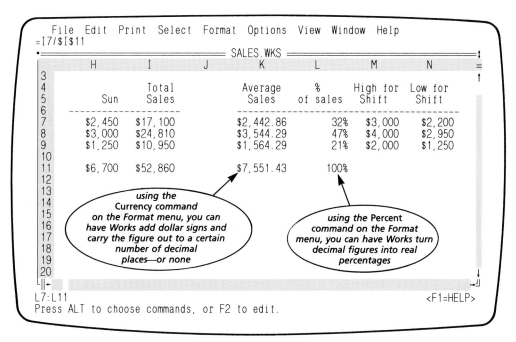

FIGURE 11-23
Currency has been formatted
with dollar signs and commas.

```
    File  Edit  Print  Select  Format  Options  View  Window  Help
 2400
 •══════════════════════════════ SALES.WKS ══════════════════════════════↨
 |       C        D        E        F        G        H        I       ≡
 |2                                                                        ↑
 |3   name:              Eric
 |4                                                            Total
 |5       Tue      Wed     Thur     Fri      Sat      Sun      Sales
 |6    ─────────────────────────────────────────────────────────────
 |7   $2,350   $2,200   $2,300   $2,400   $3,000   $2,450   $17,100
 |8   $3,700   $3,540   $3,670   $4,000   $3,950   $3,000   $24,810
 |9   $1,400   $1,500   $1,600   $2,000   $1,950   $1,250   $10,950
 |10
 |11  $7,450   $7,240   $7,570   $8,400   $8,900   $6,700   $52,860
 |12
 |13
 |14
 |15
 |16  Best Sales:                 3000
 |17  t Best Sales:               4000
 |18  t Best Sales:               2000
 |19                                                                       ↓
 └‖←                                                                      ‾↲
 B7:I11                                                          <F1=HELP>
 Press ALT to choose commands, or F2 to edit.
```

FIGURE 11-24
You can have Works format
your data for you.

```
    File  Edit  Print  Select  Format  Options  View  Window  Help
 =I7/$I$11
 •══════════════════════════════ SALES.WKS ══════════════════════════════↨
 |       H        I        J        K        L        M        N       ≡
 |3                                                                        ↑
 |4                Total            Average     %     High for  Low for
 |5       Sun      Sales             Sales   of sales  Shift     Shift
 |6    ─────────────────────────────────────────────────────────────
 |7   $2,450   $17,100           $2,442.86     32%   $3,000   $2,200
 |8   $3,000   $24,810           $3,544.29     47%   $4,000   $2,950
 |9   $1,250   $10,950           $1,564.29     21%   $2,000   $1,250
 |10
 |11  $6,700   $52,860           $7,551.43    100%
 |12
 |13
 |14
 |15
 |16
 |17
 |18
 |19
 |20                                                                       ↓
 └‖←                                                                      ‾↲
 L7:L11                                                          <F1=HELP>
 Press ALT to choose commands, or F2 to edit.
```

using the Currency command on the Format menu, you can have Works add dollar signs and carry the figure out to a certain number of decimal places—or none

using the Percent command on the Format menu, you can have Works turn decimal figures into real percentages

Column Width

Sometimes a column gets too big for its numbers. Or the numbers get so big they no longer fit. You need to shrink or widen your columns. In this spreadsheet, column J sets off the analysis from the actual sales figures, but it puts a little too much room in between. It is time to shrink it a little.

1. Highlight any cell in column J.

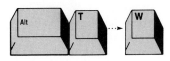

Column Width

2. Choose *Column Width* from the Format menu. You see the dialog box telling you how many characters wide that column is. The standard width is 10 characters.
3. Key 5 and press Enter. That draws the two sides a little closer together, but leaves a distinct division between them.

You're just about ready to print this spreadsheet. You want to make sure that the sales figures will all fit on one sheet of paper. You need to squeeze the last ounce of space out of those columns.

4. Highlight cells A7 through H7.
5. Choose *Column Width* from the Format menu.
6. Set the column width at 8 characters, and press Enter. The columns close up, making a much tighter presentation.

Congratulations! You've added functionality to the spreadsheet, and you have made it meaningful and legible to almost anyone who looks at it. Your formatting has made the spreadsheet easier to view. You are ready to print it out.

PRINTING A SPREADSHEET

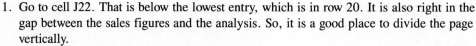

This spreadsheet is wider than the 80 characters that this standard font allows on an average 8.5-by-11-inch sheet of paper. You can tell Works what font and size to use, and what to put on each page as it prints, establishing a position at which it should break to a new page. You can also define exactly which part of the total spreadsheet you want to print, using the *Set Print Area* command. And you can add headers and footers to identify your spreadsheet to the reader.

Insert Page Break

1. Go to cell J22. That is below the lowest entry, which is in row 20. It is also right in the gap between the sales figures and the analysis. So, it is a good place to divide the page vertically.
2. Choose *Insert Page Break* from the Print menu.
3. Select *Column* and press Enter. Angle brackets appear next to the column letter, indicating that column J will begin a new page.
4. Highlight cell F22, under the best sales day figure. Choose *Insert Page Break*, and in the dialog box, select *Row* and press Enter. More angle brackets appear next to the row number 22. Now Works will know not to print anything below there on the same page with the material you have been formatting.
5. Press Ctrl-Home to return to cell A1.
6. Hold down Shift, and use the Arrow keys to highlight all the way over to column O and down to row 20.

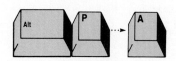

Set Print Area

7. Choose *Set Print Area* from the Print menu. Now Works knows what information you want to include when it prints.
8. To make sure that you can fit the key facts on one page, choose *Font* from the Format menu, and choose 10 points as the size. (If your printer does not offer 10 point print, stay with the preset 12).

Page Setup & Margins

9. To make more room on the page, choose *Page Setup & Margins* from the Print menu, and set the left margin to 0.5 inches, and the right margin to 0.5 inches.
10. Choose *Headers & Footers* from the Print menu. Make the header: Weekly Sales Analysis. Make the footer your name.

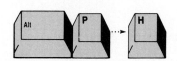

Headers & Footers

11. Make sure your printer is switched on, hooked up to your computer, and on-line.
12. Choose *Print* from the Print menu.
13. After your printing is completed, save your file as *SalesXXX.WKS* on the template disk.
14. Remove your disks, store them in a safe place, and turn off the computer.

There now! You have taken a set of ordinary numbers and used formulas and functions to analyze those numbers in a meaningful way. Along the way, you have changed the format of the labels and numbers so they can be easily understood. And now you have printed out a hard copy for Sarah Lugosi and Morris Yu. They'll be proud of you.

KEY TERMS

absolute reference   *MSW 200*
argument   *MSW 189*
ERR message   *MSW 195*
filling   *MSW 198*
format   *MSW 195*
function   *MSW 188*
range   *MSW 189*
relative reference   *MSW 202*
special label   *MSW 199*

FUNCTIONS

= AVG
= MAX
= MIN
= SUM

COMMANDS

Alt-E-E (Clear)	Alt-E-F (Fill Down)	Alt-E-I (Insert Row/Column)
Alt-T-W (Column Width)	Alt-E-R (Fill Right)	Alt-P-M (Page Setup & Margins)
Alt-E-C (Copy)	Alt-T-F (Font)	Alt-T-P (Percent)
Alt-E-S (Copy Special)	Alt-S-G (Go To)	Alt-P-P (Print)
Alt-T-U (Currency)	Alt-P-H (Headers & Footers)	Alt-P-A (Set Print Area)
Alt-E-D (Delete Row/Column)	Alt-P-I (Insert Page Break)	Alt-T-S (Style)

REVIEW QUESTIONS

1. What signals Works that you are about to enter a label?
2. How is a function different from a formula?
3. What signals the Spreadsheet that you are entering a function?
4. Do you have to enter cell references into a function or formula by entering individual characters? How else can you do this?
5. How does the Spreadsheet know that you are referring to a range of cells?
6. What symbols must be used to enclose cell references in a function? Are these symbols required in all formulas?
7. What key do you press in order to edit individual characters in a cell's contents?
8. How would you format a series of cells so that the numbers displayed dollar signs and two decimal places?

9. How should you begin a label that will start with some character other than a letter of the alphabet?
10. What is the difference between filling and copying?

APPLICATIONS

1. Open the *Fest.WKS* file from the template disk. In the previous lesson, you made several modifications to the spreadsheet and saved it with the name *FestXXX.WKS*. To ensure that you do not lose those changes, you will need to save this version under the name *FestRev.WKS*.

   Sarah Lugosi has asked you to add some formulas to this spreadsheet that will calculate additional information about travel expenses. She would like to know what percent of the total is spent each day and the highest and lowest daily totals. She also wants you to make sure the format of the new information is easy to read.

   a. Enter your name.
   b. For the department, enter: Administration
   c. Start out by entering some labels. In cell A20 enter Daily Percent. Enter Max Spent in cell A22 and Min Spent in cell A23.
   d. Now enter a formula in cell B20 that will calculate the percent of the weekly expenses for Monday. (Hint: The formula you want divides Monday's total by the week's total.)
   e. Copy cell B20 within the worksheet to cells C20 through I20 using a relative reference to Monday's value, but an absolute (no change) reference for the week's total.
   f. In cell B22, enter a function that will calculate the maximum amount from the range of cells B17 through H17.
   g. In cell B23, enter a function that will calculate the minimum amount from the range of cells B17 through H17.
   h. Format cells B20 through I20 so that the percentages appear with zero decimal places.
   i. Format cells B22 and B23 so that they display dollar amounts with zero decimal places.
   j. Save the document under the name *FestRev.WKS* and then print it out.

2. Open the *Store.WKS* file from the template disk. Morris Yu wants you to expand the spreadsheet so that it will allow for estimates of the next three months of sales.

   a. Enter your name in cell B2.
   b. Highlight the group of cells from C4 through F18, choose *Copy* from the Edit menu, highlight cell H4, and press Enter.
   c. In cell K4, change the label 1st Qtr to 2nd Qtr.
   d. Change cells H4, I4, and J4 to Month 4, Month 5, and Month 6.
   e. Format the group of cells from C5 to K18 as *Currency* with zero decimal places.
   f. Enter the amounts shown in the table below in columns H, I, and J. (Remember that you do not have to change the amounts in rows 9, 16, and 18 because they are the results of calculations.)

	MONTH 4	MONTH 5	MONTH 6
INCOME			
Tape Rentals	135	150	165
Tape Sales	15	17	19
Other Sales	9	11	13
EXPENSES			
Rent	10	10	10
Salaries	20	20	20
Overhead	5	5	5

   g. Add a header, Estimated Sales, and a footer carrying date.
   h. Save your changes as *StoreRev.WKS* and print a copy of columns H through K.

3. Open the *Drive.WKS* file from the template disk. This file is designed to calculate total and average scores for student drivers on their driving tests. It also should calculate the highest and lowest average scores. Unfortunately, none of the

formulas to make these calculations are included. You will have to enter the formulas yourself.

a. Enter your name in cell C3.

b. In column F, add formulas to calculate the total score for each student.

c. In column G, add formulas to calculate the average score for each student.

d. In cell C18, add a formula that calculates the maximum average score from all the average scores listed in column G.

e. In cell G18, add a formula that calculates the minimum average score from all the scores listed in column G.

f. Format the averages so that they include no decimal places. (Hint: Use the *Fixed* command on the Format menu.)

g. Change the name of the file to *DriveXXX.WKS*, save your changes, and print out the spreadsheet.

Creating and Using a Spreadsheet

OBJECTIVES

- Plan a new spreadsheet.
- Determine labels, numbers, and formulas.
- Design the layout of the spreadsheet.
- Understand and use what-if analysis.
- Explain other advanced Spreadsheet functions.
- Create and use a macro command.

MAKING A NEW SPREADSHEET

*I*n the last two lessons, you have used many features of the Works Spreadsheet. You know how to enter labels, numbers, dates, and formulas; how to copy and move information using both absolute and relative references; and how to edit and format a spreadsheet. That means you have all the tools you need to plan and make a new spreadsheet. In the first part of this lesson, you will do just that. In the second part, you will practice with some advanced features that make the Spreadsheet a very powerful tool for performing what-if analyses.

Planning the New Spreadsheet

Before you sit down at the computer to create a new spreadsheet, you should spend some time planning what it is that you want the spreadsheet to do. First, you should know what kind of labels you want to include, what kind of numbers you will use in calculations, and what kinds of calculations you need performed. Then you should plan where you want to put each label, number, date, and formula. Finally, you should decide how you want to format the spreadsheet—that is, how the labels and values will be displayed on the screen. You don't have to do all your planning on paper. The Spreadsheet tool makes it easy for you to change your mind and reorganize a spreadsheet file. However, it is a very big help to prepare before actually entering anything.

Sarah Lugosi has asked you to make a new spreadsheet to calculate projected revenue (sales), expenses, net income (revenue minus expenses), and profit margins over the next five years. She would like the spreadsheet to be able to project these figures for each of the stores. This will be a relatively simple spreadsheet to plan. You can start by dividing the job of building the spreadsheet into a series of smaller tasks. First you need to figure out what labels will appear on the spreadsheet, then what data someone will enter into the spreadsheet, and finally, what will be calculated, with what formulas.

Determine the Labels This spreadsheet will calculate four items: revenue, expenses, net income, and profit margins. All of these will have to be labeled on the spreadsheet. You will be calculating future amounts for these figures, so you will need some way for the user to enter the revenue growth rate and the growth rate for expenses. These items will also have to be labeled. As you come up with ideas for labels, both for data that will be collected and data that will be calculated, write them down. For this spreadsheet, you have the following items:

Revenue   Growth Rate (Revenue)
Expenses   Growth Rate (Expenses)
Net Income
Profit Margin

For the purposes of this spreadsheet, you can assume that the growth rates for revenue and expenses will be constant for all five years. However, you will need to show revenue, expenses, net income, and the profit margin for each of the five years, so you also need labels for the years.

Year 1
Year 2
Year 3
Year 4
Year 5

You know that there are three stores for which the spreadsheet will calculate sales: the main store in Palookaville and branches in Fairfax and Riverside. The easiest way to design the spreadsheet would be to have a prompt for the user to enter the name of the store for which calculations are being made—a label like this:

Store location:

This gives you enough to get started planning your spreadsheet. The next step is to see what information you need from the people who will use the spreadsheet.

Determine the Data That Will Be Entered into the Spreadsheet The user of the spreadsheet will have to enter some information into the spreadsheet to make the calculations take place. For instance, in order to calculate revenues and so forth for each year, the user will have to enter numbers for the revenue growth rate and the expenses growth rate.

The spreadsheet cannot calculate future revenues without having some figures with which to make the calculations. It needs some starting place. For this spreadsheet, that means the user will have to enter the first year's revenue and expense figures. Then the computer can take over and calculate the results for the rest of the years. So you need two additional labels to prompt for the starting information, for a total of four prompts.

First Year Revenue:
First Year Expenses:
Growth Rate (Revenue):
Growth Rate (Expenses):

The number the user enters after each of these prompts can be copied into the part of the spreadsheet used for calculations. By keeping the input separate from the calculations, you help the user see the assumptions that are used in the calculations.

Determine the Calculations the Spreadsheet Will Perform What values need to be calculated? For years two to five, the spreadsheet must calculate revenues and expenses based on the first year figures. For all the years, the spreadsheet must calculate the net income and profit margin.

You can set up the formula for these calculations using words, since you do not yet know which cells will be used for the calculations. When you make the actual spreadsheet file, you can convert these word formulas into spreadsheet formulas. These are the formulas that you will want to include:

Revenue = (Previous Year's Revenue) * (Growth Rate of Revenue)
Expenses = (Previous Year's Expenses) * (Growth Rate of Expenses)
Net Income = Revenue - Expenses
Profit Margin = Net Income / Revenue

Design the Layout of the Spreadsheet Now that you know the labels, numbers, and formulas to be included in the spreadsheet, you are ready to determine where to put everything. When you create a spreadsheet, you should begin planning the spreadsheet by sketching your plan on a piece of paper. You can use a ruled piece of paper, divide it into lettered columns, number the lines, and write down the labels and sample values that will be included on each line. This will guide you as you enter the information, so you know roughly where to put each piece of data.

For many spreadsheets, some labels naturally would appear as row labels and others as column labels. In this spreadsheet, for example, one logical layout would be to put labels for revenue, expenses, net income, and profit margin in the first column, and labels for the years in a row. Your first attempt at designing a layout might look like the example shown in Figure 12-1.

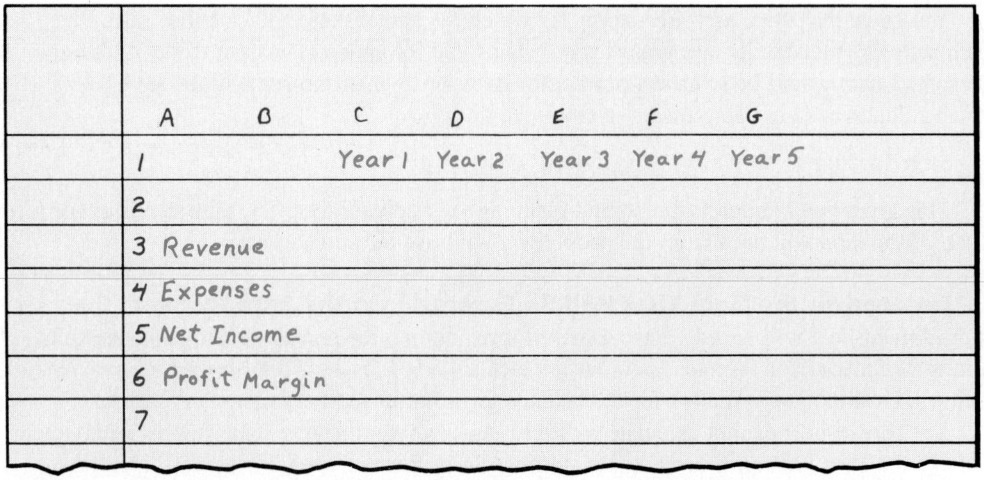

FIGURE 12-1
A first attempt at a spreadsheet layout.

Right away, you may notice something wrong with this layout. There is no title for the spreadsheet, and there is no space for prompts that tell the user what to enter. You could solve this problem by adding the spreadsheet title in the first row, then inserting several rows to make room for the prompts. Your second try at designing the spreadsheet might look like the example shown in Figure 12-2.

With a few modifications, this looks like a good layout. You might want to separate the net income from the amounts for revenue and expenses using a dashed line. Then add a blank line between net income and the profit margin, to show that the profit margin amount provides an analysis of the other information on the spreadsheet. After making these minor changes, your sample layout should look like Figure 12-3.

		A	B	C	D	E	F	G	H
1				Growth Projections					
2									
3	Store Location:								
4									
5	First Year Revenue:								
6	First Year Expenses:								
7	Growth Rate (Revenue):								
8	Growth Rate (Expenses):								
9									
10				Year 1	Year 2	Year 3	Year 4	Year 5	
11									
12	Revenue								
13	Expenses								
14	Net Income								
15	Profit Margin								
16									

◄ **FIGURE 12-2**
Adding a title and prompts.

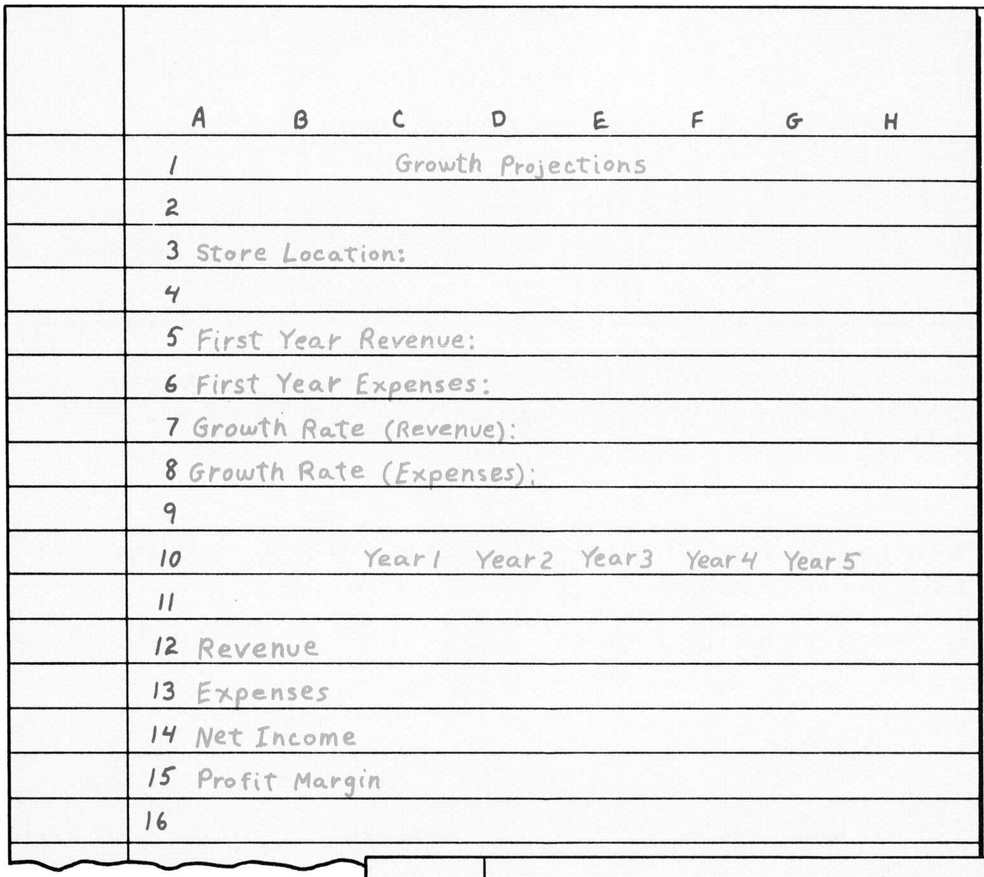

FIGURE 12-3
Modifying the layout to improve readability. ▼

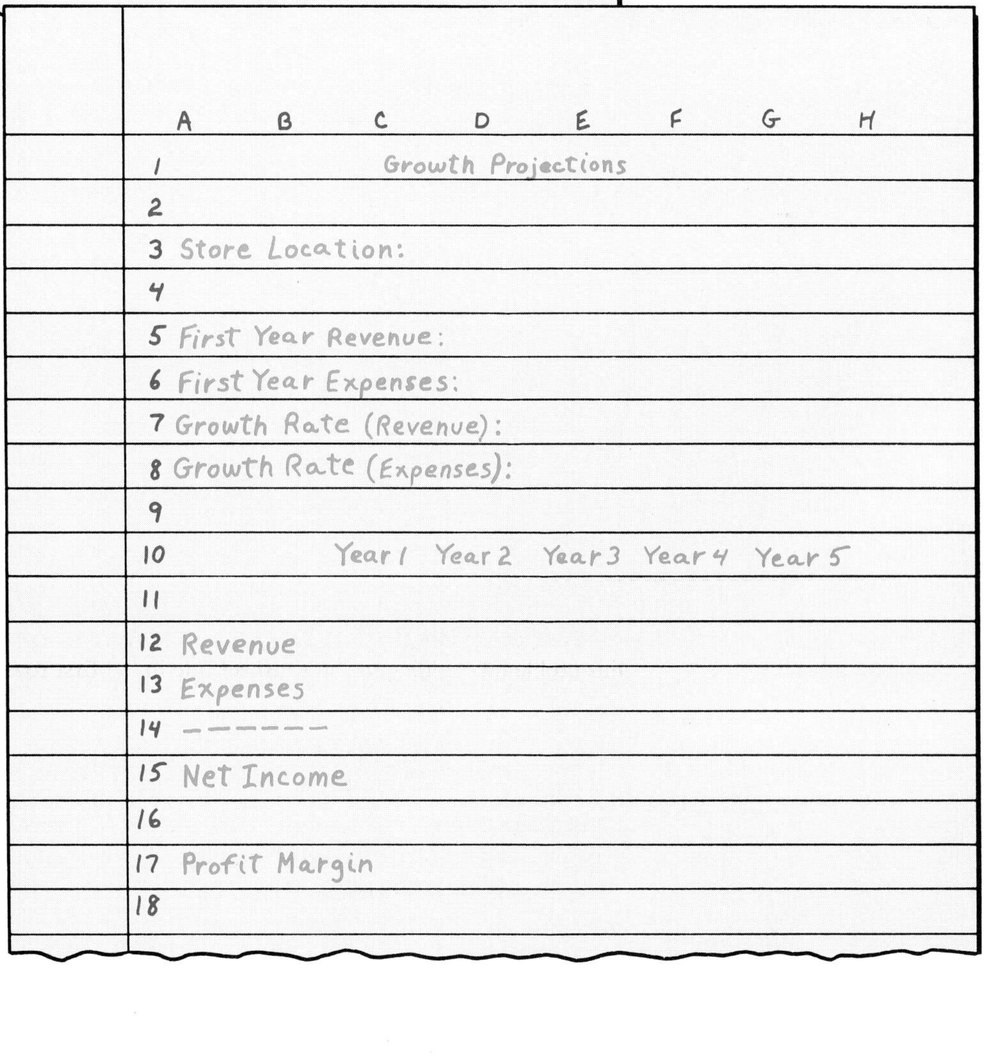

		A	B	C	D	E	F	G	H
1				Growth Projections					
2									
3	Store Location:								
4									
5	First Year Revenue:								
6	First Year Expenses:								
7	Growth Rate (Revenue):								
8	Growth Rate (Expenses):								
9									
10				Year 1	Year 2	Year 3	Year 4	Year 5	
11									
12	Revenue								
13	Expenses								
14	- - - - - -								
15	Net Income								
16									
17	Profit Margin								
18									

This sample layout gives you a good idea of where to enter each label on the spreadsheet. After you finish planning your new spreadsheet, you are ready to make a new file for it and begin entering your labels, numbers, and formulas.

Making the New File

You have already made new files for the Word Processor and Database in earlier lessons of this tutorial. The process of making a new file for a spreadsheet is very much like making those files.

1. Start Works.
2. Choose *Create New File* from the File menu.
3. In the dialog box, select *New Spreadsheet* and press Enter. You see an empty spreadsheet appear, as shown in Figure 12-4.

FIGURE 12-4
A new Spreadsheet file.

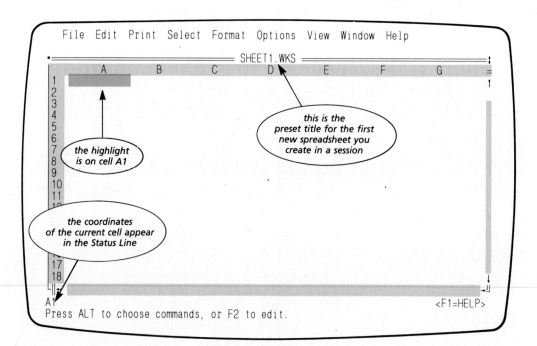

Entering Information

Normally labels are the first items you enter in a new spreadsheet. The labels tell you and other users what the numbers on the spreadsheet will mean. The labels for the prompts, of course, tell the user where to enter information that will be used in calculations.

1. Enter Growth Projections for the title in cell D1.
2. In cell A3, enter Store Location: for the first prompt.
3. Enter First Year Revenue: in cell A5.
4. Enter the other prompts:

CELL	PROMPT
A6	First Year Expenses:
A7	Growth Rate (Revenue):
A8	Growth Rate (Expenses):

5. Enter the labels for the values to be calculated in cells A12–A17 and the labels for row 10, columns C–G.

CELL	LABEL
A12	Revenue
A13	Expenses
A15	Net Income
A17	Profit Margin

CELL	LABEL
C10	Year 1
D10	Year 2
E10	Year 3
F10	Year 4
G10	Year 5

6. Use the *Save As* command to save this skeleton of your file. You should save every few minutes whenever you are working on a file, so that you will not have to start from scratch if you make a major mistake or trip over the power cord, causing the computer to forget everything it ever knew about your spreadsheet. Name the file *GrowXXX. WKS*. You will use this file again in Lesson 17 on Communications.

7. In cell A14, insert a row of ten hyphens to separate the net income from the revenue and expense figures. (Begin the label with a quotation mark, then enter the ten hyphens to fill the cell).

8. Extend the highlighting to cell G14. Use the *Fill Right* command from the Edit menu to extend the line of hyphens across the spreadsheet to G14. Your screen should look like Figure 12-5.

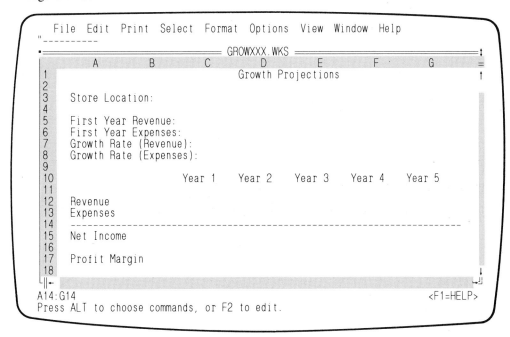

FIGURE 12-5
Entering labels on the new spreadsheet.

Now that you have entered these labels, you can begin entering the formulas. You can also enter some values to test the formulas. If the spreadsheet is correct, you can quickly copy the formulas and labels to complete the spreadsheet.

Entering Formulas

With most of the labels entered, you should enter a set of formulas in order to test whether your spreadsheet will work correctly. The following chart shows each cell that will contain a formula, explanations of the calculations, and the specific formulas necessary for the Spreadsheet to make those calculations.

CELL	CALCULATION	FORMULA
C12	Get first year revenue from D5	= D5
C13	Get first year expenses from D6	= D6
C15	Revenues minus expenses	= C12–C13
C17	Net income / revenue	= C15/C12
D12	First year revenue (C12) + (first year revenue * revenue growth rate (D7))	= C12 + (C12*D7)
D13	First year expenses (C13) + (first year expenses * expenses growth rate (D8))	= C13 + (C13*D8)

These are the basic formulas that you will use to round out the spreadsheet. All of the other formulas will be copies of these. If you are comfortable entering formulas and using both relative and absolute references, you may want to enter the formulas on your own using the chart as guidance. If you prefer step-by-step instructions, please follow these instructions:

1. In cell C12, key =D5 and press Enter. A zero appears because you have not yet put any number into cell D5.
2. In cell C13, key =D6 and press Enter. This value, too, is zero for the moment.
3. In cell C15, key =C12-C13. (You could also key the equal sign, then highlight C12, key the minus sign, and highlight C13.) Press Enter.

You are setting up the formula that subtracts expenses from revenues to find net income.

4. In cell C17, key =C15/C12 and press Enter.

Oops! That's dividing by zero, an impossibility, so you get an error message. Ignore that for now. Works is just warning you that you have no figures in cell C12, and you knew that already. You have put in place the formula for calculating the margin of profit.

5. In cell D12, key =C12+(C12*D7) and press Enter.

Cell D7 contains the expected growth rate, so this formula calculates the amount at which the revenues will grow. The asterisk stands for *multiplied by*.

6. In cell D13, key =C13+(C13*D8) and press Enter.

Cell D8 will contain the expected growth rate for expenses. Multiplying that by the first year's expenses yields the amount that expenses will grow for the second year. The formula adds that growth spurt to the first year's expenses to figure out the expenses for the second year.

7. Highlight cells C15 and D15, then choose *Fill Right* from the Edit menu to place the formula from C15 into D15, with the references changed relative to the formula's new position.

8. Highlight cells C17 and D17, then choose *Fill Right* from the Edit menu to place the formula from C17 into D17. Your screen should look like Figure 12-6.

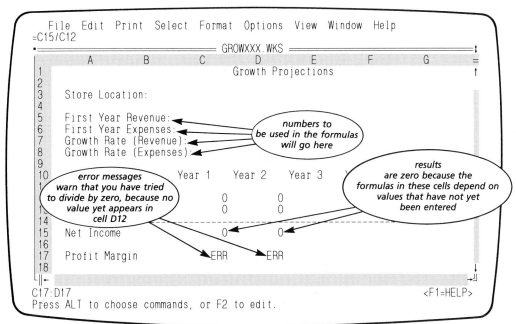

FIGURE 12-6
Entering formulas on the new spreadsheet

Testing the First Set of Formulas

Now that you have entered a set of formulas into the spreadsheet, you are ready to test them by entering some data for the store located in the city of Palookaville. The data will go into the cells following the prompts in rows 3 through 8. Sarah Lugosi has told you that she expects revenues to grow at 20 percent and expenses to grow at 10 percent a year. She also told you that first year's revenue was $400,000 while expenses were $325,000. Begin your test of the formulas by giving the spreadsheet a value to start the calculations.

1. Enter Palookaville in cell C3.
2. In cell D5, enter 400000 (which stands for $400,000).

   The first set of results appears, showing that revenues of $400,000 minus expenses of $0 gives net income of $400,000 the first year and $400,000 the second year. The error message disappears, and the profit margin appears to be 1 (meaning that 100 percent of the revenues appear to be pure profit). That would be wonderful if it were the whole story. But it is time to enter some expense figures.

3. In cell D6, enter 325000. Now the profit margin shrinks to about 19%. Now see what happens when you enter the growth rates.
4. In cell D7, enter 0.2 (meaning 20 percent). You can see that this makes revenues and net income rise in the second year.
5. In cell D8, enter 0.1 (meaning 10 percent). That completes the figures for the first and second year. Your screen should look like Figure 12-7.

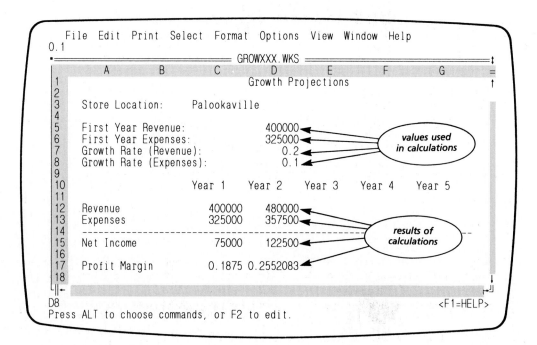

The test shows that the spreadsheet works as intended. Sometimes a test will show you that some changes are needed in the formulas to get accurate results. This test does show one change you should consider. The calculated values nearly fill up their cells. The results for later years might be even larger numbers, and those might not fit inside the same size cells.

There are two potential solutions to this problem. One would be to make the cells wider. This solution could put the Year 5 results off the edge of the screen. Then you might have to scroll back and forth to enter the first year values or the growth rates and to see the results of the changes. The other solution would be to put a note in the file saying that the values are estimates in thousands of dollars, and then enter the values without the final three zeros. Since these are estimates, not actual figures, you may not need the accuracy of having all the digits appear on the screen. Many businesses use this technique to make their financial results easier to read quickly. Use this solution to solve the problem.

1. In cell F5, enter: Estimates
2. In cell F6, enter: in thousands
3. In cell F7, enter: of dollars
4. In cell D5, enter: 400
5. In cell D6, enter: 325

Now the results appear as hundreds. The note in cells F5, F6, and F7 reminds you that these figures represent thousands—not hundreds—of dollars.

Copying and Editing

Rather than enter all the other formulas one at a time, you can copy much of the information and edit the copies where necessary. Copying can save you a lot of time and effort in creating spreadsheets. To complete the formulas for this spreadsheet, make the references absolute to the cells that contain the revenue and expenses growth rates (D7 and D8), then copy the formulas in column D to columns E through G.

1. Highlight cell D12.
2. Press F2 to edit it, and put a dollar sign ($) in front of the D and in front of the 7 to make this reference absolute. The formula should now read: =C12+(C12*$D$7)
3. Press Enter.
4. Revise the formula in cell D13 the same way, so it reads: =C13+(C13*$D$8)
5. Press Enter.
6. Highlight cells D12 through D17, then extend the highlighting to row G, for Year 5. Choose *Fill Right*. Your screen should now look like Figure 12-8.

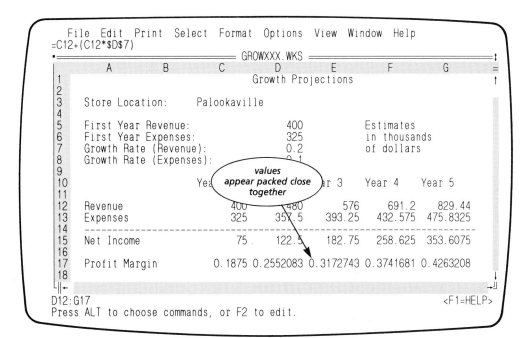

FIGURE 12-8
Copied formulas.

Congratulations! You have finished all the formulas for the spreadsheet. Notice that some of the results are so close they are almost bumping into each other. In the next section, you will solve that problem by adjusting the format.

Formatting the New Spreadsheet

Many of the values in this spreadsheet are dollar amounts. The revenue growth rate, expenses growth rate, and profit margin figures are the only values that are different; they should be displayed as percentages. In this section, you will have the Spreadsheet format both kinds of values.

1. Highlight cells D7 and D8, choose *Percent* from the Format menu, set the number of decimals to zero, and press Enter.
2. Highlight cells C17 through G17, choose *Percent* from the Format menu, set the number of decimals to zero, and press Enter.
3. Highlight cells D5 and D6, choose *Currency* from the Format menu, set the number of decimals to zero, and press Enter.
4. Highlight cells C12 to G15, choose *Currency* from the Format menu, set the number of decimals to zero, and press Enter. Now your spreadsheet will be easier to read.
5. To make sure that all your figures will show up on the same page when you print, high-

light cells C14 through G14, then choose *Column Width* from the Format menu, and set the width to 7 characters, as shown in Figure 12-9.

FIGURE 12-9
The formatted spreadsheet.

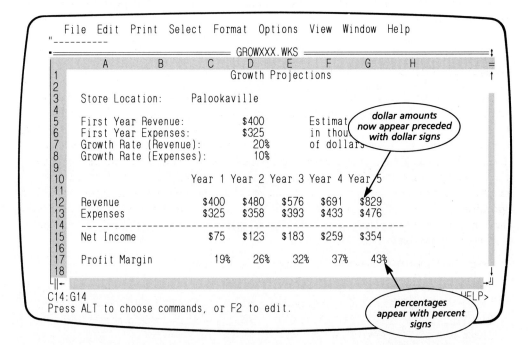

6. Choose the *Save* command from the File menu to save the updated spreadsheet.
7. Make sure that your printer has been turned on, and that it is connected to your computer and on-line. Then choose *Print* from the Print menu, and press Enter to get a printout of your spreadsheet.
8. Choose *Close* from the File menu to put away the spreadsheet for now.

Great! You have planned a new spreadsheet; laid out the labels, numbers, and formulas; formatted it; entered some test figures; and printed your first report. Now you can take a look at some of the advanced functions available with the Works Spreadsheet tool.

USING THE POWER OF WHAT-IF

Lugosi's Classic Video Store has instituted a new program to encourage the sales staff to give customers better service and increase sales. When a shift matches or exceeds their record sales for the previous week, the store will give them a bonus. If a particular shift had maximum sales last week of $3,000, and that shift sells $3,250 of merchandise today, everyone on the shift will share a bonus. Sarah Lugosi hopes that the bonus plan will get everyone excited and increase sales for the store. She developed a special spreadsheet for employees to use to see whether they will receive a bonus. The spreadsheet compares a number the employee enters (a hypothetical or actual day's sales for the shift) to last week's maximum sales and calculates a bonus. The percentage of the bonus depends on the employee's shift.

This spreadsheet lets you ponder the question, "What if...?" What if sales are $3,000 on the night shift? Will our crew get a bonus? What if we boost sales to $4,000 on the day shift? What if I change shifts? How does that affect the amount my shift has to earn to start earning a bonus?

In this part of the lesson, you will practice playing what-if. It can seem like a game, but with other spreadsheets, **what-if analysis** can help you make important decisions. You will also see how some advanced functions make it possible for a spreadsheet to work in different ways, depending on what the user enters.

Playing What-If

In this section, you will use the *Bonus.WKS* spreadsheet to see what bonus is possible for different employees working on different shifts bringing in different amounts of money. Sarah Lugosi wanted to make it possible for the night shift to earn bonuses as easily as the day shift, even though the day shift always brings in a bigger share of the business. So, she set up the *Bonus.WKS* spreadsheet to ask employees what their shift is. It calculates different bonus levels depending on the shift. When someone wants to see whether he or she might receive a bonus, the person enters his or her name, shift number, and the day's sales for that shift. The spreadsheet will tell the person what the highest day's sales were for that shift last week, what the bonus rate is for the shift's level of sales, and what the shift bonus (if any) will be. The shift bonus is split among the members of the shift.

1. Open the *Bonus.WKS* spreadsheet from the template disk.

   The spreadsheet appears on the screen, as shown in Figure 12-10. The file is often used by the employees of the store, so you may see data entered by the last person who used the file. To find out if you're due a bonus, you have to change the information currently displayed.

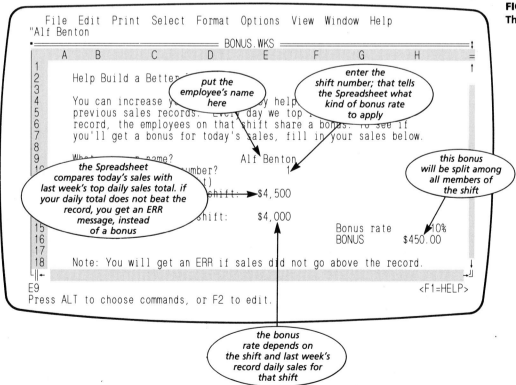

FIGURE 12-10
The Bonus spreadsheet.

2. Enter your name in cell E9, after the prompt.

   The last person who used the spreadsheet was Alf Benton, of the swing shift. You're in the night shift, from midnight to 8:00 a.m., when sales are traditionally a lot slower than from 4:00 p.m. to midnight, during the swing shift. You wonder how much bonus your shift would earn if you managed to get sales up to $4,500.

3. In cell E10, key 2 for the night shift number, and press Enter.

   When you press Enter, watch what happens to the record sales number in cell E14, the bonus rate in cell H15, and the actual shift bonus in cell H16. The record sales for your shift last week were $2,000, and $4,500 is so far above that level that you get the top bonus rate of 25%, so that your shift would end up splitting a bonus of $1,125. You begin to see some advantages to coming to work at midnight.

   Of course, your shift is not likely to reach such exalted levels. You wonder how much bonus you'd make if your shift brought in $3,000.

4. In cell E12, key 3000 and press Enter.

   The bonus rate drops to 15%, and the bonus falls to $450—still not bad for a night's work. You've been thinking about changing to the day shift. If the day shift were to earn $3,000, how much would you and your fellow employees get to split, in a bonus?

5. In cell E10, key 0 for the day shift and press Enter.

   The sales figure has not changed, but the record sales total does. In fact, it was $3,000 last week. So, the $3,000 sales for today would exactly match the record—just enough to qualify for the bonus. But the bonus rate would be the lowest—ten percent—and the amount would be $300. You wonder what would happen if you entered a sales total that was lower than last week's record.

6. In cell E12, key 2500 and press Enter.

   Oops! You wouldn't qualify for a bonus, because the sales total does not match or exceed last week's record. As a result, the Spreadsheet flashes you the ERR message. No bonus rate, and no bonus for you.

7. Play around with the shifts in cell E10. (Enter a 0 for day shift, 1 for swing shift, or 2 for night shift.)

   At the same time, play with different amounts of daily sales in cell E12. See what happens for each combination. Be careful not to enter anything in the other cells, because those contain the formulas and information that make the whole spreadsheet work. What happens when sales are only a little above the shift record? What if one shift is slightly below its record—could another shift earn a bonus on the same amount of sales? Can you find any circumstances in which different shifts end up earning the same bonus for the same number of dollars over their previous records? How much bonus would the day shift earn if they achieved sales of $5,000?

   Now that you know what the Bonus spreadsheet does, you are ready to learn how it works.

How Advanced Functions Make What-If Possible

The *Bonus.WKS* spreadsheet uses several functions that you have not seen before. The functions you have used in the previous two lessons have all generated calculations. The special functions used in the Bonus spreadsheet make choices. They choose a different course depending on the values entered by the person who is using the spreadsheet.

1. Highlight cell E14, and look in the formula bar, as shown in Figure 12-11.

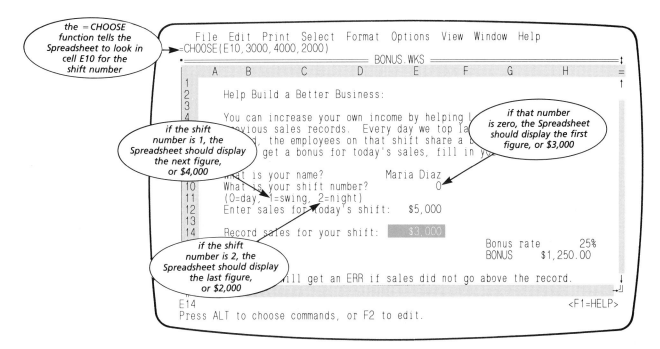

FIGURE 12-11
The =CHOOSE function.

   The **=CHOOSE** function looks in cell E10 for a value (0, 1, or 2 in this case), and depending on which value it finds there, chooses the first, second, or third of the numbers contained in the formula, right after the cell reference. Thus, the record sales for the day shift (0) were $3,000 last week; for the swing shift (1), $4,000; and for the night shift (2), $2,000. As soon as someone changes the shift number, the figure chosen and displayed by this formula will change. This is one of the ways in which the Spreadsheet can adapt to differing circumstances.

   The Spreadsheet also makes a choice about which percentage to use in calculating the shift bonus. The bonus depends on the user's shift and on the amount of the previous record sales. This kind of choice requires another kind of function, known as Vertical Lookup.

1. Use the Down Arrow to move down to row 25. This brings a table into view. You'll see how this table is used to figure the bonus rate in a moment.
2. Highlight cell H15, and look in the formula bar, as shown in Figure 12-12.

   The V in the **=VLOOKUP** function stands for vertical. You are telling the spreadsheet to look up some figures in a vertical table, that is, one made up of several columns. According to the formula, the spreadsheet should look in cell E12 for today's sales figures. That amount becomes the **lookup value**.

   The Spreadsheet then searches the left-hand column of the range of numbers mentioned next in the formula, in cells B20 through B22, looking for the largest number that is less than or equal to the lookup value. If your daily sales total was $10,000, the Spreadsheet looks at the value in cell B20 and concludes that it is indeed less than the $10,000, and not equal. But the Spreadsheet does not stop there. It looks at the number in cell B21, and

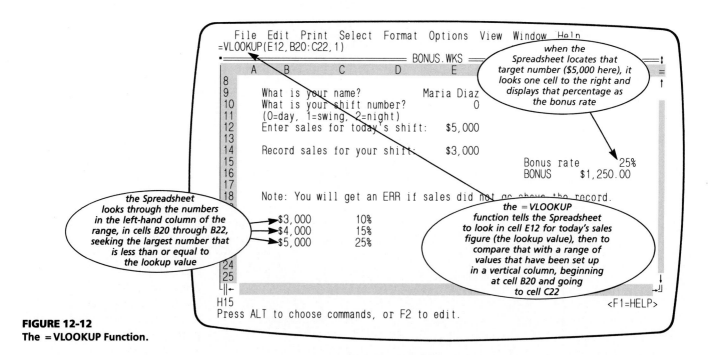

FIGURE 12-12
The = VLOOKUP Function.

finds that it too is less than the lookup value, so it goes to cell B22, and finds that even the number there is less than the lookup value. Because the number in cell B22 is the largest of the three, and is still less than the lookup value, the Spreadsheet settles on cell B22.

At this point, the last item in the formula comes into play. The 1 just means that once the Spreadsheet has located the cell containing the largest number that is less than or equal to the lookup value, the Spreadsheet should look one column to the right, and display that value as the result of all its work. The Spreadsheet displays 25% as the bonus rate in cell H15.

Notice that the values in cells B20, B21, and B22 are the result of formulas. You can see from the formula for cell B20 that the number in the cell was determined by an = CHOOSE function. The function uses the shift number in cell E10 to decide which record amount to use in the table.

3. When you have finished examining the *Bonus.WKS* spreadsheet, do not save the changes you have made to the file. Leave it open for a while.

OTHER ADVANCED FUNCTIONS

*T*he Spreadsheet offers many other functions you can use to calculate and adjust to what the user enters. Most functions start with an equal sign, then the function name, an opening parenthesis, the argument of the function (the extra information the spreadsheet needs to carry out the function), and a closing parenthesis. Many functions require several arguments. If you have more than one argument, you must separate them by commas. All the arguments must appear inside the parentheses. The table in Figure 12-13 explains some of the other functions.

Some spreadsheets have many more functions—sometimes hundreds of them. These functions allow accountants, financial analysts, engineers, scientists and others to perform extremely sophisticated analyses of situations they encounter in their work.

FUNCTION	EXAMPLE	EXPLANATION
= ABS	= ABS(C2)	Displays the absolute value of the number in the argument, whether or not it is a negative amount. This function ensures that the resulting value is always positive.
= FV	= FV(1000,9%,8)	Shows the future value of an ordinary annuity such as a savings deposit earning fixed interest at a certain rate, over a certain number of years. For instance, you deposit $1,000 and you are going to earn nine percent a year for eight years. The formula will tell you the future value of your deposit.
= IF	= IF(B2 > 10,H1,H2)	Determines whether a certain condition is true or false, then displays the value found in the first cell if true, or, if false, the value in the second cell. The argument has three parts. The first part is a simple comparison, such as B2 > 10, which asks the question: *Is the value in cell B2 larger than 10?* The second and third parts are values. If the comparison turns out to be true, the Spreadsheet displays the value that appears right after the comparison (H1 in this case). If the comparison is not true, the spreadsheet displays the last value (H2 in this case). The Spreadsheet expects that these cells will contain numbers, not labels. If it discovers a label there, it will just display a 0, meaning *Not True*, or a 1, meaning *True*. For comparisons, you can use operators such as less than (<), greater than (>), equal to (=), less than or equal to (< =), greater than or equal to (> =) and not equal to (< >).
= INT	= INT(C2)	Displays the whole number part of the number in the cell mentioned in the argument. This does not round off the number; it just takes the whole number part of the value and discards any fractions. For instance, if cell C2 contains 3.56, the result would be 3.
= PMT	= PMT(1000,9%/12,24)	Calculates the amount you will have to pay each period on a loan, or the amount you will earn each period on an investment, when you are dealing with a fixed interest rate every period or a definite number of periods. For example, if you want to buy a sofa that requires a $1,000 loan at nine percent interest per year, with monthly payments over 24 months, how much would each payment be? (You have to divide the annual interest rate by 12 to get the monthly interest rate, here.)
= ROUND	= ROUND (C12,0)	Rounds the number found in the cell to a certain number of decimal places. The argument contains the cell reference and the number of decimal places. Zero decimal places mean none; a minus number of decimal places means that the rounding applies that far to the left of the decimal place. So, *= ROUND (9678,–3)* would be 9700. *= ROUND (123.76,0)* is 124.
= SQRT	= SQRT(C2)	Displays the square root of the value found in the cell referred to in the argument. For instance, if the value in cell C2 is 16, the result would be 4.

FIGURE 12-13
Some advanced Spreadsheet functions.

MAKING UP A MACRO

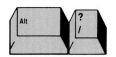

**Open Macro
Options Dialog
Box**

![A]macro is a recording of a series of keystrokes. You record the keystrokes and give them a name so that you can have Works execute all those keystrokes for you automatically. Creating a Macro is like making up your own special function. In this lesson, you will learn how to set up a macro that inserts a standard header into your document, so all your documents will have a consistent look.

1. Press Alt-/ to bring up the Macro options dialog box, as shown in Figure 12-14. (There is no *Macro* command on a menu.)

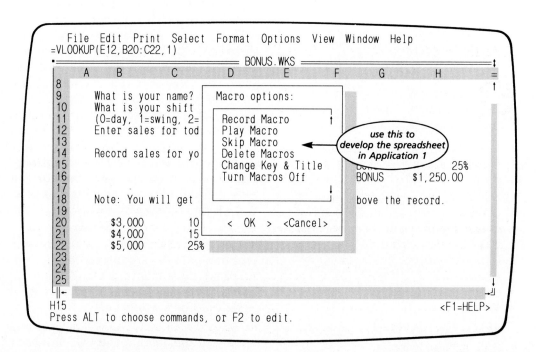

FIGURE 12-14
The Macro options dialog box.

2. The *Record Macro* option is selected, so press Enter. Works needs to know what keystroke combination you want Works to use later when you launch your macro—that is, when you have Works replay your macro, keystroke by keystroke. Press Ctrl-Insert. Works puts its own code for those two keys into the dialog box. Now you may want to give a name to your macro, so you can recognize its purpose later.
3. Press Tab to move to the Title line, then key Header, and press Enter.
4. Press Alt-P to open the Print menu, and press H to choose *Headers & Footers*.

   By the way: If you are using a mouse, abandon it while creating a macro. Works records only actual keystrokes, not mouse clicks, so anything you do with a mouse will not be recorded. For instance, you should use Alt-P to open the Print menu, and H to choose the *Headers & Footers* command, rather than pointing and clicking.

5. In the Headers & Footers dialog box, key your name on the Header line, press the spacebar five times, key &p to insert the page number, and then press the spacebar five more times, and key &d to have the current date inserted. (The page number and date do not appear until you print.) Press Enter. You have recorded your macro.
6. Press Alt-/ to bring up the Macro options dialog box.

7. *End Recording* is selected, so you can just press Enter. You have now recorded your macro. Want to test it out?

8. Choose *Headers & Footers* from the Print menu, and erase the header you find there. Now you know the document has no header.

9. Press Alt-/ to bring up the Macro options dialog box.

10. Select *Play Macro* and press Enter. You see a box with your macro header in it.

11. Select your *Header macro* and press Enter. You see the Headers & Footers dialog box flash on the screen, and then go away. You have had Works play your macro.

12. To make sure, choose *Preview* from the Print menu, and press Enter. Your header should appear at the top of your document. Press Esc to put away the Preview. Choose *Close* from the File menu, and choose not to save any of your changes.

APPLYING A MACRO TO ANOTHER DOCUMENT

nce you create a few macros, your list of macros is stored in the software, not in the particular document, so all your macros are available to you whenever you open a document.

1. On the File menu, choose *Create New File*, select *New Spreadsheet*, and press Enter.

2. In cell A1 key the number 1 2 3 and press Enter.

3. Press Alt-/ to open the Macro options dialog box.

4. Select *Play Macro* and press Enter.

5. In the box, select the *Header macro*, press Enter, and watch it flash.

6. Choose *Preview* on the Print menu and press Enter to see the results of these macros. (You must have some data in the spreadsheet for Works to place a header or footer on the document when printing or previewing.)

7. Choose *Close* from the File menu to put away the document, and choose not to save the changes. Even though you are throwing away this document, your macros are preserved by Works, and will be available to you until you choose to delete them.

Congratulations! You have created and applied a Works macro. Macros speed up your work by automating repetitive tasks.

KEY TERMS

lookup value   *MSW 229*
macro   *MSW 232*
what-if analysis   *MSW 227*

COMMAND

Alt-/ (Open Macro options dialog box)

FUNCTIONS

= ABS
= CHOOSE
= FV
= IF
= INT
= PMT
= ROUND
= SQRT
= VLOOKUP

REVIEW QUESTIONS

1. What are the steps you should go through when planning a new spreadsheet?
2. How can you tell the users what information they should enter?
3. Should you start right off setting up formulas with cell references when you are planning a spreadsheet? Why or why not?
4. Are you able to make changes to a new spreadsheet once it is complete and you have entered it into the computer? Give some examples.
5. Why should you test a new spreadsheet, and how?
6. What are some circumstances in which you might want to use the = CHOOSE function in a spreadsheet?
7. Give some examples of uses for the lookup function.
8. What function would you use if you wanted a formula to display the value 1 if the user enters an amount greater than 500, but to display a value of 0 if the user enters an amount equal to or less than 500? Write the formula, assuming the user enters the number in cell C4.

APPLICATIONS

1. Sarah Lugosi has been planning a spreadsheet to calculate how much of the store's budget is spent for different purposes. Use the rough draft of Sarah's spreadsheet in Figure 12-15 as a guide. Make a new spreadsheet file called *SpendXXX.WKS*. Enter the spreadsheet, choosing your own functions and designing your own formulas. Save the file and print a report.

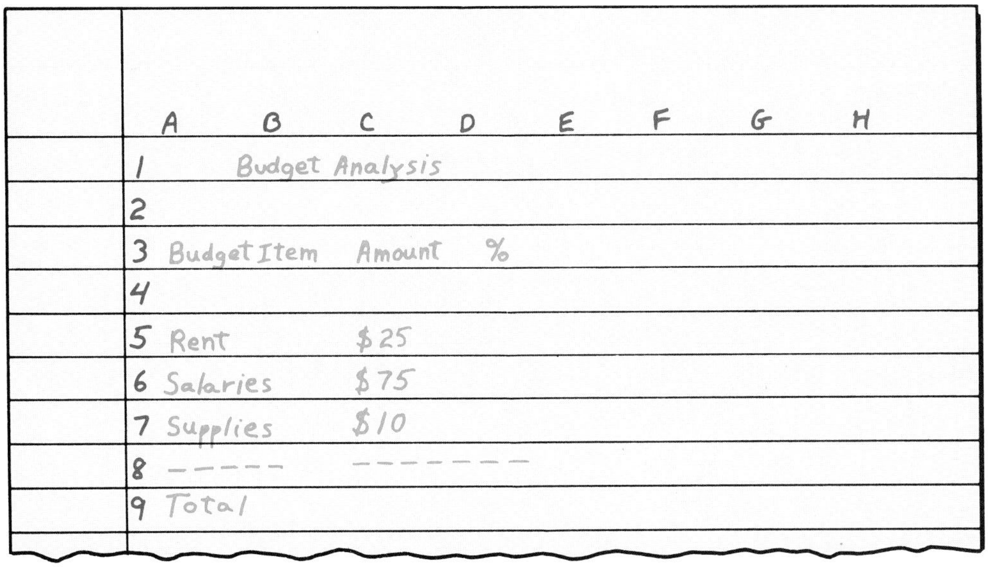

FIGURE 12-15
Rough draft budget of spending.

2. Lugosi's Classic Video Store gives potential employees a short test to see how much training they will need if they are hired. A test was given today. The results appear below. Plan a spreadsheet that lists the results for each applicant, but also shows the highest, lowest, and average scores. In addition, include a count of the number of applicants. (Use a function to accomplish this task.) Make a new spreadsheet file called *TestXXX.WKS* and enter your new spreadsheet.

Applicant	Score
Jaeger, M.	75
Juarez, F.	99
Alvin, C.	85
Kelly, C.	72
Weal, E.	98
Martin, D.	87
Wilson, B.	91

Save the file and print a report.

3. Morris Yu wants to see how the Fairfax video store will do over the next few years. He has asked you to run a few alternatives through the spreadsheet you created in this lesson and give him a summary of the results. Open the *GrowXXX.WKS* spreadsheet from the template disk and answer the following questions on a sheet of paper.

   a. Set the growth rate for revenue at 20% and the growth rate for expenses at 10%. If first year revenue is $321,000 and first year expenses are $213,000, what is the projected net income for Year 5?

   b. What would the net income be for Year 5 if the revenue growth rate drops to 8%, but everything else stays the same?

   c. What happens to the profit margin in Year 5 if the growth rate for expenses jumps up to 15% while everything else stays the same? How does the profit margin for Year 1 compare to the profit margin for Year 5? Does this show that higher sales always mean higher profits?

   d. Change the growth rate for revenue to 10% and the growth rate for expenses to 5%. Set the first year revenue to $200,000 and the first year expenses to $225,000. In what year does the chain first make a profit? How much is it?

UNIT V

Integration

Working with Charts

OBJECTIVES

- Explain the purpose of charting.
- Create a simple bar chart.
- Create a stacked bar chart.
- Create a pie chart.
- Create a line chart.

PRESENTING DATA THROUGH CHARTS

Charts translate Spreadsheet information from columns and rows of numbers into graphic shapes such as lines, thick bars, and circles. Expressing a series of numbers in a picture can help you discover patterns and trends in your information. A doctor might chart the progress of a patient's fever, from hour to hour, drawing an up-and-down zig-zag line to show the intensification and decline of the fever. A business person might use a pie chart to show how company funds are divided up among various expenses—each expense would appear as a slice of the pie. A government spokesperson might use a bar chart to compare the total amount of oil produced by different countries this year; each country's production would get its own bar, and the leader would stand out clearly. William Playfair, a nineteenth-century author who invented many of the chart types we use today, said, "Whatever can be expressed in numbers may be represented by lines," and what Playfair had to do with pen and ink, Works will do for you, with your computer and printer.

Once you have a spreadsheet, you can select the information you want charted and Works will automatically build a bar chart for you. When you choose to make a chart based on the figures in your spreadsheet, Works looks at the numbers in a special way, called a **Chart View**. The Chart View has its own menus and commands. In the Chart View, you can switch from a **bar chart** to a **pie chart** or a **line chart** just by issuing a command. You can add and refine titles and labels. In this way, you can prepare a sophisticated chart that communicates the message inherent in your numbers.

WORKING WITH BAR CHARTS

Flora Bari, the store manager, has scheduled a meeting with Sarah Lugosi to talk about scheduling staff. Flora plans to show the owner the sales figures for each day and shift. She hopes to convince Sarah Lugosi to let her put more clerks on duty during the afternoons, particularly on Saturdays, when business is heaviest.

The information the manager needs is in the *Sales.WKS* spreadsheet. She has asked you to prepare charts because the data will be much more convincing if it is presented in a visual form.

Creating a Simple Bar Chart

The first chart you make will bolster Flora's argument that the swing shift is by far the busiest time in the store. After opening the spreadsheet, you'll select the numbers and labels you want to include in the chart. Next, to switch from the Spreadsheet view to the Chart View, you'll choose *New Chart* from the View menu. Works automatically displays a bar chart on the screen. When you create a new chart, Works always displays it in the bar chart format.

1. Start up Works and open the *Sales.WKS* spreadsheet file from the template disk. Works displays the spreadsheet, as shown in Figure 13-1.

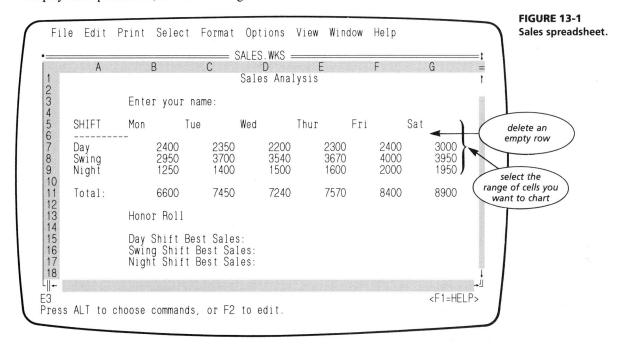

FIGURE 13-1
Sales spreadsheet.

2. Delete row 6 from the spreadsheet. Otherwise, it will be represented in the chart.
3. Highlight the range of cells from A5 to H9.

    You have selected the sales figures for every day of the week and all three shifts. You have also selected a column of row labels containing the names of the shifts and a row of column labels containing the names of the days of the week. Works will use each of these spreadsheet elements in constructing the chart.

4. From the View menu, choose *New Chart*. Works automatically creates the Bar chart shown in Figure 13-2.

Create New Chart

Looking at a Bar Chart

The Axes   The chart is laid out along a horizontal line, called the X-axis, and a vertical line, called the Y-axis. Works has marked the X-axis with a series of labels—the days of

FIGURE 13-2
A bar chart.

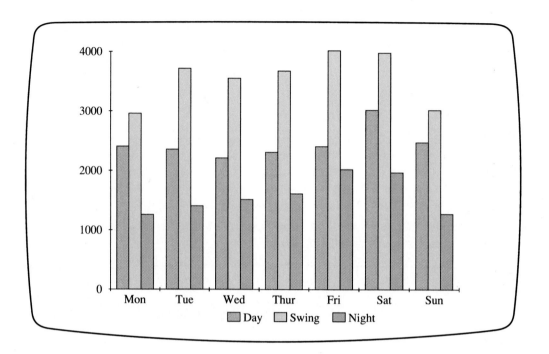

the week—using the first row you selected from the spreadsheet (A5:H5). In Works, this series of category labels is called the X-Series.

Works has created a numerical scale along the Y-axis. Based on the sales figures in the spreadsheet, which range from 1250 to 4000, Works automatically scales the Y-axis so that all the information in the spreadsheet will fit on the screen. After creating a chart, you can change the scale.

The Bars   Each figure in the spreadsheet is represented in the chart by a **bar**. The height of the bar corresponds to the magnitude of the number in the spreadsheet. For each day of the week, the spreadsheet contains figures for each of the three shifts at Lugosi's: day, swing, and night shift. So the chart has three bars for each day, one for each shift. The bars of each shift are represented by a different pattern (a different color if you have a color monitor).

The Legend   So you can understand the meaning of each bar, Works displays the patterns at the bottom of the chart, with labels that indicate what shift each pattern refers to. This is the **legend**. Works used the first column of the spreadsheet, containing the labels for each shift, to construct the chart's legend. (Works is preset to display chart legends, but someone may have turned off this option. If the legend is not displayed, press Esc to bring up the Chart View. From the Options menu, choose *Show Legends*. Then choose *Chart1* from the View menu to display the chart again.)

The Y-Series   As you scan the chart from left to right, all the bars for a single shift represent a single row of the spreadsheet. In Works, each such set is called a Y-Series. The first bar in each group represents the day shift. Together, the series of day shift bars is called the 1st Y-Series. Similarly, the series of swing shift bars is called the 2nd Y-Series, and the series of night shift bars is called the 3rd Y-Series. Works lets you display up to six Y-Series. In other words, for each category along the X-axis of the chart, you could have up to six bars, representing six rows in the spreadsheet.

You have probably noticed how much higher the bars of the 2nd Y-Series, representing the swing shift, are than the bars of either of the other two shifts. Only the bar representing the day shift on Saturday comes close to the lowest swing shift bar. This chart vividly underscores Flora's point that the most clerks need to be assigned to the swing shift. Although all the figures represented in the chart are displayed in the spreadsheet, their contrast stands out much more in the visual form of a chart than in the numerical form of the spreadsheet.

Adding Titles

You want to add titles to the chart. You will add a general title and enter your name as a subtitle. You also want to label the Y-axis so a viewer can tell what the numbers mean. (The X-axis already has labels.)

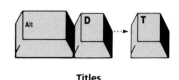

Titles

1. Press Esc to leave the chart and return to Chart View. From the Data menu, choose *Titles*. You see the dialog box shown in Figure 13-3. You can make a title and subtitle for the chart, as well as titling the chart's axes.

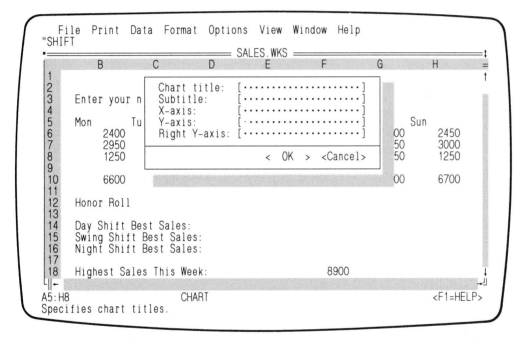

FIGURE 13-3
Titles dialog box.

2. On the Chart title line key DAILY SALES BY SHIFT. Then use the Down Arrow to move the cursor to the Subtitle line.
3. On the Subtitle line key your name.
4. Move the cursor to the Y-Axis line and key Sales in Dollars.
5. Press Enter. Works adds the titles you keyed to the chart. These changes occur behind the scenes, but you will be able to see the titles the next time you display the chart.

Formatting Titles

The type size you ordinarily use when printing text looks very small in a printed chart. If larger sizes are available on your printer, you can increase the size of all the text in the chart.

To complete this section, the printer attached to your computer must have graphic printing capabilities and a variety of fonts or type sizes. If your printer does not allow you to complete this section, you can read through the steps to learn how formatting is done.

Title Font

1. From the Format menu, choose *Title Font*. You see a dialog box similar to the one shown in Figure 13-4. (If your printer is not set up to print charts, you will see this error message: Cannot print charts with selected printer. If that happens, just press Enter to put the error message away, and skip to the next section of the tutorial.)

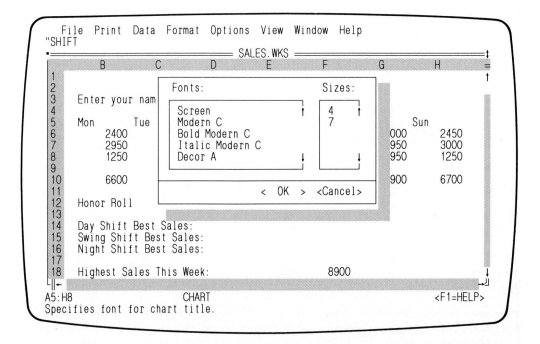

FIGURE 13-4
Fonts dialog box.

On the left, the fonts available on your printer are listed. On the right, the sizes available in the selected font are listed.

2. In the Fonts list, select a Font that comes in large sizes (20 or larger).
3. In the Sizes list, select a large size, then press Enter. When you print or preview the chart, the title will appear in the font and size you selected.
4. From the Format menu, choose *Other Fonts*. Works displays a similar dialog box.

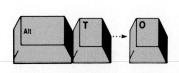

Other Font

5. Proceed as you did before to choose a font for the other text in the chart. Pick a slightly smaller size than you selected for the title (around 18). Press Enter. The **axis** labels and legend labels—all the text except for the title—will appear in the new font and size.
6. From the Options menu, choose *Show Printer Fonts*.

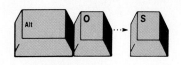

Show Printer Fonts

This command works like a toggle switch. When it is on, you see a bullet next to the command on the menu. When displaying the chart, Works will use the fonts and sizes you chose, instead of the screen font ordinarily used to display text.

7. Choose *Chart1* from the View menu to display the chart. Your finished chart should look something like the chart shown in Figure 13-5.

In addition to formatting text in a chart, you can format the data, using the **Data Format** command. The *Data Format* command lets you change the patterns (or colors) used to represent each series of bars in a bar chart. In a pie chart, you can change the patterns or colors used for the slices. In a line chart, you can change the styles of the markers and the patterns used for the lines.

Next you will make a chart to show that Saturday is the heaviest business day.

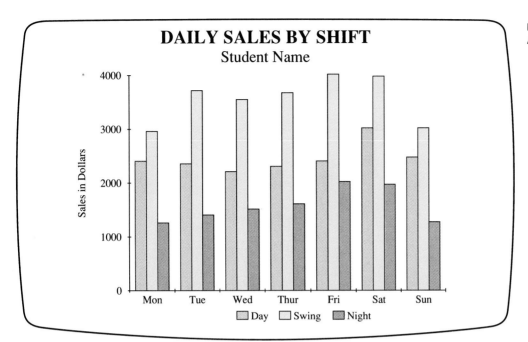

FIGURE 13-5
A titled bar chart.

Making a Stacked Bar Chart

You want a chart to show the total sales each day on all three shifts. One good way to present this information is through a **stacked bar chart** that piles the bars for each shift on top of one another. The height of the stack then indicates the day's total sales.

This chart uses the same information as the first one you made, so you will use a copy of the first chart. You will rename the first chart, copy it, and then change the copy's format to a stacked bar chart. Works lists all the chart types on the Format menu, so you can easily change a chart from one type to another by choosing the format you want.

1. To return to the Chart View, press Esc. The data you highlighted to make the first chart is still selected.
2. Choose *Charts* from the View menu. The Charts command lets you rename, delete, and copy charts. You see the Charts dialog box, as shown in Figure 13-6.

   The chart you created is listed in the dialog box as *Chart1*. Works numbers each Chart you create and lists it on the View menu, as well as in the Charts dialog box, so you can display any chart by choosing it on the View menu. The menu can list up to eight different charts. Works stores the charts with the spreadsheet when you save the spreadsheet file.

3. In the dialog box, select the *Name* option.
4. Key `Bar Chart` on the Name line, and then press Alt-R for *Rename*. The name you keyed replaces *Chart1* in the dialog box and on the View menu.
5. To make a copy of the chart, choose *Copy*. Works makes a copy of the chart and lists it as Chart1. Works copies everything in the Bar Chart, including the titles you entered and any formatting changes you made.
6. Highlight the new chart and then rename it *Totals Stack*. After you have finished, choose *Done* to put the dialog box away.
7. Open the View menu to make sure the Totals Stack chart is selected. You should see a bullet next to its name on the menu. If not, choose *Totals Stack*, and when Works displays

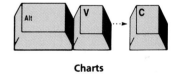

Charts

FIGURE 13-6
Charts dialog box.

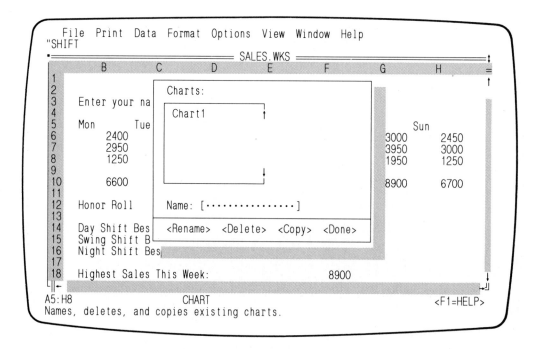

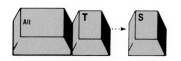

Stacked Bar Chart

the chart, press Esc to return to the Chart View. The last chart you displayed remains selected after you put it away.

8. To change the chart into a stacked bar chart, choose *Stacked Bar* from the Format menu. Behind the scenes, Works changes the format of the chart.

9. To change the title of the chart, choose *Titles* from the Data menu. Works has copied the titles from the Bar Chart and you see them in the dialog box. The Chart title is already selected.

10. Key DAILY SALES TOTALS as the Chart title, and then press Enter. You don't need to change the Subtitle or Y-Axis title. Works copied any formatting changes you made to the titles and labels of the Bar Chart, so you will not need to format any of the text in the chart.

11. To display the new chart, choose *Totals Stack* from the View menu. Works displays the chart shown in Figure 13-7.

The stacked bar chart shows at a glance how sales compare from day to day. Sarah Lugosi will readily see that business picks up during the course of the week, from the low point on Sunday to a peak on Saturday. Don't worry if the Y-Axis title appears cut off in the display. The screen does not have room to display the chart in its correct proportions. The full title will print.

Customizing a Chart

After seeing your stacked bar chart, Flora has asked you to customize the chart for additional emphasis. She wants to bring out the trend of sales from day to day and underscore how much business Lugosi's Classic Video Store is doing.

The best way to show a trend is to use a line chart. In a line chart, the numbers in a spreadsheet are represented by small markers. All the markers in a Y-Series are connected by a line, which helps to link them together like beads on a string. Looking at the chart, one's eye readily interprets the line as a trend over time. Works lets you combine a line chart with a bar chart, so you can show the trend of increased business from Sunday to Saturday by adding

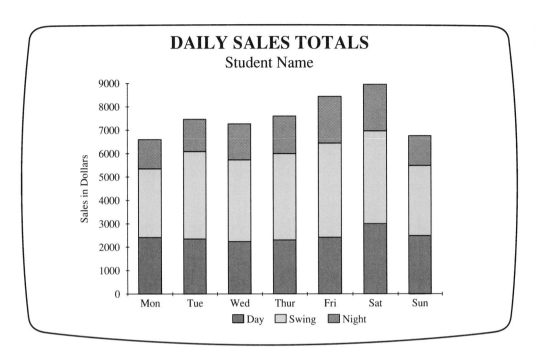

FIGURE 13-7
A stacked bar chart.

a line to the stacked bar chart. You can also emphasize the volume of business the store does by displaying numbers in the chart. You will create a chart like the one shown in Figure 13-8.

Copying a Chart

To save the trouble of formatting a new chart, you will start by making a copy of the stacked bar chart.

1. Press Esc to put away the stacked bar chart.

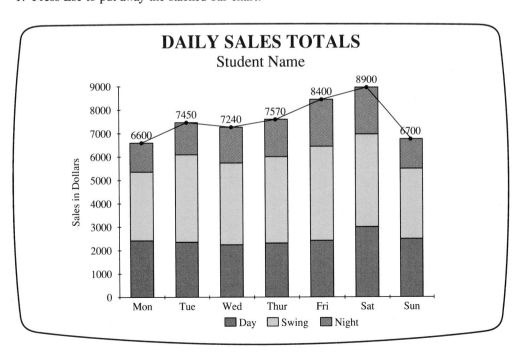

FIGURE 13-8
A mixed line and stacked bar chart.

2. Choose *Charts* from the View menu.
3. Make a copy of the Totals Stack chart.
4. Rename the new chart *Custom Totals*. Choose *Done*.

Adding a Row of Data to a Chart

The line on the chart in Figure 13-8, as well as the numbers displayed above each stacked bar, indicate the total sales for each day. The spreadsheet contains a row that lists these figures, and your first step is to add that row to the chart. Because the chart already contains three Y-Series of numbers—the figures for the Day shift, Swing shift, and Night shift—you will add the totals to the chart as the 4th Y-Series.

1. Highlight the range of cells from B10 to H10. These are the cells containing the sales totals for each day of the week.
2. From the Data menu, choose *4th Y-Series*. Although your display does not change, Works adds the cells you highlighted to the chart.

In the Chart View, Works refers to each row or column of the spreadsheet as a **series**. The Chart View lets you work with the chart by series, rather than by rows, columns, or cells.

The commands on the Data menu let you modify or build up a chart series-by-series. That lets you completely change the chart from the one Works creates automatically. For example, you just added a Y-Series to the chart. You could also use the Data menu to change the orientation of the chart so columns of data are displayed along the chart's X-axis instead of in rows.

Mixed Line & Bar

Converting a Bar to a Line

You want Works to display the series you added as a line instead of a set of bars.

1. From the Options menu, choose *Mixed Line & Bar*. Works displays the dialog box shown in Figure 13-9. The dialog box lets you select how each Y-Series in the chart is displayed.

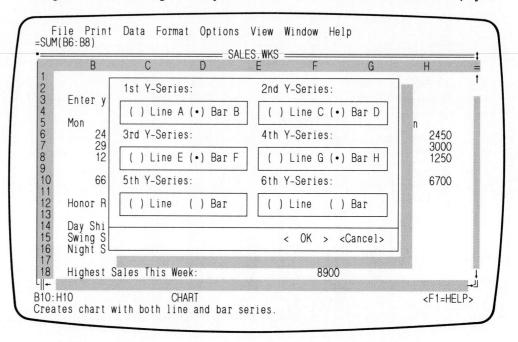

FIGURE 13-9
Mixed Line and Bar dialog box.

2. In the dialog box, change the 4th Y-Series from *Bar* to *Line* (Alt-G), and then press Enter. Works makes the change behind the scenes.

Creating Data Labels

You also want Works to display the Y-Series you added as a set of numbers above each stack. In Works, data from a spreadsheet that is displayed in a chart in numerical form is called a **data label**. To create data labels, you highlight the numbers you want Works to use as labels, and then indicate which series you want Works to apply the labels to. Because the totals in row 10 of the spreadsheet are selected already, you can skip that step.

Data Labels

1. From the Data menu, choose *Data Labels*. You see the Data Labels dialog box, shown in Figure 13-10. It lets you create data labels, delete them, or locate them in the spreadsheet.

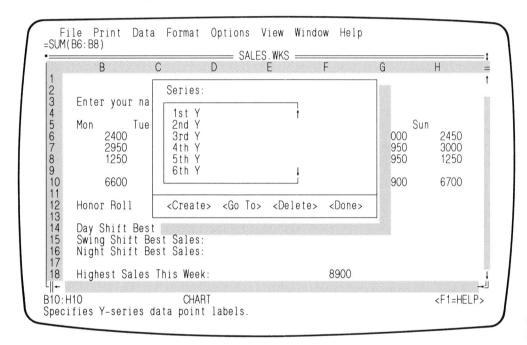

FIGURE 13-10
Data Labels dialog box.

2. Highlight *4th Y*, and choose *Create* by pressing Alt-C. The dialog box closes, and Works adds the labels to the chart behind the scenes. Now you are ready to display the chart.
3. From the View menu, choose *Custom Totals*.

   Your chart should look like the chart shown in Figure 13-8. The series depicting the Day, Swing, and Night shifts are represented by a stack of bars, as they are in the Totals Stack chart. The series depicting the total is represented by a line whose upward slope clearly shows the trend of the store's business. The numbers displayed above each bar add weight to the chart's impact.

Saving the File

Before printing the charts, save the file so the charts will be safe.

1. Press Esc to return to the Chart View.
2. To save the file, choose *Save As* from the File menu. In the Save As dialog box, change the

name of the file to *BarXXX.WKS*, replacing the X's with your initials, and save the file on the template disk. Saving the file stores all three charts you have made. Good work. You have created three charts. Even though the charts use the same data from the same spreadsheet, and even though all three are basically bar charts, they bring out different patterns of meaning in the data. Now you are ready to print the charts.

Printing the Charts

You can print a chart only if the printer attached to your computer has graphic printing capabilities. If your printer is not set up to print graphics, you will see this error message: `Cannot print charts with selected printer`
   Printing a chart can take a very long time. In order not to tie up the printer, your instructor may have you skip this section or set a special time for printing charts.
   The Custom Totals chart is already selected, so you will print it first, and then print the others.

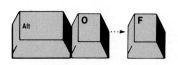

Format for Black and White

1. If you are using a color monitor, but will be printing the chart in black and white, choose *Format For B&W* from the Options menu. Works will display your chart in black and white, so you can see how it will look when printed.
2. To preview the chart, choose *Preview* from the Print menu, and press Enter to accept the preset options. Works displays a facsimile of the chart as it will appear on a page when you print it.
3. Check the titles and the labels in the legend and along the Y-axis. If they appear too large or too small, go back and use the *Title Font* and *Other Font* commands to change them. Then preview the chart again.
4. When your printer is ready, press P to print the chart. Unlike when printing a spreadsheet, your printer may take a long time to read the chart into its memory, so nothing may happen for a while. Unless you see an error message, all you need to do is wait. Your printer should begin grinding out the chart in a minute or two.
5. When the printer has released control of your computer, choose the *Bar Chart* from the View menu, and then press Esc.
6. Repeat steps 1-4 to print the Bar Chart.
7. Choose the *Totals Stack* chart from the View menu and print it.
8. Save and close the *BarXXX.WKS* file.

   Figure 13-11 shows—more or less—how the three charts look when they are printed. Because of differences between printers and the formatting changes you have made, your charts may look slightly different.

WORKING WITH PIE CHARTS

*F*lora would like to promote sales of blank video tape and other nonrental items. She thinks that movie rentals will account for too great a proportion of the store's business under the projected budget. To illustrate her argument, she has asked you to make a pie chart.
   A pie chart shows a row or column of data from a spreadsheet as a circular pie. Each number in the row or column becomes a slice of the pie. The size of each slice shows how large a portion of the whole row or column each number represents, so the pie chart is good for showing how totals are divided up. In addition to presenting each number as a slice of the pie, Works calculates and displays its percentage of the total next to each slice.

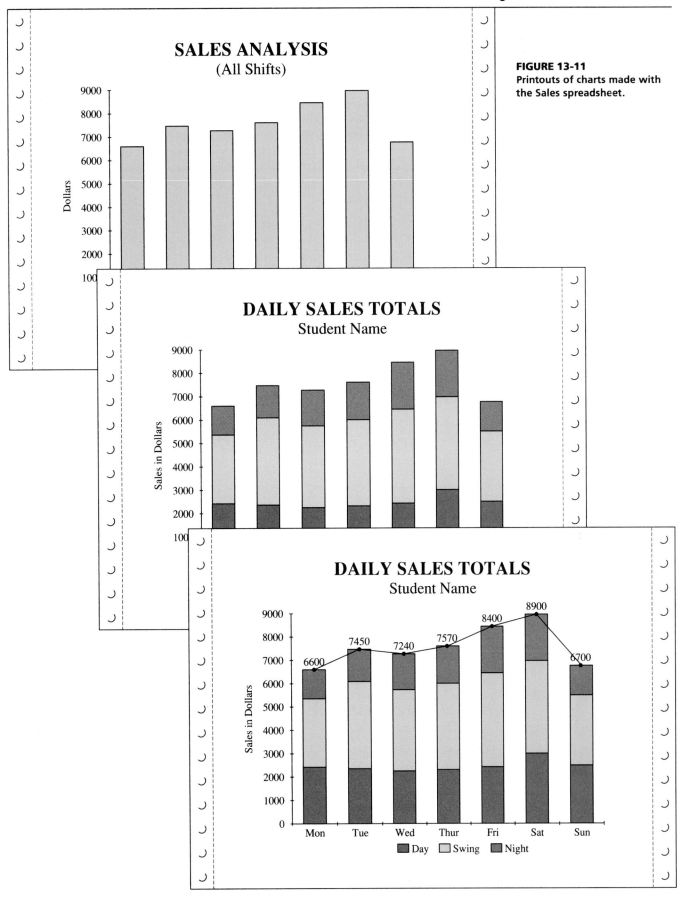

Creating a Pie Chart

The projected budget is stored in the *Store. WKS* file. You will open the file, create a new chart, and then format it as a pie chart.

The Store spreadsheet contains figures for both income and expenses, projected across three months of the store's operation. You can chart only one series of data—one column or one row of the spreadsheet—in a pie chart. For this chart, you will use the figures for the first quarter. When you create the new chart, Works displays it as a bar chart, but you can quickly change its format to a pie chart.

1. Open the *Store. WKS* file from the template disk.
2. Choose *Maximize* from the Window menu, so the Store spreadsheet fills the screen, as shown in Figure 13-12.

FIGURE 13-12
The Store spreadsheet.

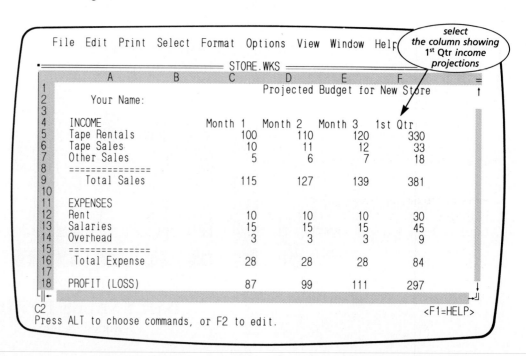

3. In the Income section of the spreadsheet, select the first quarter figures (the range F5:F7).
4. From the View menu, choose *New Chart*. Works creates Chart1 from the numbers you selected and displays them as a bar chart. Press Esc to display the Chart View.
5. Choose *Pie* from the Format menu to convert the bar chart to a pie chart.
6. To display the pie chart, choose *Chart1* from the View menu. Works displays the chart shown in Figure 13-13.

Pie Chart

Each of the three numbers you selected in the spreadsheet has become a slice of the circular pie. One is much larger than the rest. Works has labeled each slice to show its percentage of the whole.

Adding Labels

Because you selected only numbers in the spreadsheet, the chart has no labels to identify the slices. To add labels, you need to specify an X-Series. When you were making bar charts

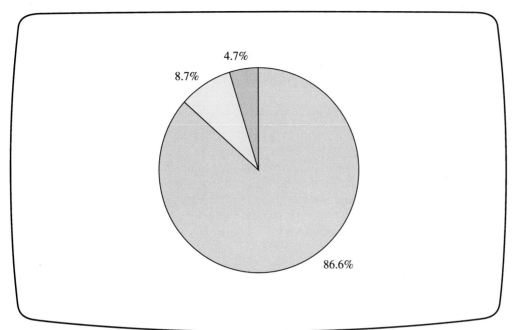

FIGURE 13-13
A new pie chart.

from the Sales spreadsheet, the X-Series contained the days of the week. In this chart, the X-Series will contain the income categories that are entered in column A of the spreadsheet.

1. Press Esc to display the Chart View.
2. Highlight the range A5:A7, containing the income category names.
3. From the Data menu, choose *X-Series*. Behind the scenes, Works defines the range of cells you selected as the chart's X-Series.
4. Choose *Chart1* from the View menu to display the pie chart again. As shown in Figure 13-14, the spreadsheet cells you chose and defined as the X-Series now label the slices of the pie.

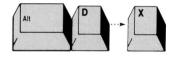

X-Series

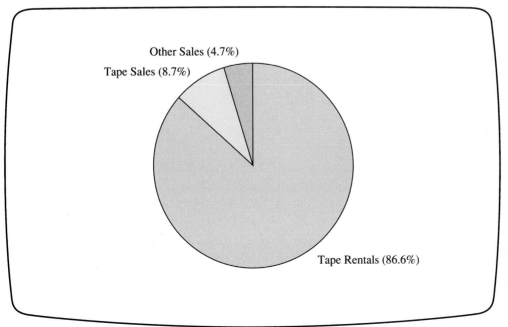

FIGURE 13-14
A labeled pie chart.

Adding Titles

Your chart needs a title.

1. Press Esc, then choose *Titles* from the Data menu.
2. Key FIRST QUARTER PROJECTED INCOME as the Chart title, key your name as the Subtitle, and then press Enter.

   These fields can contain more characters than are shown between the brackets.

3. If your printer is set up to print charts and has fonts available in large sizes, follow the same procedure you used with the bar charts to format the title and other text: Choose *Title Font* from the Format menu, and in the dialog box select a size around 20 points. Then choose *Other Font*, and select a smaller size, around 14 to 18 points. If the *Show Printer Fonts* command on the Options menu does not have a bullet next to it, choose it, so the formatting changes you have made will be displayed on the screen.

Formatting the Pie

You want to draw attention to the small slices that represent Tape Sales and Other Sales. Works lets you change the patterns or colors used to fill the slices. You will change the slice representing Tape Rentals to a sparse pattern that stands out less than the other two slices. You will also separate the two slices you are interested in from the rest of the pie to draw attention to them. This is called an **exploded pie chart**.

Data Format

1. From the Format menu, choose *Data Format*.

   Works displays the dialog box, shown in Figure 13-15, that lets you alter the colors and patterns used to chart data. *Slice 1* is selected. Lists in the dialog box show the slices in the chart, as well as the colors and patterns available to represent the selected slice.

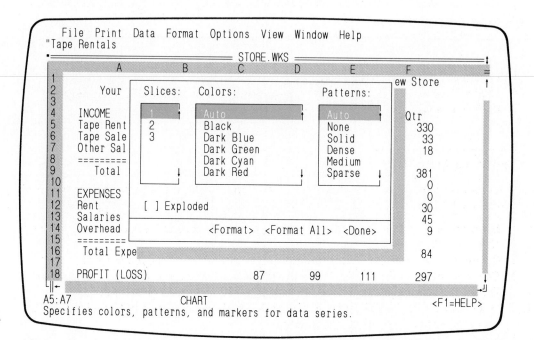

FIGURE 13-15
Data Format dialog box for pie charts.

2. In the Patterns list, select a *Sparse* pattern to represent the first slice, and then choose *Format*.
3. Highlight *Slice 2*.
4. Select the *Exploded* option, then choose *Format*.
5. Highlight *Slice 3*, choose the *Exploded* option, and then choose *Format*.
6. When you are finished, choose *Done*. You are ready to display the completed chart.
7. Choose *Chart1* from the View menu.

Works displays the finished chart, as shown in Figure 13-16. Depending on any changes you made to the format of the text, the labels of the slices may appear crowded. That appearance is a distortion of the way the computer screen displays the chart, and it will not occur when the chart is printed.

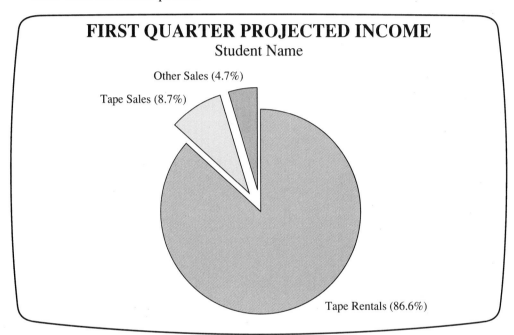

FIGURE 13-16
A formatted pie chart.

8. Press Esc to bring up the Chart View.
9. Choose *Save As* from the File menu. Change the file's name to *PieXXX.WKS*, replacing the X's with your initials, and save the file on your template disk.

Printing the Chart

If your printer is set up to print charts, print the pie chart following the procedures you used to print the bar charts.

1. If you are using a color monitor, but will be printing the chart in black and white, choose *Format For B&W* from the Options menu.
2. Choose *Preview* from the Print menu, and press Enter to accept the preset options.
3. Check the titles and the labels. If they appear too large or too small, go back and use the *Title Font* and *Other Font* commands to change them. Then preview the chart again.
4. When your printer is ready, press P to print the chart. Your printer may take a long time to read each line of the chart into its memory.
5. Save and close all of your files.

WORKING WITH LINE CHARTS

Sarah Lugosi was so pleased with the charts you made from the Sales and Store spreadsheets that she wants to use charts to attract investors to Lugosi's Classic Video Store. She has asked you to create a chart from the data in the Growth spreadsheet to show growth projections. Earlier in the lesson, you created a **mixed line and stacked bar chart**. Now you will make a chart in which all the series of data are represented by lines.

Creating a Line Chart

1. Open the *GrowXXX.WKS* spreadsheet file from the template disk. (This is a file you created in Lesson 12). You see the spreadsheet shown in Figure 13-17.

FIGURE 13-17
The Growth spreadsheet.

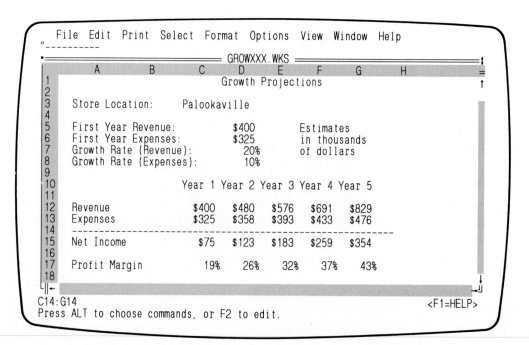

You want the chart to show the trend of revenue, expense, and income projections across the five years covered by the spreadsheet. Line charts are best for showing trends, so you will create a new chart and format it as a line chart.

2. Delete row 14 from the spreadsheet so this row of dashes will not become part of the chart.
3. Delete the empty row 11 from the chart. Otherwise Works will create a Y-Series for the blank row.
4. Select the range A10:G13. This range includes the column labels *Year 1* through *Year 5* in row 10 and the row labels in column A.
5. Create a new chart from the View menu.

Works creates a bar chart showing three series of bars representing revenue, expenses, and net income, as shown in Figure 13-18. The column headings in the first row you selected become the X-Series, creating labels along the X-axis. The row labels in the first column you selected become the labels in the legend.

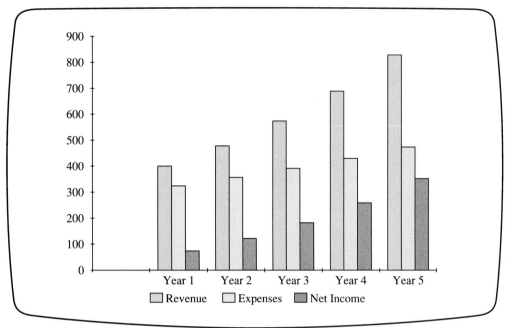

FIGURE 13-18
A Growth bar chart.

6. Press Esc to display the Chart View, and then choose *Line* from the Format menu.
7. Choose *Chart1* from the View menu. Works converts the chart to the line chart shown in Figure 13-19.

Instead of representing each number in the spreadsheet as a bar, Works represents it as a marker. The markers for each Y-Series have a distinctive shape and are connected by a line.

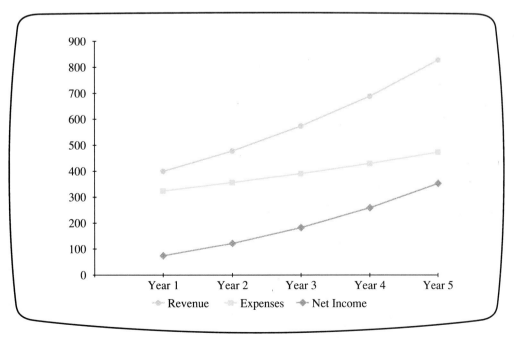

FIGURE 13-19
A Growth line chart.

Adding Grid Lines, Titles, and Formatting

Works lets you add vertical and horizontal **grid lines** to a chart. Horizontal grid lines will make the line chart easier to read. After adding the grid lines, you will title the chart, following the same procedure you used to title the charts you created earlier. Finally, you will modify the data formats to emphasize the Net Income series.

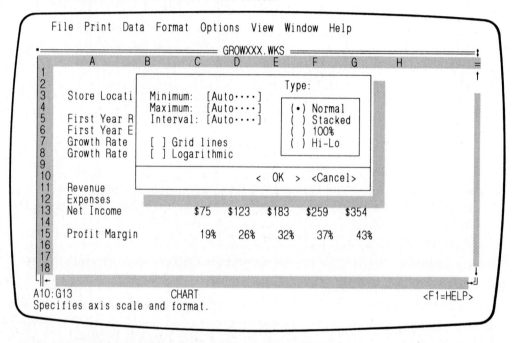

Y-Axis

1. Press Esc. From the Option menu, choose *Y-Axis*.

   You see the dialog box shown in Figure 13-20. The Y-Axis dialog box lets you change the scale Works displays on the vertical axis of the chart. Works is preset to automatically scale the chart so all the values fit on the screen.

FIGURE 13-20
The Y-Axis dialog box.

2. Choose the *Grid lines* option, and then press Enter.
3. Choose *Titles* from the Data menu. Key GROWTH PROJECTIONS as the Chart title, key your name as the Subtitle, and key Thousands of Dollars as the title for the Y-Axis. When you are done, press Enter.
4. If your printer is set up to print charts and has fonts available in large sizes, follow the same procedure you used with the charts you created earlier in the lesson to format the title and other text. Choose *Title Font* from the Format menu, and in the dialog box select a size close to 20 points. Then choose *Other Font* and select a smaller size (14 to 16 points). If the *Show Printer Fonts* command on the Options menu does not have a bullet next to it, choose it.
5. From the Format menu, choose *Data Format*. Works displays the dialog box shown in Figure 13-21.

   The Data Format dialog box lets you select the colors, patterns, and markers that Works uses to chart each series of data. Works is preset to automatically select these options. The 1st Y-Series is already selected in the dialog box, so any change you make to the colors, patterns, or markers will affect that line on the chart.

6. In the Patterns list, select *Dotted*, then select *Format*.

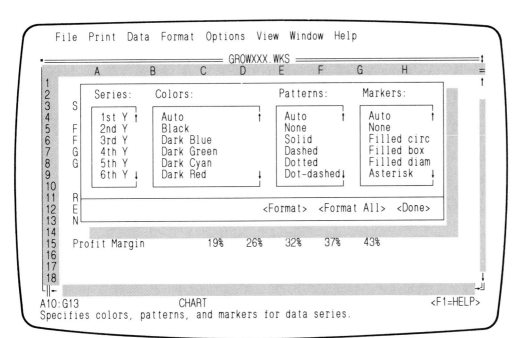

FIGURE 13-21
Data Format dialog box for line charts.

7. In the Series list, highlight *2nd Y*; select *Dotted* from the Patterns list; then select *Format*.
8. In the Series list, highlight *3rd Y*; select *Solid* from the Patterns list; press Enter; and then choose *Done*. The chart is now complete.
9. Choose *Chart1* from the View menu to display the chart, as shown in Figure 13-22.

The chart shows expenses leveling off, revenues soaring, and net income making a steady climb—clearly the growth chart of a profitable business.

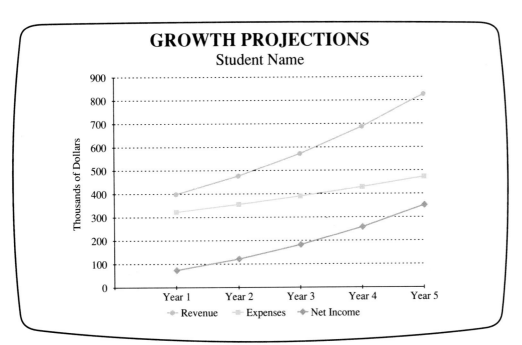

FIGURE 13-22
A formatted line chart.

Saving and Printing the Line Chart

Follow the same procedures you used earlier in the lesson to save and print the line chart.

1. Press Esc. Choose *Save As* from the File menu. Change the file's name to *LineXXX.WKS*, replacing the X's with your initials, and save the file on your template disk.
2. If you are using a color monitor, but will be printing the chart in black and white, choose *Format For B&W* from the Options menu.
3. Choose *Preview* from the Print menu, and press Enter to accept the preset options.
4. Check the titles and the labels. If they appear too large or too small, go back and use the *Title Font* and *Other Font* commands to change them. Then preview the chart again.
5. When your printer is ready, press P to print the chart. Unlike when printing a spreadsheet, your printer may take a long time to read the chart into its memory.
6. Exit Works.
7. Put your disks away safely and turn off the computer.

Congratulations! You have turned raw numbers into the major forms of charts. Works offers several other types of charts for special purposes, such as tracking the highs and lows of securities on the stock exchange. You now know enough to go ahead and experiment with some of these variations on the basic chart techniques you have already learned.

KEY TERMS

axis *MSW 242*
bar *MSW 240*
bar chart *MSW 238*
Chart View *MSW 238*
data format *MSW 242*
data label *MSW 247*
exploded pie chart *MSW 252*
grid lines *MSW 256*
legend *MSW 240*
line chart *MSW 238*
mixed line and stacked bar chart *MSW 254*
pie chart *MSW 238*
series *MSW 246*
stacked bar chart *MSW 243*

COMMANDS

Alt-T-B (Bar Chart)
Alt-V-N (Create New Chart)
Alt-V-C (Charts)
Alt-T-D (Data Format)
Alt-D-D (Data Labels)
Alt-D-1 (1st Y-Series)

Alt-O-F (Format For Black and White)
Alt-T-L (Line Chart)
Alt-O-M (Mixed Line & Bar)
Alt-T-P (Pie Chart)
Alt-T-O (Other Font)
Alt-O-S (Show Printer Fonts)

Alt-T-S (Stacked Bar Chart)
Alt-T-F (Title Font)
Alt-D-T (Titles)
Alt-O-X (X-Axis)
Alt-D-X (X-Series)
Alt-O-Y (Y-Axis)

REVIEW QUESTIONS

1. What kind of information would you put in a pie chart? a bar chart?
2. In the following table, what information would Works pick up and use as labels along the horizontal, or X-axis? How would Works create the Y-axis?

TYPE	January	February	March
Horror	20	25	35
Sci-Fi	15	18	21
Western	35	50	67

3. What does the legend provide for someone looking at your chart?
4. In the table shown in question 2, which items would become the 1st Y-Series?
5. How should you format the titles differently from other text? What steps are involved?
6. How can you create data labels?
7. What kind of information is appropriate for a line chart? How would you create a grid for a line chart?

APPLICATIONS

1. Open the *Drive.WKS* file from the template disk. This contains the test scores of people taking driving tests.
   a. Make a bar chart of all the scores.
   b. Make a stacked bar chart of all the scores.
   c. Place a grid behind the stacked bar chart, using the *Y-Axis* Option.
   d. Create a title for the chart: DRIVING SCORES. Make your name the Subtitle. Make the X-Axis title: Individual Students.
   e. Using the Options menu, create a border.
   f. Using the *Legends* command on the Data menu, assign the 1st Y-series the legend Score 1; the 2nd, Score 2; and the 3rd, Score 3.
   g. Save your file as *DrChtXXX.WKS* and print your chart.

2. Make a chart out of the shift figures for Monday, from the *Sales.WKS* file.
   a. Open the file.
   b. Choose to make a new chart.
   c. Choose *Pie* from the Format menu.
   d. Name that chart Pie.
   e. If your display is black and white, choose *Format For B&W* (Black and White) on the Options menu. Using the *Data Format* command on the Format menu, change the pattern of the 1st Y to *Dense* and the 2nd Y to *Sparse*. If your display is color, use the *Data Format* command on the Format menu to change the 1st Y pattern to *Dense* and the color to *Gray*; the 2nd Y pattern to *Sparse* and the color to *Blue*. (If you do not see these colors offered, choose *Works Settings* from Options, and set the color to *Color 1*.)
   f. Title the chart: MONDAY SALES BY SHIFT. Put your name in as Subtitle.
   g. Save the file as *MonXXX.WKS* and print the chart.

Getting Started with Integration

OBJECTIVES

- Open several files at one time.
- Arrange documents in multiple windows.
- Copy text from one Word Processor document to another.
- Copy information from one Spreadsheet file to another.

EXCHANGING INFORMATION

S arah Lugosi wants you to take some information from one document and put it into another. In earlier lessons, you have worked with one file at a time. The Copy command made it easy to copy information from one spot to another within the file. To copy some information from one file to another, you could use skills you already know: Print the first file, save and close the file, open the second file, and key the information word-for-word from the printout. That could take quite a while if you have a lot to copy. Works offers you a way to copy information from one file to another without rekeying anything.

You can open as many as eight Works files at once. The exact number of files depends on how much memory your computer has and how much memory each file occupies. Most people don't need to keep eight files open at once, but you will find it convenient sometimes to have three or four open at the same time and switch back and forth between them, without having to save and close one, then open the next. For instance, you might collect the average temperatures of Alaskan ports from the Weather Service with the Communications tool, copy those into a Spreadsheet document, create a chart based on the figures, then copy that chart into a Word Processor letter to prospective participants in a cruise. Or you might copy a list of tools from your Database and a portion of a spreadsheet showing how many of each tool you sold last month and at what rate of profit, and place both pieces of information into a Word Processor report on the tool business. You could even begin making up a list of presents for your family in the Word Processor, then copy both columns (the presents and the names of the people you want to give them to) into your Database for easier sorting and management. If you are more cost-conscious than most of us, you could then copy the final list into your spreadsheet to track your gift-giving expenses.

Information flows easily from one document to another in Works. That is because Works integrates all four of its tools. **Integrated software**, such as Works, contains more than one application and allows you to move information back and forth between one type of document and another.

In this lesson, you will learn how to copy information from one document to another within the same tool. Along the way, you will learn how to manipulate the windows that contain your documents, so you can see several documents at once. In Lesson 15, "Integrating Information," you will learn how to copy information between documents created in different tools, putting Database records, Spreadsheet figures, and a chart into a Word Processor document. Then in Lesson 16, "Creating Form Letters and Mailing Lists," you will learn how to create form letters, making the standard letter in the Word Processor, and copying names and addresses from your Database. As you print in a process known as **Mail Merge**, you integrate the names and addresses into the standard letter, creating personalized appeals to each addressee.

Opening Several Files

Works lets you open several files at once. They can all be files created in one tool, or they can be files created in different tools. Once you have opened the files, you can switch back and forth between them to check facts or to copy information.

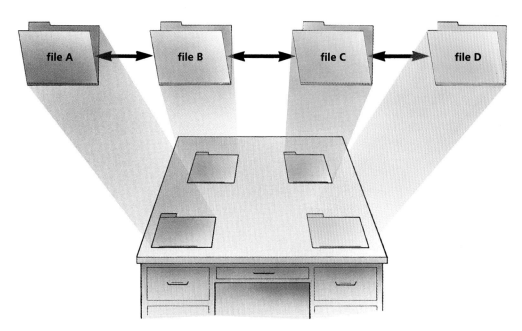

FIGURE 14-1
With several files open, you can switch easily between them.

An editor from *Famous People Magazine* called Lugosi's Classic Video Store and asked for some information about Sarah Lugosi and Morris Yu. The editor is writing an article about young entrepreneurs and would like to feature Sarah and Morris. The public relations contact at the store has written part of the letter, but she had to go out of town temporarily. She has asked you to copy Sarah Lugosi's biography from another document into the letter she has written to the editor. In addition, Sarah has asked you to copy this week's sales figures from the Sales spreadsheet into another spreadsheet she has been using to record each week's sales. You will take advantage of Works's integration to carry out these chores.

1. Start Works.
2. From the File menu, choose *Open Existing File*.
3. Select the Word Processor file *Famous.WPS* from your template disk, and press Enter. The letter to the editor, Mrs. Lenore Nudelman, appears in its own window.
4. From the File menu, choose *Open Existing File*.

5. Select the *Lugosi.WPS* file from your template disk, and press Enter.

The Lugosi biography appears in its own window in front of the window containing the letter to Mrs. Nudelman, as shown in Figure 14-2. The window in front is known as the current or active window; that is the one you can work in at the moment. But you realize you need a few more documents, and you decide to bring them into Works right now.

6. From the File menu, choose *Open Existing File*, select *Sales.WKS*, and press Enter.
7. From the File menu, choose *Open Existing File*, select *Weekly.WKS*, and press Enter. You now have four files open, one in front of the other, as shown in Figure 14-3.

FIGURE 14-2
Each file appears in its own window.

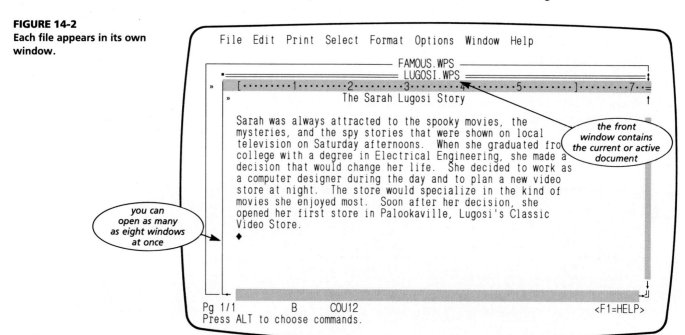

FIGURE 14-3
Four files open at once.

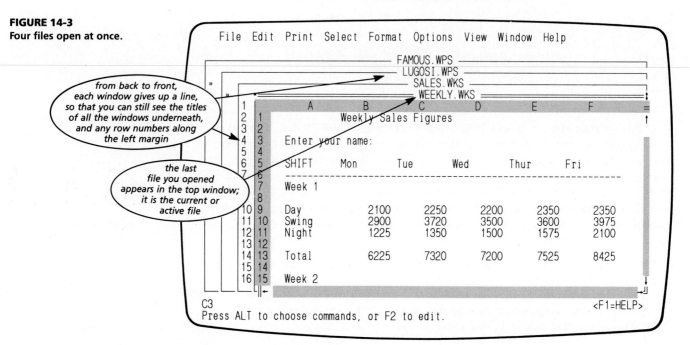

Arranging Windows

Works displays each file in its own window. At first, the windows appear one in front of the other. But you can have Works create a number of smaller windows, so that you can get a glimpse of part of each document all at once. That can be helpful when you want to get an idea of what is in each document.

1. Choose *Arrange All* from the Window menu.

   Works carves the screen up into four parts, assigning one file to each window, as in Figure 14-4. One window is active—that of the *Weekly.WKS* file. It appears in the top left-hand corner of the screen, with scroll bars and double lines around its title. The document you need to copy from is *Lugosi.WPS*, so you need to make that the active file.

Arrange All Windows

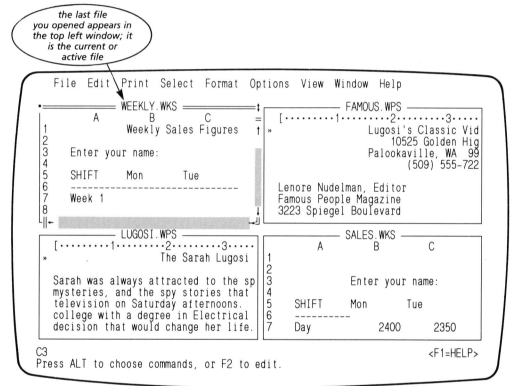

the last file you opened appears in the top left window; it is the current or active file

FIGURE 14-4
Four windows showing four files.

2. On the Window menu, choose *LUGOSI.WPS*. It becomes active. The cursor starts blinking under the *T* in *The*, in the first line. You need to get a better view of the document now.
3. Choose *Maximize* from the Window menu. The Sarah Lugosi story fills the screen. Maximizing expands the window so it takes up the maximum amount of space available.

   Copying from One Word Processor File to Another   You need to copy the biographical information about Sarah Lugosi into the letter to Lenore Nudelman at *Famous People Magazine*.

1. Skip the title, and select the whole text of Sarah's biography, from the first word, *Sarah*, to the last word, *Store*.
2. Choose *Copy* from the Edit menu. The biography is copied into the computer's memory. Now you need to switch to the letter to Mrs. Lenore Nudelman of *Famous People Magazine*.

Maximize the Size of the Current Window

3. Choose *Maximize* from the Window menu to reverse the process, shrinking the Lugosi file to its small size.
4. Choose *FAMOUS.WPS* from the Window menu. That becomes the active window.
5. Choose *Maximize* from the Window menu to enlarge the letter to full size. Read through the letter.
6. Now that you have read the letter, choose *Maximize* from the Window menu to shrink the window again.
7. Use the Down Arrow to move the cursor down to the empty line after the first paragraph (the empty line before the paragraph about Morris Yu).
8. Press Enter to place the text in that position. You have copied the Sarah Lugosi story into the letter to the magazine editor, as shown in Figure 14-5.

FIGURE 14-5
Text copied from one Word Processor document into another.

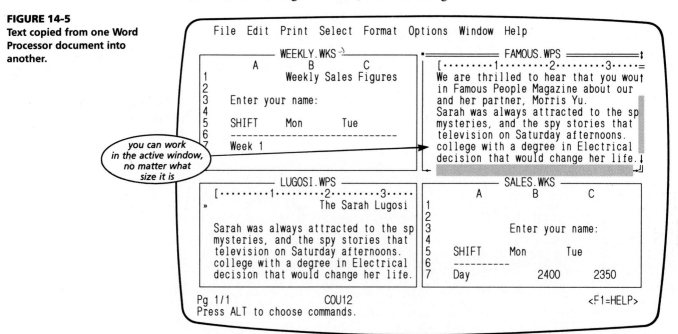

As you can see, you can work in either the miniature window or the maximum window. The size does not matter, as long as the window is the current or active window.

Congratulations! You have moved information from one Word Processor document to another, almost as easily as you could move it from one place to another within one document.

Cleaning Up After Making a Copy   Sometimes when you have placed a copy into a document, you need to make a few minor changes so that it will fit properly in its new location. For example, the new paragraph needs to be set off from the first paragraph of the letter and from the paragraph about Morris Yu.

1. Press Enter, to move the new paragraph down, leaving a blank line before it.
2. Move the cursor to the end of the paragraph, and press Enter again to set it off from the paragraph about Morris Yu.

Copying Between Two Spreadsheet Files

You have just copied information from one Word Processor file to another. In the same way, you can copy information from any document to another document created in the same tool.

For example, each week Sarah Lugosi copies the week's sales information from the Sales spreadsheet into the Weekly spreadsheet, so that she has a complete record of all sales. With the weekly spreadsheet, she can compare sales from one week to sales from all the other weeks. This will allow her to see if some seasons of the year have higher sales than others or if one day each week seems to have higher sales than other days. By analyzing the sales information, Sarah hopes to make better decisions about how to run her stores.

Moving and Resizing the Windows To make it easier to compare the information in two adjacent windows, you can move windows around and change their sizes. To put the two spreadsheets next to each other, you need to move the letter to the magazine editor out of the way, then change the size of the two windows containing the spreadsheet files to show more of each.

1. Choose *Move* from the Window menu. A box appears around the *Famous.WPS* window. You can now move it down, out of the way.
2. Press the Down Arrow twelve times, bringing the box down below the title of the *Sales.WKS* window. Press Enter. The *Famous.WPS* window drops to the bottom right corner of the screen, as shown in Figure 14-6.

Move the Current Window

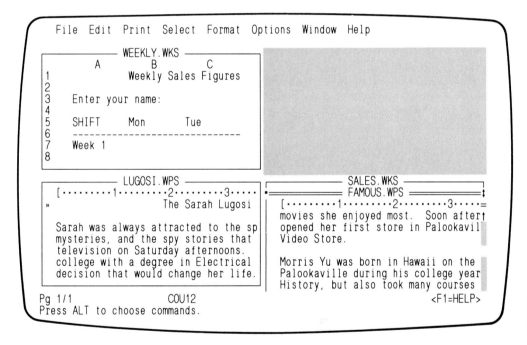

FIGURE 14-6
One window moved down in front of another.

3. Choose *SALES.WKS* from the Window menu. That activates the Sales file.
4. Choose *Move* from the Window menu.
5. Press the Up Arrow to move that window to the top of your screen. Press Enter. You now have your two spreadsheets next to each other.
6. Choose *Size* from the Window menu. This command allows you to change the size of the current window.
7. Press the Down Arrow to extend the bottom of the Sales window to the bottom of the screen. Press Enter.
8. Choose *WEEKLY.WKS* from the Window menu.
9. Choose *Size* from the Window menu, and use the Down Arrow to extend the window to the bottom of your screen. Press Enter. Your screen should now look like Figure 14-7.

Change the Size of the Current Window

FIGURE 14-7
Two windows resized.

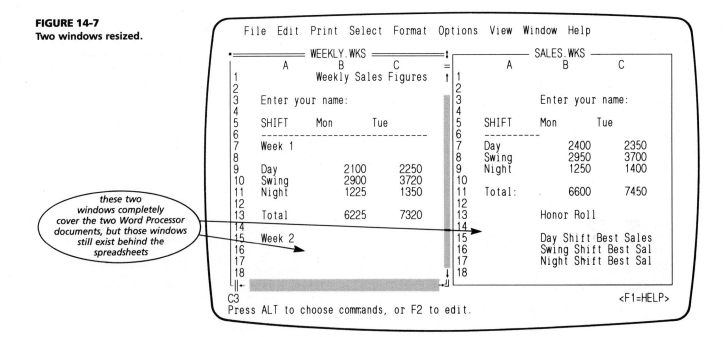

these two
windows completely
cover the two Word Processor
documents, but those windows
still exist behind the
spreadsheets

You have now set up the two windows so you can get a good look at each spreadsheet.

Copying Information   The process of copying from one Spreadsheet file to another Spreadsheet file is similar to copying from one Word Processor file to another. Sarah Lugosi has asked you to copy this week's sales figures from the *Sales.WKS* spreadsheet into the spreadsheet that will keep track of the totals for every week, *Weekly.WKS*.

1. Choose *SALES.WKS* from the Window menu to make that spreadsheet active.
2. Highlight cells A7 through H11.
3. Choose *Copy* from the Edit menu.
4. Choose *WEEKLY.WKS* from the Window menu.
5. Move the highlighting to cell A17, and press Enter. The material you highlighted in the *Sales.WKS* spreadsheet has been copied to cells A17 through H21, as shown in Figure 14-8.
6. Highlight cell B21 and look at the formula bar. Note that the formula has been adjusted to take into account the new location—in an entirely different spreadsheet.
7. Choose *Maximize* from the Window menu to see more of the Weekly totals.

Now that you have copied information from file to file, you are ready to save the revised documents and put the files away.

Closing and Saving Multiple Files

Whenever you complete some work on a file, you should save the file. In this lesson, you have not yet saved the new version of the letter to the *Famous People Magazine* editor, and you have not saved the new version of the *Weekly.WKS* spreadsheet. Better do that before the power goes out, and your computer forgets all the work you've done.

1. Choose *Save As* from the File menu.
2. Name the file *WeekXXX.WKS*, print, and save it on your template disk.
3. Choose *Close* from the File menu. You now see the maximized version of the *Sales.WKS* file. You have not made any significant change to this file, so you can just close it.

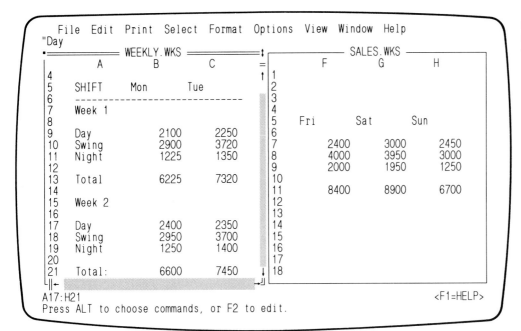

FIGURE 14-8
Copied information inserted from another spreadsheet.

4. To put away the *Sales.WKS* file, choose *Close* from the File menu. You see the Sarah Lugosi Story again. You now have only two files open, *Lugosi.WPS* and *Famous.WPS*.
5. Choose *Exit Works* from the File menu.

Oops! Works notices that you have not yet saved the new version of *Famous.WPS*. You see a warning dialog box, as shown in Figure 14-9.

FIGURE 14-9
Works keeps you from throwing away the changes you have made.

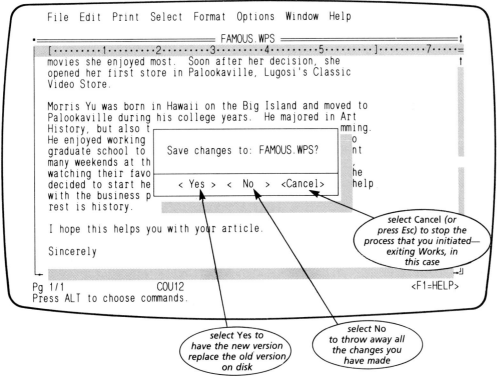

6. Press Esc to stop before you throw away the changes.

   You see the letter to Mrs. Nudelman on the screen. (The window containing the biography of Sarah Lugosi has been moved behind the letter.) Works has been designed to assure that you do not accidentally discard a document you have been working on.

7. Choose *Save As* from the File menu, give this file the name *FamoXXX.WPS*, print, and save it on the template disk.
8. Choose *Close* from the File menu. The letter disappears, and you see Sarah Lugosi's biography again.
9. Choose *Exit Works* from the File menu. Because you made no changes to the *Lugosi.WPS* file, Works does not pause this time to warn you that it is about to erase the file from the computer's memory. The screen just goes dark.
10. Remove your disks and turn off the computer.

KEY TERMS

intergrated software   *MSW 260*
mail merge   *MSW 261*

COMMANDS

Alt-W-A (Arrange All windows)
Alt-W-M (Move the current window)
Alt-W-S (Change the size of the current window)
Alt-W-X (Maximize the size of the current window)

REVIEW QUESTIONS

1. How many files can you open in Works at one time? Why would you want to have more than one file open at once?
2. How do you display all the documents at once? How can you have one document fill up the screen?
3. Does a window have to be a particular size for you to work in it? How would you go about changing the position of a window? How would you change its size?
4. How do you recognize which window is the currently active window?
5. How do you switch from one window to another? Do you have to see a window to bring it to the front and make it active?
6. What are the steps for copying from one Word Processor file to another?

APPLICATIONS

1. Morris Yu has had some trouble getting copies of a new movie to rent out to customers. He has written a little notice to customers that he would like to display in the store. He left off some information at the end of the document, because he knew the information was available in another file. He has asked you to copy the information for him, using the integration features of Works.

   a. Open two files from the template disk, *New.WPS* and then *Frank.WPS*.
   b. With *Frank.WPS* open, highlight everything except the title, then choose *Copy* from the Edit menu.
   c. Choose *NEW.WPS* from the Window menu, and move the cursor to the end of the document.
   d. Press Enter to place the material you copied.
   e. Press Enter twice more to separate the new material from the old.
   f. Print the new version of *New.WPS* and save it as *NewXXX.WPS*.
   g. Close the files.

2. Morris Yu keeps track of the week's sales of videotapes in the *Tape.WKS* file. At the end of each week, he has an employee copy the week's sales into another file that keeps track of the month's sales. He has asked you to copy one week's sales into the *April.WKS* file.

   a. Open the *April.WKS* file and then the *Tape.WKS* file from the template disk.
   b. In the *Tape.WKS* file, select cells A5 through E10, then choose *Copy* from the Edit menu.
   c. Choose *APRIL.WKS* from the Window menu.
   d. Highlight cell A15, and press Enter.
   e. Save the file as *AprilXXX.WKS*, and print a copy of the spreadsheet.

Using Integration

OBJECTIVES

- Copy information from the Database to the Word Processor.
- Copy information from the Spreadsheet to the Word Processor.
- Copy information from the Word Processor to a database.
- Exchange information between a database and a spreadsheet.
- Save a file in ASCII format for use with another program.

INTEGRATION BETWEEN APPLICATIONS

S arah Lugosi has asked you to collect some information for her. She wants to see a list of the customers who have won a free video rental as part of the promotion for the new Fairfax store. And she wants to see an analysis of the sales by shift last week in the main store. The facts you need are in two of your Works files, *Win.WDB* and *Sales.WKS*. Unfortunately Sarah has been very busy lately. So, rather than interrupt her, you are going to send her two memos summarizing the information from your database and spreadsheet files.

In Lesson 14, you copied information from one document to another within an application. In Works, you can also copy information between applications. The memos to Sarah Lugosi were written with the Word Processor. The customer records were compiled in the Database, and the sales figures were entered in the Spreadsheet. With the integration of Works, you can copy the records of the customers who won the free video rental from the Database and the sales totals from the Spreadsheet into your Word Processor documents.

An important change takes place during the process of copying into the Word Processor document. Once placed in the Word Processor document, the database records can no longer be sorted, and the spreadsheet calculations lose the ability to be recalculated. The records and values become ordinary text.

You can also move information from a Word Processor document into a Database, Spreadsheet, or Communications document. Sarah has handed you another Word Processor file called *Order.WPS*, and you will place some of the information from the order into a database for her.

Opening Several Files

In this lesson, you will work with six files: the *Memo1.WPS*, *Memo2.WPS*, and *Order.WPS* files from the Word Processor; the *Win.WDB* and *Movies.WDB* files from the Database; and the *Sales.WKS* file from the Spreadsheet.

1. Start Works.
2. Choose *Open Existing File* from the File menu, and choose *Memo1.WPS* from the template disk.
3. Open *Memo2.WPS* the same way.
4. Open *Order.WPS*.
5. Open *Sales.WKS*.
6. Open *Win.WDB*.
7. Open *Movies.WDB* as a List view. Your screen should look like Figure 15-1.

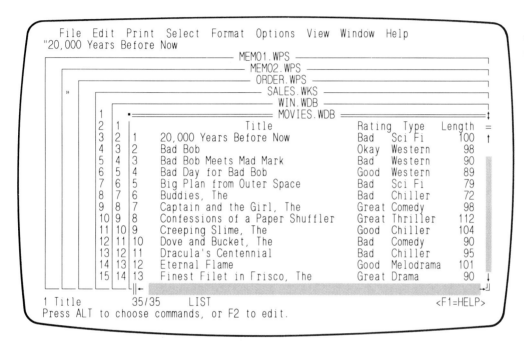

FIGURE 15-1
With several files open, you see windows in front of windows.

First you will copy some customer records from the Database file, *Win.WDB*, into *Memo1.WPS*.

Copying Records from the Database to the Word Processor

The first information Sarah wants is the list of people who won a free video rental in the recent promotion. You have that list in the *Win.WDB* file.

1. From the Window menu, choose *WIN.WDB*.
2. Choose *Maximize* from the Window menu to make the window fill the screen for easier reading.

   You know that Sarah intends to call each person individually, so she needs to know the customer's first and last name, city, and home phone number. You are looking at the records in List view, so you can make some changes to the arrangement before you copy. You need to group the fields you want to copy, so you don't bring any unnecessary information along.

3. Highlight any cell in the City field, choose *Field* from the Select menu, then choose *Move* from the Edit menu.
4. Highlight any cell in the Street field, and press Enter. That moves the City field next to the First Name field.

5. In the same way, move the Home Phone field next to and after the City field. Your list should now look like Figure 15-2.

FIGURE 15-2
Rearranging the List view to group together the information needed.

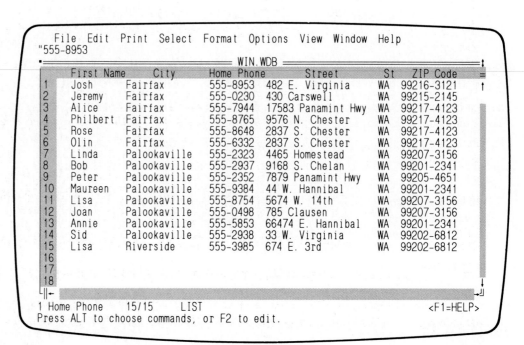

```
    File  Edit  Print  Select  Format  Options  View  Window  Help
   "555-8953
   ═══════════════════════════ WIN.WDB ═══════════════════════════
        First Name     City      Home Phone      Street        St   ZIP Code
   1    Josh          Fairfax      555-8953   482 E. Virginia   WA   99216-3121
   2    Linda         Palookaville 555-2323   4465 Homestead    WA   99207-3156
   3    Jeremy        Fairfax      555-0230   430 Carswell      WA   99215-2145
   4    Lisa          Riverside    555-3985   674 E. 3rd        WA   99202-6812
   5    Bob           Palookaville 555-2937   9168 S. Chelan    WA   99201-2341
   6    Peter         Palookaville 555-2352   7879 Panamint Hwy WA   99205-4651
   7    Maureen       Palookaville 555-9384   44 W. Hannibal    WA   99201-2341
   8    Alice         Fairfax      555-7944   17583 Panamint Hwy WA  99217-4123
   9    Lisa          Palookaville 555-8754   5674 W. 14th      WA   99207-3156
   10   Joan          Palookaville 555-0498   785 Clausen       WA   99207-3156
   11   Philbert      Fairfax      555-8765   9576 N. Chester   WA   99217-4123
   12   Rose          Fairfax      555-8648   2837 S. Chester   WA   99217-4123
   13   Olin          Fairfax      555-6332   2837 S. Chester   WA   99217-4123
   14   Annie         Palookaville 555-5853   66474 E. Hannibal WA   99201-2341
   15   Sid           Palookaville 555-2938   33 W. Virginia    WA   99202-6812
   16
   17
   18

   1 Home Phone    15/15    LIST                              <F1=HELP>
   Press ALT to choose commands, or F2 to edit.
```

Sarah Lugosi mentioned that she wants to call everyone from Fairfax first to make sure they get the news about the new store before the opening.

6. Choose *Sort Records* from the Select menu, key `City` in the *1st Field* area, and press Enter. The records appear grouped by city, with all the people from Fairfax at the top of the list, as shown in Figure 15-3.

FIGURE 15-3
Sorting records before copying.

```
    File  Edit  Print  Select  Format  Options  View  Window  Help
   "555-8953
   ═══════════════════════════ WIN.WDB ═══════════════════════════
        First Name     City      Home Phone      Street        St   ZIP Code
   1    Josh          Fairfax      555-8953   482 E. Virginia   WA   99216-3121
   2    Jeremy        Fairfax      555-0230   430 Carswell      WA   99215-2145
   3    Alice         Fairfax      555-7944   17583 Panamint Hwy WA  99217-4123
   4    Philbert      Fairfax      555-8765   9576 N. Chester   WA   99217-4123
   5    Rose          Fairfax      555-8648   2837 S. Chester   WA   99217-4123
   6    Olin          Fairfax      555-6332   2837 S. Chester   WA   99217-4123
   7    Linda         Palookaville 555-2323   4465 Homestead    WA   99207-3156
   8    Bob           Palookaville 555-2937   9168 S. Chelan    WA   99201-2341
   9    Peter         Palookaville 555-2352   7879 Panamint Hwy WA   99205-4651
   10   Maureen       Palookaville 555-9384   44 W. Hannibal    WA   99201-2341
   11   Lisa          Palookaville 555-8754   5674 W. 14th      WA   99207-3156
   12   Joan          Palookaville 555-0498   785 Clausen       WA   99207-3156
   13   Annie         Palookaville 555-5853   66474 E. Hannibal WA   99201-2341
   14   Sid           Palookaville 555-2938   33 W. Virginia    WA   99202-6812
   15   Lisa          Riverside    555-3985   674 E. 3rd        WA   99202-6812
   16
   17
   18

   1 Home Phone    15/15    LIST                              <F1=HELP>
   Press ALT to choose commands, or F2 to edit.
```

Notice that you should do as much rearranging as possible in the Database itself, where you can take advantage of the tool's ability to shift whole columns and sort records, before you bring the information into the Word Processor document. In the Word Processor, you would need to do these operations manually, one item at a time.

7. Highlight the Last Name, First Name, City, and Home Phone fields in records 1 through 15. (Start in one corner and hold down the Shift key while using the Arrow keys.) These entries contain the information you want to copy.
8. Choose *Copy* from the Edit menu.
9. Choose *MEMO1.WPS* from the Window menu.
10. Move the cursor to the space at the end of the first line, and press Enter. The selected portions of the records for the 15 winning customers drop into the memo.

   Each entry is separated from the next by a tab character. (If you do not see the tab and return characters, choose *Show All Characters* from the Options menu.) The preset tab settings in the standard Word Processor, though, are not exactly the same as the field widths in the Database, so one record has gotten out of line. Also, the list now appears on the line right after the first sentence in the memo. The list would look better if it was set off by a blank line at the beginning and end.

Cleaning Up

You often need to do a little cleaning up after copying Database records into a Word Processor document.

1. Press Enter twice to insert a blank line between the first sentence of the memo and the list.
2. Move the cursor down so it is under the *E* in *Each*, in the paragraph following the list. Press Backspace to get rid of any unnecessary space characters, then press Enter once to insert a blank line above this paragraph.

   Now the only problem is Maureen O'Connell, whose last name is so long that it extends beyond the first tab stop. So, when Works encounters the tab character after *O'Connell*, it skips to the next tab stop, pushing *Maureen* over to the column in which most customers have their city.

3. Highlight every row in the list, and choose *Tabs* from the Format menu.

   The preset placement of tab stops is every half inch along the ruler. Works has lined up the first names at 1 inch, the cities at 2 inches, and the home phone numbers at 3.5 inches. For all of the records except Maureen O'Connell's, those tab settings work fine. But you cannot change just her tab settings because you want all of the items in each column aligned.

4. Key 1 in the Position box, select *Delete*, and choose *Done*. That eliminates the first tab setting and moves the whole row of first names over, making room for *O'Connell* at last.
5. Choose *Tabs* from the Format menu, key 1.5 in the Position box, select *Insert*, and choose *Done*. That moves the first names column back a little.
6. Choose *Tabs* from the Format menu, key 2 in the Position box, select *Delete*, and choose *Done*.
7. Choose *Tabs* from the Format menu, key 3 in the Position box, select *Insert*, and choose *Done*.
8. Choose *Tabs* from the Format menu, key 5 in the Position box, select *Insert*, and choose *Done*. Your list is now spread out nicely across the page, with all the items in each column

lined up properly, as shown in Figure 15-4.

9. Key your initials after the *From:* label at the top of the memo, and key today's date after the *Date:* label.

```
   File  Edit  Print  Select  Format  Options  Window  Help
 ·═══════════════════════════ MEMO1.WPS ═══════════════════════════╤
 [·······1········2·········3········4·········5········]·······7····═
 » ·····To:···Sarah·Lugosi¶                                           ↑
   ···From:··MT¶
   ···Date:··10/22/92¶
   Subject:···Winners·of·a·Free·Video·Rental¶
   ----------------------------------------------------------¶
   ¶
   Here·are·the·customers·who·have·been·chosen·in·our·drawing.···¶
   ¶
   →Burns→       Josh→      Fairfax→      555-8953¶
   →Kravitz→     Jeremy→    Fairfax→      555-0230¶
   →Ping→        Alice→     Fairfax→      555-7944¶
   →Smith→       Philbert→  Fairfax→      555-8765¶
   →Smith→       Rose→      Fairfax→      555-8648¶
   →Trout→       Olin→      Fairfax→      555-6332¶
   →Flores→      Linda→     Palookaville→ 555-2323¶
   →Matsu→       Bob→       Palookaville→ 555-2937¶
   →Minnich→     Peter→     Palookaville→ 555-2352¶
   →O'Connell→   Maureen→   Palookaville→ 555-9384¶
   →Price→       Lisa→      Palookaville→ 555-8754¶            ↓
 ═══════════════════════════════════════════════════════════════════╝
 Pg 1/1                    CO12                          <F1=HELP>
 Press ALT to choose commands.
```

Great! You have copied information from the Database into a Word Processor document, and then cleaned it up. You are ready to save and print.

10. Choose *Save As* from the File menu, and save the memo as *Memo1XXX.WPS*, where XXX stands for your initials.

11. Make sure your printer is on, connected securely to the computer and on-line, then choose *Print* from the Print menu, and press Enter. Your memo is ready to drop in Sarah's in-basket.

12. Choose *Close* from the File menu.

Copying Information from the Spreadsheet to the Word Processor

Copying information from the Spreadsheet into the Word Processor is similar to copying records from the Database. You prepare your material in the Spreadsheet, copy it, switch to the Word Processor document, place the material, and then do a little reformatting.

1. Choose *SALES.WKS* from the Window menu.

You want the figures to be formatted as currency, and you need them closer together to fit onto the page in the Word Processor memo.

2. Highlight cells B7 through H11, choose *Currency* from the Format menu, key 0 to show no decimal places, and press Enter.

3. With the same cells selected, choose *Column Width* from the Format menu, and key 8 to make each column eight characters wide. The numbers move closer together.

You want to show Sarah how sales varied from day to day, so you intend to include a bar chart.

4. Highlight cells A5 through H9, and choose *New Chart* from the View menu. You see a bar chart like the one in Figure 15-5. (If you have a monochrome screen, you will see patterns instead of colors.)

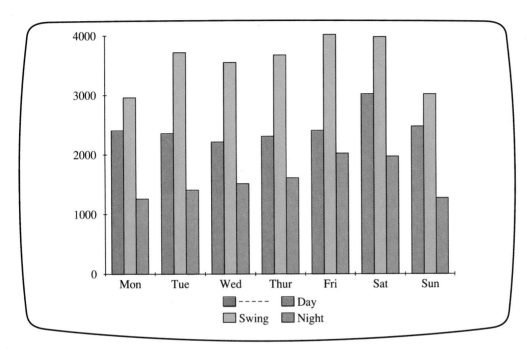

FIGURE 15-5
The bar chart shows the individual sales totals by shift for each day.

5. Press Esc to leave the chart for a moment to make some modifications.
6. Choose *Stacked Bar* from the Format menu, so that the sales figures for each shift will be combined into a single bar for the day.
7. Choose *Y-Axis* from the Options menu, select *Grid lines*, and press Enter.
8. Choose *Show Border* from the Options menu.
9. Choose *Charts* from the View menu, select *Chart1* if it is not already selected, key *Day-by-Day* in the Name box, select *Rename*, and choose *Done*.
10. To see what your chart looks like now, choose *Day-by-Day* from the View menu. It should look like Figure 15-6.

You want to show Sarah how each day's sales fits into the total sales for the week, so you need a pie chart.

11. Press Esc. Highlight cells B11 through H11, and choose *New Chart* from the View menu.
12. Press Esc, and choose *Pie* from the Format menu.
13. Choose *Show Border* from the Options menu.
14. Highlight the days of the week in cells B5 through H5, then choose *X-Series* from the Data menu to have the days labelled on the pie chart.
15. Choose *Charts* from the View menu, select *Chart1* if it is not already selected, key `Pie Slices` in the Name box, select *Rename*, and choose *Done*.
16. Choose *Pie Slices* from the View menu. Your chart should look like Figure 15-7.

You have used the Spreadsheet to format the numbers and prepare some charts. Now you are ready to copy the information into the memo.

FIGURE 15-6
The stacked bar chart combines the individual sales totals by shift into a single bar for each day. The grid lines and border make the data more attractive and easier to read.

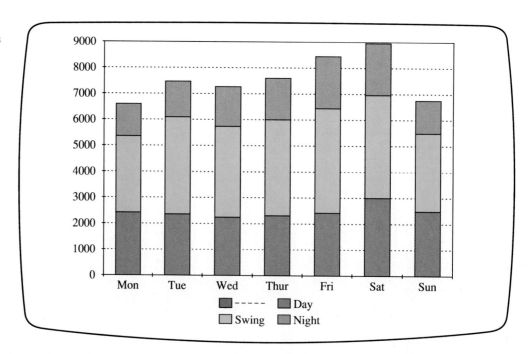

FIGURE 15-7
The pie chart shows how each day's sales contribute to the total for the week.

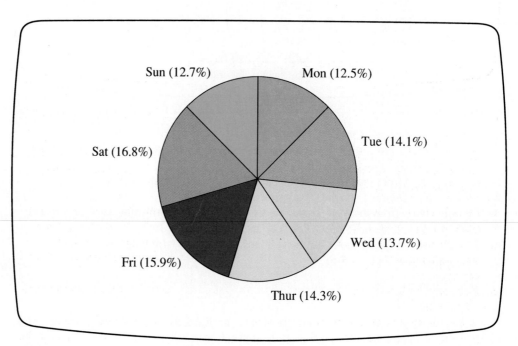

Copying

Copying numbers from the Spreadsheet is just like copying records or parts of records from the Database. Any formulas are lost, but the numbers themselves come over correctly. Charts, though, are graphic representations; they are displayed on screen as patterns of dots and colors. The Word Processor cannot display graphics; it is designed to handle text, not pictures. So, the process of copying charts into the Word Processor is a little different from copying numbers.

1. Press Esc to leave the chart.
2. Press F10 to change from the Charting menus to the Spreadsheet menus.
3. Highlight cells A5 through H11, then choose *Copy* from the Edit menu.
4. Choose *MEMO2.WPS* from the Window menu. You see the partially written memo, as shown in Figure 15-8.

```
 File  Edit  Print  Select  Format  Options  Window  Help
·══════════════════════════════════ MEMO2.WPS ═══════════════════════════════╪
  [···········1·········2·········3·········4·········5·········]·········7····═
 »  ·····To:··Sarah·Lugosi¶                                                   ↑
    ···From:··¶
    ···Date:··¶
    Subject:··Last·Week's·Sales·Figures¶
    ----------------------------------------------------------------------¶
    ¶
    Here·are·the·figures·by·shift·and·day.··I·think·the·bar·
    chart·says·it·all.··You·can·see·from·this·pie·chart·the·way·
    our·total·revenues·are·split·among·the·days·of·the·week.··¶
    ◆
                                                                             ↓
 ░░░░░░░░░░░░░░░░░░░░░░░░░░░░░░░░░░░░░░░░░░░░░░░░░░░░░░░░░░░░░░░░░░░░░░░░░░░░░░░╝
 Pg 1/1              COU12                    COPY             <F1=HELP>
 Select new location and press ENTER. Press ESC to cancel.
```

FIGURE 15-8
The memo is ready for the figures and charts from the Spreadsheet.

5. Move the cursor to the space after the first sentence, which ends with *shift and day*. Press Enter.

   The figures appear, but because the margins of the memo are narrower than those of the spreadsheet, the last column, with Sunday's figures, is wrapped around onto the next line, making a mess.

6. Press Enter two times to separate the figures from the first sentence.
7. Choose *Page Setup & Margins* from the Print menu, key 0.5 for the left margin and 0.5 for the right margin, then press Enter. Ah, that's like letting out your belt after Thanksgiving dinner. Now there is room for the Sunday figures on the right side of the page.
8. Place another blank line after the row of totals to separate them from the following paragraph of text.
9. Eliminate any spaces before the following paragraph, which begins *I think...*
10. Place the cursor after that sentence, press Enter twice, and choose *Insert Chart* from the Edit menu. You see the Insert Chart dialog box, as shown in Figure 15-9.
11. Select *Sales.WKS* by pressing the Down Arrow, then select *Day-by-Day* to bring in the stacked bar chart. Press Enter.

   The screen changes rapidly. You may need to use the Up Arrow to find out what happened. Works has not inserted the chart. It can't. The Word Processor can only display characters, not graphics. So Works has inserted a **placeholder**—a phrase that stands for your chart. When you print your memo, Works will go to your Spreadsheet, fetch the chart, and print it in this location. The placeholder reads: *chart SALES.WKS:Day-by-Day*

Insert Chart

FIGURE 15-9
The Insert Chart dialog box.

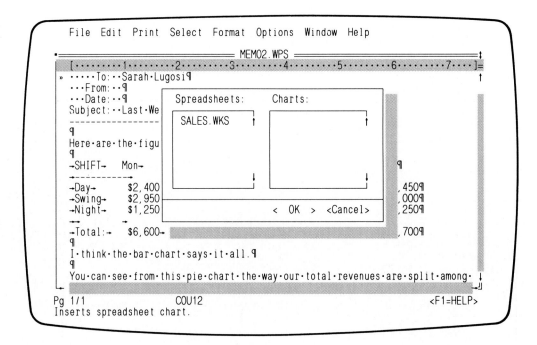

12. Eliminate any spaces before the last sentence, then move your cursor to the end of it, and use *Insert Chart* to place your pie chart called *Pie Slices*.

13. Key your initials after the *From:* label at the top of the memo, and key today's date into the date line.

14. Choose *Headers & Footers* from the Print menu, key `Sales Figures...&p` into the Footer box, and press Enter. That will put a page number on each page without interfering with the labels at the top of the memo.

15. Choose *Preview* from the Print menu, and press Enter to see how your pages will look when printed. You see a preview of page 1 first. Press Page Down to see page 2.

16. Press Esc to leave the Preview.

17. Save a copy of the memo as *Memo2XXX.WPS*, then print it out. Your pages should look like Figure 15-10.

18. Choose *SALES.WKS* from the Window menu, choose *Save As* from the File menu, rename the file *SalXXX.WKS*, and save it to your template disk.

Copying Information from the Word Processor

You can copy information from the Word Processor to any other tool in Works. To place the information into the correct fields or columns in a database or spreadsheet, though, you need to set it up in tabbed columns. Two videotapes have just come in from a vendor. You have the order you placed, and you are going to copy the information from the order into your *Movies.WDB* file to keep that list up to date.

1. Choose *ORDER.WPS* from the Window menu. You see the order Sarah sent to Central Video, as shown in Figure 15-11.

The two movies have already been set up in a table, but several of the categories that the store uses in its Movies database are missing. In order to copy information correctly into the Movies database, you need to add those fields to the Word Processor document before

FIGURE 15-10
The memo printed out with charts in place.

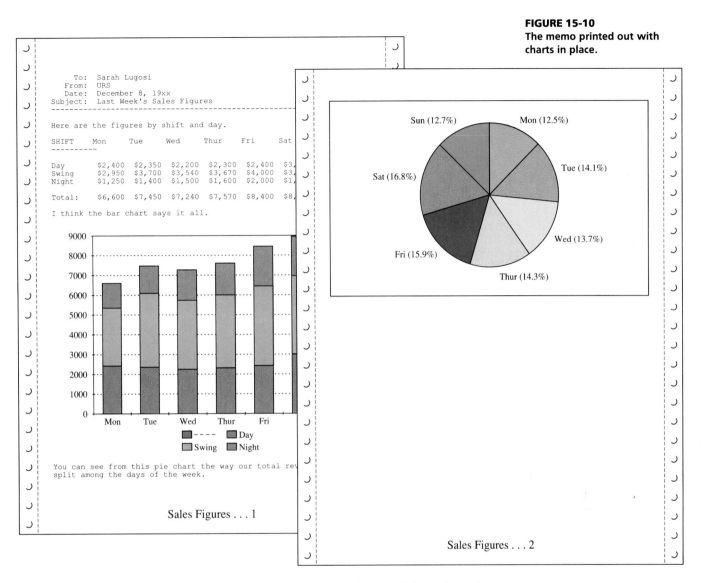

```
        To:  Sarah Lugosi
      From:  URS
      Date:  December 8, 19xx
   Subject:  Last Week's Sales Figures
   ------------------------------------------
   Here are the figures by shift and day.

   SHIFT    Mon     Tue     Wed     Thur    Fri     Sat
   -----
   Day      $2,400  $2,350  $2,200  $2,300  $2,400  $3,
   Swing    $2,950  $3,700  $3,540  $3,670  $4,000  $3,
   Night    $1,250  $1,400  $1,500  $1,600  $2,000  $1,

   Total:   $6,600  $7,450  $7,240  $7,570  $8,400  $8,

   I think the bar chart says it all.
```

You can see from this pie chart the way our total re[v]
split among the days of the week.

Sales Figures . . . 1

Sales Figures . . . 2

copying. You need to insert the Type, and then add the Rental Fee and Cost—items that Sarah did not want to bother Central Video with.

2. After the first movie title, *The Inspector & the Chicken*, press Tab, and key your rating: Yuck

3. After the length (100), press Tab and key 2, then press Tab and key 20. These represent the rental fee and cost to purchase.

4. Repeat steps 2 and 3 for *Bad Bob Rides Again*.

5. Highlight the two lines of information about the movies. (Don't select the line that says *Movie Title*....) Choose *Copy* from the Edit menu.

6. Choose *MOVIES.WDB* from the Window menu.

7. Highlight the blank entry under Title in record 36. Press Enter. The two records are added to your database, as shown in Figure 15-12.

Copying numbers or text from the Word Processor to the Spreadsheet works the same way. You just have to make sure that in the Word Processor document, you have placed the information in the same rows and columns as you expect it to fall into in the other application.

FIGURE 15-11
The original order—a Word Processor document.

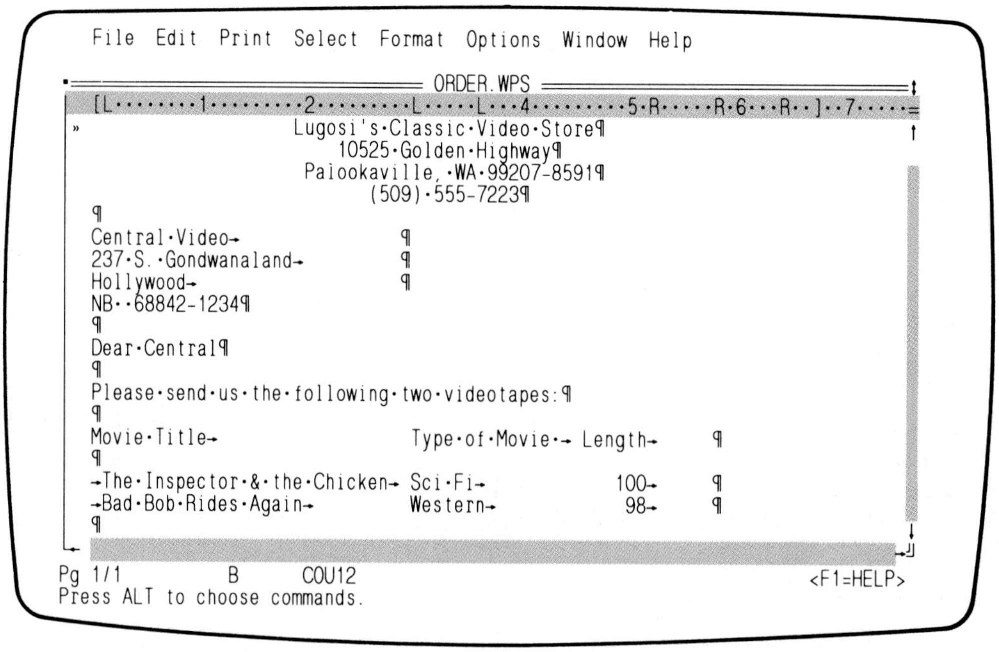

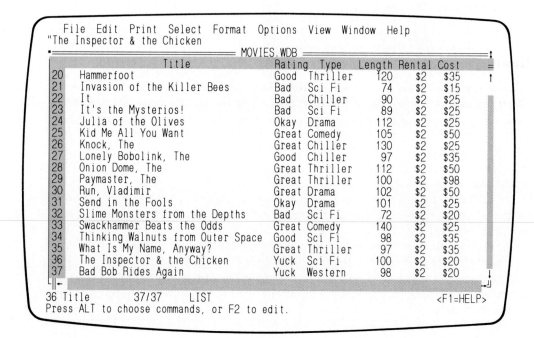

FIGURE 15-12
The expanded version of the Movies database.

Closing Some Files

You have a lot of files open now. It is time to put some of them away to make room for other work.

1. Choose *SALXXX.WPS* from the Window menu, then choose *Close* from the File menu.
2. Close *Order.WPS* and choose not to save the changes.

Copying Information from the Database to the Spreadsheet

You can copy information from the Database to any other tool in Works. To do some quick calculations, without bothering to create a real report, you can copy information from a database, place it in a spreadsheet, and perform the calculations there.

1. Choose *MOVIES.WDB* from the Window menu, then highlight the Length, Rental, and Cost columns through record 37.
2. Choose Copy from the Edit menu.
3. Choose *Create New File* from the File menu, select *New Spreadsheet*, and press Enter.
4. When the new spreadsheet appears, press Enter. The numbers pour into it.
5. In cell C5, replace *Free* with the number zero, and press Enter.
6. Highlight cell A39, then key the formula =AVG(A1:A37) and press Enter.
7. Extend the highlighting to include cells B39 and C39, then choose *Fill Right* from the Edit menu.
8. Highlight cell A39, choose *Fixed* from the Format menu, and key 0 for decimal places.
9. Highlight cells B39 and C39, choose *Currency* from the Format menu, and key 0 for decimal places.

   You now know the average length, rental price, and cost of videotapes.

10. Choose *Save As* from the File menu, name the file *AvgXXX.WKS*, and save it on your template disk. Then close the file.

Saving a File for Another Program

You can pass information from Works to many other programs, if you need to. For instance, Morris Yu has a different database program at home, and he wants to be able to read the database of winners. If his program has a **file translator** built in—a mini-program that edits your file so that the other program can display it with all the formatting as you intended—he may be able to open the *Win.WDB* file and see everything in its place, with the formatting you have set up. But if his program does not have a translator to handle Works files, you may have to save your file in ASCII.

   ASCII is short for the American Standard Code for Information Interchange, a code that assigns a number to every uppercase and lowercase letter, number, punctuation mark, and symbol in common use. ASCII does not include codes for special formatting that a particular program offers, such as boldfacing, different font sizes, borders, or centering. ASCII text is just the text, although Works can add tabs and returns, if you insist, to keep items in neat columns. So, the message gets through, but most of the formatting gets lost on the way. Graphics also disappear, because ASCII has no way of representing the thousands of individual dots that make up a chart. You can think of ASCII as the lowest common denominator—a code that any computer and any program can read and display.

1. Choose *MEMO2XXX.WPS* from the Window menu.
2. Choose *Save As*, select *Text* in the Format box, name the file *Mem2Asc*, and press Enter. You are asked if you are willing to save the file without formatting. Press Enter. The file is saved as text only.
3. Choose *Open Existing File*, and open *Mem2Asc* as a Word Processor document.

   You see that the text has been wrapped around, making a confusing jumble. You would need to spend quite a while reformatting this, but all the numbers are here. Unfortunately the two charts you originally had in the file have been discarded. Graphics are created one dot at a time, rather than one character at a time; ASCII can only handle characters, so it discards any graphics.

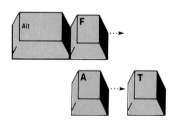

**Save Word Processor
Document as ASCII Text**

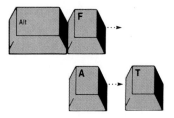

**Save Database as ASCII Text
with Tabs Between Entries**

4. Choose *Win.WDB* from the Window menu, then choose *Save As* from the File menu. Select *Text & tabs* in the Format box, name the file *WinAsc*, then press Enter. That will place tabs between entries in each row and return characters at the end of each row—a common format that many other databases can read, bringing your information into their fields.

5. Choose *Open Existing File*, select the *WinAsc* file, choose to open it as a database, choose *List* from the View menu, and you see your data arranged without field names, but still in order, as in Figure 15-13.

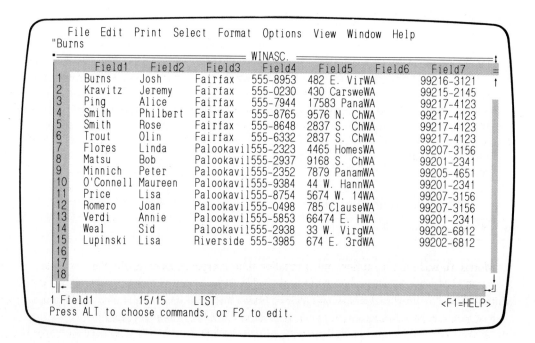

FIGURE 15-13
**The ASCII version of the
Win.WDB database.**

6. Highlight Field 5, choose *Field Width*, and set that to 20 characters. You can now see the full street address, and the state abbreviation appears clearly in its own field.

7. Choose Exit Works from the File menu. Save the changes made to *WinAsc*, but discard the changes made to *Win.WDB* and *Movies.WDB*. Since you haven't made any changes to *Mem2Asc*, this file will close automatically.

You have preserved the information and the distinction between fields, but along the way, you have lost the field names and the widths you had originally established for each field. This gives you an idea of what Morris Yu may face when he opens the ASCII version of the file in his own database application: He will need to tinker with the file a little to arrange the information so it can be easily read, but at least he will have the information. That is the virtue—and the limitation—of ASCII.

KEY TERMS

ASCII   *MSW 281*
file translator   *MSW 281*
placeholder   *MSW 277*

COMMANDS

Alt-E-I (Insert Chart)
Alt-F-A-T (Save database as ASCII text with tabs between entries)
Alt-F-A-T (Save Word Processor document as ASCII text)
F10 (Change from Charting menus to Spreadsheet menus)

REVIEW QUESTIONS

1. If you were going to copy some information from a database into a Word Processor document, what work would you do in the Database tool before copying? What kind of clean-up might be necessary in the Word Processor document after copying?
2. If you were going to copy some information from a spreadsheet into a Word Processor document, what work would you do in the Spreadsheet tool before copying? What kind of clean-up might be necessary in the Word Processor document after copying?
3. In general, what should you do in a Word Processor document before copying some information to a database?
4. What kind of information is lost when you copy from a spreadsheet into a Word Processor document?
5. Describe a situation in which you might need to save your file in ASCII. Explain what ASCII is.

APPLICATIONS

1. Morris Yu was looking at how much vacation time everyone has earned at the store. He noticed that several people have accumulated more than 80 hours of vacation. He wrote a memo to Sarah pointing this out, but he has asked you to copy the information from the Database file into the memo for him.

   a. Open two files from the template disk, *Over80.WPS* and then *Staff.WDB*.
   b. With *Staff.WDB* open, move the Vacation Hrs column over so it appears between First Name and Street.
   c. Choose *Sort Records* from the Select menu, and have the records sorted by the Vacation Hrs field.
   d. Highlight the Last Name, First Name, and Vacation Hrs of the four employees who have already earned more than 80 hours of vacation. Choose *Copy* from the Edit menu.
   e. Choose *OVER80.WPS* from the Window menu, put the cursor after the first paragraph, and press Enter to insert that information into the memo.
   f. In similar fashion, put the Last Name, First Name, and Vacation Hours of the people who are due exactly 80 hours of vacation after the second paragraph in the memo.
   g. Use the Tab key or Backspace key to clean up the spacing in the memo, so that all the names in both lists line up consistently.
   h. Add today's date; then save the file as *Ovr80XXX.WPS* and print.

2. Morris Yu keeps track of the accumulated vacation expenses for employees with more than 80 hours vacation due them; he records the totals in a spreadsheet called *Vac$.WKS*.

   a. If you are continuing from the first application, the *Ovr80XXX.WPS* file should be open; if not, open it now.
   b. Open the *Vac$.WKS* file from the template disk.
   c. Copy the material in cells A1 through G11 and place it at the end of the memo.
   d. Clean up the material you have placed in the memo.
   e. Save the file as *Ovr80XXX.WPS* and print a copy of the memo.

Creating Form Letters and Mailing Labels

OBJECTIVES

- Explain the purpose and process of creating form letters through mail merge.
- Prepare a Word Processor document for mail merge.
- Print form letters.
- Create a Word Processor document for mailing labels.
- Print mailing labels.

CREATING FORM LETTERS

L ugosi's Classic Video Store will open its new location in Fairfax in just a few weeks. Some of the original store's best customers have just won a free video rental in a contest, and Sarah Lugosi wants to urge these people to visit the new Fairfax store to pick up the videotape there. However, she does not want to send an insincere-sounding form letter that begins, *Dear Friend*. These customers have been coming to Lugosi's for a long time, and she knows them all by name, so she would like to send personalized letters to them. Sarah would like you to create a personalized letter for each of these outstanding customers, based on an original letter she has written. Rather than type a new version of the letter for each customer, you can use the mail merge features of Works to help you do the work.

How You Generate Form Letters through Mail Merge

Mail merge is a form of integration, drawing information from a database and inserting it into a standard Word Processor document. You begin with a database full of information about people—their names and addresses, their phone numbers, and possibly their special interests or situations.

Then you create a standard letter you want to send to those people. In the letter you leave holes for a person's first name, address, and any other special information you want to mention, such as a favorite hobby. In each hole, Works puts a **placeholder**—a phrase that tells the program what database to look into, and what field to examine to find the missing data.

When you print the letter, Works goes to the database you've specified, looks at the first record, finds the entry in the field, and types that entry into the form letter. Then it continues printing the form letter. When Works finishes printing the first letter, it starts a new one for the next record in the database. And it continues printing new, *personalized* letters for every person in the database.

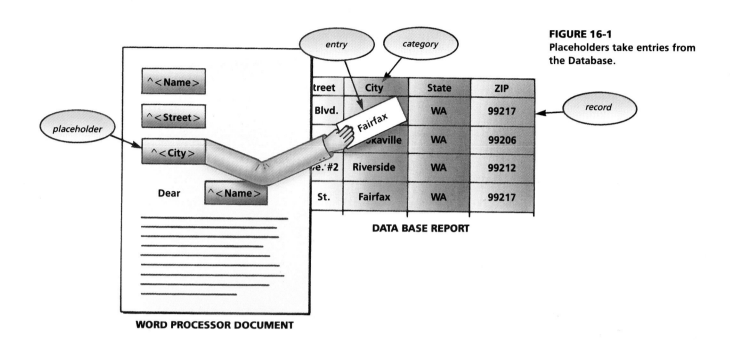

FIGURE 16-1
Placeholders take entries from the Database.

As you print the letters then, Works merges information from the database into your Word Processor document, printing one document for each record in the database. When the mail merge process is over, you have a unique letter for each customer, including the customer's name and address, plus any other personal information you chose to include.

Opening the Files for Merging

The first information you need is the list of people who won a free video rental in the recent promotion. You have that list in the *Win.WDB* file. The second document you need is Sarah Lugosi's rough draft of a letter to these people, announcing their prize and urging them to come to the new store in Fairfax to pick up the free video rental. Her letter is in the *Free.WPS* file.

1. Start Works.
2. Open *Win.WDB*. You see the list of customers who won the free video rental.
3. Open *Free.WPS*. You see Sarah's letter, with gaps left for people's names and addresses.

With the two files open, you are ready to begin making Sarah's letter ready for mail merge.

Inserting Placeholders in the Word Processor Document

Sarah has left a few blanks in her letter. You need to fill those in with personal information taken from the *Win* database.

1. Complete the date by keying the rest of this year's number.
2. Use the Down Arrow to move the cursor down four lines. That is where you want the name and address to appear, three blank lines after the date.
3. Choose *Insert Field* from the Edit menu.

Insert Field

FIGURE 16-2
The *Win* database file.

File Edit Print Select Format Options View Window Help
"Burns
WIN.WDB

	Last Name	First Name	Street	City	St	ZIP Code
1	Burns	Josh	482 E. Virginia	Fairfax	WA	99216-3121
2	Flores	Linda	4465 Homestead	Palookaville	WA	99207-3156
3	Kravitz	Jeremy	430 Carswell	Fairfax	WA	99215-2145
4	Lupinski	Lisa	674 E. 3rd	Riverside	WA	99202-6812
5	Matsu	Bob	9168 S. Chelan	Palookaville	WA	99201-2341
6	Minnich	Peter	7879 Panamint Hwy	Palookaville	WA	99205-4651
7	O'Connell	Maureen	44 W. Hannibal	Palookaville	WA	99201-2341
8	Ping	Alice	17583 Panamint Hwy	Fairfax	WA	99217-4123
9	Price	Lisa	5674 W. 14th	Palookaville	WA	99207-3156
10	Romero	Joan	785 Clausen	Palookaville	WA	99207-3156
11	Smith	Philbert	9576 N. Chester	Fairfax	WA	99217-4123
12	Smith	Rose	2837 S. Chester	Fairfax	WA	99217-4123
13	Trout	Olin	2837 S. Chester	Fairfax	WA	99217-4123
14	Verdi	Annie	66474 E. Hannibal	Palookaville	WA	99201-2341
15	Weal	Sid	33 W. Virginia	Palookaville	WA	99202-6812
16						
17						
18						

1 Last Name 15/15 LIST <F1=HELP>
Press ALT to choose commands, or F2 to edit.

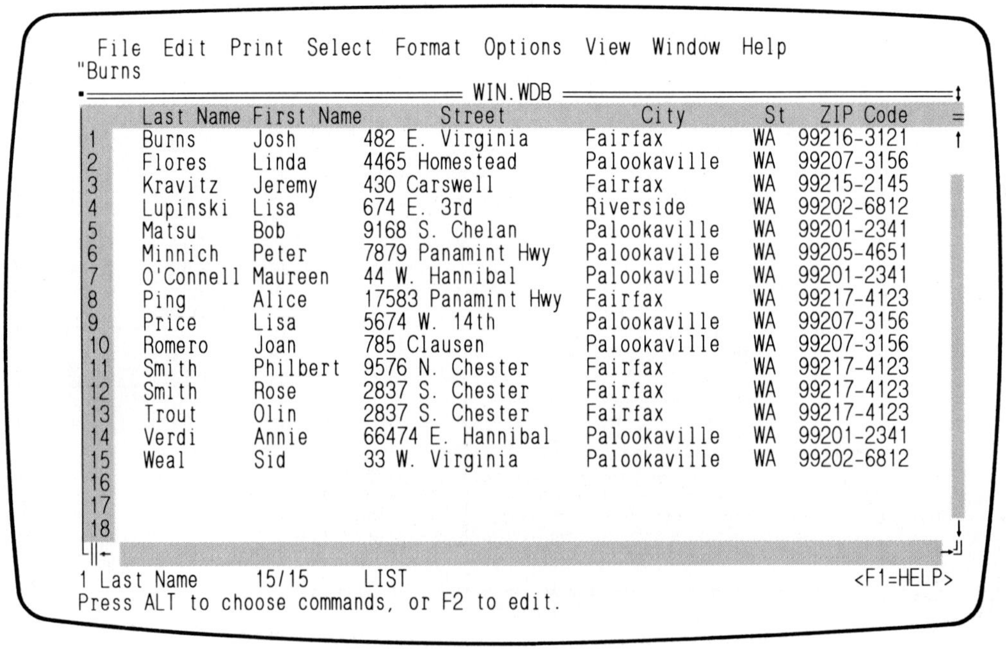

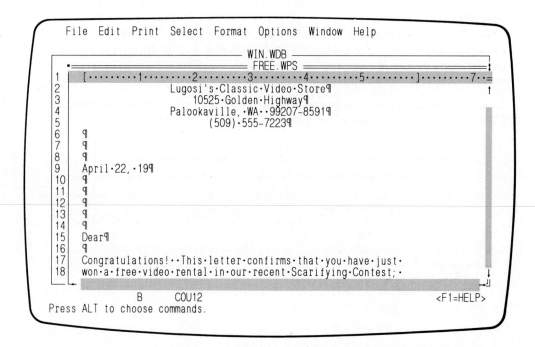

FIGURE 16-3
The *Free* word processing file.

You are going to insert information that appears in the First Name field in the Win database. You see the Insert Field dialog box, asking you which Database document to use. In the box on the left, you see a list of all the databases you currently have open; right now, you should only see *WIN.WDB* there.

4. Make sure that *WIN.WDB* is selected in the box on the left. (If necessary, use the Down Arrow to highlight it.)
5. In the Fields box, select *First Name*. Press Enter.

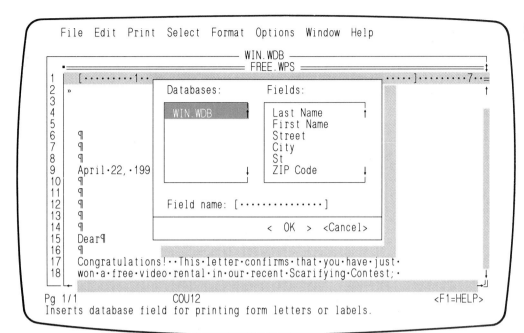

FIGURE 16-4
The Insert Field dialog box.

The dialog box disappears, and you see a placeholder containing the field name appear in your letter at the position of the cursor, as shown in Figure 16-5. The field name is surrounded with angle brackets to set it off from regular text. For now, it takes the place of the actual entry. Later, when you tell Works that you want to print the form letters using this database, the angle brackets will act as a signal telling Works to look in this field in the database for an entry, and to place that entry into the letter at this spot.

6. Press the Space Bar once to leave a space between the first name and the last name.
7. Choose *Insert Field* from the Edit menu again, select the *Last Name* field, and press Enter.

```
 File  Edit  Print  Select  Format  Options  Window  Help
 ┌────────────────────── WIN.WDB ──────────────────────┐
 ┌──────────────────────── FREE.WPS ═══════════════════╤═┐
1 [·········1·········2·········3·········4·········5·········]·········7··═
2 »                     Lugosi's·Classic·Video·Store¶                    ↑
3                          10525·Golden·Highway¶
4                       Palookaville,·WA··99207-8591¶
5                            (509)·555-7223¶
6    ¶
7    ¶
8    ¶
9    April·22,·1992¶
10   ¶
11   ¶
12   ¶
13   «First·Name»¶
14   ¶
15   Dear¶
16   ¶
17   Congratulations!··This·letter·confirms·that·you·have·just·
18   won·a·free·video·rental·in·our·recent·Scarifying·Contest;·
 └────────────────────────────────────────────────────────┘
 Pg 1/1              COU12                         <F1=HELP>
 Press ALT to choose commands.
```

FIGURE 16-5
The First Name field
placeholder.

8. Press Enter once to move to the line you will devote to the street address.
9. Choose *Insert Field* from the Edit menu again, select the *Street* field, and press Enter.
10. Press Enter once to move to the line you will devote to the city, state, and ZIP code.
11. Insert the *City* field, followed by a comma and a space.
12. Insert the *St* field, followed by two spaces.
13. Insert the *ZIP Code* field.
14. Use arrow keys to move the cursor to the space after the *r* in *Dear.*
15. Press the Space Bar once, then insert the *First Name* field again. Your letter's opening should now look like Figure 16-6.

FIGURE 16-6
The form letter with placeholders for name and address.

```
   File  Edit  Print  Select  Format  Options  Window  Help

                        ┌──────── WIN.WDB ────────
                        ════════ FREE.WPS ════════
    1  [·········1·········2·········3·········4·········5·········]·······7·=
    2  »                    Lugosi's·Classic·Video·Store¶                      ↑
    3                          10525·Golden·Highway¶
    4                       Palookaville,·WA··99207-8591¶
    5                            (509)·555-7223¶
    6     ¶
    7     ¶
    8     ¶
    9  April·22,·1992¶
   10     ¶
   11     ¶
   12     ¶
   13  «First·Name»··«Last·Name»¶
   14  «Street»¶
   15  «City»,·«St»···«ZIP·Code»¶
   16     ¶
   17  Dear·«First·Name»¶
   18     ¶

   Pg 1/1                    COU12                              <F1=HELP>
   Press ALT to choose commands.
```

Congratulations! You have turned an ordinary letter into a form letter. Now instead of having to type a new version for each person on the list, you can have Works do all that typing when it prints.

Printing Form Letters

Printing form letters is a little different from printing regular letters. You must have opened the database from which you expect Works to draw the special information for each letter. And you use a different command on the Print menu to ensure that Works recognizes the placeholders as an indication that it should replace them with entries from records in the database.

1. Make sure that your printer is on, connected securely to the computer, and on-line.
2. Check the Window menu to make sure that your *Win.WDB* file is still open. (You just opened it a little while ago, so it should be. If not, open it now, then use the Window menu to switch to the *Free.WPS* document.)
3. With the *Free.WPS* letter open and active, choose *Print Form Letters* from the Print menu. You see a dialog box asking you to specify from which database to draw information. You are going to print Sarah's letter in a special way.

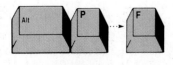

Print Form Letters

4. Make sure that *WIN.WDB* is highlighted in the dialog box, then press Enter. That tells Works to look in this database for any information needed when it is replacing the placeholders with entries from the database records.
5. Press Enter to print. Works prints one copy of the letter for the first record in the database.
6. After Works has printed three letters, press Esc to stop the printing. (You don't need to print all 15 letters now.) You are witnessing mail merge in action. Your first three letters should look like those in Figure 16-7.
7. Save your form letter as a word processing file called *FreeXXX.WPS*.

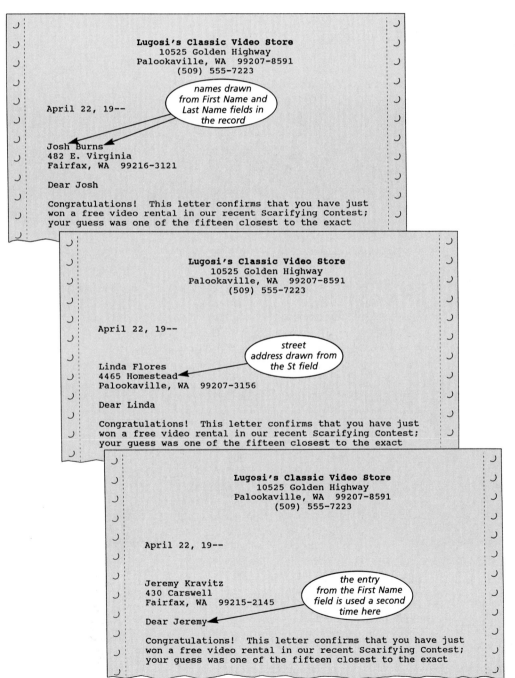

FIGURE 16-7
Each form letter is personalized with information from one record in the database.

PRINTING MAILING LABELS

Y ou have turned out some form letters through the mail merge process. You could address each envelope by hand, but Works enables you to use the same database records to create **mailing labels**. That way, instead of handwriting or typing individual envelopes for each letter, you can have Works print the labels. All you have to do is tear them off and slap them on the envelopes. Drawing your mailing labels from the Database also ensures that they are correct, because no one has to rekey anything. Fewer mistakes can creep in when you let Works take over.

Arranging the Placeholders

The process of printing mailing labels is a variation of the mail merge process you just used. First, you create a Word Processor document to contain all the mailing labels. Then you use the *Insert Field* command on the Edit menu to insert placeholders for the information you want brought over from the database document—names and addresses in this case. You format and punctuate the labels as you want. Then you choose the *Print Labels* command from the Print menu, specify the database you want used and the type of labels you are using, fit the label stock into the printer, and print.

1. Choose *Create New File* from the File menu, select *New Word Processor*, and press Enter.
2. Check the Window menu to make sure that your *Win.WDB* file is open. (If not, open it now, then switch back to your new Word Processor file.)
3. Choose *Insert Field* from the Edit menu to insert the first placeholder. You see the Insert Field dialog box, as shown earlier in Figure 16-4.
4. Make sure that *WIN.WDB* is highlighted in the Databases box; then select *First Name* in the Fields box, and press Enter.
5. Press the Space Bar once, then insert the *Last Name* placeholder.
6. Press Enter to move to a new line, then insert the *Street* placeholder.
7. Press Enter to move to a new line, then insert the *City* placeholder.
8. Key a comma, press the Space Bar once, and insert the *St* placeholder for the State abbreviation.
9. Press the Space Bar twice, then insert the ZIP Code placeholder. Your label should look like Figure 16-8 now.
10. Save your file as *Label.WPS*.

Aligning and Formatting the Placeholders

Printing on pieces of papers that contain gummed labels can be tricky. When you print, you have to tell Works the size, shape, and position of the labels on the label paper. But you do not want to have Works start printing right at the top of the label or close to the left-hand side of the label because any jiggling of the paper as it moves through the printer could mean that part of your printing misses the label, or worse, ends up on another label. To avoid these problems, you need to indent a little and put some room before your first line.

1. Highlight your entire label, and choose *Indents & Spacing* from the Format menu.
2. In the Indents & Spacing dialog box, set the Left indent to 0.5, to indent the text half an inch from the edge of the label.
3. Press Enter.

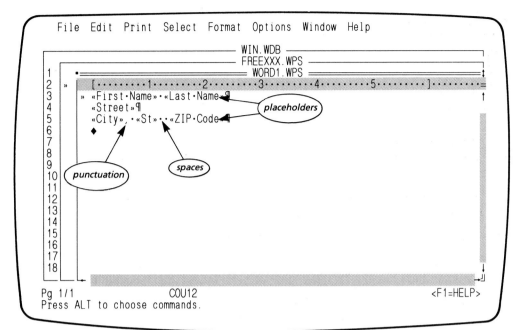

FIGURE 16-8
The basic mailing label, with placeholders for the information to be brought in from the database.

4. Highlight the first line (First Name and Last Name).
5. Choose *Indents & Spacing*, and set the *Space before paragraph* to 1 so that Works will skip down one line from the top of the label before printing. Press Enter. Your label moves down a line, as shown in Figure 16-9.
6. Highlight the entire label, and choose *Font & Style* from the Format menu. If possible, pick a font that has a size smaller than 12; then choose 10 point if available, or if 10 point is not available, anything less than 12. You want to make the type small enough so that even the longest street address in the world will fit into one line on your label.

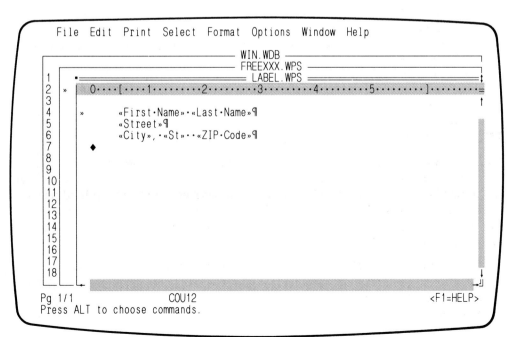

FIGURE 16-9
The label has been moved down one line and indented half an inch so it will not be printed too near the edge of the physical label.

You have only set up one label. You do not have to make up placeholders for all the labels you want to print. Works takes care of that when you tell it you intend to print labels. You will do that next.

Printing the Mailing Labels

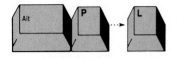

Print Labels

You are ready to print the mailing labels for the customers who guessed the approximate number of bats in the belfry in *Frankenstein's Stepsister*.

1. Choose *Print Labels* from the Print menu. You see the Print Labels dialog box, as shown in Figure 16-10.

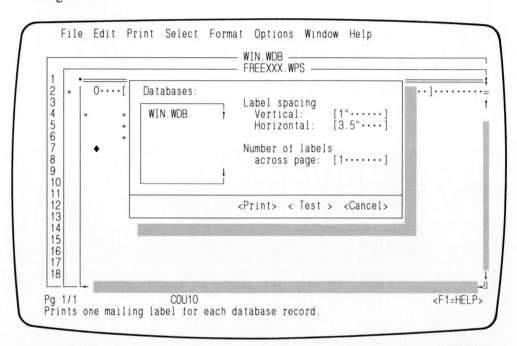

FIGURE 16-10
The Print Labels dialog box.

2. Make sure that the *WIN.WDB* database has been selected in the Databases box. That is the database from which you want to draw names and addresses for your mailing labels.

   In this dialog box, you tell Works how tall and how wide your labels are and—roughly— where they appear on an 8 1/2-by-11-inch sheet of paper. The preset options assume that you have a sheet of labels that are 1 inch high, 3.5 inches wide, and that the labels appear in a single column. But some label stock crams labels into several columns, so Works needs to know how many labels appear across an individual page. Based on the information you provide in this dialog box, Works figures out where the labels will be on the physical piece of paper.

   Once Works has mapped out where the physical labels are, it treats the left edge of each label as the left margin of a very small page; and it treats the top of the label as the top of a very small page. In effect, it is devoting a miniature page to each label.

   For now, you are just practicing, using ordinary paper to print your labels on, so you can leave the settings as they are.

   If you were using real labels, you would measure the distance from the top of one label to the top of the next label, and key that into the Vertical box. If you were using stock with more than one label across, you would measure from the left side of one label to the left side of the next label in that row, then key that distance in the Horizontal box. (If you had just one label across, and its width was different from 3.5 inches, you would key its width into the Horizontal box.)

3. Choose *Print*. You see the Page Setup & Margins dialog box. Adjust all margins to zero.

   We are assuming that the labels you are using start at the top of the page, so you key the number 0 in the Top margin box; and most labels go to the bottom of the sheet, so key the number 0 in the Bottom margin box. We are also assuming that the labels start at the left edge of the paper, so key the number 0 in the Left margin box. (On the other hand, if they begin half an inch from the top and three-quarters of an inch from the left side of the paper, you would need to take that into account by changing the top margin to 0.5, and the left margin to 0.75.)

   When printing labels, you normally do not have a header or footer, so those margins should be zero as well. You aren't inserting page numbers either, so you can ignore that option.

4. Press Enter. You see the Print dialog box. Press Enter to print.

   At the bottom of the screen, Works reports on its progress, record by record, as it merges the names and addresses from each record into this very short Word Processor document, over and over. Depending on your settings, you see one or two pages of labels come out of the printer, as shown in Figure 16-11.

5. Save your Word Processor document as *LabXXX.WPS*. That way, you can always print out the mailing labels again, without having to set the placeholders up again.

6. Close all three files.

FIGURE 16-11
Labels printed one across.

KEY TERMS

form letters   *MSW 284*
mailing labels   *MSW 290*
mail merge   *MSW 284*
placeholder   *MSW 284*

COMMANDS

Alt-E-F (Insert Field)
Alt-P-F (Print Form Letters)
Alt-P-L (Print Labels)

REVIEW QUESTIONS

1. If you were preparing a Database document to be used in creating form letters to customers of Lugosi's Classic Video Store, what fields would have to be included? Can you think of one or two other fields that might be included, just in case Sarah Lugosi wanted to notify people of specials on their favorite type of movie or on their favorite movie star?
2. Describe the main steps involved in inserting a placeholder for a person's first name into a Word Processor document. What identifies a placeholder in your document?
3. What command tells Works to insert the entry from a particular field in a particular database into your Word Processor document during printing?
4. When you are generating form letters during the mail merge process, what is Works doing behind the scenes, as it prints?
5. If you are drawing information from a 100-record database to create a series of mailing labels, how many labels will you get? Explain why that is the case.

APPLICATIONS

1. Morris Yu wants to confirm that the *Win.WDB* database contains the correct phone numbers for all the winners. You need to add a sentence to the *FreeXXX.WPS* letter and drop in a placeholder referring to the Home Phone field in the database.
   a. Open two files from the template disk, *Win.WDB* and *FreeXXX.WPS*.
   b. At the end of the letter, place the cursor on the *S* in *Sincerely*.
   c. Key the following sentences: Your name has now been entered in the Horror of Horrors super-contest. If you win, we will call you right away.
   d. Press Enter twice to separate that paragraph from *Sincerely*.
   e. Move to the end of Sarah Lugosi's name, press Enter twice, and key: PS: We want to make sure we have your correct phone number; here is the number we have on record for you: . Please call us if that is not correct.
   f. Use the arrow key to move the cursor two spaces after the colon, then use the Insert Field command to put a placeholder for the Home Phone field there.
   g. Print the first three form letters and save your revised version of *FreeXXX.WPS* as *PhoneXXX.WPS*.
   h. Close the files.

2. Sarah Lugosi has decided to automate the way she notifies employees that it's time to plan vacation.
   a. Open the *Staff.WDB* file.

b. Sort the records by Vacation Hrs.

c. Highlight the Vacation Hrs field.

d. Choose *Query* from the View menu, key >=80 in the Vacation Hrs field, and press Enter.

e. Choose *List* from the View menu. You see the records that show 80 or more vacation hours.

f. Create a new Word Processor file.

g. Press the Space Bar five times, then key: To: followed by two spaces.

h. Using the *Insert Field* command from the Edit menu, and choosing *STAFF.WDB*, insert a placeholder for the employee's first name; then a space, and another placeholder for the employee's last name. Then press Enter.

i. Press the Space Bar three times, then key: From: Sarah and Morris

j. Press Enter and key: Subject: Vacation Hours

k. Press Enter, then press the Space Bar three times, and key Date: followed by two spaces.

l. Key today's date, and press Enter three times.

m. Key: You must be working really hard! You have accumulated

n. Press the Space Bar once, then insert a placeholder for the Vacation Hrs field. (Remember to use STAFF.WDB.)

o. Press the Space Bar again, then key: vacation hours this year. Please make plans to take your vacation soon. You have earned it!

p. Choose Print Form Letters from the Print menu, select the *STAFF.WDB* database, and press Enter to print eight form letters.

q. Close *Staff.WDB*, and do not save any changes.

r. Save your memo under the name *80HrsXXX.WPS*.

UNIT VI

Communications

Getting Started with Communications

OBJECTIVES

- Explain what equipment you need for communications between computers.
- Set up a Communications file.
- Connect and disconnect.
- Understand how to send and receive text and files.

COMMUNICATIONS BASICS

Works helps you exchange information with other people using personal computers; with businesses such as banks, retail stores, airlines, and hotels; and with services that provide information on topics such as the weather, the stock market, airline schedules, ecology, medicine, agriculture, and the law.

You may have a report you need to send to someone in an office a thousand miles away. You could print the report, put it in an envelope, and mail it. A few days later, if you are lucky, the other person would get the mail and read your report. But think how much faster you could get a response if you sent the report over the telephone lines in the time it takes to make an average phone call. Your message would be delivered in minutes, not days.

Communications from one computer to another speed up the transfer of all kinds of information. Sometimes we are on the receiving end. We may receive letters and memos over the telephone lines or—in a large office—directly, via a cable that links together the computers sitting on the desks of every employee. **Electronic mail**—mail that comes over wires rather than in paper envelopes—moves faster than regular mail.

Sometimes we want to reach out for some facts stored on a database in another state or another nation. Such databases are created and maintained by companies that sell information; the companies are known, collectively, as **information services**. You can subscribe to an information service. Then when you need a fact, you can have Works dial the computer that stores that database and query that database as if it were somehow open on your own computer. You can collect information from that database—facts that aren't even available in a regular library yet, numbers that record yesterday's sales, or the latest medical breakthrough. You are billed for the time you use the service, plus a premium for the more valuable information, but in many cases, the ability to get that information immediately is more important than the cost.

You can also dial another person's computer directly and type messages back and forth. A more convenient way to exchange views with other individuals is the electronic **bulletin board**, a kind of party line for computers. You can key in a message to someone else, and the recipient can respond immediately; or you can join extended discussions where you post a question, and other people post their answers over the next few days. When you return, you collect all their ideas at once, and if you wish, continue the dialog.

In this chapter, you will learn how to start a communications session. A **session** is, literally, the time during which you are sitting down at the computer communicating. The term applies specifically to the experience you have from the moment you start communicating with another computer to the time you disconnect. You do not have to have communications equipment to follow this lesson. You will see how to make the connection and how to send and receive short messages, blocks of text, and files.

SETTING UP YOUR EQUIPMENT

Before your computer can communicate with another, there must be some kind of a line connecting them. The simplest line would be a cable plugged into each computer. Like the cable connecting your computer with your printer, such a cable can carry information at a very high speed.

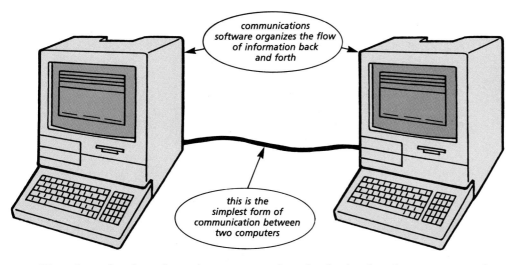

communications software organizes the flow of information back and forth

this is the simplest form of communication between two computers

FIGURE 17-1
A direct cable connects two computers.

Not quite as fast, but a lot easier to use, are the twisted pair wires that carry your voice along ordinary phone lines and the coaxial cables that bunch together hundreds and thousands of messages at the same time. Much more efficient than the cable between two personal computers are fiber optics, in which hundreds of thousands of voice messages move at the speed of light along delicate cables.

In order to communicate over the phone lines, beginning with the twisted pair wires in your own wall, for instance, and possibly whizzing out through fiber optics to a communication satellite and back down on the other side of a continent, you need a communications device known as a **modem**. The modem makes it possible to send signals from a computer over a phone line. In effect, the modem translates from the digital information used in the computer (a series of on or off signals) to the analog information that can be sent along the phone lines. Analog information comes in a series of waves. The modem attached to your computer modulates the information in your report into a sound or analog signal; and the modem attached to the recipient's computer demodulates those sounds or analog signals, turning them back into dots and dits, or digital information that a computer can understand, as shown in Figure 17-2.

FIGURE 17-2
A modem translates from digital to analog signals and back again.

A modem can be installed inside your computer, or it can sit next to the computer, connected to the computer by a cable that conveys data and connected to the phone jack by a standard phone line. It sits between the computer and the phone lines, translating back and forth.

Modems come in various sizes, brands, shapes, and speeds. Works has been preset to work with a kind of modem called **Hayes-compatible**. That means the modem follows standards set by the Hayes company in making their modems; the majority of modems available today are Hayes-compatible. You will learn more about the features of modems later in this chapter.

A modem obeys commands sent to it from your computer. You can enter these commands yourself, or—more conveniently—you can have Works issue the instructions. Typical instructions tell the modem to dial a certain phone number, turn up the volume so you can hear the dial tone, try again if the line is busy, or hang up after ten tries. Part of what you do when you start communication is to tell Works which instructions you want sent to the modem.

SETTING UP A COMMUNICATIONS FILE

*T*he phone lines have just been installed at the new store in Fairfax. Sarah Lugosi has asked you to send a file over to Morris Yu, who is getting the computers set up in preparation for the Grand Opening. In the past, you would have put the file on a diskette, gone outside, and driven across town to hand-deliver the disk. Now though, Sarah has asked you to telecommunicate it, so you can get back to work on the floor, helping customers. Your first job is to open a Communications file.

Whenever you want to communicate with another computer, you open a Communications file. This file contains the instructions and the information Works needs in order to make contact with the other computer and to maintain the give-and-take of communication without error.

In the Communications file, you enter the phone number you want to call; you set a number of options controlling the actual flow of information (its speed and format, for instance); and you identify the characteristics of your computer when it acts as a terminal. A **terminal** was originally just the monitor and the keyboard at the end or terminus of a long stretch of cable coming from a mainframe computer. The idea of a terminal has been extended to include a personal computer when it is being used to communicate with another computer, whether or not that other computer is a mainframe. Naturally there are several types of terminal, and one type does not talk easily with another.

The settings your computer uses *must* match the ones used by the computer at the other end of the cable or phone lines. You learn those settings from the individual, business, or information service at the other end. If the settings do not match, communication may falter. You may not get through at all. Your messages may come through in gibberish. Or you may see strings of words fly past you on the screen, never to be seen again. In the complex world of communications, you will find there are many surprises. Works helps you sidestep most of these pitfalls, though.

By the way: In this lesson, you do not need a modem, and you will not actually be sending and receiving information over the phone lines. You will be exploring the Communications tool and practicing.

Setting up the Phone Connection

Works will instruct the modem to dial the telephone number for you—and it will keep dialing if it encounters a problem on the line. But you have to tell Works what number to call and what kind of telephone system you are using.

1. Start Works.
2. Choose *Create New File*, select a *New Communications* file, and press Enter. You see the new file, which contains no text, as shown in Figure 17-3.
3. Choose *Phone* from the Options menu. You see the Phone dialog box, as illustrated in Figure 17-4.

   Lugosi's Classic Video Store has a small phone system with ten lines. To get an outside line, you have to dial 9.

4. Key: 9 ,

   The 9 gets you an outside line. The comma tells the modem to wait until it hears a dial tone.

   Fairfax is not far away, but the new store happens to be in a different area code. In Palookaville, you must dial a 1 before the area code.

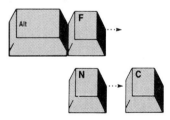

Create New Communications File

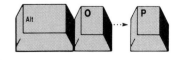

Phone

FIGURE 17-3
A new Communications file.

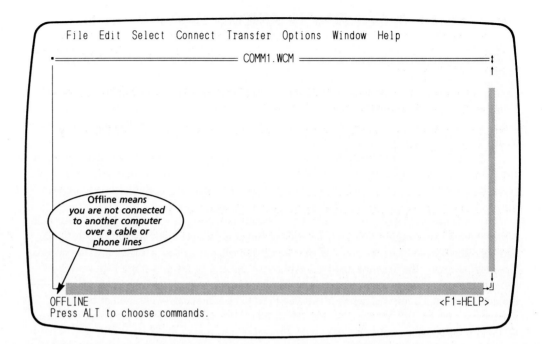

FIGURE 17-4
The Phone dialog box.

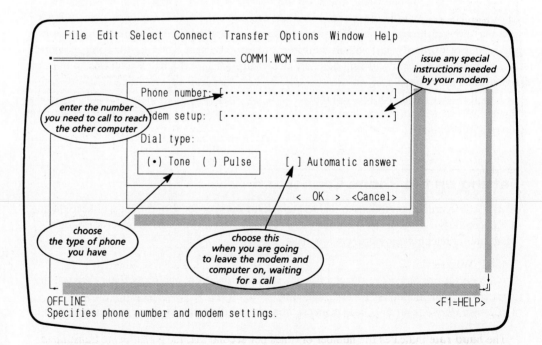

5. Key: 1(000)555-1212

You do not actually have to key the hyphens and parentheses, but you may, and most people include them to make the phone number easier to read.

You are using a Hayes-compatible modem, and you have no special instructions for it, so you can skip the Modem setup box.

The phone system in your store consists of push-button phones that make tones when you press the buttons. The *Tone* Dial type has already been selected, so you leave that untouched. (The alternative, a rotary-dial system, is the old-fashioned wheel with holes for your fingers. When you dial that way, and you hear the clicks and ratchetings, the phone is sending out a series of pulses.)

You are not expecting someone else to be sending you a message late tonight, so you do not need to select *Automatic answer* right now.

6. Press Enter. You have specified the phone number you want the modem to dial during this communications session.

Defining the Speed and Format of Communication

Now you need to make sure that your computer will send out information at the speed the other computer expects and in a format it can understand.

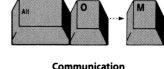

Communication

1. Choose *Communication* from the Options menu. You see the Communication dialog box, as shown in Figure 17-5.

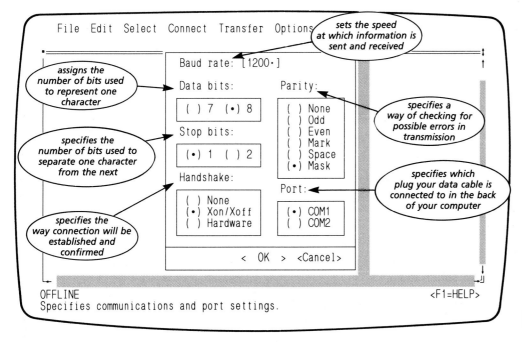

FIGURE 17-5
The Communication dialog box.

2. You know that Morris Yu will be using a 2400 baud modem at the new store, just like the one you have connected to your computer. So key 2400 in the Baud rate box.

The **baud rate** indicates the number of times per second that the signal being transmitted changes. At 2400 baud, each change in signal transmits a single **bit** of information—a yes or a no, an on or an off, a 1 or a 0. Some of those bits are used to represent a single character, such as the letter L. Because those bits convey information, they are known as **data bits**.

3. Leave the Data bits option set to *8*.

One or two bits mark the beginning of the stream of data bits or the end; these are known as **stop bits**. You and Morris have agreed to use one stop bit, not two.

4. Leave the Stop bits box set to *1*.

In the flow of bits, another bit is occasionally used to check for possible errors; that is known as the **parity bit**. If you consider the bits that are being sent as a string of 1's and 0's, and you know that there will always be eight data bits and one stop bit, then the software in your computer can add up those nine 1's or 0's and get a total. That total is either odd or even. If you are using the Even Parity system, and you get an odd total, you add a 1 as the parity bit, to make the final total come out even. If you get an even total to begin with, you just add a 0 to make the final total come out even. At the other end of the line, the other computer has been told to check for Even Parity as well. It adds up the first nine of the 1's and 0's, gets a total, and decides whether that is even or odd. Then it adds the parity bit, and makes sure that the final total is even. If not, it suspects an error in transmission and displays an asterisk, instead of a character, as a warning to you. If Works encounters a series of errors in transmission, the software tells the modem to break off the communication and start over, to get it right.

The other methods of parity checking are variations of this method, except for Mask, which ignores the other computer's parity setting altogether.

5. Set Parity to *Even*.

At the beginning of a communication session, some software expects to "shake hands" with the software at the other end as a kind of agreement to start communicating. A traditional **handshake** involves sending two characters, one known as Xon, the next as Xoff. That sequence is distinct enough to be usable as a unique code indicating: *we are linked*. Hardware has its own ways of shaking hands. Morris Yu has left word that you should use *Xon/Xoff*.

6. Leave Handshake set to *Xon/Xoff*.

The last box, Port, refers to the computer's actual **port** or connector from which your data cable runs to the modem. The two ports suggested in the box are designed for Communication.

7. Leave Port set to *COM1*. Press Enter. You have made sure that your communication settings are the same as those of Morris Yu, so your two computers will be able to send and receive information without confusion.

Specifying the Type of Terminal

The terminal settings control the way your computer responds to information you enter or receive. Works comes with these options preset for a standard personal computer. In general, you should leave them as they are and start communicating. If you encounter difficulties, come back to this dialog box, make one change, and then try again until you solve the problem.

1. Choose *Terminal* from the Options menu. You see the Terminal dialog box.
2. Leave Terminal set to *VT52*.

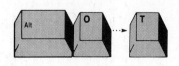

Terminal

The Terminal box allows you to decide what kind of terminal your personal computer should act like. **VT52** (or Video Terminal 52) is the most common type of terminal for a personal computer to imitate. Occasionally, if you are communicating with an old mainframe or minicomputer, you may need to imitate an **ANSI** terminal, which is based on standards adopted by the American National Standards Institute.

3. Select *Medium* as the buffer size.

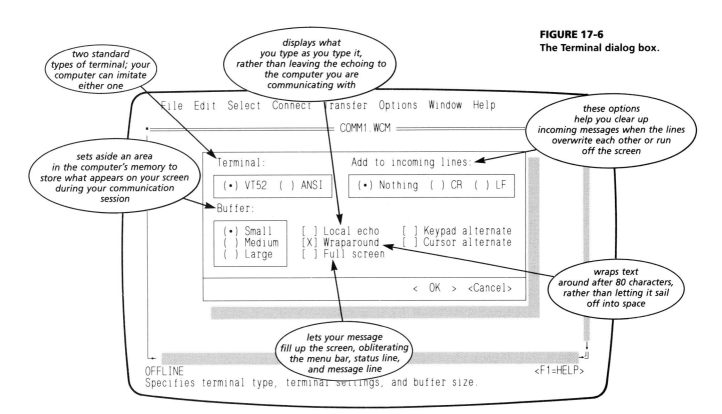

FIGURE 17-6
The Terminal dialog box.

A **buffer** is a temporary holding place in the computer's memory. The small buffer holds 100 lines; the medium, 300 lines; and the large, 750 lines. If you receive more lines than your buffer can hold, the computer throws away the earlier lines to make room for the new ones. By choosing *Medium*, you are ensuring that you will not lose any of the exchange between you and Morris Yu.

4. Leave the other options as they are.

You do not need to add anything to incoming lines, at least at first. Later, when you are actually receiving information sent by Morris, you may see all the text appear on the top line, with each new line overwriting the one before it. That would mean that Morris's computer is not sending the signal to your computer telling it, *Move down to the next line, and start typing again.* That code is called a **Line Feed**, or LF. If the lines do not begin at the left side of the screen, Morris's computer is not sending another character, called CR, for **Carriage Return**. For now though, you must assume that like most communications software, Morris Yu's version of Works will send both line feeds and carriage returns, so you will be able to read the text easily on your screen. Leave this box set so your computer will add nothing to incoming lines.

Normally when you type something, your computer displays each character on your screen. That process is known as echoing; essentially, the computer echoes back to you what you type. When you are connected to another computer and telecommunicating, you must rely on the other computer to echo back what you type, so it will show up on your screen. If for some reason the other computer has not been set to do so, you have to ask your own computer to do it for you at your own desk; that's what the **Local echo** option does for you. Leave it off for now.

The **Wraparound** option ensures that any incoming line with more than 80 characters will "wrap" around to the next line. In this way, you can be sure you will be able to see whatever messages come in, without some of the text shooting off into space on the right. Leave *Wraparound* selected. The **Full Screen** option is exciting but dangerous. If you select this option, Works removes the menu bar, status line, and message line from your screen, so that your messages fill up the screen. To return to a normal display, you must choose *Terminal* from the Option menu and reset this option, but of course the menu is no longer visible. You have to remember the keys to press: Alt-O-T. So, do not select *Full Screen*.

The alternate ways of using the numeric keypad and the arrow keys (for cursor movement) are rarely needed, and you can leave these options off.

5. Having been very careful not to change anything but the Buffer, press Enter.

COMMUNICATING

Y ou have just talked with Morris Yu on the phone. He has turned on his computer, started Works, created a new Communications file, and set his computer to answer automatically, as soon as his modem hears your call come in. You're ready to telecommunicate.

Connecting and Disconnecting

When you want to make contact with another computer, you tell Works how to make the connection, and Works dispatches all the necessary instructions, including the phone number the modem should dial.

By the way: During this lesson, you may be warned at some moment that your settings are not valid. Unfortunately, Works cannot always figure out that the modem does not exist, and that the problem is in the hardware, not in your settings. Works may also warn you that it has discovered a break in the transmission. If this happens, press Enter, and if you are connected, quickly disconnect by choosing *Connect* on the Connect menu.

Also, the Communications Tool expects you to use the keyboard to issue commands. Do not try to use your mouse while connecting or disconnecting.

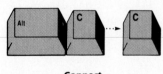

Connect

1. Choose *Connect* from the Connect menu.

   On the screen, you should see the numbers, 9,1(000)555-1212, meaning that Works has just told the modem to dial that number and that the modem attempted to dial that number. You may also see the letters ATDT in front of the phone number. The cursor is blinking, waiting for some response from the other computer. At the bottom of the screen, a clock begins ticking, so you can keep track of the amount of time you are connected. (With many information services, you are billed by **connect time**.) Your screen should look like Figure 17-7. If you do not see the text on your screen, choose *Terminal* from the Options menu, and set *Local echo* on.

   Because you are not actually dialing out through a modem, you will not get any response from Morris. But let's pretend that you have gotten some message like, Is that you? Morris here. Over.

2. Key: Yes, it's me. Am about to send GROWTH file. Over.

   What you key overwrites the message that Works had displayed, telling you that it was trying to dial the phone number. Now you know that Morris will be ready to receive the file.

Send File

3. Choose *Send File* from the Transfer menu. You see the Send File dialog box, as shown in Figure 17-8.

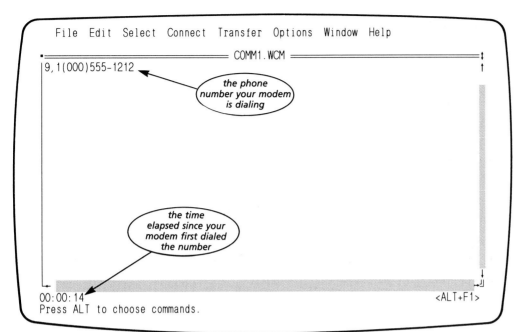

FIGURE 17-7
The beginning of a connection.

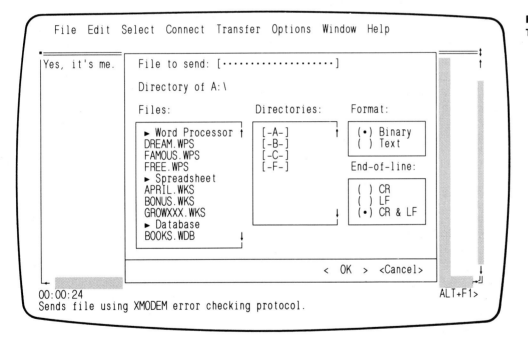

FIGURE 17-8
The Send File dialog box.

4. Select the *GrowXXX.WKS* file, a file you created and stored on your template disk. Leave the Format set to *Binary*, and the End-of-line set to *CR & LF*.

A **binary file** is a formatted file or a piece of software. If you were sending a file you saved in ASCII, that is, with only text and no formatting, you would select *Text* as the format.

If you do not know what the other computer will be doing about text when it reaches the end of a line, you can be sure that every line starts at the left edge of the screen by having your computer send both a Carriage Return (sends the cursor back to the left edge of the screen) and a Line Feed (sends the cursor down to the next line to start again).

At the bottom of the screen, you see a message indicating that Works will send the file using the **XMODEM** error checking protocol. A protocol is a conventional way of doing things—a routine. The XMODEM method is more sophisticated and faster than the Parity method you encountered in the Communication dialog box.

5. Press Enter. You see a status dialog box, like that in Figure 17-9.

FIGURE 17-9
The status box.

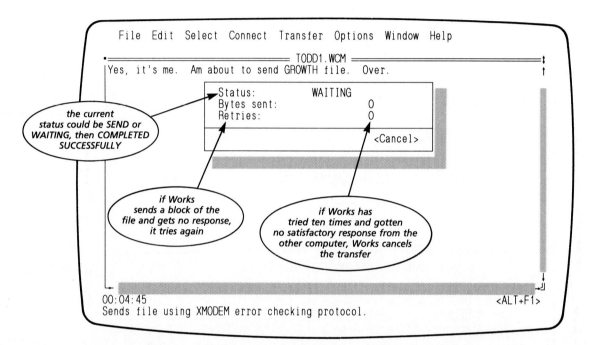

At the moment, your computer is WAITING, so it has not yet sent any bytes of information. (A **byte** is eight bits.) Works now begins to try, try, and try again. Watch the seconds tick by in the status line, as Works tries a few more times. After nine Retries, Works gives up and announces that the transfer has ended. Actually, nothing has been transferred; Works just gave up. If you had been successful in transferring the file, Works would have displayed a message telling you that it had completed the transfer.

6. Press Enter to clear the dialog box.
7. Choose *Connect* again from the Connect menu to disconnect. You are asked if it is really OK to disconnect. Press Enter. After a few seconds, the time disappears in the status line, to be replaced with the message, OFFLINE.

You are offline because you are not connected, or on-line. Your words are not pouring across the phone lines. If you were impatient to reach Morris, you could choose the *Dial again* command from the Connect menu.

8. Choose *Save As* from the File menu. Name the file *YuXXX.WCM*. (*WCM* is Works' extension for a Communications file.) Save the file on your template disk.

Saving a Communications file is a little different from saving another Works file. Later, when you close the file, the text in the window will disappear. What remains in the file are all the settings you chose and the phone number. That way, when you open the file again, you can call Morris Yu immediately just by choosing *Connect* on the Connect menu. And the window will be empty, waiting for you to send and receive messages.

9. Choose *Close* from the File menu.

Receiving

Morris Yu just called you on another line and told you that the file came through. Now he wants to send you a file. You need to reopen your Communications file called *YuXXX.WCM* because it contains the settings that match his computer.

1. Open the Communications file you just saved and closed, *YuXXX.WCM*. You see a dialog box asking you whether you want to connect to the other computer, as shown in Figure 17-10. Notice that none of the text that used to be in the window has been preserved.

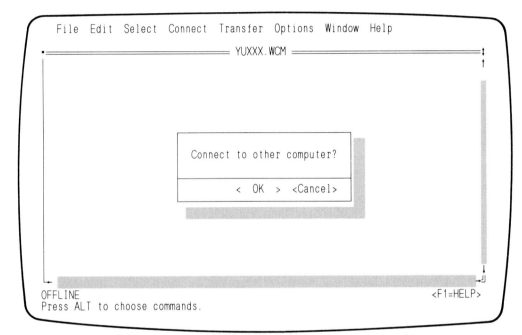

File Edit Select Connect Transfer Options Window Help

YUXXX.WCM

Connect to other computer?

<   OK   >   <Cancel>

OFFLINE   <F1=HELP>
Press ALT to choose commands.

FIGURE 17-10
When you open a Communications file you previously saved, Works assumes you want to connect to the other computer.

2. Press Enter to make connection with Morris Yu's computer. You see the phone number spelled out, which means your computer has attempted to dial that number.

   Morris Yu wants to keep track of the on-line conversation—the exchange of messages between the two of you—so he has asked you to capture the text.

3. Choose *Capture Text* from the Transfer menu. You see a dialog box allowing you to name a file that will contain the text and specify where to save it.

Capture Text

4. Save the file as *CaptXXX.WCM* on your template disk. From now on, whatever text appears on your screen will flow right into that file. Later, Morris Yu will be able to open it and read through it.

   Imagine that you have successfully established a connection with his computer.

5. Key the message: Ready to capture text. Over.

   Your message overwrites the phone number. Imagine that Morris Yu's message appears on your screen: Get ready to receive file. Over.

6. Choose *Receive File* from the Transfer menu. You see another file-handling dialog box. Save the file as *InXXX.WCM* on your template disk. Press Enter.

Receive File

   Now Works knows where to save the file as it comes in and what name to assign to it. Because the file is formatted, you leave the *Binary* option selected.

In a moment, you get the news that the transfer has ended with zero bytes received after nine retries.

7. Press Enter to accept the bad news.

8. Choose *End Capture Text* from the Transfer menu. That closes the *CaptXXX.WCM* file.

9. Choose *Close* from the File menu. Works warns you that closing the Communications file means disconnecting from the other computer. That is okay, so press Enter.

10. To use the text that you captured, you need to open the *CaptXXX.WCM* file as a Word Processor document. Use the *Open Existing File* command to do that. You see the text you typed at the top of the window, as in Figure 17-11.

End Capture Text

FIGURE 17-11
Text captured during a communications session can be opened and edited in a Word Processor document.

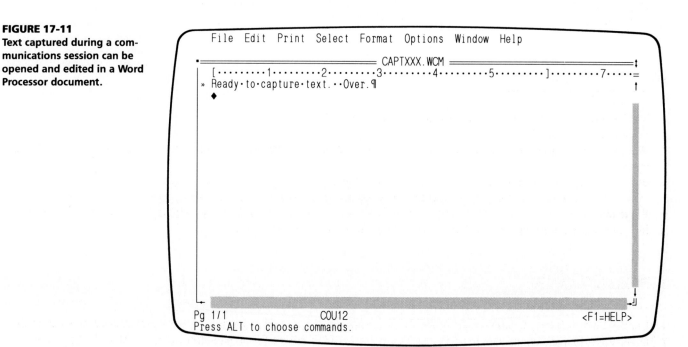

Congratulations! You have walked through the steps of capturing text and receiving a file. Even though we have practiced without a modem, you have explored the major activities in Communications.

KEY TERMS

ANSI   *MSW 304*
baud rate   *MSW 303*
binary file   *MSW 307*
bit   *MSW 303*
buffer   *MSW 305*
bulletin board   *MSW 299*
byte   *MSW 308*
Carriage Return   *MSW 305*
communications   *MSW 298*

connect time   *MSW 306*
data bit   *MSW 303*
electronic mail   *MSW 298*
full screen   *MSW 306*
handshake   *MSW 304*
Hayes-compatible   *MSW 300*
information services   *MSW 298*
Line Feed   *MSW 305*
local echo   *MSW 305*

modem   *MSW 299*
parity bit   *MSW 304*
port   *MSW 304*
session   *MSW 299*
stop bit   *MSW 303*
terminal   *MSW 301*
VT52   *MSW 304*
wraparound   *MSW 305*
XMODEM   *MSW 308*

COMMANDS

Alt-T-C (Capture Text)
Alt-O-M (Communication)
Alt-C-C (Connect)
Alt-F-N-C (Create New Communications file)
Alt-T-E (End Capture Text)
Alt-O-P (Phone)
Alt-T-R (Receive File)
Alt-T-S (Send File)
Alt-O-T (Terminal)

REVIEW QUESTIONS

1. What are the major activities people use communications for?
2. What does a modem do?
3. What is the purpose of opening a Communications file? What is the purpose of the Terminal, Communication, and Phone options?
4. Explain the options available in the Communication dialog box.
5. What kind of information can you send and receive, when connected to another personal computer?
6. What are some of the ways that the actions of saving, closing, and opening a Communications file are different from saving, closing, and opening another type of Works file, such as a Word Processor document?

APPLICATIONS

1. Reread Chapter 9, "Data Communications," in the front section of this book (pages 9.1 through 9.20). Using some of the information in that chapter and the ideas described in this chapter, describe the path that a message would follow as it leaves your computer at Lugosi's Classic Video Store, and goes over the phone lines to appear on the screen of Morris Yu's computer at the new branch store in Fairfax.
2. Morris Yu has subscribed to an information service, Videorama. The service has sent a description of the settings you need to use to connect to the service. Morris has asked you to create a Communications file for connecting to Videorama, using the following information to set the options in the Terminal, Communication, and Phone dialog boxes.

   a. You will need to add Carriage Returns or Line Feeds to the text that comes from Videorama.
   b. The service uses no parity checking and no handshake protocol.
   c. The most efficient baud rate to use is 2400.
   d. The local Palookaville access number for Videorama is (509) 555-1212. You have to dial 9 to get an outside line, and wait for a few seconds until you get the dial tone before you dial the rest of the number. (Because the access number is local, you do not need to include the area code in the Phone dialog box.)
   e. Save the Communications file as *Video.WCM*, then close it.

Quick Reference to Microsoft Works Commands

Some of the commands that are listed in this section do not have page references. These commands were not used in any of the applications in this book, but they are listed for your reference.

Command or Function	Operation	Page

Works Options

Alt-O-A	Alarm Clock	MSW 29
Alt-O-C	Calculator	MSW 28
Alt-/	Open Macro options dialog box	MSW 232
Alt-O-W	Works Settings	MSW 27

File Handling Commands

Alt-F-C	Close	MSW 26
Alt-F-N	Create New File	MSW 21
Alt-F-X	Exit Works	MSW 32
Alt-F-F	File Management	MSW 27
Alt-H-H	Help Index	MSW 29
Alt-F-O	Open Existing File	MSW 26
Alt-F-S	Save File	MSW 26
Alt-F-A	Save As	MSW 42
Alt-F-A-T	Save database as ASCII text with tabs between entries	MSW 282
Alt-F-A-T	Save Word Processor document as ASCII text	MSW 281

Help Commands

F1	Ask for Immediate Help	MSW 21
Alt-H-G	Getting Started	MSW 30
Alt-H-H	Help Index	MSW 29
Alt-H-K	Keyboard Help	MSW 31
Alt-H-U	Using Help	MSW 29

Print Commands

Alt-P-H	Headers and Footers	MSW 78
Alt-P-I	Insert Page Break	MSW 75
Alt-P-M	Page Setup & Margins	MSW 75
Alt-P-V	Preview	MSW 79
Alt-P-P	Print	MSW 44
Alt-P-S	Printer Setup	MSW 43
Alt-P-F	Print Form Letters	MSW 288

Command or Function	Operation	Page
Alt-P-L	Print Labels	MSW 292
Alt-P-A	Set Print Area in Spreadsheet	MSW 212

Window Commands

Alt-W-A	Arrange All	MSW 263
Alt-W-X	Maximize	MSW 263
Alt-W-M	Move	MSW 265
Alt-W-S	Size	MSW 265
Alt-W-T	Split	

Word Processor Tool

Alt-T-C	Align text in the center	MSW 67
Alt-T-L	Align text to the left	
Alt-T-R	Align text to the right	
Backspace	Back up over a character, deleting it	MSW 38
Alt-T-B	Bold	MSW 73
Alt-T-O	Borders	MSW 70
Alt-T-C	Center	MSW 67
Ctrl-C	Center	MSW 68
Alt-O-S	Check Spelling	MSW 60
Alt-E-C	Copy text	MSW 56
Alt-E-S	Copy Special	MSW 72
Alt-E-D	Delete text	MSW 56
Alt-T-D	Double Space	MSW 73
Alt-E-T	Footnote	MSW 59
Alt-T-F	Font & Style	MSW 73
Alt-S-G	Go To	
Ctrl-End	Go to end of document	MSW 41
Ctrl-Home	Go to start of document	MSW 40
Alt-T-A	Indents & Spacing	MSW 69
Alt-E-P	Insert Special	
Alt-E-F	Insert Field	MSW 285
Alt-E-I	Insert Chart	MSW 277
Alt-T-J	Justified	MSW 71
Alt-T-I	Italic	
Alt-E-M	Move text	MSW 56
Ctrl-Up Arrow	Move to first character in line, or up a line	MSW 40
Home	Move to first character in line	MSW 40
Alt-T-N	Normal Paragraph	MSW 67
&p	Page number in Header or Footer	MSW 78
Alt-T-P	Plain Text	
Alt-S-R	Replace	MSW 54
Alt-S-S	Search	MSW 52
Alt-S-E	Select Text	
Alt-S-A	Select All	
Alt-O-L	Show All Characters	MSW 38
Alt-T-S	Single Space	
Alt-O-R	Show Ruler	MSW 75

Command or Function	Operation	Page
Alt-T-T	Tabs	MSW 57
Alt-O-T	Thesaurus	MSW 55
&d	Today's Date in Header or Footer	MSW 78
Alt-O-Y	Typing Replaces Selection	MSW 53
Alt-T-U	Underline	

Database Tool

Command or Function	Operation	Page
Alt-S-Q	Apply Query	
Alt-S-E	Cells	MSW 108
Alt-E-E	Clear	MSW 105
Alt-T-C	Comma Format	
Alt-E-C	Copy	MSW 107
(field name): Enter	Create Field	MSW 126
Alt-T-U	Currency Format	MSW 129
Alt-E-D	Delete Record/Field	MSW 109
Alt-V-Q then Alt-E-L	Delete Query	MSW 100
Alt-S-F	Field (select column)	
Alt-E-N	Field Name	MSW 145
Alt-T-Z	Field Size	MSW 131
Alt-T-W	Field Width	MSW 135
Alt-E-F	Fill Down	MSW 108
Alt-E-R	Fill Right	MSW 108
Alt-E-S	Fill Series	MSW 134
Alt-T-X	Fixed Format	
Alt-T-F	Font	MSW 163
Alt-V-F	Form	MSW 91
Alt-T-G	General Format	
Ctrl-PgDn	Go down one screen's worth of records in List View	MSW 88
Alt-S-G	Go To	MSW 89
Ctrl-Home	Go to the first entry in the first record	MSW 89
Home	Go to the first entry in the record	MSW 91
Ctrl-End	Go to the last entry in the last record	MSW 89
Ctrl-Right Arrow	Go to the last entry in the record	MSW 91
End	Go to the last entry in the current record	
Ctrl-PgUp	Go up one screen's worth of records in List View	MSW 89
Alt-S-H	Hide Record	
Ctrl-;	Insert Date	MSW 128
Alt-E-O	Insert Field Contents (after viewing report)	MSW 166
Alt-E-N	Insert Field Name (after viewing report)	MSW 165
Alt-E-S	Insert Field Summary (after viewing report)	MSW 155
Alt-E-I	Insert Record/Field	MSW 110
Alt-V-1	Listing (a report definition)	MSW 114
Alt-V-L	List View	MSW 90
Alt-E-M or F3	Move	MSW 131
Tab	Next Field (at end of record selects first field of next record)	MSW 129
Alt-V-N	New Report	MSW 148
Alt-T-P	Percent Format	
Shift-F7	Repeat copying an entry	MSW 107
Alt-V-R	Reports View	MSW 161
F10	Return to previous view from Query window	MSW 98

Command or Function	Operation	Page
F2	Revise or edit an entry	MSW 91
Alt-S-O	Row	MSW 158
Alt-V-Q	Query View	MSW 97
Alt-S-S	Search	MSW 94
Alt-S-A	Select All	
Alt-S-E	Select Cells	
Alt-S-F	Select Field	MSW 132
Alt-S-R	Select Record	
Alt-S-L	Show All Records	MSW 97
Alt-T-N	Show Field Name	MSW 138
Alt-S-O	Sort Records	MSW 93
Alt-T-S	Style	MSW 139
Alt-S-W	Switch Hidden Records	MSW 98
Alt-T-T	Time/Date	MSW 152

Spreadsheet Tool

Command or Function	Operation	Page
Alt-V-C	Charts	MSW 243
Alt-E-E	Clear	MSW 205
Alt-T-W	Column Width	MSW 212
Alt-T-C	Comma Format	
Alt-T-U	Currency Format	MSW 210
Alt-E-D	Delete Row/Column	MSW 207
F2	Edit contents of formula bar	MSW 176
Ctrl-semicolon	Enter current date	MSW 181
Alt-E-F	Fill Down	MSW 203
Alt-E-R	Fill Right	MSW 199
Alt-T-X	Fixed Format	
Alt-T-F	Font	MSW 212
Alt-T-G	General Format	
Alt-S-G	Go To	MSW 189
Alt-E-I	Insert Row/Column	MSW 207
Home	Move to first entry in row	MSW 179
End	Move to last entry in row	MSW 179
Ctrl-End	Move to last entry you made in spreadsheet	MSW 179
Ctrl-Down Arrow	Move down to next entry	MSW 179
Ctrl-Right Arrow	Move right to next entry	
Alt-V-N	New Chart	MSW 239
Alt-T-P	Percent Format	MSW 210
Enter	Place contents of formula bar into cell	MSW 176
Ctrl-Home	Return to cell A1	MSW 180
Alt-V-S	Return to Spreadsheet	
Alt-S-S	Search	
Alt-S-A	Select All	
Alt-S-C	Select Column	
Alt-S-E	Select Cells	
Alt-S-R	Select Row	
Alt-P-A	Set Print Area	MSW 185
Alt-S-O	Sort Rows	
Alt-T-S	Style Format	MSW 209

Command or Function	Operation	Page
Functions		
= ABS	Absolute value	MSW 231
= CHOOSE	Choose	MSW 229
= FV	Future Value	MSW 231
IF	If	MSW 231
INT	Interest	MSW 231
PMT	Payment due	MSW 231
ROUND	Rounding	MSW 231
SQRT	Square root	MSW 231
VLOOKUP	Vertical Lookup	MSW 229

Charting Tool

Alt-T-B	Bar Chart	MSW 239
Alt-V-N	Create New Chart	MSW 239
Alt-V-C	Charts	MSW 243
Alt-T-D	Data Format	MSW 242
Alt-D-D	Data Labels	MSW 247
Alt-D-1	1st Y-Series	MSW 240
Alt-O-F	Format for Black and White	MSW 248
Alt-D-L	Legends	MSW 240
Alt-T-L	Line Chart	MSW 254
Alt-O-M	Mixed Line & Bar	MSW 246
Alt-T-O	Other Font	MSW 242
Alt-O-S	Show Printer Fonts	MSW 242
Alt-T-S	Stacked Bar Chart	MSW 243
Alt-T-F	Title Font	MSW 242
Alt-D-T	Titles	MSW 241
Alt-O-X	X-Axis	MSW 239
Alt-D-X	X-Series	MSW 251
Alt-O-Y	Y-Axis	MSW 239

Communications Tool

Alt-T-C	Capture Text	MSW 309
Alt-O-M	Communication	MSW 303
Alt-C-C	Connect	MSW 306
Alt-F-N-C	Create New Communications File	MSW 301
Alt-C-D	Dial Again	MSW 308
Alt-O-P	Phone	MSW 301
Alt-T-R	Receive File	MSW 309
Alt-T-S	Send File	MSW 306
Alt-O-T	Terminal	MSW 304

Learning to Use Microsoft Works Index

Acknowledgments

The following organizations donated materials used for research and photographs for use in this book. We thank them.

3Com Corp.; 3M Company; ACCO International, Inc.; Accurex Corp.; Acme Visible Records; ADAC Laboratories; Adage, Inc.; Addisk, Inc.; Adobe Systems, Inc.; Advanced Computer Communications; Advanced Matrix Technology, Inc.; Agricultural Software Consultants; Aim Technology; Aldus Corp.; All Easy Software Corp.; Allied Corp.; Amdahl Corp.; Amdek Corp.; American Laser Systems, Inc.; American Software; AMP, Inc.; Analog Devices; Anderson Jacobsen; Apollo Computer, Inc.; Apple Computer, Inc.; Applicon, Inc.; Applied Data Research, Inc.; Armor Systems, Inc.; Ashton-Tate; Ask Computer Systems, Inc.; AST Research, Inc.; AT&T Bell Laboratories; Atchison, Topeka and Santa Fe Railway Co.; Atek Information Services, Inc.; Auto-Trol Technology Corp.; Autodesk, Inc.; Automated Insurance Resource Systems, Inc.; Aydin Corp.; BancTec, Inc.; Bank of America; BASF Corp. Information Systems; Bates Manufacturing Co.; BBN Software Products; BDT Products, Inc.; Beagle Bros.; Beehive International; Bell & Howell Co.; Bishop Graphic, Inc.; BR Intec Corp.; Broderbund Software, Inc.; Brother International Corp.; Bruning Computer Graphics; Buttonware, Inc.; CADAM, Inc.; Cadlogic Systems Corp.; Caere Corp.; CalComp; Camwil, Inc.; Canon USA, Inc.; Century Analysis, Inc.; Chrislin Industries, Inc.; Chromatics, Inc.; Chrysler Motors, Inc.; Cincinnati Milacron, Inc.; Cincom Systems, Inc.; Cipher Data Products, Inc.; Claris Corp.; Cognotronics Corp.; Coin Financial Systems, Inc.; Cole, Layer, Trumble Co.; Command Technology Corp.; Compaq Computer Corp.; CompuScan, Inc.; Computer Associates; Computer Methods Corp.; Computer Museum, Boston; Computer Power Products; Computer Power, Inc.; Computer Support Group; ComputerLand; Computervision Corp.; ComputorEdge Magazine; Control Applications; Control Data Corp.; Convergent Technologies, Inc.; Corning Glass Works; CPT Corp.; Cray Research, Inc.; Cullinet Software; Cummins-Allison Corp.; Cylix Communications Corporation; Dartmouth College News Service; Data General Corp.; Datacopy Corp.; Datagram Corp.; Datapoint Corp.; Dataproducts Corp.; Daytronic Corp.; DBX; Delco Associates, Inc.; Dest Corp.; Develcon, Inc.; Diebold, Inc.; Digital Equipment Corp.; Dorf & Stanton Communications, Inc.; Drexler Technology Corp.; Eastman Kodak Company; ElectroCom Automation, Inc.; Electrohome Ltd.; Electronic Arts; Electronic Form Systems; Emerson Electric Co.; Emulex Corp.; Engineered Data Products; Epson America, Inc.; Esprit Systems, Inc.; Evans & Sutherland; Everex Systems, Inc.; Eye Communication Systems, Inc.; Fellowes Manufacturing Co.; Firestone Tire & Rubber Co.; Forney Engineering Co.; Fortune Systems Corp.; Fujitsu of America, Inc.; Gandalf Technologies, Inc.; General Electric Co.; General Meters Corp.; General Motors Corp.; General Robotics Corp.; GenRad, Inc.; Geber Systems Technology, Inc.; Gould, Inc.; GRiD Systems Corp.; Harris Corp.; Harris/3M; Haworth, Inc.; Hayes Microcomputer Products, Inc.; HEI, Inc.; Heidelberg West; Hercules Computer Technology; Hewlett-Packard Co.; Hitachi America Ltd.; Honeywell Bull, Inc.; Hughes Aircraft Co.; Hunt Manufacturing Co.; ICS Computer Products; Imunelec, Inc.; Index Technology; Industrial Data Terminals Corp.; Information Builders; Information Design, Inc.; Infotron Systems Corp.; InfoWorld Publishing, Inc.; Intecolor Corp.; Integrated Marketing Corp.; Integrated Software Systems Corp.; Intel Corp.; Interface Group, Inc.; Intermec Corp.; Internal Revenue Service; International Business Machines Corp.; International Mailing Systems; International Power Machines; Intertec Diversified Systems, Inc.; Ioline Corp.; ITT Information Systems; Jax International; Jet Propulsion Laboratory/California Institute of Technology; John Fluke Manufacturing Co., Inc.; Kao Corp. of America; Kaypro Corp.; Krueger, Inc.; Kurta Corp.; L/F Technologies, Inc.; Lear Siegler, Inc.; Liberty Electronics; Lockheed Corp.; Logical Business Machines; Logitech, Inc.; Lotus Development Corp.; LXE Division of Electromagnetic Sciences, Inc.; Management Science America, Inc.; Maxell Corp. of America; Maxtor Corp.; MBI, Inc.; McDonnell Douglas Computer Systems, Inc.; MDS Qantel, Inc.; Mead Data Central; Memorex Corp.; Mentor Graphics Corp.; Message Processing Systems, Inc.; MICOM Systems, Inc.; Micro Display Systems, Inc.; Microcomputer Accessories, Inc.; Micrografx, Inc.; Micron Technology, Inc.; MicroPro International Corp.; Microsoft Corp.; Microtek; Mini-Computer Business Applications, Inc.; Minolta Corp.; Modular Computer Systems, Inc.; Moore Business Forms, Inc.; Motorola, Inc.; Mountain Computer, Inc.; MSI Data Corp.; NASA; National Semiconductor Corp.; NCR Corp.; NEC America, Inc.; NEC Home Electronics; NEC Information Systems, Inc.; Neuron Data, Inc.; Norman Magnetics, Inc.; Norsk Data; Northern Telecom, Inc.; Novation, Inc.; Okidata; Olivetti USA; Oracle Corp.; Packard Bell; Panafax Corp.; Panasonic Industrial Co.; Panel Concepts, Inc.; Paperback Software; Paradyne Corp.; Penril DataComm; Perception Technology; Pertec Peripherals Corp.; Photo & Sound Co.; Pitney Bowes; Plus Development Corp.; Polaroid Corp.; Prentice Corp.; Princeton Graphics Systems; Princeton University; Printronix; Promethus Products, Inc.; Pyramid Technology; Quadram Corp.; Quality Micro Systems; Questronics, Inc.; Quicksoft, Inc.; Racal-Milgo; Racal-Vadic; Radio Shack, A Division of Tandy Corp.; RB Graphic Supply Co.; RCA; Reliance Plastics & Packaging Division; Ring King Visibles, Inc.; Rockwell International; Royal Seating Corp.; Sato Corp.; Schlage Electronics; Scientific Atlanta; Scientific Calculations, Inc.; Scotland Rack, Ltd.; Seagate Technology; Shaffstall Corp.; Sharp Electronics Corp.; Siecor Corp. of America; Siemens Information Systems, Inc.; Silicon Graphics; Sony Corp. of America; Soricon Corp.; Spectra Physics; Spectragraphics Corp.; SRI International; STB Systems, Inc.; Steelcase, Inc.; Storage Technology Corp.; Summagraphics Corp.; Sun Microsystems, Inc.; Sunol Systems; Symbolics, Inc.; Synergistics, Inc.; Syntrex, Inc.; T/Maker Co.; TAB Products Co.; Talaris Systems, Inc.; Tallgrass Technologies; Tandem Computers, Inc.; Tandon Corp.; Tangent Technologies; TDA, Inc.; Tecmar, Inc.; Telematics; Telenet Communications Corp.; Telenova, Inc.; TeleVideo Systems, Inc.; Telex Communications, Inc.; Telex Computer Products, Inc.; Teltone Corp.; Texas Instruments, Inc.; Thomson Information Systems Corp.; Thunderware, Inc.; Toor Furniture Corp.; Topaz, Inc.; TOPS, a division of Sun Microsystems, Inc.; Toshiba America, Inc.; Totec Co. Ltd.; U.S. Department of the Navy; U.S. Postal Service; UIS, Inc.; Ungermann-Bass, Inc.; Unisys Corp.; Universal Data Systems; Varityper; Ven-Tel, Inc.; Vermont Microsystems; Versatec; Verticom, Inc.; Video-7, Inc.; Viking; Votan; Voxtron Systems, Inc.; Wandel & Goltermann, Inc.; Wang Laboratories, Inc.; Weber Marking Systems, Inc.; Western Digital Corp.; Western Graphtec, Inc.; Westinghouse Furniture Systems; WordPerfect Corp.; Wyse Technology; Xerox Corp.; Xtra Business Systems; Z-Soft Corp.; Zehntel, Inc.; Zenith Data Systems; Ziff-Davis Publishing Co.

Photo Credits

Chapter 1

Page 1.1 H. Armstrong Roberts/Camerique / **1-1** Photo Network/Michael Manheim / **1-2, 1-3** International Business Machines Corp. / **1-4** Wyse Technology / **1-8** (a) Compaq Computer Corp.; (b) NCR Corp.; (c) International Business Machines Corp.; (d) Cray Research, Inc.; (e) Paul Shambroom / **1-10** Curtis Fukuda / **1-15** Hewlett-Packard Co. / **1-16** Honeywell Bull, Inc. / **1-17** Modular Computer Systems, Inc. / **1-18** Hewlett-Packard Company / **1-19** Coin Financial Systems / **1-20** Control Data Corp. / **1-21** Racal-Milgo / **1-22** McDonnell Douglas Automation Co. / **1-23** Intertec Diversified Systems / **1-24** Racal-Milgo / **1-25** Management Science America / **Page 1.25** Top: United Press International; Bottom: (left) Carl Howard; (center) Iowa State University; (right) Princeton University / **Page 1.26** Top: U.S. Department of the Navy; Bottom: (both) / International Business Machines Corp. / **Page 1.27** Top: (left) International Business Machines Corp.; (right both) Intel Corp.; Bottom: (left) Dartmouth College News Service; (right) Digital Equipment Corp. / **Page 1.28** Top: (left both) International Business Machines Corp.; (right) Ira Wyman; Bottom: (left) The Computer Museum, Boston; (right) Apple Computer, Inc. / **Page 1.29** Top: (left) Microsoft Corp.; (right both) Lotus Development Corp.; Bottom: International Business Machines Corp. / **Page 1.30** Top: International Business Machines Corp.; Bottom: Compaq Computer Corp.

Chapter 2

Page 2.1 P. Skrivan/H. Armstrong Roberts / **2-1** (a,b,d) Curtis Fukuda; (c) Ashton-Tate / **2-2** (left) Curtis Fukuda; (right) Hewlett-Packard Co. / **2-12** (left) Curtis Fukuda; (right) Lotus Development Corp. / **2-14** International Business Machines Corp. / **2-21** Curtis Fukuda / **2-29** Compaq Computer Corp. / **2-30** Radio Shack, A Division of Tandy Corp. / **2-31** Electrohome Ltd. / **2-32** Aldus Corp. / **2-33** Claris Corp. / **2-34** Curtis Fukuda / **2-35** (top both, bottom left) Curtis Fukuda; (bottom right) TDA, Inc. / **Page 2.20** MicroPro International Corp. / **Page 2.21** (both) Ashton-Tate / **Page 2.22** Polaroid Corp.

Chapter 3

Page 3.1 Gary Gladstone/Image Bank

Chapter 4

Page 4.1 Texas Instruments, Inc. / **4-2** Curtis Fukuda / **4-3** (left) Wyse Technology; (right) Apollo Computer, Inc. / **4-4** Wyse Technology / **4-5** International Business Machines Corp. / **4-6** (top) Logitech, Inc.; (bottom) Curtis Fukuda / **4-7** Logitech, Inc. / **4-8** Compaq Computer Corp. / **4-9** Diebold, Inc. / **4-10** Adage, Inc. / **4-11** Lear Siegler, Inc. / **4-12** CalComp / **4-13** Computervision Corp. / **4-14** Texas Instruments, Inc. / **4-16** NCR Corp. / **4-17** Soricon Corp. / **4-20** Caere Corp. / **4-21** (both) Spectra Physics / **4-22** AST Research, Inc. / **4-23** Wang Laboratories, Inc. / **4-24** LXE Division of Electromagnetic Sciences, Inc. / **4-25** Motorola, Inc. / **4-33** Curtis Fukuda / **4-37** Mohawk Data Sciences Corp. / **4-44** Acme Visible Records

Chapter 5

Page 5.1 Micron Technology, Inc. / **5-18** Intel Corp. / **5-20** NCR Comten, Inc. / **Page 5.17** (1), (2), (3) Intel Corp. / **Page 5.18** (4), (5) Siltec Corp.; (6), (7), (8) Intel Corp. / **Page 5.19** (9) Intel Corp.; (10) National Semiconductor Corp.; (11) International Business Machines Corp.; (12) AT&T Bell Laboratories; (13) 3M Company

Chapter 6

Page 6.1 Eastman Kodak Co. / **6-1** Xerox Corp. / **6-6** Micrografx, Inc. / **6-7** International Business Machine Corp.; / **6-8** Micrografx, Inc. / **6-11** (left) Storage Technology Corp.; (right) Atchison, Topeka and Santa Fe Railway Co. / **6-12** Epson America, Inc. / **6-13** (both) Printronix / **6-14** DataProducts Corp. / **6-18** Okidata / **6-19** Beagle Bros. / **6-20** Radio Shack, A Division of Tandy Corp. / **6-22** International Business Machines Corp. / **6-24** Hewlett-Packard Co. / **6-26** McDonnell Douglas Automation Co. / **6-27** Dataproducts Corp. / **6-28** Xerox Corp. / **6-29** Beehive International / **6-32** Toshiba America, Inc. / **6-33** Radio Shack, A Division of Tandy Corp. / **6-36** (left) Applicon, Inc.; (right) Evans & Sutherland / **6-38** Hewlett-Packard Co. / **6-39** (both) CalComp

Chapter 7

Page 7.1 Michael Salas/Image Bank / **7-2, 7-3** Curtis Fukuda / **7-5** Kao Corp. of America / **7-12** Hewlett-Packard Co. / **7-13** (both) Plus Development Corp. / **7-14** Seagate Technology / **7-16** Plus Development Corp. / **7-17** Curtis Fukuda / **7-18** Everex Systems, Inc. / **7-19** NNC Electronics / **7-20** International Business Machines Corp. / **7-21** Lockheed Corp. / **7-24** (top) Hewlett-Packard Co.; (bottom) Curtis Fukuda / **7-27** Hewlett-Packard Co. / **7-28** Curtis Fukuda / **7-32** (left) 3M Company; (right) Drexler Technology Corp. / **7-33** Hitachi America Ltd. / **7-34, 7-35** Storage Technology Corp.

Chapter 8

Page 8.1 © Brett Froomer 1988 / **8-17** Hewlett-Packard Co.

Chapter 9

Page 9.1 Lou Jones/Image Bank / **9-2** BR Intec Corp. / **9-3** Corning Glass Works / **9-4** Siecor Corp. of America / **9-5** Gregory Heisler/Image Bank / **9-6** Hewlett-Packard Co. / **9-7** NASA / **9-16, 9-17** Hayes Microcomputer Products, Inc. / **9-18** Panasonic Industrial Co. / **9-20** International Business Machines Corp. / **9-21** Hayes Microcomputer Products, Inc. / **9-25** Bank of America

Chapter 10

Page 10.1 AT&T Archives / **10-9** UIS, Inc. / **10-11** International Business Machines Corp. / **10-12** Apple Computer, Inc.

Chapter 11

Page 11.1 American Software / **11-2** (c) Adobe Systems, Inc. All rights reserved. / **11-3** T/Maker Co. / **11-4** WordPerfect Corp. / **11-5** TOPS, A Division of Sun Microsystems, Inc. / **11-6** Computer Associates / **11-7** Ziff-Davis Publishing Co. / **11-11** InfoWorld Publishing, Inc. / **11-12— 11-14** Curtis Fukuda

Chapter 12

Page 12.1 Kay Chernush/Image Bank / **12-1** Internal Revenue Service / **12-2** Hewlett-Packard Co. / **12-3** Integrated Software Systems Corp. / **12-4** Neuron Data, Inc. / **12-18** Curtis Fukuda / **12-19** American Software / **12-20** Walter Bibikow/Image Bank / **12-21** Curtis Fukuda

Chapter 13

Page 13.1 Curtis Fukuda / **13-12** U.S. Department of the Navy / **13-26, 13-27** Oracle Corp.

Chapter 14

Page 14.1 Compaq Computer Corp. / **14-1** Radio Shack, A Division of Tandy Corp. / **14-2** © 1988 Christopher Springmann / **14-4** ComputerLand / **14-5** Radio Shack, A Division of Tandy Corp. / **14-6** Cullinet Software / **14-12** Interface Group, Inc. /

Chapter 15

Page 15.1 Don Carroll/Image Bank / **15-1** (top to bottom) Radio Shack, A Division of Tandy Corp.; Claris Corp.; Lotus Development Corp.; Compaq Computer Corp.; Hewlett-Packard Co. / **15-2** Canon USA, Inc. / **15-3** NEC America, Inc. / **15-4** Apollo Computer, Inc. / **15-5** NASA / **15-6** General Motors Corp. / **15-8** (both) Broderbund Software, Inc. / **15-9** Electronic Arts / **15-11** Quicksoft, Inc.

Cover: Art direction and design by Alexander Atkins Design / **Photo(s):** Tim Davis Photography.

Learning to Use Microsoft Works

Page MSW 1 © Clayton J. Price / **MSW 5, MSW 7** (bottom) Video store courtesy Marc Cohen and Bob Zemsky/Premier Video Inc. / **MSW 11** Courtesy of Hayes Microcomputer Products, Inc.

Computer Concepts Index

The index for Introduction to DOS is on page DOS 32.

The index for Learning to Use Microsoft Works is on page MSW 317.

Access arms: Mechanical arms that hold one or more read/write heads; used in hard disk drives.
and hard disk storage, 7.9

Access time: The time required to access and retrieve data on a floppy disk.
defined, 5.15, 7.7–8

Actuator (See Access arms)

Adding records, 8.7–8.8

Ada: A language used by the Department of Defense that is designed to be portable (usable on different computers) and easy to maintain; named after Augusta Ada Byron.

Alpha numeric, 3.4

American National Standards Institute (ANSI)
and program flowcharts, 13.6

American Standard Code for Information Interchange (See ASCII)

Analog signal: A signal used on communications lines that consists of a single, continuous electrical wave. Compare with digital signal.
and data communications, 9.9

Analysis: In information system development, the separation of a system into its parts to determine how the system works, combined with the development of a proposed solution to system problems.
defined, 12.6 detailed system, 12.7–9
example of, 12.10
feasibility study, 12.9–10
preliminary investigation, 12.7

ANSI (See American National Standards Institute)

Application generators: Programs that produce other programs based on input, output, and processing specifications from the user.
and program development, 13.18

Application software package: Computer programs that perform common business or personal tasks; purchased from software vendors or stores, 1.10
commercial, 11.2
example of, 1.12–15
general, 11.3–6
microcomputer, 1.10–15, 15.11
operating system and, 10.4
purchasing guidelines, 2.18
system software vs., 10.2
types of, 1.11

Arithmetic/logic unit: The part of the CPU that performs arithmetic and logic operations.
CPU and, 5.3
instruction execution and, 5.10

Arithmetic operations: Numeric calculations such as addition, subtraction, multiplication, and division.
in CPU, 5.3
defined, 1.7
example of, 3.9–10

Arrow keys, 4.5

Artificial intelligence: Methods of simulating aspects of human reasoning with computers.
and expert systems, 12.4

ASCII (American Standard Code for Information Interchange): The most widely used computer code for representing characters.
data representation and, 5.5–6
floppy disk storage and, 7.7

Assembly language: Similar to machine language, but uses abbreviations for machine instructions called mnemonics or symbolic operation codes that are easier for humans to work with.
defined, 13.12–13

Asynchronous transmission mode: Data communication method in which individual characters (made up of bits) are transmitted at irregular intervals, for instance as they are entered by a user.
defined, 9.10

Attribute: A field in a relational database.
defined, 8.13

Automated office: Describes the use of computers, facsimile machines, and electronic communications to make office work more efficient.
information processing trends and, 15.2
summary of, 15.5

Auxiliary storage: Stores programs and data when they are not being processed; similar to a filing cabinet.
defined, 7.2
direct-access storage devices, 7.12
disk cartridges, 7.10
file organization methods, 8.3–7
floppy disks, 7.4–8
hard card, 7.9
hard disks, 1.7, 7.8–10
in information processing cycle, 3.3
magnetic disks, 7.12–14
magnetic tape, 7.14–17
mass storage devices, 7.18
on microcomputers, 7.4–12
on medium and large computers, 7.12–17
networks and, 9.15
optical, 7.17–18
solid-state devices, 7.18
types of, 1.17–18, 7.19
user needs and, 7.3

Auxiliary storage unit: Computer hardware used to store instructions and data when they are not being used in the main memory of the computer.
defined, 1.7 (See also Auxiliary storage)

Backup of data files, 3.6
disks and, 7.11–12
magnetic tape and, 1.17, 7.15
reasons for, 7.9, 7.21
sequential files and, 8.4

Bandwidth: The range of frequencies that a communications channel can carry.
and transmission rates, 9.11

Banking, and data processing, 4.10

Bar chart: A common form of graphical display of information in which data is represented by vertical or horizontal bars.
advantages of, 6.4
graphics and, 2.14

Baseband: A type of coaxial cable that carries only one signal at a time, 9.4

BASIC (Beginner's All-purpose Symbolic Instructional Code): A commonly used high-level programming language.
described, 13.15

Batch control: The technique of balancing numeric data to a predetermined total to check the accuracy of data input.
and batch processing, 4.24

Batch processing: Data is collected and at some later time, all the data that has been gathered is processed as a group or batch.
applications for, 3.16
batch control and, 4.24
combined with interactive processing, 3.18
compared with interactive processing, 3.16
data entry for, 4.23–24
defined, 3.16
example of, 3.16–17
offline data entry and, 4.24
source documents and, 4.24

Baud rate: The number of times per second that a data communications signal changes; with each change, one or more bits can be transmitted.
and data transmission, 9.12

Benchmark test: A test that measures the time it takes for particular software or hardware to process a set of transactions.
and software evaluation, 11.10

Bidirectional printing: A form of printing in which the print head can print both when moving left to right and when moving right to left.
and printer features, 6.8

Binary number system bit
representation and, 5.5
described, 5.8–9

Bit: An element of a byte that can represent either of two values, "on" or "off".
defined, 5.5

Bit-mapped display: A type of screen used for graphics in which the number of addressable locations corresponds to the number of dots (pixels) that can be illuminated. Also called dot-addressable display.
and display methods, 6.17

Bits per inch (bpi): A measure of the recording density of a disk.
and floppy disk storage, 7.7

Bits per second (bps): A measure of the speed of data transmission; the number of bits transmitted in one second.
and transmission rate, 9.12

Blocked records: A method of organizing records on magnetic tape into groups called blocks for easier access.
and storage, 7.16

Bold: Bold characters are displayed on a screen with greater brightness than the surrounding text.
defined, 6.15

Booting: The process of loading the operating system into main memory of the computer.
described, 10.3–4

Bottom-up design: Design approach that focuses on the data, particularly the output, of a system.
and information system development, 12.11

Broadband: Describes coaxial cable that can carry multiple signals at one time.
defined, 9.4